Doing Educational Research (Second Edition)

Bold Visions in Educational Research
Volume 47

Series Editors:

Kenneth Tobin, *The Graduate Center, City University of New York, USA*
Carolyne Ali-Khan, *College of Education & Human Services, University of North Florida, USA*

Co-founding Editor:

Joe Kincheloe (with Kenneth Tobin)

Editorial Board:

Barry Down, *School of Education, Murdoch University, Australia*
Daniel L. Dinsmore, *University of North Florida, USA*
Gene Fellner, *Lehman College, College of Staten Island, USA*
L. Earle Reybold, *College of Education and Human Development, George Mason University, USA*
Stephen Ritchie, *School of Education, Murdoch University, Australia*

Scope:
Bold Visions in Educational Research is international in scope and includes books from two areas: *teaching and learning to teach* and *research methods in education*. Each area contains multi-authored handbooks of approximately 200,000 words and monographs (authored and edited collections) of approximately 130,000 words. All books are scholarly, written to engage specified readers and catalyze changes in policies and practices. Defining characteristics of books in the series are their explicit uses of theory and associated methodologies to address important problems. We invite books from across a theoretical and methodological spectrum from scholars employing quantitative, statistical, experimental, ethnographic, semiotic, hermeneutic, historical, ethnomethodological, phenomenological, case studies, action, cultural studies, content analysis, rhetorical, deconstructive, critical, literary, aesthetic and other research methods.

Books on *teaching and learning to teach* focus on any of the curriculum areas (e.g., literacy, science, mathematics, social science), in and out of school settings, and points along the age continuum (pre K to adult). The purpose of books on *research methods in education* is **not** to present generalized and abstract procedures but to show how research is undertaken, highlighting the particulars that pertain to a study. Each book brings to the foreground those details that must be considered at every step on the way to doing a good study. The goal is **not** to show how generalizable methods are but to present rich descriptions to show how research is enacted. The books focus on methodology, within a context of substantive results so that methods, theory, and the processes leading to empirical analyses and outcomes are juxtaposed. In this way method is not reified, but is explored within well-described contexts and the emergent research outcomes. Three illustrative examples of books are those that allow proponents of particular perspectives to interact and debate, comprehensive handbooks where leading scholars explore particular genres of inquiry in detail, and introductory texts to particular educational research methods/issues of interest to novice researchers.

Doing Educational Research (Second Edition)

A Handbook

Edited by

Kenneth Tobin
The Graduate Center, City University of New York, USA

and

Shirley R. Steinberg
University of Calgary, Canada

SENSE PUBLISHERS
ROTTERDAM / BOSTON / TAIPEI

A C.I.P. record for this book is available from the Library of Congress.

ISBN 978-94-6300-074-1 (paperback)
ISBN 978-94-6300-075-8 (hardback)
ISBN 978-94-6300-076-5 (e-book)

Published by: Sense Publishers,
P.O. Box 21858,
3001 AW Rotterdam,
The Netherlands
https://www.sensepublishers.com/

Cover image by Moey Hewitt

Moey Hewitt is an artist from Cocoa Beach, Florida, and is currently pursuing a Bachelor of Fine Arts degree in painting at the University of Central Florida. She designed the cover for *Regenerating the Philosophy of Education: Whatever Happened to Soul?*, edited by Joe L. Kincheloe and Randall Hewitt. Her email is moeyhewitt@yahoo.com

Chapter 2 is reprinted here with kind permission of Springer. Originally published as: Kincheloe, J. L., & Tobin, K. (2009). The much exaggerated death of positivism. *Cultural Studies of Science Education, 4*, 513-528. DOI 10.1007/s11422-009-9178-5.

Printed on acid-free paper

All rights reserved © 2015 Sense Publishers

No part of this work may be reproduced, stored in a retrieval system, or transmitted in any form or by any means, electronic, mechanical, photocopying, microfilming, recording or otherwise, without written permission from the Publisher, with the exception of any material supplied specifically for the purpose of being entered and executed on a computer system, for exclusive use by the purchaser of the work.

CONTENTS

Foreword: Pearls of Wisdom ... ix
Joe L. Kincheloe

Foreword to the Second Edition: Contributing to an Art of Educational Research ... xxxix
Kenneth Tobin and Shirley R. Steinberg

I Introduction

1 Doing Educational Research in a Complex World ... 3
Joe L. Kincheloe and Kenneth Tobin

2 The Much Exaggerated Death of Positivism ... 15
Joe L. Kincheloe and Kenneth Tobin

3 Qualitative Research in Classrooms: Pushing the Boundaries of Theory and Methodology ... 33
Kenneth Tobin

II Ways of Doing Educational Research

4 Research as Bricolage: Embracing Relationality, Multiplicity and Complexity ... 79
Kathleen S. Berry

5 Proposing a Multiplicity of Meanings: Research Bricolage and Cultural Pedagogy ... 111
Shirley R. Steinberg

6 Philosophical and Historical Research ... 133
Barbara Thayer-Bacon and Diana Moyer

7 Researching with Children: Dialogic Approaches to Participatory Research ... 151
Christina Siry

8 "Can't You Just Know?": Critical Research as Praxis ... 167
Tricia M. Kress

CONTENTS

9	A Multilectical Approach to Research in Inner City Schools *Gene Fellner*	181
10	Conversation Analysis: Deconstructing Societal Relations in the Making *Wolff-Michael Roth*	199
11	On Hermeneutics: "Over and above Our Wanting and Doing" *David W. Jardine*	235
12	Motion-Sensing Phenomenology *Rebecca J. Lloyd and Stephen J. Smith*	255
13	Critical Historiography *Joe L. Kincheloe*	279
14	Liberation, Mice Elves and Navel Gazing: Examining the Ins and Outs of Autoethnography *Carolyne Ali-Khan*	293
15	Educating Desire: An Impressionist Tale of Alcoholics Anonymous *Peter Waldman*	321
16	To Your Health! Heuristics and Deep Breathing as Mindfulness Promoting Interventions in Educational Context *Malgorzata Powietrzynska*	339
17	Using Photovoice as a Critical Youth Participatory Method in Environmental Education Research *Marissa E. Bellino*	367
18	Arts-based Educational Methodology: An Impossible Possibility? *Mark Vicars*	383
19	Speculations on Qualities of Difficult Knowledge in Teaching and Learning: An Experiment in Psychoanalytic Research *Alice J. Pitt and Deborah P. Britzman*	395

III Reflections: After Doing the Research

20	Limits of Knowledge in the Physical Sciences *Phil Francis Carspecken*	421

21 From *Scientific Research in Education* to the "Open Science" 455
    Movement: Science as Touchstone and Buzzword
    Cheryl Holzmeyer and John Willinsky

    Contributors 473

    Index 479

JOE L. KINCHELOE

FOREWORD

Pearls of Wisdom

Ken: Joe Kincheloe and I worked together at the Graduate Center of CUNY from fall, 2003 until he left for a distinguished Canada chair position at McGill University in fall, 2005. We talked endlessly about research and had a vision of producing a scholarly text that addressed the logics of inquiry. This vision became manifest in *Doing Educational Research* (2006), or, as my students refer to it: the Red Book!

We resolved almost immediately to do a second edition, based on our success of using the book as a graduate text. We had already identified ways to improve the revised edition when a rather negative review was published in Education Researcher. The editors of the journal was somewhat apologized about the Tanner of the review and spoke with us about writing a rejoinder. We needed no encouragement to rejoin and feverishly worked on a manuscript. To our surprise, the full editorial board of the Journal declined to accept the manuscript because they did not publish rejoinders for book reviews. However, we had a polished manuscript and were in the process of submitting it for publication when Joe died in Kingston, Jamaica on December 19, 2008 at the age of 58 years. In the context of his death, I decided to publish the article in *Cultural Studies of Science Education*, as a testimonial to his impact on educational research. The article is as republished, with permission of Springer, as chapter 2 of this revised edition of *Doing Educational Research*.

One of the changes we had agreed to in creating a second edition of the Red Book was a series of Editors' Introductions to each chapter. We divided the chapters and Joe quickly wrote his set. These are published here as sections of this Foreword. Of course, some of the Introductions authored by Joe related to chapters that were not republished or revised in this second edition. We have included these introductions following those that are referenced to chapters that appear in this revised volume. Joe's insights and genius are reflected in these pieces and we regard this Foreword as an appropriate forum to publish this work that otherwise would not be available to the scholarly community. Also, we decided to include, as the final section of the Foreword, a segment of a chapter that was written by Joe, but was not re-published in this volume.

Shirley: Joe had very few mates. Ken Tobin was his mate. After Joe moved to the CUNY Grad Centre from Penn State (via Brooklyn College), he began thinking about whom he should attempt to recruit to become the third full time professor in the new Urban Education Program. It took little effort to realize Tobin was the perfect choice. Not only did Ken successfully get offered the position, but he and Barbara bought a house about 3 blocks from us. Many are the flashbacks of Ken picking up Joe and their very loud, laughing walks to the train on the way to Manhattan. Almost as frequently, the two would come back with Aussie/Tennessee embellished stories of the two very out-of-place urban interlopers and whatever they experienced or saw on the train. The two of them lived auto-ethnographies wherever they went; this, coupled with their great intellects and fondness for one another, created a dynamic duo devoted to their students, their scholarship, their friendship, and laughter. This book was a major part of their collaboration.

ON KENNETH TOBIN'S CHAPTER

The first chapter on doing educational research authored by my co-editor, Kenneth Tobin, is an exemplary introduction to the specific ways an adept researcher comes to change his approach to research, in the process coming up with a powerful set of insights into the problems and possibilities of educational inquiry. Ken's adept use autobiography to illustrate not "the way" but a range of possible approaches to classroom research grants all readers insight into the power of personal narratives in not only research itself but also in the effort to teach individuals how to become researchers. As a young researcher of the learning environments of science classrooms, Tobin found that he did not have the research tools he needed to gain a larger sense of what was happening in science classrooms. Tobin found the effort to make sense of the complexities of classroom life with empirical variables to be reductionist and decontextualized.

Like the other authors in this book, Ken found that positivistic approaches to knowledge production are profoundly limited and account for very narrow dimensions of human experience. By not examining a phenomenon within the framework of historical consciousness, reductionist research loses sight of the contexts and processes from which data cannot be removed. In this decontextualized setting crypto-positivism loses the ability to understand the way that phenomena and human consciousness are inscribed by culture and power – a deficiency that results in a lack of understanding of the way their own positions are socio-cultural and historical constructions. This leads to a form of ideological naiveté that allows such researchers to unconsciously reflect dominant cultural values and ideologies. Thus, in the name of reason and human progress such scholars (many times, unconsciously) sustain the power asymmetries of the status quo with its race, class, gender, sexual, colonial, and religious hierarchies. Logical procedure and methodological correctness (rigor) take precedence over the complex dynamics of producing usable and ethical knowledge.

Thus, the trouble with positivistic rigor is multidimensional. Its foundations, as so many from Western and non-Western locales have argued over the past several decades, are shaky and crumbling. For example, it is simply no longer possible to accept the foundational notion of objectivity when we know so much about the complex and vital relationship between knower and known. A rigorous positivistic model of decision-making that explains phenomena and provides solutions to problems emerging from them without involving the researcher/policy maker is misleading from its inception. Such a model gives the impression that the data and answers provided are not culturally or ideologically inscribed. That which is covertly subjective is whitewashed in a way that presents it as neutral. The abstract certainties that positivists produce in this context in the name of rigor possess great oppressive potential in their erasure of their investment in the issues in question. Rigor in the positivistic cosmos ensures neutrality. Researchers remove the complex human element from the process, thus making sure that our knowledge is uncontaminated. After all these years it is still hard for me to comprehend that this argument persists decade after decade.

But whatever difficulty I may have, such perspectives continue to survive and thrive. Ken ran into them at both the beginning of his career and also, unfortunately, in his present efforts to research classrooms and teach doctoral students this complicated skill. Rigorous thinking in the positivistic sense is a mode of cognition based on an unproblematized use of reason. The only concession to subjectivity in this process that many positivists are willing to tolerate involves attending to psychological pathologies that undermine one's ability to be completely rational. Outside of this realm of psychological health, the relationship between self, rationality, and objective knowledge and decision-making is irrelevant on the reductionist landscape. Thus, we are back to what the positivistic tradition omits, the complex contextual, process-oriented, and ideological factors at work in any analysis and research process. As Ken recognized the way reductionist classroom research was stripped down and isolated from its natural setting, he found himself writing more and more about the contextual factors: the macro-social forces, the impact of race, social class, and state and national mandates. To help him make sense of these forces, Tobin had to gain a profound understanding of social theory, diverse modes of research, multiple voices, and diverse participants in his projects.

In this chapter readers clearly understand how these diverse ways of seeing helped Ken grasp the deficit perspectives permeating the view of inner-city students and urban education in general. Again the author's autobiographical narrative grants us powerful insights into the ways a world-renown scientist, science educator, and researcher of science education in urban settings does his work. This is, of course, what many other approaches to teaching individuals how to become researchers do not do – provide autobiographical insights and examples of what the researcher was thinking as he or she was designing and conducting research. Such narrative respects the dignity of the reader by not laying out a step-by-step cookbook of how to do research. All researchers have their own ways of researching and the idea that there is one correct way to engage in classroom research is the height of positivism. Knowing there are multiple ways to accomplish the task, Tobin asks two main questions of the phenomena he is studying: "what is going on here?" and "why is this happening?"

Such ostensibly simple questions separate Tobin's research from more reductionist counterparts. The hermeneutic question – why is this happening? –

demands forms of rigor swept under the rug by crypto-positivists. It is with this interpretive question and the effort to use the information produced to improve schooling that researchers earn their stripes. Such explanations go far beyond the mimetic pictures of classrooms produced by researchers who believe they can provide a complete and verifiable account of an event. Critical interpretive research involves conversing informally, Tobin tells us, with students as lessons progress. Ken follows up such dialogue with formal interviews that emphasize the "what" and "why" questions referenced above. Ken makes sure that the students he chooses to be interviewed are not picked randomly. Here Tobin uses the concept of opposites: after choosing one person to interview, Ken's works to make the next selection as different from the first pick as possible. The process continues with selections based on who has perspectives worth knowing about what Ken wants to learn next. The process Tobin describes is fascinating and edifying to anyone who is or seeks to be a researcher.

With this in mind Tobin challenges traditional reductionist practice by maintaining that he never goes into his research on classrooms with solidified ideas about what a research project will reveal. A critical pedagogical researcher, for example, who has already decided how power plays out in a particular social situation or classroom setting has made a profound mistake, because power in its complexity will operate in diverse ways given the idiosyncrasy of the contexts of which it is a part. As Tobin so aptly puts it, research that begins with a set of assumptions about what is to be gained from the process finds that "such ideas can serve as templates that filter data and confirm a priori expectations." I have seen far too much research of all varieties and ideological persuasions fall into this trap.

Keeping himself open to new ideas, new theoretical and methodological lenses, Ken insists that his complex classroom research meet one more central criterion: research with human subjects must benefit the students, teachers, and other individuals involved in the inquiry not only in the future but also as the research is being conducted. I have talked at length with Ken about research in which he has been involved, and one dimension he always deems essential involves the ways his work benefits himself as a teacher-researcher and all people involved in whatever capacity with the research. If these benefits are not identifiable, Ken is simply not satisfied with what he has done. Using Egon Guba's and Yvonna Lincoln's notion of ontological authenticity, Tobin asks how those involved with the study change their perceptions of the socio-cultural dynamics shaping the phenomenon under analysis as well as the phenomenon itself. How does the research change who the participants are and the conceptual matrixes they bring to their work?

In this context Tobin induces readers to consider the way their own perceptual frameworks are changed and how this changes their descriptions and interpretations. What is the relationship between these theoretical frameworks and the final information produced? As we explore this questions with which Ken confronts us, we move into a new epistemological, ontological, and ideological territory – a terrain where objects in the mimetic researcher's rearview mirror may be more complex than we ever imagined. This issue of the benefits of research and the ontological changes it brings about cannot be separated from Ken's profound concern with the ethics of research with human subjects – a topic on which he is a trusted expert. Using the guidance of the Belmont Report – prepared by the National Commission for the Protection of Human Subjects of Biomedical and Behavioral Research in 1979 – Tobin discusses the foundational ethical precepts for conducting ethical research with human subjects.

Here Tobin provides a great service for all researchers and students of research about the nature of ethical research and the diverse problems one encounters in working with human subjects committees. Tobin documents how he has dealt with the crypto-positivistic impulse of some committees to ask for research questions and researcher hypotheses before the research commences. In this context Tobin concludes that these are requests he can as a researcher live with as long he can show how his initial conceptions changed as the research was being conducted. This illustration of how researcher perspectives change during the research process is a central dimension of Guba and Lincoln's ontological authenticity. In this ontological context Ken asks: how did the participants in my research project and I as the researcher change as the project proceeded? The answers to such a question are central to the research on classrooms that Tobin conducts. They are important to any effort to engage in rigorous, complex, critical research in general.

Another important aspect of Tobin's chapter involves how he illustrates the complex, non-reductionist aspect of his research for his readers. After searching for what he calls "patterns of coherence" in the data he has collected, Ken explores the contradictions that do not fit the patterns he has delineated. Instead of engaging a positivistic epistemology that explains such incongruities as errors, Tobin views them as propitious moments where deeper insight into the data can be gained into the domain under study. This is such an important understanding for researchers who have been taught to erase such contradictions in the quest for final truth. Bringing together patterns of coherence with these conflicts, Tobin gains a more textured view of the phenomenon under study. Through an appreciation of the relationship between the patterns and the contradictions, he gains a greater sense of the way coherence and conflict work together to help shape a thicker view of things-in-the-world.

The compelling nature of this interaction of coherence and conflict illustrates the importance of conducting research at diverse levels – in this context Tobin refers to microscopic, mesoscopic, and macroscopic domains of research. From his macro-social theoretical insights to his videotape microanalyses, Ken promotes the value of these diverse perspectives. In relation to the notion of diverse perspectives one of the most important dimensions of Tobin's classroom research involves his compelling use of students as researchers. No only does he gain students' valuable perspectives on what is going on in the teaching and learning process, but he also engages students in observing and doing research. There are few pedagogies more powerful than this. Tobin is careful to view students in classroom research not simply as sources of information but also as researchers in their own right. Student researchers attend the meetings of Ken's research teams, they learn the theoretical underpinnings of the research project, they work to understand the nature of research design, and they find that they too grow ontologically as a result of their involvement in the research process.

Ken Tobin's chapter is profoundly valuable in our effort to develop new, more rigorous forms of critical complex research. Contributing to a new epistemology and ontology – and the research they help us construct – Tobin helps young (and not so young) classroom researchers obtain the tools to get beyond the reduction valves of positivism. Such epistemological and ontological spigots exclude so many dimensions of the world from our purview and understanding. In this new context we are better prepared to transcend the normalized pictures of reality that dominant ideologies and positivism work to construct. In an era of complexification, of hyperreality where information exponentially increases, the power of dominant ideology is magnified, surveillance techniques for regulating teacher and student actions abound, and new media help develop new forms of social discipline and resistance, the need for new levels of insight into these issues has never been greater. Indeed, the nature of education and schooling in the coming decades will be profoundly shaped by how successful we are in developing and deploying these new forms of knowledge work. Tobin's chapter provides us a compelling insight into a central dimension of this effort.

ON KATHLEEN BERRY'S CHAPTER

Kathleen Berry provides a powerful introduction to the use of bricolage in educational research. Berry and I have worked together on the concept of the bricolage, co-authoring the book, *Rigour and complexity in educational research: Conceptualizing the bricolage* (2004). I have long argued that Kathy Berry is one of the most gifted pedagogical and research-oriented thinkers operating in contemporary North America. The following chapter helps illustrate this assertion. As she introduces readers to the bricolage, Berry maintains that since she embraced the use of the bricolage she has felt as if she were thrust back into the middle of the paradigmatic wars many thought were over. The rise of crypto-positivism in its evidence-based guise placed Berry and her students in situations where colleagues demanded a single methodology – rejecting in the process an effort to employ a more rigorous, more theoretically savvy mode of knowledge production for the reductionist comfort of the "one correct way." This is profoundly discouraging to Berry and myself, as it illustrates a regressive backlash against the insights we have developed about the social construction of knowledge and knowledge production and dominant power's ability to covertly infiltrate such processes in a way that promotes its own interests.

As bricoleurs bring multiple theoretical lenses and research designs to the process of educational inquiry, Berry contends that a key dimension of this multiperspectival process involves situating oneself in the inquiry. How am I (the researcher) positioned in the study, Kathy asks, and how does this affect the knowledge I produce. A researcher who conducts a rigorous form of research understands the forces that shape what we think we know about the world. In the process we come to understand how much we don't know about and don't experience in the socio-educational cosmos. Thus, what crypto-positivist researchers label reality is actually more like a belief about what the world is – a conviction grounded on passing glimpses.

Such researchers don't seem to keep in mind that a human view of the world is always truncated by our vantage point and the nature of our consciousness and unconsciousness – as Berry knows all too well. This is why a critical complex theory of mind and consciousness are so important in good research in general and in the bricolage in particular: in such a context we can better understand the way subjectivity/identity are socially constructed and the process by which we come to see ourselves and the world. The critical complex theory of mind and consciousness Shirley Steinberg and I have worked on over the last fifteen years, postformalism, provides a socio-political, spatio-temporal analysis of consciousness that allows us to see more dimensions of the ways our consciousness – and, thus, our knowledge – is limited. This critical complex mode of studying mind and consciousness is central to the bricolage.

Unlike bricoleurs and postformalists, positivist researchers operate as if the construction of the mind of the researcher has simply nothing to do with the knowledge that is produced. Just as long as the mental mirror that reflects the real world is not cracked, the mind has very little to do with the positivistic/reductionist knowledge production process. Obviously, the bricolage maintains that the mind has far more to do with the production of knowledge than has typically been admitted by the positivists. What we call reality exists in the intersection of the universe with the mind – a key dimension of what the bricolage studies. The fact that we don't have the olfactory sense of dogs or the cognitive radar of bats doesn't mean that what such creatures perceive about their reality doesn't exist.

This, however, is exactly how many positivist researchers function. If a phenomenon doesn't lend itself to perception by the way our minds presently work, then the phenomenon is dismissed. In such situations bricoleurs maintain that the positivist refusal to employ diverse epistemologies, ontologies, and research designs that allow us to bring the phenomenon into our range of perception is a form of parochial anti-intellectualism. Because it did not conform to the kind of perception needed for empirical scientific investigation, consciousness, behavioral psychologist, B.F. Skinner asserted, didn't exist. The central role of mind in helping to construct the universe is in the positivist context summarily eliminated. The ties between knower and known are severed. Berry and other bricoleurs work to address this unacceptable state of affairs.

In positivism and its contemporary crypto-positivist expression the meaning of an observation is transmitted from sensory perception directly to the passive receiver – the researcher. The bricolage confronts such reductionism in the name of good scholarship. Meaning in the crypto-positivist epistemological/ontological framework resides in phenomena themselves and the job of the researcher is simply to capture that meaning and relay it to the readers of their research. Bricoleurs such as Kathy Berry see this process of meaning making not as an objective procedure of researching and then relaying the meaning of a phenomenon but more as a negotiated process between the viewer and the entity under observation – a negotiation that is better accomplished with a variety of perspectives and theoretical orientations. What the phenomenon means is neither objectively predetermined nor entirely open to any imagined interpretation. The place the observer occupies in the web of reality, the values she holds, the epistemological, ontological, ideological and other perspectives she either consciously or unconsciously embraces all help shape how a particular entity is viewed and interpreted. Indeed, after Einstein, quantum mechanics, Heisenberg, and Maturana and Varela the idea that meaning resides simply in the phenomenon itself seems archaic.

Operating in the spirit of quantum theory, bricoleurs posit that the phenomena of the world never have fixed, set meanings. What this suggests in the everyday lived world of the researcher is that physical and social phenomena don't have an eternal Platonic form, a permanent spatial arrangement that persists as time passes. This is where the complexity theoretical notion of process enters the bricolage's understanding of objectivity vis-à-vis epistemology and ontology. As a part of larger contexts and processes, the phenomena of the world are always changing, ever in process in an act of becoming. This is one of the major points positivism has always missed: things change, people change via patterns that play out over long periods of time. Indeed, when positivist researchers attempt to observe an entity in a single snapshot ignoring its historical construction and future possibilities of what it could be – not to mention what surrounds it outside the frame of the picture – they get a highly distorted view of the entity.

These are not simply arcane philosophical notions that have relevance only if an individual takes a philosophy of science course. The epistemological and ontological concepts developed here and in Kathy's chapter shape what we think we know about the world. They help construct our ideological views of who we are, what the world is, and how human suffering and oppression continue unabated in contemporary life on Earth. The crypto-positivism that attempts to dismiss these questions in the name of just doing research in a monolithic method has to be addressed if we are to advance our ability to understand and change the world. As I get older, I become increasingly weary of crypto-positivistic arguments that such insights don't matter in the education of researchers. This is why Berry characterizes the next moment in Norman Denzin and Yvonna Lincoln's (2005) timeline of qualitative research as belonging to the bricolage. I agree with Kathy and argue that the progression to the bricolage is already happening under a variety of names as a compelling effort to produce better, highly informed research.

The repertoire of discourses/resources on which bricoleurs can draw, Berry maintains, increases every day and every year. Thus, as bricoleurs we read in and are conversant with diverse fields, various manifestations of high and popular culture, and knowledge sources from academic information to video, television, and cyberspace. As bricoleurs, we have no choice – we have to know a lot, study hard, and work to compare differing theoretical dynamics and diverse perspectives throughout our lives. It takes a tremendous commitment to be a bricoleur – one's education as a researcher doesn't simply end at the completion of one's formal education. To fulfill such a commitment, Kathy tells us, takes a special commitment – a "rhapsodic intellect." A rhapsodic intellect she tells readers so eloquently, is grounded on "passion for new knowledge and insights" and "compassion for others." These allegiances help construct the sustainable battery from which bricoleurs draw energy for the complex task ahead of them.

The bricolage, Berry insists, involves the creative task of constructing knowledge emerging from diverse perspectives, fresh questions, and artful interpretation. Such bricolage-produced knowledge is dangerous no doubt, as it exposes the hidden consequences of dominant power in education, the contradictions and asymmetries that are typically overlooked in crypto-positivist research. To accomplish such a task, Berry maintains that bricoleurs must view the issues in question from the vantage point of diverse contexts – the social, cultural, historical, economic, political, etc. Indeed, this contextualizing impulse is a central dimension of the bricolage. As we view a phenomenon from numerous horizons, we begin to see it in completely different ways. Our acquaintance with these diverse perspectives sets us up to provide fresh insights into a variety of events.

As we reflect on Kenneth Tobin's chapter 2 in the context of Berry's explication of the bricolage, we can begin to see the ways that Ken's multiple lenses into classroom research allow him to gain new insights into the interactions of students and teachers. Thus, bricoleurs acting in the spirit of multilogicality ask how is this student's life and relationship to learning connected to dominant political, epistemological, ontological, cultural, and economic forces. What is the relationship here? Who is privileged by these relationships? Who is oppressed by them? What is my relationship as a researcher to these dynamics? How does this relationship affect the way I view the situation? This is why the bricolage is so central to any form of critical research – it provides us new tools and strategies to answer such questions. In a participatory manner it engages interviewees in ask such questions, bringing about ontological changes not only among readers of the research but participants in it as well. Hopefully, these ontological changes lead to larger structural and ideological transformations as well.

In this larger conversation Berry discusses the ways researchers might enter the bricolage. Through a variety of point of entry texts (POETs), a group of researchers might examine a classroom practice, a particular book, a curriculum, or a movie using a diverse array of theoretical perspectives, methodological approaches, and interpretive strategies. Such tools can help problematize traditional perceptions of such "texts" in ways that create emancipatory insights and critical complex modes of consciousness. Such new ways of seeing expose the ways both cultural education and schooling can become modes of social control, regulation, and classification that lead to great injustice. When such analysis is conducted rigorously, bricoleurs can begin to understand the ever-morphing nature of power and the ways it produces both agency and oppression. As Berry maintains, we gain a deeper insight into these processes by appreciating both what we see about a particular phenomenon and what is invisible to our "commonsense" modes of perception.

Thus, we learn from Berry's compelling chapter on the bricolage that we simply cannot become viable researchers who produce compelling and transformative knowledge unless we appreciate the numerous and varied socio-political and conceptual structures that shape the research act. As we engage in such analysis we gain a new vantage point on the means by which such frameworks prop up the needs of oppressive power. Diverse power blocs deploy these frameworks to develop what appear to be levelheaded practices that often shape the lives of the poor, the racially marginalized, women, the colonized, and other peoples in profoundly damaging ways. I have stood before people deemed to be reasonable and ethical in public and private schools, universities, colleges of education, and many other venues who constructed policies that unabashedly exerted a disastrous effect on the least powerful members of the communities of which these policy makers were involved. In these and other contexts we witness the results of egregiously flawed research strategies and epistemologies that are structured to dismiss particular contextual factors such as the welfare of marginalized peoples from consideration in the knowledge production process. Kathy Berry helps us overcome these unfortunate tendencies of hegemonic forms of inquiry.

ON SHIRLEY STEINBERG'S CHAPTER

Shirley Steinberg continues Kathleen Berry's discussion of the bricolage. Here Steinberg argues that a bricoleur's research should be a "complex collage" tying together the researcher's theoretical lenses, images, insights, and interpretations of the interconnections between texts, social justice, the social context in which these dynamics are situated, and its effects on those who come into contact with it. Like Berry, Steinberg situates the bricolage in a critical theoretical context, as a tool in the critical pedagogue's repertoire that helps her expose the oppressive effects of power. Steinberg, like all critical bricoleurs, understands that all research is partial and lacking in diverse ways. While bricoleurs are not so naïve that they attempt to *complete* research by opening new perspectives on the process, they do make an effort to broaden their vantage points through the power of cultural, theoretical, and methodological difference. While such efforts extend our understanding on a phenomenon or a pedagogical process, Steinberg is quick to point out that bricoleurs do not gain some God-like view – no matter how hard we may try, bricoleurs' perspectives are also partial. Instead of fighting this incompleteness, bricoleurs accept it, in the process promoting a humble view of the world that understands the limitations of all inquiry.

Thus, Steinberg's bricolage represents an effort to carry on knowledge production with the realization that knowledge is contingent and always open to change when someone asks new questions from a different perspective. This presents crypto-positivism with an "in its face" challenge. The correspondence epistemology of old and new versions of positivism certify data that accurately reflect the correspondence between the knowledge the research puts on paper and the one true version of "real things." The reductionist quest for certainty in this context overcomes good sense. The critical complex epistemology promoted by Steinberg's and Berry's bricolage questions the declaration that there exists one fixed external world of real things that will be seen by everybody from every

FOREWORD: PEARLS OF WISDOM

spatio-temporal location in the same way if they simply employ the correct research methodology. Such doubt in the infallibility of positivist science scares the hell out of true believers in the objectivity of mainstream research – I think this is one of the reasons they sometimes react so vehemently to the bricolage. On one level such positivist fear is puzzling in light of the tendency for all of the greatest advances in twentieth century science to question reductionism and to promote the complexity of all research practices. The correspondence epistemology of positivism was kneed in the guts by Einstein's Special and General Theories of Relativity, quantum mechanics, Werner Heisenberg's uncertainty principle, Humberto Maturana's and Francisco Varela's theory of emergence as complexity intensifies in biological systems, the insights of literary theorists into the imprecision of language employed in scientific research and its often hidden effects, just to mention a few challenges of the last century.

In light of such complex insights many scholars from physics, biology, and sociology to education now understand that scientific certainty is more fleeting a notion than once so confidently was assumed. With this in mind it is necessary to note that a critical complex bricolage-grounded approach to research delivers a blunt invitation for knowledge workers and educators to account for the dangerous weaknesses displayed by traditional positivism and its crypto-positivistic contemporary manifestation. In a twenty-first century world of perpetual war and elitist social and educational policies, critical bricoleurs such as Shirley Steinberg view this "call for accountability" as a mode of scholarly decolonization – an effort to reinstate the ethical dimension of educational research. A critical form of research validity asks how the research in question has helped us understand the causes of human suffering and how it has enabled action to address it. Indeed, Shirley in her discussion of "doing the bricolage" illustrates how crypto-positivism is a form of epistemological colonialism designed to support dominant power blocs including the political economic and sometimes military neo-colonialism that the U.S. and its Western allies have unleashed against the world.

In its epistemological sophistication, the bricolage stands up against this episto-oppression. Epistemological colonialism operates to invalidate the information constructed by peoples from oppressed locales and replace them with Eurocentric crypto-positivistic knowledges – all in the geo-political and economic interests of the wealthiest peoples from North America, Australia, New Zealand, Europe, and their co-conspirators in other parts of the world. Indeed, in the standardized educational cosmos of the twenty-first century U.S.-led Western empire, one of the central dimensions of schooling involves colonizing student minds with this imperial impulse. Critical evaluations of such colonial forms of knowledge production have emanated, of course, from colonized countries and from numerous Western scholars.

Such researchers have systematically outlined the inadequacies of Western ways of seeing and their socio-political and pedagogical effects. Bricoleurs in education – no matter what they are studying – have much to learn from such critiques. It is essential to human welfare, educational legitimacy, and the well being of the planet itself that educational researchers understand the effects of this epistemology of correspondence and the variety of ways it is deployed to exacerbate human oppression and pathological educational practices. Steinberg leads the way in this process with her delineation of how the bricolage operates. At the end of the first decade of the twenty-first century, bricoleurs can't help but sense that while the planet burns and Western patriarchal free marketers pour gas onto the fire, crypto-positivist researchers fiddle with the production of trivial, deracinated, decontextualized, and faux-depoliticized data.

In this socio-political, epistemological, and ontological context Shirley provides insights into the way she engages the bricolage. After transcribing her notes on the text in question, Steinberg reads through her data set allowing themes and motifs to materialize. Coding her emerging concepts with colored pencils, she watches macro-themes emerge turning her original motifs into micro-themes. One of the many dangers of traditional "how-to-do-research books" involves this coding process. The quality of one's coding is contingent on conceptual frames and ways of seeing that researchers bring to this aspect of the process. To simply view this – as many educators of researchers do – as a technical act carried on outside of the epistemological, ontological, ideological, cultural and many other dimensions mentioned by Steinberg and the other authors in this book *is a form of mis-education.* Here is a key dimension of a critical complex research as informed by the bricolage: research is not a mechanical process of following proper steps. Research is a scholarly, creative act that must be improvised in light of a wide range of insights. There is no correct way to perform any form of research – we have to be able to reflect, think on our feet, change course abruptly, and bring in numerous insights from our general education and our life experiences. To do otherwise is to dumb down the process.

In this rigorous research context Steinberg focuses much attention on the interpretive process in the bricolage. She understands that in a Heideggerian (grounded on the epistemological/ontological work of Martin Heidegger) sense living, being in the world, always involves a hermeneutic interpretation of the world and self. Thus, we must always as critical ethical beings actively engage in the process of understanding how our place and time in the world – in the social and temporal web of reality – is always shaping our actions and thoughts. This process is a central dimension of the bricolage's counter-positivistic and counter-hegemonic research act. Indeed, it may be fair to argue that contemporary crypto-positivistic researchers emphasize the production of knowledge over the nature of our being in the world. If this is the case, then the effort to understand who we are and how our location in the web of reality shapes both our selfhood and the knowledge we produce about the world is not a high priority in twenty-first century Western research. There is no way to separate knowing and being, implying that particular phenomena can only be understood when the knower has become aware of her context and the way it shapes her conceptual lens.

If we bring in diverse individuals to view the mundane contexts in which we live and the ways they affect our ways of seeing, there is little doubt they will show us things about ourselves and our world that are completely surrounding us but yet invisible to our eyes. A key concept emerges at this point: although knowing and being-in-the-world are inseparable, human beings have the agency to understand the relationship in a way that allows them to act in defiance of any final, deterministic influences of such a relationship. We are not prisoners of the processes and contexts that shape us. Indeed, the in process, fluid, ever changing, emergent nature of the world makes critical agency more possible that we could have previously imagined. As critical theorist Walter Benjamin (1968) maintained in *Illuminations*, language plays a powerful role in helping construct the nature of the world. In this context it is central to note that language helps shape, and therefore it can help reshape the nature of human consciousness. Yet, another factor is identified that provides possibility and hope that researchers don't have to be trapped in the immediacy of the contexts and processes that help shape them. Bricoleurs such as Steinberg take advantage of this opportunity.

Bricoleurs know that context and process are powerful but not deterministic forces in the world. It is fascinating what we can find out about researchers and ourselves as we come to understand the impact of ontological assumptions, discursive practices, conceptual frameworks, and epistemes on knowledge work. When we gain the ability to appreciate these dynamics, we have made a giant step in our effort to both understand the typically hidden dimensions of the research process and also take more power over our own destiny. We are interpretive beings no doubt, but we can always get better at the process of interpretation. As we hone our hermeneutics we gain a firmer grasp on the social role of knowledge – how knowledge hookworms its way into us, in the process changing us. From this vantage point we can discern the way knowledge exerts its ontological power.

This transgressive, nay ideologically intoxicating perspective of the critical bricolage, can free us from the hegemony of dominant power and its hypnotic consumerist trance. With this knowledge and the critical affect that accompanies it, bricoleurs can never become researchers who can be bought and sold to the highest corporate bidder – degraded objects of exchange. Our consciousness is elevated – we are empowered to create knowledges that matter, to reframe the purposes of school in light of new perspectives on what it attempts to do, to expose and help end human suffering. Crypto-positivist lessons on becoming a researcher avoid connecting educational research to the purposes of education in a democratic society. Critical complex bricoleurs with these notions in mind understand that there is never a disconnection between educational research and the purposes of one's pedagogy. If the purpose of our pedagogy is to gain new cognitive abilities, to see the world in emancipatory ways, to understand the hidden forces that shape what happens in various societies, to gain empowerment to re-shape the nature of our lives and the lives of our communities, and to gain the civic literacy and courage to fight oppression, then how we conduct our research cannot remain unaffected.

If an educator's purpose is to pass along a body of traditional knowledges many of which are simply untrue in order to raise standardized test scores, then the nature and purposes of her research cannot be unaltered. If one embraces such a purpose, then developing more exacting ways of testing students might be a key dimension of her research agenda.

Indeed, being situated does not undermine our ethical compass, our social commitments, our sense of higher purpose, or the ineffable willpower that motivate advocates of the bricolage. Steinberg knows the direction in which she wants to travel, she has a critical vision of where she might go. Here, bricoleurs understand the political ethics of their own ontological and epistemological stance. They are made aware once again of the inseparability of their political, pedagogical, and research strategies. Understanding selfhood and its construction is a key missing dimension to both doing educational research and teaching people to do educational research. The self is always in a process of revising and readjusting. It is never stable and we never know exactly where it is located – Francisco Varela (1999) refers to this as the virtuality of the self. Varela's conception of the virtual self *emerges* out of a complex matrix of relationships. Because of its ever in process, ever-evolving nature as a thing-in-relationship, the virtual self possesses no describable central processing mechanism, no "situation room" where activities are organized and coordinated – the dynamics that shape it are widely distributed in the physical and social worlds. Bricoleurs Steinberg and Berry know that as critical complex researchers they must understand how the self works in the research process. They must take advantage of its capacity for change.

ON BARBARA THAYER-BACON'S AND DIANA MOYER'S CHAPTER

Barbara Thayer-Bacon and Diana Moyer present a dynamic introduction to research in the philosophy and history of education. Once again it is important to contextualize this chapter in terms of the hegemonic epistemological world of educational research. Thayer-Bacon and Moyer argue that norms of physical science with their rules for explanation are still considered the standard in educational research. In this superior position many practitioners of such types of inquiry look at historical, philosophical, literary studies, interpretive, and critical designs as inferior forms of research. Many of the types of research delineated in *Doing Educational Research: A Handbook* including Thayer-Bacon's and Moyer's philosophical and historical work are dismissed by the narrow-minded crypto-positivists. Bringing philosophical and historical ways of producing knowledge into contemporary educational research is a battle worth fighting. It is simply absurd that contributors to this handbook, including Thayer-Bacon and Moyer, produce high quality scholarship that too often is not respected in educational circles.

It is even more obnoxious that when we point out the oppressive dimensions of such epistemological arrogance, we are charged with confrontational language and being uncivil. According to the crypto-positivist position those of us who do non-positivistic research should just keep quiet when we find ourselves and many of our brilliant colleagues being denied tenure and not being reappointed because we and/or they are not really doing rigorous research. I am very, very tired of such malicious, parochial, and ideologically and intellectually indefensible policies. We cannot remain silent in the face of such oppressive and hegemonic actions. Crypto-positivists can destroy the lives of brilliant young researchers, but those of us coming from different paradigms must not speak with indignation and anger about such ludicrous practices. We must make sure that historical, philosophical, literary, interpretive, and critical modes of inquiry are included in the research courses offered in colleges/faculties of education. While we do not want to fight the research wars once again, we cannot retreat from the positivistic gauntlet that has been thrown on the ground beside us.

Thayer-Bacon and Moyer understand that philosophical and historical research cannot produce the modes of prediction and control demanded by an imperial reductionist research establishment. As we move farther and farther down the road of No Child Left Behind and the type of "evidence-based data" its standardized and test-driven practices demand, the conversation about research becomes narrower and narrower. Thayer-Bacon and Moyer quote the National Research Council's *Scientific Research in Education* that categorizes philosophical and historical research as "other approaches" that could be used to supplement *real* scientific research. At least the authors of the book admit that an educator might use such modes of research – there are numerous crypto-positivistic educators who see no reason at all to engage in such types of knowledge work. In one university where I was a professor, one of my colleagues who was well-known and well-respected as a philosopher of education found that the tenure committee in his department had ruled against him because in their words "there is no such thing as research in philosophy – thus, he has conducted no research."

This positivistic hegemony reveals itself in numerous fields as those whose research falls under the umbrella of scientism with its alleged disinterestedness, mimetic forms of data production, and replicability receive the vast majority of research grants and institutional perks. In these situations there emerges a tendency on the part of university leaders to use this positivist mode of research as the exclusive model of what research should be. In relation to the huge financial allotments given to such research, critical complex types of social, psychological, and educational inquiry – such as philosophical and historical studies – pale in fiscal comparison. Recently, I was told by a representative from a national educational research organization that the critical pedagogical research that my colleagues in that field and I do is not really empirical research. Thus, a critical complex, multiperspectival, multimethodological understanding of research demands that we examine the nature of the disciplines and the knowledge work they promote, reassess the criteria for evaluating scholarship in a way that removes knowledge work from the positivist hierarchy, and develop new modes of understanding the ways that research agendas are set and whose interests they serve. It really is time that positivists stopped bullying researchers coming from different epistemological backgrounds.

The implicit values that shape university and other institutional policies around conceptions of research must be made explicit and the metaphysics on which they are grounded exposed. Power's presence – no matter whether it takes the form of whiteness, class elitism, patriarchy, colonialism, heterosexism, abilism, religious prejudice – in the creation of knowledge is omnipresent. It is the 1153-pound bull moose in the room about which oftentimes no one dares speak. I cannot help but laugh – after a thirty year career as a professor in higher education marked by positivists who have attempted to deny my critical, philosophical, social theoretically-oriented colleagues tenure – when such positivist scholars demand that we temper our rhetoric about issues surrounding research and epistemology. The laugh is dry and sarcastic. I have to immediately visualize the marginalized children oppressed by dominant forms of power who have always motivated me to continue my teaching and research in education. Their images in my mind's eye flood out the cynical and nihilistic feelings that envelop me in such situations.

I have yet to see or hear about a non-positivist researcher attempting to deny tenure to a positivist researcher on the grounds of the type of research he or she employs. (Of course, I hope I never do, for these are not the grounds on which academic reward should or should not be granted.) It is fascinating that such "rigorous" scholars who often sit on research ethics committees, dissertation review committees, and other governing boards cannot discern the difference between certain forms of educational research coming from teacher research, action research, participatory action research, etc. and propositional knowledge and mimetic knowledges about education. The ability to distinguish between different types of knowledges that come from different types of questions, epistemologies, ontologies, and purposes is essential to any researcher working in education or any other domain of study. Yet, in far too many academic programs in colleges/ faculties of education and elsewhere such discernment is simply not taught.

Without the ability to understand different types of knowledges and how they relate to divergent questions, scholars will continue to operate from a monological perspective that dismisses powerful research traditions such as philosophy and history. They will continue to deny research funding to scholars such as Thayer-Bacon and Moyer. Indeed, as Thayer-Bacon describes her effort to explain what a philosophical argument is to her students, the power of scientistic hegemony to determine what is and even what sounds like research rears its head. To students under the spell of such hegemony, philosophical arguments sound like mere opinion not based on empirical, verifiable fact. The reductionism and arbitrariness of such positivistic determination of "the truth" is not usually taught to such students. They are ensnared in the positivist trap – in the name of rigor they dismiss some of the most powerful ways of producing knowledge that presently exist.

Indeed, as the authors maintain, philosophical arguments don't attempt to do the same thing as positivistic research. As philosophical arguments make the case for what should be – a key dimension of any educational knowledge work – philosophers draw upon their intuition, creativity, imagination, and educational background to support the positions they advocate. This is certainly one of the most rigorous and demanding jobs in scholarship. The fact that it would not be recognized as such and as a valuable form of research is unacceptable. Indeed, any scholar doing any form of research could profoundly profit from a detailed knowledge of such philosophical dynamics. In previous work I have made the argument for the importance of philosophical research in educational inquiry in general and the bricolage in particular. While many researchers have been very complementary in regard to such work, many of the crypto-positivistic reviewers have ridiculed such a position. They find it ridiculous that philosophical analysis would even be used in a discussion about doing educational research – a manifestation, the argument goes, of a sophomoric perspective. The ad hominem vehemence of this reaction to such a position may be telling in and of itself. Given the crypto-positivist lack of familiarity with such a discourse, they have accused proponents of promoting an esoteric and elitist language when we/they speak of such issues. As long as we speak of "my tradition" our language is open and accessible; when we speak of a "tradition different than mine" your language is arcane and inaccessible. As one might guess, I am not impressed by such arguments.

I have often used the phrase philosophical research to denote the use of various philosophical tools to help clarify the process of inquiry and provide insight into the assumptions on which it conceptually rests. Informed by Thayer-Bacon's and Moyer's conception of philosophical research, researchers become smarter, more self-reflective about their own role and the role of researchers in general in the knowledge-and reality-creating process. An appreciation of complexity, of course, demands such insights, as it insists on an understanding that conceptual categories are human constructions and posits that such categorization exerts a profound impact on modes of perception and human action itself.

The mode of philosophical consciousness advocated here helps researchers bracket their own subjectivity as researchers in ways that force the intersection of notions such as researcher "invention" and researcher "discovery." The bricolage makes use of philosophical research into the boundary between the social world and the narrative representation of it. Such explorations provide profound and often unrecognized knowledge about what exactly is produced when researchers describe the social world. Rigor, I assert, is impossible without such knowledge and discernment. Exploring this complex, ever shifting boundary between the social world and the narrative representation of it, philosophically-informed researchers begin to document the specific influences of life history, lived context, race, class, gender and sexuality on researchers and the knowledge they produce.

These aspects of philosophical research help the researcher highlight the ethical, epistemological, ontological, and political features of the research process and the knowledge it produces. Such tasks might be described as a form of research concerned with conceptual clarification. For example, what does it mean to exist in history? To live and operate as a social and historical subject? How do researchers begin the process of exploring such dynamics? How do the ways researchers conceptualize these features shape the research process and the knowledge it produces? How do social theoretical choices and assumptions affect these issues? All of these questions point to the role of science as first and foremost a cultural activity. Abstract and objective procedural and methodological protocols come to be viewed as the socially constructed entities that they are. Thus, researchers are freed from reductionist conventions in ways that facilitate their moves not to an anything-goes model of research but to a genuinely rigorous, informed multiperspectival way of exploring the lived world.

What researchers are exploring in this philosophical mode of inquiry is the nature and effects of the social construction of knowledge, understanding, and human subjectivity. Realizing the dramatic limitations of so-called objectivist assumptions about the knowledge production process, philosophical researchers struggle to specify the ways perspectives are shaped by social, cultural, political, ideological, discursive, and disciplinary forces. Understanding the specifics of this construction process helps researchers aware of complexity choose and develop the methodological, theoretical, and interpretive tools they need to address the depictions of the world that emerge from it. In the context of the philosophical inquiry as conceptual clarification the researcher comes to understand that the objectivist view of knowledge assumes that meaning in the world exists separately from an individual's experience. In such an objectivist context the research act simply involves identifying external objective reality and reflecting it in the research narrative. Such reductionism and its concurrent distortion is exactly what rigorous research seeks to avoid.

In the same anti-reductionist vein Thayer-Bacon and Moyer work to conceptualize a historical mode of research that understands the profound difficulty with depicting history as "it really was." No matter how we cut it, historical research always requires interpretation by the historian. As the authors point out: "even the seemingly transparent issue of historical 'fact' is fraught with difficulty." In this context educational historians must be particularly careful about imposing a pseudo order on historical data, a "false coherence" that will often work to legitimize existing power relations.

Power renders certain historical narratives to be commonsensical and, therefore, resonant with asymmetrical power relationships – with oppression. As critical complex historians construct information about the past, they concurrently produce insights about the way history is shaped by power and dominant culture. In this context Thayer-Bacon and Moyer help us appreciate the notion that learning to be an educational historian requires more than simply learning a set of historical research strategies. In order to appreciate the socio-political construction of a society's historical understandings, historians have to understand social theoretical, cultural, and philosophical insights. The path to becoming a critical complex historian is longer and more demanding than a more technicist and reductionist boulevard.

While many scholars believe that positivism is an epistemological and ontological position found only in the physical sciences and quantitative modes of research, what we are maintaining here is that elements of positivism inscribe research of all kinds. As one who was educated in my doctoral program as a historian, I recognized early on that even historians could be influenced by these positivistic dynamics. Some historians – both past and present – have assumed that their objective task has involved presenting the final truth about the past. The numerous obstacles concerning the objectivity of the sources one has to deal with in historical research were glossed over as historians claimed their chronicles to be an objective rendering of a historical event or era. What mattered to such historians was not the process of knowing and the way the knower entered into that process –

the important aspect of research was the *known*. Thus, a critical complex form of research always takes knower and known – and their intricate relationship – into account when producing or studying the production of knowledge.

When philosophical and historical research are examined together as part of a larger effort to understand education in ways that reveal particular tendencies and trends in the way public knowledge production and schooling work, powerful insights can be gained. This is exactly what Thayer-Bacon and Moyer do in this chapter, in the process providing the reader with compelling new ways of understanding the dynamics of the pedagogical process. After reading this essay, one will be upset to learn that courses in philosophical and historical analyses of education are found less and less often in teacher education programs and as modes of understanding education. This is a tragic trend that must be reversed in the coming years. Thayer-Bacon and Moyer show us the power of these discourses when guided by capable and creative scholars.

ON PHIL FRANCIS CARSPECKEN'S CHAPTER

Phil Francis Carspecken provides a powerful epistemological, ontological, and ideological analysis of twenty-first century educational research that resonates with and extends many of the concepts that appear in previous chapters. Carspecken maintains that a virulent form of scientistic (defined as the notion that the epistemological/ontological constructs and methodologies of the physical sciences are the only legitimate forms of science no matter what a researcher is studying) ideology has reemerged in Western social and educational research. This notion resonates with the emergence of what has previously been described in this book as crypto-positivism. Carspecken's chapter involves an analysis of what is presupposed but unstated in such a rigid notion of educational research. Such an analysis is essential in the last years of the first decade of the twenty-first century, as many governmental and other agencies have openly stated that only research that fits the mold of the physical sciences will be funded and/or used in educational policymaking.

In crypto-positivistic/scientistic research one of the most important unstated assumptions permeating all of its belief structures involves the notion of substance. In the lexicon of the philosophy of science, substance is something that can exist in isolation, unconnected to anything else. Substance in this Western ontological context is what makes up all things. Thus, all things (even in the social, psychological, and educational domains) can be studied in the same way we study the substance of biology, cells, or chemistry, solids and gases. Throughout the twentieth century, however, researchers began to find more and more domains where traditional physical scientific notions of substance did not work – for example, in the study of consciousness, in the quantum domain of sub-atomic particles, in social frameworks, etc. The study of the phenomena raised profound ontological issues, which we are still attempting to understand. Indeed, an analysis of these ontological concerns raises a conceptual window through which we can crawl to gain fresh insights on the issues that motivate the attacks of crypto-positivists on diverse forms of research delineated in this book.

In this context Phil takes us into an important domain of analysis where we gain a deeper insight into the nature of scientism and its relation to crypto-positivism. Traditional positivism was obsessed with measurements and predictions of measurements. In the larger scientific community, especially among many philosophers of science, a notion of semantic realism gradually came to replace a measurement-oriented positivism. Semantic realism expanded the definition of empiricism to allow for the admission of data that cannot be observed in traditional ways – this is what Carspecken means when he refers to "excess content." When educational researchers point to the "death of positivism," it is this move in the philosophy of science they typically point to as proof of positivism's passing. While it is the case that a form of semantic realism has gained ascendance over traditional positivism in these circles, it is also apparent that in contemporary educational and psychological science elements of positivism are alive and well in modes of evidence-based research that always involve measurement of academic performance and cognitive ability. In this context such notions are treated the same way as substances are taken up in traditional modes of biology and chemistry and also in Newtonian physics.

Thus, Phil maintains in this context that formally speaking, much contemporary science operates in a space characterized by tension between scientific realism and positivism. Scientific realism posits that the phenomena of the world exist objectively, that is, unconnected to the mind of the perceiver. Those things that are not observable, realism maintains, are constructed in the same way as things that are more easily observable. Thus, regardless of whether we associate scientism with positivism or scientific realism, both constructions rely on the ontological notion that all phenomena consist of substance. This is a central tenet of Carspecken's argument in this chapter – a concept that is profoundly valuable to any epistemological/ontological understanding of a critical complex mode of research.

Indeed, the ontological rubber hits the research road in Phil's chapter when he argues that the inner experience of human beings (most of the time central in studies of the social, psychological, and educational domains) cannot be researched and analyzed in the same way that outer experience (the domain of many dimensions – not all – of the physical sciences) can. Thus, in this context selfhood, consciousness, and the notion of the "I" cannot be studied in traditional ways by the natural/physical sciences because such concepts are not substances. Research, Carspecken warns, must be very careful with these concepts, as "inner-sense" is produced intersubjectively (by diverse people interacting) and differs from culture to culture.

Returning to Carspecken's concern with preexisting (*a priori*) constructs and concepts in the ideological, epistemological, and ontological domains, Phil asks how much such assumptions shape the knowledge researchers produce. If the scientistic belief that everything is made up of substance rests at the foundation of research, then a quest for objective depictions of the phenomena of the world is

FOREWORD: PEARLS OF WISDOM

presupposed in such inquiry. Such preexisting assumptions shape what researchers are going to find before they begin their research. Since the experience of human beings is multidimensional and is not made up simply of experiences of phenomena in the physical universe, Phil maintains that the preexisting notions of substance and objectivity are not useful in this context.

Instead, scientific research on human phenomena such as education has operated by shredding human experience of its subjective features and restricting its study to its "objective" features – for example, I.Q. testing. What we get in such studies is a profoundly reduced view of humanness and the complexity of the human experience. Such perspectives have shaped the way the world has viewed consciousness, thinking, teaching and learning, etc. In the scientific universe of crypto-positivism and realism psychologists operating in this epistemological/ontological realm, for example, sincerely believe that one day consciousness will be understood via a physical theory that traces its origins to particle physics. In such research nothing will be left unknown about the physicality of consciousness, and with such knowledge psychologists will be able to predict accurately what humans will do next.

A compelling feature of Carspecken's chapter involves this epistemological/ontological investigation of complexity theory's notion of emergence. Emergence involves the notion that in complex systems patterns, configurations, and characteristics develop that cannot be sufficiently accounted for by alluding to the system's original properties and relationships. For example, none of the properties of a thunderstorm could be used to predict the emergence of a tornado. We only know that tornadoes emerge from particular types of thunderstorms by observing them over the years. Carspecken posits that emergence is grounded on the notion that the whole can be greater than the sum of the parts, in the process wondering which phenomena should be called emergent and which should not since there are so many types of processes that are labeled as such. In the case of educational research, Carspecken asserts that the type of emergence that is most relevant involves the emergence of subjectivity or consciousness.

Reflecting the larger concerns of his chapter and certainly of *Doing Educational Research: A Handbook* in general, Carspecken maintains that most research into the emergence of subjectivity/consciousness is positioned securely in the context of scientific ways of seeing. In my work on postformalism (a critical theory of cognition that understands mind as an emergent social construction in a larger context informed by power) Carspecken's questions about the crypto-positivistic/realist dimensions of emergence theory are profound and must be addressed. When we view the emergence of consciousness in light of a critical complex conception of the social construction of self and a critical ontological notion of self-production, we begin to gain a deeper understanding of the way networks of power and other concerns help shape contemporary selfhood. Concurrently, in a postformal understanding of consciousness analysts understand the capacity of the individual to reshape who she is and how she operates in the world.

As we understand the concept of an emergent consciousness, educational and psychological researchers begin to appreciate the pedagogical possibilities it opens – but only if we get beyond the scientific notions of consciousness as substance. For a critical complex notion of the emergence of consciousness to sophisticate our understanding of selfhood and thus teaching and learning, it must be viewed as a hermeneutic concept that transcends the notion of scientism. This complex hermeneutic notion of the self is far more supple and malleable, more amenable to transformation and growth than social, psychological, and educational researchers had ever envisaged. This characteristic of selfhood, no matter what socio-political and ideological space from which one operates, can be mobilized for great help to the critical struggle or manipulated for great detriment. With the possibility of an evolving selfhood in mind, critical complex researchers approach inquiry with a renewed appreciation of the possibility, the use-value of their work.

Such researchers know that notwithstanding the influence of cognitive determinists maneuvering under the banner of scientism and its reductionist concept of I.Q., humans can learn to become more intelligent and discerning. As they understand how to and engage in making themselves smarter, they come to realize that selfhood is a far more amazing marvel than previously understood. Appreciating complexity theory's notion of emergence but ever careful to heed Carspecken's warnings about the scientific articulation of the concept, critical complex researchers recognize that no self is without perspective – to exist is to bring a standpoint to lived situations. Emergence as a hermeneutic construct is an amazing and promising property of the physical, biological, social, psychological, and educational world. With a non-substance-oriented emergence in mind we realize that as we come to better understand our own and other people's perspectives, even newer and deeper insights emerge.

Such understandings applied to self-knowledge require a detailed monitoring of our subjectivity – a key point made by all the authors of this book. In such an analytical context we nurture a meta-awareness of the diverse connections we forge to divergent dimensions of the social and physical worlds in which we operate. Key to this process is the isolation and the release of an egocentrism that blinds humans to the virtual and relational dimensions of our selfhood. In such a context individuals can work to catalyze the emergence of new and more vital forms of selfhood – and in turn new types of community. This tendency for emergence occurs at all levels of reality, and the notion of the individual mind is much more complex, relational, and distributed than we once thought. Thus, researchers have to understand this emergent dynamic at all levels of their research – in the formation of their own selfhood, the consciousness of their research subjects, the social dynamics that they are studying, and the interpretation of their findings. Indeed, critical complex researchers are always looking for that point when things-in-relationship move to a new level of interaction, in the process producing new socio-cultural, political, economic, psychological, and pedagogical dynamics previously lost in the isolation of crypto-positivism and realism and their notion of substance existing in isolation from other dimensions of the world and the mind of the perceiver – i.e., a thing-in-itself.

In my notion of a critical ontology these ideas are central. In order to gain new levels of insight, humans have to understand the complexity of their own construction so they can remake themselves. Consider how far we have cognitively traveled when we first gain the initial stages of self-consciousness. Imagine how much farther we will have traveled when we become conscious of how this self-consciousness can be used for cognitive growth and insight into the way we are induced to see the phenomena of the world in a particular way. Thus, our growth, our becoming is a fundamental dimension of learning how to be a rigorous researcher. Unfortunately, this is one the aspects of learning to be a researcher that is typically ignored in research courses. As individuals become researchers, the quality of their work will always depend on the knowledges, experiences, and intellectual skills they bring to the task. There is simply no way around this. Knowing the seven steps for producing ethnography will not help if an intellectual foundation such as the one delineated by Carspecken is not appreciated.

Sometimes learning to become a researcher produces a pedagogical moment that moves students of research to gain new insights into the social, historical, and philosophical questions that are so central to the process of inquiry. As we gain these emergent new insights we begin to understand the fallibilities of what crypto-positivism/realism represented as finite and limited. Nothing can limit the possibilities of a critical complex consciousness – a force that can help shape the universe and the social order is nothing to be carelessly dismissed. Imagining what else such a consciousness can do is the first step in making such constructions a reality. Critical complexity is directly concerned with imagining new ways of seeing the world and using such insights to reshape it in more just, creative, and interesting ways. As our conception of consciousness, research, and criticality morphs from a noun to something more like a verb, we move to a new domain. If consciousness is a verb then how do we reconceptualize research and knowledge production? We quickly return to the critical theoretical concept that critical research is designed to expose the relationship between "what is" and "what could be."

In such a notion substance has nothing to do with the synergy of the relationship, with the emergence of a new level of organizational complexity. As with consciousness, we cannot experience "what could be" through our senses. Concepts and attitudes in scientistic configurations are treated as variables in empirical studies and located in a set of correlational or causal relations. This relegation of such phenomena to the designation of substance is profoundly misleading, as such an act deletes an entire realm of ontological phenomena that shape the astounding nature of psychological activity, social dynamics, and human being in general. In this profoundly important province, Phil maintains that the cause-effect nature of scientism, so central in the crypto-positivist and realist world, inflicts great harm on efforts to appreciate the domain of meaning, culture, social relations, pedagogy, and inquiry into pedagogy. In many ways Carspecken at this point guides us down the Cartesian River to the heart of positivistic darkness – the scientistic domain that demands that we gain a far more rigorous and epistemologically/ontologically appropriate set of precepts for doing educational research.

Thus, we come to the main theme of Carspecken's brilliant chapter: the limits of the knowledge that can be produced by scientism. "If a theory of everything really could explain *everything*," Phil asks, "then it could it explain its own production as a theory?" If it could, then a scientistic/crypto-positivist/realist epistemology and ontology would support a mode of research that answered all our questions, told us all we need to know about education while precisely predicting the outcomes of particular educational objectives, curricular designs, and pedagogical methodologies. Obviously, it can't do this because of the profound complexity of such dynamics. This is so important for researchers, educators, policy makers, politicians, and citizens to understand in an era marked, as Phil puts it, by the "growth of particularly virulent form of scientistic ideology." Carspecken's rigorous analysis of this epistemological and ontological cancer is central, obviously, to the larger concerns of *Doing Educational Research: A Handbook.*

Indeed, contrary to scientistic/crypto-positivist logic, the critical complex refusal to believe that we can operate from what the Greeks called the Archimedean point – the place from which we could see the world objectivity and in its totality – does not destroy the value of the knowledge we produce. It merely overthrows the notion that any discourse can provide a final criticism of positivism and the knowledge it produces. Our critical complex criticism is not absolute; it is provided at a historical moment and a socio-cultural location – and that matters. What are we to do about the embeddedness of the self in the research project? The answer is to rigorously study the construction of selfhood, the socio-cultural and political relations of the knower, in the process bringing our understanding of the knower back to her inseparable relationship with the known. Carspecken's critique of scientism profoundly helps us perform these tasks – currently so unappreciated if not feared by the sirens of scientism and the proponents of an insidious positivism.

Cultural location, for example, profoundly matters in this context. For example, how does the way a North American researcher from Charlottetown, Prince Edward Island views diversity differ from the perspective of an individual from the Sami peoples of northern Scandinavia? The difference of worldviews and ways of seeing and being of these two individuals can help us understand how divergent conceptual frameworks can change what we see about the world. Thus, we can see how important it is in cross-cultural research – and really any inquiry for that matter – for the researcher to listen carefully to her research subjects and position them as co-researchers operating as respected observers of the world. The power of difference, of alterity in these research situations becomes one of the greatest tools in the critical complex researcher's, the bricoleur's, and Carspecken's critical ethnographer's toolbox. It provides the researcher with not only a fresh view of the topic under study but also, of course, a unique look at her selfhood and the ways she sees the world. In this way educational researchers quickly come to see the limits of the methods of scientism and their ability to "explain everything."

A theory of everything could not be isolated, Carspecken maintains, from the restrictions imposed from the beginning by the multidimensional complexity of humanness, language, and everyday practice. In this context Phil asks if in such a scientistic theory, would we have to explain the detailed process of producing theories and the subjective role that human consciousness would play in such a process. Such efforts, of course, are undermined by the pesky realization that humans are concurrently observers of nature and entities that are observed. This subjective role involves the consciousness of the researcher, and consciousness simply cannot be seriously studied by scientific realists, crypto-positivists, or proponents of scientism. I agree with Carspecken – this presents scientific psychological and educational researchers with a serious problem. Indeed, it excludes them from a rigorous examination of most of the central questions of education.

In this context painted so adeptly by Carspecken, critical complex researchers understand both the possibilities and limits of research. While there is no limit as to where our research can take us, there are limitations around the ability of research simply to provide a true reflection of reality. The concept of rationality is used to cover up what we don't know about the world, about the moment in which we are living. Using reason and positivistic notions of universal, eternal truth, scientific reductionists place their faith in the findings of science. Critical complex researchers may see the same phenomenon that crypto-positivists observe, but criticalists have an extensive set of conceptual tools to discern the contexts and processes of which it is a part. With such knowledge they can begin to not only rethink the meaning(s) of the phenomenon in question but the uses to which such understandings can be put. Thus, their understanding of complexity undermines what they can say for *certain* about the phenomenon, but the same insights can enhance the possibilities of what can be done with the knowledge they produce about it.

At the heart of the crypto-positivism's/scientism's successful effort to undermine complexity is the notion of causal determinism. If we know the forces that are shaping a situation, then we can predict its future – if positivists know a student's I.Q., for example, then they can confidently predict how she will do in her academic future. As I have written elsewhere, numerous scientists in a variety of areas have argued over the last century that with just a little more time and research, we will no longer need to conduct any further inquiry into a phenomenon because we will know everything about it (a tacit theory of everything) – including its past, present, and future. Thus, reductionism triumphs in such an epistemological construction, as substance-based science claims a transcendent position in regard to the production of truth. Such reductionists are hell-bent on winning the race to certainty and in this context are contemptuous of the ambiguity produced by critical complexity. When it comes to human phenomena such as the mind, we begin to realize that there is nothing at this historical point we know of that is more complex. It takes great conceit to believe that we can know all about it and even place a number – an I.Q. of 118 – on its capacity to function. In a few years this will be viewed as a primitive form of psychological science comparable to nineteenth century phrenology.

The effort to overcome scientific reductionism's "know-it-allism" demands Phil's more rigorous insights into epistemology and ontology. And, of course, such views of knowledge and being-in-the-world necessitate new, more rigorous modes of research that are capable of attending to complexity. This, Carspecken knows, is easier said than done, as efforts to embrace the complexity of the lived world while in the process producing knowledge that is focused on the creativity and vibrancy of its interpretation and the pragmatic nature of its applicability to problem solving are profoundly difficult in rationalistic and reductionist educational institutions. When faculties/colleges of education are grounded on modes of instrumental/technical rationality – focused exclusively on "how" questions as opposed to "why" questions – then modes of scientism and crypto-positivism continue to flourish with all their reductionist and hegemonic inclinations. Innovative scholars such as Carspecken are relegated to the peripheries of educational research. We cannot at this perilous time in educational history and world history in general allow this to happen.

RADICAL LISTENING

Ken: Joe's comments on Greg Martin's, lisahunter's, and Peter McLaren's chapter in the Red Book contained an amazing piece on radical listening – a construct that was "so Joe"! One of Joe's many commendable attributes, a distinctive feature, was the way in which he listened attentively to what was being said by others. He had the capacity to listen for meaning without using the time to frame what his next turn of talk would be. He followed the train of talk and his initial contributions were focused on making sense and ascertaining the possibilities of what was being suggested. He was quick to see the affordances in others' ideas. Even though the chapter that the following introduction was written for is not read published in the second edition of the Handbook, the text that Joe prepared makes a substantial contribution to the literature and is included below.

Critical action research is one method of engaging in the difficult and often unrewarded task of "doing justice." When educators engage in such research they are confronting the various forms of oppression that hurt students and teachers all around the world. Critical action research allows teachers, students, and parents to confront the cruel practices of dominant power by taking part in a study of how they function – actions that are typically difficult for many to identify, as they operate incognito in the guise of validated educational practices. A key aspect of critical action research involves the notion of radical listening. Such a concept involves those engaged in the research listening to and learning from those who have been marginalized by diverse power blocs.
– White people to the non-white
– men to women
– the well-to-do to the poor
– heterosexuals to homosexuals
– colonizers to colonized
– Christians to people from other religious backgrounds

– able bodied people to individuals with disabilities

In this context radical listeners attend to the perspectives of the marginalized in a way that helps them understand the causes of and ways of ending oppression and suffering. While it is a mistake to ever romanticize (or exoticize) the perspectives of the marginalized, there are still many exciting secrets to be gained from subjugated knowledges that can change the lives of critical action researchers and the lives of the subjugated. How does one's positional superiority vis-à-vis power shape or misshape the consciousness of people from dominant locations in the web of power? How do certain forms of scientific and curriculum knowledge become engaged in the perpetuation of colonialism and marginalization?

The radical listening of critical action research places researchers from colonializing societies on a road to respecting and learning from diverse forms of knowledge. It helps marginalized people reassert the validity of their own data and gain more control over the research being conducted about them. Both of these goals resonate well with the critical complex attempt to learn from subjugated knowledges. Such learning is so important to the reconstruction of Western consciousness in a more just and humble manner, as well as in the effort of critical researchers to gain excluded levels of awareness, to appreciate the fissures and defects of positivist ways of seeing, and to reframe their view of self, other, and world. In such a praxiological context we are far more capable as critical complex researchers of reinventing the world in a way that attacks the causes of human suffering.

All critical participatory research explores the way the knower is implicated in what is known, the inseparability of the researcher from what is researched, and the "interested" nature of all knowledge produced. When positivists fail to appreciate the forces that shape the consciousness of the researcher, they are less able to appreciate the nature of how particular knowledge was created and how particular perspectives took shape. The process of their construction reveals so much about not only the quality but also the reason such knowledge came to exist in the first place. Thus, the positivist use of the term, objectivity, often hides many of the ideological, cultural, and colonial biases that are always present in the production of knowledge.

It is amazing on numerous levels that positivist researchers claim a god-like perspective on the world, as they are able to see all things from no particular point in time or space. Obviously, such an erasure of the positionality of the researcher is problematic. One of the first and most basic questions a critical action researcher must ask involves what are we to do about the researcher's embeddedness in the research process. While the answer to such a question is quite involved, the one thing that can be said succinctly at this juncture is that critical complexity does not accept the positivists' objectivist "solution" of simply ignoring it. In the crypto-positivist world in which we now operate, critical participatory action research comes across to many hegemonized scholars as a great mystery. If we – the positivist experts – have the methodology to produce "the truth" about an educational situation, why do we need the cooperation and participation of the "ignorant"? Such positivistic arrogance must be confronted and exposed for what it is.

Contesting positivist arrogance and the oppressive rituals such ways of thinking support, the authors maintain, demands research methods capable of critique. Such critique, unfortunately, is almost always met with mainstream retaliation. Henry Giroux recently reminded me in this context that critical scholars/researchers have been vilified and harassed in the field of education since critical pedagogy came into existence in the late 1970s and early 1980s. As I listened to Henry make this statement, I realized that many of us operating in the critical domain often become so accustomed to such a reality that we find it difficult to imagine a different situation. It simply becomes an expected part of our everyday lives. Yet, researchers working from critical standpoints know they must continue – they must keep on producing modes of critical action research that situate their studies in the matrix of dominant power blocs in ways that specify the way power mediates knowledge. In this way they are equipped to expose the ways that the pedagogical practices of everyday life are related to these larger political and ideological forces.

One of the great tragedies of twenty-first century life involves the realization that at the same time as we are coming to understand the unfathomable possibilities of human consciousness, dominant power works to regulate the lives of individuals in ways that are not in their interests. Of course, this is an intricately complex process, and power both wins and loses efforts to ensnare individuals in its disciplinary net. It is safe to say, however, that dominant power's operations work enough of the time for power wielders to continue to spend hundreds of billions of dollars to induce people to do things that are in opposition to everyone's and everything's well being. Power works best when no one knows what it's doing or that it's power at work. This is why it's so important to look behind the imperial drapes, make sense of what we see, and expose the mass media delusions crafted by the pimps who promote corporate greed and ideological indoctrination by disempowered teachers in standardized schools as good things.

Western power wielders came to understand in the eighteenth and nineteenth centuries that it was much more effective to develop systems of truth and discipline that would help people "regulate" themselves than to physically coerce them to obey the mandates of power. Internal regulation simply worked better than external coercion – it elicited less resentment and resistance. In this system of internal regulation, dominant power enters into the body where it shapes affect, attitudes, and interests in a way that resonates with the requirements of hegemonic power blocs. Such a thanocentric view of the individual as an object to be manipulated illustrates the ethical and ontological poverty of contemporary Western life – a way of life it is spreading around the planet at an alarming rate. Schools, of course, in this hegemonic struggle become primary battlefields for the hearts and minds of teachers and students.

The existence of these Western hegemonic regulatory systems makes it profoundly important that critical researchers view these frameworks from as many perspectives as possible – diverse cultural perspectives in particular. People from social and cultural backgrounds different than ourselves can usually see the implicit conceptual frameworks that shape our consciousness and activities better than we can. Critical complex researchers take advantage of this epistemological gift and seek out the perspectives of those who come from divergent places in the web of reality. Listening carefully to the perspectives of peoples from diverse cultural backgrounds can uncover assumptions we make in our research that changes us forever. Our ethnocentrism, cultural arrogance, racial and colonial privilege can be more clearly seen through the eyes and ears of individuals who have been victimized by such orientations.

Western epistemologies and research methods see such a tiny dimension of what is occurring in the world. It's as if traditional positivist epistemology relied on the measurements of a thermometer to tell us about the nature of the physical world or I.Q. to reveal the workings of the mind. Compared to what is possible as we gain new insights from diverse and yet unimagined social, cultural, and psychological locales, the positivist reality that grounds the "commonsense" of contemporary Western life is rather thin and denuded. When we add to this the aforementioned arrogance of many positivists that leads them to believe that other ways of seeing and producing knowledge are inferior and even primitive in relation to mainstream Western science, the problem intensifies. From the perspective of many non-Westerners, the positivistic correspondence epistemology produces not a "realistic" mirror image of reality but more a funhouse mirror with bizarrely and often humorously distorted images.

As I radically listened to members of the Rosebud Sioux Tribe (the Sicangu People) of South Dakota discuss their encounters with many mainstream Western anthropologists, I was (and still am) fascinated by the way they had suffered for generations from the bizarre pictures painted of them in this scholarly context. I also gained great insight, as tribal members with great humor told stories of Western anthropological misconceptions of them. "The Sioux are a taciturn and humorless people," the anthropologists wrote. "Obviously," several members of the tribe told me, "they didn't get that we were making fun of them the whole time they were studying us." A positivist correspondence epistemology? No, more an epistemological funhouse mirror. A key aspect of becoming a good researcher, not to mention a critical action researcher, involves understanding these dynamics. It involves freeing ourselves from the umbilical relation to dominant power and its misleading epistemologies. Although positivists vehemently deny the importance of such dynamics, we believe they are central to the research process – especially, of course, if we value social justice and the recognition of oppression.

Consider positivistic pronouncements about the dismissal of the role of the researcher, the view of human input into research as a contamination of the process of inquiry in light of these ideas. If the correct methodological steps are followed, the researcher is simply not a part of the research process. The only role for the researcher is "troll at the bridge," the one who simply makes sure the proper steps are followed. In the positivistic mind-set the cultural location of the observer is irrelevant, for if we just follow the 39 steps faithfully (rigorously) we will all see the same reality. Even though positivists often speak loudly about the ethics of research, the idea of valuing the unique and powerful insights of those people they research and treating subjects as co-researchers is viewed as an assault on the expertise of the "trained researcher." It is the ethical and ideological duty of the critical complex researcher to assess the designs and methodologies of mainstream research in light of the power structures and the insidious ways such frameworks shape the knowledge produced in these circumstances. This is the study of the politics of knowledge, the analysis of how power asymmetries shape the production and reception of all knowledge that is produced as well as how it is used in the world.

This doesn't even get into the more traditional domain of knowledge politics that includes the important investigation of how research priorities and the ideological interests of funding agencies can affect what issues are studied and which ones are not. In a recent conversation with Peter McLaren, he told me he was very upset about his lack of funded research. Of course, I understand his frustration and as I told him, we produce knowledge that scares away the main funding agencies. Scholars who have operated in think tanks or higher education have all heard the phrase, "researchers have to follow the money." Sometimes the researchers who live by this mantra end up in bed with some pretty unsavory operators with less than pristine motives.

As they awaken on the "morning after," some (not all) of these researchers begin to understand this dimension of the power-knowledge relationship – that power is not only a restrictive but also a productive force that constructs ways of seeing and being. Positivists and their covert operatives in contemporary domain – the crypto-positivists – need to be seen more often as the "natives under study." In this context they can read about the ways they are perceived by diverse others who may help awake them from their dominant Western cultural trance. At this juncture they can begin to understand the social construction of their own selfhood and the ways they have been hegemonized by the dominant politics of knowledge and the ideologies of dominant power.

KENNETH TOBIN AND SHIRLEY R. STEINBERG

FOREWORD TO SECOND EDITION

Contributing to an Art of Educational Research

From the moment we envisioned *Doing Educational Research* we embraced the idea of bricolage, that educational research and practice could benefit from the use of diverse methodologies and associated methods. Our standpoint was polysemic and we valued difference as a resource for learning. In fact, we anticipated that different methodologies would provide different lenses into social lives, affording insights into diverse framings of what was happening and why it was happening. Also we were acutely aware that any set of frameworks would illuminate social life in particular ways, affording certain insights and possibilities while obscuring others. A tacit understanding we shared, as editors and scholars, was that no perspective and its associated framework would provide a unique view of truth. Furthermore, we did not insist that methodologies used in research needed to be commensurable. Indeed, polysemia acknowledged the desirability of going beyond tolerating difference or merely understanding others' standpoints. On the contrary, we regarded difference as a resource for creating an expansive system of knowing education.

In this second edition of *Doing Educational Research* we move further along the pathways of understanding and expanding the logics of educational research. The 21 chapters of the book do not present techniques for researchers, but instead delve into systems of logic that underpin what we do and can do in educational research. As a set, the Handbook created in this second edition eschews oversimplified categorical ways of teaching and learning educational research – as methods courses such as quantitative, qualitative, and mixed methods. Instead, we argue for thoughtful, emergent forms of inquiry that are nuanced, caring, and aware of the transcendent nature of what we learn, what we seek to know, and what we claim to know.

In the spirit of contributing to an art of educational research we offer the second edition of *Doing Educational Research*, as a contribution to an ongoing conversation that precedes our lives and careers as educational researchers – a conversation that will continue for as long as humanity seeks to understand, through research, what we know and can do. It is a privilege to participate in this conversation and we invite readers to join us in a project we regard as critical and expansive.

Ken: Following the death of Joe Kincheloe I decided to publish an article that he and I co-authored in *Cultural Studies of Science Education,* as an acknowledgement of Joe's contributions to the sociocultural turn in science education. When Wolff-Michael Roth and I considered proposing to create a new science education journal, Joe supported the idea with enthusiasm. As it happened, the article, concerning the exaggerated death of positivism, was catalyzed by a review of the first edition of *Doing Educational Research*. Among other points of critique, the book reviewers adopted a standpoint that the anti-positivist tenor of *Doing Educational Research* was inappropriate and biased. In contrast, we felt strongly that mainstream wisdom in educational research and policy was saturated by a common sense that embraced positivism. We referred to this as cryptopositivism.

When Shirley Steinberg and I agreed to edit a second edition of *Doing Educational Research*, affectionately referred to as the Red Book, we obtained permission to republish "The exaggerated death of positivism" as a chapter in the revised edition. In the chapter we argue that approaches to research in the social sciences often embrace schema that are consistent with positivism, even though it is widely held that positivism is discredited and essentially dead. Accordingly, many of the methods used in present day scholarship are supported by tenets of positivism, and are sources of hegemony. We exhort researchers to employ reflexive methods to identify the epistemologies, ontologies and axiologies that are salient in their scholarship and, when necessary, transform practices such that forms of oppression associated with crypto-positivism are identified and extinguished.

It is now more than eight years since the first edition of the Red Book was published. Joe and Ken felt strongly that there ought to be a graduate level educational research publication that explored in depth the logics of inquiry. The book we envisioned would present a diverse range of methodologies and associated methods. We felt it important to provide alternatives to positivism and highlight their affordances. After a few years we were well pleased with the book and had used it in a variety of our classes. We felt that it was time for a second edition, editing some chapters, deleting some, and adding others. It was not that any of the deleted chapters were in any way inappropriate for the Red Book. We felt that already there were strong reasons to feature the scholarship of a new breed of scholars who were working beyond the boundaries of positivism and might stimulate others to innovate and create fresh, bold visions through educational research. Hence in the second edition of *Doing Educational Research*, we revised 11 chapters and added 10 new chapters (including the exaggerated death). In the remainder of this Foreword to the Second Edition, we include abstracts written by the new chapter authors to orientate readers to what follows.

Christina Siry, from the University of Luxembourg, draws on the UN Convention on the Rights of Child, which outlines children's right to have their views taken seriously on matters that affect them. Chapter 7 examines approaches to participatory research with children. Several different methods are explored through an overview of research in the field of education, including interviews, visual representations, and pedagogical documentation. The necessity of dialogue is elaborated through a discussion of the ethics of working towards multiple perspectives in participatory work with children, and a central argument put forward involves the value of creating knowledge for action.

In chapter 8 Tricia Kress (University of Massachusetts, Boston), uses critical pedagogy and her own research about urban high school youth in the Boston region of the USA, who participated in an after school research club, as lenses to provoke questions about the epistemological, ontological and axiological dimensions of educational research. Kress interrogates the roots of Western, positivist thought underlying typical conceptions of research vis-à-vis concepts such as subject-object relationships, proximity, dialogue, conscientização, and praxis. Tricia examines the relationships between knowledge and power, the researcher's self in relation to those he or she researches, the role of the body and lived experience in research, and how researchers' values are revealed through the ways in which they choose to work with minoritized youth.

Gene Fellner (College of Staten Island, New York) is a professional artist and literacy educator. Gene notes that the official lenses through which students are assessed are often overly narrow, privileging quantitative evaluations of student abilities. Too frequently, these lenses exclude the voices of students themselves and data that though not quantifiable might contradict the statistical measures highlighted in official school transcripts. In chapter 9 Fellner applies multilectics to a study of Justin, an underperforming seventh grader in an underperforming school. In so doing he illuminates many of Justin's strengths, which are not visible in the transcripts that represent him. Multilectics joins the concept of Marxist-Hegelian dialectics with the concept of multiplicity – multiplicity of voices (polyphony), meanings (polysemy), lenses, levels of observation (macro, meso and micro), and modes of communication (verbal and non verbal).

Carolyne Ali-Khan, presently at the University of North Florida, examines the ins and outs of autoethnography in chapter 14. Carolyne explains how and why autoethnography is important to educational research. She positions autoethnography as a liberating rather than domesticating pedagogy. In the chapter she examines the aims and affordances of autoethnography, discusses ways it has been used, and provides examples of a variety of different types of autoethnographies. Carolyne delves into questions about autoethnography as a research method and teaching tool and in a second section she provides a thematically organized annotated bibliography of a variety of autoethnographic work.

In chapter 15 Peter Waldman provides a gripping impressionist tale of an open meeting of Alcoholics Anonymous (AA) using his own voice as an imagined first-person-present of an addicted, angst-ridden narrator. He provides an imagined present because the tale is about the past and is recalled through memories and interpretations of texts. The identity conflict he experiences during an AA meeting is a paradoxical position of marginalization within an already marginalized group. This dramatized positionality is the engine that propels the narrative forward more so than a plotted beginning, middle and end, which is the narrative logic of the life story in AA, and more so than the meeting itinerary which is arbitrary for the reader unfamiliar with AA. There is another narrator's voice, too, another first person 'me' mingling with Peter's addicted past that is present in the text: a present/future self, an educational researcher with a small pile of notions requiring exegesis and a decades long AA member for a research participant.

Malgorzata Powietrzynska, a recent graduate from the Graduate Center of CUNY, describes the logics of her mindfulness-focused research against a backdrop of the current state of the field in the educational setting. In chapter 16 Malgorzata addresses the ongoing debate over which methodological paradigms are appropriate for conducting studies involving contemplative states. Development and enactment of interventions is presented as vital to conducting authentic inquiry. She discusses in depth two mindfulness-based interventions – breathing meditation and heuristics – and presents a case study to illustrate the workings of the two interventions. Ethical issues that may arise in mindfulness-based research are also considered.

Marissa Bellino, the author of chapter 17 (currently a doctoral student in urban education from the Graduate Center of CUNY), describes how photovoice evolved in her environmental science classroom from a research method to a methodology. She discusses her emerging critical identity and shares how it mapped onto the photovoice process during two years, addressing specifically her shifts in thinking about the nature of research. Included are some of the participatory methods utilized in conjunction with photovoice as a means of exploring young people's senses of place. Data from a second year of photovoice are explored with a focus on the multiple ways data were utilized by students to generate research topics, narratives, and critical presentations about their urban environment. Marissa concludes by addressing implications of using photovoice in reframing environmental education as more local and relevant to the lives of young people and expansive ways to think about research.

Mark Vicars, from Melbourne, Australia, sets out to 'trouble' how research on teaching and learning gets done. In chapter 18 he draws on experiences of re/presenting diversity and divergence in educational studies; articulating a performative and artful praxis as a productive site of and for re/presenting resistance(s) to pedagogies of the normal. Troubling method remains a risky endeavor within the academy. Over the last decade, research funding requirements and rubrics have framed and increasingly narrowed possibilities for methodological diversity and discussion in educational research. Mark shows how the rigorous rising of method has rewarded normative method/ological 'dispositions, positions and position-takings …' (Luke and Carrington 2002, p. 2) and by un/doing method one can easily become haunted by the tensions of transgression.

In the final chapter of *Doing Educational Research*, Stanford researchers Cheryl Holzmeyer and John Willinsky argue that the publication of the National Academy of Sciences' report *Scientific Research in Education* (2002) catalyzed a spectrum of critical commentary on the meanings of "scientific" research, among education scholars and beyond. Simultaneously, new online academic publication infrastructures and the open access movement suggested possibilities for more direct public engagement with education research. However, these possibilities remained inextricable from fraught epistemological and ethical questions about the terms of engagement with research, in academia and beyond. Since then, broader "open science" initiatives have emerged, enabled by the Internet and digital platforms. Though framed in capacious and universal terms, many open science initiatives are devoted to epistemological projects that embody narrow, particular, positivist approaches to "scientific" and "evidence-based" research – to the exclusion or marginalization of many other kinds of evidence and knowledge. These include qualitative, interpretive and community-based participatory research, as well as different kinds of local knowledge. This chapter argues that research dissemination practices, including online publication infrastructures and "open science" initiatives, are constituted together with knowledge hierarchies. "Open science" initiatives are simultaneously technical *and social*; they are inevitably value-laden, in ways that do not serve all types of scholarship equally. This point underscores the need to foster critical interventions and community-based collaborations on behalf of public, democratic scholarship underpinned by multiple social epistemologies, alongside publishing and beyond new information technology infrastructures.

REFERENCES

Luke, A., & Carrington, V. (2002). Globalisation, literacy curriculum practice. In R. Fisher, M. Lewis, & G. Brooks (Eds.), *Raising standards in literacy* (pp. 231-50). London: Routledge.

Shavelson, R. J., & Towne, L. (Eds.). (2002). *Scientific research in education*. Washington, DC: National Academy Press.

I. INTRODUCTION

JOE L. KINCHELOE AND KENNETH TOBIN

1. DOING EDUCATIONAL RESEARCH IN A COMPLEX WORLD

The last half of the first decade of the twenty-first century is a strange time for educators. Many of the gains many of us thought we had made twenty years ago are under assault and many of the epistemological fights for the benefits of multiple ways of doing educational research in which we were forced to engage in the 1980s are breaking out again. The right-wing recovery movement – a reeducation of the public to accept Eurocentric and often male ways of both being and seeing – has shaped everything from the corporatization of the public space, the social positioning of poor people and people of color, the politics of public knowledge to the ways we conceptualize and validate research about education.

Indeed, it is a strange and challenging time. It is in such a Zeitgeist that we have put together *Doing Educational Research*. After having lived through this last 25 years, we have come to believe that a book dealing with diverse, innovative, challenging, and rigorous ways of conducting educational research that is both thought-provoking and practical is sorely needed. To accomplish this task, we have brought together some of the most innovative minds in contemporary educational research. We believe that the combined efforts of these scholars have produced a unique and highly usable text that will work to engage new generations of scholars while reinvigorating mature researchers in the complications and vagaries of doing educational research.

We find educational research intrinsically exciting and even mysterious. No matter how much the mavens of evidence-based inquiry in right-wing movements may insist that there is one right way to produce educational research, we are convinced of the power of multiple ways of seeing the world – the educational world in particular.

We believe that there are yet unexplored domains of human consciousness, cognition, teaching and learning. While we make no claim that we have achieved some transcendent way of approaching knowledge – not by a long shot – we do believe that some of the ideas and concepts explored here may lead the wisest among us to new domains of human thinking, exploring, being, and doing.

A STARTING POINT FOR RECONCEPTUALIZING EDUCATIONAL RESEARCH

We construct *Doing Educational Research*, thus, as a starting point for something much greater than what is produced here. In the finest critical tradition the authors writing here initiate an exploration of what could be: new exciting ways of understanding educational phenomena, being students of the world, and changing those aspects of education that bring about injustice, pain, and suffering. Indeed, we believe in the power of the ideas the authors of this book delineate in their chapters, and in this context, we sense we are still in the early stages of a journey that will eventually change the basic ways we conceptualize both the act of knowledge production and the process of teaching and learning.

Employing these diverse ways of seeing and making meaning delineated in the following chapters, educational researchers begin to discern interconnections between ideas, physical objects, political decisions, social circumstances, and the teaching and learning processes that have been previously ignored. A complex critical mode of educational research is aware of many different perspectives, the vantage points of diverse disciplines of knowledge (e.g., history, philosophy, economics, psychology, literary criticism, sociology, etc.) and transdisciplinary ways of seeing such as cultural studies. Educational researchers informed by these multiple perspectives understand relations between values and different interpretations of the world in general and education in particular. They understand the way one's location in the world or position in the web of reality (e.g., one's race, class, gender, sexuality, religion, ideology, epistemology, etc.) helps shape how one sees self and world. Educational researchers who do not understand these dynamics of positionality (the way one is situated in the world) and their impact on the questions we ask of education, schooling, politics, etc. are babes in the research woods. Their claims of objectivity fall on fallow ground.

The researchers who have written the following chapters understand these issues and work to follow them to new research spaces and intellectual places. With this in mind we want our readers to accompany our authors on these journeys. Indeed, we want them to recognize and understand the benefits of diverse ways of thinking and understanding the world and the cosmos of education. While we deeply respect those who have come before us and have helped us get where we are, we are ambitious – we want to go farther into the epistemological and ontological fog. While important benefits have historically come from educational research, past practice in the domain and the contemporary regressive efforts to reclaim the worst of such ways of researching are insufficient to the task of improving education.

Not only is there more to learn, more to be addressed, more to do, contemporary educational researchers must have the skill and will to fend off the regressive purveyors of one-truth, monological, and reductionistic ways of viewing education. In this context the researchers who crafted this book provide alternatives to the arrogance of positivist reductionism with a radical humility, a fallibilism, an awareness of the complexity of our task. We are aware of how little we know about the immensity of it all, but we push on. We view ourselves and our ways of seeing in the light of new horizons and new contexts, in the process recognizing previously unnoticed connections. Such connections alert us to new dimensions of what we are capable of engaging – the ones we previously missed. Critical, yet humble, we push for something better.

BEYOND HYPERRATIONALITY: INTO A NEW DOMAIN OF CRITICALITY AND COMPLEXITY

Obviously, one of our most important concerns in this volume is to avoid the surge of hyperrationality and the instrumental rationality that characterizes it. Such a rationality involves an obsession with means rather than ends, method, procedure, and efficiency rather than an effort to understand the world so we can better serve the needs of human beings. As this hyperrationality limits questions to "how to" rather than "why should," we are reminded of the meticulous Nazi medical researcher obsessed with recording and analyzing the "cephalic index" (the shape of one's head) of those entering Hitler's death camps while ignoring the moral implications of genocide. Concurrently, we understand that resistance to such hyperrationalism does not necessitate the embrace of an irrationality characterized by a nihilism and relativism that offer no hope for scholarly growth or ethical action. In *Doing Educational Research* we avoid these untenable extremes and search for new and more compelling modes of reason – in other words, new forms of knowledge production that allow us to understand more so that we can engage in empowered action for our individual and social good.

As you read the following chapters, one begins to understand that all of the authors in this volume are searching for something better, are attempting to move into a new domain of educational research. All of them are concerned with the role of the self in research, the role of relationship(s) and multiple contexts in understanding pedagogical phenomena. With these concerns at the front burner of our consciousness, we attempt to blaze new trails into the epistemological (the branch of philosophy that deals with knowledge) and ontological domains (the branch of philosophy that deals with the nature of being in the world). In the epistemological domain we begin to realize that knowledge is stripped of its meaning when it stands alone. This holds profound implications in education and research because more positivistic forms of educational science have studied the world in a way that isolates the object of study, abstracts it from the contexts and interrelationships that give it meaning. Thus, to be a critical researcher that takes the complexity of the lived world into account, we have to study the world "in context." All of the authors here agree that we have to search for the interrelationships and contexts that give knowledge meaning while avoiding reliance upon decontextualized study.

Operating in the ontological realm educational researchers understand that to be in the world is to operate in context, in relation to other entities. Western Cartesian (coming from the tradition of the scientific method delineated by Rene Descartes in the 1600s) science has traditionally seen the basic building blocks of the universe as things-in-themselves. What much recent research in physics, biology, social science, the humanities, and cognitive science has posited involves the idea that relationships not things-in-themselves are the most basic properties of things in the world. In the ontological realm this would include human beings themselves. To *be* in the world is to be in relationship. People are not abstract individuals who live as fragments, in isolation from one another.

Humans come to be who they are and change who they are as a result of their interrelationships, their connections to the social sphere. They learn to think and talk via the socially constructed languages, deport themselves via cultural norms in their communities, and take care of themselves by imitating significant others in their immediate environment. Race, class, gender, sexual, religious, geographical, and place affiliations exert powerful influences on how they see themselves and their relation to the world. To be human is to be in relation to .... And, importantly, for those engaging in educational research, we understand that to be human is to possess the power to change, to be smarter than we now are, to engage in praxis – transformative action informed by the insights gained from our inquiry.

As most of us know by now, many observers have come to the conclusion that the simplicity of Cartesian rationalism and mainstream forms of educational knowledge production has not met our needs. This is the realization that is being challenged by those who would attempt to recover the infallibility of Western traditions. The web of reality is composed of too many variables to be taken into account and controlled. Scientist Illya Prigogene (Prigogene and Stengers 1984) labels this multitude of variables, "extraneous perturbations," meaning that one extraneous variable in an educational experiment can produce an expanding, exponential effect. So-called inconsequential entities can have a profound effect in a complex nonlinear universe. The shape of the physical and social world depends on the smallest part. The part, in a sense, is the whole, for via the action of any particular part, the whole in the form of transformative change may be seen. To exclude such considerations is to miss the nature of the interactions that constitute reality. The development of a reconceptualization of educational research does not mean that we simplistically reject all empirical science. It does mean, however, that we conceive of such scientific ways of seeing as one perspective in the complex web we refer to as reality.

ACCOUNTING FOR THE COMPLEXITY OF THE EDUCATIONAL COSMOS

All of the authors of *Doing Educational Research* attempt in their own way to account for this complexity and develop ways of seeing and being that avoid reductionism. As educational research comes to recognize the complexity of the lived world with its maze of uncontrollable variables, irrationality, non-linearity, and unpredictable interaction of wholes and parts, they begin to also see the interpretative dimension of reality. Educators have been "scammed" by a science that offers a monological process of making sense of the world. Critical researchers who appreciate the depth of this complexity maintain that we must possess and be able to deploy multiple methods of producing knowledge of the world. I (Joe Kincheloe) – borrowing from Norman Denzin and Yvonna Lincoln, Claude Levi-Strauss and Jacques Derrida – have referred to this elsewhere as the bricolage (Kincheloe 2001, 2005; Kincheloe and Berry 2004). Kathleen Berry and Shirley Steinberg extend our understanding of the bricolage in their chapters in this volume.

Such methods provide us diverse perspectives on similar events and alert us to various relationships between events. In this complex context we understand that even when we use diverse methods to produce multiple perspectives on the world, different observers will produce different interpretations of what they perceive. Given different values, different ideologies, and different positions in the web of reality, different individuals will interpret what is happening differently. We never stand alone in the world, especially when we produce knowledge. We are connected and constantly affected by such connections in every step of the research act. Understanding these aspects of the connections between the knower and the known modifies the very way we approach knowledge, research design, research method, and interpretation.

When inquiry is conceptualized as a complex process we begin to understand that research is not something employed by solitary negotiators operating on their own. Educational researchers use language developed by others, live in specific contexts with particular ways of being and ways of thinking about thinking, have access to some knowledges and not others, and live and operate in a circumstance shaped by particular dominant ideological perspectives. In its effort to deal with previously neglected complexity, the view of research offered here appreciates the need to understand these contextual factors and account for them. Connected, critical researchers sensitive to the complexity of the lived world are not isolated individuals but people who understand the nature of their socio-cultural context as well as their overt and occluded relationships with others. Without such understandings of their own contextual embeddedness, individuals are not capable of understanding from where the prejudices and predispositions they bring to the research act originate. Any educational research that attempts to deal with the complexity of the lived world must address these contextual dynamics.

The editors and authors of *Doing Educational Research* maintain that these, social, philosophical, political and pedagogical theoretical knowledges are essential to the development of a rigorous and complex mode of educational research capable of lifting us to a new intellectual, agency-enhancing, action-based domain. In the social theoretical domain, for example, we might ask how does the existence of socio-economic inequality along the axes of race, class, gender, sexuality, physical ability, religion, and language influence the way we approach research. What happens to our research when we bring an understanding of power and justice to our analytical table? What is the effect of social theoretical insight on the subjectivity and context-dependency of knowledge production? Might, for example, the knowledge emerging here help shape the way we answer questions about the curriculum? About school purpose? About strategies for reform? About the control of knowledge? About the disturbing covert political agendas that motivate the research and research policies of particular political and educational leaders?

So-called evidence-based research and hyperrationalistic modes of positivist inquiry do not help us answer such questions. How does evidence-based research help us answer questions, about the purpose of schools? Social theory viewed in relation to pedagogical theory in this context profoundly enhances the ability of educators as critical thinkers to evaluate the worth of particular educational purposes, public knowledge policies, articulations of curriculum, and evaluation practices. Indeed, as you read the various chapters of *Doing Educational Research*, it becomes increasingly obvious the importance each of the authors places on such social theoretical insights. The editors and authors believe that these theoretical modes help educational researchers – as well as teachers and students – escape the well regulated and administered world that unbridled rationalism works to construct. Critical, connected researchers sensitive to the complexity of socio-educational reality use these theoretical tools to sidestep new models of social control that put a chokehold on individual and social freedom. They use these tools to enhance their own and other individuals' agency.

As we engage in research to enhance our agency to fight the power of oppression in its contemporary hydra-headed forms, the researchers operating here draw upon a critical complex theory of epistemology to provide insight into the nature of pedagogical knowledge. Rejecting hyperrationalistic notions that there is a monolithic knowable world explained by positivist science, an epistemology of complexity views the cosmos as a human construction – a social creation. The world is "officially" what dominant groups of humans perceive it to be. This complicates our notion of theory. Positivistic/rationalistic theories were simple to the extent that they claimed truth-value on the basis of how they corresponded to *true* reality. More complex, counter-positivistic theories study the various philosophical and social groundings of diverse theories, learn from them, and understand the social construction of them all. In the theoretical speculations grounding our research, we take this understanding of social construction and add the critical theoretical, hermeneutical, feminist, and fallibilist dimensions. Our pluralistic and multiperspectival orientation is omnipresent, as we seek benefits from a variety of social, cultural, philosophical, and theoretical positions.

In other work I (Joe Kincheloe) have used the term critical constructivism (2005) to denote my epistemological perspective and postformalism (Kincheloe and Steinberg 1993) to denote my cognitive theoretical orientation. A short description of critical constructivism might be helpful at this point to ground the theoretical maneuvers operating in this reconceptualization of critical thinking. An epistemology of constructivism has maintained that nothing represents a neutral perspective, in the process shaking the epistemological foundations of modernist Cartesian grand narratives. Indeed, no truly objective way of seeing exists. Nothing exists before consciousness shapes it into something we can perceive.

What appears as objective reality is merely what our mind constructs, what we are accustomed to seeing. The knowledge that the world yields has to be interpreted by men and women who are part of that world. Whether we are attempting to understand the music of West Africa, the art of Marcel Duchamp, the social theory of Max Horkheimer, the epistles on indigenous knowledge of George Dei, the curriculum theory of William Pinar, or the insights into hermeneutics of David Jardine, the constructivist principle tacitly remains. For example, most analysts don't realize that the theory of perspective developed by fifteenth-century artists constituted a scientific convention. It was simply one way of portraying space and held no *absolute* validity. Thus, the structures and phenomena we observe in the physical world are nothing more than creations of our measuring and categorizing mind.

A critical constructivist epistemology forces educational researchers to ask:
− Does much of the research conducted in the field of education simply reflect the context, values, and assumptions of researchers?
− In light of such constructions, what is really meant by the construct objectivity?
− By what processes are our constructions of the world shaped?
− Are our psychosocial dispositions beyond our conscious control?
− Do we simply surrender our perceptions to the determinations of our environment, and our social, cultural context?
− What does this process of construction have to do with the education of pedagogical researchers

DIVERSITY AND EDUCATIONAL RESEARCH:
THE POWER OF CONTEXTUALIZATION

Researchers who understand complexity understand why we ask these questions; they understand that knowledge producers, teachers, and students perceive the world from a center located within themselves, shaped by the social and cultural context in which they operate, and framed by languages that contain within them tacit views of the world. As they dig deeper into the contexts surrounding the construction of self and the lived world of education broadly defined as well as schooling, research sensitive to complexity find that students from different racial, ethnic, and class locations will relate to education in different ways. They learn from their studies that if students who fall far from the middle class, white, English speaking mainstream are not provided assistance by insightful teachers, they will often become the victims of decontextualized ways of producing knowledge about education. Critical researchers aware of these complex dynamics understand that such students will not fail because of some inability or lack of intelligence but because of a set of forces unleashed by their relation to what is often labeled the "common culture." Indeed, we learn that the more educators use the term, common culture, in an unexamined way, the more those students who fall outside of its boundaries will fail.

Researchers who understand this contextual complexity appreciate the notion that Western culture and Western colonized cultures do not present a homogeneous way of life but a domain of difference shaped by unequal power relations. They understand that they must act on an appreciation of the way these differences shape people's relationships to various institutions. If everyone is seen as a part of some narrow articulation of a common culture, then those who don't fit the mainstream criteria will find themselves looking into the society's institution as unworthy outsiders. Critical complex researchers work to understand these important social tendencies, make sure that steps are taken to include everyone in a high quality education, and avoid the deficitism that emerges when such ways of seeing are disregarded.

The way these factors play out in the everyday life of school is multidimensional, complex, and always significant. When classroom instruction is driven by technical standards with their fragmented factoids, the same pedagogical actions take place repeatedly without regard for who succeeds and who fails – in particular, what social groups succeed or fail over time. A creative way of merely delivering content, no matter how ingenious it may be, still works to produce much the same results as long as the epistemological assumptions are the same. Thus, to avoid falling into these age-old traps, researchers must help educational leaders, politicians, and teachers understand both the social context that shapes learners and the epistemological context that molds the way knowledge is viewed and thus educational goals are forged in the classroom. Such contextual awarenesses provide teachers with a monitoring system that allows them a cognizance of the multidimensional effects of their pedagogy.

The ability to employ contextualization in the pursuit of multiple perspectives is an important skill promoted by the researchers the editors and authors of *Doing Educational Research*. As researchers begin to discern the multiple perspectives that always surround any topic, they examine such viewpoints in relation to one another. The insights derived from such an activity lead directly to new ways of seeing and appreciating the complexity of the cosmos. In this context we believe that our approaches to research are particularly important in this disturbing era where standardized curricula are being implemented in numerous national and local educational systems.

When such policies are pursued – on the basis of reductionistic, decontextualized, epistemologically naïve research – the ability of teachers to develop pedagogies for their unique students is subverted. In such decontextualized situations teachers are disempowered – teaching itself is deprofessionalized. The prerogative of master teachers to act on their knowledge of and participation in critical and complex research in a way that accounts for the multiple contexts of schooling and its students is undermined. Their capacity to study the contexts in which knowledge is produced and validated is subverted. In such simplified standards-based, test-driven classrooms, it doesn't matter who students are or what their specific needs may be – the curriculum has already been mandated on the basis of pseudo-rigorous research. The views of research presented in this volume can help researchers, teachers, and other individuals begin to free us from this ever-worsening pedagogical/epistemological crisis.

In this contemporary quagmire of regressive knowledge production, teaching and learning are becoming less immediate, less connected to the conditions of the community, less involved with what motivates students, less concerned with moral and ethical issues in the life of the school, less connected with other bodies of knowledge produced in different situations, less aware of the ideological motivations that drive educational and political leaders. Moreover, the rationalistic policies emerging from this decontextualized and misleading research about education remove schooling even further from the socio-economic and cultural changes surrounding it. As the capital driven, global information society changes the nature of jobs and the tools required for them – not to mention the need for new citizenship skills in a new transnational knowledge order – teachers and students drift along in low-level memory work far removed from the commerce of everyday life. The educational researchers writing in *Doing Educational Research* understand the context of socio-economic, political, and cultural change, so that teachers and students can keep ahead of it and help direct it in positive, democratic, and just ways.

Educational reforms based on decontextualized, rationalistic research remove teachers and students from an understanding of the compelling intellectual and political issues of the day. This is a fatal pedagogical mistake as it sets up a dichotomy between school and the "real world." Such a division will always undermine motivation, as teachers and students come to see the mandated activities of school as trivial and irrelevant. Critical complex researchers understand that to be able to integrate these understandings into their pedagogies, all educators must appreciate the way the world has changed in the last few decades. The rate of socio-economic, political, and cultural change has accelerated and in this process identities are no longer as stable as individuals are bombarded with information to the point of incomprehensibility. Traditional forms of problem solving where variables are limited and are assumed to act in predictable ways are less useful in an era marked by the complexity of multiple causality and as many have termed it, chaos. With globalization and new forms of information production and communication individuals in various fields have been confronted with more ill structured and divergent problems, cultural misunderstandings and value conflicts, and problems of power inequities. It is apparent that rigorous educational research would include an understanding of this new context and the forms of knowledge, skills, and cognitive abilities needed to deal with it successfully.

Critical research aware of the complexity of these new contexts understand that even the era of images and pictorial representations ushered in by television has never been adequately addressed – if addressed at all – by mainstream educational research and integrated into schooling. Media literacy, a set of skills so central to citizenship and an understanding of the contemporary world, is provided little respect in the mainstream educational knowledge climate of the last half of the first decade of the twenty-first century. When such imagery is not integrated with hypertext and cyberspace schools fall even further behind cultural and informational change. Those students who are conversant with such dynamics learn about them on their non-school time. While their insights and abilities often border on genius, there are still many aspects of the contemporary techno-electronic landscape that are missed by such students.

Nevertheless, the technological abilities obtained by such students exacerbates the gulf between the haves and have nots in alarming ways. Technical rationalistic educational policies that emphasize memorization of data are devised as if we are still living in an oral culture. The cognitive and pedagogical processes required by such decontextualized policies hearken back to medieval schooling where students memorized texts because there was so little literature in print. The editors and authors of *Doing Educational Research* understand both the importance of these new developments in communications and the necessity of devising new methods of researching their complex roles in the contemporary education and schooling.

In the context of cyberspace we possess less and less knowledge of the cultural location, the human contributions, the socio-political and economic interests that shape information. In those few classrooms where students are asked who produced the data they downloaded off the Internet the night before, they are often at a loss to answer such a query. They have never considered such a question or its multi-dimensional implications. Information in such situations has lost its borders, it moves and flows in the non-linear and instantaneous ways that human thought operates. Traditional forms of knowledge as it is researched in reductionistic designs and as it is organized in books and official interpretations are undermined in this new context. A subversive element implicitly operates that challenges the informational status quo but at the same time allows power wielders who control informational pipelines to covertly promote data that serves their economic, social, and political interests. Obviously, such a dangerous reality demands new forms of knowledge work and educational inquiry. In an era where the power of economic institutions – especially in relation to control of information – has risen to unprecedented heights the development of our ability to delineate the hidden interests of the knowledge cyber-technology provides us so abundantly is crucial to the future of democratic education. The need for innovative and rigorous forms of educational research has never been greater.

EDUCATION RESEARCH AS COURSE REQUIREMENTS

Traditionally graduate studies have involved research and were regarded as research degrees. Indeed, when I (Ken) was involved in higher education in Australia, advanced degrees that involved coursework (such as honors and masters degrees) were regarded as inferior to those that were research-only degrees. Of course many students who started out on research-only degrees floundered at the beginning, especially if they were not connected to a research group to provide scaffolding associated with how to do and learn from research, what to read, and how to present what you learn from research. Research groups also provided for participation in various forms of peer review and dissemination at brown bag seminars and more formal colloquia. In the sciences research groups have a long history that continues to the present time. In contrast, this was not such a tradition in education where individual researchers often worked independently throughout their career. Perhaps in education it was easier to see a rationale for two trends that have profound impacts on graduate degrees in education – the mergence of coursework as a partial fulfillment of degree requirements and the creation of methods courses designed to teach the foundations of educational research.

In particular circumstances both of these trends make sense – especially if degree candidates cannot participate conveniently in appropriate research groups. However, as is often the case with institutionalization of such trends, rules are created to specify the authorized pathways for obtaining a degree and standards come to be defined in terms of adherence to the rules. Hence, in doctoral and masters degrees students may be required to take courses in specified areas irrespective of the knowledge they need to attain their scholarly goals and undertake research in a chosen area. Also, method is separated from the substantive research focus and many universities embrace a bankrupt dichotomy of qualitative and quantitative research methods, stipulating that all students should take at least one course in each area.

In compiling this Handbook we did not envision it only as a textbook in qualitative methods courses – though it may find uses in research methods courses. The chapter authors raise issues of epistemology and ontology that are germane to the doing of educational research by individual researchers and research groups. Every chapter serves as an introduction to learn more about the issues it raises and thereby is a foundation for deeper learning to support inquiry in education. For many educational researchers it makes more sense to pursue deeper studies through focused reading in the areas we explore in the Handbook rather than stipulating that graduate students take a time out to study methods that are not relevant to their scholarly interests. Ironically, the tendency to specify particular methods in educational research is not found in the same way in the sciences where it would be unthinkable that, for example, the mass spectrometry group would become adept at electro fluorescent spectroscopy or that theoretical physicists would do any required laboratory methods.

The issues raised in the chapters of the Handbook are germane to the practice of educational research wherever it is undertaken and, in the spirit of bricolage, complementary methods are explored that have the potential to add value to ongoing investigations as well as to serve as an aid to planning research. Furthermore, the issues addressed in the Handbook can comprise a critical framework for review of research and the associated claims; including policies and practices that truncate the agency of scholars in the name of higher standards. Not the least of these is the regression toward prescribed standards for educational research – standards that embrace an oversimplified grasp of the natural sciences and adherence to positivism and causal relationships between over-reduced social systems defined in terms of variables.

REFERENCES

Kincheloe, J. (2001). Describing the bricolage: Conceptualizing a new rigor in qualitative research. *Qualitative Inquiry, 7*, 679-692.

Kincheloe, J. (2005a). On to the next level: Continuing the conceptualization of the bricolage. *Qualitative Inquiry, 11*, 323-350.

Kincheloe, J. (2005b). *Critical constructivism*. New York: Peter Lang.

Kincheloe J., & Berry K. (2004). *Rigor and complexity in educational research: Conceptualizing the bricolage*. London: Open University Press.

Kincheloe, J., & Steinberg S. (1993). A tentative description of post-formal thinking: The critical confrontation with cognitive theory. *Harvard Educational Review, 63*, 296-320.

Prigogene, I., & Stengers I. (1984). *Order out of chaos*. New York: Basic Books.

JOE L. KINCHELOE AND KENNETH TOBIN

2. THE MUCH EXAGGERATED DEATH OF POSITIVISM[1]

Over the past three decades all educational researchers know that there has been great controversy around the nature of knowledge production and research as well as the politics of knowledge. One of the common themes of this debate over knowledge involves the assertion that positivism is dead, a discredited epistemology that has been replaced by more contemporary and updated philosophies of research. The main thesis of this essay is that such an assumption is misleading and can be quite dangerous in supporting modes of research that provide distorted pictures of the educational world, promote particular values and worldviews, and often harm individuals who suffer marginalized status around diverse axes of power – e.g., race, class, gender, sexuality, religion, relation to colonialism, etc. A central dimension of our argument is that many of the tenets of positivism are so embedded within Western culture, academia, and the world of education in particular that they are often invisible to researchers and those who consume their research. Various points in this debate have been published in many journals and books on numerous occasions. Thus, we will attempt to address the issue in the context of "where we are now" – in the Zeitgeist and social context of the contemporary era.

It is not unimportant that, for at least a decade we have witnessed in North America a long brewing regressive rejection of progressive values and are operating in the midst of a neo-conservative, militaristic, socio-political fog. What we often refer to as Western reason has not served us well in relation to a variety of issues including our geo-political strategies, environmental policies, economic frameworks that transform human beings from interconnected community members to "fiscal entities," and test-driven educational reforms that standardize pedagogy and curriculum in ways that deprofessionalize teaching and exclude diverse knowledges that might challenge the status quo. We have often argued that the epistemology that supports such a dehumanizing and oppressive form of reason is a contemporary form of positivism. This "undead" positivism never operates in the name of positivism, and like a zombie walks the socio-political and educational landscape shaping the way we think, what we see in the world, and, of course, how

---

[1] Reprinted with permission of Springer. Originally published as: Kincheloe, J. L., & Tobin, K. (2009). The much exaggerated death of positivism. *Cultural Studies of Science Education*, *4*, 513-528. DOI 10.1007/s11422-009-9178-5.

we produce knowledge. A central part of this crypto-positivism is adherence to a scientific method derived from the natural sciences and deemed necessary for a rigorous social science. Ironically, even though many social scientists embrace scientism, today's scientists and philosophers of science do not endorse the dated and misconstrued methods of science that the social sciences have appropriated. That many scientists have moved on is evident in the following excerpt from an Op-Ed piece written by Paul Davies (2007) in the New York Times:

> A second reason that the laws of physics have now been brought within the scope of scientific inquiry is the realization that what we long regarded as absolute and universal laws might not be truly fundamental at all, but more like local bylaws. They could vary from place to place on a mega-cosmic scale. A God's-eye view might reveal a vast patchwork quilt of universes, each with its own distinctive set of bylaws. In this "multiverse," life will arise only in those patches with bio-friendly bylaws, so it is no surprise that we find ourselves in a Goldilocks universe — one that is just right for life. We have selected it by our very existence. (¶. 8)

Within the philosophy literature and in the academic lifeworld there is ample evidence of many of the tenets of positivism being applied with and without conscious awareness. Larry Laudan (1996) noted that "… what has doomed postpositivism to amount to little more than a hiccup in the history of epistemology is the fact that it has carried to their natural conclusion several tendencies *indigenous to positivism* itself – tendencies that, once one sees their full spelling out, turn out to be wholly self-defeating" (p. 6).

In this contemporary Zeitgeist, scholars who embrace this unnamed, crypto-positivism and the damage it supports often garner praise as rigorous scholars. Those who "call out" the existence of the contemporary version of positivism are sometimes accused of name-calling, promoting a straw man [sic] argument (as something that is dead, positivism is invoked for unspecified but nefarious motives), and even embracing a form of paranoia. Indeed, the discussion of positivism, the culture of positivism, and its impact on contemporary educational research takes place on an epistemological minefield. How we might approach such an explosive topic in a way that engages dialogue and not polarization is a difficult and perplexing matter. For what we are discussing are ways of seeing the world that are often times profoundly in opposition to one another. As a cultural practice as well as a formal logic of inquiry, positivism and the debate surrounding it takes on emotional/affective dimensions that can lead to great anger. Many of us have served on search committees, for example, where differences around epistemological assumptions became overtly contentious and profoundly hurtful to young, unprotected faculty caught in the maelstrom. At many educational conferences proponents of dissimilar epistemological perspectives have become virtually segregated, as scholars avoid the conflicts generated by such differences.

DEFINING POSITIVISM: DESCRIBING THE UNDEAD

In the 1820s Auguste Comte endorsed scientific reasoning as a method of progressive discovery and accumulation of knowledge leading to a general law for all social science. There was confidence that the employment of a scientific method utilizing induction and deduction would produce generalizable laws for social science. There was even an effort to identify laws to unify social and natural sciences. The emergence of Comtean positivism can be understood in terms of the history of philosophical thought, including the works of Plato, Socrates, Galileo, Descartes, and the spread of democracy, acceptance of reasoned argument as a resource for deciding what was, what is, and what can be, and the Renaissance. It was assumed that the natural and social worlds could be understood and improved by using reason and systematic observation; that is, the use of scientific reasoning could enhance social progress and the human condition by emulating the successes of science and scientists from Galileo onwards. Observing, experimenting, and predicting were among the processes thought to constitute a scientific method that would lead to an understanding of social life in terms of causal, invariable, and universal laws and the interrelations among them. Using positivism involved posing salient research questions, identifying important variables, obtaining measures for participants on all variables, and analyzing data to produce causal relationships between variables. Empiricism was positivism's backbone as it evolved and thrived.

At the turn of the twentieth century many leading philosophers and educators undertook research in the social sciences using a variety of empiricist epistemologies, including logical positivism, behaviorism, instrumentalism and pragmatism. The development of these theories was no doubt interdependent as scholars of the time worked together and interacted face-to-face and through publications and participation in professional meetings. For example, at the beginning of the century John Broadus Watson went to the University of Chicago to study with John Dewey. Apparently he did not fully understand Dewey and sought advisors in psychology and physiology. Watson's development of behaviorism was consistent with John Locke's empiricism and the collective influence of two physiologists Jacques Loeb and Henry Donaldson, James Angell (psychologist), and Dewey (philosopher). Based on footnotes in Watson's 1913 paper on behaviorism there is no doubt that he engaged in debate over salient issues with prominent scholars such as Edward Thorndike and others. Even though behaviorism was developed mainly within psychology and in the United States, other empiricist theories emerged at the same time and no doubt scholars of this epoch learned from one another by participating in face-to-face interactions and through the published literature, conference presentations, and ripple effects associated with "word of mouth."

Many of the tenets of empiricism are consistent with scientism, a position that the methods of science can and should be applied in the social sciences to obtain social truths. These schemas are not necessarily used consciously and serve as an ideology that saturates professional practices in many facets of education. Alfred

Schutz (1964) critiqued the assumptions of logical empiricism and theories that invoke scientism, noting that:

> all forms of naturalism and logical empiricism simply take for granted this social reality, which is the proper object of the social sciences. Intersubjectivity, interaction, intercommunication, and language are simply presupposed as the unclarified foundation of these theories. They assume, as it were, that the social scientist has already solved his fundamental problem, before the scientific inquiry starts. (p. 53)

During the twentieth century positivism was a dominant philosophy used to make sense of natural and social science. Many scholars made sense of their work using the tenets of empiricism and derivative philosophies, such as positivism, behaviorism, pragmatism and instrumentalism. Pragmatists and instrumentalists, such as Charles Sanders Peirce, William James and Dewey employed some of the tenets of Comtean positivism during an epoch (e.g., Laudan 1996) when logical positivism, developed within the Vienna Circle, endeavored to "express all true statements about the world in a single scientific language" (Bronowski 1974, p. 627). Logical positivism, which is a form of empiricism, embraced verifiability, a premise that something is meaningful if and only if it is verifiable empirically. Concepts of knowledge are wholly or partly based on experience through the senses and introspection.

Despite its remarkable success, logical positivism had some formidable opponents. For example, Jacob Bronowski noted that Alfred Tarski successfully refuted the master narrative idea and Karl Popper insisted in his philosophy and life "that there is no final sanction and authority for knowledge, even in science; that only that is knowledge which is free to change and grow; and that a condition for its growth is the challenge by independent minds" (p. 627). Bronowski continued "there is no model in the mind of God towards which knowledge moves, and yet it moves from lower to higher forms by a process of natural selection which discards the errors, and step by step elevates those mutations that fit the world" (p. 627).

Early in the twentieth century Watson launched behaviorism (Watson 1913), which greatly impacted both psychology and education, especially in the United States. Because behaviorism and logical positivism are forms of empiricism they share tenets and are often confused. From a behaviorist perspective, psychology is an objective experimental branch of natural science with a theoretical goal of predicting and controlling behavior. There is almost a preoccupation with method as a means of replicating results, and thereby identifying reproducible outcomes. The sources of behavior are external, belonging to the environment. A defining characteristic of behaviorism is a rejection of introspection and consciousness. If mental terms or concepts are used they are to be translated into behavioral concepts. Causal regularities, laws and functional relations that govern the formation of associations are identified through experimentation in order to predict how behavior changes and the environment changes. Because different forms of behaviorism developed at about the same time as logical positivism was being honed and other forms of empiricism were developing, there is evidence of cross-fertilization between different theories, with shared tenets as well as differences.

Lawrence Stenhouse, a British scholar, was greatly concerned that behaviorism was an ideology that saturated school curricula of the 1960s and, as such, it was essential for teachers to be researchers in their own classrooms in order to identify oppression of students due to an ideology of empiricism. His stance launched the teacher as researcher movement in England and drew attention to the potential danger of the ideology of behaviorism as a source of hegemony.

It is now more than twenty years since Denis Phillips explored the extent to which positivism was dead (Phillips 1983). It is apparent from Phillips' analyses that there is confusion about what positivism is, which theorists are aligned with positivism, and the ways in which positivism evolved during its reign as the gold standard framework for natural and then social science. Salient in Phillips (2005) and Laudan (1996) is that many tenets of Comtean and logical positivism pervaded thinking from the early nineteenth century onwards. This is vividly illustrated with examples depicting how scholars who attacked positivism, such as Thomas Kuhn, Paul Feyerabend and Willard Van Orman Quine, adopted tenets of positivism while arguing against positivism.

Even today Plato's "clear sky of eternal ideas" (Cooper 1997) are elevated to a significant extent over other ways of knowing, especially when it comes to considerations about the purposes of research. As Hannah Arendt argued in the *Human Condition*, a pervasive tendency to privilege theoretical ways of knowing over all other ways of knowing is historically constituted (Arendt 1958). Accordingly, journal editors, peer reviewers, and research project officers from funding agencies might judge research on the premise that the production of theoretical knowledge is the only acceptable goal, or at least the most important goal.

Comtean positivism embraced the use of the scientific method as a means to produce social truths. The tenets of the scientific method now serve in many quarters as referents used to judge the value of research in social science. Similarly, as different genres of empiricism differentiated during the early twentieth century, a common core was accepted, virtually without debate and served as a mainstream ideology; an unquestioned set of referents underpinning research in the social sciences. Because the ongoing and widespread use of these tenets is usually unexamined we refer to them collectively as crypto-positivism, acknowledging that the tenets we identify below apply not only to logical positivists, but also to other branches of empiricism. We opt for crypto-positivism because many of the tenets appear to have arisen in Comtean positivism and the milieu of European thought in the early to mid nineteenth century. Despite the efforts of heavyweights such as Karl Popper to kill logical positivism, and dramatic counter movements in sociology, cultural studies and cultural anthropology, the center of mass that represents informed public opinion remains saturated by an ideology of crypto-positivism.

When scholars including Theodor Adorno (1973) and Max Horkheimer (1974) from the Frankfurt School of Critical Theory examined these dimensions of empiricism and positivism, they understood the ways that such objectivist epistemological orientations dismissed the value of historically contextualizing knowledge while concurrently problematizing the epistemological, ontological, and ideological assumptions embedded within it. In the critical theoretical analysis of this issue, knowledge producers in these aforementioned objectivist traditions simply do not possess the ability to discern the nature and impact of their own philosophical and socio-political assumptions on the knowledge they produced. Thus, to the scholars of the Frankfurt School the objectivist notion of neutral knowledge produced by the scientific method served to limit scholarly actions that would allow researchers to better understand the way they had been influenced by the dominant norms and values of their culture.

When such norms and values go undetected, they exert a profound influence on what passes as objective and rigorous knowledge and what does not. And, importantly, such "validated knowledge" operates insidiously to prop up the status quo. Henry Giroux (1997), picking up where Adorno and Horkheimer left off, argues that these objectivist forms of research and knowledge work have produced a "culture of positivism" that accounts for a range of reductionistic and dominant ideology-based epistemological practices that continue to operate in contemporary research. It is fascinating how this culture of positivism with its scientific kinship ties to behaviorism, logical empiricism, and instrumentalism has been able to deny its own existence while concurrently exerting a powerful influence.

The epistemology of positivism identifies knowledge as worthwhile to the degree that it describes objective information that corresponds to or reflects the world. Joe Kincheloe (2008) has used the acronym FIDUROD to specify the mechanistic and reductionistic dynamics that shape contemporary manifestations of this culture of positivism. The following six epistemological (with ontological dimensions) assumptions are found in positivistic research.

Formal – produced by rigid adherence to a particular research methodology that never changes no matter what new circumstances are encountered, no matter how much these new circumstances might lend themselves to rethinking the mode of inquiry one is using. This methodology can be taught to students of research in a step-by-step process.

Intractable – grounded on the ontological assumption that the world is basically an inert, static entity. What we find today about, say, childhood will be true in all circumstances and will remain true indefinitely. Here childhood (in the same manner as limestone or the chemical composition of salt) is assumed to be a fixed, never changing concept. Of course, such an epistemological stance doesn't account for the ever-changing nature of the world and the observers who study it. The notion that human beings and social, cultural, political, and educational phenomena are always in process, changing in new historical times and circumstances is not important in this positivistic context.

Decontextualized – constructed by researchers who have removed a phenomenon from the diverse contexts of which it is a part and that grant it meaning. Without these contexts – e.g., the lived world of a student who takes an I.Q. test – the knowledge produced is distorted as it gives a misleading partial picture. The I.Q. tested student may come from a home where her parents were not first English language speakers, characterized by dire poverty where most energies are directed toward survival not school performance. Might these contextual factors make a difference in the girl's I.Q. test scores? Do they have anything to do with some genetic, inherited notion of intelligence? Studies of any type from the quantitative to the qualitative and everything in between can be decontextualized in the same way.

Universalistic – what inquirers discover when strictly following the correct epistemology and the research methods it supports applies to all domains of the world and the universe. In pre-Einsteinian physics, for example, gravity was assumed to remain constant in all domains of the cosmos. Einstein's work in the General Theory of Relativity undermines the universality of gravity as it delineates special circumstances where Sir Issac Newton's notion of gravity does not work as he postulated – black holes, for example, where nothing can escape the depression in space caused by the concentrated mass of the black hole. There are countless examples one could provide in the social, psychological, and educational sciences to illustrate this same concept. A central dimension here is the decontextualization that comes from colonialism—both traditionally and in its new, reconfigured format—that decontextualizes knowledge produced in colonial centers of power by dominant power blocs that dismiss and degrade the knowledges and well being of marginalized, colonized groups.

Reductionistic – focusing on those dynamics that lend themselves most easily to measurement, research/knowledge produced in this context fails to account for the multitude of factors that shape the nature of knowledge produced: the belief and value structure of the researcher, the structural forces that create particular ideological and cultural climates in which the research process operates, the discursive practices of the research community involved in the process, the perspective of numerous individuals from other cultural settings about the phenomenon in question, to name only a few. Such reductionism provides a parochial, limited, and deceptive body of knowledge. In the name of objectivity and neutrality an ethnocentric, patriarchal, or class biased mode of research can be produced.

One Dimensional – shaped by the belief that there is one true reality that can be discovered and completely described by following the correct research methods. Such an epistemological orientation tacitly posits that the Western waking dimension of human consciousness is the only state worthy of study and use in our daily existence. Thus, the reality that Westerners have depicted via their knowledge production that follows the step-by-step methodology of positivism is a certified reflection of the way the world really is. Anyone that would suggest differently has been labeled as deranged, anti-American, an enemy of Western civilization, or at least a bad scholar (e.g., Harding 1998).

THE DANGER OF MONOLOGICAL WAYS OF SEEING THE EDUCATIONAL WORLD: THE POWER OF HIDDEN POSITIVISM

As these insidious modes of positivism creep into research practices, they work to promote a belief that what we perceive about the world in our unexamined first glance is simply "what is." It is profoundly difficult to escape this culturally conditioned way of seeing that simply takes for granted the veracity of the Western gaze as well as dominant sociocultural ways of being in the world. All epistemologies, all logics of inquiry are grounded upon a particular view of the world whether the researcher is conscious of it or not. One of the main reasons that we are so interested in the positivist zombie in contemporary research is that it integrates these socially and culturally inscribed worldviews into knowledge production in often an undetected manner. Knowledge is a far more slippery and complex concept than researchers traditionally assume. In its complexity countless assumptions about the "proper" way of producing it slip by undetected in the research process, in the attempt to validate knowledge, and in situations where we teach individuals to be researchers.

This slipperiness of knowledge is well illustrated by positivist-based objectivist claims to the separation of the knower and the known, specifically the researcher and the researched. In this transcendent space the researcher stands outside of history and culture producing uncomplicated and validated knowledge that is generalizable to different places and different times. Teachers often tell educational researchers that their knowledge is more slippery than they think, for the validated "best practices" developed in research studies A and B don't have much significance for Ms. Soto teaching on the Navajo Reservation in Arizona. This separation of knower and known, this objective stance of the inquirer tacitly gives researchers the erroneous impression that they can produce neutral and value-free information about a pedagogical phenomenon (e.g., Faulconer and Williams 1985). Not only educational professionals but also people in Western culture and around the world have been misled by the universal truth claims of crypto-positivist research. The claims don't match what we actually get with such knowledge.

This mismatch of claim and what we get is complicated and profoundly important in the thesis of this essay. We both believe that there should be diversity in the ways that knowledge is produced and greater toleration and respect for multiple methodologies and designs. At the same time, we assert that researchers producing any form of knowledge should understand and make it clear to their audiences the nature of the knowledge they are producing. This is where the ghost of positivism plays such a problematic role. As it hovers over and haunts contemporary knowledge work, positivism induces researchers to discount the value of examining the nature of the knowledge one produces and the forces at work in shaping the inquiry process. As scholars of the past three or four decades have explored these dynamics, they have produced a wide variety of insights into the specific ways – ways frequently hidden in the folds of power and mundane cultural routine – such factors operate. Simply, we have learned a great deal about how values influence researchers and their research. This not only concerns the production of viable research (Elmesky and Tobin 2005), but also the ways that our knowledge contributes to enhancing human agency in the face of the growing strength of the oppressive practices of capital and other forms of oppression (Nelson 2000).

THE POWER OF EUROCENTRISM: POSITIVISM AS A PART OF A LARGER OPPRESSIVE MATRIX

From the perspective of many Islamic scholars (e.g., Said 1979) (and of course many other scholars from around the world) the power of Europe and its scientific knowledge was won at the expense of the "non-Western other." In this tradition scholars operating under the flag of positivist objectivity have proclaimed the inferiority of Muslims and many other Asians, Africans, Latin Americans, the progeny of such peoples now living in the West, and indigenous peoples from all over the world. To those who would argue that this is a practice of a previous historical era, we would direct them to recent research on Islamic and Latin American peoples (e.g., Huntington 2004) and Africans with their average I.Q. of 75 (Herrnstein and Murray 1994). It is fascinating in the context to study the history of Western produced positivist knowledges in education and a variety of fields as compared to the indigenous knowledges constructed by people with an intimate knowledge of a particular locale.

Whether one is reading about social and educational research and practices in Maori scholar Linda T. Smith's (1999) *Decolonizing methodologies: Research and indigenous peoples*, the grassroots knowledge of African farmers in Guy Gran's (1986) *Beyond African famines: Whose knowledge matters?*, or the genius of indigenous Andean peoples in South America in Frederique Apffel-Marglin's (1995) *Development or decolonialization in the Andes?*, analysts begin to understand the limits of Western positivistic knowledge as they look at comparisons of the efficacy of Western knowledges vis-à-vis indigenous knowledges in these multicultural contexts. In these same contexts scholars begin to understand the role of Western produced positivist knowledges in oppression, as diverse "others" are positioned as inferiors in positivist knowledge systems. Controlled by Western academic interests individuals from poor backgrounds around the world are defined by Western research. Too often such oppressed peoples play no role in the defining of themselves (Weiler 2004). Thus, positivism is inseparable from the belief in the superiority of Western ways of seeing and being – with positivism "we" found the correct method to discern the truth about the world.

We can see this quite clearly in many contemporary Western studies of indigenous knowledge. Indeed, the historical process of Europeanization with its colonial perspectives toward indigeneity continues to operate despite both insightful and misguided attempts to thwart it. In this context an ethnocentric

Western positivist-oriented science claims a value for indigenous ways of seeing as an "ethnoscience." Western scientists maintain that much can be learned from a number of ethnosciences including ethnobotany, ethnopharmacology, ethnomedicine, ethnocosmology, and ethnoastronomy. The concept discursively situates indigenous knowledge systems as ways of knowing that are culturally grounded, simultaneously representing Western science as "not culturally grounded" – reflecting the positivist framework it is transcultural and universal. Thus, in the process of ascribing worth to indigenous knowledge, such analysis implicitly relegates it to a lower order of knowledge production. Also, to speak of indigenous knowledge systems in Western terms such as botany, pharmacology, medicine, etc., is to inadvertently fragment knowledge systems in ways that subvert the holism of indigenous ways of understanding the world (Hess 1995).

In this Western positivistic gaze, indigenous knowledge is tacitly decontextualized, severed of the cultural connections that grant it meaning to its indigenous producers, archived and classified in Western databases, and eventually used in scientific projects that may operate against the interests of indigenous peoples. All of this takes place in the name of Western scientific concessions to the importance of the information generated by local peoples. Arun Agrawal (1995) labels this archival project as *ex situ* conservation – a process that removes it from peoples' lives. Such indigenous knowledge is always changing in relation to the changing needs of its producers, *ex situ* conservation destroys the dynamic quality of such information. Despite their overt valorization of indigenous knowledge, these Western scientific archivists refuse to accept the worthiness of "raw" indigenous knowledge – upon collection Western scientists insist on testing its validity via Western scientific testing (Grande 2004). As Marcel Viergever (1999) maintains, this archival project and the scientific validation that accompanies it illustrate the positivistic disregard of the need to protect and perpetuate the cultural systems that produce dynamic indigenous knowledge. In this context, Western proclamations of valorization ring hollow, as positivist ethnocentrism exposes itself.

POSITIVISM, TEMPORALITY, AND COMPLEXITY: TIME HAS COME TODAY

Arendt (2004) argued that at the moment a so-called universal and eternal truth is brought into the lived world of human beings, it becomes temporal and thus no longer occupies such a lofty transcultural and transhistorical status. This is to contend that once any phenomenon enters into the commerce of human events, it is changed and continues changing as its context(s) and even those who perceive it change. Thus, positivist knowledge about social, psychological, and educational phenomena whether they are researched by statisticians or ethnographers removes such events from their historical and cultural locations. The concept of time is highly problematic in positivist-influenced accounts of socio-educational behavior. In the positivist research context objects under study are taken on faith to be fixed, static, atemporal phenomena. In the course of study these atemporal entities are assumed to exist in cause-effect relationships. Except for the notion of time implicit in causal ordering (if A caused B then A temporally preceded B), positivist studies remove the influence of the past and the future in the present. Time, as it is experienced in social life (e.g., Bergson 1910), is beyond the theoretical ouvres of positivism, as are the emotions of experience.

Where a school stands in history, we maintain, is profoundly important in understanding what is happening there today. Where political and educational leaders think schools should be going in the future exerts a major impact on what researchers are viewing in their study of, say, classroom practices. Positivist atemporality in research produces a view of the school in question that is significantly different from one where such dynamics of time are taken into account. In this ontological and epistemological context we draw upon the work of both Gilles Deleuze (1994) and Alfred North Whitehead (1929/1978). Both Deleuze and Whitehead promoted a temporal ontology maintaining that no entity comes into being out of nothing. Even though the phenomenon emerges from preexisting realities, it surfaces in a novel manner involving the uniqueness of the relationship it develops with what came before and what will come after it. Whitehead contended that single incidents of becoming are "occasions."

These occasions are connected in space and time and when seen in such interrelationships become a nexus. From these initial understandings we move into the process-orientation of Whitehead's ontology, as the world is structured by a series of events that at the macro-level become a process. Deleuze (1993) maintains that Whitehead's insight in this context represents a radical break from the way we typically look at temporality in Western thought. As the positivist impulse moved researchers to view the single atemporal thing-in-itself, Whitehead's process-based lenses viewed events in spatio-temporal relationships. The world itself and the world of research are no longer the same with these realizations. The cosmos in which we operate is not made of intractable entities but ever-evolving events; verbs begin to gain as much importance as positivistic nouns; processes begin to trump substances.

These are not arcane philosophical musings – these ontological/epistemological insights profoundly shape how we perceive the world, ourselves, our relation to the world, education, and the production of knowledge. We are all in the process of becoming – everything we study is in the process of becoming something new and unique. Every thing-in-itself designated by positivism is a temporal event viewed by reductionist researchers as a static phenomenon. A child, a teacher, a school, a curriculum, what is deemed essential knowledge are always event-like in that they keep changing in relationship with unexpected dimensions of physical, social, political, and other dimensions of the world. Events or things-in-relationship are the definitive constituents of the world around us. Such a realization forces us to understand the way positivism undermines an understanding of this level of the socio-educational world's complexity, its political implications, the value dynamics involved in the process of studying it. The epistemologies, ontologies, and multiple research methodologies we embrace understand that educational phenomena are situated in environments constructed by their temporal interactions with the other dynamics in the web of reality (see Tobin and Kincheloe 2006).

PERSISTENT OBJECTIVISM: THE NEUTRAL OBSERVER

We carefully observe the ways that researchers are taught in quantitative and qualitative methods courses. Too often, the issues we are dealing are rarely discussed, as some professors of research focus on providing "practical" step-by-step methods of "how to do research" complete with didactic guidance on how to follow the pre-given steps correctly. In such contexts the cultivation of the sociological imagination of the student-research, the appreciation of the complexity of interpretive process, and the understanding of epistemological, ontological, and ideological assumptions implicit in particular research designs are deemed not simply irrelevant but as impediments to learning to become a rigorous researcher. Often, when we have talked to students (and colleagues who once were students) who raised such questions in positivist-inscribed research methods classes, they tell about the myriad ways they have been punished for raising such "irrelevant" issues.

One of these irrelevant issues involves the nature of objectivity and the role of the self in the research process. Western researchers and those they have influenced around the world of all methodological stripes have had difficulty appreciating their own temporal location and their involvement in cultural, economic, political, and social matrixes often not apparent to the naked eye. Historians, sociologists, and philosophers of science from Western societies, critical/feminist scholars, as well as non-Western analysts have produced a body of work over the last few decades revealing how much "objective" science is tacitly linked to the social forces and power dynamics of its Zeitgeist (see Sandra Harding 1998 for an expansion of this theme). An educational science that eschews ways of seeing that understand these dynamics and then charges more critical and complex research approaches with setting up a bogeyman of positivist objectivism is operating as a hegemonic force that supports an oppressive status quo. In this positivist context, the only alternatives for educational researchers that exist are either a hard objective stance or a soft subjective position that involves no real empirical data and produces pseudo-knowledges emerging from the imagination of the researcher.

Responding to such a false dichotomy, Sandra Harding (2004) argues that – if we want to use such a term as objectivity – understanding the diverse forces that shape researchers and the knowledge they produce actually constitutes a stronger form of objectivity than the decontextualized positivistic notion. Knowing such factors, she argues, alerts us to the various ways that knowledge is unconsciously distorted and fitted to the interests of dominant power. Such a claim is an anathema to the impulses of positivism, for "the social" by definition exists outside the boundaries of objective science. Indeed, in a positivist framework the mind is separate from both the physical and social world of phenomena, and anytime this boundary is crossed in the research process the objectivity of the inquiry is contaminated. An uncontaminated process in this context produces undistorted mental pictures that correspond to actual reality (Allen 2000). Objectivist research design exists to make sure that this mimetic process occurs. Hopefully, despite the resurgence of crypto-positivist methodologies, many educational researchers understand the problematic nature of such epistemological, ontological, and cognitive assumptions.

The idea that there exists in the atemporal ether a true meaning of a phenomenon is baffling, as we observe an ever changing and interacting educational world in process. The meaning of an educational event is always in the process of negotiation among divergent researchers, emic and etic observers, and various other parties. Such a meaning is never completely open or determined, as diverse constraints shape differing interpretations. Thus, the meanings of educational policies or classroom practices never simply speak for themselves. The sociocultural and ideological frameworks researchers bring to the process always influence the meanings different individuals make. In a crypto-positivist world the message is transmitted that such hermeneutic dynamics are impediments to the "real business" of research: to represent the world "as it is."

TRAVERSING CRYPTO-POSITIVISM'S TRANSCULTURAL AND TRANSHISTORICAL NETHER DOMAIN

Positivist researchers and their contemporary progeny-in-denial lost sight of the epistemological and ontological processes connecting the knower and the known. The knower was disembodied and like a deprofessionalized teacher in a contemporary corporatized school was given a script of steps to follow regardless of context. Thus, in some ways positivist inscribed research with its step-by-step methods are deskilling to researchers, as they induce them to ignore the complex analyses of the various contexts and processes of which they themselves and the phenomena and individuals they study are a part. This relationship between the subjectivity of the author and the research produced is an issue that cannot be ignored. Whenever it is disregarded the result is a caricature of the claims of positivist objectivity that serves to suppress the sociocultural, ideological, and personal issues that help construct the outcomes of research (Thayer-Bacon 2003).

Thus, neo-positivist educational research continues the objectivist tradition of viewing everything from a transcultural, transhistorical nowhere. When we have attempted to work with neo-positivist researchers, our argument that it is important to situate ourselves ideologically, culturally, pedagogically, epistemologically, and ontologically so our readers will know from what locations we are entering the conversation has not been meet with great enthusiasm. "Why in the world would we need to do that?" such researchers ask. Since they often believe that they are presenting the objective truth from the privileged position of a spatial and temporal nowhere, such disclosure seems rather fatuous. Thus, the question remains: what are we to do with the fact that our selfhood is deeply embedded in the research process? With this question at the front of our consciousness in the complex ontology and epistemology advocated here, we begin to realize that the quality, the viability of the information we produce does not depend on an objective correspondence to the "objective reality" "out there."

Instead, it has to do with numerous understandings of the ways knowledge production operates, the nature of the constructed self, the role of socio-political and epistemological and ontological frameworks in which we all operate, and the relationship between these dynamics and the spatio-temporal processes that we are researching. Understanding, describing, and even critiquing the existing state of affairs does not mean we must retreat to the positivist land of nowhere. We can understand, describe, and critique but always from a specific time and location. Because of the limitations of these spatial and temporal dynamics, we must be open and humble about our inadequacies as producers of knowledge (e.g., Clark 2001). While we believe that such a task is profoundly rigorous and takes much study and practice to do well, we do not believe that it can be reduced to a simple step-by-step, connect-the-dots procedure. Thus, unlike the crypto-positivists we are calling for a new rigor in educational research that, we assert, demands more of those who claim the mantle of scholar.

In this rigorous and *complex* context the self-knowledge we seek as researchers does not suggest some narcissistic turn inward, but a part of the larger effort to gain deeper insight into the spatial and temporal process of knowledge production. Neither is it a solipsistic retreat from engagement in the world but an effort to connect the knower to the world in the process of understanding the outcomes of such relationships. Such relationships, of course, involve values and normative dynamics. From a political economic standpoint they are part of a larger politics of knowledge that is so vital in a time when knowledge work, knowledge workers, universities, and institutes in which educational research is conducted are for sale to the highest corporate bidder (Steinberg and Kincheloe 2006). Indeed, it is an effort to construct a critical, independent, democratic mode of engaging in research that understands the way dominant power constantly operates to overtly and covertly shape the outcomes of educational research.

POSITIVISM PLACE: THE WORLD THAT POWER FORGOT

Crypto-positivism is a pervasive ideology that permeates many educational practices that connect with research. For example, peer review of manuscripts submitted for publication, proposals submitted for funding or for presentation at annual meetings of organizations such as AERA, and the creation of "what works" databases are examples of fields in which tenets of crypto-positivism are frequently used to justify decisions. Also, the reading of educational research may be filtered through the crypto-positivistic lenses. Phillips (2005, p. 584) noted that policy researchers appear to be guided by some of the tenets of positivism.

> Educational policies are, logically, causal recipes – 'if it is desired to produce effect or result R, then introduce treatment or programme P' – but in order for an educational agency to be justified in imposing this policy, strong or reliable evidence must be available that P will reliably produce result R. This logic is what grounds the powerful movement in both North America and the UK that marches under the banner of 'evidence based policy and practice.'

Based on our educational experiences, which cover the 1960s through the present, we have myriad examples of crypto-positivism shaping educational practices. The following example is provided as one illustration. Most institutions have an Institutional Review Board (IRB) that consists of qualified peers to review research with human subjects. The Belmont Report (1979), which addresses three general principles: respect, beneficence, and justice, guide the responsibilities of the IRB. Proposals to the IRB should show clearly how the research design respects human participants by maximizing their autonomy to make choices about their participation, that there is a balance favoring the benefits associated with being involved in research compared to the harms from being involved, and that the practices involved in doing research and distributing the benefits and harms are equitable.

A proposal to the IRB should address ways in which human subjects will be recruited to participate in a study, what they will be told as part of an informed consent process, how they can exercise autonomy during the conduct of a study, and benefits and harms associated with being involved, withdrawing, and staying involved. Details should be provided on the scope of the study, defining the boundaries of what the study is about and being precise about where the study will take place and its duration. Assurances also should be given about anonymity and confidentiality and the ways in which data will be stored, used, made available to others, and protected from tampering. If the data are to become part of a database this should be made clear and if data will be destroyed at a particular time the dates should be specified.

Recently a doctoral candidate proposed an ethnography of the emotions experienced within an upper class family when a child from the family is categorized as learning disabled. The proposal attracted a great deal of attention from the IRB and during a period of several months the graduate student was required to answer aggressive questions that threatened to disallow the research based on numerous premises, many of which embraced tenets that were also a part of positivism and, more generally, empiricism. The following paragraph is an example of numerous issues identified by the IRB, to which the graduate student was required to respond.

> Because the PI is involved with only one family he needs to reduce the claims he makes for the research's potential contribution to generalizable knowledge, both in his application and in the consent forms. His involvement with one family is not research in the sense of "a systematic investigation (the gathering and analysis of information) designed to develop or contribute to generalizable knowledge." Rather, it more closely resembles a biographical study, which contributes to understanding through in-depth study at the expense of generalizability. Ultimately the PI should remove any language implying that we will be able to conclude anything definitive about "upper class parents' experiences." At most the study might suggest directions for further research with people fitting these criteria.

The IRB's argument is consistent with many of the tenets of empiricism, defining research as empirical, having the goal of producing generalizable knowledge. Generalizability is focused on sampling a sufficient number of cases, researching the sample and generalizing to a population. Intensive studies are regarded as producing in depth understandings, which are presumed to be not generalizable and hence the activity is not considered to be research. The IRB then took an astonishing step in requiring the graduate student to remove any language about benefits implied that anything definitive could be learned from this activity, which was regarded as less than research.

One of the key aspects of contemporary crypto-positivism involves the continuation of this erasure of power as part of the research process. Simply put, the domains of epistemology and knowledge production cannot be removed from the larger politics of knowledge. Multiple forms of power help construct the knowledge production process on many different levels, and it is in such a context that we view *external* political influences in a neo-colonialistic, corporate-driven, globalized imperial world. In distinction from many analyses of dominant power's influence on research, we contend that such external influences of power – e.g., institutes that support research projects that legitimate corporate influences in school and society – make up only one dimension of power's influence on educational inquiry. Power also affects research in an *internal* manner as well, as it helps shape assumptions concerning the epistemology, methodologies, and designs of positivist inquiry. In this internal process dominant power operates like a quantum force, in that its exact position is always obscure and difficult to find in one specific province of scientific research.

As with so many other dimensions of the socio-political world, power operates as an unseen network, working best when it is hidden from those people and practices it affects. For example, when issues of the spatio-temporal location of the researcher or the multiple historical and sociocultural contexts in which an educational phenomenon are dismissed as dynamics that contaminate the research act, dominant power casts its spell. The power of the crypto-positivist ideology is not perceived as oppressive and its role in quashing research is not acknowledged; instead, the tenets of crypto-positivism are regarded as forces for objectivity, protecting the sanctity of the research process from politicized poison. In its underground social mycelia, dominant power positions those of us who would ask questions of the objective location of positivist researchers and research designs as dangerous ideologues who no longer believe in empirical "truth." We are divisive agents who are guilty of name-calling and incendiary rhetoric. In this conceptual framework as long as knowledge producers support dominant power – no matter how much human suffering it may help perpetuate – they are viewed as reasonable and neutral moderates. Challengers to such power are irrational and disruptive "episto-paths."

In this hidden positivist place it is essential that contemporary educational researchers listen carefully to diverse voices – from other conceptual frameworks and other sociocultural settings. Often because of their location in social space and associated standpoints, those who are different from mainstream researchers can distinguish the tacit epistemologies and ontologies that go unnoticed by those who employ them. Individuals coming from diverse locations can provide profound insights into the way these tacit beliefs about knowledge and being shape the outcomes of crypto-positivist research and the actions they engender. Crypto-positivism is an insidious, harmful force that at once denies its own existence while vilifying those who point it out. We have not reached the "end of epistemology," for there is much analysis, conversation, and debate that must take place around these issues in the coming years.

REFERENCES

Adorno, T. (1973). *Negative dialectics.* NY: The Seabury Press.
Agrawal, A. (1995). Indigenous and scientific knowledge: Some critical comments. *Indigenous Knowledge and Development Monitor, 3*(3), 3-6.
Allen, M. (2000). *Voice of reason.* Retrieved December 05, 2007, from http://www.curtin.edu.au/learn/unit/10846/arrow/vorall.htm
Apffel-Marglin, F. (1995). Development or decolonialization in the Andes? *Interculture: International Journal of Intercultural and Transdisciplinary Research, 28* (1), 3-17.
Arendt, H. (1958). *The human condition.* Chicago: The University of Chicago Press.
Arendt, H. (2004). Philosophy and politics. *Social Research, 71,* 427-454.
Belmont Report. (1979). *Ethical principles and guidelines for the protection of human subjects of research.* Washington, DC: The National Commission for the Protection of Human Subjects of Biomedical and Behavioral Research. Retrieved December 6, 2007, from http://ohsr.od.nih.gov/guidelines/belmont.html
Bergson, H. (1910). *Time and free will: An essay on the immediate data of consciousness* (Trans. F. L. Pogson). London: George Allen and Unwin.
Bronowski, J. (1974). Humanism and the growth of knowledge. In P. A. Schilpp, *The philosophy of Karl Popper* (Book 1) (pp. 606-629). La Salle, IL: The Open Court Publishing Co.
Clark, C. (2001). Surely teaching hypertext in the composition classroom qualifies as a feminist pedagogy? Retrieved December 05, 2007, from http://english.ttu.edu/kairos/6.2/coverweb/gender/clark/index.htm
Cooper, J. M. (1997). (Ed.). *Plato: Complete works.* Indianapolis: Hackett Publishing Co.
Davies, P. (2007). Taking science on faith. *New York Times* (Op-Ed, November 24).
Deleuze, G. (1993). *The Fold: Leibniz and the baroque* (Trans. T. Conley). Minneapolis: University of Minnesota Press.
Deleuze, G. (1994). *Difference and repetition.* Trans. P. Patton. NY: Columbia University Press.
Elmesky, R., & Tobin, K. (2005). Expanding our understandings of urban science education by expanding the roles of students as researchers. *Journal of Research in Science Teaching, 42,* 807-828.
Faulconer, J., & Williams, R. (1985). Temporality in human action: An alternative to positivism and historicism. *American Psychologist. 40,* 1179-1188.
Giroux, H. (1997). *Pedagogy and the politics of hope: Theory, culture, and schooling.* Boulder, CO: Westview.
Gran, G. (1986). Beyond African famines: Whose knowledge matters? *Alternatives, 11,* 275-296.
Grande, S. (2004). *Red pedagogy: Native American social and political thought.* Boulder, CO: Rowman and Littlefield.
Harding, S. (1998). *Is science multicultural? Postcolonialisms, feminisms, and epistemologies.* Bloomington, IN: Indiana University Press.
Harding, S. (Ed.) (2004). *The feminist standpoint theory reader: Intellectual and political controversies.* New York: Routledge.
Herrnstein, R., & Murray, C. (1994). *The bell curve: Intelligence and class structure in America.* New York: The Free Press.
Hess, D. (1995). *Science and technology in a multicultural world: The cultural politics of facts and artifacts.* New York: Columbia University Press.

Horkheimer, M. (1974). *Critique of instrumental reason*. NY: Seabury Press.

Huntington, S. (2004). *Who are we? The challenge to America's national identity*. NY: Simon and Schuster.

Kincheloe, J. L. (2008). *Knowledge and critical pedagogy: An introduction*. Dordrecht: Springer.

Laudan, L. (1996). *Beyond positivism and relativism: theory, method and evidence*. Boulder: Westview Press.

Nelson, L. (2000). Feminist epistemology as and in practice. *Newsletter on Feminism and Philosophy*. *99*(2). Retrieved December 05, 2007, from http://ww.apa.udel.edu/apa/publications/newsletter//v99n2

Phillips, D. C. (1983). After the wake: Postpositivistic educational thought. *Educational Researcher*, *12*(5), 4-12.

Phillips, D. C. (2005). The contested nature of empirical educational research (and why philosophy of education offers little help). *Journal of Philosophy of Education, 39*, 577-597.

Said, E. (1979). *Orientalism*. NY: Vintage Books.

Schutz, A. (1964). *Collected papers II: Studies in social theory* (A. Brodersen, editor). The Hague: Martinus Nijhoff.

Smith, L. (1999). *Decolonizing methodologies: Research and indigenous people*. New York: Zed.

Steinberg, S. & Kincheloe, J. (Eds.) (2006). *What you don't know about schools*. New York: Palgrave.

Thayer-Bacon, B. (2003). *Relational "(e)pistemologies."* New York: Peter Lang.

Tobin, K., & Kincheloe, J. (Eds.). (2006). *Doing educational research: A handbook*. Rotterdam: Sense Publishers.

Viergever, M. (1999). Indigenous knowledge: An interpretation of views from indigenous peoples. In L. Semali & J. Kincheloe (Eds.), *What is indigenous knowledge? Voices from the academy* (pp. 333-359). Bristol, PA: Falmer Press.

Watson, J. B. (1913). Psychology as the behaviorist views it. *Psychological Review, 20*, 158-177.

Weiler, H. (2004). Challenging the orthodoxies of knowledge: Epistemological, structural, and political implications for higher education. Retrieved December 05, 2007, from http://www.stanford.edu/~weiler/unesco_paper_124.pdf

Whitehead, A. (1929/1978). *Process and reality*. New York: Free Press.

KENNETH TOBIN

3. QUALITATIVE RESEARCH IN CLASSROOMS

Pushing the Boundaries of Theory and Methodology

My first studies of science classrooms, undertaken in Australia and the United States were quasi-experiments and involved investigations of the relationships between teaching and science achievement. For more than a decade I participated in a program of research that explored verbal interactions, teacher and student participation in science classes, and achievement. I was also interested in learning environments and issues such as formal reasoning ability and locus of control.[1] Although I felt that I was learning a great deal from this research, I experienced several sources of frustration. First, making sense of teaching and learning in terms of variables was extremely reductionist and my research involved large sets of variables and complex statistical algorithms (unconvincing processes of breaking down and packing together – never quite capturing an elusive whole). In many instances the most salient features of classroom life seemed to be outside of the statistical model and I found myself writing more and more about what I referred to in those days as context – the factors I had not identified a priori; that were surely shaping what happened in the classes in which I was an observer. Second, macroscopic social forces, such as race, social class, equity and policy mandates were not represented convincingly as quantified variables, even when multivariate approaches allowed me to represent such factors with clusters of variables. Furthermore, macro social forces, such as poverty and stipulations for high stakes tests, seemed to be overwhelmingly important in comparison to within-school and -classroom variables (e.g., how questions were posed and answered). I sought an approach that was amenable to understanding how learning in science classes occurred within a complex social system in which what happened within schools and classrooms was saturated by macroscopic forces such as race, social class and state and national level policies. Third, I wanted to employ a methodology that was more closely aligned with the ways in which scientists do science, when they are involved in explorations of new areas in which there is much to be learned. I wanted to explore and probe macro social forces that could be described and interpreted without a need to reduce and quantify. My search for a new approach was deeply theoretical and the transformations from quasi experiments to interpretive forms of inquiry were not revolutionary in the sense that there was an abrupt shift. Instead, over a 10-year period my methodology evolved to be consistent with sociocultural theory, using collective forms of qualitative inquiry to build understandings of social life; informed by multiple voices, diverse participants, and dialectical relationships that seek to transcend part-whole dichotomies.

ABOUT THIS CHAPTER

Research in classrooms focuses on better understanding teaching and learning, using what is learned to create and sustain improved learning environments. The methodology I present in this chapter is grounded in sociocultural theory and an ethical stance that obligates me to adhere to criteria that acknowledge that, while education research is central to effective practice, it is a privilege and must be undertaken in ways that meet four authenticity criteria, which I describe later in the chapter. The remainder of this chapter contains seven sections. First, I address the necessity for research with human subjects to be ethically sound, undertaken with the informed consent of all participants. In subsequent sections I review participant observer forms of research, how to make sense of data resources, involving students as researchers, undertaking auto/ethnography and auto/biography, and incorporating microanalyses into critical ethnography. Finally, I conclude the chapter with discussions about judging whether or not a study meets the criteria for high quality, authenticity and credibility, doing research at different grain sizes, and generalizability.

RESEARCH WITH HUMAN SUBJECTS

When I commenced education research in 1973 there was no necessity to obtain approval from an Institutional Review Board (IRB) or its equivalent for research with human subjects. However, because of many high profile ethical problems with research involving human subjects (mainly in the sciences), peer review processes have been established in most countries to protect the rights of human subjects involved in research. Here I address the central issues associated with obtaining and maintaining informed consent of participants in a study and enacting ethical research practices.

Negotiating Entry

My first step in getting involved in research is to talk to teachers about the possibilities before I have worked out all the details. Initial contacts are oral and open ended, allowing the participants opportunities to make suggestions. My purposes in doing this are to ascertain whether the teacher is comfortable with what I have in mind and to provide opportunities for her[2] to make suggestions about possible foci, likely participants, and the duration of the study. For example, Donovan, a first year science teacher from an inner city high school, frequently complained to me about his students and the school. He and I were serving together on an advisory group assembled by the regional coordinator from an urban school district. Based on numerous conversations in and out of the group Donovan and I agreed to coteach his science classes. Since the regional coordinator was present during many of our conversations she encouraged our collaboration and facilitated the necessary permissions from the school district.

Donovan and I made an appointment with his principal and requested her consent for us to coteach Donovan's classes and approach the school district and the university IRBs for permission to undertake a longitudinal study of the teaching and learning of science. The principal was highly enthusiastic, gave her approval, and came with us to discuss our proposal with the coordinator of the *Incentive* small learning community, one of 10 small schools within a larger school of about 2,000 students. I took notes and promised that prior to seeking formal approval to undertake the project I'd write a draft incorporating their suggestions and get further input from them. Subsequently, the classroom teacher, principal, and small learning community coordinator all agreed to a multi-phase project involving coteaching and then, subject to the research being formally approved, coteaching with research.

Getting Started

Although we had agreed to coteach, Donovan preferred to enact a peripheral role, observing my teaching and struggles to succeed. Even though it did not work out as intended, coteaching was important because it allowed me to begin teaching, get to know students, co-plan lessons with Donovan, and videotape lessons so that we could critically examine our teaching and the students' learning, and identify changes we'd like to make. The videotaping and associated analyses were not done for research purposes, but with the goal of improving learning environments. Even so, the students and their parents or guardians had to give their permission to be videotaped, using the standard permission forms employed by the school district when the purposes of videotaping are for instructional improvement. Approvals to videotape for the purposes of instructional improvement and professional development allowed us to focus on the priority of student learning, afforded me gaining valuable experience of this classroom and school, and provided all of us with experiences and time to become comfortable with our interactions being videotaped. Coteaching and videotaping became a part of what was regarded as normal practice in Donovan's science class, a fact that was highlighted in the proposal to the IRB – since the research did not require a significant change to the practices already approved by parents/guardians, school, and district.

During this period of about six weeks the IRB approvals needed to do research were being prepared by us and reviewed by panels in the university and school district. These were submitted simultaneously despite the contradiction that the approval of each was contingent on approval of the other.

A critical issue was when to commence videotaping and how to deal with the situation of students not returning parental consent forms. We discussed the issue with the principal and agreed to a procedure that allowed us to start once a reasonable proportion of the consent forms were returned. In this instance, one student did not assent to being videotaped and the parent/guardian consent forms were returned over a period of two weeks. Once we had received more than a third of the signed consent forms we started videotaping, taking precautions not to inadvertently capture images of students for whom consent had not been obtained. We asked students to assist us by avoiding movement into the line of the camera. Even though we were videotaping we did not change other aspects of what might be regarded as normal classroom practice. For example, seating arrangements were not changed to make it easier to avoid videotaping particular students. Our primary goal was to ensure that no students were disadvantaged by our decision to use video resources to improve our teaching and the benefits of videotaping interactions were shared among all participants.

Initially we placed the camera at the side of the classroom, focusing on the coteachers and only zooming in on students whose consent forms were returned. However, when all consent forms were on file the coteachers hand-held a small digital camera or positioned it on a desk to capture different forms of interaction as they unfolded.

From Instructional Improvement to Research

My perspectives on obtaining approval for undertaking research with human subjects are guided by the Belmont Report (1979), which addressed three general principles: respect, beneficence, and justice. Proposals to the IRB should show clearly how the research respects human participants by maximizing their autonomy to make choices about their participation, that there is a balance favoring the benefits associated with being involved in research compared to the harms from being involved, and that the practices involved in doing the research and distributing the benefits and harms are equitable.

The proposal to the IRB should address the ways in which human subjects will be recruited to participate in the study, what they will be told as part of the informed consent process, how they can exercise their autonomy during the conduct of the study, and the benefits and harms associated with being involved, withdrawing, and staying involved. Details should be provided on the scope of the study, defining the boundaries of what the study is about and being precise about where the study will take place and its duration. Assurances also should be given about anonymity and confidentiality and the ways in which data will be stored, used, made available to others, and protected from tampering. If the data are to become part of a database this should be made clear and if data will be destroyed at a particular time the dates should be specified.

Once our proposal was written, and Donovan agreed to it, we obtained letters of support from the regional coordinator, school principal, and small learning community coordinator. I then prepared informed consent protocols to be signed by the people we would invite to be involved. In this study the primary participants were high school students who were less than 18 years of age, and therefore could not consent. Accordingly, we produced two forms, one to obtain consent from parents/guardians and the other for students to assent to be involved in the study. Only students who signed an assent form were given a consent form to take to their parents/guardians.

> Good morning. I am Dr. Ken Tobin from the Graduate Center of the City University of New York. I am a researcher who focuses on improving the quality of learning and teaching science and mathematics in urban schools.
>
> Today I'd like to invite you to get involved in a study that will involve me, your teacher, and three other teachers and their classes. Being involved in the research will involve me coming to your class about once a week and carefully watching what happens, taking videotape of what happens, and using audiotapes to record what is said in whole class and small group settings. I will do my best to assist your teacher to teach you science and when I can I will help your teacher to respond to questions and assist with teaching the lesson.
>
> In addition to watching science lessons your teacher and I will study the work you produce in class and we may ask you questions about what happens and why certain things happen the way they do. We may invite you to be interviewed and you can fill out a short form to request an interview with your teacher or me. Anything you say will be kept confidential and we will never use your actual name in anything you write. You will be asked to let us have a name we would use in our writing about what we learn.
>
> I will watch the videotapes and select parts that interest me. I will then analyze these tapes. Usually I will write my impressions of what happens, and analyze how the teacher interacts with students and how the students interact with one another. I will study how the teacher and students talk to one another. I will examine the loudness and pitch of sentences and words and I will see how pauses are used in the talk of the teacher and students.
>
> I will discuss what I learn from the research with students in interviews and in small groups that I call cogenerative dialogues. During interviews I may use video clips, which will vary in length from 30 seconds to 2 minutes in length. If your images are in the video clip I will ask your permission to use the video clip.
>
> About once a month I will select short video clips to show to the whole class so that I can discuss what I see together and work out how to improve the quality of teaching and learning science. I want these discussions to be serious and we should all show respect for one another and not make fun of anyone who is shown in the video clip. If your image is in the video clip I plan to use I will ask your permission.
>
> As part of this study I will look at your performance on quizzes and tests so that I can see how your involvement and work relates to your achievement in science.
>
> If you agree to be involved in the study you should sign the assent form and then take a consent form for a parent or guardian to sign. When I have both forms signed I will copy them and give you a copy of each. The forms have a place for you to show whether or not you agree to have what you say recorded and for me to videotape you during the class.
>
> You can decide at any time not to be involved in the study. To indicate your decision to withdraw you would let your teacher or me know and at that time I would not audiotape you, interview you, or use any video images of you in the research.

Figure 3.1. Sample recruitment script to be presented orally (not read).

Because coteaching, videotaping, and conversations about instructional practice were part of the normal day in Donovan's classes there were no additional burdens placed on participants as a result of this study. Accordingly, we were able to apply for what is referred to as expedited review from the IRB – a request that was approved by the IRB Chair, allowing the proposal to be reviewed by two members of the IRB and the committee chair. Because of Donovan's official relationship with the students I was designated to collect the assent and consent forms to minimize feelings of coercion for people to be involved in the study.

CONSENT FOR MINOR TO PARTICIPATE IN RESEARCH

Title of the Study: Use of research to improve the quality of science education in an urban high school.

Invitation to Participate: Your child is being asked to participate in this research because he/she is a student in a school that has agreed to participate in a study of the teaching and learning of science in an urban high school.

Purpose: This study seeks to enhance science education in urban schools. The study will explore how students' learning of science is affected by teaching and the ways in which your child and other students participate in the class.

Procedures: During this study your child may be videotaped or audiotaped. He/she may be asked to take part in interviews. In addition, test scores and school records may be accessed. Selected excerpts from the videotapes will be used in the dissemination of what is learned from this study.

Risks: Except for the embarrassment of seeing him- or herself on videotape segments shown to the class there are no potentially harmful risks related to participating in this study. Your child's images will not be shown to the whole class without first obtaining his or her permission.

Benefits: As a result of participation, your child's awareness about school and learning may be increased, particularly in science. The study provides students with valuable insights into different approaches and practices in teaching and learning science.

Withdrawal: Participation in the study is voluntary and if your child decides to participate, he or she can withdraw without any penalty at any time. Participation in the study is not a factor in determining your child's grade or standing in any course.

Alternatives: You may choose not to allow your child to participate in this study. If so, he/she will not be videotaped, audiotaped, or interviewed, and no references to him/her will be made in the reporting of this study.

Compensation: Your child receives no financial compensation for his/her participation.

Confidentiality: All information collected in this study will be kept private and your child will not be identified by name. The researcher will keep the audio- and videotapes from this study in a locked filing cabinet. Only the researchers will have access to these tapes.

Subject Rights: If you have questions about your child's rights as a participant in this study, you can contact the IRB Administrator, Gotham City University, (367) 373-2724, IRB@gcu.edu.

Conclusion: You have been given the opportunity to ask questions and have had them answered to your satisfaction. You have read and understand the consent form. You agree to allow _____ to participate in this research. Upon signing below, you will receive a copy of the consent form.

I agree for my child to be videotaped _____ (Initial)	Yes	No
I agree for my child to be audiotaped _____ (Initial)	Yes	No

Name Parent/Guardian	Signature	Date

Figure 3.2. Sample consent form for the participation of minors.

The IRB required an example of the script I would use to recruit participants in the study. Although I did not intend to read to students and other potential participants I informed the IRB that the text of the script contained below in Figure 3.1 contained the essence of what I would say to possible participants.

After a statement like the one in the script is presented orally to students they would be advised about how to get involved in the research should they have an interest in participation. Involvement requires understanding fully what is involved, that is informed consent, and a signed willingness to participate. If the participants are less than 18 years of age they are not able to consent to be involved and a two stage process is needed – assent from the student and consent from the parent/guardian.

CONSENT OF PARENT OR GUARDIAN

I am Ken Tobin, a professor in Urban Education at the Graduate Center of the City University of New York. I am doing research in New York City public schools in an effort to learn more about how to improve the quality of teaching and learning science. I can be reached at (737) 327-3437. Alternatively you can email me at ktobin@gcu.edu.

You have previously consented for your child to be involved in a study of the teaching and learning of science at his or her school. As part of this research I have used videotape to explore how learning happens as the teacher and students interact with one another and materials from the classroom. I want to use short segments of the video to educate others about what I have learned from the research. Your child's image is included in one or more of the short excerpts I want to use in meetings with science teachers and with researchers at professional meetings throughout the world.

I am requesting permission to use your child's image for the purposes of professional development for teachers and disseminating what I have learned from the research. You can view the videotape at the school or request a compact disk or digital videodisk containing the images for which I am requesting your permission.

If you have questions about your about your rights as a participant in this study, you can contact IRB Administrator, Gotham City University, (737) 327-3437, IRB@gcu.edu.

Please read the following, select Yes or No to indicate your preferences, and sign below.

Circle Yes or No as appropriate:
I allow you to use the video segments that contain my child's images:	Yes	No
I would like to view the video segments at school:	Yes	No
I would like a CD or DVD containing the video segments:	Yes	No

I give permission for you to use video clips that include the image of _____ (insert child's name) in professional development activities with teachers and meetings of researchers to let others know what has been learned from the research.
Print name: _____ Date: _____
Signature: _____

Figure 3.3. Informed consent protocol for additional uses of videotape.

There are numerous ways in which potential participants can be informed about the purposes of a study. The process starts with an explanation like the one provided in Figure 3.1. The next step can involve distributing assent forms to an entire class, explaining what the various sections mean and allowing those who are willing to participate to complete them. A potential problem is that some students might feel coerced into participation by peer pressure – the classroom providing a context in which students might be influenced one way or the other by the presence of peers and perhaps the teacher. For this reason I prefer to meet with students one-on-one in an office away from the classroom. I can then speak to them about the study, answer questions, assure them that participation is voluntary, and distribute the consent forms to students who assent. Figure 3.2 contains an example of an informed consent protocol to be signed by a parent/guardian.

Additional informed consent protocols were needed for the adults participating in the study, in this case other teachers who were colleagues of Donovan's, school and small learning community administrators, parents and guardians, non-teaching assistants, and school police. Also, because I would use videotape for a variety of purposes I prepared an additional consent form for these purposes. It is provided above in Figure 3.3.

Sharing Opportunities to Participate

Name: _____ Email address: _____

Please check any that apply and put your request for an interview in the box at the back of the room.

I would like to be interviewed about the science class from _____ (write the day or date).
I would like to be interviewed about what generally happens in my science classroom.
I would like to be interviewed about my participation in science.
I would like to be interviewed about the teaching of science.
I would like to be interviewed about why we do science and what science might be like.

Figure 3.4. Protocol to request an interview.

In interpretive research it is customary to speak to students informally about what they are doing and why they are doing it. Informal interviews take the form of conversations and can occur as a lesson unfolds. Usually, the conversations are quiet and relatively short. Efforts are made not to disadvantage any students by taking too much of the time of the person being interviewed or by distracting others. Informal interviews are augmented by formal interviews with students selected to provide insights into what is happening and why it is happening. Interviews might also be set up for students to check on what is being learned from a study and to get participants' perspectives on the patterns of coherence and the contradictions that have been noted. In the selection of participants from a stakeholder group (e.g., students), I use a process that involves the use of opposites. I never use random selection. The participants are chosen because their perspectives are judged to be worth knowing and of value to the research. I select someone who has something to contribute to the study. Having selected a first person to interview, I then select a second who is as different from the first as possible. In this way participants are selected serially based on their differences from one another and contingently – based on what I'd like to learn next. However, there may be participants who want to be interviewed and do not get selected.

Accordingly, to be fair, I use a process to allow students to request to be interviewed by filling out a form (Figure 3.4) that is available at the back of the classroom. In this way participants are not prevented from experiencing the benefits of being interviewed in a study (and if there is harm from being interviewed it is shared out).

Negotiation of Approval

I ran into difficulties with the IRB when I moved to a new institution and did not understand the culture of the peer group at my new university. Whereas there was a special IRB panel to review education research at my previous university, here there was just one panel for all research in the social sciences. Two issues caused me most concern, essentially because I did not understand the difference between writing a proposal for a funding agency and writing one for IRB approval. An initial stumbling block concerned an IRB request for research questions and hypotheses. My knee-jerk reaction was that the request reflected an epistemological position that I rejected because in ethnography the questions are broad and only narrow down as the study progresses. Usually I do not write hypotheses and focus on identifying patterns and associated contradictions that relate to what is happening and why it is happening. However it is clear that my knee-jerk thoughts are wrong. The IRB wants to know what a researcher will study and what she expects to learn from the research. Their request makes sense if the IRB is to do its work of peer review. Providing the information also makes sense from the perspective of good ethnography since it provides a baseline for what Guba and Lincoln refer to as ontological authenticity (discussed in the next section of this chapter), whereby a researcher is obliged to show that her initial constructions change as a result of doing the research (Guba and Lincoln 1989). Hence, providing the IRB with hypotheses is a first step in establishing that a qualitative study has ontological authenticity.

The questions you provide to the IRB should be broad and cover the domain of your research interests. For each broad question also provide five more specific questions to explicate the likely areas in which the study will be undertaken. Hypothesize on the likely answers to these specific questions – based on what you know now. Nobody will hold you accountable for these answers. By responding in this way I define the scope of my study and the boundaries for which I am seeking approval. If, in the course of doing the research, I stray from within those boundaries, I need to seek additional approval from the IRB. This can prove to be extremely important in the event that a participant or her guardian complains about some aspect of the research. You want to be sure that what you do has been approved by the IRB – so your predictions are important. For example, one of my graduate students recently undertook research with middle school students in inner city schools. One of the students she interviewed raised the question of sexual harassment and the researcher decided to ask other participants about sexual harassment in her interviews. Almost immediately there was a protest from a

> Thanks for taking the time to speak to me this afternoon. I now have a clear idea of some of the concerns you have about my proposed research "Use of research to improve the quality of urban science education."
>
> The ethnography planned for each of the four case studies is longitudinal and researchers will examine the ways in which the teachers and students interact when science is taught in regular classroom settings and when the teacher and students interact in cogenerative dialogues. Past research in urban high schools, in Philadelphia, suggests that the students learn to interact with one another and the teacher in cogenerative dialogues and build new procedures for interacting with peers and the teacher. Similarly, the teacher learns to successfully interact with students, listen and learn from them, and effectively deal with their ways of interacting. Cogenerative dialogues are safe spaces in which to learn new ways of interacting across differences in age, ethnicity, social class, and gender. Key to previous research and this proposed study is that once these new ways of interacting are learned the teacher and students are then able to enact what they have been learned in actual lessons. Not only that, the students can become leaders in initiating interactions with peers and the teacher.
>
> We regard cogenerative dialogues as a professional development activity in which teachers and students can accept shared responsibility of the quality of teaching and learning, and by regularly meeting they can learn to interact successfully with one another. We will study what happens in the cogenerative dialogues intensively. As I explain in the materials I sent you we will use a variety of qualitative data sources to ascertain what is happening in the cogenerative dialogues and why that is happening. By undertaking analyses on a weekly basis through until the end of the year we will be able to identify patterns of change in the ways in which the teacher and students interact. We will explore patterns and associated contradictions using ethnography and then we will examine interactions using microanalysis. The microanalysis will enable us to explore the ways in which the teacher and students use their voice, gesture and body movement and orientation. We will explore which interactions have successful outcomes and which do not. Evidence of improvement will be sought in longitudinal studies that are undertaken weekly.
>
> In parallel we will explore the ways in which the same students involved in the cogenerative dialogues participate in regular science classrooms. We will look to see if patterns from the cogenerative dialogue are evident in the classroom and vice versa. We will also ascertain the extent to which new interaction styles developed in cogenerative dialogues transfer to the classroom.
>
> A question we discussed on the telephone is how will we know if we are successful. The criteria for success will emerge from discussion between all the teacher researchers. We will meet at least once a week as a group and will discuss what is happening in the classroom and design procedures to be used in the forthcoming week to test how robust our claims for success are. We will also search strenuously for contradictions to any claim that is made. Some of the criteria for deciding whether positive environments are occurring will include criteria such as the following:
> Higher levels of student engagement. Higher levels of attendance. Higher levels of synchrony in the interactions involving student<-> student and student<->teacher. Higher quality of teacher and student discourse as evident in solicitations, responses, reactions, and structuring.
> Standard procedures of discourse analysis will be used and advanced technological tools, such as PRAAT, will allow us to measure such characteristics of speech as pauses, frequency of utterances and the amplitude of utterances.
>
> There are many more examples of what would constitute higher quality teaching and learning. I am very experienced in such analyses and since 1973 have been involved continuously in qualitative and quantitative studies of teaching and learning. The bottom line is in higher quality learning environments and higher achievement in science – including high stakes tests like the Regents' exams. I also expect more students to go on to college and expand their career options as a result of being involved in the study.
>
> The four case studies in the first year involve a middle school, a new high school, a high school for relatively high performing students, and a school for students who have been expelled from their previous school because of violence to a teacher (i.e., a last chance school).
>
> I hope I have addressed all of the points you raised in the telephone conversation. If you have further questions I will be happy to respond to them.

Figure 3.5. An email response to questions raised by a school district IRB.

concerned parent, pointing out that she had not been informed that questions about sex were part of the research. The topic was beyond the scope of the informed consent and had not been approved by the IRB.

The above incident was quickly resolved, but served as a wake up call for me. It is important in seeking IRB approval that careful attention is given to identifying the likely areas of interest that will arise and to identify the places in which the research will be undertaken. If changes happen as a study unfolds then the IRB should be informed and a decision should be taken about whether or not the informed consent protocols need to be changed.

After I had obtained the official approval from the university IRB, the school district IRB asked me additional questions to clarify the scope of the study. These requests occurred in a telephone conversation with the committee chair and a follow-up email message confirmed what we agreed to in writing. With the common use of email I regard it as important to consolidate into one document the original proposal together with subsequent questions and answers, so that IRBs, researchers, and participants are clear on what has been agreed. The letter in Figure 3.5 provides an example of my responses to queries raised by the school district IRB coordinator during a telephone conversation.

AUTHENTICITY CRITERIA

What criteria can be used to judge whether or not high quality ethnography has been planned and undertaken? Different researchers will adopt different stances, however, I use the four criteria advocated by Guba and Lincoln – recognizing that education research with human subjects must benefit those who are involved in the study and that researchers have a responsibility to those who agree to be involved that benefits will not be realized only in the future, but will also lead to improvements as the research is enacted.

Criterion 1: Learning from a Study

Although it is customary for researchers to engage in programmatic research in which each successive study builds on what was learned previously, it is important that they do not commence a study with preconceived ideas about what will be learned. The danger is that such ideas can serve as templates that filter data and confirm a priori expectations. To guard against this occurring researchers can document the progressive changes in their understandings and the foci of their research. The intention is that researchers learn from the data and associated analyses. Evidence of learning from the study would include a changing trajectory of answers to a research question, possibly through the inclusion of nuances and the identification of contradictions to patterns of coherence. Of course the patterns themselves could change over time and the initial constructions could become contradictions to those patterns. While learning from a study it is important to obtain and retain diverse perspectives of participants who are located in different social spaces by virtue of such factors as race, social class, gender and first language. In the remainder of this chapter I refer to participants in these different social spaces as stakeholder groups. Hence in meeting criterion 1 it is important for researchers to show how research questions are answered for different stakeholder groups – how the answers evolve over time, are nuanced for different participants, and incorporate contradictions.

Ontological authenticity relates to the ways in which participants in the study alter their perceptions of the nature of social life, as it pertains to the research foci. The role of the researcher is to document these changing perceptions. Traditionally researchers, including those within my group, have focused on documenting their own changing ontologies. One important way to do this is to undertake auto/ethnography and dedicate a significant part of the writing of a study to the documentation of changing ontologies and making sense of such changes in relation to what is learned from a study.

An important part of the analysis of a researcher's changing ontology is an examination of the changes that occur in the theoretical underpinnings of a study and the associated changes in the methodologies employed. It can then be shown how changes in the frameworks alter the ways in which social life is illuminated and represented in descriptions and explorations. In this way, changes in the theoretical underpinnings of a study can be linked to the realities presented as outcomes of a study. Perhaps, as a further emphasis on the relationships between theoretical frames, research questions, and methodology it can be shown that decisions to employ one set of theoretical constructs rather than another not only illuminates social life differently by highlighting certain features, but also obscures others. For example, in research on teaching and learning a decision to theorize learning as cultural production brings into focus such issues as cultural reproduction (of the canon), cultural transformation, and cultural fluency, including conscious and unconscious ways of knowing. At the same time issues associated with conceptual change may be shaded from view. Also, opting to use Sewell and Bourdieu as starting points for conceptualizing culture led us to adapt our methodology to search for patterns in social life that have thin coherence and are interconnected with contradictions. The purpose of our research then was not to explain away the contradictions, but to understand them as an expected part of social life that together with the patterns of thin coherence were central in what we could learn from a study and perhaps would have to address in efforts to improve the quality of learning environments.

Concerns about ontological authenticity should extend beyond university-based researchers to include each of the salient stakeholder groups. To what extent do stakeholders construct their lived lives in the fields of study in ontologically changed ways? If ethnography is to be critical in ways that catalyze and sustain desirable changes, from the perspectives of stakeholders, then the ways in which stakeholders enact and perceive social life ought to change as a result of the research. Enduring transformation, for the better, might be sustained if fresh theoretical and empirical lenses are acquired for making sense of teaching and learning and the ways in which participants successfully interact to produce learning.[3]

Criterion 2: Educating Stakeholders about the Unfolding Outcomes

In a process of informing stakeholders about what is learned from a study it is important to educate each stakeholder group about the nuances of a study, what is learned from the different stakeholder groups, assisting them to understand the patterns of coherence and contradictions. This criterion can be addressed in a number of ways and the process can be continuous. Within the framework of negotiated agreements, anonymity, and confidentiality, the unfolding outcomes of a study can be made available to participants on a website that can be accessed at their personal convenience. Depending on how public these findings should be, the website could be password protected with access limited to researchers and participants.

Clearly, educative authenticity is at the heart of ontological authenticity and is seen as an essential step in sustaining beneficial changes due to research in classrooms. Not only is it important to obtain rich descriptions of what is happening and why it is happening, but also to ensure that all stakeholder groups understand how others experience and make sense of reality. If issues of equity and oppression in classrooms are to be addressed effectively through research an effective program of educating all stakeholder groups about the constructions of others seems central.

Criterion 3: Research Should Catalyze Improvements

Researchers have an obligation to educate all participants in ways that afford improvements in regard to what is learned from a study. Accordingly, to the extent possible, situations of disadvantage, inequity, and oppression are addressed in ways that expand the collective agency of stakeholder groups. Hence, the results of a study are expected to change over time as adjustments are made by stakeholders to create and sustain environments in which all stakeholder groups can meet their goals. If this is to occur it might be necessary for representatives of each stakeholder group to meet to discuss the unfolding results of a study and negotiate changes to produce desirable goals and outcomes. Ideally, the participants in such discussions would assume a shared responsibility for enacting agreed to changes.

Just as criterion 2 (i.e., educative authenticity) was related to authenticity criteria 1 and 3, so is this criterion related to the others. Research is not a privilege to benefit researchers alone. Instead there is a tax to be paid for the privilege of doing research and that is to act in ways that catalyze desirable changes, not just for the well positioned within the fields of study; but also for all participants. Scholars such as Lather (1993) and Kincheloe and McLaren (1994) refer to the centrality of research catalyzing positive changes for the participants involved in a study. As a quality criterion, researchers should structure a study so that all participants are educated by what is learned in a study and can then use what they learn agentically; to improve the quality of their social lives in the fields in which they participate.

Criterion 4: Assist all Individuals to Benefit from the Research

Even though the steps taken to educate stakeholder groups and catalyze positive changes to the learning environments will expand the agency of most participants there will be some who cannot make the changes needed to reduce their disadvantage. Accordingly, researchers have an obligation to help those participants who are unable to help themselves or whose disadvantage continues as the study proceeds. That is, the researchers provide additional structures for those individuals for whom the efforts to educate them and catalyze worthwhile changes were not enough.

For example, a pattern that we observed was that African American males were underachieving in science compared to their female counterparts. This was partly due to the sporadic attendance of some youth who were suspended from class and school for a variety of reasons. Despite the principal, coordinators of schools within a school, and teachers knowing about this trend, when Shakeem was suspended from school and had to transfer to another school because of his high frequency of suspension I intervened with the principal; making a case for allowing him to continue at the school because he did not want to go to a new school and a change of schools would further disadvantage him. Fortunately the principal agreed to my request and Shakeem was permitted to stay at the school. In this instance the principal, a Black female, recognized that the enforcement of the rule would needlessly disadvantage Shakeem. Similarly, when Tyrone was suspended for 5 days, essentially because his mother could not come to the school for a compulsory conference, I asked the principal if she would waive the rules for Tyrone and consider changing a school policy that was keeping urban youth out of the school.

The Bottom Line on Authenticity

Although I dealt with the four authenticity criteria in a linear way, it is apparent to me that this is yet another example of factors that constitute a whole – they are dialectically related. I do not envision a researcher claiming that classroom research is authentic or credible based on just one or two of the authenticity criteria. Because each is constituted in a whole, the quality of a study can be judged in terms of the ways in which each of the four criteria is addressed and accomplished.

DATA RESOURCES

Interpretive research is a form of participant observation that has the goal of ascertaining what is happening and why it is happening from the perspectives of the participants in the fields of study. Hence, as culture is enacted within fields, the researcher describes what happens in terms of the emergent patterns and associated contradictions. To do this, the researcher visits the field regularly, becomes a participant observer, a visitor to the field with a set of roles that other participants need to understand and accept. The presence of the researcher (as a participant observer) changes what happens because his or her presence, and associated practices and schema, alter the structure of the field and hence the agency of all participants. Accordingly, as participants appropriate the dynamic structures introduced by the researcher, different forms of culture are produced and enacted than would be the case if the researcher were not present. Although the roles of the researcher inevitably change as she becomes more familiar with the fields of study and is known by the participants, it is important that all participants are aware of the roles to be enacted, accept them, and are apprised of changes as they occur.

In my research described earlier, I negotiated with the school principal, the coordinator of the small learning community in which the study was to occur, and the science teacher that I would coteach with Donovan. The students understood that I was a professor from the university and that I would serve as a coteacher when I came to their class to do research. Enacting the role of coteacher gives me close access to the students' praxis as learners and also to the teaching praxis of my fellow coteacher. I am also able to access multiple data resources, an important criterion in ethnographic research. Accordingly, students knew that I would observe, take notes, videotape what happened, photograph their work, speak to them about their work during the class and, as necessary, teach individuals, small groups and, if called upon by the teacher, the whole class. Students did not hesitate to ask me for assistance. In this way I was a coteacher, usually involved in peripheral roles that occasionally became more central. By having a form of participation that was active I had access to the unfolding production of teaching and learning. My practices and associated schema were part of the dynamic structure of the classroom and were structured by it as well.

A problem associated with me being a "coteacher as researcher" is my inability to create field notes as the lesson progresses. I use two approaches to address this limitation. One is to speak into the microphone of the camera, which I hold in my hand as I move around the classroom, thereby catching what happens (in the direction of the lens) in terms of video and audio. The second is to speak my descriptions and interpretations – things to pay attention to – into a hand held digital recorder, in my case iTalk connected to an iPod. Rather than reading back over field notes written during a lesson I can play back my recorded comments and, as I watch the video replay, I can take those comments into account as I make sense of the data.

During a lesson I routinely speak to students, usually recording what they have to say through the microphone on the camera. Often this is accomplished as the camera points elsewhere, making the speakers less conscious of being recorded. If I feel the necessity to have video and audio I usually ask permission of the student to shoot the video as well as have a short conversation. When I talk to students, either informally or formally I make a point of trying to structure the interactions such that students speak for longer than me. To the extent possible I want to capture their perspectives on teaching and learning and the many relationships that are central in my research – such as agency|structure, individual|collective, and practices|schema. When I first introduce the study I let them know that when I interact with them I want them to speak until they "run out of gas."

The other piece of technology I carry with me as part of my ethnographer's toolkit is a Nikon Coolpix 4600, a digital camera with a 512 MB memory card that can be used to take high quality pictures of artifacts used during teaching and learning. In effect this replaces a photocopier in that I can photograph student work, chalkboard inscriptions, the layout of the class, the uses of equipment and materials and capture the ways in which particular resources are used during the lesson. These digital images are of high quality and, as a slide show, are a way for me to quickly reconstruct the key features of a lesson. When I use the digital camera I usually set the videocamera on a desk or table, leaving it to record events as I capture specific high quality images.

Analytic Memoranda

As soon as possible after coteaching a lesson I endeavor to write analytic memoranda, with and without the assistance of video replay. An example of an analytic memorandum is provided in Figure 3.6.

Analytic memoranda are used as data resources and can be used as evidence to support patterns of coherence or contradictions to those patterns. Another use of analytic memoranda is to give a copy to participants to see whether they correct and elaborate on the text and to highlight areas of agreement and disagreement. Hence, analytic memoranda are generative and interpretive resources.

MAKING SENSE OF THE DATA RESOURCES

A critical part of interpretive research, as I do it, is to stay on top of the data analysis. Hence, as soon after being in the field as possible, it is important to answer the two main questions of interpretive research, namely, what is going on here? – and why is that happening? In formulating responses my methodology guides me to search for patterns of coherence in the data and associated contradictions. Once I identify patterns and contradictions I want to be able to describe both in terms of examples, what I refer to as vignettes, or little stories. I do not expect the patterns of coherence to be thick, just systems of practices and schema that tend to cohere and always contradictions, or inconsistencies with those patterns. Accordingly, I do not try to explain away the contradictions as error, but seek to understand them along with the patterns of coherence. I am guided theoretically by William Sewell's ideas on culture, whereby culture is enacted as patterns of practices and schema that have thin coherence; dialectically interconnected with contradictions (Sewell 1999). Hence, in an important sense, the patterns of coherence and the contradictions represent a whole, or to think of it another way, when culture is enacted, patterns of coherence and contradictions are mutually constitutive – that is, each mediates the other.

the periodic table or to its probable valence. She asked many questions about why the correct formula for magnesium bromide contained two atoms of bromine. In my efforts to explain how she could write chemical formulae for each of the reactants and products as a first step into the given problems Kamica became frustrated and began to write a letter about how much she disliked chemistry. With 20 minutes still to go it was a struggle for me to connect with Kamica.

Several of the students had their heads on the desk. Aaron could be aroused and he told me that he did not know what to do. Once I had taught him what to do he stayed on task for most of the rest of the lesson. Another African American male looked menacingly at me when I aroused him. "I have a headache man. Don't mess with me," he snarled. Remembering Tyrone's advice of not messing with students who did not want to be taught I quickly moved away to deal with other students who were interested in receiving assistance. The male sitting near to Kamica was rarely at school. When he too complained about not being taught the material I asked him why he was absent so much. His response was not at all rational and he then indicated that he did not like chemistry and since failure was no stranger to him he was not concerned at the thought of failing the course. Throughout the 75 minutes he toyed with the problems but made no serious commitment either to learn or work his way through any of the problems. I had a sense that he would have engaged if I could have given him a set of problems that he could be successful at.

The lesson reinforced how the students can manage book-focused activities. It was relatively easy to move from student to student and to keep them quiet and moderately active. However, connecting to what the students could do was a challenge in this activity. At any time that I tried to teach to the whole class the students switched off and hardly paid attention at all. When I worked with them one on one they appreciated the effort usually and were prepared to work in this way for as long as I was prepared to teach them.

The students were unable to navigate a textbook and searched through their notes to find what they needed to solve the problems. If they did not have notes on a given topic they were of the opinion that we had not covered it in class. To avoid the problem of having them spend so much time on writing notes I had been giving them handout sheets from the first day I taught them. I did not see any of these notes being used as a resource. For me this raises the question of what students regard as resources to support their own learning. Although I invited students to work together to solve the problems there was no apparent take up of this offer. The students seemed to want to work alone and any conversations were social rather than substantive.

The lesson ended with an invitation for the students to complete up to number 11 for homework. From my standpoint this was a compromise. I had initially set a target of 50 problems to be completed. The rationale offered by Donovan for the reduced target was that the first 11 problems provided both the reactants and the products whereas the final 39 only provided the reactants, leaving students to work out the products as well as to balance the equation. Reluctantly I agreed with this reduced assignment even though I felt privately that in 75 minutes of class time it ought to have been possible to complete the entire 50 problems and do other work as well. I am greatly disturbed that students can accomplish so little in a double period of chemistry and then we adjust our expectations downward with an inevitable outcome being the addition of fuel to the cycle of social reproduction.

As I walked down the hallway to exit the building I encountered at least five students from my class who were absent from the first period. The issue of truancy and absence from class is a major problem that influences the extent to which a coherent program can be planned and enacted. How is it possible to plan for instruction when on the average a student will only attend for three-fifths of the classes in a given week?

Figure 3.6. An example of an analytic memorandum.

So, where to start? If I have digital audio messages I begin there, by playing them through, so that I can pick up my memory joggers, recorded while I was in the field. Usually my recorded comments impel me toward particular tasks and perhaps lead me to focus on specific events and examine the evidence for identified patterns or contradictions. Once I have dealt with my oral remarks I like to review the videotape. I find it best to watch the tape having first imported it into iMovie. Once it has been imported and saved, as an iMovie file on a 500 GB external hard drive, I watch it in real time and use my computer to make notes. If something catches my interest or if complex interactions occur, I play the tape back, over and over if necessary and when salient vignettes occur I clip them, so that they exist as discrete entities. On the first pass through I do not delete any of the images – I simply break down the file into smaller segments and write notes about the patterns and contradictions I notice.

As I identify patterns of coherence (often called assertions) and associated contradictions I make a note of the evidence to go with each. At this time I make decisions about whether or not to show particular clips to the participants either as a whole class, in cogenerative dialogues, or to individuals such as selected students and the teacher. Usually the clips I select range in duration from 30 seconds to 3 minutes. If I decide to show selected clips to the participants I save them as QuickTime files and store them on a DVD or CD ROM. To the extent possible I like to write interpretive memoranda based on my initial review of the tape. The interpretive memoranda will connect what I am learning to what I have learned previously from the study, to the theoretical framework, and to what others have learned. Usually the others will be from my research group and close associates.

These initial analyses and interpretations help to focus what happens next in my research and also provide a basis for me to get feedback on my tentative findings from participants and peers who are not directly involved in the research. The process of discussing what I have learned with participants and asking for their input on my interpretations is called member checking. I do not privilege the interpretations of any particular participant, but want to get input from a range of them as additional data to provide nuances to what I have learned. Member checking might lead me to change my mind, or more often, to elaborate what I have learned from a study to include additional patterns of coherence and contradictions, or to consider alternative interpretations as contradictions to my claims. Whatever happens I keep a record so that over time I can explore the trajectory of my changing understandings – a key authenticity criterion.

Once a week I schedule a meeting of my research group. Usually each person in the group is involved in his or her own research and we come together to discuss what we are learning and thereby learn from one another's ongoing research. Also we share our foci and methodologies. For example, at the present time my research group is tiered, the base group consisting of four colleagues who are doing research in their own classes and me. Each month the base group meets for three consecutive weeks on Wednesday evening for two hours. Each person in this group takes a turn at leading the research group until, over a five meeting cycle, all researchers have had an opportunity to lead and get focused feedback on their research. This is called peer debriefing and its purpose is to enrich a study through the critical insights of peers.

A second tier consists of the base group plus two other research groups, which undertake research in New York City. The first and second tiers meet on Friday once a month and each month we rotate the meeting venue – the host researchers leading the conversation about our research. This meeting of the larger group is also a form of peer debriefing allowing for even more disparate perspectives to inform our studies.

A third tier is distributed nationally and internationally and consists of colleagues who are undertaking similar research to that being undertaken in the first and second tiers. Some scholars in this network participate in many of the tier 1 and 2 meetings, either by traveling to New York City or by videoconferencing using iChat. In this way valued perspectives enrich our research on a regular basis. In fact, the uses of videoconferencing afford important conversations within and across the tiers.

As I learn from my study I make sure that I have sufficiently compelling data to support the patterns of coherence and the associated contradictions. I want all claims to be nuanced and illustrated with vignettes, narratives of what I experienced as a researcher. For any pattern of coherence, or claim I want to make about the study, I expect to have multiple data sources. That is, I do not want to make a claim that is based only on interview, or just on my impressions of one short excerpt from videotape. Hence, as a pattern and its associated contradictions begin to emerge I examine the design of the study to ensure that I get more data resources to address the pattern and associated contradictions. When I call for multiple data resources I mean that the data assembled to support coherence and contradictions should be compelling, supported by evidence that is appropriate for the claim.

INVOLVING STUDENTS AS RESEARCHERS

The use of students as researchers provides a way to obtain their perspectives on what is salient in terms of school, teaching, learning and myriad other issues. Having identified foci for research they can provide insights into what is happening and why it is happening, in terms of patterns of coherence and contradictions. Especially since we began doing research in urban high schools we have utilized numerous student researchers and their expertise has benefited the research. Elsewhere Rowhea Elmesky and I provided a detailed account of the ways in which we have expanded the roles of students in our research (Elmesky and Tobin 2005). Here I provide some windows into their roles, how they enacted them, and what use we made of their intellectual work.

Initially the key idea in using student researchers was to obtain their answer to the question of how to better teach kids like me on a lesson-by-lesson basis. This role then expanded to allow student researchers to interview their peers. I was astonished by the work of Tyrone in this regard. He took the task very seriously and prepared for his interviews by coming to my methods classes to hear what issues we spoke about and browsing through the bookshelves in my office to get insights into issues that were central to urban education. For example, without prompting from me he perused a book that addressed Fordham and Ogbu's ideas about acting white and then proceeded to interview a number of his peers about the construct (Fordham and Ogbu 1986).

The battle for me has been to include the student researchers as researchers and not regard them as data resources enacting different roles. Accordingly, we schedule research meetings with the student researchers to discuss our research in relation to theory and methodology. As the student researchers begin to understand the theoretical underpinnings they can connect with the research and identify and produce resources that would not otherwise inform the research. Their development as scholars is no different than any other researcher – that is university and teacher researchers. What tends to hold them back is a tendency for some of us to reify traditional student-adult power differences. For example, some of our most successful teacher-researchers, such as Alex, had difficulty in dealing with the expanded roles of student researchers, such as Shakeem. As researchers we welcomed Shakeem's perspectives on teaching and learning; however, as a teacher Alex regarded some of them as brash and disrespectful. Also, when Shakeem returned to his classroom his critical discourse about what was happening was sometimes regarded as "out of line." Being a student researcher allows students to produce new culture that can transform their identities and roles in many facets of their lifeworlds. As student researchers learn to use their voices to identify new sources of inequity and to advocate new roles and activities it is not surprising that the traditional power brokers might resist these new forms of culture. The potential for student researchers to encounter difficulties because of their changed agency and identity ought to be closely monitored to ensure they do not encounter serious problems.

Interviewing Peers

When student researchers interview their peers the peer-to-peer talk seems to be distinctively different than occurs when an adult, like me, conducts an interview. My approach has been to talk to the student researchers about conducting interviews and let them decide how many students to interview, whom to interview, and what to ask. Whether or not follow up interviews are desirable also is left to the student researcher to decide. I encourage student researchers to write a brief analytic memorandum about each interview, focusing on what was done and what was learned. The student researcher then transcribes the interview, which is recorded on a small hand held digital recorder.

In terms of the mechanics of doing an interview I usually discuss the place of the interview with the student researcher, the optimal length, and the ways to avoid interrupting responses with questions. The heuristic we use and advise student researchers to use is to let the persons being interviewed know that they should consider questions as invitations to discuss issues that are important to them, especially things that happen commonly in their class and contradictions. The persons being interviewed should talk for as long as they want to, until they run out of gas. When they let the student researcher know they are out of gas (using the timeout signal from sports) the turn at talk can transfer to the student researcher who can then ask for clarification, elaboration, or pose a fresh question.

The following transcript is from an audiotape made by Tyrone as he listened to the playback of an interview with Amirah. Tyrone was fluent orally and we obtained much richer interpretations when he audiotaped his interpretations. In Tyrone's case we did not consider it good use of his time to transcribe interviews. Accordingly, we oriented his researcher roles to his interests and capabilities. Of course when we needed his assistance to decipher parts of an interview his insider knowledge was invaluable.

> All in all, I think that was a good interview I had with Amirah because she stated a lot of good points. And she had a lot of things to get off of her head. I think it's good that a lot of …. I think a lot of people should be talking to Amirah. Not actually interviewing, not actually talking about school, but actually trying to get her to express her feelings on certain things because she has good feelings and good ideas and good thoughts. Plus she has a lot in her head. And I think some of the things need to be let off of her head, and maybe she'll be able to calm down and act like a child again. Because even though she's a teenager, and she's almost grown, she's acting a little older than she is. And she feel as though that's the right way to be. I feel as though it's good to act a little older than your age, but you're still supposed to act your age and have fun. You're not supposed to just be a 16-year-old acting like you're a 34-year-old like you've got to maintain two jobs and ten kids. She has to be able to lay back and relax sometimes. And I feel as though she feel as though she can't do it that way.

Tyrone's insights into Amirah incorporate an insider perspective that nobody else on our research team had. As an African American youth who is growing up in poverty, he recognized Amirah's necessity to fend for herself because at the age of 3, within a few months her single supporting mother died and then just a few months later, her guardian grandmother also died. Now raised by her cousin, Amirah has the responsibilities of home duties, and providing food and clothing for herself and others in the home. At home and in her neighborhood Amirah has the responsibilities of an adult and yet at school she is required to be compliant and is treated as a child. Not surprisingly, Amirah is very resistant to efforts of teachers to control her and suspicious of efforts to create collaborative activities in which she can coparticipate. Tyrone's interpretation of his interview with Amirah contained perspectives that have significant implications for the ways in which we structure classes in urban schools, interact with urban youth, and make sense of what we regard as their resistance to enacted curricula.

Doing Urban Ethnography

One of the early ways we involved student researchers was to ask them to undertake ethnography of sounds of the city. We provided them with audio and video recording equipment and invited them to record sounds in different parts of the city, such as on busy street corners, in fast flowing traffic, in parks, in stores, on a building site, and on bustling sidewalks. After a discussion about what was happening and why, the students used iMovie and QuickTime Pro as tools to produce a movie, to capture what they learned from their ethnography. To us, their movie and the processes that led to its production were salient windows into their perspectives on science and its intersections with an aspect of urban life. Foci for other video ethnographies undertaken by student researchers included the shopping mall, rapping in the 'hood, going to church, my family, and homework.

In a similar vein we have taught high school youth an elective course on public interest anthropology, whereby they learned how to do ethnography and then undertook a study of their neighborhoods, exploring issues of salience to the residents. These ethnographies provide compelling insights into the neighborhoods in which urban schools are situated and can inform the foci and interpretations of ongoing research that focuses primarily on what is happening in classrooms.

Video Vignettes

As an alternative to one of the coteachers identifying video vignettes for analysis and discussion we regularly asked students to identify and analyze clips that were salient to our research. The video vignette and associated analyses then were discussed critically during a research meeting. The following is an example of a written critique of a video vignette identified by student researchers from Ms. Bonds' science class.

Ms. Bonds Boring (January 16 2003)

The way she was teaching was appalling. She just sat on the table and lectured the students. As you can see the students are very uninterested and are not listening. As a student I know that that isn't an effective way to teach the class. Ms. Bonds was also lacking power. I say this because earlier in the clip the students were out of control and very rambunctious and when she said stop they ignored her. There was only one student who was actually paying attention. Later on in the clip she started yelling and shouting commands and instructions at the class. Yelling to your class isn't effective because it will just be an invitation for that student to be impertinent to you and to be resistant towards you. A student may also sense that the teacher doesn't care if she/he yells at the student.

Although the above interpretations are harsh for Ms. Bonds to read she welcomed the feedback, along with some earlier comments from student researchers that she was "stiff, white, standin'." In effect the student researchers identified a potential connection between a teacher's verve and the interest and focus of students. Students tended to shut down whether Ms. Bonds stood straight and talked at them or sat on her desk and talked at them. Consistently the student researchers selected examples of ineffective teaching as those in which the teacher was relatively immobile. In contrast, examples of good teaching were those in which the teacher showed oral fluency and moved her body energetically. Another key point in this analysis of the vignette is the senselessness of a teacher's efforts to establish control over students (rather than creating collaborative rituals) and especially acting in ways that are disrespectful and likely to catalyze forms of resistance.

The student researchers are wonderful storytellers and can produce autoethnographies and autobiographies – especially using video and audio media. We also had a great deal of success in asking student researchers to document their 'autobiographies, for example, as science learners, in written form. The following is an example from Natasia:

> As the years go by it seems that I have done worst in sciences, the reason being my attention span and tolerance for being ideal. When I say "my attention span" I mean that when I get bored I acquire a short attention span. When this occurs I tend to sleep, disrupt the class, talk to the other students and other things of that nature, therefore my work doesn't get completed. When I say my "tolerance for being ideal" I mean my zero tolerance for having nothing to do. This only happens when I finish my work before the rest of the class and then I have nothing to do. I absolutely dislike to have nothing to do, in this case my work would sometimes get misplaced or destroyed or very seldom turned in. It is in this case, that the only work that would get turned in is the work turned in as soon as it is completed. The other work get lost because it is mixed up in all of the junk that I have, by this point, taken out trying to find something to occupy myself with. These, in the long run, cause my grade to fall to a near failing grade. Not the best reasons, but the reasons nonetheless.
>
> I not bored in all of my science class, just chemistry and physics. Chemistry bores me be cause I had had it after I had had biochemistry which is much more in-depth than chemistry. To me chemistry is more bookwork than anything. Where as biochemistry is more lab work to me, it was fun. Physics is boring to me because all it is just a group of measurements that you will never in life use again in life. Physics is one of theses class that you really don't needs but you have to take it because they said so.
>
> The only two challenges that I have in my science class now is drawing the pictures for the magnitude and displacement, and stay awake in class.
>
> In my science class no one helps me well other then to tell me to stay awake in class. But my friends help me to stay on task as far as homework, now. Other than the usual, there's nothing much to say about homework. We don't really get much of if it, but we do get homework, and sometimes it useful and sometimes it not.

Natasia's narrative raises some crucial points that also arose in other parts of our research. As a grade nine youth Natasia was clearly the leader in her class and had quick insights into the biological sciences, especially genetics. In the four years of high school Natasia struggled to succeed despite the fact that she wanted to be a doctor, had a strong interest in science and studied at least one and often two science courses a year. Issues addressed in her narrative include the lack of challenge in school science, catering for talented students, connecting studies to the interests and perceived relevance of students, sequencing science courses, the role of homework, and ways in which teachers and other students can provide support for learning.

Making PowerPoint Presentations

Student researchers are routinely asked to prepare PowerPoint presentations to support oral presentations they will make at research meetings and to stakeholder groups like peers and teachers. The students create presentations that include text, graphics, illustrations, digital images, and short video clips. Such presentations serve multiple purposes such as viably presenting student researchers' perspectives, allowing student researchers to become technologically fluent, and providing a context for interactive exchanges about research.

Students as Teachers and Teacher Educators

As we undertook research in urban classrooms we have been responsive to requests by school administrators and teachers to offer a variety of options to benefit the students and hence the school. For example, we have provided elective credit for student researchers to teach science to children in a nearby middle school. We worked out a plan with the principals and other administrators and the science teachers from the two schools. According to the plan a group of high school students would meet with our researchers on Mon, Tues to plan what they would teach on Wed and Thurs and then on Fri the group would meet to review what they had learned from their experiences and how to make improvements for next week. We divided the middle school class of about 30 students into five groups, each taught by two high school student researchers. In a semester we typically taught two five-week units to the middle school students. This activity created many foci for intensive research, including our teaching of the student researchers on Monday and Tues, the students' coteaching on Wed and Thurs and the critical analyses and research undertaken on Friday. In addition, we were most interested to see how the experiences of teaching others afforded the learning of science and the emergence of new roles as learners in the student researchers' other classes.

Obviously there are many potential foci for research in just the peer teaching activity described above. In this example, the school requested the activity and as a research team we did not have the resources to study it to fully realize the potential of the data resources that were accessible to us. Importantly we had to limit the scope of what we researched and focus our efforts on doing the activity successfully, being sure to answer the broad questions of what is happening and why is it happening. However, it is also important not to privilege the sort of research I do over the sorts undertaken by the teacher and student researchers. Although I was not collecting data resources at the micro level to support my research agenda, the students and teachers undertook research to improve the quality of the activity and to learn what might be retained from this study for enactment in the forthcoming semesters and years. In terms of the authenticity criteria all participants in the peer teaching activity were guided by and achieved all four of them. Students, teachers, administrators and university researchers learned enough from the study to be able to describe what happens and make suggestions on what should happen in the future. Furthermore, if challenged in any point there were compelling data to support claims.

On a regular basis we arrange for the student researchers to interact one-on-one with small groups of prospective teachers in their methods classes and as an expert panel. In this way they disseminate what has been learned from our research in ways that can potentially impact practice. Even though student researchers have coauthored papers and book chapters with other researchers, their roles as teacher educators and when they use PowerPoint presentations (as described above) are the most authentic ways we have used to allow them to present their voices in credible and authentic ways. Obviously, such presentations also serve as data resources for ongoing analyses and interpretations. In addition, the following testimony from a candidate science teacher suggests she found the information provided by the panel of urban youth to be of considerable value.

> You were all great! I know I, personally, learned a lot (probably more than you think we all did). I am new to the Philly public school system, and I just want to say that you have helped to alter my perspective on the school system. All of you were articulate, candid, and well spoken. You also helped me to see some of the things that can make me a better teacher (being caring, but not overbearing; or to be sure to approach the students before calling the parents; and many other things).

Just as we have expanded the roles of students to allow them to contribute to key aspects of education, it is feasible to expand the roles of parents, school administrators, and members of the community. Appealing pathways for getting them involved as coresearchers are coteaching and cogenerative dialogues.

AUTO/ETHNOGRAPHY AND AUTO/BIOGRAPHY

It seemed to me that much of the research in urban education was premised on deficit perspectives of the school systems, the teachers and the students. While I acknowledge that unbridled optimism is unlikely to catalyze the improvements in urban education that we all would like to see, I am equally sure that describing a flawed landscape and producing policies to hold participants accountable for the flaws will not produce improvements of the required magnitude. Accordingly, when I faced mounting contradictions about urban science education I resolved to undertake auto/ethnography – to learn from ethnography of my own efforts to teach science in inner city schools. These initial efforts were followed up by studies of others' teaching, however in a context in which I cotaught with regular urban science teachers.

When I began my research in urban schools in 1998 I didn't set out to do auto/ethnography – but with hindsight it was exactly the right thing to do. The problem for me was that I had just moved to Philadelphia and the schools in the inner city were unlike any I had ever experienced in my lengthy career as a teacher and researcher. The first hint that there was something wrong came in the form of complaints from my science methods students who felt that what I was teaching them "didn't work." I felt that what I was teaching was solid and that they were just not up to the task of teaching in urban schools. When I observed Donovan teach at City High – the supervisor of one of my student teachers – I did not regard him as effective. My perspectives were external, distant, and laden with deficits. As I previously described, Donovan agreed to coteach with me – however, he did not do that, leaving me instead to go it alone. I did not mind since I was confident of success. What a shock to me when I found that I was unsuccessful.

Autobiographies and the stories about how I taught and why I did what I did flowed in narrative form. Naturally the stories incorporated an historical perspective that brought the different cultures of suburban and rural students in Australian schools in the 1960s and 1970s into juxtaposition with urban youth in the 1990s and 2000s. Through a variety of theoretical lenses the research showed that my teaching, which I felt to be effective in Australian high schools several decades earlier, could not adapt to the culture of the students and provide the structures needed to expand their agency and afford their learning of science. When this study began my research group was relatively small, consisting of a doctoral student, a student teacher, and several high school students who served as researchers. Donovan was a researcher too, but it took him some time to assume that role. So, making sense of the data resources was very difficult in the first six weeks or so. I had field notes, videotape, many formal and informal interviews, and regular conversations with Donovan. I was puzzled by the way in which the students refused to show me respect and virtually ignored me when I spoke to them. They would not cooperate with me and often put their heads down as if to sleep in my class. If I pushed too hard they responded aggressively and I was clearly out of my depth. To make matters worse, they had difficulty understanding my Australian accent and I found it impossible to understand their dialect. The learning environments in the class were dysfunctional from my perspective and I did not have the tools to create and sustain productive learning environments.

I was emotionally involved in ways I did not think possible. I had trouble sleeping and often felt so frustrated that I became angry with myself. I prepared for many hours each night and purchased materials to enrich the learning environment and build the curriculum around lab activities. To no avail – each day brought its new wave of failures to report to my close colleague Wolff-Michael Roth. Having a critical colleague to shed light on what was happening was fruitful. In those days we interacted many times a day using email – now we use iChat.[4] Even though Michael had not at that time been a researcher in urban schools of Philadelphia, he had deep theoretical insights that greatly shaped my ways of making sense of what was happening. He was sympathetic, but also a critical friend – exactly what Guba and Lincoln meant by peer debriefing. As I offered my accounts of what was happening he mentioned alternative theoretical ways to think about my experiences. I am sure that I was not as open to his suggestions as I should have been. However, two comments he made were highly influential in shaping my research and providing a foundation for much of the work we did in our urban education research. These pertained to focusing the curriculum on students' interests rather than my perceptions of what students would be interested in, and my failures to succeed being an example of a breach of habitus.

Students' Interests as a Focus for Curriculum

I was convinced that I would succeed as a teacher if the students were interested in science. Like most teachers I felt that I had to cover the state and school district standards and so I worked from them to plan a lab centered approach in which students also talked and read a lot about science. I found myself relying heavily on what and how I taught in Australia up until 1974 when I became a university teacher educator. I was confident that, as David Hawkins had noted in his classic paper *Messing about in Science* (Hawkins 1965), the students would be curious about science and use inquiry as a basis for learning. Michael pointed out to me that each of the units I designed was built around my sense of what the students were interested in rather than what they said they were interested in. Although this is quite a difference in orientation I did not see the difference initially. I felt that if I designed labs that were interesting students would create interests in new aspects of science, and learn. The following is an excerpt from an autobiography, one of many written in conjunction with this study.

> I was determined to enact a science curriculum that was libratory and potentially transformative in the sense that, by virtue of their participation and learning, students would have a better appreciation of their world, enhanced opportunities for advanced study in science, and increased choices for career placement and training (Barton 1997). I wanted to enact a curriculum that the students would perceive as interesting, relevant to their lives, and useful. To the extent possible I wanted the students to have choices in what they would study and where they would study it. I predicted that they would enjoy doing science if the program was based on investigations and I had a preference for the activities to involve real world problem solving. Although I would focus on inquiry as a means to develop deep understandings of science subject matter the critical defining characteristic of my approach to the science curriculum would be deep learning whereby students would pursue areas of interest in detail and, in so doing, employ a multitude of resources to support their learning.
>
> Even though I began to teach with a transformative/libratory agenda I was by no means sure of how to proceed with the teaching of consecutive units on chemistry and physics. I intended to use a multi-faceted approach. For example, I wanted students to read about contemporary science and thought they could access science from journals, newspapers, magazines, and the Internet. To accommodate my initial thoughts on what the enacted curriculum might be like I requested that my class be scheduled for two days

in a computer lab and three in a science room that would support a range of activity types, including investigations.

I planned to begin with an activity sequence on chromatography, examining the dyes from M & Ms and Skittles because those items of candy were potentially interesting to students, involved simple materials with which they were familiar, and could easily connect to a unit on food and nutrition. While studying food coloring and the relative safety of different dyes I believed we also could study the chemical constituents of the foods consumed by students in various meals. As part of a unit on food and nutrition I considered that students might grow sprouts, radishes, and other edible plants. Also, within the chemistry course, I thought they might grow fast plants, study life cycles, and learn how to grow nutritious plants, such as corn, in relatively quick time. I did not expect that these activities would replace chemistry but set a context in which concepts of chemistry could be explicated.

Narrative accounts like this can be used in a publication as a vignette – thick descriptions that provide detailed accounts of my experiences in a holistic, unfolding sense that is well-captured by narratives.

Peer Debriefing

I wrote several papers that were published and in the process applied sociocultural theory to make sense of my experience. By publishing with a student teacher, doctoral student and one of the high school students I was learning from their perspectives and in the papers made sure that their perspectives were retained. However it was in my first autobiographical piece from this study that Michael, as a peer reviewer, made the comment that my habitus was being breached. I did not like to read that at first because it seemed to impugn my teaching – yet in hindsight it was a critical review that allowed the research to progress in leaps and bounds. Once I realized that my teaching, as praxis, was not working as I intended I began to see that, in becoming conscious of what was happening, my teaching lacked fluency and was not timely, anticipatory or appropriate. This realization drew attention to the ontological characteristics of teaching and focused attention back on how I was implementing my methods course. Clearly there were major contradictions between my experiences in teaching at City High and how I was expecting my student teachers to learn to teach.

Writing papers and presenting them at national meetings opened the door for peer debriefing and when I returned from the April meetings I was determined to coteach with Donovan, rather than always be the central teacher. From that point onward the classes were much more productive and the doctoral student also got involved in coteaching. With more teachers the students were able to expand their agencies and learn more science and the coteachers were able to experience more teaching and learn to teach by being at one another's elbows. As coteachers we also were coresearchers and had direct access to important experiences associated with learning to teach, teaching science, and learning science. From this point onwards all of my research in urban science classes employed a methodology of coteaching.

Learning from the Literature

A key resource at any stage of research is the research and theorizing of others. In my urban research there are three good examples of the ways in which others' scholarship made a profound difference to the focus and practice of my research. The first example of a central resource was a pair of publications by a colleague of mine from the sociology department at the University of Pennsylvania. Elijah Anderson had written two books, *Streetwise* (Anderson 1990) and *Code of the Street* (Anderson 1999). In these books he wrote about the culture of African American youth in West Philadelphia. In particular, he wrote about the poverty extant in this part of the city and the ways in which respect assumes the place of a currency. Respect had to be shown and it had to be earned. I read with great fervor and built new lenses for making sense of my autobiography and making sense of what people were telling me about my teaching and their learning. The students were earning respect among themselves by showing their disrespect for me. Anderson laid out a culture that was foreign to me and as I gleaned insights into it, I was able to make sense of what had happened in my class and then to educate others about what I was learning and even to catalyze changes in the learning environments of the classes I taught.

My involvement in sociocultural theory was somewhat ad hoc, often related to the citations of colleagues and their recommendations about which scholars and works were germane to my research. Of course, doctoral students were a wonderful source of new ideas and resources to study. However, in the early 1990s I realized my reading needed to be much more systematic and I decided to study a course in African American psychology and then two doctoral-level courses in theoretical sociology. These courses allowed me to identify new ways of looking at my research, which was deeply influenced by Wade Boykin's ideas about African American dispositions and the triple quandary faced by participants from minority ethnic and racial groups (Boykin 1986). An even greater emphasis was due to William Sewell's perspectives on culture, structure and agency (Sewell 1992 1999). Direct outcomes of my re-education were dramatic changes in focus and methodology, especially in my uses of microanalysis to augment what I referred to then as critical ethnography.

My entrée into microanalysis placed a strong focus on interactions of participants with structures (i.e., resources). My theoretical framework, which was essentially post-Bourdieusian, did not successfully connect interactions with the creation of productive learning environments. Regina Smardon, and later Stacy Olitsky, took courses from Randall Collins, who was completing a book on *Interaction Ritual Chains* (Collins 2004). They introduced me to his theoretical framework and immediately we saw applications in our research. Over a period of years we incorporated Collins's sociology of emotions into our theoretical framework to produce a coherent theory that afforded research across the micro, meso, and macro levels of social life.

Incorporating Microanalysis into Critical Ethnography

During my studies of others' teaching and the associated learning environments I incorporated critical ethnography as I described earlier and microanalysis, based on the uses of videotape. In the next section I focus on the methodology employed in microanalysis using two studies undertaken by Alex (Tobin 2006a) and Victoria (Tobin 2006b) respectively. As I have done previously, I use excerpts from a paper written about this research to make salient points.

Microanalysis involves the use of videotape to examine practices in detail by replaying excerpts and manipulating the replay speed to search for patterns and associated contradictions. I use the iMovie application to produce and analyze videoclips. For users of the Windows Operating system the applications I have found most useful are QuickTime Pro and Studio Mediasuite (version 10 by Pinnacle). Transana is a cross-platform application that many researchers use[5].

What's Happening?

When I do microanalyses I explore agency|structure relationships in detail. First, I address the general question of "what is happening?" and then undertake a detailed analysis of "why is that happening?." In the following example, the answer to what is happening is referenced to the practices of key participants during a selected vignette. How do you decide whether or not a vignette is salient? I watch videotape and identify episodes that are relevant to the research questions. The episode should depict either a good example of what tends to happen or a contradiction to what usually happens. The first thing I do is to write a short description of what the episode represents – for example, in this episode a female shows unusually intense engagement in a dissection lab. It is unusual in that most students participate in sporadic ways and are easily distracted. Also, it is often the case that males are more often engaged than females. The amount and quality of the engagement make this episode quite salient to the roles of urban youth in lab activities that connect directly to their interests and in which they have the autonomy to choose what, how, when and with whom. Also salient in this episode is the central role of Alex, the science teacher. In contrast to what is often advocated vis a vis the role of a teacher in a lab, Alex enacts his roles in a very central way, exhibiting his competence in science fluently and showing students what and how to participate. When he joins students he does so with purpose and structures their experiences so that they can participate autonomously in his absence.

The selection of an episode is followed by detailed analysis that focuses on the unfolding agency|structure relationships in terms of verbal and non-verbal interactions among selected participants. The analyses involve the production of a transcript that includes details of the words spoken as a function of time, body movements and the appropriation of resources.

Science in the *Science Education and Technology* small learning community was taught in a former shop room – a large room in the basement of City High. My initial impression, based on entry to the classroom, was how different the classroom felt and looked. There were no students seated in the desks where whole class interactions usually occurred and Alex was nowhere to be seen. Clusters of students were interacting at workbenches dispersed throughout the large classroom. At the dissection table four students were examining the latex gloves, dissection kits, and aprons. As they got themselves ready to start their dissections Alex emerged from the storeroom with a frog, still in a plastic bag. As Kareem, one of the students, placed the frog on the dissecting tray, Alex began to interact with the students about their roles and the resources they could use to support their learning. In addition to the lab equipment and materials the resources available to support the students' learning included manuals for the organisms they were to dissect, a computer connected to the Internet with a high-speed T1 line, reference books, peers, and Alex.

During an eight-minute vignette selected from the beginning of a lesson Alex came to the dissection group on four occasions. His first visit to the group was brisk, lasting less than a minute. While he was with the group he explained what equipment was available for them to use and reviewed the division of labor that the group might adopt. He negotiated with Katrina who had dissected a frog yesterday and discussed what she needed to include in a report on the dissection of a starfish. He suggested to her that she dissect a grasshopper today, adjacent to the other three students in the group, who would dissect a frog. Alex listened attentively to Katrina and requests for equipment from the others in the group. Then he explained to them the value of doing their dissections close to one another, thereby affording comparisons of the structures of the two organisms that were very different from one another. He then left the group purposefully, to get what they needed from the storeroom. Immediately, the group commenced various forms of participation.

Within a minute Alex returned to the group with a grasshopper to be dissected. As he arrived the two females requested gloves, since Katrina did not yet have any and Samantha's gloves were too small. Alex affirmed that he would get them and, noticing Katrina pull back the frog's outer skin with her fingers, discussed safety and explained that students should treat the animal with respect, using a probe to hold back the skin, lift organs and so forth. As Alex spoke to the students they stopped what they were doing and oriented their heads to listen to him. After explaining to them how to use the probe he volunteered to give them his dissection kit, which contained a greater array of scalpels and dissection tools. After 50 seconds with the group Alex left with the comment "go to work!"

From the moment Alex arrived at the group he was an active participant. He interacted with Katrina and Darnell and challenged what they were doing and why they were doing it. Based on his experience he knew they would want to cut and remove the organs without a plan and so he asked questions that would pique their curiosity, directing them to other resources so that they would know what to look for, in determining the sex of their frog for example. Alex showed his knowledge of the anatomy of the frog and at the same time made it clear to the students that they would decide what to do and when and how to do it. That is, through his verbal and non-verbal practices Alex expanded the agency of all three students who remained in the group during the above interactions. Figure 3.7 shows the orientation of the four participants in this episode.

Figure 3.7. The participants lean forward to interact about dissecting a frog.

Utterances and Time as Resources

As an example of how verbal interactions are used as a resource, I provide a transcript of a segment of a frog dissection in which Alex interacts with Katrina and Darnell. The conventions I use are similar to those employed by Roth (2005) and are printed using Courier font, because each character is assigned equal spacing, making it possible to vertically align speech utterances that occur at the same time.

The following transcript[6] depicts fast talk and fluent action as participants use gestures, tool manipulation, and body sways to interact successfully with one another and material resources. Chains of verbal and non-verbal interactions are in synchrony and produce successful outcomes and obvious signs of enjoyment, interest and sustained involvement from all participants.

```
1. Katrina: These two things
2. Darnell: =Well what about it?
(1.4)
3. Katrina: Let's find out where it's going
(0.6)
4. Alex: See but that's why you cut things. Well. You, make a
decision.
```

5. Katrina: =It's coming. It's got. It's got. I think it's coming this way.
6. Darnell: =It's the smaller thing. It's right there.
7. Alex: =Where?
8. Darnell: =This.
9. Alex: =Yeah. The end of it is called the cloaca. That's probably gonna be the gall bladder. But you figure that out.
(0.8)
10. Alex: Take. Start taking organs off from the top end then. Right?
11. Darnell: =Are you serious?
12. Katrina: =Can we cut it here? (0.4) Can we cut it here?
13. Darnell: =No. No. You're going to cut its gender loops
14. Alex: =Awright. Let me tell you.
15. Katrina: =I'm cutting it.
16. Darnell: =No. You're not.
17. Alex: =First of all, do you know if it's a female or a male?
(0.5)
18. Darnell: Yep.
(0.8)
19. Alex: That's a question for you
20. Darnell: =I don't see nuthin' there so I guess ((points to the groin))
21. Alex: =Well if it's in there on the bottom there. If it's a female you know (1.1) actually on the end of that website it'll tell you what to do to figure out if it's a male or a female. I think it's a male to tell you the truth.
(0.6)
22. Alex: I need to go fro:m
23. Katrina: =Can I cut it around here?
(0.3)
24. Alex: I I don't know.
(0.8)
25. Eventually you might want to cut here but I don't know if you want to cut here yet.
(0.8)
26. Right. (0.2) See. (0.3) Do the organs first and then find out
(1.3)
27. Darnell: Why for?
28. Alex: =Because the opening for the anus is going to be different for from everybody. Right?
29. Darnell: =Awright.
30. Alex: =Now what are you doing with your hand?
(0.5)
31. Katrina: Me?
(0.4)
32. Alex: Yeah.
(0.5)
33. Katrina: I'm doing what I can.
(1.2)
34. Alex: Okay. What's your plan? What are you guys gonna do? What and why are you doing what you're doing? Right now you're just exploring and just poking around?
35. Darnell: =Yeah. [I'm not. I'm not
36. Katrina: [I'm finding that You see this rough thing attach with this?
37. Alex: =Hm. Hm.

38. Katrina: =allow me to see if this one prefer that it makes it um um
(1.2)
39. Alex: You wanna see how the opening goes from the mouth to over there. Right?
40. Katrina: =Hm. Hm.
41. Alex: =Right?
(0.9)
42. Darnell: Awright. I take this out from right here?
(0.7)
43. Katrina: Oh. It's [the heart?
44. Darnell: [I can dig deeper down in there?
(0.2)
45. Alex: Yeah. (0.4) Did you want to remove the liver?
46. Darnell: =Yeah.
47. Alex: =So what I'd say before you do that, go on the website and see if it suggests a cut because they'll suggest to you how to cut and where to cut to get the liver out easily and not destroy anything else. Okay?
((Darnell leaves to access the website))
(0.6)
48. Alex: Put your aprons on, both of you. Put aprons on you won't stink. (0.5) ((Alex strides away from the group)) Aprons are over there. So you won't stink when you go home. ((Both girls move to get aprons and Alex leaves to interact with another group))

Alex spoke for 22 of the 48 moves and in so doing provided suggestions for dissecting the frog (moves 10, 25, 26, 39, 45), asked questions to create a focus (moves 21, 47), showed evidence of interest and curiosity (moves 7, 28), suggested resources for the students to access (moves 21, 47), affirmed the autonomy of students (move 4), used canonical knowledge (move 9), challenged students (move 34), showed uncertainty (move 24), and emphasized safety (move 48). Only 1 of the 22 verbal moves focused on what not to do and was likely to create negative emotional energy (move 48). On this occasion Alex waited until there was a transition and Darnell had moved off before he spoke firmly, briskly stressing what had to be done and alluding to an earlier joke about avoiding the "stinking up" of clothing due to splashing of the formaldehyde used to preserve the frog.

Katrina was central in the dissection because of her prior experience, knowledge, and where she sat – directly in front of the dissecting tray with the others on either side of her. Since Katrina had the dissecting tools throughout the interaction it is no surprise that 9 of her 12 verbal moves consisted of talk about the organism. Of the other 3 verbal moves, one was clarifying, one was explaining, and the third affirmed an agreement. Hence Katrina's talk was an extension of her manipulation of the dissecting tools and her gestures, many of which pointed to specific organs.

Darnell was between Katrina and Alex and interacted with both of them, often providing short verbal affirmations to acknowledge what they had said. Sometimes these took the form of acknowledgement (move 18), agreement (moves 29, 46) and disagreement (moves 13, 16). Also, because he had dissection tools in his hand, many of his verbal moves were about the frog (moves 6, 8, 20, 42, 44). Other verbal moves involved challenging Katrina (move 2), expressing surprise (move

11), raising a query (move 27), and explaining (move 35). None of his turns at talk were especially long, the longest being six to eight words about the organism being dissected.

Pam was silent and attentive throughout the interaction, observing how to use the dissection tools and listening to Katrina and Alex. Her attention was intensive and at times she leant forward to observe closely. Pam's head moves and body orientation and sways were in synchrony with the dynamic structure of the frog dissection. Her participation appeared to be an active form of observation. As soon as Pam collected her apron she was ready to assume Katrina's place as the central person involved in dissecting the frog.

The pauses in the transcribed episode ranged from immeasurable to 1.4 seconds. Few pauses exceeded 1 second. In fact, the transcript shows many instances of overlapping speech and speaker exchanges that were not separated by a discernible pause. Twenty-seven of the 48 moves were separated by immeasurable pauses of 0.1 seconds or less. My interpretation is that the participants were coparticipating and maintained brisk interchanges that added to rather than detracted from making sense of the task at hand – to dissect the frog and learn about its anatomy. The longer pauses occur between and within moves. The distinction is somewhat arbitrary since I could have created a new move whenever a pause of more than 0.2 seconds occurred. I did not, however, preferring to change moves with speaker or when the semantic focus changed. Fourteen pauses separated different speakers. That is, pauses were resources for changing speaker, affording the agency of speakers and presumably the listeners as well. I analyzed these interactions to see if there were patterns. Five of the 14 pauses followed an utterance from Alex, three to Darnell (0.5, 1.3, 0.9) and two to Katrina (0.5, 0.5). Four of the speaker exchanges involved Darnell, transferring twice to Katrina (1.4, 0.7) and twice to Alex (0.8, 0.2). The remaining five transfers were from Katrina to Alex (0.6, 0.3, 0.4, 1.2, 1.2). This trend more than likely reflects Alex's central role in creating structures to allow students to be autonomous in proceeding with the dissection in his absence. Katrina spoke about the frog and when she paused for a sufficient time Alex followed up with the verbal moves previously described. The transfers associated with pauses of 1.2 seconds were salient in the interaction in that in each case Alex spoke for longer, the first calling for a group plan and the second suggesting a procedure they might follow in their dissection of the frog. Even though these verbal moves followed Katrina's comments, they were directed at Darnell and Pam who would have to create the plan and in a short time assume full responsibility for dissecting the frog[7].

Eleven discernible pauses were not associated with a change of speaker. These pauses ranged from a low of 0.2 to a high of 1.1. With one exception all of these discernible pauses occurred in Alex's speech. Katrina showed the group where to cut, paused for 0.4 seconds, and then asked if she could cut an organ in a particular spot. In all other instances, it was Alex who used discernible pauses and retained a turn at talk. On most occasions, and for all speakers other than Alex, discernible pauses signaled the end of a turn at talk.

There is a high degree of synchrony among the participants as Katrina, Darnell and Alex interact and Pam leans forward to observe. Katrina and Darnell continue to use the dissecting tools as they verbally interact with Alex and ascertain how to structure the dissection of the frog. Figure 3.8 shows the coordination of Katrina's and Darnell's hands as they examine various organs and discuss how to proceed. The ungloved hand of Alex points to the cloaca (move 9) as he identifies what is possibly the gall bladder. Interaction chains involving Alex, Katrina and Darnell are in synchrony, mutually constituting a dynamic structure that affords individual and collective agency of all participants.

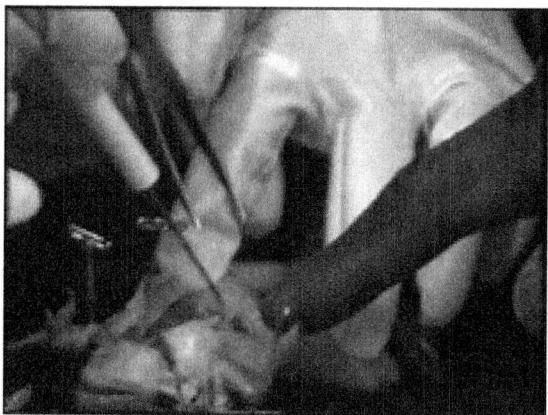

Figure 3.8. As Alex points, Katrina and Darnell use a probe and forceps to explore the frog's organs synchronously.

The analyses suggest that sense making during interactions about a material object, this time a frog's organs, extend far beyond talk, and that the meaning arises from more than the spoken words; requiring (in this case) a frog and the tools, gestures and body orientations used to create and sustain focus among participants. The transcript shows that the talk flows quickly from speaker to speaker, with short turns at talk, and some overlapping speech. The speech structures the interactions, contributing to meaning making in many ways as the purposes of dissecting the frog become clearer and emerge from the unfolding experiences. These interactions are not rehearsed or a result of careful planning by any of the participants. Alex has experience of teaching dissection to other classes and students within this class and in previous years he has enacted dissection activities in his classes. However, what happens in this vignette is similar to what has happened before and unique in the ways in which participants interact with one another and appropriate structures to meet their goals – which change from the first to the 47th turn at talk.

Pitch and Amplitude of Utterances

In the above analysis I did not explore the intonation of the voice or variations in the amplitude within and between speakers. PRAAT is a cross-platform tool that can be used to analyze audio files to provide measures of variables such as time, pitch and amplitude of utterances (Boersma and Weenink 2006). I usually export the sound from iMovie or QuickTime Pro, as an AIF file, which can be read into PRAAT and is ready for analysis. Because PRAAT provides plots of pitch and amplitude against time (for example) we can examine variations in pitch and amplitude as a function of time.

In a study of the ways in which teachers were able to adapt their culture to align with that of the students, Victoria (teacher) and Mirabelle (student) were involved in a series of interactions in which emotions were salient. Victoria was showing the class how to obtain information about chemical valence from the periodic table. Mirabelle listened to Victoria and then attempted to provide an alternative model for valence. Victoria did not accept the model as viable and the exchange between Victoria, Mirabelle and several of her classmates involved many examples of cultural alignment and misalignment. Data resources include a transcript, analyses of the audio file to obtain measures of time, pitch and amplitude, and analyses of a video to obtain descriptions of gestures and body movements.

```
Victoria:    Look at the placement on (83 dB, 294 Hz) the table
             (0.3) of the element. So that's the trick for
             figuring out the valence electrons. ((Mirabelle
             raises her hand.)) Yes Mirabelle.
             (0.1)
Mirabelle:   I figured out (79 dB, 233 Hz) a system way you can
             remember. (0.8) [How many val- valence electrons?
Victoria     [yeah. So this is the trick. The placement on the
             table↑ is how you can remember how many electrons
             there are. (1.2) So now it's two boxes over?
             (0.7)
Mirabelle:   I'm not talkin' about that.
             (0.6)
Victoria:    What are you talking about? (77 dB, 227 Hz)
             (0.9)
Mirabelle:   Arright. (75 dB, 213 Hz)
             (0.6)
Victoria:    You just said placement for valence electrons
             [so that's the trick.
Mirabelle:   [Yeah, there's another way you can figure it out.
             (1.2)
Victoria:    This is (79 dB, 321 Hz) the way to do this.
```

Victoria reviews valence of elements in terms of electron configuration and the placement of elements on the periodic table. She wants students to be able to look at the group in which the element is placed and predict its valence. She refers to this as a "trick for figuring out valence electrons." Mirabelle, seated at the end of the second of three rows, raises her hand and volunteers that she has "figured out a way you can remember how many valence electrons." However, before she can complete her sentence, Victoria speaks in overlapping speech that "Yeah. This is the trick."

As Victoria continues to explain how to figure out valence from the periodic table Mirabelle interrupts her to emphasize that she is speaking about something different. Numerous non-verbal interactions between students communicate solidarity among them. At 30 seconds, as Victoria says, "This *is* the way to do this." Tasha, the student sitting adjacent to Mirabelle, turns her head toward her, smiling broadly as she makes eye contact. Victoria's statement is a challenge to Mirabelle and the way she says it, raising intensity and pitch, may have created a resonant structure for Mirabelle and other students in the class. Heads turn, attention is focused on Mirabelle, and there is anticipation about what is to follow. Mirabelle inclines her head to one side, makes eye contact with Tasha, and smiles. As others in the class turn their heads they too have supportive expressions on their faces, although they do not appear to make direct eye contact with Mirabelle. The head turns and eye gaze of many students suggest that Mirabelle's explanation is a mutual focus for them. Mirabelle's explanation is loud, expressive and rhythmic and she uses her right arm to gesture toward the periodic table and the teacher, pointing at times with her index finger and at other times spreading her fingers for emphasis (Figure 3.9). The student researchers recognize this as typical of how Mirabelle interacts when challenged in out-of-school settings, one of them characterizing it as bullying.

The following excerpt from my analytic notes provides a glimpse into the interactions featuring Tasha, Mirabelle and Stacy (seated in the front row) in the first five seconds of the episode.

> Tasha was in synch with Mirabelle in several ways. The two females turned their heads toward each other and smiled broadly at one another. Also as Mirabelle gestured toward the periodic table Tasha gestured at about the same frequency and each held a focus that was evident in eye gaze and head tilt. Stacy turned to look at Mirabelle and as she made eye contact with her, Tasha smiled and also turned to look at Mirabelle. The look on Stacy's face is one of empathy.
>
> In the first five seconds there is other non-verbal evidence of mutual focus. Students in the front row orient themselves either to look at Mirabelle or to watch the periodic table as they listen to her oral presentation.

The interaction sequence is characterized by several breaches when Victoria and Mirabelle speak at the same time and in opposition to one another. The intensity and pitch analyses show that Victoria speaks loudly and at a fairly high pitch as she explains about valence electrons to the whole class. When called upon Mirabelle speaks discernibly softer, 4 dB less intense and at a slightly lower frequency. Nonetheless, for a student speaking to a teacher the initial statement is relatively loud. After she completes her first explanation of what she wants to say she pauses for 0.8 seconds. This pause then becomes a resource for Victoria to take back the turn at talk. However, it is also a resource for Mirabelle to continue with her turn at talk. Accordingly, there is overlapping speech as Victoria reiterates her trick for calculating valence. Her turn at talk contains a relatively long pause of more than a second and even though Mirabelle attempts to interrupt, her effort is not loud and her hand partly covers her mouth. Victoria continues and after a pause of 0.7 seconds Mirabelle steps in, and informs the teacher that she is not talking about that. A rapid exchange occurs until Mirabelle makes it clear that she is proposing an alternative model. Mirabelle's assertion is followed by a pause of more than a second, after which Victoria is emphatic, raising her voice to 79 dB, noticeably above Mirabelle's previous turns at talk, which peak at approximately 75 dB.

Figure 3.9. The spatial orientation of the students.

Both speakers showed signs of frustration and there is a hint of anger from both of them. Mirabelle cannot locate spaces to explain her model for valence in Victoria's stream of talk. At the same time Victoria is focused on explaining to all students a way to quickly find out the valence, especially if they need to know to respond to a test question. Whereas Victoria has the symbolic capital of being the teacher, Mirabelle is supported by structures associated with solidarity among at least several peers. Hence, even though Victoria is emphatic that her way is the right way, Mirabelle uses her agency to make a case for an alternative model for valence.

DOING HIGH QUALITY RESEARCH IN CLASSROOMS

Qualitative research is an investigation of cultural enactment that describes what happens in terms of patterns that have thin coherence and contradictions to those patterns. These patterns are pieces of evidence that "hang together" and are deemed to have salience to the research. Some of the places in which patterns can be seen are in interactions among participants, schema of a field, and the participants' practices. My preference is to describe an identified pattern, and provide evidence for the pattern in the form of thick description, included in a vignette. To the extent possible multiple data resources should support each claim. It is not sufficient to identify and describe the patterns of coherence and ignore the contradictions. Special efforts should be made to identify contradictions, understand what they represent, and illustrate them with vignettes.

At a very basic level the patterns of coherence and contradictions are regarded as assertions about social life in the fields involved in a study. Similarly, they might be regarded as answers to research questions. Intellectual efforts to explain why patterns of coherence and contradictions occur should connect to the theoretical framework that underpins a study and to the empirical and theoretical works undertaken by a researcher and others. Explanations of why phenomena occur are theoretical and should elaborate on what was known prior to the study. Citations to other studies and scholarly works should be substantive and not symbolic. That is, a citation should include an explicit connection of what is learned in a study to salient aspects of the cited works. What should be clear is what has been learned from a particular study, its implications, and what needs to be done next.

Obtaining evidence for claims necessitates prolonged engagement and the use of multiple grain sizes for analyses. Roth uses a zoom lens as a metaphor for thinking about the process. For me the key to effective classroom research is learning from coparticipation in the classroom as curricula are enacted. Making sense of these experiences is the initial step in a process that employs mesoscopic analyses in which time is not manipulated. The data resources for such analyses include field notes, analytic memoranda, video replay, transcripts of conversations, including interviews, and digital photos of artifacts such as students' work, blackboard inscriptions and wall charts. My interest, in teaching and learning, focuses on the ways in which teachers and students access and appropriate, that is interact, with classroom structures. Hence, as I intensively analyze the all data resources my interest is in interactions of selected participants with social, material and symbolic resources. On the basis of these intensive analyses patterns and associated contradictions emerge. The point to emphasize here is that the patterns and contradictions are based on mesoscopic analyses.

Theoretically, evidence for any claims at the mesoscopic level should be available at the microscopic level. Of course, such evidence would be confirming and disconfirming, with the confirming instances constituting a pattern that has thin coherence. Based on my theoretical framework for cultural enactment, any pattern of thin coherence would be dialectically related to contradictions and my search would involve the identification of evidence for coherence and contradictions at the microscopic level. In this context the question of what would be a salient video clip is referenced to the mesoscopic claim. A useful episode to analyze microscopically would be one that depicts a particular instance of a pattern I have identified or contradictions to that pattern.

Returning to the metaphor of zooming, it is also possible to zoom out, which, in this case suggests a macroscopic or multi-field analysis. The macroscopic issue, in this instance, is whether or not claims made based on mesoscopic analyses are evident in other fields – that is at other times, in other types of activities associated with this class (e.g., whole class interactive; small group; individualized; labs; field trips), and in classes with different participants (e.g., same teacher with different students; same students with different teacher; different teacher and different students). In making macroscopic claims it is useful not only to project forward, but also to look backwards and situate claims historically. Also, by looking at other classes and, if relevant, other parts of the school (e.g., hallways, lunchroom, entrance foyer), claims can be made about the extent to which patterns apply in other fields. Over time it is useful to examine how culture associated with fields outside of the school permeate the porous boundaries of the school fields (e.g., such as a science classroom). It goes without saying that macroscopic analyses would explore the extent to which culture produced in a classroom permeates fields outside of the classroom, since it is assumed that education will make a positive difference on social life writ large. Hence it is within the ambit of classroom researchers to undertake studies that span the micro-, meso- and macroscopic levels of social life, building understandings of cultural production, as reproduction and transformation.

Having laid out the terrain I conclude with a cautionary note. It is always best to focus on quality and the scope of a study must be referenced to the resources available to support high quality scholarship. Whatever is planned and done should be done well, quality is a first criterion, and it has been my experience that researchers (even senior researchers) err on the side of attempting to do too much. Hence, at the planning stage of a study, identify the boundaries and, as the study unfolds, re-examine earlier decisions to ensure that what is done meets the authenticity criteria and that all claims are nuanced – paying attention to contradictions and supporting claims with compelling evidence, describing how much of it there is, and providing salient examples with thick descriptions. When I have clearly described what I have learned in a study it is for readers to decide if they are convinced and whether any of what I have learned is applicable to and has implications for their professional activities.

ACKNOWLEDGEMENTS

The research in this book is supported in part by the National Science Foundation under Grant Nos. REC-0107022 and DUE-0427570. Any opinions, findings, and conclusions or recommendations expressed in this chapter are those of the authors and do not necessarily reflect the views of the National Science Foundation.

NOTES

[1] The extent to which participants assume control for what happens or attribute control to others
[2] Female pronouns are used when male or female forms could be used.

[3] Based on questions and comments by Joe Kincheloe at a recent doctoral defense I decided to add to what I had originally written in this section.
[4] iChat is a videoconferencing application that runs on Macintosh computers
[5] http://www.transana.org/
[6] I use transcription conventions employed by Roth (2005).

[	beginning of overlapping talk or gesture;
=	equal sign at the beginning of turn indicates no gap between two speakers;
(2.1)	elapsed time in tenths of a second; sound intensity (dB) and pitch (Hz) also are in parentheses.
::	colons indicate lengthening of the preceding phoneme, approximately one tenth of a second for each colon used;
–	a dash indicates sudden stop in talk;
↑↓	arrows indicate shifts to higher or lower pitch in the immediately following utterance part;
°uh hu°	utterances surrounded by degree signs are less loud than the surrounding talk;
(())	double parentheses (italicized) are used to enclose comments and descriptions.

[7] Katrina would soon leave to dissect a grasshopper.

REFERENCES

Anderson, E. (1990). *Streetwise: Race, class, and change in an urban community*. Chicago: University of Chicago Press.

Anderson, E. (1999). *Code of the street: Decency, violence and the moral life of the inner city*. New York: W.W. Norton.

Belmont Report. (1978). *Ethical principles and guidelines for the protection of human subjects of research*. Washington, DC: The National Commission for the Protection of Human Subjects of Biomedical and Behavioral Research. Retrieved March 4, 2006, from http://ohsr.od.nih.gov/guidelines/belmont.html

Boersma, P., & Weenink, D. (2006). *Praat: Doing phonetics by computer* (Version 4.3.27) [Computer program]. Retrieved March 4, 2006, from http://www.praat.org/

Boykin, A. W. (1986). The triple quandary and the schooling of Afro-American Children. In U. Neisser (Ed.), *The school achievement of minority children: New perspectives* (pp. 57-92). Hillsdale, NJ: Erlbaum.

Collins, R. (2004). *Interaction ritual chains*. Princeton, NJ: Princeton University Press.

Elmesky, R., & Tobin, K. (2005). Expanding our understandings of urban science education by expanding the roles of students as researchers. *Journal of Research in Science Teaching, 42*, 807-828.

Fordham, S., & Ogbu, J. U. (1986). Black students' school success: Coping with the "burden of 'acting White.'" *The Urban Review, 18*, 176-206.

Guba, E., & Lincoln, Y. S. (1989). *Fourth generation evaluation*. Beverly Hills, CA: Sage.

Hawkins, D. (1965). Messing about in science. *Science and Children 2*(5), 5-9.

Kincheloe, J. L., & McLaren, P. L. (1994). Rethinking critical theory and qualitative research. In N. K. Denzin & Y. S. Lincoln (Eds.), *Handbook of qualitative research* (pp. 138-157). Thousand Oaks, CA: Sage.

Lather, P. A. (1993). Fertile obsession – Validity after poststructuralism. *Sociological Quarterly, 34*, 673-693

Roth, W-M. (2005). *Doing qualitative research: Praxis of method*. Rotterdam: Sense Publishers.

Sewell, W. H. (1992). A theory of structure: Duality, agency and transformation. *American Journal of Sociology, 98*, 1-29.

Sewell, W. H. (1999). The concept(s) of culture. In V. E. Bonell & L. Hunt (Eds.), *Beyond the cultural turn* (pp. 35-61). Berkeley: University of California Press.
Tobin, K. (2006a, January). *Structuring success in science labs.* Paper presented at the annual Hawaii International Conference on Education, Honolulu, HI.
Tobin, K. (2006b). Aligning the cultures of teaching and learning science in urban high schools. *Cultural Studies of Science Education, 1* (DOI: 10.1007/s11422-005-9008-3).

II WAYS OF DOING EDUCATIONAL RESEARCH

KATHLEEN S. BERRY

4. RESEARCH AS BRICOLAGE

Embracing Relationality, Multiplicity and Complexity

Bricolage: The processes by which … societies construct language and myth

Claude Levis-Strauss (1966)

The activity of borrowing from one's own textual heritage whatever is needed to produce new and different texts, with an emphasis on intertextual borrowing for the purposes of textual construction

Derrida (in McLerran and Patin 1997)

It has been six years since my chapter on bricolage as research was published. Since then retirement and the new worlds of thoughts, people, and geographical cultures have created new knowledge and values for my work as a bricoleur. And as a bricoleur in life and theoretical development for research, the complexity and rigour continues. In spite of retirement, just when I thought simplicity would be the rule of the day, I find life gets even more complex – that is, if 'you live it to the fullest' (with rigour and rhapsodic intellect). In retrospect, my past as a university professor governed by academic expectations and frameworks seemed so simple. Why? Because the borders were clearly defined, reward and punishment was obvious, and academic freedom was hegemonic – power meant follow the regulated society of the ivy tower. Don't get me wrong, I loved that life I; sometimes resisted dominant powers, sometimes crept through the gaps but mainly followed the taken-for-granted protocols. How does a critical pedagogue teach in such an environment and push the boundaries of innovative research such as bricolage? That was the purpose of writing the first edition of this chapter.

In re-reading my chapter of the first edition, and in re-writing for the second edition, I tried to do it as a writerly text; that type of reading where you write back to the author, in this case, myself. In a writerly text as I understand, incorrectly perhaps, and as a critical pedagogue and a bricoleur, you use the tools available or needed (as Monsieur Gallant does) to dismantle the knowledge and values that are erasured, reproduce established knowledge and truths, regurgitate hegemonic power/discourse and other aspects of critical bricolage perhaps as was produced in the first edition. With these features in mind, I kept the roots of the original chapter because of the raw, organic nature of the where, how and why of "getting started" both in theory and practice. To create a writerly text, I used italics inserted into the original text to indicate a re-thinking, re-questioning and re-doing of engaging the bricolage as a means of doing research in this digital, postmodern world. The italic insertions might produce discomfort for the reader; no flow or traditional paragraph structure and so forth as expected in modern writing, be it fiction, non-fiction or even traditional academic writing. If that happens while you are reading, I successfully have employed one of the many 'tools' for writing in a manner befitting bricolage. Emily Ashton, a brilliant critical postmodern researcher, would use the hypertext capabilities of a computer, inserting cross references and intertextuality in a manner compatible with bricolage (see Landow, 2006, for a comprehensive work on hypertext and critical theory).

PROLOGUE TO RESEARCH AS BRICOLAGE

As the use of traditional dominant quantitative and qualitative methodologies comes into question, a framework is needed so novice and seasoned researchers can manage the complexities of doing research in the postmodern era. *In his introduction to chapter 3, Joe Kincheloe discusses this binary opposition between qualitative and quantitative. Hopefully those arguments are slowly disappearing and both are useful to the application of the bricolage: in other words, used but dismantled by the host of 'discourses and methodologies available to do so. That is, to expose hidden truths, knowledge and powers in the familiar to reveal 'other' and 'Other's.'* With this in mind, I would like to elaborate on the concept of *bricolage* as a way of researching human activities, relationships and cultures. Bricolage is fast becoming a key way of rethinking what counts as research and how to conduct research. My intention in this chapter is to supply an introductory stance to a changing body of knowledge and methodologies about research. Further discussions on possible ways to begin and continue through the complexity of a research process using bricolage are included. To complete the research cycle of employing bricolage, possible innovations on recording and reporting will be shared towards the end of this chapter. Words that appear in the glossary are **bolded**. Clarification of some terms is kept in the context of the text in [squared brackets].

My French Acadian neighbors know what bricolage means when I ask them. "Oh yes," they reply, "It's like when the carpenter who builds a house and *uses anything he (she) has handy to get the job done.*" Another neighbor builds birdhouses as a hobby and calls himself (in French), un bricoleur. He *uses scraps* of leftover wood from large scale projects to create the most unique and charming birdhouses and *notes that no two ever look the same.* I watch Monsieur Gallant *collect scraps of metal, wood, tossed out chairs and other furniture*; extract *assorted* nails from moldings; *gather* nuts, bolts and screws *of all shapes and sizes* from the ground around construction sites and drive around in his pickup on garbage days to select *odds and ends* of 'the other person's junk.' I ask him what he is going to do with all these materials. "*Buildin*' a cabin on my little private island," he giggles. "But M. Gallant," I observe, "nothing matches and how do you know what you need or what it's going to look like? Do you have a plan? Do you use everything? What do you do with the leftovers?" He shrugs his shoulders, "Uh? I don't use everything, just what I need. No plan, I just get started and then depending on what I've got available decides what way I'm going to build it, what shape it will take. And the leftovers? – I just use them for the next job, ya' never know what I'll use them for the next time." Daringly, as the academic, I ask, "Es tu un bricoleur?" "Mais oui – of course!"

These anecdotes help me to understand what is meant by bricolage when applied to the field of research and what is meant when researchers are called bricoleurs. Several key features of bricolage include: "using the tools at hand"; "many different tools"; "collecting different parts from different sources"; creative, unique and no two look the same"; "no blueprint on how to build/construct the object (*the knowledge* – my italics)"; "don't know in advance what shape the building (*text/knowledge/research*) will take"; and "you don't use all the parts." *It might be wise/helpful to post these fragmented cliches in the front of you as the process of bricolage unfolds. It will act as a visual contract when you engage in bricolage and avoid slippage into traditional monological research and writing.*

Introduced into the field of research by the French anthropologist Levis-Strauss in *The Savage Mind (*1966*)*, adopted by Denzin and Lincoln (1994) in *The Handbook for Qualitative Research* and developed further by Kincheloe and Berry (2004) in their book *Rigour and Complexity in Educational Research*, bricolage is gradually addressing a growing concern about what counts as and how to do research in an age of postmodernism, other postdiscourses and digital technologies. At a time when the discourses of emancipation, inclusiveness, social justice, plurality, multiplicity, diversity, complexity and chaos are entering academic circles and mainstream communication media, a way of incorporating these discourses and their complementary practices requires new research questions, tools, processes and ways of reporting. Bricolage offers the potential to do so.

Some of the common questions asked by both novice and seasoned researchers unfamiliar with bricolage are:
– What is it?
– Where does it fit in the field of research?
– Why use it instead of other types of research?
– How do you get started?
– How do I know what to do if there are no explicit directions?
– How do you know what 'tool' to use/select from all that information?
– How do you write it up?
– How do you report it?
– How do I know if it will be an acceptable way of researching?

Many, but not all, of these questions and concerns are addressed throughout the chapter. Here are some of the concerns when there is a degree of familiarity:
– Too much for beginning researchers
– Too messy
– No depth
– No focus

- Lacking logic and evidence/proof
- Too bulky/lengthy to include everything

THE HISTORICAL AND POLITICAL CONTEXT OF BRICOLAGE

Although Kuhn (1970) led the way for thinking about research and scientific breakthroughs as a sociological process of normal and revolutionary sciences respectively, what has emerged over the past two decades still tends to support a monological process of conducting research in the arts, humanities, social sciences and, specifically in the context of my world, education. Contemporary research theorists and practitioners alike have developed a host of new research methodologies but still tend to think in terms of totalizing frameworks. Research processes and methodologies seem self contained, individualistic, singularly applied, isolated from one another or merely laid out in a block pattern similar to that suggested by Denzin and Lincoln (1994, 2000, 2005) in their introductory chapter under the heading *Qualitative Research as Bricoleur and Quilt Maker*. Researchers as quilters may become astute at doing one or a few types of research but use the principles and practices in a manner that strongly hints at authority and objectivity, neither of which are conditions for postmodern sensibilities or bricolage. *Caution is warned here in selecting what metaphor/s you use to conceptualize research using bricolage. I am a quilter. I find that most quilters use very structured, traditional approaches mainly by following a set pattern and merely changing the color scheme. Be aware that the metaphors you choose, may indeed be locking you into a familiar monological approach.*

It might be a human trait to want manageable, workable, familiar structures and guidelines to frame the research process and product. So most researchers, needless to say, grasp at different metaphors such as quilt maker, collage artist, film montage, and potpourri to help conceptualise what bricolage means as a way of researching. In chapter five of Kincheloe and Berry (2004), to image the process of research as bricolage, I used several metaphoric and mapping devices such as trees and forest [foregrounding-backgrounding]; transparent overheads [each layer contains multiple theoretical, methodological, interpretive, political and narrative discourses, styles and perspectives]; DVD menu selections and hypertexting. In the end, the image that worked best for me was the map of Lorenz's butterfly effect (p. 112) borrowed from theories of chaos and complexity (Prigogine and Stengers 1984). *Again, any of these metaphors need careful scrutiny for slippage into the familiar, linear, etc.*

Positivistic and other traditional research designs tend to work with a singular, linear, step-by-step structure with certain features such as rationality [critical bricoleurs ask whose rationality and what counts as rationality?]; significance, limitations, literature review/background to the study [not usually a discussion of the theories employed in the study as bricolage demands]; one kind of design and methodology [thus one kind of research and analysis]. Bricolage, however, works with elements of randomness, spontaneity, self-organization, far-from-equilibrium conditions, feedback looping, and bifurcations, all features of the world of chaos and complexity. In addition, poststructuralists, feminist perspectives, and researchers working with other post-multiple discourses, and a host of various narrative structures, create and borrow features from multiple sites befitting bricolage; in a manner similar to *intertextuality*. Bricoleurs struggle to avoid a monological, single path or method. This is where novice and seasoned researchers need to unlearn as much as learn about research when engaging bricolage.

Much of the discussion and many of the examples in this chapter are drawn from my work with MEd and PhD graduate students over the past few years in our attempt to make sense of why bricolage, what and when to use bricolage, and how to do bricolage yet maintain the expectations and quality of academic and scholarly work. My work as a professor of multiple literacies with both undergraduate and graduate students also adds to my understanding of how to do bricolage as a means of research. Overriding all this knowledge gained from experience is my forty years of teaching, twenty-five of those at the university level. With this background, I feel I have lived through a historical account of changing theories and practices of what counts as research in the social sciences, arts and humanities including education. A personal contextualization of that history might clarify how I came to be located in the field of research as a bricoleur [one who uses bricolage] – a use of *narrative* bricolage, so to speak.

For contemporary research content and processes such as bricolage, identifying how and why the researcher is positioned in the study is a must. Shifting positionalities [based on place, time, gender, race, class, sexuality etc.] from which a researcher reads, writes, analyzes, indicate a recognition of the part played by the socializing texts of scholarly discourses, academic expectations and contexts throughout time and space. I have listed my personal research history by dates to coincide with that of Denzin and Lincoln (2000, 2005). They are calling the dominant research periods historical 'moments' of research and claim the different moments overlap and operate simultaneously. It is noted that even from the second edition published in 2000 to the third edition in 2005, the authors have added four historical moments, which reflect the fast-paced changes occurring in the field of educational research. In addition to the extra moments, fourteen new topics have been added to the 2005 edition, which are reflective of the changing landscape of what counts as research and the increase in research 'tools' available for a bricoleur.

I tell this story as a narrative account of not only how I came to be positioned as a bricoleur in the historical and political contexts of doing research but as an individual subjected to the contexts of societal, institutional and Western civilizational notions of what counts as research. Furthermore, using bricolage to do research requires a wide and deep knowledge of multiple *theories* and *methodologies*; multiple ways to collect, describe, construct, analyze, and *interpret* the object of the research study; and finally multiple ways to *narrate* (tell the story about) the relationships, struggles, conflicts, and complex world of the study that maintains the integrity and reality of the subjects. The purpose of research as bricolage involves providing new knowledge, insights, ideas, practices, structures that move towards social justice, inclusiveness, diversity, plurality and so forth.

And all of these elements of the bricolage need to be connected and interconnected to the historical, intellectual and political landscape in which the research occurs. Relationality instigates social action at more than just the personal level.

THE MAKING OF A BRICOLEUR

Denzin and Lincoln (2000, 2005) call the first historical moment of research *the traditional* which covers a period from approximately 1900 to 1950. I feel that period of logical positivism, objectivity and scientific rationality still exists today (remember they claim these moments overlap). I was introduced to research through this traditional moment. In the 1960s, while studying for a BA in sociology with minors in psychology and geography, I had to take courses in both quantitative and qualitative research methodologies. I remember the lab experiments in psychology and the isolation of variables that might contaminate the findings. There was the perennial case study methodology about how to interview research subjects and how to remain objective throughout the interview and in the interpretation of the data. I obviously remember the discourse that shaped what counted as research; variables, standard deviation, contamination, control and experimental group and placebo. I will never forget standing on a street corner of Toronto fulfilling a research mini-assignment in sociology. Dressed one day in hippie garb and looking quite disheveled, I asked directions to a local bookstore and a colleague recorded passer-by's reaction and responses – everything from ignoring me to 'get a job slob.' A few days later, dressed in a three-piece pantsuit and with a manicured appearance, I made the same request for directions while the same colleague recorded the responses. The passer-bys seemed more helpful with even offers to escort me to the bookstore. The purpose was to answer the research question, *Do people stereotype based on a person's appearance*? The professor's feedback to the mini-research mentioned problems about researcher's bias, lack of control of the variables and how my descriptive passages were interesting but too subjective and irrelevant to the findings. *Bricolage research would overlap this simple mini-research project to perhaps include other ways of conducting the research, multiple readings yet still include the original work. More importantly, the professor could have had the student asking different questions (at the time, he and I knew that people stereotyped based on appearance) so why confirm the knowledge? Perhaps different sets of questions and different research approaches such as phenomenology would have moved the research forward into social action. How individuals experience the 'lived' world of stereotypes – bring in the narrative bricolage; What are the institutional and societal discourses and policies of, for example, business and media that generates and maintains stereotypes based on appearance?*

The second historical moment that Denzin and Lincoln (2000, 2005) identify is *the modern* ranging from the 1950s to the 1970s. In the 1970s, while taking honours courses in marine ecology, synergy (I still don't know what it means), microbiology, Canadian history, drama and various other disciplines (my entry into blurred genres and interdisciplinary studies but the academy still wanted to know "what the h..." my major was) and continuing to teach in elementary schools (where blurred disciplinary borders tried to exist), I was required to approach my studies with a broader lens than just that of clinical, laboratory type research. Although scientific objectivity and other traditional research methods were still expected in some courses, I was introduced to modern research fields such as descriptive observation [borrowed from anthropology] and naturalistic settings (even in observing swamp life as ecological) where subjectivity and narrative records counted. Professors versed in research approaches of the time, emphasised the interrelationships between knowledge of one phenomenon/object/subject of the study and another. In marine ecology courses two different professors taught research about marine life in two different ways. One professor insisted that quantitative measurements of insect life, bird life, plant life, fish life and the levels of oxygen in the water gave a picture of the swamp. He had us reduce the complexity, interactive relationships, and the shifting dynamics at the micro and macro levels to isolated batches of numbers and averages [the traditionalist approach]. Another professor had each student go into the swamp with hip waders and stand in the water for approximately 10 minutes, slowly rotating and making observations from the different viewpoints. We had been informed beforehand about what possibilities to look for but he left us enough space to bring in our own observations. After 10 minutes, the students reported their observations from each individual standpoint. It was impossible to reduce the complexity of swamp life to mere numbers, averages and isolated, decontextualized knowledge. Perhaps my propensity towards personal, subjective, descriptive storytelling biased my observations. However, I still carry with me the ecological knowledge produced in the latter approach as a favored way to do research. It is not that one way is better than the other one, it is just that each research approach produces different knowledge, tells a different story and in different ways – a *major principle of research employing bricolage. I like to think that the latter professor created research allowing for rhapsodic intellect to move us into research as play, discovering the wonder and complexity of the swamp – just like children finding new worlds.*

My work as a teacher was beginning to show signs of modern research techniques in schools through focus groups, action research and shared narratives. These activities plus asking classroom teachers to share their everyday observations and anecdotal documentation of the theory (literacy) and how it was enacted in actual practice and, in turn, informed the theoreticians [praxis] was given credence and legitimized by both school administrators and university professors. Although Denzin and Lincoln (2000 2005) call the third historical moment from 1970 to 1986 the time of **blurred genres**, I was not at the university level so I wasn't aware of the formalized field of research during this stretch of time.

From 1980 to 1987, I pursued a MEd and PhD in education. This time period crosses over the third and fourth designation of Denzin and Lincoln's (2000, 2005) historical moments, blurred genres (1970-1986) and **crisis of representation.** Graduate students were expected to include two mandatory generalist courses in research which included mainly a study of quantitative methodologies with the usual qualitative uses of case study, ethnography, in-depth interviews and anecdotal questionnaires. But with a visionary advisor *like David Dillon who was able to convince a Dean's committee otherwise*, I was able to substitute the two mandatory courses for one in the anthropology department [study of the patterns/everyday rituals of a culture in naturalistic settings, everything from the cultures of 'Other,' wolf culture to classroom culture]. The other substituted research course was hermeneutic **phenomenology** with Max van Manen and many of his colleagues including those using a Marxist or Existentialist or Psychological approach to phenomenology. *In and of themselves, each of these theoretical and methodological areas of phenomenology produces different questions, different stories, different discourses, different findings and so forth yet all claim doing phenomenology. If two or more were employed, revealed conflicting and opposition findings, which one is the 'proper' one? If conducting the research as bricolage, several if not all would be engaged in the research and the conflicts would be exposed and valued as knowledge. Now that means rigour and complexity if you get 'the drift' of bricolage.*

Introduced to new research methodologies, I felt equipped to begin my graduate research studies. A major obstacle, however, presented itself. The politics of what counted as research at that time (1980-1987) made it difficult to proceed without further barriers including thesis committee membership, institutional history and funding agencies. Firstly, committee members versed in anthropological and phenomenological methodologies were sparse or, in many cases, resistant to these approaches. Secondly, the history of research in the institution of higher learning and research policy guidelines had, over time, secured and legitimized certain kinds of research, mainly quantitative, while pooh-poohing or rejecting others. Writing research proposals that used phenomenology were met, except for a few leaders in the field such as van Manen (1990), with resistance and skepticism. Thirdly, as an example that confirms the politics of research, representatives from the major Canadian funding agency for research in the social sciences and humanities (which included educational research) told graduate students they had limited to nil chance of being funded if their research was ethnographic. In fact, they clearly stated that national funding committees and government agencies looked mainly for quantitative and objective methodologies and were hesitant to fund proposals using qualitative methodologies – something about "too subjective" and "not measurable" rang throughout the room. Not only does this demonstrate the politics of research but also clearly suggests that the traditional notions of what counts as research are still prevalent throughout all historical moments and exist at all cultural, societal and institutional levels of research. An indication that the politics of research are constantly shifting is exemplified in a recent (2005) policy statement by the same national funding agency that frowned on qualitative research twenty years earlier. The agency's focus has shifted from a Funding Council to a Knowledge Council and it seeks innovative approaches to research. Perhaps bricolage will fit that demand?

Throughout the late 1980s to 2005, as a university professor and researcher, I read widely in several theories and research methodologies and, along with colleagues, introduced graduate students to the same. In the late 1980s, ethnographic research gradually became more acceptable and predominate at both the institutional and national levels and, for many researchers, funded. Personal narratives, focus groups and action research started to enter research discourses and practices. I remember my first conscious introduction to the word **postmodernism** in 1991 at the home of Joe Kincheloe and Shirley Steinberg. I had picked up two books from their shelves; one academic (Lash 1989) and one fictional (Carter 1990). Both were gateways into postmodernism and revisionist writing for me [Carter rewrote the Red Riding fairy tale from a feminist perspective, although there are many critiques of her work as feminist writing]. Entry into the multiple theories, discourses and practices that a bricoleur can use to construct the research is different each time and for each person.

From approximately 1991 to the present I have been introduced to, introduced students to, taught and written about several ways to do research. From the late 1980s to 2006, my knowledge and practice (and the issues and conflicts) about doing research include: Feminist research [from first wave to Marxist and poststructural feminism]; poststructuralism [claims language is an unstable system of referents; the slippery slope of language and signifiers]; postcolonialism [challenges research as Euro-American imperialism and the inherited power and crisis of representing the Other from a colonialist perspective]; semiotics [a study of the signs, symbols, signifiers and what meanings are attached to them – in critical studies as signs of power]; poststructuralist semiotics [how the meanings of symbols and signifiers shift in different historical and political contexts] and Foucault's archeological genealogy [digging through the layers of discourses that shape knowledge and gain power; how they connect to the historical, intellectual, cultural contexts of the time that construct certain practices and not others]. Researchers like myself (because of years in the field of research and experience) have available a host of tools and several other ways of thinking about research especially as a critical theorist and pedagogue [a person who studies, teaches and practices about power relations, social justice, inclusiveness, plurality, diversity and so forth]. I have dabbled with phenomenography when graduate students ask what it is because a colleague asked them to do this kind of research. I explore other fields and regions of research depending on the questions asked of the research object and what 'research tools' will be needed to construct knowledge for social justice. I challenge what counts as research at any given time and place; whose research counts and gets funded and why.

It appears that from the late 1980s to the time of writing the original chapter in 2006 that I passed through several historical moments of what counts as research. According to Denzin and Lincoln's (2005) recent edition of their handbook on qualitative research, those moments are: the fifth moment – *postmodern*, 1990-1995 [a period of experimentation and challenge to modern research methodologies in particular logical positivism, objectivity and scientific rationality; new forms of text building such as hypertext that provide a possible formatting for writing research as bricolage; texts/research becomes writerly, in other words, the reader writes back to the author to challenge or change the text]; the sixth moment – *post-experimental inquiry*, 1995-2000; and the seventh moment from 2000 to 2004 – the *methodologically contested* present. Since I formally and institutionally donned the mantle of bricoleur in 2002, there are many times when I feel I am reliving the traditional and methodologically contested moments again in what is known as the eighth moment and identified as the *fractured future* 2005 – a period that "confronts the methodological backlash of evidence-based social movements, moral discourses and the development of sacred textualities" (3). For example, when one of my students employed the bricolage for his study, between his struggle to find a form that was creative yet scholarly and colleagues' complaints about the student not using a singular methodology to report his work, and the questions about proof [evidence-based], and no literature review of his field of study (there was but it appeared as a theoretical bricolage as a review of the theories he used to interpret his research), he and I experienced the phenomenological [experience as lived] and political backlash described above as the fractured future.

What has this lengthy, personal journey through the fields of research to do with bricolage? I would characterize the ninth moment of research as belonging to bricolage. This moment for me is a gathering of all the past moments and has been fluttering (*the butterfly effect*) for the past three decades to create chaos in the field of research. It is my way of leading you through some of the multiple tools [theories, histories, methodologies, stories and politics] that a researcher can access when using bricolage. Granted I have a forty-year span to draw from but as novice bricoleurs know, the repertoire builds from day to day and year to year. This is where rigour comes into play when doing research as bricolage instead of following a prescribed format and step-by-step single methodology. Bricoleurs read a lot of theories and methodologies that will be added to their research toolbox when needed. They read a lot of academic materials in their field but as disciplinary boundaries blur and interdisciplinary studies seep into each other, bricoleurs read in and are familiar with many fields; from high to popular culture; from the sciences to the arts and humanities; from academic journals and reports to film, theater, Internet and other digital technologies.

The most difficult aspect of doing research as bricolage is the writing; that is, how to shape and format a text that avoids the linear, reductionist structure of traditional research thesis or report. I encourage students to read poststructuralist, revisionist, postcolonial and postmodern fiction in addition to watching films that might help fracture traditional research reporting structures and dissemination processes. From these forms, bricoleurs can borrow a host of both traditional narrative conventions such as irony, parody, foreshadowing, split text, overlapping narratives and unfamiliar ways of storytelling such as those in postmodern fiction and films.

HOW DOES A NOVICE BRICOLEUR GET STARTED?

It seems when university students and professors embark on a research journey through the complexity and multiplicity of doing bricolage; the major concerns are where and how do we start? With no familiar structure, with no explicit directions as were available in traditional and modern research processes and practices, bricoleurs need a starting point. And, like bricolage, there are many. In keeping with the possible ninth moment of research, the plurality and diversity of starting points in bricolage must remain forefront. But given this statement, novice bricoleurs and even seasoned researchers ask; "How do I get started." The following activities and discussions are only suggestions but at the same time drawn from experience and possibilities. As bricoleurs become more articulate about their work, I assume there will be volumes of books on just 'getting started.'

Research Background

Start from what you know and where you are. Students and researchers, even novice ones, do not come to the research process without some knowledge, formally or informally, of what counts as research. Researchers are not blank slates and have been asking questions and doing research since birth. The research may not have been named or institutionalised as is the case with academic research but was done as curiosity and wonderment. The trick is to keep *rhapsodic intellect* alive and not feel bogged down with intellectual paralysis throughout the research. If you do, take it as a stumbling block that all researchers and writers are confronted with constantly. Let passion for new knowledge and insights keep you focused. Let compassion for others drive you forward. *And surround yourself with advisors/mentors/courses that encourage and support the rigour and complexity demanded of bricolage.*

To practice what I've just preached, I suggest that professors and students brainstorm what they already know about research and put headings such as in Figure 4.1 (please note this is not an actual example but a composite taken from a beginning research course).

From this chart (and there are other ways to construct it) comes a variety of possible discussions, pedagogical practices, and paths to follow when doing research as bricolage. A picture of the research profile from the course members makes 'the getting started' transparent in addition to constructing a contingent, big picture of where we are coming from (as if gathering the historical moments from 1900 to 1995 in one chart). As you can see from only five members in a class of twenty or more there is already a variety of research backgrounds that are available from the bricolage toolbox. The task for the professor and other students is to discuss the limitations, similarities and conflicts between the different areas of the profile. The discussions are not meant as a debate about which research period or practice is best – they are intended to initiate dialogue to show differences between and within each research moment. In this way, budding bricoleurs come to

Name	Already Knows This About Research	What Conventions	What Historical Moment	Why So	What Questions Does It Ask	What Results
Bill	quantitative	Statistics Mean Deviation T-Scores	Traditional Modern	Scientific Objectivity	How Much? Norms	Measurement percentage numbers rating
Linda	Feminist Research	Discourse Analysis of Texts	Crisis of Representation	Problematic how Women are Represented	Ones that challenge dominant patriarchal worlds, practices	Transformation of society's knowledge about women, valuing women's worlds
Joy	Race Studies	Deconstructs texts as racialized, colonialized, whiteness	Postmodernism, Crisis of Representation	Challenges authority and shaping devices of whiteness and euro-colonialism	Ones that challenge the invisible powers of colonial ideas and practices that marginalize colonized peoples	Insights about marginalization of people based on race
Mike	Ethnography	Observation key informant	Modern	Studies other cultures	What are the Patterns of Behavior? Rituals of this culture? Mythology? Social Structures?	Knowledge about other cultures

Figure 4.1. Brainstorming chart.

understand how each research approach or period constructs certain knowledge [epistemology], about being human and relationships [ontology], self, society, values, practices and social action. Furthermore, the discussions should expose the assumptions in each area of the grid. Each area trains the researcher to see, read and interpret in certain ways yet neglects many other ways of seeing the world being researched. Opening the fields of research for discussion such as in Figure 4.1, evoke dialogue as a stepping-stone for moving into bricolage.

In addition to charts and other formatting, I have used large different colored file cards for each different activity/discussion previously mentioned and that follows. As the students' knowledge and practices about doing bricolage expand though participation in each of the activities, the colored-coded file cards produce a visual map of the multiplicity and complexity of doing research as bricolage – a non-computerized hypertext, so to speak. I also find the file cards help the novice learn what's involved (and me too!) in research as bricolage when they come to do their own individual research. The cards can be shuffled, moved around, laid on top of one another (blurred genres perhaps?), packed up at the end of class and brought out before beginning the next activity. Unlike an actual computer hypertext model, the students get to see the process and history of research as bricolage.

Each time I do this, it evokes different ways to proceed, different use of 'tools,' different ways to start, and different reasons for using certain 'tools' and not others. In addition, playing with the ideas, knowledge, questions etc. on the file cards prepares the novice bricoleurs for using features of complexity and multiplicity which research as bricolage demands. The features of complexity (in italicized words) unfold when students can: 1) mix and match cards at different moments (*randomness* but with purpose); 2) come to a point where they have to decide which route to follow next (*bifurcations*); 3) take advantage of serendipitous moments when someone has a modest or major epiphany (*spontaneity*); 4) from the group discussions, use someone else's comments, questions, conflicts and suggestions to change or modify or rethink their thinking and in turn have those people rethink (*feedback looping*); and 5) challenge, disrupt, and interrupt when consensus sets in, rock the boat and upset familiar thinking, preconceived ideas and categories, don't take for granted ideas, knowledge that is espoused as common sense, natural, and normal (practice creating *far-from-equilibrium* conditions). There are no step-by step procedures or methods to follow, no preconceived format, no familiar structure but only the respect for difference and the desire to continue constructing new knowledge and possibilities, to pull from other places and times when needed (*self-organization*). The flexibility and structuring devices of the file cards or hypertext programming allow many students and even seasoned researchers to shift from a positivist world of research to the unfamiliar territory of using bricolage. Novice bricoleurs relearn how to play and live in a ludic, postmodern world, not as shallow intellectualism but as intelligent, differently informed social theorists and activists.

Expanding the Bricolage Toolbox

From these dialogic discussions, it seems fitting that the tools for doing bricolage need to be expanded to a point of exhaustion (dependent on time, space and institutional expectations) when heading for the ninth historical moment of research. Added to their background knowledge, novice bricoleurs need to access multiple theories [theoretical bricolage], research genres and conventions [methodological bricolage], ways to interpret [interpretive bricolage] and ways of reporting/telling the story [narrative bricolage]. Kincheloe and Berry (2004) list a plethora of possible regions to explore with multiple sub-areas included. The regions (115-127), to name a few, include:
- multiple critical socio-theoretical discourses
- traditional and contemporary research genres/methodologies and their analytical tools
- cultural/social positionalities
- disciplinary/interdisciplinary departmentalization of knowledge
- philosophical domains
- modes of power
- narratological strategies
- dismantling western grand narratives
- contexts of human activity
- accessing different sources of knowledge
- archeological genealogy
- axiology
- semiotic readings
- a brief encyclopaedia of discourses
- othering

Many other books and Internet sources list similar and additional regions such as Denzin and Lincoln's 5th edition (2005) of *The Sage Handbook of Qualitative Research*. As mentioned previously in this chapter, they added "fourteen totally new topics between 2000 and 2005, including, among others, indigenous research, ... critical and performance ethnography, arts-based inquiry, narrative inquiry, Foucault, the ethics and strategies of on-line research, cultural and investigative poetics and the politics of evaluation" (amazon.com – accessed 9/20/05). A bricoleur's toolbox is starting to spill over with choices. *The difficulty is choosing the tool that produces conflicting knowledge to the dominant; new knowledge not yet considered valued in the current research findings as the knowledge is constructed through the different tools available to the bricoleur. Choosing from the vastness of the bricolage needs a sense of freedom to do so. M Gallant was free to build his cabin from a host of choices.*

One glance at this list of potential regions tends to turn many future bricoleurs away from entering the multiple doors of bricolage. One way to revive confidence is to have each novice take on an area and/or sub-area not part of anybody's background discussed in #1 (Research Background) and report back to the others. Each novice takes on 'the mantle of an expert' in a particular area. This mantle is not 'an expert' but beginning an apprenticeship into becoming a bricoleur. Nobody at this point in the initiation can claim actual expertise in an area. Beginners can be rough around the edges hopefully not imprisoned by grades and the politics of research but learning in the spirit of collegiality and play.

At many universities in Europe, both at the undergraduate and graduate level, a student is considered a reader in an area or areas. Instead of course work, the student is given an extensive book list (nowadays other sources of knowledge such as the Internet would be part of the list) by one professor in the area/s; reads them, writes a paper to present at a seminar with several professors and students of differing theoretical and disciplinary backgrounds. At the seminar, attendees make suggestions and critique the individual's work. Then the 'reader' gets another list of books, reads and rereads, writes and rewrites, presents and continues this process several times before completion in that area. Overlapping this process, the student receives feedback on an individual basis from a supervising professor and from colleagues. For the purpose of nurturing bricoleurs, perhaps thinking of them as 'readers' and using this process of seminars is similar to what is meant by each student responsible for a specific theory, methodology and such. As I reflect on this idea, however, I realize that I have appropriated a colonial model that is exclusive of different ways of increasing the tools for apprentice bricoleurs. Here's where one 'reader' might be asked to read Smith's *Decolonizing Methodologies* (2001), and challenge my notions of research as well as my idea of the teaching and learning process. Bricolage is as much about conflict of ideologies, theories, methodologies, discourses and practices as it is about multiplicity of those areas. *Problematising, making problematic is quite different than identifying a problem. The latter is static, an object, a noun whereas problematising suggests process, action, verb and never ending. Problematising the discourse, knowledge, methodology etc. is a major adage of bricolage.*

When the novices report back to each other, it is not a case, however, of just reporting the knowledge and practices for their region/sub-area. Bricolage is not about amassing a host of tools. It is about using the available tools as bits and pieces to construct new knowledge; but as knowledge that exposes complicity, contradiction and conflict about the world under scrutiny. Added to the critique of knowledge and the regions reported are sets of questions and issues that build on the background knowledge produced by discussions such as in Figure 4.1. Further discussions should include:

a) how each region/sub-area (including the multiplicity of the bricolage) claims authority to speak as knowledge, as legitimised research

b) what discourse, assumptions, practices, strategies are generated by each area

c) what those discourses, assumptions, practices, etc. claim counts as research

d) what promises each region makes about why and how it serves the individual, society, institutions and the micro and macro world that does or does not construct knowledge for inclusiveness, diversity, plurality and social justice

e) a critique of how each theory, methodology, region etc. problematises or makes claims that: *generalise* [knowledge of this study can be transferred to other situations and cultures etc. and the results will be the same]; *universalise* [we all are the same, we belong to the human race]; *naturalise* [it's natural to be like that; i.e. boys will be boys as legitimising certain behaviors]; *pathologise* [people living in poverty don't want to get off welfare]; *essentialise* [a research study and discourse that makes claims that speak for all – women, middle classed, aboriginals etc.]; *neutralise* [differences based on class, race, gender, religion are not made problematic, left out to be politically safe]; *normalise* [there is something, someone gets to be defined as normal and against which others are considered abnormal, initiates research that takes action to make others like those who count as normal]; *reduce* [eliminates the complexity, fluctuations, variables and dynamics of human activity for purposes of objectivity and 'hard science'], *assimilate* [where difference is blended into the mainstream because they want to be like the mainstream]; and *erase* [eliminates certain truths and knowledge by romanticising or not talking about the complexity of human activities, agency and relationships by not telling the unromantic, horrid, actual aspects of humanity, like Disney's take on fairy tales]

f) challenges/questions/resistances to any theory, methodology, interpretations, narratives [grand and petite, local and global, national and international], research and researchers etc. to claims of absolute truth, meaning, and knowledge [for example, I was raised on the totalising knowledge of the King James Bible, the way I must live and accept as absolute truth. But when I challenged the grand narrative of patriarchy in that text with feminist discourse I had to leave the church]

g) personal responses to the research genre/area, to its assumptions, claims, discourses, etc. based on your positionality in relation to the region being discussed. For example, when Diane who is multi-racial (of African, White European, Chinese and Caribbean descent) and I, mono-racial (of white European descent), discuss a film or book, we are located as racially different and see/read the text differently. Constructs/representations of race that I take for granted, she notices as misrepresentations and contradictions and as erasure and essentializsing the Other

h) a brief discussion of the terminology in your own words with actual personal and local examples specific to each of the different areas. (Kincheloe (2002) did this with a graduate research class and they found it to be a very useful exercise for understanding the multiplicity and chaos of bricolage)

i) a writing process workshop approach which, similar to what was mentioned previously when a 'reader' presents a seminar, includes writing draft essays (not the typical reduced five paragraph type but 'real' essays like those in *Harpers, The Atlantic* and *New Yorker* for example). When each student presents his/her area of the bricolage, including further readings in the area, a draft essay is distributed to the other members of the seminar in paper, CD or on-line format. Each member then responds to the draft essay by writing back; that is, from his/her positionality, using the specific area in which he/she read. For example, if the draft essay were in semiotics; the responses to the draft are from all the other areas in which each student was a reader. Again, it is not writing back to the author to report the information of the specific fields but to set up challenges, contradictions, conflicts, purposes, concrete examples, questions that, for example, ethnography/ethnographers might have for a semiotician about the different theories, methodologies, strategies, interpretations, and ways of reporting the knowledge work as research. In addition, if research using bricolage is about researching for inclusion, diversity, plurality, complexity, multiplicity and social justice, then the responses from colleagues must also reflect these purposes. The original draft is handed back to the author with notes in the margins, in the empty spaces and so forth.

The processes mentioned above in a) to i) are excellent opportunities for rehearsing the thinking, reading and writing processes and practices that a bricoleur will meet when engaged in using bricolage as research. These are also opportunities to introduce novices to the ideas and discourse of the hermeneutic circle of interpretation; another tool for bricoleurs to include in their repertoire. Other discussions and ways of introducing novices to the principles and processes of bricolage are also possible. One book I use in teaching bricolage and in my critical literacies classes is Tyson's (1999) *Critical Theory Today*. In it, there are multiple readings of The Great Gatsby (Fitzgerald) based on several theoretical discourses such as: Psychoanalytic Criticism, Marxist Criticism, Feminist Criticism, Reader –Response Criticism, Lesbian, Gay, and Queer Criticism and Postcolonial and African American Criticism. Novice bricoleurs find the different readings of the same text are very helpful especially the questions presented at the end of each theory. *I have always argued for a university course on formulating questions. Most students, myself included, are heavily versed in the types of questions emanating from Bloom's Taxonomy. Again I find categories such as Bloom's levels of questioning limiting and irrelevant to anything remotely considered a question. I sometimes spent several classes of a research course trying to create questions for every theory, methodology, research findings, and so forth. One time I took a photo (could be any text) and had each student attempt to generate a list of questions depending on their selected area of expertise. For example, what questions would an Existential phenomenologist ask of this photo? a Social Anthropologist? an Educational Psychologist? a businessperson? a politician? a teacher? an administrator? and the list goes on. I definitely bring in*

Foucault's questioning (see Kincheloe and Berry 2004) and encourage students to listen to an expert questioner such as Charlie Rose (on public television stations). These types of classes are among my most favourite to conduct.

When Denzin and Lincoln (2000) and Kincheloe and Berry (2004) presented possible arrangements for research as bricolage, they collapsed the multiplicity under five areas: the *theoretical* bricolage; the *methodological* bricolage, the *interpretative* bricolage, the *narrative* bricolage and the *political* bricolage. I am assuming this categorization is done so for the purposes of academic criteria of what counts as research and as a way of organising the complexity and huge amounts of content available for doing this kind of research. The danger in these categorizations might defeat the purposes of engaging some of the major principles of bricolage, such as profiling the interconnectivity, conflicts, resistances, silences, complexity, the political and historical conditions between new knowledge and insights to human activities, relationships of power and conditions of exclusions, inequities and social injustices. One student, for example, used these five areas for his thesis format/structure to fulfil the academy's criteria for what counts as research. What happened seemed to crush the purpose of the multiplicity and complexity in bricolage. His thesis read like a typical empirical study, linear in structure and redundant in content as it was a mere summary of some of the 'tools,' such as postmodernism and poststructuralism that he tried to apply to his research. In fact, he simply applied several post-discourses in addition to four other theoretical and methodological areas to his text being researched. It read like an encyclopedic rehash of the areas he selected instead of creating new knowledge for inclusion and social justice. Please let it be known, however, that he was not responsible for this situation but his supervisor – me. In trying to meet traditional academic criteria and introduce research as bricolage, I was caught between two moments of research –the modern and bricolage. The student became caught also. This moment represents a good example of the politics of research in the academy. *A critical bricoleur always challenges categorisations as reductive and slippage into the traditional rationality that Kincheloe himself has argued against. The five categories might be helpful but again must be problematised as any good bricoleur should do.*

From the discussions, beginning researchers may wish to chart out or create visual images/metaphors (such as the butterfly effect in Kincheloe and Berry 2004, p. 112) or create a DVD hypertext as a means to show the interrelationships, multiplicity, complexity, conflicts and contradictions between and within a region/area. Whatever means are used to image the various fields, keep in mind the purpose is to expand the bricoleur's knowledge [epistemology] for later use when constructing new knowledge through research. An understanding of the history and content of multiple theories, methods and techniques, their overlaps and limitations, their similarities and conflicting discourses should help the bricoleur to see how each region creates its own set of questions, focuses, processes and practices.

In traditional and modern research moments, researchers use paradigms and conceptual frameworks to guide their research process. Paradigms represent a fixed body of knowledge and a particular belief system, a way to view the world such as Newton's theory of gravity. Einstein challenged that system and using metaphors drawn from images and perceptions outside of Newton's world and the scientific rationality of the time to create a scientific revolution and a paradigmatic shift in knowledge about the world. Bricolage works with 'bits and pieces' of theoretical, methodological and interpretive paradigms. It works with scattered parts, overlaps and conflicts between paradigms. In other words, the novice learns what each 'tool' does and can do thus creating a host of possibilities (not mere facts and information) from which to select when conducting his/her individual research. The researcher practices bricolage with guidance and feedback about how and when to use the different aspects of the field when needed.

Learning to Problematize

When novice researchers have an initial understanding of the complexity and multiplicity of using bricolage, they can use the various parts to apply to any **text** to be researched. But to move beyond simply cutting and pasting the parts together in a collage-like manner, bricoleurs must know why and how to problematise the details of the research text including all the relational elements. Since a major principle of bricolage and of other more recent historical research moments is the shift from problem-based/problem-solving research to problematising/social action research, students need to recognise the difference between the two and the implications for using bricolage.

McLerran and Patin (1997) define the term problematic as "derived from the writings of Marxist theorist Louis Althusser and used to designate theoretical and/or ideological formations. It can also be used to refer to rather large and wide-ranging belief systems." As Fedory (2005) notes, problem is a noun and problematising is a verb; the former suggests object, the latter motion (6). Problematising seems to have entered the discourse of research as a response to the thinking and practices of the **scientific method**. The term problematising certainly is important to several research moments since blurred genres and especially important to social action research and thus bricolage. It means the bricoleur faces the challenge of problematising every detail before, during and after the completion of the research process.

In problem-based research, assumptions about knowledge, truth and meaning are **aporia**, what already counts prior to conducting the research. Problem-based/solving research finds out if something exists or doesn't exist, whether someone is abled or disabled and how to solve the problem. Problem based research isolates the object of the study from the multiplicity and complexity in which the object of study is situated. It treats the object of study, whether an issue, question, group of people, testing techniques, knowledge or community development as a fixed entity. Thus the end result is data that has answers or conclusions for problem solving; features of research belonging to the scientific method. Granted there are problems that need to be solved immediately, for a long time or forever. The leaky roof presents a problem. Repair it and fix the problem.

Having one arm is a problem but isn't solved by assuming or taking-for-granted the world that one armed people live in.

Having one arm is *problematic* when that person faces a world planned, designed, and meant for two armed people. That's me. I belong to the culture of one armed people. To problematise our world doesn't mean it will solve the problems of being one armed. What problematising asks is for the world to be transformed in many different ways, at many different levels, and in the many different situations and times we encounter everyday, as do two armed people. The subjects of the research are not seen as problems to be fixed but the world they live in is problematised. Why? To transform the world so we can live with equity, inclusion, agency, plurality, and social justice at all levels of society, institutions as do two armed people. Substitute any difference in the place of the world of one-armed people and you have the shift to problematising.

In the process of becoming a bricoleur, novices begin to recognise that problematising includes the complexity and multiplicity, to name a few, of human relationships, of discourses that shape relationships of knowledge and power, of structuring the world at the individual, societal, institutional and civilizational levels, of the shifting individual, historical, intellectual, social, economic and political experiences at local and global levels. Problematising is done in order to rethink and re-see not solve. To rethink and re-see the world leads to transforming the policies, discourses and practices of exclusion, inequities and social injustices – research for Social Action. Actually, for bricoleurs, everything and everyone in the world is problematised. Once introduced to the term, many novices think this activity means a negative stance in the world ("You're always soooooo negative Kathy and you're trying to teach us to be the same"). Immediately that tends to suggest they are still working with the binarism of positive/negative. When I work with novices to problematise the binarism itself, the gradual realisation of the difference between problem and problematising becomes 'slightly' understood with granules of resistance (perhaps from a novice's long term familiarity and unexamined working relationship with logical positivism and its production of binarisms?). But discussions about binary opposition are, for me, a **segue** from problem-based research to problematizing.

Learning to problematize the world follows on the previous activities in #1 and #2. Assuming apprentice bricoleurs have accessed a wealth of research tools to use, and have delineated the premises, purposes and practices for contradictions, conflicts and so forth, the practice of problematising moves them further into the cracks and gaps in knowledge produced by research throughout all historical moments including bricolage. The following, in no specific order, are suggestions for learning to problematize the worlds to be researched.

a) Bring a poster or magazine/photograph/picture/classic piece of art (the types of texts are unlimited but I find a visual text is easiest to start with). Ask what each student's specific bricolage 'tool' would say is problematic about the text. Some students will say what is right/wrong, good/bad, positive/negative about the text according to their individual region of the bricolage they are applying. Then mention that these are **binarisms** and will be discussed later as problematic in and of themselves. One way I charted this activity of learning to problematise is have each student write on a large colored file card what each particular bricolage theory, method, interpretation etc. would say is problematic and post it around the visual text. A variety of points will emerge but the focus remains on problematising the text as the purpose of the activity.

b) The previous activity in (a) usually generates a plethora of binarisms. Novice bricoleurs need to problematise the use of these words when they appear at any time before and during the research process. Have one or two people record words that arise from the problematising of the text such as right/wrong, good/bad, male/female, us/them, positive/negative and the many other words that can be paired with an oppositional word. For example, students may say: the house in the picture is middle classed; poor people in the picture deserve to be poor; the picture depicts a man and a woman in a loving relationship – that's normal; the children are acting bad; and that's natural for boys to play sports. These are perhaps obvious and weak examples but it is not hard to find texts where the binarisms can be spotted and problematised. Newspapers, curriculum guides, conversations, television shows and the world are packed with binarisms. The task for the bricoleur is to problematise them. They set up unequal representations and relationships and privilege one side of the binarism as being normal, natural, right, true and so forth and the other side abnormal, unnatural, wrong or disabled. Binarisms describe social situations. They govern social policies, testing practices, job employment, evaluation criteria, and actions. They shape who gets to be called a reader and who doesn't. I have even worked on the binarisms in fairy tales with elementary and secondary students. Bricoleurs are continuously problematising binary oppositions that appear in research texts as if normalised and legitimised categorizations of the human condition, relationships, practices and agency. Practice in problematising binarisms is part of the learning process for novice bricoleurs and even seasoned researchers.

c) What to problematise? – everything and everybody. Why problematise? – to avoid reducing the complexity of the world for the sake of control, management, objectivity, classification, and the production, maintenance and circulation of inequities, exclusions, and social injustices based on difference in gender, race, class, age, body, religion, education, sexuality and so forth. How to problematise more than the surface and obvious levels of the text and recognition of the invisible agendas of power is just a small part of the knowledge a bricoleur uses when doing research. They also learn to recognise that at different historical, intellectual, cultural, and political times and places, what is identified as problematic is constantly shifting and undulating. In addition, problematising what's not part of the text and what is invisible in the text is as important as what is there.

That's why problematising adds to the rigour of doing bricolage. Each historical, intellectual, social, and political period has specific needs for problematising the research text and its constituents. Thus, problematising the worlds/texts/issues /events etc. to be researched requires an additional recognition of connectivity with the world of the text with the world outside the text. The students could bring to the class a variety of texts and practice problematising them and the world in which they are located. Ask not just what is problematic but also why it is problematic for inclusion, social justice and agency. Students might find this activity exhaustive and endless but certainly can sense the complexity and multiplicity of doing research as bricolage. I find problematising is the ground from which the research text grows in purpose and directs the bricoleur to what tools to use and when. *Incorporate your autobiographical positionality in problematising any text – ask how did I come to know, believe, value the truths, facts and ideas generated by this text that reveals how you come to think/read/ about the topic/question as you do.*

Learning to Contextualize, Situate and De-centre

Contextualization is another major aspect of doing bricolage. Whereas traditional and modern research used only the research text itself as the context, bricoleurs expand the research beyond itself to a multitude of contexts. Because bricolage considers research to be a complex act embedded in and contested by a host of social, intellectual, historical, economic, institutional, local, global and political beliefs, values and relationships, it is imperative that contextualization plays a major part in the bricoleur's construction of knowledge through research. A bricoleur asks how the world being researched is connected to the policies, structures, discourses, and practices of the dominant political, economic, institutional, intellectual and other powers that govern social activity. Even the responses, for example, of subjects talking about the topic being researched have to be taken outside the interview context and analysis.

In bricolage, the responses can not be reduced to categories, classifications, numbers or themes in the manner that most research using interviews does. Bricoleurs frame their questions not just to evoke conversation but to push the topic under scrutiny beyond the immediate context and link the responses to other contexts which visibly or invisibly shaped or influenced the interviewee's knowledge, beliefs and actions. The links are reminiscent of a hypertext image in which, as one response is elicited, the bricoleur 'clicks' on the response and moves it to another context. The bricoleur might be asking a single mother living in conditions of poverty how she teaches her child at home to read. She responds that she doesn't have the time or money to do so. The bricoleur hears her response as blaming herself, blaming the individual, pathologising the realities of mothers living in conditions of poverty. Sensitive to the limits of a single and individual context and recognition that the individual is embedded in several other larger and more powerful contexts, the bricoleur begins to frame questions that move the interviewee to think beyond the boundaries of the individual context. Linking the individual's experiences and understandings to, for example, the historical, societal, institutional, religious, economic, and political contexts and re-linking each of these with each other; linking this mother's context with the contexts of her neighbourhood, surrounding neighbourhoods and with the neighbourhood schools reveals the relationships and interrelationships that exist for single mothers living in conditions of poverty. What is missed by reporting just the context of the individual interviewees – *reducing* their world to categories, themes, generalisations and seeing them as the problem – is problematic for a bricoleur. Problematic because it leaves the responsibility for transformation and struggle in the hands of the individuals instead of society, institutions and other contexts in which the women live their lives. Keeping responsibility at the individual level also removes hope for change. A different kind of knowledge than individual knowledge alone could is obtained by showing how the conditions of poverty are linked to the policies and practices of society and institutions in historical, economic and political contexts of time and space.

Simultaneously as relationality, multiplicity and complexity are unfolding through the connectivity by the bricoleur of the interviewee's responses, the personal can not be lost to the abstractness of academic discourse and so forth. This is a situation where the bricoleur turns to another tool to keep the personal vibrantly present. The bricoleur might, for example, feel that when showing the relationality between the interviewee's life and, let's say, an institutional policy, he/she inserts, as a phenomenologist would, an eidetic [vivid] description or variation from the interviews.

Furthermore, a bricoleur might use the 'tools' of Foucault's archeological genealogy and critical discourse analysis to get the job done.' Granted the introduction of a new tool from the theoretical and methodological bricolage adds to the complexity of knowledge and interpretation of the initial interviews but also adds new knowledge and insights to the research study that might be overlooked or erased by de-contextualization or reduced contextualization. The spontaneous insight to use Foucault's theory and the methodologies of critical discourse analysis of the initial interviews is just one of many possibilities the bricoleur could use but could not have planned ahead of time that this serendipity would occur.

Contextualising in the manner described above also requires a situating and decentering on the part of the researcher. While contextualising is about connecting and contesting the different contexts relevant to the research, situating is about presenting the autobiographical aspects (what I call the critical ethno-biographical bricolage) that indicate how the bricoleur came to be situated in the research study and influences the process of selecting, choosing, speaking, interviewing, observing, interpreting and telling the story. Situating is not about remaining objective or isolating one's biases, a trait of logical positivism, but identifying what the socialising texts of the bricoleur's life are that locates her/him in the research in a particular way with certain knowledge, beliefs, and values related to the research.

If we use the example above of the interviews with single mothers living in conditions of poverty, there is no question that a researcher enters the interviews with previous knowledge and beliefs that shaped what he/she already thinks/knows about the topic. Situating examines not only the bricoleur's taken-for-granted assumptions about the topic but the established and unexamined 'common sense' knowledge and beliefs of the society, institutions, media and cultural artifacts related to the topic. The countless number of socializing texts (tools) and processes ranging from oral to printed; family to media, from birth to date and multiple other texts adds another dimension to the knowledge, interpretation and understanding of the research as bricolage. Also a bricoleur must consider how the research is written and read in relation to the constructs of gender, race, class, sexuality, religion and other constructs of culture. In other words, how the bricoleur and the research subjects are situated in the research by gender, race, class and other different cultural constructs shapes the knowledge produced.

Identification of how the researcher is situated in the study requires a decentering on the part of the researcher especially during the interpretive and narrative processes of bricolage. Decentering from the research subjectively situates the researcher in the research but allows a distancing for objective observations and perspectives. On the one hand, bricolage allows subjective input to the research with such conventions as first person, multivocal perspectives, and non-reduced personal narratives. In fact, similar to The Orchid Thief by Susan Orlean or the more recent version of the film Moulin Rouge, authors using bricolage write themselves into the text as active participants in the construction of knowledge, allowing personal opinion and reflective moments to interrupt the objective flow of the text (writing, viewing, reading). Here is a good example of bricolage borrowing conventions from other sources and disrupting the text to have the readers challenge their own thinking and the topic being examined. On the other hand, decentering forces the bricoleur to be sensitive to the research subjects' position in the research and not misrepresent them as, for example, inactive, disenfranchised, lazy, or apathetic. A researcher who is privileged by class and/or gender, race (a concern of postcolonial, race and whiteness studies) needs to decenter from those positions especially when researching subjects who are not privileged by dominant cultural constructs.

Further complexity is added when the bricoleur also situates the study in related fields and other research studies (called background literature or review of the literature in traditional and modern research). However, instead of listing the studies and their findings to prove they have read in the field, bricoleurs situate where their study stands in relation to the other studies. The main purpose of situating instead of reviewing the literature is to uncover the historical and political agendas of the background literature as research legitimised by logical positivism and scientific rationality. If indeed, the research and literature of related studies is found to be located in traditional and modern research moments, without question, bricolage problematises these studies and the knowledge they produced. To reiterate, the point is that bricoleurs tell a different, not necessarily better, story than traditional and modern research literature.

As novice bricoleurs practice contextualising, situating and decentering as dynamic parts of the research process, they build a knowledge base for and understanding of what is meant by engaging complexity and multiplicity. When a research class as a group applies bricolage to a single text (such as a poster, a visual/artwork, a familiar book, a film, a TV show, newscast or other media text), the principles and processes discussed to this point in the chapter act as a rehearsal for when each bricoleur conducts his/her own research. To practice problematising, contextualising, situating, and decentering, there are many great examples in postcolonial fiction and revisionist writing such as Angela Carter's *Bloody Chamber* mentioned earlier. I have suggested that novice bricoleurs read the traditional canonised *Robinson Crusoe* by Daniel Dafoe as an example of a text that privileges and legitimises European knowledge, history, values and practices. Then I have them read *Friday* by Michael Tournier, a revisionist writing of Robinson Crusoe. In Tournier's text, without direct reference he problematises, re-situates and decenters the position of Crusoe in Dafoe's book as representative of European powers. The emerging bricoleurs search the pages for examples of the premises listed previously in #4 in addition to asking what their respective theoretical, methodological and interpretive areas of bricolage would problematise and/or say about the books. In a manner of speaking, others may want or need to introduce novices to bricolage in different ways and for different reasons. These suggestions are only a few of many possible ways. And yes, there is more.

Learning about Intertextuality

To create a research text, bricoleurs borrow from other texts. Thus it seems wise for bricoleurs to learn about intertextuality, a literary idea "coined by Julie Kristeva … and employed in structuralist, poststructuralist, semiotic, deconstructive, postcolonial, Marxist, feminist and psychoanalytical theories" (Allen 2000), as just some of the regions employed in the theoretical bricolage. Although the term has many different meanings, it is useful to employ some of its major principles and practices for the purposes of doing bricolage. Since bricolage borrows from many theories, methodologies, interpretive practices and narrative conventions, an understanding of intertextuality is considered helpful.

At this point in the discussion on doing research as bricolage, a delineation of some of the major principles of intertextuality should demonstrate for the novice the connections to doing bricolage as multiplicity and complexity. Some of the premises (taken from Allen 2000 and with modifications to connect to bricolage) include the assertions that texts in an intertextual context

a) lack any kind of independent meaning (thus contextualising etc. in bricolage)
b) create [research] which plunges us into a network of textual relations (in bricolage, theoretical, methodological, societal, institutional, local, global relationships)
c) are part of a process of moving between a variety of texts (in bricolage, borrowing and using when needed)
d) practice theoretical [and methodological] intervention and debate (problematises in bricolage).
e) replace assertions of objectivity, scientific rigor, methodological stability and positivistic rationality (monologism) with an emphasis on uncertainty, indeterminacy, non-communicability, subjectivity, desire, pleasure and play
f) disrupt notions of stable meaning and objective interpretations

g) challenge long-held assumptions concerning the role of the author in the production of meaning (bricolage problematises researcher, literature reviews, common sense, normalisations, etc.)
h) lead [researchers] and readers on to new textual relations (a purpose of bricolage)
i) help authors create and readers discover multiple meanings in the research text (the attempt of bricolage to avoid positivistic reductionism)
j) celebrate plurality (Barthes); others see this as problematic and not necessarily liberatory
k) are concerned with marginalised and oppressed communities
l) are used to reflect and transform [knowledge, beliefs, values, practices] of society and human relations
m) mix already established styles and practices (bricoleurs mix theories, methodologies, narrative styles etc. to get the job done)
n) foreground notions of relationality, interconnectedness, and interdependence
o) promote a relationality that may involve the radical plurality of the sign; the relation between signs and texts and cultural [historical, political, intellectual, theoretical, discourse] texts; and, extremely important to research as bricolage, the transformative relation between the final research text and another text [practices of society, institutions, policy, curriculum, testing, inclusion, equity and social justice
p) support a new vision of society, authorship and reading, researching and research
q) resist ingrained notions of originality, uniqueness, singularity, and autonomy.

This is by no means the only available or exhaustive list of premises on intertextuality and their relationship to doing research as bricolage. The list serves as another way of introducing future bricoleurs to the multiple principles and practices (tools) available to use when enacting research as bricolage.

To practice intertextuality, I use films, especially those drawn from popular culture (as most people in a class have seen them) as they can be shared easily in a class and, in a shorter period of time, cover several of the premises of intertextuality. The Shrek 1 and 2 films both provide very simple and basic examples of texts within texts or texts that cross over into other texts. To understand most of the humor in the two Shrek films, the viewer has to recognize texts that lie outside the movie itself; a premise that texts have no independent meaning (see (a) above). To obtain meaning out of Shrek, the viewer has to know several European nursery rhymes (problematic for culturally different students), watch/read other texts such as the TV game show *The Price is Right* to get what Donkey (Donk-a, important here to know whose voice it is – Eddie Murphy's – and why it is pronounced this way) meant by "giving the cat the Bob Barker Treatment" (Bob Barker, the host always ends the show with "Remember to help control the pet population, have your pet spayed or neutered"). One viewer, who is homosexual, pointed out several examples of homophobia and signifiers of homosexuality which several heterosexual viewers could not assign meaning to in their first viewing of the movie. A poster in the film (which is set a long time ago in Far Far Away Land) is of Stonehenge Night Club – a gay night club in London, England. There is one scene in which the three main characters are driving down the main street of Far Far Away Land; a street filled with shops from days of yore but with Arthurian twists on names from Hollywood's Rodeo Drive. In that scene alone, viewers would have to know past and present times in addition to Arthurian legends, European fairy tales, the names of modern day stores but with names merged with medieval shops. This is a very small sample of how many texts from outside the film are important to the film's success. More importantly for bricoleurs is how the film's intertextuality "plunges us into a network of textual relations," and "moves us between texts" in different times and places.

Intertextuality exists in newspapers, television newscasts, religious texts, magazines, school disciplinary textbooks, history books, photographs, academic journals, personal experiences, autobiographies, fiction and non-fiction books. In one university class I taught intertextuality using texts about Iraq and American relations. Each student was to bring in any five texts they thought relevant to this topic but none produced after 9/11. They went on a one week scavenger hunt for materials. Each student could not bring in any two texts of the five that were of the same media or date. One week later, the classroom was filled with boxes of materials and every one of us was surprised at the variety. The sources of materials above were collected plus a father's war medals; books on oil production and trading; an interview with a Canadian peace keeper; maps on the shifting borders of the Middle East with colored-coded explanations; editorials from magazines as far back as 1930s; a Koran; a Christian bible; clippings from different political journals and banking newsletters.

Then there were discussions on why the selection and how connected to Iraqian-American relations. Then we referred to different lists of premises and questions asked by different theories and methodologies in the bricolage toolbox, problematising, contextualising and those of intertextuality. Then all the tables in the classroom are placed together to provide a space to begin mapping out the bricolage. In the center of the table is a huge poster with the words [A Map of Iraqian-American Relations]. This becomes our point of entry text (POET) from which all other texts are connected and hypertexted. Each time we refer to a premise or question, we also returned to one of the texts collected and place it on our huge bricolage map using different color-coded file cards, different colors of string, post-em stickers, overheads and a wad of other materials that can be written on, moved, organised differently, stretched, connected and layered. As we discuss the texts, the relationships, premises and questions the map unfolds in a fashion similar to a Jackson Pollock painting and reminiscent of the model of complexity in Lorenz's Butterfly Effect.

Bricoleurs, both novice and seasoned, gradually see the emergence of new knowledge, insights and connections. Eventually we become overwhelmed by the complexity and multiplicity as the connections grow and continue to grow. In order to organise but not totalise the complexity and multiplicity we decide on a stopping point. Then decisions are made, to name a few, about: what to keep in the map or toss aside for the moment; how to organise the map for meaning; how to recognise what counts as new knowledge or conflict and contradictions in ideologies and practices; if we actually have a variety of perspectives, opinions, references, conflicting and complicit ideologies; what connections we made that would perhaps speak to different audience/readers and evoke rethinking their thinking and changing practices; and what political actions and discourses could be challenged and used to "make a difference" in the world (one student's comment). This activity is an accumulation of what novice researchers have learned to this point about research as bricolage.

Just getting started, practicing the thinking and the processes of complexity, including multiplicity and making hypertext connections and relationships between texts and discourses is a vast undertaking. The practice of building the 'tools' as a group/class, applying them to first a single text and then multiple texts seems a good way of introducing beginners to doing research as bricolage – a preparation for the ninth moment of research history. From here they can go to their individual research projects with some sense of what it means to engage relationality, complexity and multiplicity through bricolage. But the most difficult questions remain – How do I format this complexity so it can be 'read' by others? How do I organise the messiness and process of bricolage into a final product for dissemination?

Learning to Self-organize the Messiness

A major tenant of complexity theory in the sciences and deconstruction in the arts is the ability to self organize. When I was starting to write my Masters thesis, my advisor David Dillon said instead of following the formula given in a research writing class, the typical 5 chapter/5 paragraph format go to the library read these thesis as ways to rethink the structure of your thesis. It worked. I was able to build the structure from examples in English department (writing as a novel), from the Media department examples of student produced films and of course the traditional 5 chapter-5 paragraph format. The difficult task was to put together a committee in educational research that would accept the unfamiliar format. That was 1982. Since that period, it seems that those committees are more willing to 'step outside the' familiar. In 2012, Emily Ashton did her Masters thesis as a series of articles. Her PhD will most likely be even more different?

If there is a point in which I myself almost give up on bricolage is when it comes to organising the messiness into a 'readable' but writerly text. I wonder how I can move the novices beyond the formulas of positivism, scientific rationality and methodology; beyond traditional and modern ways of constructing texts; and decentering the dominance of printed text especially with academic criteria, expectations and structures looming over both the head of myself and the students doing research. After finishing the Iraqian-American activity, several students answered, in part, those questions for me; they were not, however, graduate students bound by thesis expectations (again the politics of research). When at least ten out of thirty students submitted their final assignment on a CD ROM as hypertext, I knew they were of a different generation than I. The CDs were laden with the content, connections, and multiplicity we had practiced in class. I was able to click on different texts, print excerpts from magazines, newspapers, academic journals, music, visuals, interviews, polls, quotes, and go from each of them to theoretical discussions that problematised, interconnected, challenged, and contextualised. One student used split screen conventions to show the conflict between two reports on Iraqian-American relations with her own interpretations and analysis of the discourse in each.

Another student used his life as the son of Canadian military parents as his point of entry text and used the digital technology of a DVD. From there he developed a hypertext narrative that used the personal but connected it to historical and political texts. He very clearly showed how the personal is political; how he was socialised by the military contexts and texts in which he was exposed to certain knowledge and beliefs about Iraqian-American relations. He inserted memories from childhood conversations (more like lectures he noted) he had with parents and other military personnel. He disrupted these texts with newspaper clippings written at approximately the same time of his memories. He included vivid descriptions (the phenomenological strategy of eidetic description, reduction, and variation of the lived experience) of the physical abuse from his father overlaid with transparent magazine photos of Iraqian and American military scenes concurrent with his memories of personal abuse. This student was very well read and a student of history. He accessed passages on the topic from textbooks he was asked to read in history courses at both the secondary and university levels of education. It was frightening how one-sided and objective the knowledge was which he remembered as having to regurgitate in assignments and exams. He pointed out the lack of multiple perspectives and sources; the same and only textbook for all students and usually written by one or two authors. I still carry the work of this student with me today. As I write this example of bricolage, in no way it is as important as the student himself and his impact on my life. I only hope I can honour him as a person by using his work to inform my work as a bricoleur.

Many other sources (narrative tools) are available that might help the novice and seasoned researcher organise the *narrative* bricolage; help him/her use different tools to self-organise the messiness of bricolage into a final text for readers/viewers/listeners without resorting to traditional academic structures of reporting. Another example and one that was very useful for many students learning to do research was using Kincheloe's book *The Sign of the Burger* (2002). He used bricolage to research MacDonald's as a culture of power. After reading the book, students and I use it to scrutinise for content and form. We ask how does he include, theories, methodologies and interpretations that maintain research integrity through using bricolage? Does he avoid positivism, scientific methodology and rationality, and objective reductionism? How did he or did he remain truthful to the promises of bricolage as engaging relationality, complexity and multiplicity? And finally how did he tell the story as narrative bricolage?

There are other examples of bricolage texts but using a single text such as Kincheloe's helps to clarify how to organise the messiness of bricolage.

I have mentioned before how I use postmodern, poststructural and postcolonial writers of fiction to help students organise the messiness. Students and I have examined films on DVD's such as, to name a few, Pulp Fiction, Run Lola Run, Memento, Like Water For Chocolate, The Hours, Shrek, Adaptation and many others that disrupt traditional, linear monological narratives. We have read scripts for plays that incorporate multi-voiced, multi-perspective conventions such as those written by Anna Deavere Smith. Students will sometimes combine medias that range from reading texts, to television clips to live performances and photographs.

IN CLOSING

As I share discussions about bricolage with colleagues, undergraduate and graduate students, I still sense the nervousness and hesitancy to use bricolage to do research. I am amazed, however, that those same colleagues and students are very comfortable using Web, Internet and different hypertext programs. They can access and produce more texts in an hour than traditional research technologies could in a lifetime. Mind you, accessing and producing texts is not necessarily doing research as bricolage. Bricoleurs keep in mind major principles of relationality, multiplicity, complexity and, most importantly, criticality for social action and justice. I have alluded to the politics of doing research as bricolage especially in academia. Hopefully, however, academia begins to look differently at what counts as research. Bricolage offers that potential.

When Ken Tobin emailed me about including my first edition chapter, I replied "I'd like to do an additional chapter for the second edition just on Foucault and implications for Doing Educational Research." Then several events happened to question my request. Foucault, for me, expanded the theories and methodologies of doing educational research. But his works were not enough. I needed more and different questions and views. Why? Because several parents and teachers, amazingly in both Canada and U.S.A., when they met me (as a former teacher and professor) would bombard me with how their 'kids,' students had asbergers, ADHD, and a host of other behaviours that fall on the "spectrum of autism." They quote research about frontal lobes, about inoculations, about genetic makeup of boys (most diagnosed group), Oprah, Cosmopolitan, how Ritalin has helped and on and on. The cause and effect discourse of these diagnoses are so circulated, maintained and pervasive especially by psychologists, society, by institutions ranging from media to medical, from education to business it becomes difficult if not impossible to discuss or argue other ways to knowing about and relating to these children. I try and insert other ways, other questions, other ways. I try to problematise the dominant discourses and practice that categorise these children. I attempt to bring in the problem with their cause and effects – who create that a certain effect is caused by ...? Do you see maybe there are causes not listed by certain experts and why did those experts and not others get to say what the 'problem' is? What research looks at the social, economic, personal, cultural, modern conditions that has created this rise in diagnosis of so many children (mainly boys)? Is it nature or nurture? Most of the time I divert the conversation to the weather or new dishes to cook. These are friends. I want to keep my friends so I back down. I want so badly to do research on these 'spectrums of autism' using bricolage. Maybe then I can insert new knowledge that releases both the adults and children from the box of hegemonic discourse, policies and practices that seems to govern (governmentality) from Foucault's panopticon. If not me, maybe researchers who engage the bricolage?

GLOSSARY OF TERMS

aporia – impassable path, a contradiction of the logic or sense and the rhetoric in a text

blurred genres – where the distinct borders between research methods, disciplines, and strategies fade into and over one another

butterfly effect – Lorenz's theory of chaos and complexity which he metaphorically frames as the butterfly effect; that is if a butterfly flaps it wings in Brazil, it causes a tornado in Kansas *(and now he might just be right – tornados occurring in the world where they never in recorded weather history had happened before – in my youth, I read it was Dorothy's shoes!)*

crisis of representation – 1986-1990, research more reflexive, called into question issues of gender race etc. and challenged older models of truth and meaning

intertextuality – a relation between two or more texts in which one text is echoed or included in another (McLerran and Patin 1997). Allen (2000) defines the term to mean a text that does not lack any kind of independent meaning but borrows from previous systems, codes and traditions of other texts and cultures thus moving from the independent text into a network of textual relations (1). In bricolage, the research text borrows from many other texts (see glossary for the meaning of **texts**).

monological – one way only of thinking about the research, one logic; but whose counts?

phenomenology – studies the pre-conceptual, pre-linguistic experiences of life as lived; hermeneutics is used to bring the experience to language while still maintaining the experience 'as lived'

postmodernism – privileges no single authority/grand narrative such as patriarchy, middle class values, Euro-American white race, Christianity, Colonialism, capitalism and others especially those constructed during modernist era

rhapsodic intellect – the joy, excitement of working serendipitously and towards epiphanies

segue – a transition from one way of thinking/doing to another way

scientific method – a way of researching that dominates the natural and physical sciences and includes the principles of logical positivism, objectivity, reductionism and scientific rationality

text – a system that produces meaning, beliefs, values and knowledge such as an oral text, a printed or visual text, a research study, a classroom, a policy document, a theory, a culture, an institution and so on. Original meaning, a tissue, a woven fabric

totalizing framework – a right way to do a particular kind of research; i.e., ethnography

variables – the exceptions, other perspectives, polyphonic, polylogical, and polyoptic approaches that are eliminated in traditional and modern research because they interfere with or contaminate objectivity, the truth, the data

REFERENCES

Allen, G. (2000). *Intertextuality*. New York, NY: Routledge.
Carter, A. (1990). *The bloody chamber*. England: Penguin.
Denzin N. K., & Lincoln, Y. S. (Eds). (1994. 2000. 2005). *The handbook of qualitative research* (1st, 2nd, 3rd editions respectively). Thousand Oaks, CA: Sage.
Fedory, Z. (2005). *Dismantling the grade nine visual arts curriculum using bricolage*. Unpublished MEd thesis. University of New Brunswick, Canada.
Kincheloe, J. L. (2002). *The sign of the burger: McDonald's and the culture of power*. Philadelphia, PA: Temple University Press.
Kincheloe, J. L., & Berry, K. S. (2004). *Rigour and complexity in educational research: Conceptualizing the bricolage*. London: Open University Press.
Kuhn, T. S. (1970). *The structure of scientific revolutions*. Chicago: University of Chicago Press.
Landow, G.P. (2006). *Hypertext 3.0: Critical theory and new media in an era of globalization*. Baltimore, MD: The John Hopkins University Press.
Lash, S. (1989). *Sociology of postmodernism*. New York: Routledge.
Levi-Strauss, C. (1966). *The savage mind*. Chicago, IL: University of Chicago Press.
Manen, M., van (1990). *Researching lived experience: Human science for an action sensitive pedagogy*. London: Althouse Press.
McLerran, J., & Patin, T. (1997). *Artwords: A glossary of contemporary art theory*. Westport, CT: Greenwood.
Prigogine, I., & Stengers, I. (1984). *Order out of chaos: Man's new dialogue with nature*. New York: Bantam Books.
Smith, L.T. (2001). *Decolonizing methodologies: Research and indigenous peoples*. New York: Zed Books.
SSHRC (Social Sciences and Humanities Research Council of Canada). (2005). *Knowledge council: SSHRC 2006-2011*. web/about/publications/strategic_plan_e.pdf.
Tyson, L. (1999). *Critical theory today: A user-friendly guide*. New York, NY: Garland.

SHIRLEY R. STEINBERG

5. PROPOSING A MULTIPLICITY OF MEANINGS

Research Bricolage and Cultural Pedagogy

In the contemporary information environment of the twenty-first century-so aptly named hyperreality by Jean Baudrillard, knowledge takes on a different shape and quality. What appears to be commonsense dissipates slowly into the ether, as electronic media refract the world in ways that benefit the purveyors of power. We have never seen anything like this before, a new world – new forms of social regulation, new forms of disinformation, and new modes of hegemony and ideology. In such a cyber/mediated jungle new modes of research are absolutely necessary. This chapter proposes a form of critical cultural studies research that explores what I refer to as cultural pedagogy. Cultural pedagogy is the educational dimension of hyperreality, as learning migrates into new socio-cultural and political spaces. In these pages, I will focus my attention on my research with film, specifically on *doing educational research* with a bricolage of methods leading to tentative interpretations. Relating to the hyperreality of the times, I am asserting that the notion of one orthodox methodology cannot achieve a rich text and present a multiplicity of meanings: essential components in contemporary research.

CRITICAL CULTURAL STUDIES

Observing that the study of culture can be fragmented between the disciplines, those who advocate cultural studies look at an interdisciplinary approach, that which transcends any one field. Additionally, a critical cultural studies does not commit a qualitative evaluation of culture by a definition of "high" or "low" culture, and culture may be the most ambiguous and complex term to define in the domain of the social sciences and humanities. Arthur Asa Berger (1995) estimates that anthropologists alone have offered more than one hundred definitions of culture. At the risk of great reductionism, I use the term in this chapter to signify behavior patterns socially acquired and transmitted by the use of social symbols such as language, art, science, morals, values, belief systems, politics, and many more. Educators are directly implicated in the analysis of culture (or should be) in that culture is transmitted by the processes of teaching and learning, whether formally (schools) or informally (by wider social processes, e.g., popular culture). This pedagogical dynamic within all culture is a central concern of this chapter. Indeed, culture is inseparable from the human ability to be acculturated, to learn, to employ language and symbols.

Culture, in this chapter, involves specifically its deployment in connection with the arts. This is where we move into the social territory traditionally referred to as elite or high culture, and popular culture. Individuals who attend symphonies, read the "great books," enjoy the ballet, are steeped in elite culture – or as it is often phrased, "are cultured." Referring to "low" culture, many scholars assert that the artifacts that grew within a local or regional movement are indeed low. Fitting neither into a category of low or high culture is mass culture. Cultural theorists do not agree on any one definition for each type of culture. However, Dwight MacDonald summarizes the difference between the three, and the propensity of all types of culture to become political:

> Folk art grew from below. It was a spontaneous, autochthonous expression of the people, shaped by themselves, pretty much without the benefit of High Culture, to suit their own needs. Mass Culture is imposed from above. It is fabricated by technicians hired by businessmen; its audiences are passive consumers, their participation limited to the choice between buying and not buying .... Folk Art was the people's own institution, their private little garden walled off from the great formal park of their master's High Culture. But Mass Culture breaks down the wall, integrating the masses into a debased form of High Culture and thus becoming an instrument of political domination. (MacDonald 1957, p. 60)

Within critical cultural studies it is maintained that the boundary between elite/high culture and popular/low culture is blurring. Such occurrence holds important ramifications for those interested in pedagogy (Berger 1995). The study of culture, for the purpose of this chapter, is not to delineate the "level" or "type" of culture invoked by popular films, but to discuss the pedagogical, sociological and political themes within the films. Consequently, a debate as to the "quality" of popular culture or its place in the light of elite culture will not be undertaken. I will use the term popular culture to define what is readily available to the public as a form of enjoyment and consumption.

Popular culture defies easy definition. It can be defined as the culture of ordinary people – TV shows, movies, records, radio, foods, fashions, magazines, and other artifacts that figure in our everyday lives (Berger 1995). Often analysts maintain that such artifacts are mass-mediated and consumed by large numbers of individuals on a continuing basis. Such phenomena are often viewed condescendingly by academicians as unworthy of scholarly analysis. As addressed in this chapter, the aesthetic dynamics of popular culture are not the focus; rather the social, political, and pedagogical messages contained in popular culture and their effects are viewed as some of the most important influences in the contemporary era. In this context the study of popular culture is connected with the sociology of everyday life and the interaction and interconnection of this micro-domain with macro-socio-political and structural forces. Thus, the popular domain – as ambiguous and ever-shifting as it may be – takes on unprecedented importance in the electronically-saturated contemporary era.

CREATING A CULTURAL PEDAGOGY

Cultural studies and pedagogy involves education and acculturation that takes place at a variety of cultural locations including but not limited to formal educational institutions. Cultural studies scholars extend our notion of cultural pedagogy, focusing their attention on the complex interactions of power, knowledge, identity, and politics. Issues of cultural pedagogy that arise in this context include:

1) the complex relationship between power and knowledge.
2) the ways knowledge is produced, accepted, and rejected.
3) what individuals claim to know and the process by which they come to know it.
4) the nature of cultural/political authority and its relation to the dialectic of empowerment and domination.
5) the way individuals receive dominant representations and encodings of the world – are they assimilated, internalized, resisted, or transformed?
6) the manner in which individuals negotiate their relationship with the "official story," the legitimate canon.
7) the means by which the official and legitimated narrative positions students and citizens to make sense of their personal experience.
8) the process by which pleasure is derived from engagement with the dominant culture – an investment that produces meaning and formulates affect.
9) the methods by which cultural differences along lines of race, class, gender, national origin, religion, and geographical place are encoded in consciousness and processed by individuals.
10) the ways scientific rationality shapes consciousness in schools and the culture at large.

It is with the above issues in mind that I create my bricolage.

The attempt to delineate a universal research method for the study of the cultural curriculum and cultural pedagogy is a futile quest. The critical research of cultural studies and cultural pedagogy can make no guarantee about what questions will be important in different contexts; thus, no one method should be promoted over others – at the same time, none can be eliminated without examination. Ethnography, textual analysis, semiotics, deconstruction, critical hermeneutics, interviews, psychoanalysis, content analysis, survey research, and phenomenology simply initiate a list of research methods an educational scholar might bring to the table. Such an eclectic view of research has been labeled *bricolage* by several scholars. A term attributed to Claude Levi-Strauss (1966), bricolage (use of a tool box) bricolage involves taking research strategies from a variety of scholarly disciplines and traditions as they are needed in the unfolding context of the research situation. Such an action is pragmatic and strategic, demanding self-consciousness and awareness of context from the researcher. The *bricoleur*, the researcher who employs bricolage, must be able to orchestrate a plethora of diverse tasks including interviewing and observing, to historiographical analysis, to self-monitoring and intrapersonal understanding.

The text produced by this research process of bricolage should be a complex collage, as it weaves together the scholar's images, insights, and interpretations of the relationship between the popular cultural text, critical questions of justice, the social context that produced it, and its effect on youth and the cultural curriculum (Kincheloe and Berry 2004). Using theoretical and conceptual frames drawn from critical theory, poststructuralism, postmodern epistemologies, feminism, psychoanalysis, hermeneutics, recovery theory and other traditions, bricolage interprets, critiques, and deconstructs the text in question. Because scientific research has traditionally offered only a partial vision of the reality it seeks to explore, pedagogical bricoleurs attempt to widen their perspectives through methodological diversity. In no way, however, do they claim that as the result of the multiperspectival bricolage they have gained "the grand view" – from their poststructuralist perspective they understand that all inquiry is limited and incomplete. Humble in this knowledge, the bricoleur attempts to gain expanded insight via historical contextualization, multiple theoretical groundings, and a diversity of knowledge by collecting and interpreting methodologies (Kincheloe 2005; Steinberg 2007, 2012).

Theoretical bricolage compensates for the blindness of relying on one model of reading a cultural text. Bricolage does not draw upon diverse theoretical /methodological traditions simply for the sake of diversity. Rather, it uses the different approaches to inform and critique each other. A critical theoretical analysis of popular culture, for example, that is informed by psychoanalysis will be different than one that relies only on the sociological dimension of the text under analysis. Such an interpretive process subverts the tendency of knowledge producers to slip into the position that their interpretation is the "right one" (Kincheloe 2005). As we study the pedagogy of film, we are able to position it not only in historical, socio-political, and economic context but in relation to other films on a particular topic, with similar themes, or identified with a particular genre – for example, the films of John Hughes concerning middle-class male misbehavior. Expanding our ways of seeing with diverse perspectives we begin to grasp the ideological dimensions of films that often fall through the cracks. A more specific focus on how particular methodologies may be used in this popular cultural/film context may be in order.

CRITICALIZING ETHNOGRAPHY

Critical ethnography is an example of a critical research methodology that can be used within the bricolage. Ethnography is often described as the most basic form of social research: the analysis of events as they evolve in their natural setting. While ethnographers disagree about the relative importance of each purpose, ethnography attempts to gain knowledge about a cultural setting, to identify patterns of social interaction, and to develop holistic interpretations of societies and social institutions. Thus, typical educational ethnographies attempt to understand the nature of schools and other educational agencies in these ways, seeking to appreciate the social processes that move educational events. Ethnography attempts to make explicit the social processes one takes for granted as a culture member. The culture could be as broad as the study of an ethnic culture or as narrow as the middle-class white male culture of misbehavior. The critical ethnographer of education seeks to describe the concrete experiences of everyday school/educational life and the social patterns, the deep structures that support it (Hammersley and Atkinson 1983). In a bricolage, ethnography can be used in a variety of ways to gain insight into film. The most traditional involves audience studies where ethnographers observe and interview film audiences. John Fiske (1993) began his book, *Power Works, Power Plays,* using such a methodology, as he observed and interviewed a group of homeless men in a shelter as they watched the movie, *Die Hard.* What was the nature of the interrelationship between the viewers and the text? What did the men's responses to the film tell us about their selfimages? What did the men's responses tell us about film viewing in general and its ideological effects? Fiske's effort to answer these questions – to interpret his data – constitutes much of the content of the book.

In addition to such "audiencing" ethnographies, scholars can use ethnographic methods to explore the characters and cultures portrayed within the film and their relation to social dynamics outside the texts. Gaining knowledge about the "film culture" provides insight into the ideological orientations of film makers and entertainment corporations. Through the identification of patterns of cultural expression and social interaction, researchers can begin to specify the ideological dynamics at work. As socio-political processes are exposed, hidden agendas and tacit assumptions can be highlighted so as to provide new appreciations of the power of film to both reflect and shape culture. Poststructuralist forms of ethnography have focused on the discontinuities, contradictions, and inconsistencies of cultural expression and human action. As opposed to more modernist forms of ethnography, poststructuralist methods refuse to reconcile the asymmetries once and for all. The poststructuralist dimension of ethnography highlights the tendency of classical ethnography to privilege a dominant narrative and a unitary, privileged vantage point. In the effort to connect knower and known, the poststructuralist ethnographer proposes a dialogue between researcher and researched that attempts to smash traditional hierarchical relations between them (Atkinson and Hammersley 1994).

In this critical process the modernist notion of ethnography as an instrument of enlightenment and civilization of the "native" *objects* of study is overthrown. Poststructuralist ethnographies are texts to be argued over, the meaning of texts is never "natural" but are constructed by circumstance and inscribed by context (Aronowitz 1993). A film never stands alone as an object of study in poststructuralist ethnography. Seen as a living part of culture and history, the film takes on new meaning and circumstances and contexts change. How different the movie, *The Green Berets* (1968) looked to the young audience that viewed it in the late 1960s and early 1970s than it does to young people viewing it in the 21st Century. More young people of the present eara, adopting a conservative stance may positively resonate with the ideological intentions of the film makers than did young, anti-war viewers of the era in which it was produced. Indeed, the notion of radical and revolutionary youth has been revised in contemporary society. Circumstance and context must always be accounted for in critical poststructuralist ethnography. In this context poststructuralist ethnography informs and is informed by feminist and minority researchers concerned with the status quo of apologetics of film and traditional ethnography itself.

USING CONTENT ANALYSIS

Traditionally a content analysis could be considered methodical and quantitative in nature. The important issue about literally analyzing text is to allow the text to open and present themes for the researcher. Following is a method I have used with success in first, analyzing text, and second, in letting the textual analysis speak to me and suggest the themes that can be included. The content analysis then becomes an authentic interpretive analysis that precludes preliminary hypotheses, and instead waits to allow the data to speak for themselves in muli-layered ways. The analysis especially lends itself to research in film, written text, visual text (comics, photography, etc.). It then becomes ready for the critical hermeneutic interpretation, which is my tentative research goal.

In addition to such ethnographic analysis critical educational scholars use other methods of studying the social dynamics and effects of film. Douglas Kellner (1995) performs content analyses of film reviews and criticisms in the process gaining new vantage points out the ways that film texts become embedded in popular discourses. The "mode of reception" study was promoted by the Frankfurt School critical theorist, Walter Benjamin (Kellner 1995). Appropriating Benjamin's methodology, literary critics and theorists developed literary reception research that continues to contribute innovative ways of exploring textual effects. Distributed throughout Aaron Gresson's analysis of *Forrest Gump* is the discussion of the film by various critics and the news media. Beginning with the traditional "thumbs up" or "thumbs down" types of articles and moving to more esoteric and scholarly discussion, Gresson is able to trace themes relating back to his original suggestion of the recovery of whiteness and maleness in film (Gresson 1996). In this context, various research methodologies can be added to the bricolage, in the process providing ever more nuanced forms of insight into popular cultural texts.

Semiotics plays an invaluable role in the methodological pantheon with its focus on codes and signs that contribute to individuals' attempts to derive meaning from their surroundings. Educational researchers can use semiotic methods to gain insights into the social dynamics moving classroom events. Classrooms are full of codes calling out for semiotic analysis. Not only are classrooms saturated with codes and signs but they are characterized by rituals and conventions that are rarely questioned. The ways teachers, students, and administrators dress; pupils' language when speaking to teachers as compared to conversations with classmates; graffiti in a middle school restroom; systems of rules of behavior; the uses of bells and the intercom in schools; memos sent to parents; and the nature of the local community's conversation about school athletics are only a few of the topics an educational semiotician could study.

OBSERVATION

Contrary to notions that qualitative research dealing with popular culture is vacuous and without rigor, I submit my methodology in the spirit of academic scholarship and indeed, a poststructuralist, feminist, pedagogical research in which I am not seeking answers, but seeking questions, questions and more questions in which to make sense of the world of youth and of education. In their *Handbook of Qualitative Research,* Norm Denzin and Yvonna Lincoln (2005) discuss their union of poststructural/postmodernist cultural research (Denzin) and constructivist /pedagogical research (Lincoln). They contend that traditional research stops short of boundary crossing within interpretation. Observing that "over the past two decades, a quiet methodological revolution has been taking place in the social sciences" (1994, p. ix) Denzin and Lincoln define this revolution as the "blurring" of the boundaries within disciplinary research. As I discuss my methods and objectives in my research, keep in mind that I want to make "noise" in this so-called "quiet" revolution. In fact, I question whether or not it has ever been quiet. Certainly there have been attempts to silence the noise caused by radical qualitative research – silence in the denial of the politicization of the research of pedagogy; however, my qualitative predecessors have worked long and hard in the legitimization of the discipline. The word *rigor* seems to rear its ugly head at methodological junctures. I assert here that my research is indeed rigorous, challenging and constantly changing. Unlike a statistical formula, an organized hypothesis and a proven theorem, I am not beginning with any assumptions other than the one that popular culture must be studied. My thoughts about my subjects and my expectations in my observations changed each time I analyzed and recorded (for lack of a better word) *data.* It was within this discovery and rediscovery that I found rigor and challenge. It is within this context that I present my *literal method of interpretation.* I assert that rigorous scripting, recording and viewing/re-viewing (or consuming/re-consuming) is essential for critical hermeneutical research, and it is this process I delineate here (Steinberg 2007, 2012).

The postmodern condition has also re-determined and re-defined the actual research methods and practices that we use. No longer, as in earlier cultural research, do we view a film at the theater, go to the typewriter and write a response and review. We have the tools of hyperreality, through portability, films are readily available in VHS, DVD, and iMovie, consequently, we are able to view, then script, interpret, re-interpret, then problematize our interpretations as we attempt to make meaning from the text. Unlike viewer/historians of the past, we are able to re-visit an event, a text, and look for the tacit assumptions that reside within each signifier, floating signifier, code and ideology presented within the film.

"MAKING" THE BRICOLAGE

In order to be able to re-visit and re-view text, I found it essential to have access to videotapes of the films I wished to discuss. Wherever possible, I have avoided even alluding to films still in the theater as I feel they are available for a shallow interpretation at best (unless, of course, one owns his or her own theater). Along with the video tapes, I needed a video recorder, television and a good remote control. Other "equipment" I needed was an unlimited amount of colored pencils, ruled notebooks and a pen. However, on review of these methods, I feel that the use of a laptop computer while viewing could have or would have enhanced and possibly quickened the recording method.

In the manner of traditional ethnography, I used scripting as my form of recording. I wrote constantly through each film, usually filling up my notebooks after two films. I wrote quickly, and intuitively. I cannot delineate *what* to record. I can only describe that I recorded *everything* that made me think, consequently I relied on my own pedagogical intuition in my records. The use of the remote was essential in being able to rewind and record exact dialogue or to view a scene closely. In some films, I recorded no dialogue, only impressions of the scenery or music or cinematography. In most films I did record dialogue, discerning it as the salient data that would eventually be entered into my hermeneutical interpretations and discussions.

Each film took many hours to watch and re-watch. When I felt comfortable that I had scripted enough to begin my transcriptions, I transcribed the notebooks into wordprocessed form. Using phrases, I typed my entries going down each page as I had originally written them. After completing the transcription of all of the films, I read through the entire set of data. As I examined this completed set of scripting, themes and motifs started to emerge. As they began to repeat themselves, I wrote down my impressions of their emergence, *named* them as separate entities. After my first reading of the data, I used the colored pencils to code each theme/motif that I wanted to pursue. Underlining each item with a different color, macro-themes began to emerge, as the micro-themes seemed coalesced under the auspices of larger themes. Analyzing all the pages of scripting, I discovered additional themes each time. In many instances there would be three or four different colors under a certain situation or dialogue indicating an overlap among the themes.

A note: Not appear a "Luddite," I want to clarify that I chose to use both video and DVD to use in my work. I feel organically connected to the materials in this way, as an audience participant. This is my quirk. However, those with the technical abilities and equipment will find this method quite easy to do digitally using competent software.

Both visually and intuitively, I began the task of arranging micro-themes and placing them within the macro-themes. Given the thematic crossover, it was important to not essentialize any situation or dialogue and limit it to only one "category." I kept in mind that through my choice of bricolage, that I was not adhering to one method of interpretation, consequently it was important to record and underline each micro-theme every time it emerged in all macro-categories.

FILM RESEARCH

As this is a chapter discussing critical cultural pedagogical research methods, I chose to not use traditional methods of film theory and criticism (which are often not criticalized). I will delineate three terms that I used within my bricolage. As a bricoleur, I cut and pasted what I felt was significant and examined the multiple meanings that emerged. Traditional film criticism, as in any form of sociological research, has categories and philosophies attached to methods of interpretation of audiences and of text. And, as in traditional research, this criticism essentializes and closes itself off to the boundary crossing to which Denzin and Lincoln have chosen to blur. By taking each interpretative method and applying it to a film bricolage, I was able to use film criticism and theory to my advantage in my critical hermeneutical readings.

Traditional film criticism "reads" film in many ways. The most compelling methods and classifications involve concepts such as 1) *auteurism* 2) *montage* and 3) *genre*. Each term has value in critical hermeneutics, however, using them in a unilateral deconstruction would limit interpretation to a dogmatic ideological framework established by the original researcher.

Auteurism

As the name suggests, auteurism refers to the authorship of the text. As in a Derridian deconstruction, the text becomes the only artifact examined, and unlike a Derridian deconstruction, the text in relationship to the author/creator is the essential interpretation. The entire act of meaning making in auteurism is restricted to who the author is, his or her positionality, and tacit and overt agendas in regard to the text. While I would be unable to discount the inclusion of auteurism in interpreting film text, in no way would I be comfortable limiting the interpretation to this narrow theory. In the case of the writer/director, John Hughes – on whose films I rely heavily in my research – I cannot discount the fact that he is a white, middle-class male, and a baby boomer from Chicago. Further discovery of his own background and education *can* inform me about him and "where he comes from." However, to allow auteurism to define the purpose of his films, for example: Ferris Bueller *is* John Hughes or Hughes's plotlines revolve around his own personal agenda for humiliating adults would direct and possibly limit my interpretation(s). Robin Wood (1995) insists that limiting film theory to auteurism adds to the propensity of inconclusive, inaccurate research that insists "on its own particular polarization" (p. 59).

Montage

Like auteurism, montage relies on one lens through which to view a text. Unlike auteurism, montage examines the intent of the editor in the analysis of the "essential creative act" of film making (Wood 1995). While auteur theory exclusively read the act of the author as the textual interpretation, montage theory introduces the notion that the cutting room floor becomes the site for the decisive interpretative act. Once again, one cannot ignore the possible intent of the film editor and/or cinematographer, however, to limit interpretation to montage at the expense of any other aspect of film criticism and theory would once again limit the thickness of the interpretation.

Genre

In the traditional literary manner, the concept of genre is used to define and classify texts into manageable categories which immediately allow the interpreter to draw conclusions and make expected observations. For instance, when we refer to the Western as a genre, it is easy to imagine horses, Indians, pioneers and a white cowboy on a majestic horse. Within genre theory we are able to find familiar Western themes of patriarchy, white supremacy and colonialism without much effort. If we refer to *film noir*, we easily picture the frames of shadowy figures, a femme fatale and a Bogartesque antihero engaged in questionable activities. Once again, a prevailing theme of patriarchy emerges without question. Consider the l950s sci-fi genre – a white, middle-upper-class scientist who goes against the odds to defeat an alien invader – back to patriarchy, colonialism, and so forth. Exclusive reliance on genre theory determines in advance which themes will be analyzed and which will not – again the possibility of new interpretations is truncated. Categorizing texts aids us in the ability to place films on the shelf, to place books in the library and to choose different genres in which to research. However, the discussion of genre should be used only to name in a general sense, the macro-category of film that the researcher chooses to interpret. The catch, is that the genre must be determined and defined by each researcher in the context of his or her own research. Consequently, what I view as a western, may indeed be viewed as a political satire to one researcher and a classic to another.

With the use of auteurism, montage and genre, I have combined the qualitative method of bricolage using critical ethnography, semiotics, feminist theory and critical hermeneutics to interpret my research

USING FEMINIST RESEARCH TO INFORM THE BRICOLAGE

Another important aspect of the bricolage involves feminist research with its subversion of the principle of neutral, hierarchical, and estranged interaction between researcher and researched (Clough,1992). It is important that no one body of feminist theory exists. Three forms of feminist analysis have dominated the feminist critique:
1) liberal feminism has focused on gender stereotyping and bias. While such analyses have provided valuable insights, liberal feminism in general has failed to engage issues of power. As a result the position has been hard pressed to make sense of social reality with its subtle interactions of power, ideology, and culture – an interaction that needs to be analyzed in the larger effort to understand both the oppression of women and male privilege (Rosneau 1992);

2) radical feminism has maintained that the subjugation of women is the most important form of oppression in that it is grounded on specific biological differences between men and women. In radical feminism concerns with race and class are more rejected than ignored, as radical feminists maintain the irrelevance of such categories in the study of women's oppression;
3) the form of feminist theory privileged in my research is critical poststructuralist feminism. This articulation of feminism asserts that feminism is the quintessential postmodern discourse. As feminists focus on and affirm that which is absent and/or peripheral in modernist ways of seeing, they ground the poststructuralist critique in lived reality, in the material world (Kipnis 1988). As critical poststructuralist feminists challenge modernist patriarchal exclusions, they analyze the connections between an unjust class structure and the oppression of women (Rosneau 1992). Often, they contend, male domination of women is concretized on the terrain of class – e.g., the feminization of poverty and the growth in the number of women who are homeless over the last fifteen years (Kincheloe and Steinberg 1997).

In this poststructuralist feminist context research can no longer be seen as a cold, rational process. Feminist research injects feeling, empathy, and the body into the act of inquiry, blurring the distinction between knower and known, viewer and viewed – looking at truth as a *process* of construction in which knowers and viewers play an active role, and embedding passion into the bricolage. Researchers in this context see themselves as passionate scholars who connect themselves emotionally to what they are seeking to know and understand. Modernist researchers often weeded out the self, denying their intuitions and inner voices, in the process producing restricted and object-like interpretations of socio-educational events. Using the traditional definitions, these object-like interpretations were certain and scientific; feminist self-grounded inquiries were inferior, merely impressionistic, and journalistic (Reinharz 1992). Rejecting the authority of the certainty of science, feminist researchers charged that the so-called objectivity of modernist science was nothing more than a signifier for the denial of social and ethical responsibility, ideological passivity, and the acceptance of privileged socio-political position of the researcher. Thus, feminist theorists argued that modernist pseudo-objectivity demands the separation of thought and feeling, the devaluation of any perspective maintained with emotional conviction. Feeling is designated as an inferior form of human consciousness – those who rely on thought or logic operating within this framework can justify their repression of those associated with emotion or feeling. Feminist theorists have pointed out that the thought-feeling hierarchy is one of the structures historically used by men to oppress women (Walby 1990). In intimate heterosexual relationships if a man is able to present his position in an argument as the rational viewpoint and the woman's position as an emotional perspective, then he has won the argument – his is the voice worth hearing.

Drawing from feminist researchers, critical poststructuralists have learned that inquiry should be informed by our "humanness," that we can use the human as a research instrument. From this perspective inquiry begins with researchers drawing upon their own experience. Such an educational researcher is a human being studying other human beings focusing on their inner world of experience. Utilizing his or her own empathetic understandings, the observer can watch educational phenomena from within – that is, the observer can know directly, he or she can watch and experience. In the process the private is made public. Not only do we get closer to the private experience of students, teachers, and administrators and the effect of these experiences on the public domain, but we also gain access to the private experience of the researcher and the effect of that experience on the public description the researcher presents of the phenomena observed (Reinharz 1992). Thus not only do we learn about the educational world that surrounds us, but we gain new insights into the private world within us – the world of our constructed subjectivity. By revealing what can be learned from the every-day, the mundane, feminist scholars have opened a whole new area of inquiry and insight. They have uncovered the existence of silences and absences where traditional scholars had seen only "what was there." When the feminist critique is deployed within the methodological diversity of the bricolage, new forms of insight into educational and social affairs as well as the cultural curriculum emerge.

CONNECTING RESEARCH TO SOCIAL THEORY

In examining social dynamics of media/popular culture via the research methodologies of ethnography and semiotics and the political and epistemological concerns of poststructuralist feminism, an effort is made to connect research to the domain of social theory. Indeed, theory is very important in the bricolage of critical poststructuralist research. Theory involves the conceptual matrix analysts use to make sense of the world. Theory, whether it is held consciously or unconsciously, works as a filter through which researchers approach information, designate facts, identify problems, and devise solutions to their problems. Different theoretical frameworks, therefore, privilege different ways of seeing the world in general or the domain of popular culture in particular (Kincheloe 2001). The theory behind a critical poststructuralist way of seeing recognizes these theoretical dynamics, especially the potential tyranny that accompanies theoretical speculation. The problem that has undermined the traditional critical project of understanding and changing the inequality plaguing modernist societies has involved the production of a theory that was too totalizing (all encompassing) and rigid to grasp the *complexity* described here. Critical poststructuralist theory is committed to a theoretical stance that guarantees the individual or community the capacity to make meaning and to act independently. Any theory acceptable to critical poststructuralists, thus, must take into account local divergence. This is not to adopt a position that insists researchers allow phenomena to speak for themselves. Theory in this context is a resource that can be used to generate a dialogue with a phenomenon; it is always contingent and it never whispers the answers to the researcher in advance (Grossberg 1995). Theory does not travel well from one context to another. Indeed theory's usefulness is always mitigated by context.

Such a locally sensitive theoretical position allows bricolage research a space from which to view movies and popular cultural phenomena that maintains an oppositional but not a totalizing and deterministic interpretive strategy (Smith 1989). Such a strategy searches for manifestations of domination and resistance in popular texts in light of larger questions of democracy (Kellner 1995). Drawing upon the theoretical work of the Frankfurt School of Critical Theory, the concept of immanent critique helps us understand this oppositional dynamic. Critical theory, according to Max Horkheimer, attempts to expose and assess the breach between reality and ideas or "what is" and "what could be." Within capitalist society, Horkheimer maintained, there is an inherent contradiction between the bourgeois order's words and deeds. The more the power bloc speaks of justice, equality, and freedom, the more it fails under its own standards. Immanent critique, therefore, attempts to evaluate cultural production "from within," on the basis of the standards of its producers. In this way it hopes to avoid the accusation that its concepts inflict superfluous criteria of evaluation on those it investigates. Employing such a theoretical critique, critical theorists hope to generate a new understanding of the cultural phenomenon in question – an understanding that is able to articulate both the contradictions and possibilities contained with it (Held 1980).

INTERPRETATION THROUGH CRITICAL HERMENEUTICS

I ground my research in the hermeneutical tradition and its concern with both the process of understanding the meaning of various texts and the production of strategies for textual interpretation. Traditionally concerned with the interpretation of religious texts and canonical scriptures within their social and historical context, hermeneutics, after the scientific revolution of the European Enlightenment, emerged as the tradition that challenged the increasingly powerful shibboleths of the empirical scientific tradition. One of the central assertions of hermeneutics is that research and analysis of any variety involves an awareness of one's own consciousness and the values residing tacitly within it. Such values and the predispositions they support, hermeneuts maintained, unconsciously shape the nature of any project of inquiry. Such profound arguments, unfortunately, exerted little influence on their scientific contemporaries, as they held fast to their science of verification, the notion of objectivity, and the absurdity of the need for self-analysis on the part of the researcher (Kincheloe 2005).

Central to the hermeneutic method is an appreciation of the complexity and ambiguity of human life in general and the pedagogical process in particular. Hermeneutics attempts to return lived experience and meaning making to their original difficulty. In this context, words and images are relegated to the realm of the living with all the possibility for change such a state implies. Words and images to the hermeneutical analyst are not dead and static but alive and dynamic. Such a reality, of course, complicates the process of interpretation but concurrently provides a far more textured picture of human experience. The Greek root of hermeneutics, *hermeneuenin,* refers to the messenger god Hermes. Such an etymology well fits hermeneutics' ambiguous inscription, as Hermes was often a trickster in his official role of translator of divine messages to human beings. Interpretation is never simple and straight-forward – humans in the Greek myths learned this lesson frequently at the hands of their deceptive messenger. This lesson is not lost in twentieth century hermeneutics, as analysts focus their attention on the sediments of meaning and the variety of intentions that surround social, political, and educational artifacts. Transcending the scientific empirical need for final proof and certainty, hermeneuts celebrate the irony of interpretation in the ambiguous lived world. Framing the methods of such interpretation as both analytic and intuitive, hermeneutics pushes the boundaries of human understanding in a manner more consonant with the contradictory nature of the world around us.

The Nature of Hermeneutic Interpretation

Hermeneutics insists that in social/educational science there is only interpretation, no matter how vociferously empirical scientists may argue that the facts speak for themselves. The hermeneutic act of interpretation involves in its most elemental articulation making sense of what has been observed in a way that communicates understanding. Not only is human science merely an act of interpretation, but hermeneutics contends that perception itself is an act of interpretation. Thus, the quest for understanding is a fundamental feature of human existence, as encounter with the unfamiliar always demands the attempt to make meaning, to make sense – but such is also the case with the familiar. Indeed, as in the study of commonly known popular movies, we come to find that sometimes the familiar may be seen as the most strange. Thus, it should not be surprising that even the so-called objective writings of qualitative research are interpretations, not value-free descriptions (Denzin 1994).

Learning from the hermeneutic tradition and the postmodern critique, critical researchers have begun to re-examine textual claims to authority. No pristine interpretation exists – indeed, no methodology, social or educational theory, and discursive form can claim a privileged position that enables the production of authoritative knowledge. Researchers must always speak/write about the world in terms of something else in the world. As creatures of the world, we are oriented to it in a way that prevents us from grounding our theories and perspectives outside of it. Thus, whether we like it or not we are all destined as interpreters to analyze from within its boundaries and blinders. Within these limitations, however, the interpretations emerging from the hermeneutic process can still move us to new levels of understanding, appreciations that allow us to "live our way" into an experience described to us. Despite the impediments of context hermeneutical researchers can transcend the inadequacies of thin descriptions of decontextualized facts and produce thick descriptions of social/pedagogical texts characterized by the context of its production, the intentions of its producers, and the meanings mobilized in the process of its construction. The production of such thick descriptions /interpretations follows no step-by-step blueprint or mechanical formula. As with any art form, hermeneutical analysis can be learned only in the

Deweyan sense – by doing it. Researchers in this context practice the art by grappling with the text to be understood, telling its story in relation to its contextual dynamics and other texts first to themselves and then to a public audience (Kincheloe 2005).

Thoughts about Hermeneutical Methods of Interpretation

These concerns with the nature of hermeneutical interpretation come under the category of philosophical hermeneutics. Working in this domain scholars attempt to think through and clarify the conditions under which interpretation and understanding take place. The following analysis moves more in the direction of normative hermeneutics in that it raises questions about the purposes and procedures of interpretation. In its critical theory-driven cultural studies context the purpose of hermeneutical analysis employed in this research is to provide understanding of particular cultural and educational phenomena of contemporary life. Drawing upon the Frankfurt School's goal of theorizing the driving forces of the present moment, critical hermeneutics is used to develop a form of cultural criticism that sets the stage for a future politics/pedagogy of emancipation. Hermeneutical researchers operating with these objectives build bridges between reader and text, text and its producer, historical context and present, and one particular social circumstance and another. Accomplishing such interpretive tasks is a difficult endeavor, and scholars interested in normative hermeneutics push aspiring hermeneuts to trace the bridge-building process employed by successful interpreters of culture and pedagogy (Kincheloe 2005).

Grounded by this hermeneutical bridge-building, critical social analysts in a hermeneutical circle (a process of analysis where interpreters seek the historical and social dynamics that shape textual interpretation) engage in the back and forth of studying parts in relation to the whole and the whole in relation to parts. No final interpretation is sought in this context, as the activity of the circle proceeds with no need for closure (Kincheloe 2005). This movement of whole to parts is combined with an analytical flow between abstract and concrete. Such dynamics often tie interpretation to the interplay of larger social forces (the general) to the everyday lives of individuals (the particular). A critical hermeneutics brings the concrete, the parts, the particular into focus, but in a manner that grounds it (them) contextually in a larger understanding of the social forces, the whole, the abstract (the general) that grounds it (them). Focus on the parts is the dynamic that brings the particular into focus, sharpening our understanding of the individual in light of the social and psychological forces that shape him or her. The parts and the unique places they occupy ground hermeneutical ways of seeing by providing the contextualization of the particular – a perspective often erased in modernist science's search for abstract generalizations (Kincheloe 2005).

The give and take of the hermeneutical circle induces analysts to review existing conceptual matrixes in light of new understandings. Here preconceptions are reconsidered and reconceptualized so as to provide a new way of exploring a particular text. Making use of an author's insights hermeneutically does not mean replicating his or her response to the original question. In the hermeneutical process the author's answer is valuable only if it catalyzes the production of a new question for our consideration in the effort to make sense of a particular textual phenomenon (Gallagher 1992). In this context participants in the hermeneutical circle must be wary of critical techniques of textual defamiliarization that have become cliched. For example, feminist criticisms of Barbie's figure and its construction of the image of ideal woman became such conventions in popular cultural analysis that other readings of Barbie were suppressed (Steinberg 2004). Critical hermeneutical analysts in this and many other cases have to introduce new forms of analysis to the hermeneutical circle – to defamiliarize conventional defamiliarizations – in order to achieve deeper levels of understanding (Berger 1995).

Within the hermeneutical circle we many develop new metaphors to shape our analysis in ways that break us out of familiar modes. For example, thinking of movies as mass-mediated dreams may help us reconceptualize the interpretive act as a psychoanalytic form of dream study. In this way, educational scholars could examine psychoanalytical work in the analysis of dream symbolization for insights into their studies of the pedagogy of popular culture and the meanings it helps individuals make via its visual images and narratives. As researchers apply these new metaphors in the hermeneutic circle, they must be aware of the implicit metaphors analysts continuously bring to the interpretive process (Berger 1995). Such metaphors are shaped by the socio-historical era, the culture, and the linguistic context in which the interpreter operates. Such awareness is an important feature that must be introduced into the give and take of the hermeneutical circle. As John Dewey wrote almost a century ago, individuals adopt the values and perspectives of their social groups in a manner that such factors come to shape their views of the world. Indeed, the values and perspectives of the group help determine what is deemed important and what is not, what is granted attention and what is ignored. Hermeneutical analysts are aware of such interpretational dynamics and make sure they are included in the search for understanding (Berger 1995).

Situating Interpretation

Researchers who fail to take Dewey's point into account operate at the mercy of unexamined assumptions. Since all interpretation is historically and culturally situated, it befalls the lot of hermeneutical analysts to study the ways both interpreters (often the analysts themselves) and the object of interpretation are constructed by their time and place. In this context the importance of social theory emerges. In this research critical social theory is injected into the hermeneutic circle to facilitate an understanding of the hidden structures and tacit cultural dynamics that insidiously inscribe social meanings and values (Kellner 1995). This social and historical situating of interpreter and text is an extremely complex enterprise that demands a nuanced analysis of the impact of hegemonic and ideological forces that connect the micro-dynamics of everyday life with the macro-dynamics of structures of white supremacy, patriarchy, and class elitism. The central hermeneutic aspect of this work will involve the interaction between the cultural curriculum and these situating socio-historical structures.

When these aspects of the interpretation process are taken into account, analysts begin to understand Hans-Georg Gadamer's contention that social frames of reference influence researchers' questions which, in turn, shape the nature of interpretation itself. In light of this situating process the modernist notion that a social text has one valid interpretation evaporates into thin air. Researchers, whether they admit it or not, always have a point of view, a disciplinary orientation, a social or political group with which they identify (Kincheloe 2005). Thus, the point, critical hermeneuts argue, is not for researchers to shed all worldly affiliations but to identify them and understand their impact on the ways they approach social and educational phenomena. Gadamer labels these world affiliations of researchers their "horizons" and deems the hermeneutic act of interpretation the "fusion of horizons." When researchers engage in the fusion of horizons they enter the tradition of the text. Here they study the conditions of its production and the circle of previous interpretations. In this manner they begin to uncover the ways the text has attempted to represent truth (Berger 1995).

In the critical hermeneutical tradition these analyses of the ways interpretation is situated are considered central to the critical project. Researchers like all human beings, critical analysts argue, make history and live their lives within structures of meaning they have not necessarily chosen for themselves. Understanding this, critical hermeneuts realize that a central aspect of their cultural pedagogical analysis involves dissecting the ways people connect their everyday experiences to the cultural representations of such experiences. Such work involves the unraveling of the ideological codings embedded in these cultural representations. This unraveling is complicated by the taken-for-grantedness of the meanings promoted in these representations and the typically undetected ways these meanings are circulated into everyday life (Denzin 1992). The better the analyst, the better he or she can expose these meanings in the domain of the "what-goes-without-saying" – in this research those features of the media curriculum that are not addressed, that don't elicit comment.

At this historical juncture – the postmodern condition or hyperreality, as it has been labeled – electronic modes of communication become extremely important to the production of meanings and representations that culturally situate human beings in general and textual interpretations in particular. In many ways it can be argued that the postmodern condition produces a second hand culture, filtered and pre-formed in the marketplace and constantly communicated via popular cultural and mass media. Critical analysts understand that the pedagogical effects of such a *media*ted culture can range from the political/ideological to the cognitive/epistemological. For example, the situating effects of print media tend to promote a form of linearity that encourages rationality, continuity, and uniformity, on the other hand, electronic media promote a non-linear immediacy that may encourage more emotional responses that lead individuals in very different directions. Thus, the situating influence and pedagogical impact of electronic media of the postmodern condition must be assessed by those who study the pedagogical process and, most importantly in this context, the research process itself (Kincheloe 2005).

CRITICAL HERMENEUTICS

Understanding the forces that situate interpretation, critical hermeneutics is suspicious of any model of interpretation that claims to reveal the final truth, the essence of a text or any form of experience. Critical hermeneutics is more comfortable with interpretive approaches that assume that the meaning of human experience can never be fully disclosed – neither to the researcher nor even to the human that experienced it. Since language is always slippery with its meanings ever "in process," critical hermeneuts understand that interpretations will never be linguistically unproblematic, will never be direct representations, critical hermeneutics seeks to understand how textual practices such as scientific research and classical theory work to maintain existing power relations and to support extant power structures (Denzin 1992). This research draws, of course, on the latter model of interpretation with its treatment of the personal as political. Critical hermeneutics grounds a critical pedagogy that attempts to connect the everyday troubles individuals face to public issues of power, justice, and democracy. Typically, within the realm of the cultural curriculum critical hermeneutics has deconstructed popular cultural texts that promote demeaning stereotypes of the disempowered (Denzin 1992). In this research, critical hermeneutics will be deployed differently in relation to popular cultural texts, as it examines popular movies that reinforce an ideology of privilege and entitlement for empowered members of the society – in this case, white, middle/upper-class males.

In its ability to render the personal political, critical hermeneutics provides a methodology for arousing a critical consciousness through the analysis of the generative themes of the present era. Such generative themes form the basis of the cultural curriculum of popular culture (Peters and Lankshear 1994). Within the academy there is still resistance to the idea that movies, TV, and popular music are intricately involved in the most important political, economic, and cultural battles of the contemporary epoch. Critical hermeneutics recognizes this centrality of popular culture and seek to uncover the ways it impedes and advances the struggle for a democratic society (Kincheloe 2005). Appreciating the material effects of media culture, critical hermeneutics trace the ways movies position audiences politically in ways that not only shape their political beliefs but also formulate their identities. In this context, Paulo Freire's contribution to the development of a critical hermeneutics is especially valuable. Understanding that the generative themes of a culture are central features in a critical social analysis, Freire assumes that the interpretive process is both an ontological and an epistemological act. It is ontological on the level that our vocation as humans, the foundation of our being, is grounded on the hermeneutical task of interpreting the world so we can become more fully human. It is epistemological in the sense that critical hermeneutics offers us a method for investigating the conditions of our existence and the generative themes that shape it. In this context we gain the prowess to both live with a purpose and operate with the ability to perform evaluative acts in naming the culture around us. In the postmodern condition the pedagogical effects of popular culture have often been left unnamed, allowing our exploration of the shaping of our own humanness to go unexplored in this strange new social context. Critical hermeneutics address this vacuum (Kincheloe 2005).

Critical hermeneutics names the world as a part of a larger effort to evaluate it and make it better. Knowing this, it is easy to understand why critical hermeneutics focuses on domination and its negation, emancipation. Domination limits self-direction and democratic community building while emancipation enables it. Domination, legitimated as it is by ideology, is decoded by critical hermeneuts who help individuals discover the ways they have been entangled in the ideological process. The exposé and critique of ideology is one of critical hermeneutics' main objectives in its effort to make the world better. As long as the various purveyors of ideology obstruct our vision, our effort to live in democratic communities will be thwarted (Gallagher 1992). Power wielders with race, class, and gender privilege have access to the resources that allow them to promote ideologies and representations in ways individuals without such privilege cannot. Resources such as entertainment and communication industries are used to shape consciousness and construct subjectivity (Kincheloe 2005; Steinberg 2010).

THE PRODUCTION OF SUBJECTIVITY AND CULTURAL PEDAGOGY IN CRITICAL HERMENEUTICS

Those who operate outside the critical tradition often fail to understand that the critical hermeneutical concern with popular culture in the postmodern condition is not a matter of aesthetics but an issue of socio-political impact. In light of the focus of this research on the cultural curriculum and cultural pedagogy, a key aspect of this socio-political impact involves the socialization of youth. Those same outsiders sometimes look down their noses at the popular texts chosen for interpretation in the critical context, arguing that cultural productions such as *Fast Times at Ridgemont High,* for example, doesn't deserve the attention critical scholarship might devote to it. Critical hermeneuts maintain that all popular culture that is consumed and makes an impact on an audience is worthy of study regardless of the aesthetic judgments elite cultural scholars might offer (Berger 1995). In the case of a movie like *Fast Times at Ridgemont High,* it is important to critical analysts because it is both inscribed with profound cultural meanings and so many people have watched it. In its interest in oppression and emancipation, self-direction, personal freedom, and democratic community building, critical hermeneutics knows that popular texts such as movies shape the production of subjectivity; it also understands that such a process can be understood only with an appreciation of the socio-historical and political context that supports it (Ellis and Flaherty 1992).

Norm Denzin (1992) is extremely helpful in developing this articulation of critical hermeneutics, drawing on the sociological genius of C. Wright Mills and his "sociological imagination." A key interest of this tradition, which Denzin carries into the contemporary era, involves unearthing the connections among material existence, communications processes, cultural patterns, and the formation of human consciousness. This articulation of a critical hermeneutics has much to learn from Denzin and Mills and their concern with subjectivity/consciousness, their understanding that cultural productions of various types hold compelling consequences for humans. Denzin is obsessed with the way individuals make sense of their everyday lives in particular cultural contexts by constructing stories (narratives) that, in turn, help define their identities. Employing a careful reading of Denzin, a critical hermeneut can gain insight into how cultural texts help create a human subject. How, Denzin wants to know, do individuals connect their lived experiences to the cultural representations of these same experiences (Denzin 1992)?

Following this line of thought a critical hermeneutics concerned with the pedagogical issue of identity formation seeks cultural experiences that induce crises of consciousness when an individual's identity is profoundly challenged. Such moments are extremely important to any pedagogy, for it is in such instants of urgency that dramatic transformations occur (Denzin 1992). In this research it is argued that such moments are not uncommon in individual interactions with popular texts and that the results of such experiences can be either oppressive or liberatory in nature. Indeed, some pedagogical experiences may be characterized as rational processes but they almost always involve a strong emotional component. Too often in mainstream research this emotional dynamic has been to some degree neglected by logocentric social science (Ellis and Flaherty 1992). A critical hermeneutics aware of such cultural pedagogical dynamics will empower individuals to make sense of their popular cultural experiences and provide them with specific tools of social interpretation. Such abilities will allow them to avoid the manipulative ideologies of popular cultural texts in an emancipatory manner that helps them consciously construct their own identities. Critical social and educational analysis demands such abilities in its efforts to provide transformative insights into the many meanings produced and deployed in the media-saturated postmodern landscape (Kellner 1995).

CONCLUSION

This chapter describes the way that cultural studies can be used with a bricolaged approach; combining critical research methods in order to critically interpret film, in this case, for a cultural pedagogical reading. As one who self-defines herself as abstract random, with a strange penchant for organization, I believe that cultural studies is best read through an approach that does not limit itself to one research method.

REFERENCES

Aronowitz, S. (1993). *Roll over Beethoven: The return of cultural strife*. Hanover, New Hampshire, NH: Wesleyan University Press.

Atkinson, P. & Hammersley, M. (1994). Ethnography and participant observation. In N. Denzin and Lincoln, Y. (eds.), *Handbook of qualitative research*. (pp. 83-97). Thousand Oaks, CA: Sage.

Berger, A. (1995). *Cultural criticism: A primer of key concepts*. Thousand Oaks, CA: Sage.

Clough, P. (1992). *The end(s) of ethnography: From realism to social criticism*. Newbury Park, CA: Sage.

Collins, J. (1990). *Architectures of excess: Cultural life in the information age*. New York: Routledge.

Denzin, N. (1992). *Symbolic interactionism and cultural studies: The politics of interpretation*. Cambridge, MA: Blackwell.

Denzin, N. (1994). The art and politics of interpretation. In N. Denzin & Y. Lincoln (Eds.), *Handbook of qualitative research* (pp. 500-515). Thousand Oaks, CA: Sage.

Denzin, N., & Lincoln, Y. (2005). *The Sage handbook of qualitative research* (3rd edition). Thousand Oaks, CA: Sages

Ellis, C. & Flaherty, M. (1992). An agenda for the interpretation of lived experience. In C. Ellis and Flaherty, M. (eds.), *Investigating subjectivity: Research on lived experience* (pp. 1-16). Newbury Park, CA: Sage.

Fiske, J. (1993). *Power plays, power works*. New York, NY: Verso.

Gallagher, S. (1992). *Hermeneutics and education*. Albany, NY: SUNY Press.

Gresson, A. (1996). Postmodern America and the multicultural crisis: Reading *Forrest Gump* as the call back to whiteness. *Taboo: The Journal of Culture and Education*, Spring, 11-34.

Grossberg, L. (1995). What's in a name (one more time)? *Taboo: The Journal of Culture and Education*, Spring, 1-37.

Hammersley, M., & Atkinson, P. (1983). *Ethnography: Principles in practice*. New York, NY: Tavistock.

Held, D. (1980). *Introduction to critical theory*. Berkeley, CA: University of California Press.

Kellner, D. (1995). *Media culture: Cultural studies, identity and politics between the modern and the postmodern*. New York, NY: Routledge.

Kincheloe, J. (2001). Describing the bricolage: Conceptualizing a new rigour in qualitative research. *Qualitative Inquiry*, 7, 679-692.

Kincheloe, J. (2005). On to the next level: Continuing the conceptualization of the bricolage. In *Qualitative Inquiry*, 11, 323-350.

Kincheloe, J., & Berry, K. (2004). *Rigour and complexity in educational research: Conceptualizing the bricolage*. London: Open University Press.

Kincheloe, J. & Steinberg, S. (1997). *Changing multiculturalism*. London: Open University Press.

Kipnis, L. (1992). Feminism: The political conscience of postmodernism. In A. Ross (Ed.), *Universal abandon? The politics of postmodernism* (pp. 149-166) Minneapolis: University of Minnesota Press.

Levi-Strauss, C. (1966). *The savage mind*. Chicago: University of Chicago Press.

MacDonald, D. (1957). A theory of mass culture. In B. Rosenberg & D. White (Eds.), *Mass culture* (pp. 59-73). Glencoe: Free Press.

Peters, M., & Lankshear, C. (1994). Education and hermenetics: A Freirean interpretation. In P. McLaren & C. Lankshear (Eds.), *Politics of liberation: Paths from Freire*. (pp.173-192). New York, NY: Routledge.

Reinharz, S. (1992). *Feminist methods in social research*. New York: Oxford University Press.

Rosneau, P. (1992). *Postmodernism and the social sciences: Insights, inroads, and intrusion*. Princeton: Princeton University Press.

Smith, P. (1989). Pedagogy and the popular-cultural-commodity text. In H. Giroux & R. Simon (Eds.), *Popular culture: Schooling and everyday life*. (pp. 31-46). Granby, MA: Bergin and Garvey.

Steinberg, S. R. (2007). Hollywood's curriculum of Muslims and Arabs in two acts. In D. Macedo & S. R. Steinberg (Eds.), *Media literacy: A reader* (pp. 299-315). New York: Peter Lang Publishing.

Steinberg, S. R. (2010). Not the real thing: A history of Hollywood's TV families. In M. Marsh & T. Turner-Vorbeck (Eds.), *(Mis)understanding families: Learning from real families in our schools* (pp. 37-52). New York: Teachers College Press.

Steinberg, S. R. (2012). What's critical about qualitative research? In S. R. Steinberg & G. S. Cannella (Eds.), *Critical qualitative research reader* (pp. ix-x). New York: Peter Lang Publishing.

Steinberg, S. R. (2004 1997). The bitch who has everything. In S. Steinberg & J. Kincheloe (Eds.), *Kinderculture: The corporate construction of childhood* (pp. 207-218). Boulder, CO: Westview Press.

Walby, S. (1990). Theorizing patriarchy. *Utne Reader, 64* (July/August), 63-66.

Wood, R. (1995). Ideology, genre, auteur. In B. Grant (Ed.), *Film genre reader II* (pp. 59-73). Austin, TX: University of Texas Press.

FILMOGRAPHY

Die Hard 1988. John McTiernan, Director.
Fast Times at Ridgemont High 1982. Amy Heckerling, Director.
Forrest Gump 1994. Robert Zemeckis, Director.
Ferris Bueller's Day Off 1986. John Hughes, Director.
The Green Berets 1968, Ray Kellogg and John Wayne, Directors.

BARBARA THAYER-BACON AND DIANA MOYER

6. PHILOSOPHICAL AND HISTORICAL RESEARCH

We write this essay as colleagues who work in the same program, Cultural Studies of Education, that is located in a department that is home to a very eclectic group of scholars, including people in instructional technology, health and safety, curriculum, research and assessment. We all participate in a seminar for our department where we come together and meet the new PhD student cohort and we try to explain to them what our programs entail and the kinds of research we do. As can be imagined, with such a diverse group of scholars, there is a variety of forms of research going on in our department, including filmmaking, program assessment, learning motivation, technology implementation, theory writing, and public health promotion.

Such a diverse array of programs brings logistical and conceptual challenges to the students and faculty. But it also offers our students a unique opportunity to see different research traditions presented in relation to one another. We attempt to use philosophy and history of education to broaden students' knowledge of educational research and theory. Most of our students are familiar with the quantitative /qualitative distinction and some of the methods associated with each. They have seen examples in journals, talked to peers who are planning to do an ethnography or survey, and can visualize themselves within a narrowly defined quantitative or qualitative tradition. In contrast, students' connection with philosophical and historical research is rare or marked by misperceptions. In the absence of more familiar and tangible products such as taped interviews, field sites, or chi-squares, alternative forms of research can appear abstract and disconnected from educational practice.

As might be expected, our filmmaker in the department has to make the case that what he does counts as research, that making a film is a creative endeavor that produces a product (a film), and it is just as difficult, time consuming, and has much the same possible scholarly significance as the writing of a book, report, or article, or the publishing of a how-to manual. That our filmmaker has to make the case for his artistic work to be recognized as a form of research is a sign of a problem we want to discuss in relation to our own research work. The problem is that science holds sway in academia presently and scientific research is the norm used to define educational research. Science has the highest status and other forms of scholarly endeavors such as artistic work are viewed as the exceptions that prove the norm is scientific scholarship.

In cultural studies the concept hegemony, originally developed by Antonio Gramsci (1971), is used to explain what happens when one group of people or one way of thinking is so powerful that it is considered "natural" and "normal" and what others may do or think that is contrary or different is considered "unnatural" or "abnormal," if it is even recognized at all. Included in the concept of hegemony is the idea that when something is considered the norm, it holds powerful sway on all people's lives, such that people who don't meet the standard of the norm will view themselves as lacking, or inferior, or deviant, and they will discipline themselves to try to fit the norm. Gramsci noticed that in his country, Italy, people were often voting for policies or politicians who actually represented policy positions that were harmful to the people voting. Gramsci tried to understand why people would vote for something or someone that is harmful to them (such as regressive sale tax laws). He developed the concept of hegemony to explain this phenomenon. People will vote for policies that actually only help the rich and powerful, but they do so with the hope that it might help them as well, and because they accept the norms of the rich and powerful as their own. Not only will they vote for policies that are harmful to them, they will police what others do and pressure them to vote the same way.

We want to argue that science and scientific forms of argumentation are considered the norm in research, and other forms of arguments that are not scientific are considered inferior forms of research, if they are even recognized as research at all. Policing action is taking place regularly to make sure faculty are doing scientific research and those who aren't don't get published, funded, tenured, or promoted. This hegemonic situation applies to educational research as well. Students are taught in educational research courses on how to do quantitative and qualitative research, both of which are scientific forms of research, but philosophical arguments often are not even considered a form of research and are not included in their course curriculum. Historical research does get recognition as a form of research, under the broad umbrella of qualitative research, but is often seen as a humanities discipline with little to offer students in the social sciences. Students are required to learn statistics to graduate, so that they can make sense of a quantitative study and determine if it is sound or not, but they are not required to learn logic, so they can make a well reasoned argument and critique others' arguments for their soundness and fruitfulness.

We will discuss our various fields of study below as we explain what historical and philosophical research is, against the norm of scientific research. But it is important to notice right from the beginning that we are working in a situation where we are not the norm, and often feel like we must defend our very existence, given the current conditions within which we work. One of the things that makes both of our fields of study so interesting to examine, in contrast to work in film for example, is that history and philosophy are two fields of study that have been around a long time. They are not new to the academy, like instructional technology is. In colleges of arts and sciences, history and philosophy are two departments that are mainstays and have been visible in universities from their very beginnings. Philosophers and historians enjoyed prestige and status for their scholarship at one point in time. Yet today they are barely visible, and find themselves having to survive on starvation diets, while their colleagues over in the sciences receive tremendous support in a variety of ways. It is the hard sciences that receive grants that help them buy new equipment and hire graduate assistants, as well as more faculty. The sciences are located in the nicest buildings, and the scientists receive the highest salaries and teach the least number of courses. They are the ones in the news and the ones whose names are mentioned when university presidents talk about their faculty's research work.

Philosophical and historical scholarship had status that has been lost to science. Along with that status, they had hegemonic power as well in their heyday. Even today, without the status that science enjoys, we can still see examples of hegemony within our fields of study. Both historians and philosophers of education work to advance educational practice and thereby reject the model of research for its own sake. This practitioner-orientated work is not held in as high regard as "pure" philosophy or history, which is viewed as unencumbered by the need for applicability. We can see the evidence of these claims by how seldom "pure" philosophers cite philosophers of education's scholarship in their own work, whereas philosophers of education regularly cite "pure" philosopher's work. Similarly, historians located in history departments sometimes dismiss educational history as "presentist" in its use of history to address current educational issues. Historians of education attempt to speak to both the past and present while satisfying the disciplinary expectations of history and education (Donato and Lazerson 2000).

We write this essay in an effort to help others understand that the scholarly work we do represents various forms of research. Research is a concept that is continually in need of reexamining, for it is a growing, changing concept in a constant state of flux. What we would like to write about is the kind of research we do within our specific fields of study within the cultural studies program. We both do different kinds of research, yet we find that our paths often cross, not only because we are sometimes interested in similar topics and issues, but we also find we often cite the same sources and apply similar forms of analysis with our work. We understand what each other does much better than our colleagues in our department or college understand what we do, let alone their students. We hope this effort will help to make our work "visible" and have it "count" as research, and maybe we will even succeed in convincing some budding scholars of the exciting possibilities within our fields of study, and they will come and join forces with us, over on the outskirts of educational research.

PHILOSOPHICAL ARGUMENTS

I (Barbara Thayer-Bacon) teach a course titled, Philosophy of Education, CS 526, that is a nuts-and-bolts, how-to course on theory writing.[1] We learn how to read a theoretical argument, describe it, interpret it, and evaluate it. We practice the steps on how to do this with six essays over the course of the semester. In the end the students have learned how to write what philosophers call an "epistemic commentary" or what conferences will present as "replies" to a conference paper. I am very proud to be able to say that at the University of Tennessee this course counts as a research course that graduate students can take. That was not the case at my previous university. Before I arrived at UT another colleague of mine in philosophy of sport, Bill Morgan, had already made the case that a course he taught for sports studies students on philosophical argumentation should count as a research course. I was able to have my course easily added to the list of possibilities. I also teach a second level theory writing course for doctoral students who want to write a philosophical dissertation. But my focus here will be on the first level course that students from all over our college now take. The last several times I have taught the course, it has been full. The students are spreading the word, "This course counts for the research requirement, and it will help you be a better reader, writer, and thinker." I am so glad the word is out! I want to argue that it will also help the students be better *researchers*, even if they do not write a philosophical argument for a thesis or dissertation.

Arguments

The first thing I have to address in CS 526 is what a philosophical argument is, in contrast to scientific arguments, and other types of arguments such as testimonial arguments. Each time I watch the students struggle with trying to understand what a philosophical argument is, I am reminded how powerfully strong the hegemony is that science holds over what counts as research today. Philosophical arguments sound to students like hearsay, or what some have labeled "b.s." or "crap," just an author's opinion on the topic. If it is not trying to establish a fact and it is not warranted by verifiable, observable data, it must not be research, or at best, it is bad research. I share with my students a true story: a friend of mine was taking a research course somewhere in Ohio toward earning her masters degree, not where I worked. I believe the focus of the course was on quantitative research, but it could have included qualitative research. Either way, it was definitely a scientific research course. My friend's professor used out-of-context pieces of a published essay by me to show his students an example of "bad research." The professor was making the case that my discussion of another philosopher's ideas was an example of an appeal to authority. My friend was shocked, first to discover that she knew the author of the example her professor was using, but also to find that he was using my work as an example of what not to do, when she had taken courses with me and held a different opinion of my work. I asked my friend if her professor had acknowledged to his students that my work was philosophical, not scientific. She said no. And then I explained to her why what he did is not only unfair, in terms of pulling out pieces of an argument rather than looking at the entire argument, but also because it is unfair to judge a philosophical argument based on scientific standards, and vice versa.

Philosophical arguments do not try to accomplish the same goal as scientific arguments, and they are not warranted in the same manner. Scientific arguments try to establish facts. They are warranted by verifiable, observable data. We judge whether or not it is good science by looking at the quality of the data collected and the methods used for collecting the data. Philosophical arguments try to establish norms and standards. They don't try to make the case for what is (that's science); they try to make the case for *what should be ideally*. Philosophical arguments try to make the case for what is the best, the right, the good, the beautiful, the fair and just, the true. These are arguments that are warranted by reasons, using logic to make their case. We judge whether or not it is good philosophy by looking at the soundness of the logic and the fruitfulness of the argument. I have argued elsewhere that philosophers don't just rely on reason, as their essential tool for making an argument, but that they use other tools that are just as important: intuition, emotions, imagination, and their communicating and relating skills (Thayer-Bacon 2000). However, it is still the case that philosophers use all of these tools to help them develop reasons to make the case for what should be ideally. We may use a variety of styles of arguments, where some of us use formal logic to establish our claims, and others use a narrative style of argument, for example, but all of us warrant our arguments with reasons. Reasons are the "data" for a philosophical argument.

When philosophers try to make the case for what should be, what's called a normative argument, we aren't trying to say, "This is what I think should be." That would be an argument based on personal opinion that others may take or leave as valuable or b.s. The response to such an argument is likely, "Well you may believe that, and you're entitled to your opinion, but that's not what I believe, and I don't have to listen to you." Or, "so what?" Instead, philosophers are trying to say, "This is what we all should agree to, not because it is what I think, but because it is right, or good, or just." When philosophers say, "we all should agree to this," they mean "all people throughout time," not just Americans, or people from the 21st century, but all of us, across time and across our various cultures and settings. For example, philosophers have argued that all people should be treated with dignity and respect (Locke) and that women are equal to men and are equally capable of leading a country/state (Plato). If a philosopher is trying to make a normative argument that is universal, it only takes one counterexample to prove them wrong. That is a very tough standard for a philosophical argument to have to hold up to. In science, if the data I collect are verifiable and repeatable, if others can do the same experiment and get the same results, then I can begin to consider that I have managed to establish a fact. The more tests I make that return with the same results, the better. But, I don't have to keep testing my data until the end of time. Philosophical arguments are open to continual reexamination and continual amending and extending, they do not go out of date. This is why people still consider today what Plato and Aristotle argued, and we still find their ideas worthy of reconsideration.

As soon as I attempt to try to define what a philosophical argument is, which by the way is something philosophers do – try to define key concepts and look at basic assumptions embedded within those definitions – I am vulnerable to criticisms by other philosophers. We don't all agree on what philosophy's role is, and the kind of arguments philosophers can make. We don't all agree on what the limits are for philosophical arguments. And, we certainly don't agree on how to go about making a good philosophical argument. Some philosophers argue that the problems of the world have been solved, but our problems today are really due to misunderstandings and miscommunications with each other due to the ambiguity of language. They describe the role of philosophers as one of clarifying our obtuse language and they apply a method for doing this that has been labeled "language analysis." Analytic philosophers use logic to clarify the meaning of terms. Other philosophers, such as pragmatists, argue that philosophers' roles are to be prophets, poets, and soothsayers, helping us solve human problems that exist through a greater understanding of our social context, and helping us imagine new possibilities. Pragmatists seek to heal the dualisms we have created over time. They may use an historical approach, as Dewey did, and compare the development of ideas over time as a way of exposing the splits that have developed, between theory and practice or the mind and the body, for example, to help us heal them. Still others, postmodernists, argue that the role of the philosopher is dangerously similar to legislative and police work, where what are established as the rules and standards for a good philosophical arguments are then used to police people's thoughts and keep out unwanted views, which become labeled as "irrational" or "illogical."

Given all the ways we disagree with each other and the varieties of ways we approach our task, we still agree that philosophers work with ideas and that they seek to establish normative claims. And, we also agree that this is important work that is different from science. Scientists try to establish what is. Philosophers try to get us to think about what would be the ideal way to be. Philosophical arguments are not bound by what is, for example, how much time is available and how much money. Theirs is the world of possibilities, what could be, and they are only limited by their imaginations, emotions, intuitions, and reasoning to help them consider what those possibilities are. Philosophers don't go out and interview people and collect samples of their writings. They don't need to apply for research funding to send out survey mailings or to visit an archival collection at a particular site. Philosophers need time to think about ideas. They gather their own experiences, read what others have argued about those ideas, discuss their thoughts with others who are currently working on similar ideas, and write down their ideas, all as ways to help them clarify their own thinking. What could be more fun?

When I worked at my first university, there were research funds available for faculty to apply for, but I could never figure out how to get those funds. This was because what I did was not recognized as research. My colleagues applied for the funds to help pay for things such as mailings, but I didn't need funds to collect data as scientists do, I needed the research funds to help me travel to conferences where I could discuss my ideas with others and I needed the funds to give me more time to think. I applied for these funds annually to no avail. I even requested meeting with the college committee to try to make the case for what I needed, under the category of research funds. They didn't change their minds. One of my colleagues who served on the research funds committee started teasing me by asking me if I was doing research when he would see me standing at the elevator waiting for it to arrive. I would laugh and say, "You bet. I'm thinking about the ideas I'm working on."

When I went to apply for a sabbatical at this same university, I was advised by my college-level colleagues who had served on the university-wide committee not to write up my sabbatical as a desire to do research, but as a request for faculty development. My colleagues read my proposal and knew that it would not be recognized as research across the campus. This is because what I wanted to do was go to Teachers College at Columbia University and read and discuss my ideas with other philosophers of education located there. For a philosopher, that is what we do as researchers. But for scholars who only define research as quantitative or qualitative collection of data that is observable and verifiable, as science, working with ideas is not recognized as data collection. Because I wanted the sabbatical, I swallowed my pride and asked for a faculty development leave, which I was granted, but once again I was forced to face the hegemony of a scientific definition of research. I wondered, how can I be hired to be a researcher, even tenured and promoted, and not have the work I do be recognized as research? What a strange world we live in! Hegemony is not rational though, as Gramsci realized, it does not make sense.

Reasons

When philosophers try to explain their ideas to others, they use all sorts of examples to help illustrate what they mean. They may turn to nature and compare their ideas to bees (Plato), or to farming (Dewey). They may turn to fictional stories (Plato's "ring story" in the *Republic* 1979) and literature (Nussbaum's use of Greek tragedies and other classic Euro-western literature in her narrative arguments 1992) to help them, or today you might find them turning to film (Blum 2000), rock 'n roll lyrics (Thayer-Bacon 1998), and even television shows such as "The Simpsons" and "South Park" (Hostetler 2005). Philosophers have the freedom to use anything to help explain their ideas, for what matters are the ideas, and the examples are meant to serve as illustration to help explain the ideas. Again, what could be more fun? This is the poetic side of philosophy.

One of the ways to criticize a philosophical argument is to look at the examples used and determine if they work well or not. Do they add clarity (exactness) and help explain the ideas or do they make things more confusing? Do they include more than what the key idea includes (exclusivity) or are they too limiting (extendabilty)? While we evaluate each other's examples in terms of whether or not they work well, we do not try to place limits on what can be used for examples, for what is important to consider are the ideas. For philosophers, our focus is: What is the central claim the scholar is trying to make and has s/he supported that claim with good reasons?

While philosophers may use anything for examples, we are limited only by our experiences and our abilities to use our imagination, intuition, emotions, and reason, still, we do use certain kinds of reasons to structure our arguments. Reasons play different kinds of roles in an argument. *Need reasons* usually come at the beginning of a philosophical argument as their job is to establish that there is a problem in need of solving. Need reasons try to get us to see that there is a need to look at an issue, and think about it. The philosopher's first task is to convince us that we need to think about such-and-such. "Why should I even bother to think about this?" Need reasons answer that question.

Once the philosopher has established a need, her next task is to justify what s/he intends to argue. S/he has to make the case that what s/he will claim is the solution, the answer, the way things should be. The argument is not meant to establish, this is how things are (once again, that's science), the argument is meant to establish, this is how things should be ideally. How things are right now is often described as a way to make the case that there is a problem we need to address. And, how things are can be used to justify how things should be.

For example, suppose I want to look at how we define democracy in the USA as a way of trying to address the educational problem in our schools of exclusion and/or lack of success of children who come from collective, communitarian cultures, such as Native Americans, Mexican Americans, and African Americans. This is my current research project, which I call the C.A.R.E. Project (culturally aware, anti-racist, relationally focused, educational communities) (Thayer-Bacon, 2008, 2013). First I need to establish that there is a problem, and I can do that by giving drop out rates, test scores, number of students attending and graduating from college, for example. Then I need to look at the history of how democracy has been defined, trace its roots as a concept, and look at its underlying assumptions. Then I need to show how this conception of democracy is expressed in our schools. And, I need to examine the three collective cultures I named and determine if they share the same underlying assumptions, or others, and what these are. What I have discovered is that democracy in the USA is based on Locke's (1960/1823) and Rousseau's (1968/1762) concepts of democracy and both of them start with an assumption of individualism. Classical liberal democracy assumes individualism and this assumption is expressed in the USA's public school design. Yet, individualism is logically contrary to collective cultures that start with an assumption of group identity. A student who comes from a collective culture and attends a school based on individualism is put in the position of having to choose between either losing his/her family values in order to be successful in school or giving up on being successful in school in order to maintain her family values. It is an either/or logical problem. I want to argue for a pluralistic, relational democracy that begins with an assumption of transactional relationships, that I influence the group and the group influences me and we both are affected and changed by each other. It is a both/and logical approach to democracy. The reasons I give to justify my claims are what I call *justifying reasons*.

Philosophers don't limit themselves to how things are or have been in their reasoning. They also try to think about what would be the consequences of changing how we describe things, or changing our ways of doing things. They offer us warnings about how things are going to get worse if we don't change and embrace their central claim and follow their recommendations and they offer us predictions of what will be the benefits of embracing their argument and following their advice. These are *consequential reasons*. They are not as strong in supporting the central claims as need reasons and justifying reasons because they are not based on the past or what is, but are based on the future and what could be. The future is a prediction, we don't know for sure if what we predict will come to pass. Our predicted consequences might happen, but then again they might not. There could be unforeseen variables that we can't account for that change what occurs. This is the soothsaying side of philosophy, the prophesizing. Consequential reasons help us anticipate the results of reaching our ideals, and think deeply about whether or not we really want those results. These kinds of reasons serve an important role in helping us determine if this argument is fruitful or not. But there is no way to test them out for certainty, as the future is not here yet.

Evaluation

How do we evaluate philosophical arguments? We said science was warranted by verifiable, observable data and we know that the way to check scientific arguments is to look at the data. This should tip us off that since philosophical arguments are warranted by reasons and logic, the way to evaluate them is by going back and looking at the reasons given, and the way they are put together. Are there any gaps in the reasoning? How is the argument arranged and connected together? If there are problems with the chaining of the ideas, how well they connect together, then there is a syntax problem that will affect the soundness of the logic. *Syntactic evaluation* has to do with judging the form (structure) of the argument.

What about the terms that are used? Are they well defined and is their meaning clear? Do they meet the criteria of exactness, exclusivity, exhaustiveness, external coherence, and extendability? If the terms are used in ways that are problematic this will effect the semantics of the argument, the meaning. Semantic problems lead to an argument that is not logically sound too. Sometimes the problems can be minor and easily fixed. However, sometimes they can be significant and they will affect the validity of the argument. *Semantic evaluation* judges the meaning of the argument.

Philosophical arguments are also judged on pragmatic grounds. *Pragmatic evaluation* judges how well is the central claim supported? How well do the reasons work (operative soundness)? Does the author give enough need reasons and justifying reasons to support the central claim, or could the argument use more? Does the author rely mainly on consequential reasons, which are weaker, or does the author offer enough need and justifying reasons along with consequential reasons? Maybe the author offers only need and justifying reasons, does this limit the range of the argument and its fruitfulness? Not only do we insist that philosophical arguments are logically sound, but we also judge them on their *fruitfulness*, if they are valuable and beneficial or not. A philosopher can offer an argument that is logically sound but has no impact on our lives. Then we will all feel disappointed and wonder, "So what? What this author has to offer does not contribute in any way to improving the human condition." Philosophical arguments are normative arguments that hope to contribute to a better world. They are arguments that hope to establish ideals that can guide us and help us make decisions today to help us reach our aims. They help us understand changes we need to make to reach our goals.

Have I convinced you yet that philosophical arguments are not just b.s. or crap? That they are held to rigorous standards and are not easily defended? Are you beginning to understand that they are important and have something significant to offer to research, even though they are not scientific arguments? I hope so! I hope for even more though, that you may be intrigued and actually want to further explore the possibilities of philosophical research. Come on over and join us on the outskirts of educational research! Whether you do so or not, at least now you know that there are other kinds of arguments besides scientific ones and they have a different role to play in educational research. This does not mean scientific work is not valuable or important as a form of research, but that scientific work is not the only kind of research there is. My argument is that philosophical work is also a form of research that has a valuable and important contribution to make. When I apply for grants, which I do so regularly without much success, my hope is that I can now refer reviewers to this essay to help them avoid imposing scientific criteria on a philosophical argument and instead judge the proposal for research using philosophical criteria. Maybe then, the next time I apply for a sabbatical I can ask for it on research grounds, and say that I want to go talk to some key scholars in New Zealand about New Zealand's concept of bi-cultural democracy and compare it to my idea of relational, pluralistic democracies-always-in-the-making, as well as read what others have to say on the topic, to help me clarify my own thinking, and my request will be granted because my work is valued for its possible significant contribution to educational research.

HISTORICAL RESEARCH

The natural sciences continue to serve as the exemplar of legitimate research. Barbara Thayer-Bacon's experiences powerfully illustrate the difficulties of pursuing research that diverges from the norm of science. As an educational historian, I (Diana Moyer) have faced fewer of these challenges. The scientific model heavily influenced the development of historical research and education historians benefit from the discipline's long alliance with science. Traditionally, grant reviewers and peers in other fields rarely questioned that historical inquiry was a valid form of research. But debates over history as science or art and the proliferation of nonrepresentational historical approaches challenge historical writing as a form of research.

History and philosophy of education employ very different research methods. Despite these differences, both fields fit uneasily within the norms of educational research. The direction of current research policy further marginalizes historical and philosophical inquiry as outside the norms of legitimate inquiry. I anticipate a move toward using narrowly defined norms of scientific research to evaluate historical projects. If that occurs, historians will face very similar barriers to those philosophers have encountered for years.

We hope this combined discussion will explain the methods of our research and add to the visibility of historical and philosophical research within education. We also aim to challenge the scientific hegemony that constricts what counts as legitimate educational research. My discussion addresses procedures that ground historical inquiry, history's contributions to qualitative research, and its divided status as both science and art. Some would argue that questioning the appropriateness of the scientific model undermines history's legitimacy. I see the debates over written history's ability to represent the past as strengthening, rather than diminishing, historical inquiry's value as a form of research.

Perceptions of History

Students enter my graduate History of American Education course with a variety of experiences with studying the past. Some praise high school teachers who dressed in period clothing or used role-play to make history exciting and relevant. Others equate history with memorized dates and names disconnected from social and cultural practices. Some students enroll in the course looking for historical insight into ongoing problems such as racial segregation in schools and the slow pace of educational change.

On the first day of class, I give my student several pages of quotes on the topic of history. Some of the quotations are familiar, others humorous or provocative. Regardless of tone or author, I select quotes that touch on larger questions about the writing and purpose of history. As illustrated below, people have debated the meaning of history for centuries.

"History is written by the victors." Source Unknown

"Those who cannot remember the past are condemned to repeat it." George Santayana

"History is the best medicine for a sick mind, for in history you have a record of the infinite variety of human experience plainly set out for all to see, and in that record you can find for yourself and your country both examples and warnings: fine things to take as models, base things rotten through and through to avoid." Livy

"History is but a pack of tricks we play on the dead." Voltaire

"History, real solemn history, I cannot be interested in .... I read it a little as a duty; but it tells me nothing that does not either vex or weary me. The quarrels of popes and kings, with wars and pestilences in every page; the men all so good for nothing, and hardly any women at all – it is very tiresome." Catherine Morland in *Northanger Abbey* by Jane Austen

"Historical evidence has special functions. It lends weight and depth to evidence which, if culled only from contemporary life, might seem frail. And, by portraying the movements of men over time, it shows the possibility of change." Howard Zinn

I use these contrasting quotes to encourage students to reflect on their own assumptions about the meaning and significance of history. Beginning the course in this way underscores the importance of reading history critically. I want students to learn about the historical development of schooling while also reflecting on the types of questions implied in the quotes above. Should the goal of history be to guide action? Should history be used to address contemporary political concerns? Does history reinforce the views of those in power? All these questions speak to larger issues of historical research.

Researching History

Most people see history as a window to the past. We pick up a history book or turn on educational programming to learn more about the what, where, and why of past events. The finished products of historical research, however, tend to obscure the subjective choices that led to the final conclusions. A well-written history can lull us into thinking that it is the only possible story. The goal of the following discussion is to help nonhistorians understand two aspects of the process of historical research: 1) the sources that serve as evidence and 2) the relationship between what occurred in the past and what historians write about the past.

Historical research can conjure up the figure of a lone scholar poring over faded papers. Given the importance of archival research in historical study, this popular image of the historian is not without merit. The historian's main concern is locating primary sources – texts produced during the time period under study.[2] The number and type of sources can vary depending on the topic, source availability, and consistency with existing research. Sources might be numerical, narrative, graphic, or auditory. Quantitative historians might use labor patterns, census records, or literacy rates. Other common sources include letters, oral histories, speeches, institutional records, diaries, newspapers, and photographs. Given the sheer volume of information, historians rely heavily on the archivists and librarians who preserve and catalogue primary source materials. These are the individuals who organize primary sources into collections housed by libraries, universities, museums, and historical associations.

For example, some of the primary sources I used in researching the 1930s educator and administrator Elsie Ripley Clapp, I obtained easily. My university library owned copies of her book, *Community Schools in Action*, and her articles in the journal *Progressive Education*. Other sources required trips to the repositories where they were housed. I viewed materials such as her unpublished manuscripts, letters she wrote to John Dewey, and her scrapbook of newspaper clippings on site at the Special Collections of Southern Illinois University.

If history were simply the accumulation of facts concerning dates, events, and people of the past, it stands to reason that each new source would bring us closer to the truth. But as with other forms of qualitative research, historical methods include both empirical data and researcher perspective. Despite 19th century historian Leopold von Ranke's urging for a scientific history that simply "showed how it really was," writing about the past always involves interpretation. Historical projects may vary by type (e.g., social, cultural, intellectual, political, military, etc.), theoretical orientation, guiding questions, and goals. Even the seemingly transparent issue of historical "fact" is fraught with difficulty. Evidence may offer conflicting perspectives and sources such as letters and oral histories may be difficult to authenticate.[3]

The subjectivity of historical sources extends beyond individual judgment. Larger social and political norms influence what is documented, what is preserved and the topics deemed worthy of study. Without external verification to adjudicate among multiple perspectives, it may seem that history is an art of persuasion rather than evidence. If historians are not neutral gatherers of fact are they, as quoted above, merely authors of "tricks … on the dead?"

Most historians reject having to choose between fiction and fact in describing historical research. Carr, for example, described historical research as embedded in the time and place of its creation. He wrote:

> The facts of history never come to us 'pure,' since they do not and cannot exist in a pure form: they are always refracted through the mind of the recorder – Study the historian before you begin to study the facts – When you read a work of history, always listen out for the buzzing. If you can detect none, either you are tone deaf or your historian is a dull dog. (1961, pp. 25-26)

Readers used to more transparent forms of qualitative research may quickly despair of tone deafness when encountering history. Compared to many other fields, historians have largely neglected issues of methodological reflexivity (McDonald 1996). Readers accustomed to authors' self-disclosure about their identity, connections with participants, and research mistakes may find it difficult to distinguish the "buzzing" of interpretation that reveals the historian behind the narrative curtain.

The field of historiography, the study of the methods and theory of writing history, is one avenue for learning the characteristics that define different approaches to history.[4] Books that provide an overview of different traditions combined with examples help illustrate the connection between historians' theoretical frameworks and their research assumptions.[5] A quick scan of the historiography literature reveals that the implications of postmodernism for historical practice continue to inspire controversy. A central issue of the debate is whether historical writing corresponds to a real past or is the historian's construction (Iggers 1997).

Joan Scott and Gertrude Himmelfarb, for example, approach history with radically different assumptions about objectivity and the impact of postmodernism on the discipline. Scott sees traditional historical narratives as imposing false coherence on the past to legitimize power differences. For Scott, historians have the dual responsibility of providing knowledge about the past and revealing the processes of historical construction (1988). Historical narratives should acknowledge the role of power, bias, and suppression in their creation (Abelson, Abraham and Murphy 1989).

Gertrude Himmelfarb, in contrast, writes extensively on postmodernism's damage to the historical profession (2004). She also reminds advocates of the "linguistic turn" that historians questioned the fallibility of representing the past long before Foucault and Derrida. Himmelfarb parts paths with Scott most dramatically on the use of race, class, and gender as interpretative frames. For Himmelfarb, these categories politicize history and distort the past with the ideologies of the present.

I think it is important to understanding the points of contention between Scott and Himmelfarb. The danger is that students will see historical scholarship as comprising only two incompatible approaches from which they must choose. There are numerous epistemological and methodological perspectives that inform history. Despite the tendency of books on historiography to divide historical frameworks into rigid categories, approaches often defy easy classification.

My research reflects Scott much more than Himmelfarb. Her emphasis on power in shaping historical knowledge is consistent with my integration of cultural studies and history of education. I see history as vital to understanding issues such as why the vast majority of teachers are white women and how gender influences educational theory and practice. One of the ways I do this is by analyzing the categories and interpretations historians use to make sense of the past. For example, in researching progressive education of the 1930s, I was particularly interested in the role of gender in classifications of educators as "child-centered" or "social reconstructionist" (Moyer 2001). Historians' descriptions (or lack of mention) of the work of Elsie Ripley Clapp highlighted the role of historical writing in reinforcing gender norms.

History and Educational Research

Knowledge of the past contributes to a variety of forms of educational research. Rousmaniere (2004) asks all educational researchers to reflect on how a historical perspective might contribute to their work. Whether one is doing an ethnography of a single school or analyzing national policy, historical context provides insight into institutional cultures and offers a long-term view of school/community relations. Recognizing qualitative researchers' justifiable reluctance to add to their project with a historical "detour," Placier makes a persuasive case for the value of historical context in understanding the present (1998, p. 320). Reviewing several qualitative junior high/middle school studies, she explains the role of historical research in understanding how a school arrived at its present circumstances, the school's link to broader educational trends, and its past experiences with reform.

Researchers today have far more options for incorporating history than in 1998 when Placier published on the value of history. The rapid move to digitizing materials for online access and increasingly sophisticated search engines has greatly expanded the accessibility of primary sources. Nonhistorians in particular have new opportunities for incorporating a range of historical materials into their teaching and research. For example, websites such as the Library of Congress

American Memory collection (http://memory.loc.gov/ammem/index.html) offers over nine millions items documenting American history and culture.

The breadth of online searches can range from a single website or institution to international access. Harvard University's OASIS (Online Archival Search Information System) is a finding aid for the University's nineteen different repositories. ArchivesUSA encompasses over 5,500 repositories and more than 154,000 collections of primary source material across the United States. A search in ArchivesUSA for Elsie Ripley Clapp, for example, shows one collection bearing her name located in the Special Collection of Morris Library at Southern Illinois University at Carbondale. The search result includes a brief description of the collection, the dates that the materials in the collection span, and the size of the collection.

Print and online source directories, like any finding aid, have their limitations. They don't include all collections and one may not be able to find relevant materials depending on the match between the indexing and the search terms. Many databases also restrict access to those affiliated with institutions that have paid the subscription cost. Even more significantly, online directories such as ArchivesUSA continue to follow the norms of print materials and have not kept pace with the move toward digitization. The directories are online and searchable but are defined by traditional archival practices. ArchivesUSA assumes materials are indexed and stored as boxed folders and housed in traditional repositories such as universities, museums, and historical societies.

Digitization and online access of historical sources brings previously unknown opportunities and responsibilities (Giakoumatou 2005). Formerly the province of large manuscript repositories, housing and sharing sources can be done by individuals and small groups via the internet. But accompanying this expanded accessibility are new issues of preservation, authentification, and the limitations of online search technology. Efforts such as the 2002 Workshop on Research Challenges in Digital Archiving and Long-term Preservation, are working for more flexible, reliable digital preservation and less labor-intensive methods of organizing and evaluating digital collections (NSF 2003).

Can History Guide Future Action?

One of the quotes that began this discussion was Santayana's warning about repeating the past mistakes. His cyclical view of history mirrors the pendulum swings of educational reform. Educators stand witness to the numerous fluctuations between traditional versus progressive methods, high standards versus accessibility, and local versus national control. Educational "reform" often seems like recycling rather than innovation. Was Hegel correct that "We learn from history that we never learn anything from history?"

Studies of educational reform offer a more complex picture than repetition of the same approaches and debates. Each time has its own unique circumstances that alter the cycle. The success of educational practices is contextual and responsive to specific circumstances (Kliebard 2002). Contrary to the current emphasis on scientifically tested, generalizable "best practices," the lessons of history are that one cannot transcend the specifics of time and place. The history of education tells us much, though, about the enduring faith in the power of education to change society. Historical perspectives on educational reform teach us that reform movements are much larger than what happens in schools (Cuban 1993). Domestic and international circumstances such as unemployment and trade deficits trigger talk of educational crises regardless of stable test scores and graduation rates. History teaches us that educational change and demands for reform are intertwined with broader economic and social interests.

CONCLUSION

History and philosophy cannot meet the standards of science based models of prediction and control. The push for a narrowly defined research base for educational practice, threatens the future of both philosophy and history of education.[6] The National Research Council publication, *Scientific Research in Education* (2001), categorizes our fields as the "other" that solidifies the dominance of experimental science. Historical, philosophical, and literary studies are mentioned on one page as the "other approaches" that might serve as supplements to scientific research (p. 26). The pairing with literature is significant, for it underscores the dismissal of all three areas as restricted to the realm of values and ideologies. We hope our joint venture challenges such dismissals and the shortsightedness of collapsing the categories of valid educational research.

As can be seen in our above discussions, we do not do the same work, nor do we write in the same manner, and yet we both recognize the value and importance of each other's field of study, and how our work contributes significantly to each other's individual research projects. History helps us understand our current educational research within a larger context, and protects us from repeating ourselves, so that the work we do really is original research. Philosophy helps us analyze the basic categories we use to define our research as ontological categories that are never truly value free. Both fields of study insist that we carefully scrutinize researchers and the work they do, as we are always situated knowers embedded within a larger context. We can never claim to have a God's eye view of Truth, a view from everywhere, as science wants to claim (and traditional philosophy has wanted to claim as well); our views are always limited, from somewhere, thus underscoring the need for multiple perspectives, and for others to be included in the conversation. It is very dangerous indeed, for scientific research to deceive itself into thinking it doesn't need history and philosophy to help it critique itself. Without history and philosophy, scientific research risks arrogance and deception, which will lead not to possible truths and better understanding, but instead to its own demise.

NOTES

[1] I want to give credit to Professor Emeritus George Maccia, one of my major professors in the philosophy of education program at Indiana University, for what I describe as CS 526. George taught me a philosophy of education course on theory writing that has served as my inspiration and model, and I am very much indebted to him for the description of philosophical arguments that follows.

[2] For an introduction to identifying primary sources and finding them online see http://www.lib.washington.edu/subject/History/RUSA/

[3] There are numerous guides on locating and evaluating sources. See, for example, Howell and Prevenier (2001). An example of a guide for students in disciplines other than history is Startt and Sloan (2003).

[4] A useful introduction to historiography that explores the implications of postmodernism is Appleby, Hunt and Jacob (1994).

[5] See Green and Troup (1999) and Tosh (2000).

[6] For a discussion of the political implications of the NRC reports on research see Lather (2003), sponsored by AERA Special Interest Group: Qualitative Research Chicago, April 2003. Paper accessed at www.coe.ohio-state.edu/plather/ and Scientism and Scientificity in the Rage for Accountability: A Feminist Deconstruction. Paper presented at the American Educational Research Association annual convention, April 11-15, 2005, Montreal, Canada.

REFERENCES

Abelson, E., Abraham, D. & Murphy, M. (1989). Interview with Joan Scott. *Radical History Review, 45,* 41-59.

Appleby, J., Hunt, J., & Jacob, M. (1994). *Telling the truth about history.* New York: W. W. Norton & Company.

Becker, C. (1931). Everyman his own historian. *American Historical Review, 37,* 221-236.

Blum, L. (2000). Universal values and particular identities in anti-racist education. In R. Curren (Ed.), *Philosophy of education 1999* (pp. 70-77). Urbana, IL: Philosophy of Education Society.

Carr, E. H. (1961). *What is history?* New York: Vintage Books.

Center for Education. (2001). *Scientific research in education.* Accessed at http://www.nap.edu/books/0309082919/html/R1.html

Donato, R., & Lazerson, M. (2000). New directions in American educational history: Problems and prospects. *Educational Researcher, 29,* 4-15.

Giakoumatou, T. (2005). *When history becomes digitalized.* Elearn ingeropa.info. http://www.elearningeuropa.info/index.php?page=doc&doc_id=6793&doclng=6&menuzone=2. Accessed December 12, 2005.

Gramsci, A. (1971). *Selections from the prison notebooks* (Q. Hoare and G. Nowell Smith, Trans. and Eds.). London: Lawrence & Wishart.

Green, A., & Troup, K. (Eds.). (1999). *The houses of history: A critical reader in twentieth-century history and theory.* New York: New York University Press.

Himmelfarb, G. (2004). *The new history and the old: Critical essays and reappraisals* (Revised ed). Cambridge, MA: Harvard University Press.

Hostetler, K. (August/September, 2005). What is "good" educational research? *Educational Researcher, 34,* 16-21.

Howell, M., & Prevenier, W. (2001). *From reliable sources: An introduction to historical methods.* Ithaca, NY: Cornell University Press.

Iggers, G. (1997). *Historiography in the 20th century: From scientific objectivity to the postmodern challenge.* Hanover, NH: Wesleyen University Press.

Kliebard, H. M. (2002). *Changing course: American curriculum reform in the 20th century*. New York: Teachers College Press.

Lather, P. (2005, April). *Scientism and scientificity in the rage for accountability: A feminist deconstruction*. Paper presented at the American Educational Research Association annual convention, Montreal, Canada.

Lather, P. (2003, April). *This IS your father's paradigm: Government intrusion and the case of qualitative research in education*. Guba Lecture, sponsored by AERA Special Interest Group: Qualitative Research Chicago, IL.

Lerner, G. (1997). *Why history matters*. New York: Oxford University Press.

Locke, J. (1960). *The second treatise on government*. Cambridge: Cambridge University Press. (Original work published 1823).

MacDonald, T.J. (1996). Introduction. In T. J. MacDonald, (Ed.), *The historic turn in the human sciences*. Ann Arbor, MI: University of Michigan Press.

Moyer, D. (2001). *'Sentimentalists and radicals': The role of gender in the construction of progressive education in the 1930s*. Unpublished doctoral dissertation, Ohio State University.

National Science Foundation. (2003). *It's about time: Research challenges in digital archiving and long-term preservation* (Nowell Smith, Trans. and Eds.). London: Lawrence & Wishart.

Nussbaum, M. (1992). *Love's knowledge*. New York: Oxford University Press.

Placier, M. (1998). Uses of history in present-day qualitative studies of schools: The case of the junior high school. *Qualitative Studies in Education, 11*, 303-322.

Plato. (1979). *Republic* (R. Larson, Ed. and Trans.). Arlington Heights, IL: Harlan Davidson.

Rousmaniere, K. (2004). Historical research. In K. deMarrais & S. D. Lapan (Eds.), *Foundations for research: Methods of inquiry in education and the social sciences* (pp. 31-50). Mahwah, NJ: Lawrence Erlbaum Associates.

Rousseau, J. J. (1968). *The social contract* (M. Cranston, Trans.). Harmondsworth: Penguin Books. (Original work published 1762).

Scott, J. (1988). *Gender and the politics of history*. New York: Columbia University Press.

Startt, J. D., & Sloan, W. D. (2003). *Historical methods in mass communication* (Rev. ed.). Northport, AL: Vision Press.

Thayer-Bacon, B. (1998). The power of caring. *Philosophical Studies in Education*, 1-32.

Thayer-Bacon, B. (2000). *Transforming critical thinking: Thinking constructively*. New York: Teachers College Press.

Thayer-Bacon, B. (2008). *Beyond liberal democracy in schools: The power of pluralism*. Foreword by Maxine Greene. New York: Teachers College Press.

Thayer-Bacon, B. (2013). *Democracies always in the making: Historical and current philosophical issues for education*. Lanham, MD: Rowman & Littlefield Publishers, Inc.

Tosh, J. (Ed.). (2000). *Historians on history*. Harlow, England: Longman.

Tyack, D., & Cuban, L. (1995). *Tinkering toward utopia: A century of public school reform*. Cambridge, MA: Harvard University Press.

CHRISTINA SIRY

7. RESEARCHING WITH CHILDREN

Dialogic Approaches to Participatory Research

> "Every child has the right to say what they think in all matters affecting them, and to have their views taken seriously."
>
> (Article 12, UN Convention on the Rights of the Child)

The United Nations Convention on the Rights of the Child came into effect in 1990, and as of the middle of 2014, this human rights treaty has been ratified by most members of the United Nations.[1] As is indicated by the title, this treaty outlines the rights of a child, including the civil, political, economic, social, health, and cultural rights of children. A central point is that the child's view must be considered and taken into account in all matters affecting her.[2] It is the notion of children having both the *right* to say what they think, as well as the *right* to have those views taken seriously that is critical to this chapter. Educational research is a process of knowledge construction, and children have the right to express their perspectives in this process *and* to have these perspectives taken seriously. As such, this chapter is about one approach to constructing knowledge about children's experiences and perspectives – that of researching *with* children, rather than *on* or *about* children.

Research in the social sciences is a dialogic, as well as relational, undertaking (Riecken, Strong-Wilson, Conibear, Michel, and Riecken 2004). In educational settings, the relational aspect of engaging in the research process is a central, ethical, consideration to working with children. This chapter opens with *The Rights of the Child*, and begins with the assumption that research with children ought to be built upon a foundation of children as active participants in constructing knowledge about teaching and learning. My overall aim is to reflect upon the use of participatory research structures with children and to elaborate several possibilities for producing research together with children. Central questions that guide the sections that follow include; whose knowledges and experiences can, and should, be made visible in educational research? How can children's experiences, perspectives, and understandings be central to the production of research? Who participates in and constructs these research processes? What can we (researchers and participants) learn when we engage in participatory research?

WHY RESEARCH *WITH* CHILDREN

Framing Notions of 'Participatory'

Participatory: providing the opportunity for people to be involved in deciding how something is done.[3]

At its essence, participatory practice implies that the participants are involved in the *decision-making* processes of constructing knowledge through research. Approaches that include participants in the process of deciding how research will be carried out have gained acceptance in the field of educational research over the past several decades. The history of research paradigms in education that work towards being participatory can be traced back indirectly to the origins of action research in the 1940s (e.g., Lewin 1946), or more directly to the label of 'participatory' that was applied to research in the 1970s (Hansen, Ramstead, Richer, Smith, and Stratton 2001). One can find the term "participatory" applied to research in a wide variety of ways; participatory action research (PAR, e.g., McIntyre 2008), community-based participatory research (CBPR, e.g., Hacker 2013), and participatory learning and action (PLA, e.g., Chambers 2007), among others. One of the main distinctions that identifies an approach as participatory is where power is located within the research process (Cornwall and Jewkes 1995). Participatory research is extremely fluid and emergent. With this in mind, this chapter is not intended to be a "how-to" chapter in any sense of the word. Nor is it intended to be an exhaustive examination of all of the ways in which to involve children as active participants in the educational research process. Rather, it will present an exploration of arguments for participatory approaches and an elaboration of the different ways in which researchers, including myself, use such approaches in their work with children. Through this exploration I seek to examine ways in which participatory approaches have been used with children in educational research and problematize the notion of 'participatory research' with children. For simplicity's sake, I will refer to research done in classrooms, however, I would like to point out that the approaches explored herein extend to both in- and out-of-school settings, such as informal educational contexts including the home, before- and after-school care, and outdoor and community based experiences.

Situating the Need for Children's Participation in Research

Writing in the field of health research almost 20 years ago, Cornwall and Jewkes explained that while conventional research "tends to generate 'knowledge for understanding,' which may be independent of its use in planning or implementation, most participatory research focuses on 'knowledge for action'" (1995, p. 1667). If this distinction is extended to educational research, there is a relationship that is created between research and pedagogy – one that implies that what is learned from research ought to inform the pedagogical, relational, aspects of working with children. I write this as a researcher working in the field of science education, and in particular, I focus on the teaching and learning of science in elementary and early childhood classrooms. This relationship between research and pedagogy that emerges from creating 'knowledge for action' is one that grounds the work that I do, and is by extension a perspective that grounds the need for engaging in research with participants in educational settings. My work has led me to believe that what researchers learn from research carried out together with the participants can, and should, inform the pedagogy of a given place.

Children are not often asked about their participation in the process of research (Hill 2006), and they typically do not have the possibility to speak for themselves in the research process (Christensen and James 2000). As such, children can be underrepresented, and marginalized, in the decision-making processes that unfold in researching in classrooms. This omission of children's participation in research about their own lives can be considered a consequence of researchers (and society's) belief that children are not able to participate actively in making important decisions that can impact their lives (Langhout and Thomas 2010). "Silence is created when those who are the subjects of research have little or no power in the constructions about them, no access to texts, and no avenues into the corridors of knowledge-production power" (Lincoln 1993, p. 32). Engaging children in the process of research provides for a space in which respectful, relational interactions can emerge, and ideally these will unfold into a cacophony that pushes back on the silences created by marginalization and underrepresentation of participants. As individuals, we engage in experiences leading to different interpretations and we emerge with different perspectives, as we are each situated differently in time and space. Participatory research in schools is one way to shine a light on the differences that we each experience in order to inform the actions that occur in classrooms. By engaging in research with participants, we can be privileged to learn about their specific insights into experiences – and when it is with children, we gain particular perspectives into their unique insights emerging from their positionality as children within society. Such multivocal, polysemic data creation has the potential to lead us to new ways of understanding, and as such, hopefully to new ways of action and potential transformation.

Going from Part to Whole and Back Again

How do we work towards representing, and understanding, people's experiences? Can we even ever truly understand a situation as others experience it? While we can never capture all the complexities of a given moment, we can work towards learning about, and appreciating, the distinctive differences in how we all experience social life. Research that is participatory and collaborative with children can highlight multiple subjectivities. A variety of perspectives can come to light and be used to create meaning out of complexity.

As a cultural studies researcher, I draw on hermeneutic approaches to make sense of social life. Hermeneutics is the art of understanding, as well as the theory of interpreting. There is a distinct difference between describing events that happen through research, and trying to understand them interpretively. This difference is critical to thinking about participatory approaches. As already introduced, participatory is defined as providing the opportunity for people to be involved in deciding how something is done.[2] This decision making process implies a level of situated understanding that is owned by the participants involved. Through hermeneutics we can work towards understanding, and this understanding is primarily the process of coming to an understanding *with others* (Warnke 1987). Hermeneutics requires that understanding be built up from an understanding of the parts that come together to create the whole. This is precisely what can be worked towards in research conducted with children. In such approaches we can work towards understanding what a given experience is, for example, and also try to understand *why* it has occurred. To do this, one must place the events within the differing contexts in order to better understand them. This is quite a complex process, and it necessitates working towards an understanding of the individual experience as well as collective perspectives. Through this process, one can emerge with research that is sensitive to localized contexts and individual experiences, and then engage in hermeneutic interpretation to make sense of it through our own situated perspectives and also through the contextualized presentation of the experience from the participants. But how can we do this in work with children?

CHILDREN'S 'VOICE' IN RESEARCH

Research literature that argues for repositioning children as active participants in educational research typically advocates for seeking children's 'voice' in the research process. "The two beliefs in and about children and young people – their capacity to speak, and their right to do so – come together in the notion of 'voice'" (Thomson 2000, p. 2). However, seeking children's voice in the process of research is not unproblematic. Incorporating voice is much more than gathering children's words. It implies opening up "spaces and minds not only to the sound but also to the presence and power of students" (Cook-Sather 2006, p. 363). Spaces need to be created so that students' perspectives and ideas can be heard, but simply listening to students is not enough to create any 'knowledge for action,' as introduced earlier. Voice needs to be not only elicited, but also heard, and acted upon. What children have to say should matter. Eliciting, hearing and acting upon children's voices ought to done with extreme care, and these efforts need to be positioned as "another step in an ongoing struggle to find meeting places for teachers and students and for researchers and students from which to effect cultural shifts that support a repositioning of students" (Cook-Sather 2006, p. 361).

In this section, I present several of the main ways in which children's voice, perspectives, and understandings have been elicited for teaching and research. The distinction between teaching and research in early childhood context is a blurry one (Clark 2005), as tools developed for teaching can inform research, and vice versa. Mindful of this, I often go between the two in my writing about these processes. In what follows, I focus on three main ways in which others have attempted to create spaces for children's 'voice' in their research; interviews and focus groups; visual representations; and pedagogical documentation. After presenting a brief overview of these predominant ways in which researchers work to include participatory tools into research, I elaborate on the necessity of dialogue, and listening, as I raise questions concerning the centrality of 'voice' and 'rights' of children in educational research.

Eliciting Children's Perspectives in Interviews and Focus Groups

In research with children at the elementary and early childhood levels, one common approach to seek children's perspectives and participation in the research process is through interviews and focus group discussions. Typically groups of children and the researchers meet for discussions structured to elicit children's views, but these conversations can also provide spaces for discussing the research process itself. In particular, group conversations can serve to create forums for children to discuss matters central to the research, including situating children to have input on the agenda of the research (Greig, Taylor, and MacKay 2007). Darbyshire, MacDougall, and Schiller (2005) utilized focus groups with children between the ages of 4-12, with the main purpose of enabling and allowing "the children to discuss and articulate 'in their own words' their perceptions, understandings and experiences" as related to the study's purpose. After a review of the concerns in the literature regarding engaging in focus group discussions with young children, Darbyshire and colleagues organized their approach to support children in engaging in conversation with each other about the focus of the discussion. They found that flexibility on behalf of the moderators of the conversations was critical to the success of the experience, and they created an informal environment for the conversations by using activity areas near the classroom (rather than meeting inside the classroom).

Slightly distinctive from focus groups is the use of interviews with children as a part of the research process. With young children, unstructured, or semi-structured, interviews are most typical, and rather than situate the research process within the more formal interview style, many researchers have chosen to gather data resources by engaging in a "conversation with a purpose" with children (Siraj-Blatchford 2001, p. 225). An open conversation can lead to the direction of wherever both parties in the conversation take it. Conversations are more fluid and have perhaps a more participatory approach than an interview. It has been suggested that research conversations enable the researcher to "hand over" the agenda to the children (Mayall 2008, p. 121), as the children are positioned to have control over the topics and pace of discussions. It has been noted that through more informal exchanges, individually, in pairs, or in a small group, there can be an attempt to partly address issues of power, and also to have trust and rapport built over time (Connolly 2008) as children are positioned to raise concerns, make suggestions, and share ideas.

Seeking Visual Representations of Children's Perspectives

Researchers have also adopted strategies to support participatory involvement by children in the process of data creation by including a variety of visual representations of children's perspectives. Mapping, drawing, and photographing are several of the central ways in which visual representations of children's perspectives can be incorporated in the process of engaging in research. Mapping is used as a technique to elicit children's perceptions of their environment (Morrow 2003). With mapping, children are encouraged to draw a map that that represents a given environment; e.g., an environment they would like to participate in (Darbeyshire, MacDougall, and Schiller 2005), one that they might like to play in (Jansson 2013) or a space that is familiar to them (Einarsdottir 2005). Mapping has been found to enable children to graphically portray spaces in their lives and site themselves within their environment (Darbeyshire, MacDougall, and Schiller 2005). Other forms of drawing can also be included in participatory research processes as a visual representation of children's perspectives and points of view. Drawing can situate children to express their emotions, difficult issues, or complex ideas in ways that might not be preferred in a verbal exchange (Hunleth 2011). In one of the research projects that I have engaged in, children chose to utilize photos of classroom moments as central documentation on sheets of paper. These photos were printed out and then used as a start upon which to illustrate, and later narrate, their understandings and experiences within science investigations (e.g., Siry 2013). From these discussions, teachers and students together constructed a variety of investigations to explore their science questions (e.g., Siry and Max 2013).

Another way for participants to engage in the creation and eventual analysis of data is through photography. Using the camera to create knowledge with children can be done through the use of photovoice. Originally developed within the field of public health and community development (e.g., Wang and Burris 1994), this approach involves participants in the taking of photographs to represent their circumstances, and then narratives are created by the participants from their photographs. At its essence, photovoice is a methodology for action research, as one intention is to involve participants in policy changes or programmatic improvements (Hurworth 2012). In education, photovoice has been used with secondary school students and pre- and in-service teachers in a variety of settings. For example, researchers have found that through photovoice they can initiate dialogue in different community settings (e.g., Sharma 2010), learn about students' content area conceptions (e.g., Harkness and Stallworth 2013) and promote healthy lifestyle choices with adolescents (Brazg, Bekemeier, Spigner, and Huebner 2011). At the elementary school level, photovoice is gaining popularity as a participatory approach to documenting and analyzing experiences and perspectives with children. Photovoice has been used with English Language Learners to document their instructional experiences (e.g., Graziano 2011) and their contexts (Ali-Khan and Siry 2013).

Regardless of whether it is via drawing, mapping or photography, however, important to remember is that the images that are generated by participants need to be handled with care, in that they are created within a context and a relationship (White and Drew 2011). As such, they are merely one representation of reality (Sharma 2010) and the construction of meaning from these data sources is fluid and incomplete. This can certainly be said about any data source, but photos and drawing can be seductive as representations, and researchers must take care to emphasize that there can be multiple, diverse interpretations of the same drawing or photo.

Documenting Understandings Collaboratively

Recent work in the field of early childhood education has examined tools for eliciting students' perspectives and understandings as guides for teaching and assessing. A quite common direction for this is through a variety of approaches for pedagogical documentation. Pedagogical documentation is perhaps most known in early childhood circles from the perspectives of the Reggio Emilia approach from Italy (e.g., Dahlberg 2012), in which teachers "routinely take notes and photographs and make tape recordings of group discussions and children's play" (Gandini 1996, p. 82). These serve as documentation of children's work, and these photographs and transcriptions of children's talk taken by the teachers are combined with products produced by the children. These forms of documentation come together to represent the children's experiences. Another approach to pedagogical documentation that is commonly seen in the literature at the early childhood level is Learning Stories (e.g., Carr and Lee 2012). Learning Stories is a method that has been developed to work towards documenting children's learning through narrative 'stories' that teachers write based on their observations of their students, and it has been used as an approach for assessing children's understandings; for assessment *for* learning (rather than *of* learning). Learning Stories was developed as a pedagogical tool for teachers, yet it is also used in research (e.g., Daniels 2013). These are both examples of tools that can situate teachers and children within the research process as well as within the process of teaching and learning.

These have been used in particular within research studies to examine teachers' perspectives on students' experiences. Typically these forms of documentation are created by teachers, together with children, and they are used for assessment of children's learning, experiences, or understandings. An example of a similar tool, but one that that was developed specifically for researching *with* young children, is the Mosaic Approach. This was developed as part of a study that sought to find a methodology to include young children's perspectives in the evaluation of early childhood services (Clark 2005). As the name implies, it brings together a variety of different pieces to create an image of children's experiences and contexts. There are two stages to the multi-method Mosaic Approach, beginning with the children and the adults gathering the documentation, and in the second stage the information is put together for dialogue and interpretation (Clark and Moss 2001). The term "mosaic" comes from the multiple pieces that come together in this approach to exploring children's perspectives of their child care settings. In fact, several of the tools mentioned above are integrated in this approach, beginning with observation and conferencing with the child and moving onto cameras and mapping.

DIALOGUE AS CENTRAL TO RESEARCHING TOGETHER

The previous section is intended to provide a brief overview of three common approaches to developing participatory research structures with children. These are certainly not the only ways in which children can be central participants in the production of research, as researchers have used a wide variety of other approaches, including drama (e.g., Christensen and James 2000), cartooning (e.g., Cameron and Theron 2013) and many more. Whether it is in group discussions, visual documentation of experiences by children, pedagogical documentation by children and teachers, or other forms of participatory documentation, one critical requirement for all of these approaches is that they are grounded on a foundation of dialogue. Dialogue between children, children and researchers, children and teachers, and teachers and researchers; all of these forms of dialogue (and the listening that is implied by true dialogue) are necessary to create interactions that sustain the process of researching *together*. "Genuine dialogue requires the deliberate creation of opportunity for initiative-sharing and collaboration" (Carr and Lee 2012, p. 5).

Each of the approaches of participatory work with children lead the participants and the researchers to work towards interpretation of experiences. The process of interpretation can be seen as being situated among differing 'horizons.' In this view, a horizon "is a range of vision that includes everything that can be seen from a particular vantage point" (Gadamer 1975/ 2011, p. 301). In other words, horizons are essentially a representation of how far a person can understand, based upon their own situated perspectives. Participatory research has been suggested as best viewed as a 'fusion' of horizons (Hansen, Ramstead, Richer, Smith, and Stratton 2001), in that different perspectives come together in a process to create a representation of an experience. This fusion requires "the creation of narratives in multiple forms ... with multiple voices represented" (Lincoln 1993, p. 31), and it is in providing a variety of dialogic opportunities for participation in the research process that multiple voices can be represented, and acted upon. This seeking of polyvocality, and the polysemicity that it implies, can also bring together the researcher and the participants in a more horizontal relationship, as the people who are the focus of the research are put in a new light. Power relations must be made visible and analysed through reflexive discussions between participants and researchers (Barker and Weller 2003). While the imbalance of power in educational research can perhaps never be completely equalized, dialogue creates a space to unpack some of the issues that arise in the participatory research relationship and reveal a variety of different perspectives, positions, and differing realities. In addition to providing multiple perspectives within research, participatory research approaches can lead to creating research structures collaboratively with children, which can support children in gaining "more control of the resources that affect their lives" (Langhout and Thomas 2010, p. 61).

Storytelling in Dialogue and with Documentation

Educational research is a journey – one that we can engage in through a variety of directions; each of which provides us with different stories to tell, and ways to make sense of what we experience. The relation between the knower and the known can be viewed as a "most problematic one and anything but independent in cultural studies...there is no way of hearing, seeing, or representing the world of others that is absolutely, universally valid or correct" (Van Maanen 1988/2011, p. 35). As an advocate for involving our participants as much as possible, it is the dialogic, relational aspect of engaging in the research process that is most critical to me. In my work with young children, the act of collecting data resources and identifying points for further analysis is often done collaboratively with children. Through dialogue, we identify moments that are interesting for further interpretation. In this way, "the development of dialogic research is educative for those being researched" (Fielding, p. 305). Whether through group discussions, visual documentation, or pedagogical documentation, there are spaces created for active engagement in the process of generating knowledge; ideally, knowledge for action. With young children, the knowledge that emerges often emerges in a narrative, story telling format. "We are a storytelling species. Storytelling is in our blood. We think in story form, speak in story form, and bring meaning to our lives through story "(Atkinson 2007, p. 224). One way that storytelling forms can emerge is in the layering of visual documentation with narrative documentation. Participants become the creators of visual documentation, which can become the central part for dialogic exchanges. The tools that support children's communication symbolically, through photographs or drawings, can serve as a catalyst for dialogue (Clark and Moss 2001). Participatory inquiries extend to curriculum, teaching, and research. Such approaches to research, and teaching, can present a challenge for more normative forms of teaching, as learners may often 'know' in ways that are outside the knowing of the teacher (Lovat 2003). As such, listening within a dialogic encounter is critical. Regarding the use of photos and drawings, there is a potential problem that can emerge without this critical component of dialogue, and that is that "having children take photographs and then having only adults 'interpret' (or possibly misinterpret) them is potentially an adultist approach to research on children" (Darbyshire, MacDougall, and Schiller 2005, p. 429). To try to avoid such situations, it is important to facilitate an approach in which the children can be positioned in a way to explore and elaborate their ideas and experiences through dialogue.

Making Meaning through Dialogic, Participatory Processes

Research is a way of making meaning and of understanding. In the hermeneutic tradition introduced earlier, it is a bridging of parts to wholes. A central part of this process is considering the pluralistic meanings that are given to actions and moments by those who are participating in them. A related consideration is of the diverse, multifaceted meanings that are given to children's productions, whether written, drawn, painted, acted, etc. It is not sufficient to have children 'participate' by creating an array of data resources such as photos, drawings, etc. Rather, the analysis of these texts is one critical aspect for making meaning, and it is in the dialogic process that the diverse meanings embedded in the texts can emerge in a way that is sensitive to context and to the individuals. This became clear to me in a  very straightforward manner, when one of my own children worked for days on creating a surprise gift for me some years ago on Mothers Day. When the day finally arrived, he very proudly handed me a wrapped box, in which was a painting that he had made for me. I opened the gift, and for a moment I was speechless at what my 6 year old had created for me. "*Thank you so much for this beautiful artwork*," I said, "*I will frame it and put it in a special place.*" "*Do you really like it mom?*" He said in a sweet, soft voice, while looking at the painting. This was the first time he had created artwork that combined drawing and painting, and clearly he was very proud of his masterpiece. "*Oh, yes honey. It's the most beautiful cat I have ever seen*" I gushed at him. "*CAT?? It's not a cat mommy. It's a white wolf!*" he explained with a certain degree of indignation. To him it was obvious that it was a wolf. There was no cat. You might look at this painting and also see a cat, or a wolf, or something totally different. The point of this short anecdote is that to me, it was very clearly a cat. However, to him, as the creator of the artwork, it represented a wolf. I have often wondered since that time how many times in my work with children I see cats, when there are wolves that are intended. Writing about drawing as a research method, Mitchell and her colleagues have stressed that "the drawer's context (both present and past) must colour what is drawn, how it is drawn, and what the drawing represents" (2013, p. 25). This historically contextualized emergence of meanings as embedded in, and emergent from, drawings extends to participatory documentation of all types. Some have chosen to use the metaphor of an onion in working towards contextualized research (e.g., Mac Naughton, Rolfe, and Siraj-Blatchford 2010), as there are multiple layered meanings that are to be uncovered in research, and these are positioned by the differing viewpoints and experiences of our participants. These viewpoints, experiences, perspectives, and meanings are central to situate in participatory work, and can also, within a reflexive process, ideally bring participants and researchers to an understanding and an appreciation of differences in perspectives and meanings.

SOME CAUTIONS AND HOPES

The tools we adopt for our research do not automatically create a participatory process (Waller and Bitou 2011). We cannot assume that there is an equal opportunity to participate in the research process simply because research structures have been created to seek participation (Hansen, Ramstead, Richter, Smith, and Stratton 2001). These authors elaborate the "trap" of what they refer to as "pseudo-democracy" – when equality and participation are assumed, rather than reflected upon and questioned (p. 317). Even with studies that might be structured to facilitate significant opportunity to participate in the research process, a variety of constraints can emerge that impact the possibilities for children to be *actually* active participants. If there is such active participation, there still are some "hard questions" that need to be asked (Kincheloe 2009, p. 119), as researchers ought to use caution that the approach does not romanticize and essentialize the perspective of the child participants, and that simple notions of participation not become new, hegemonic, forces that actually serve to exclude the views of the children (Kincheloe 2009).

Ethics of Dialogic, Participatory Research with Children

There are complex ethical issues in working with participatory approaches with children. "Researchers need to provide a complex mix of technical, creative, and critical support to move young people from consumers to producers of media" (Haw 2008, p. 206). Earlier in this chapter I mentioned that a central component of participatory research is in where the power lies to engage in decision making within the research process. Many of the tools I have touched upon in the chapter can certainly be useful for generating data resources, but that does not mean that they reconstruct any power relationships or situate children in a position to engage in a decision-making process. In research with children, this is a very delicate situation, and there are several dilemmas that arise. First is that there is a consideration of the power of the adult / child relationship. "Though power differences are present in all research encounters, these differences can be more pronounced in child–adult research where age differences (in addition to all other social differences) are also present, as well as socially sanctioned adult responsibilities towards children that inevitably shape the encounters" (Spyrou 2011, p. 161). Second is that there is the power of interpretation that needs to be unpacked. If the interpretation of children's perspectives are typically made by the adult, thus these are no longer through the child's point of view (Waller and Bitou 2011).

Engaging in social science research is both a dialogical as well as a relational act, and as such, it necessitates a careful focus on ethics throughout the process (Riecken, Strong-Wilson, Conibear, Michel and Riecken 2004). Further, "caution is needed in assuming that power relations can be changed through the elicitation of student talk" (Arnot and Reay 2007, p. 311). Although we must heed this assumption, it is in working towards respectful relationships that the possibility for true dialogue can emerge, in which the locus of power can shift. Working towards more equitable relationships in research requires redefining the traditional research relationships (Grieshaber 2010), and time and support are required to build relationships (Phillips, Berg, Rodriguez, and Morgan 2010). A research design that supports relationships can help support research in becoming dialogic. Through dialogue there emerges the possibility to develop the research agenda collaboratively with participants and also later to analyze data with participants. Many of the tools mentioned herein are intended to shift the power within the research and teaching relationships. Tools such as photovoice have been shown to change the role of the teacher to being a role of facilitation, which in turn has been discussed as enabling more trust and healthy relationships grounded on a basis of dialogue (Warne, Snyder, and Gillander Gadin 2012).

Hearing Multiple Voices

Writing about visual and arts-based methodologies, Mitchell explains that designs that use the visual "raise many new questions and suggest new blurrings of boundaries" (2012, p. 293). Different individuals may have different expectations of what an outcome of such a process should be based on their situated, historically constituted perspectives. Teachers, parents, researchers, and of course, the children, often have an expectation of what should emerge from 'research,' and so it is important to allow for the construction of a variety of possible outcomes. This needs to be done from the perspective of the participants, and the researchers (and teachers) must allow for the spaces for children to be able to this on their own accord and to their own directions. A central part of participatory approaches to research is that children should be recognized as the experts that they are; as they are experts on their own lives. As Hendrick (2000, p. 55) posits, "Only when the mentality of adultism has been overcome will it be possible to hear a more authentic and, probably, unsettling set of voices." However, it is important to point out that participatory research is built upon a foundation of respect; one that is "respectful of children's views and also of their silences" (Clark and Moss 2001, p. 7). Thus a critical part of participatory research with children is to provide a space for their voices and action, but also to allow space for silences to remain if participants find them fruitful or necessary.

Children are not only entitled to provide their voice in the matters that affect them, but they have the right to have their perspectives heard and acted upon. This requires a new set of relationships in many educational contexts. "Openness, trust, and reciprocity between researcher and researched may involve unlearning and relearning old habits and behaviors and most certainly mandates new relationships between the two" (Lincoln 1993, p. 42). The approaches I have introduced herein call allow for building new relationships and facilitate eliciting, hearing, and acting upon children's perspectives, questions, ideas, and experiences. This is knowledge for action. In the creation of knowledge for action, I am left with a hope. A hope for action and for transformation that can work towards educational contexts that are truly sensitive to the needs, perspectives, and wishes of those that are central to the process of teaching and learning; the children.

NOTES

[1] Three exceptions are Somalia, South Sudan and the United States, although Somalia and South Sudan have recently agreed to ratify the convention. *The Economist* (2013, October 6).
[2] I use the female pronouns when referring to either gender.
[3] http://www.merriam-webster.com/dictionary/participatory

REFERENCES

Ali-Khan, C., & Siry, C. (2014). Sharing seeing: Exploring photo-elicitation with children in two different cultural contexts. *Teaching and Teacher Education, 37*, 194-207.

Arnot, M. & Reay, D. (2007). A sociology of pedagogic voice: Power, inequality and pupil consultation. *Discourse: Studies in the Cultural Politics of Education, (28)*3, 311-325.

Atkinson, (2007). The life story interview as a bridge in narrative inquiry. In D.J. Clandinin (Ed.) *Handbook of narrative inquiry: Mapping a methodology* (pp. 224-245). Thousand Oaks: Sage Publications.

Barker, J. & Weller, S. (2003). "Is it fun?" Developing children centred research methods. *International Journal of Sociology and Social Work, 23*(1/2), 33-58.

Brazg, T., Bekemeier, B., Spigner, C., & Huebner, C. E. (2011). Our community in focus. The use of photovoice for youth-driven substance abuse assessment and health promotion. *Health Promotion Practice, 12*, 502-511.

Cameron, C.A., & Theron, L. (2013). With pictures and words I can show you: Cartoons portray resilient migrant teenagers' journeys. In L. Theron, C. Mitchell, A. Smith, & J. Stuart (Eds.), *Picturing research: Drawing as visual methodology,* (pp. 205-217). Rotterdam: Sense Publishers.

Carr, M., & Lee, W. (2012). *Learning stories: Constructing learner identities in early education.* Sage.

Chambers, R. (2007). *From PRA to PLA and pluralism: Practice and theory.* IDS Working Paper, 286, Institute of Development Studies, Brighton. Accessed on December 21, 2013 from: http://opendocs.ids.ac.uk/opendocs/bitstream/handle/123456789/660/Wp286%20web.pdf?sequence=1

Christensen, P., James, A. (2000). *Research with children.* Falmer Press; London.

Clark, A. (2005). Ways of seeing: using the Mosaic approach to listen to young children's perspectives. In A. Clark, Kjørholt & P. Moss (Eds.), *Beyond listening. Children's perspectives on early childhood services.* (pp. 29-49). Bristol: Policy Press.

Clark, A., & Moss, P. (2001). *Listening to young children: The Mosaic approach.* London: National Children's Bureau for the Joseph Rowntree Foundation.

Connolly, P. (2008). Race, gender, and critical reflexivity in research with young children. In P. Christensen & A. James (Eds.), *Research with children: Perspectives and practices* (pp. 173-188). New York: Routledge.

Cook-Sather, A. (2006). Sound, presence, and power: "Student voice" in educational research and reform. *Curriculum Inquiry, 36*(4), 359-390.

Cornwall, A., & Jewkes, R. (1995). What is participatory research? *Social Science Medicine, (41)*12, 1667-1676.

Dahlberg, G. (2012). Pedagogical documentation: A practice for negotiation and democracy. In C. Edwards, L. Gandini, & G. Forman (Eds.), *The hundred languages of children: The Reggio Emilia experience in transformation* (3rd ed., pp. 225-231). Oxford: Praeger.

Daniels, K. (2013). Supporting the development of positive dispositions and learner identities: An action research study into the impact and potential of developing photographic learning stories in the

Early Years. *Education 3-13: International Journal of Primary, Elementary and Early Years Education, 41*(3), 300-315.

Darbyshire, P., MacDougall, C., & Schiller, W. (2005). Multiple methods in qualitative research with children: More insight or just more? *Qualitative Research, 5*, 417-436.

Einarsdottir, J. (2005). Playschool in pictures: Children's photographs as research method. *Early Child Development and Care, 175*(6). 523-541.

Fielding, M. (2004). Transformative approaches to student voice: Theoretical underpinnings, recalcitrant realities. *British Educational Research Journal, 30*(2), 295-311.

Gadamer, H-G. (1975/2011). *Truth and method.* London: Continuum.

Gandini, L. (1993). Fundamentals of the Reggio Emilia approach to early childhood education. *Young Children, 49*(1), 4-8.

Graziano, K. J. (2011). Working with English language learners: Preservice teachers and photovoice. *International Journal of Multicultural Education, 13*(1), 1-19.

Greig, A., Taylor, J., & MacKay, T. (2007). *Doing research with children* (2nd ed.). London: Sage.

Grieshaber, S. (2010). Equity and research design. In G. MacNaughton, S. A. Rolfe, & I. Siraj-Blatchford (Eds.), *Doing early childhood research: International perspectives on theory and practice* (2nd ed., pp. 177-192). New York: MacGraw Hill.

Hacker, K. (2013). *Community-based participatory research.* Los Angeles: Sage.

Hansen, H., Ramstead, J., Richer, St., Smith, S., & Stratton, M. (2001). Unpacking participatory research in education. *Interchange, (32)*3, 295-322.

Harkness, S. S., & Stallworth, J. (2013). Photovoice: Understanding high school females' conceptions of mathematics and learning mathematics. *Educational Studies in Mathematics, 84*(3), 329-347.

Haw, K. (2008). "Voice" and video: Seen, heard, and listened to? In P. Thomson (Ed.), *Doing visual research with children and young people* (pp. 192-207). UK: Routledge.

Hendrick, H. (2000). The child as social actor in historical sources. Problems of identification and interpretation. In P. Christensen & A. James (Eds.), *Research with children: Perspectives and practices* (pp. 36-61). London: Falmer Press.

Hill, M. (2006). Children's voices on ways of having a voice. *Childhood, 13*(1), 69-89.

Hunleth, J. (2011). Beyond *on* or *with:* Questioning power dynamics and knowledge production in 'child-oriented' research methodology. *Childhood, 18*(1), 81-93.

Hurworth, R. (2012). Techniques to assist with interviewing. In J. Arthur, M. Waring, R. Coe, & L. Hedges (Eds.), *Research methods and methodologies in education* (pp. 177-185). Thousand Oaks: Sage.

Jansson, M. (2013). Children's perspectives on playground use as basis for children's participation in local play space management. *Local Environment: The International Journal of Justice and Sustainability.* Advance online publication: DOI:10.1080/13549839.2013.857646

Kincheloe, J. (2009). Critical complexity and Participatory Action Research. Decolonizing "democratic" knowledge production. In D. Kapoor & S. Jordan (Eds.), *Education, Participatory Action Research, and social change: International perspectives* (pp. 107-121). New York: Palgrave MacMillan.

Langhout, R. D., & Thomas, E. (2010). Imagining Participatory Action Research with children: An introduction. *American Journal of Community Psychology, 46*, 60-66.

Lewin, K. (1946). Action research and minority problems. *Journal of Social Issues, (2)*, 34-46.

Lincoln, Y. (1993). I and thou: method, voice, and roles in research with the Silenced. In D. McLaughlin & W. G. Tierney (Eds.), *Naming silenced lives: Personal narratives and processes of educational change* (pp. 29-47). New York, Routledge.

Lovat, T. (2013). Jurgen Habermas: Education's reluctant hero. In M. Murphy (Ed.), *Social theory and educational research: Understanding Foucault, Habermas, Derrida and Bourdieu* (pp. 69-83). London: Routledge.

MacNaughton, G., Rolfe, S., & Siraj-Blatchford, I. (2010). *Doing early childhood research: International perspectives on theory and practice* (2nd ed.). New York: Open University Press.

Mayall, B. (2008). Conversations with children: Working with generational issues. In P. Christensen & A. James (Eds.). *Research with children: Perspectives and practices.* (p. 109-124). New York: Routledge.

McIntyre, A. (2008). *Participatory action research.* Los Angeles: Sage.

Mitchell, C. (2012). *Visual methodologies and social change.* In J. Arthur, M. Waring, R. Coe & L. Hedges (Eds.) *Research methods and methodologies in education,* (pp. 290-295). Thousand Oaks: Sage.

Mitchell, C., Theron, L., Stuart, J., Smith, A., & Campbell, Z. (2013). Drawings as research method. In L. Theron, C. Mitchell, A. Smith, and J. Stuart (Eds.) (2013). *Picturing research: Drawing as visual methodology,* (p. 19-35). Rotterdam: Sense Publishers.

Morrow, V. (2003). "No Ball Games": Children's views of their urban environments. *Journal of Epidemiology and Community Health, 57*(4), 234.

Phillips, E.N., Berg, M.J., Rodriguez, C., & Morgan, D. (2010). A case study of Participatory Action Research in a public New England middle school: Empowerment, constraints, and challenges. *American Journal of Community Psychology, 46,* 179-194.

Riecken, T., Strong-Wilson, T., Conibear, F., Michel, C. & Riecken, J. (2004). Connecting, Speaking, Listening: Toward an Ethics of Voice with/in Participatory Action Research. [57 paragraphs]. *Forum Qualitative Sozialforschung / Forum: Qualitative Social Research, 6*(1), Art. 26, http://nbn-resolving.de/urn:nbn:de:0114-fqs0501260.

Sharma, M. (2010). Photovoice in alcohol and drug education. *Journal of Alcohol and Drug Education, 54*(1), 3-6.

Siraj-Blatchford, J. (2010). Surveys and questionnaires: An evaluative case study. In G. MacNaughton, S.A. Rolfe, & I. Siraj-Blatchford. *Doing early childhood research: International perspectives on theory and practice, 2nd edition.* (p. 223-238). New York: MacGraw Hill.

Siry, C. (2013). Exploring the complexities of children's inquiries in science: Knowledge production through participatory practices. *Research in Science Education* Advance online publication. DOI: 10.1007/s11165-013-9364-z

Siry, C. and Max. C. (2013). The collective construction of a science unit: Framing curricula as emergent from Kindergarteners' wonderings. *Science Education,* 97 (6), 878-902.

Spyrou, S. (2011). The limits of children's voices: From authenticity to critical, reflexive, representation. *Childhood, 18,* (2), p. 151-165

The Economist (2013, October 6). Retrieved December 20, 2013 from: The Economist explains blog: http://www.economist.com/blogs/economist-explains/2013/10/economist-explains-2

Thomson, P. (2008). Children and young people' voices in visual research. In P. Thomson (Ed.). Doing research with children and young people, (pp. 1-20). UK: Routledge.

United Nations. (1989) *United Nations Convention on the Rights of the Child.* Geneva: United Nations.

Van Maanen, J. (1988 / 2011). *Tales of the field: On writing ethnography,* 2 edition. Chicago: University of Chicago Press.

Waller, T. & Bitou, A. (2011). Research with children: Three challenges for participatory research in early childhood. *European Early Childhood Education Research Journal, 19,*(1), 5-20.

Wang, C., & Burris, M. A. (1994). Empowerment through Photo Novella: Portraits of participation. *Health Education & Behavior, 21*(2), 171-186.

Warne, M., Snyder, K, & Gillander Gadin, K. (2012). Photovoice: An opportunity and challenge for students' genuine participation. *Health Promotion International,*

Warnke, G. (1987). *Gadamer: Hermeneutics, tradition, and reason.* Stanford: Stanford University Press.

White, J., & Drew, S. (2011). Collecting data or creating meaning? Troubling authenticity in ethnographic research. *Qualitative Research Journal, 11*(1), 3-11.

TRICIA M. KRESS

8. "CAN'T YOU JUST KNOW?"

Critical Research as Praxis

THE TROUBLE WITH "EXPERT" KNOWLEDGE

Tricia: I think what you're saying is probably what most people think. You know, that you go to school and eventually you get to the point where you know enough that you can create knowledge, but the way that I see it is that we can create knowledge anyway. All people can create knowledge, we've just been taught not to.

Spock: Like when you write things down. Isn't that, like, I dunno. Like I get what you're saying like it's happening all the time, like just sitting here like thinking […] or like, you recorded it so we created it, but if that [video camera] wasn't there, then when I left, it would just exist for me and you.

Tricia: … but it exists for me and you, and that's exactly it …

(Spock, individual interview)

According to Bauer (1994), people often think that doing research is about seeking out and discovering facts. As we become insiders in the social science world, however, we quickly discover that this is only partly the case, despite the lessons we learn about how to design and conduct sound research in graduate school. As academics, a good part of what we do for a living involves performing the role of "the expert researcher" and building upon a collective base of "expert" knowledge by demonstrating how much we know about the intellectual traditions in which we work and by using information we collect from other people and the world to prove that our interpretations of the inner workings of the social world are true (or close to it) (Kress 2011a). For those of us who work with marginalized communities and who conduct critical research in the name of social justice, this can be a troubling contradiction between what we believe and how we are compelled to act in our professional lives (Kress 2011c). As a critical researcher, I would like to say that I was clever enough to have figured this out on my own. Even better, I could show that I am educated in this school of thought by citing prominent scholars like Bauer (1994), Polayni (1969), McLaren (1988) and Kincheloe (2005) who have written about this phenomenon. But, that's not really how I came to this understanding, at least, not entirely. Instead, sitting in my university office, surrounded by at least 100 books written by other "expert researchers," most of which I had read (the important parts of them, anyway), I learned this lesson by talking with a 17-year-old high school student who assigned herself the pseudonym "Spock" (Kress 2012).

When I began working with the Young Researchers Club (YRC), a group of urban high school students who conducted critical social research in an after school club, at the same time I was struggling to resolve the tension between the two words I had strung together to signify myself – "critical researcher." In my conversations with the YRC, I was repeatedly compelled to see myself and my academic job through their eyes, thereby forcing me to reconsider my livelihood and my role as "expert researcher" (Kress 2011c). Over the course of the semester in which we worked together, Spock especially talked with me at length about her understanding of knowledge, and how some people's knowledge is validated while others' is not. She even pointed out to me, "no offense, but, like, I thought that [producing knowledge] was, like, *your* job" (Spock, individual interview). One afternoon, she reflected on her school experiences and how the structuring of knowledge plays out in day-to-day life in school.

> [I]n our English class, when you're trying to establish that you're an expert you usually quote other people, which, aren't you just establishing that they're experts, and that you just know what they said? […] So is there any other way to establish that you're an expert in something without using other people's work? … Can't you just know? (Spock, individual interview)

At 17, Spock already understood (and questioned) how in U.S. society, and in academic work in particular, all knowledge is not considered equal, and the knowledge of "experts" holds more weight. If you are able to link your knowledge to "expert" knowledge, then your knowledge will also hold more weight. Although Spock did not have the academic vocabulary, literature base, or empirical evidence with which to support her position, notable critical scholars have said what amounts to the same thing. For example, McLaren (1988) explains, "Every form of knowledge can be located within specific power relations; as time passes certain forms of knowledge are transformed by ruling groups as 'regimes of truth'" (pp. xvii-xviii). Spock, an urban teenager in a "failing" high school, and Peter McLaren, a world-renowned scholar of critical pedagogy, see eye-to-eye on this issue, yet McLaren is the expert while Spock is invisible. In this example, we see the interconnectedness of knowledge and power: Given her position as an urban minoritized youth in an underperforming school, Spock's words are less visible and hold less social value than McLaren's because she, and therefore her knowledge, is not linked to a regime of power. McLaren, on the other hand, can say nearly the same thing as Spock, and people will listen and take notice (critical academics will, at least), largely in part because of his long-standing connections to high profile academic institutions and publishing outlets.

In this chapter, by using my experiences with Spock and the Young Researchers as exemplars, my goal is to bring to the surface the ways in which research, in this case about education, is often underpinned by "common sense" features of Western constructions of reality. When left unexamined, these structures of knowledge will necessarily shape how Western researchers see those with whom we work and the ways we endeavor to do research, often to the disadvantage of marginalized groups. As a philosophy of learning, critical pedagogy encourages educators to consider how our work can be conducted in oppressive or liberating ways and to change oppressive circumstances so that education can be humanizing. Notably, it encourages a critical examination of ourselves in relation to our students and a reconceptualization of learning environments to be nonhierarchical, such that learners and teachers inquire about the world together and share in the production of knowledge through critical inquiry about their lived realities (Kress, DeGennaro and Paugh 2013). While critical pedagogy is not typically considered a research methodology, the fit of its application for researchers who strive to be critical in our work with oppressed groups is readily apparent in a number of the fundamental ideas that undergird the philosophy, namely: subjectivity/objectivity, dialogue, praxis and conscientização. By exploring the epistemological, ontological and axiological dimensions of Western research vis-à-vis critical pedagogy, my goal is to initiate a conversation about the possibilities for alternative ways of seeing and doing research if we engage in critical pedagogy as a research praxis.

TOWARD AN EMBODIED KNOWING: RECONNECTING THE KNOWER AND THE KNOWN

Spock's question, "Can't you just know?" continues to haunt me as I write this chapter. In seeking to resolve the tension between critical and research, many of my conversations with Spock were focused on what it means to know and how knowledge is structured in relation to power arrangements in society. But by choosing epistemology as our starting point, I believe I missed the mark as a fledgling critical researcher. The problem is, by looking first at epistemology, I did not fully consider what "just knowing" might actually mean to Spock, a lower-income, young woman of color. At the time when I was working with the Young Researchers, Spock was a high school senior. Ethnically, Spock identifies herself as half Irish and half Dominican, and she speaks fluent Spanish. She assumed a lot of responsibility at home by taking care of her younger sibling and paying the family's utility bills via her afterschool job. In my experience working with Spock, she was an exceptional critical and analytic thinker. She was a key member of the school debate team, and she would often debate with her father and her older brother at home. Other students who participated in debate looked up to her and she would often help them with the researching and writing of their debate speeches. She was very interested in discussing social issues and keenly attuned to conversations about social justice. Yet, in school she sometimes struggled, not because she had difficulty with understanding the content of her coursework, but because she felt so much of her school education was "a joke." When she was in classes that engaged her in learning about real world matters that were relevant in her life, where she felt challenged, and where she respected the teacher and felt respected in turn, she excelled. In other classes where she felt she was treated "like an idiot," she either didn't attend, didn't participate, or became oppositional toward the teacher. Much of Spock's frustration emerged from her first-hand knowledge that she was receiving an inequitable education. Prior to attending Urban High School (where she and I met), she attended Suburban High, which had more course offerings and better facilities and resources. It also had a wealthier and Whiter student body. Spock was painfully aware of the disadvantages that often went along with being a low-income student of color, and she knew that these disadvantages had nothing to do with how knowledgeable she was.

In Paulo Freire's (2007) *Pedagogy of the Oppressed* epistemology is important, but the mind was not his sole preoccupation. In fact, through the lens of critical pedagogy, privileging the student's mind over his or her body is precisely where we get into trouble. Cartesian duality, which I refer to as the mind-body split (Kress 2011a), is fundamental to modern-positivist thinking. By privileging epistemology over ontology, by not fully considering the ontological dimensions of Spock's lived experience in relation to her question, I was unknowingly reproducing this same line of thinking that troubled me. Kincheloe (2010) explains, positivism "is an epistemological position that promotes what it calls objective scientific knowledge produced in rigorous adherence to the scientific method. Positivism identifies knowledge as worthwhile to the degree that it describes objective information that corresponds to or reflects the world" (p. 22). Spawned in the Age of Enlightenment in Europe, positivism is inextricable from the underlying philosophy that frames Western epistemology and Western beliefs about the nature of the world and everyday life (Smith 1999); it privileges objectivity over subjectivity and the (ostensibly) rational disembodied mind over the tacit ways of knowing of the body (Polayni 1969). From the positivist perspective, the lived experience of the body is irrelevant; the body is simply an instrument for collecting data to discover truths about the underlying order of the natural world. Modern-positivist thinking also undergirds contemporary Western science; as Polayni (1969) explains, "for the last three hundred years the progress of science has increasingly controlled the outlook of man on the universe, and has profoundly modified (for better or worse) the accepted meaning of human existence" (p. 64). When mind is divorced from body, knowledge is removed from the person who created it and the socio-cultural-historical context within which the knowledge was developed.

Those of us raised in Western culture often take modern-positivism for granted to the point where this belief system is invisible to us. Axiological questions about power and whose interests are served within this belief system are avoided, while the knowledge generated becomes solidified as inarguable "objective fact." Other forms of knowing (e.g., embodied, intuitive, relational, spiritual) are thus regarded as inferior, if not foolish, thereby ghettoizing entire people's knowledge systems into an epistemological trash heap of "unproven," "mythical," or "archaic" folklore (Kress, Malott and Porfilio 2013). The erasure of the body is critical to the maintenance of the hegemony of Western epistemology because gathering objective, "rational," "evidence-based," scientific knowledge, untainted by the sensations and emotions of the body and one's values and beliefs inculcated through cultural systems, is considered the only reliable way of finding the underlying truth about how the world works. One must remove himself or herself from the world in order to see the world from a distance, as if he or she were examining an organism on a slide under a microscope. Ontologically speaking, this is a very specific way of understanding the nature of being in the world. It is assumed that it is not only possible but also desirable to remove ourselves from the world and the knowledge and value systems that have formed us in order to observe it from afar. Knowledge is not to be trusted if it emerges from one's subjective experience. In this line of thinking, the answer to Spock's question, "can't you just know?" is invariably, "no." Any knowledge she has gained through her experiences in the world is unreliable, unless she can provide scholarly or empirical evidence to demonstrate its trustworthiness.

While critical pedagogy is not concerned with science and research per se, Paulo Freire's writings about pedagogy challenged educational models that emerge from a modern-positivist orientation and reflect the above-described philosophy. This type of education, which he called the "banking" model, serves as a tool for the domination of subordinated groups by disallowing learners from creating and naming their own alternative truths drawn from their lived experiences (Kress 2011a). Freire's description of a radical (i.e., critical) pedagogy differed from banking because he posited that learners should learn to read both *the word and the world*. This necessarily involves the experiences of the body. While Freire acknowledged that there is indeed an objective reality that exists outside human perception (he was not a relativist), he asserted that one cannot come to know reality outside of his or her subjective experience in the world. In the banking model, learners are taught to read the word *without* reading the world; the word is assumed to have a fixed meaning when removed from its context. Under the guise of the neutrality of "fact," learners receive the word as a story of how the world works; the very same power blocs that oppress them bestow this story upon them. Yet, through critical questioning, the objectivity of the word is belied as it is linked to the maintenance of the existing unequal socio-economic order. As Giroux (1988) explains, if learners are to develop the knowledge and skills to transform circumstances of oppression, they

> need to understand how subjectivities are produced and regulated through historically produced social forms and how these forms carry and embody particular interests. At the core of this position is the need to develop modes of inquiry that not only investigate how experience is shaped, lived and endured within particular social forms such as schools, but also how certain apparatuses of power produce forms of knowledge that legitimate a particular kind of truth and way of life. (p. xxxv)

Consider, for example, in the United States the story of meritocracy, which says, "if you work hard, you will succeed; everyone has an equal chance at the American Dream." Through critical questioning, learners from subordinated groups may begin to demystify this story by asking if this holds true in their lives and the lives of people they know; if not, why not? Is it because they or their families do not work hard? Is it because wealthier and more powerful people work harder? If their reality contradicts the story of meritocracy, they may choose to further investigate why this is the case by researching labor, wealth distribution, educational opportunities and the intersections with race, class and gender in the United States.

For Freire, banking education suppresses the subjugated knowledges of the oppressed by preventing them from critically examining their lived realities, including the bodily experiences of economic and social inequality, which reveal the fictitious nature of a dominant ideology that touts equal opportunity. As he explains,

> Any situation in which some individuals prevent others from engaging in the process of inquiry is one of violence. The means used are not important; to alienate human beings from their own decision-making is to change them into objects. (Freire 2007, p. 85)

By denying the individual bodies and experiential knowledge of students in classrooms, students are objectified and manipulated; like filing cabinets, they are treated as receptacles for storing information until they are asked to produce it at the behest of the teacher. Treating people as if they are objects (i.e., receptacles) is, in Freire's terms, an act of "dehumanization." Pedagogy that is used to dehumanize another person is an act of violence and oppression. A student like Spock who refuses to be objectified and manipulated is disadvantaged by and sometimes punished within the banking learning environment (Kress 2012). In contrast, a humanizing pedagogy would engage learners like Spock in their totality, as knowledgeable, contextualized, raced, classed, and gendered bodies and minds, and encourage them to critically inquire about the world so that they can act upon it and change it. If we are to apply this to the act of research, the researcher cannot regard the researched as mere wells of information from which to draw data. Research that simply extracts information from the heads of others, just like education that simply deposits information into the heads of others, is dehumanizing. The people we research with are living, feeling, complex people who should be engaged with as such; this means valuing the knowledge they bring from their lived, bodily, experiences and honoring them as partners in the inquiry process (Kress 2011c).

PROXIMITY, DIALOGUE AND CONSCIENTIZAÇÃO

The more I got to know Spock and the other Young Researchers as individuals, the more I understood that too often, research tends to paint urban youth as caricatures that represent an aggregate group (Kress 2012). Consider, for example, the amount of "achievement gap" literature that presents lower income and minority students as failing and lagging behind their wealthier and Whiter counterparts (Kress 2011b). On the flipside, there is another trend to demonstrate the successes of these groups of students, despite unlikely odds. Kincheloe (1997) asserts that the stories we tell when we share our research are not objective fact for all time. Rather, they are social constructions (which he calls "fiction formulas") that are specific to the particular person who is interpreting the data and the context in which he or she is formulating interpretations. The research stories that are shared by Western researchers may even mimic literary genres that are endemic to Western canonical literature. The aforementioned are examples of how urban youth could be represented as if their lives were literary tragedies or romances (i.e., heroic tales). After telling these same stories for so long, the research literature homogenizes urban youth, and the complexity of individual students' lives are erased. The stories are then crystallized as "common sense," much like the moral of a fable. The simplicity of these stories is seductive, and it is easy for them to color the ways we look at and understand how to work with urban youth (Goldstein 2008). The preconceived notions we hold are informed, in part, by these social myths and will guide our hands in shaping learning environments, designing research projects, and sharing research findings.

I was first made aware of this in a conversation I had one day with Zulu, Spock's debate partner. After a YRC meeting, I gave him a ride to my university where he was enrolled in an undergraduate Calculus class. I mentioned to him that the Dean of my college thought the work the YRC was doing was very sophisticated. Zulu responded to me by saying, "I never thought of it as sophisticated, it's just what we do." This revealed to me that Zulu perceived himself and his peers differently than my Dean and, to a degree, I did. I encountered a similar situation with Kirk, the captain of the YRC, who pointed out that I seemed surprised when he told me that he and Zulu were taking a university Calculus class. While I believed that I held an asset-based view of the youth, they showed me that I still harbored underlying deficit views because I saw their work in the YRC and their university classes as exceptional; whereas, for them, this was typical. This forced me to question where these assumptions came from, and why exceptional was not considered typical for these youth. It is easy to speak about the importance of seeing people as individuals and valuing the assets they bring to the learning environment or the research process, but this requires a change in how we view others in our work. If we allow ourselves to see through others' eyes, we can begin to reveal the underlying values that inform our work, even if we are unaware of them ourselves. To do this, however, we need to shorten the distance between us and our students and research participants. The further we are from each other, the more our students or research participants will appear to be a faceless mass. Greene (1995) describes this as "seeing things big" when we are up close and personal or "seeing things small" from a far away distance. When we see things small, we may be able to see more of the world. As if looking down at a city from an airplane, we can describe sweeping trends, boundaries of territory, and contours of land masses, but we cannot hear the sounds of traffic, nor smell the food sold by street vendors, nor see the lines on people's faces after a hard day of work. When we see things big, we may not be able to see the entire city-scape, but we can see the texture and nuance of people's lives, hear the quickness and volume of their speech patterns, and be exposed to the layers of meaning they make in their lives.

In the modern-positivist paradigm, educators and researchers may conduct their work in the name of equality and justice; however, intrinsic to this way of knowing and being is a valuing of *distance*. This is built into the basic "rules" of Western

Enlightenment thought (Smith 1999), and it emerges in education and research as quality control criteria. For example, in the banking classroom, a student's personal experience with the issue at hand may appear to be relevant to him or her, but in the context of a multiple choice exam, it is unimportant and can get in the way of selecting pre-determined "correct" answers. One only needs to know about the issue in a decontextualized and general way for the purposes of the demonstration of mastery. Therefore, distance is encouraged, and students are *dis*couraged from learning vis-à-vis their personal experiences. Likewise, in positivist research, one cannot be objective if he or she is close to the object under investigation; closeness or intimacy leaves the positivist researcher open to potential biases, again, distance is encouraged. Researchers will use techniques such as inter-rater reliability and "bracketing" of personal experience to protect against researcher bias, in much the same way that a lab technician might use sterilization techniques or surgical gloves to guard against outside contamination. In this school of thought, one's proximity to the object under study translates into where he or she falls within the hierarchical structuring of knowledge (and associated knowers): the closer one is to an issue, the less reliable his or her knowledge. This means that a man or woman who lives through poverty is not considered an expert on poverty until he or she has used another expert's knowledge or tools drawn from the scientific method to create distance between him or her and the issue of poverty. In effect, the researcher of poverty who has not experienced poverty but creates the proper distance and gathers sound data via methodological techniques is deemed more knowledgeable because his or her knowledge is untainted by emotion and preconceived notions garnered through an experienced intimacy (i.e., closeness) with the issue itself.

From a critical pedagogical perspective, this hierarchical arrangement, enforced via proximity, is oppressive because the students and the researched are prevented from naming their worlds through the education or research act. The teacher and researcher are the sole arbiters of what constitutes reality or fact, despite the socially constructed nature of *all* reality and fact, including theirs. In education, if students are not allowed to interpret information in relation to their own experiences, what they learn in school my ring hollow, or like Spock, they may reject the learning environment. Similarly, positivist quality control techniques in the research process cannot prevent the research data from being skewed from the outset. When the researcher's knowledge construction processes are left unexamined he or she will still conceptualize the object of inquiry in relation to his or her interpretations of the world, which are necessarily informed by his or her location in the web of reality. In both cases, the tentative nature of truth is brought to the forefront by understanding inquiry (learning or research) as an interpretive process (Kincheloe 2005) that cannot be corralled by distal quality control methods. When teaching or researching critically, teacher and students or researcher and researched will instead seek closeness in order to engage in a process of dialogue. The knowledge developed in close proximity can be compared with knowledge gained from a distance, and new questions can be raised about the nature of knowledge (whose knowledge? what knowledge? for whom? why?) and truth (whose truth? what truth? for whom? why?), in order to develop new self|other|world awareness (i.e., conscientização).

For Freire (2007) dialogue is not simply talk; in dialoguing with each other, that is, truly hearing each other as equals, we can learn to see ourselves, each other, and the world differently. In effect, we participate in transforming the world as we begin to reconstruct what we perceive and, therefore, how we engage in the world with others (Kress 2011a). Freire (2007) explains dialogue as

> the encounter between men, mediated by the world, in order to name the world …. If it is in speaking their word that people, by naming the world, transform it, dialogue imposes itself as the way by which they achieve significance as human beings. Dialogue is thus an existential necessity. (p. 88)

In a dialogical educational environment, learners are not taught at; teachers and learners develop non-hierarchical relationships where they engage in inquiring about the world together (Kress and Patrissy 2014). This does not mean that the teacher cannot be more knowledgeable about or have more experience with some things than the students, but a critical pedagogical perspective recognizes that students too have knowledge and experiences and everyone in the learning environment can therefore be a co-learner. If we extend this notion of dialogue to the research act, we are compelled to research *with* not *on* our participants because even as we are researching about them, they are also researching about us as all of us engage in researching about the world.

One such means of doing this might be to use a research approach like Youth Participatory Action Research (YPAR); however, dialogical research should not simply be reduced to a particular research genre or technique – it is an orientation to how one approaches his or her work with others. For example, in my auto|ethnographic work with the Young Researchers (Kress 2011b; Kress 2011c; Kress 2012), I began to listen more closely to what Spock and the others were telling me about their relationships with school adults and with me. I allowed their cues to guide me in how to engage with them and where to focus my attention during the data collection and analysis processes. This required a tremendous amount of humility, reflexivity, and flexibility. Zulu and Kirk opened my eyes to how the gazes of adults like me may structure their lived experiences according to who we understand them to be as members of a fictitious group, rather than for who they are and what they bring to the table as individuals. I found I needed to make concessions about the after school learning/research environment and my expectations of what I would be writing about at the end of our time working together. For instance, I had intended on writing about how the YRC students identified as intellectuals in that specific learning environment. However, I shifted my focus when I learned that Spock, Zulu and Kirk identified themselves as intellectuals in nearly all aspects of their lives, but many school adults did not identify them in the same way. This compelled me to follow a path I had not anticipated when I designed the project: I began investigating the meaning behind this contradiction and how it shaped the students' experiences with in-school and after-school learning environments designed by adults, myself included.

EMBRACING THE TENSION: CRITICAL RESEARCH AS PRAXIS

When I began working with the YRC, I entered into their world with lofty goals for us. I wanted the students to conduct critical social research (complete with theoretical frameworks) that emerged from their own interests; I wanted to guide them in presenting their findings to school adults; and I wanted to co-author with at least one of them about our experiences together. Given all that I had read about conducting research with urban youth, I believed these activities could develop into powerful findings to share with academics and school adults. Week-by-week, I met with the YRC to talk about critical social theory and research design. I also met with Spock separately every other week in order to co-author with her. As the weeks passed, I genuinely enjoyed spending time with the YRC, and I was pleased with the research they were conducting. I was especially fond of my conversations with Spock. But I was also anxious because the time went by so quickly, and by the end of the semester, we had only accomplished one of my research goals. Each student had designed and conducted a research project, but only a few had begun analyzing their data, and none of them had completed their findings. Spock and I had a number of fruitful conversations, but we did not actually get to the point where we were able to co-author together. In hindsight, I suppose, I was a bit too ambitious, and the researcher in me felt like a failure because I did not accomplish what I had set out to. And yet, at the same time, I *did* feel good about what we had accomplished together. Even now, I think about the last day we met as a group. It was a sunny and warm spring afternoon, and it just seemed wrong for us to be inside the dreary brick building surrounded by books and blackboards. There was so much work that still needed to be done, but as a group, we decided to go outside instead. We sat on the grass next to the baseball field; we ate tortilla chips, salsa and gummy candies, and washed it down with warm soda; we tossed around a tennis ball; and we talked about life outside of and after high school (most of the students were graduating seniors). After days like those, I wrestled with the inner tension of feeling good about sharing a treasured moment with the students, while not being a "good" researcher. Despite the fact that we were learning really interesting things about ourselves, each other, and the world, I still felt I had compromised my academic goals.

I now recognize this tension as a necessary part of critical research praxis (Kress 2011a); through reflection and action, I was beginning to think about my research and my relationship with the students differently, a process Kincheloe (2005) calls transformation. I see this as the emergence of conscientização through dialogue. Freire (2007) explains, "Through dialogue, the teacher-of-the-students and the students-of-the-teacher cease to exist and a new term emerges: teacher-student with students-teachers" (p. 80). In my work with the YRC, I felt my position as researcher-of-the-researched slipping sideways while the students came to stand beside me as co-inquirers of the world. Once this researcher/researched relationship changed, I was no longer sure who I was as a researcher. I find McLaren's (1988) critique of academic social science appropriate here:

> the social conscience of the scholar too often is supplanted by the will to power, the desire for security within the academy, personal success, and recognition. Scholarly research is thus compromised as it becomes assimilated into the status quo of the discipline, is written more and more for one's peers rather than the general public, and is judged according to the empirical rigor of its arguments and the (misplaced) concept of scientific neutrality. (p. xviii)

As a pre-tenured faculty member, conducting and sharing "sound research" that "makes an impact" on the field is not just an aspiration, it is necessary for survival in the academy. My expectations as a critical researcher were also formed in relation to other critical research I had been exposed to, so I thought I had a sense of what "good" critical research that engages youth looks like. "Good" research is systematic and "clean" and it makes a difference in the lives of youth. Each day my work with the YRC felt less like "research" and more like we were simply spending time together, getting to know each other while we philosophized about the world. It was not terribly systematic or clean, but it did make a difference for them and me.

The notion of praxis is perhaps one of the most vital, yet elusive, concepts in critical pedagogy. For Freire, praxis is not something you know or do; praxis is a way of living in a continual state of "uncompleteness" (Winchell and Kress 2013). It is intimately connected to inquiry about self, other and the world. As Freire (2007) explains, "For apart from inquiry, apart from praxis, individuals cannot be truly human. Knowledge emerges through invention and re-invention, through the restless, impatient, continuing, hopeful inquiry human beings pursue in the world, with the world, and with each other" (p. 72). Praxis has little to do with procedure; instead, it is an inquisitive, humble, and *listening* disposition toward life in which we are always co-inquirers alongside others. Our agendas are no longer ours alone; once we enter into a dialogical relationship with others, we must begin to consider our goals in relation to theirs. And for me, sometimes this meant sitting on the lawn, eating snacks and tossing a tennis ball while enjoying the spring sunshine, "research" be damned: "Embracing this type of praxis means a radical reorientation of who we are as teachers [researchers], a reorientation that is rooted in our becoming as social beings in relationship with others and the world around us" (Winchell and Kress 2013, p. 152). As we change our dispositions, we also change the very purpose of our work; "especially in relation to justice, interconnectedness, and even love" (Kincheloe 2005, p. 94). As I gained a clearer sense of who I was in relation to the Young Researchers, I began to realize "Dispassionate, objective, systematic pursuit of knowledge is profoundly unnatural" (Bauer 1994, p. 147). I needed to be fully alive in my work, even when my academic common sense told me otherwise and the tension of praxis was especially strong. Yet, engaging in this struggle is precisely the point of critical pedagogy. For Freire, the key to any liberatory praxis means embodying a love of life and humanity in our work, which means accepting life's tensions and celebrating our differences. In his words, "If I do not love the world – if I do not love life – if I do not love people – I cannot enter into dialogue" (Freire 2007, p. 90). I would extend this for the critical researcher and say that to love the world, to love life, and to love others is to engage fully in the moment, and taking a cue from Spock, to allow ourselves to "just know."

REFERENCES

Bauer, H. H. (1994). *Scientific literacy and the myth of the scientific method.* Urbana, IL: University of Illinois Press.

Freire, P. (2007). *Pedagogy of the oppressed* (30th anniversary ed.). New York, NY: Continuum.

Giroux, H. (1988). *Teachers as intellectuals: Toward a critical pedagogy of learning.* Westport, CT: Bergin & Garvey.

Giroux, H., & Penna, A. (1988). Social education in the classroom: The dynamics of the hidden curriculum. In H. Giroux (Ed.), *Teachers as intellectuals: Toward a critical pedagogy of learning* (pp. 22-42). Westport, CT: Bergin & Garvey.

Goldstein, R. A. (2007). Who you think I am is not necessarily who I think I am: The multiple positionalities of urban student identities. In J. L. Kincheloe & k. hayes (Eds.), *Teaching city kids: Understanding and appreciating them* (pp. 97-108). New York, NY: Peter Lang.

Greene, M. (1995). *Releasing the imagination: Essays on education, the arts, and social change.* San Francisco, CA: Jossey-Bass.

Kincheloe, J. L. (1997). Fiction formulas: Critical constructivism and the representation of reality. In W. B. Tierney & Y. S. Lincoln (Eds.), *Representation and the text: Reframing the narrative voice* (pp. 57-79). Albany, NY: State University of New York Press.

Kincheloe, J. L. (2005). *Critical constructivism primer.* New York, NY: Peter Lang.

Kincheloe, J. L. (2010). *Knowledge and critical pedagogy: An introduction.* Dordrecht, The Netherlands: Springer.

Kress, T. M. (2011a). *Critical praxis research: Breathing life into research methods for teachers.* Dordrecht, The Netherlands: Springer.

Kress, T. M. (2011b). High achievement in an unaccredited, 'failing' school. *The Journal of the Imagination in Language, Learning and Teaching, 9,* 23-29.

Kress, T. M. (2011c). Stepping out of the academic brew: Using critical research to break down hierarchies of knowledge production. *The International Journal of Qualitative Studies in Education, 24*(3), 267-283.

Kress, T. M. (2012). Beyond caricature: Illustrating the identities of an urban learner. *PowerPlay: A Journal of Educational Justice, 4*(1), 1-28.

Kress, T. M., DeGennaro, D., & Paugh, P. (2013). Critical pedagogy: "Under the radar" and "off the grid." *The International Journal of Critical Pedagogy, 4*(2), 5-13.

Kress, T. M., Malott, C., & Porfilio, B. (2013). Seizing the "moment": Critical researchers challenging status quo retrenchment. In T. M. Kress, C. Malott, & B. Porfilio (Eds.), *Challenging status quo retrenchment: New directions in critical research* (pp. vii-xiii). Charlotte, NC: Information Age.

Kress, T. & Patrissy, P. (2014). Hope–faith–fortitude–> praxis: Retheorizing schooling with Erich Fromm. In S. J. Miri, R. Lake, & T. Kress, (Eds.), *Reclaiming the sane society: Essays on Erich Fromm's thought* (pp. 203-214). Rotterdam, The Netherlands: Sense Publishers.

McLaren, P. (1988). Forward: Critical theory and the meaning of hope. In H. Giroux (Ed.), *Teachers as intellectuals: Toward a critical pedagogy of learning* (pp. ix-xxi). Westport, CT: Bergin & Garvey.

Smith, L. T. (1999). *Decolonizing methodologies: Research and indigenous peoples.* New York, NY: Zed Books.

Winchell, M., & Kress, T. (2013). Living with/in the tensions: Freire's praxis in a high-stakes world. In R. Lake & T. Kress (Eds.), *Paulo Freire's intellectual roots: Toward historicity in praxis* (pp. 145-168). New York, NY: Bloomsbury.

GENE FELLNER

9. A MULTILECTICAL APPROACH TO RESEARCH IN INNER CITY SCHOOLS

BROADENING THE LENSES THROUGH WHICH WE SEE OUR STUDENTS

Justin, seen at left, is thirteen-years old. Even though the photo is distorted and altered to prevent identification, the smile on his face and the folds around his laughing eyes are mostly intact. In this representation of him, though it freezes a dynamic moment and separates it from its context, Justin is present, joyful and clearly interacting with someone. The photograph was taken after Justin finished reading his memoir, and it provides evidence that he can be exuberant, engaged and friendly. As we will see, there are other types of evidence – transcripts of conversations, videos of classroom interactions, writing he has done – that represent him as intelligent, insight-ful, witty, reflective, ambitious and as a respected classroom leader. Yet, the school system represents Justin as a 160 out of a possible 300; a seventh grader who reads at a third grade level; a disciplinary problem who has accumulated latenesses and absences and a number of suspensions. According to school data that so strikingly contradicts the image we have from the photograph, Justin is a loser, a loose cannon, disobedient, and in these and other ways undifferentiated from many of his peers who are more or less in the same statistical boat. If Justin has any intelligence at all you would not know it from the numbers that officially represent him. He is young, Black, male, failing and delinquent, constructs that are often merged together in discourse about education. As represented to the outside world by school transcripts, he is one more example of class and racial failure who will vanish into the statistical heap. The protagonist in Ralph Ellison's classic, *Invisible Man,* declares, "I am invisible, you understand, simply because people refuse to see me" (p. 3). Many of our youth, and disproportionately our inner city youth, go through their elementary and secondary schools largely invisible to those who have the power to assess them. A 13-year old in a school not far from Justin's wrote, "I feel like I live in a fog. The only one who can see me is my dog." The author of those lines depicts her condition in the scribble below.

We need new ways of looking at our students and of assessing them, ways that illuminate their multidimensionality and shine the light on the fullness of their character and abilities in a manner that amplifies their possibilities for academic success. The current lenses and ideological frameworks that guide official representations of students, especially poor youth of color, tend to elevate their weaknesses over their strengths and often ignore their strengths entirely. They reify only a narrow range of abilities and they make inadequate attempts to value the experiences of our students, to see the world through their eyes.

One serious limit of the lenses is their failure to prioritize the emotional components of learning. Thus official pedagogy rarely provides the emotional scaffold that might begin to mitigate the formidable economic obstacles and related conditions that often accompany inner city students to school (though teachers, individually, often attempt to do so). Furthermore, methods of teaching and the methodologies that legitimize them often demean cultural ways of communicating that stray from the accepted norm (Gee 1996); these are often misunderstood as signs of ignorance or disobedience in school settings or are correctly interpreted as acts of rebellion without recognizing the framework which makes rebellion reasonable however self-defeating it may be in the long run. In the process, policy and perception recursively reinforce each other, calcifying categories of failure, bleak visions and dismal trajectories for students who arrive at school with skill sets and values that often do not align with those that are officially sanctioned.

In this chapter, I propose a multilectical approach to educational policy and to teaching and learning that rejects the narrow framework through which students are judged. Though I focus on the inner city students I have worked with, a multilectical approach to education could serve students from all social classes. Multilectics (Fellner 2013) is a methodology that joins the Marxist-Hegelian dialectical process with the concept of multiplicity – multiplicity of perspectives (voices and meanings), of modes (spoken and non-spoken ways of communicating), of mediating conditions and of vantage points of observation all recursively interacting with each other. From a multilectical standpoint, Justin's voice is as important as the voices of those who judge him. From a multilectical frame of reference, what Justin does and what he says is seen as mediated by what others say and do (those in authority, his peers), and his world in school cannot be perceived apart from his cultural background, his economic condition, and the values and historical ties that bind him to family, friends, community and nation. I choose to observe and analyze through a multilectical lens because social life is complex – it is dynamically driven by contradictions and nuance.

Marxist-Hegelian dialectics theorizes that "every historically developed form," because it embraces contradictions, is "in a fluid state" (Marx 1990, p. 103). The dialectic, writes Marx, "in its positive understanding of what exists" includes "a simultaneous recognition of its negation." If what exists embodies its contradiction, it cannot be stable; it is always in a "transient" (p. 103) state. It is a contradiction that so many are poor and unsuccessful in a country with so much wealth and achievement. It is a contradiction that many of those whose histories in the United States predate the arrival of most immigrants remain members of an economic underclass. The stability of the educational status quo is threatened by these contradictions, and challenged by the vision of what education, at its best, could be.

A weakness of the Marxist dialectic lies in its tendency to view contradictions as dualistic rather than as nuanced and multiple. Though traditional Marxist theory is inspiring and optimistic, its teleological certainty makes no allowance for contingency. Furthermore, its general representation of human beings as stereotyped "personifications of economic categories" and of every individual as not "responsible for relations whose creature he remains, socially speaking, however much he may subjectively raise himself above them" (Marx 1990, p. 92) leaves little room for men and women, collectively, to transform the trajectory of their lives.

The fluid dynamic of Marxist-Hegelian dialectics is essential to a multilectic methodology, but its reliance on certainty and stereotype contradicts it. Multilectics rejects the rigidity of categorical constraints and the predetermination of "outcomes." It holds that human beings construct social and economic structures and so they can transform them as well. Multilectics rejects the very idea that any individual can be represented solely by economic characteristics or be unable, a priori, to transcend the categorical limits into which she was born. While multilectics acknowledges the formidable power and endurance of class and racial categories, it sees these macro structures as always mediated by the meso-level beat of daily life and the relationships we form with each other. Simultaneously, macro and meso structures are mediated by what transpires during unconsciously enacted events. These micro level interactions (gesture, eye contact, facial expression, prosody, laughter, silence) saturate everything we do just as powerfully as do the structures that identify us as belonging to a particular class and race. Though we separate for purposes of analysis macro-, meso-, and microlevel activity, they are all so enmeshed in one another that true separation is impossible. Randall Collins (1981) writes, "Micro and macro are relative terms both in time and space, and the distinction itself may be regarded as a pair of continuous variables" (p. 987). Ken Tobin (2006), also writing about the essentially borderless relationship between macro, meso and micro phenomena writes, "what happened within schools and classrooms was saturated by macroscopic forces such as race, social class and state and national level policies" (p. 15). Both micro and macro forces infuse everything we do.

What might multilectics look like when applied to Justin and how might it inform pedagogical theory and practice?

MULTILECTICALLY INTERPRETING CLASSROOM EVENTS

Frames 1-7 = 2.8 seconds   Frame 8 = 1.4 seconds

In the 4.2 second sequence above, a seventh-grade teacher, Mr. C., has just asked students to raise their hands if they are ready to write an argument relating to the Bill of Rights. Justin begins to emerge from his seat (#2, notice the top of his head beginning to appear, barely visible, in the lower right corner) and then approaches the teacher, making bodily contact with him and mimicking his gesture. What is not visible in image 6, because it is a still outtake from a moving picture, is that Justin not only makes physical contact with Mr. C. but actually and deliberately body-bumps him, causing his upper body to sway backwards. The effects of this action can be seen over frames 6 and 7. In frame 6, Mr. C. is leaning toward his left but once he is bumped (frame 7), his body is jolted into a more erect position.

These video outtakes, torn from their social, cultural and historical context and interpreted monosemically, can be used as evidence to substantiate dominant narratives about school dysfunction within our inner city public schools. According to this interpretation, Justin's words and gestures are that of an unruly student. They demonstrate disrespect for and mockery of teachers and physical aggression, both causes for disciplinary measures. They demonstrate a teacher's inability to maintain proper decorum. The narrative, placed solely within the context of statistical evidence that elevate Justin's academic weakness over all other data, intensifies the severity of the deficit lens. Indeed the visual story and the statistical one reaffirm and inspire each other, they comprise the substance of what we mostly hear about public schools in poor Black and Hispanic communities, locating fault in students or teachers but not within the multiple layers of interactions that comprise a multilectical world.

Even the theories of scholars who reject causal narratives might agree that the above outtakes reflect school dysfunction though their analyses are much more nuanced and socioculturally anchored than are the often-prevailing and deficit-infused narratives. Maryann Dickar (2008) building on Mikhail Bakhtin (1984), might interpret Justin's act of mockery as strategic, used by underperforming classroom leaders to shift attention away from their academic weaknesses. By stealing the limelight from the teacher and generating general laughter among his peers, Justin gains recognition and respect (from other students) that otherwise eludes him in school and places the teacher in a seemingly untenable position. If Mr. C. punishes Justin for his physical and verbal interruption, he may be seen as overreacting to what the students view as a basically good-humored attempt at producing levity. If Mr. C. does not discipline Justin, he allows his authority to be diminished and, potentially, cedes control to the students. Bakhtin (1984) writes that the "temporary suspension... of hierarchical rank" (p. 10) is associated with carnivalesque laughter and, quotes the radical 19th century Russian thinker A. I. Herzen, "laughter contains something revolutionary.... Only equals may laugh" (p. 92) and "Fear ... is defeated by laughter" (p. 47). Laughter mitigates the alienation and fear that many low performing students feel in school; this may be especially true for failing students who have street "cred" and need to maintain it.

Through a lens informed by John Ogbu's (1986) theories on caste-like peoples, Justin's confrontation with the teacher seems a maybe stereotypical enactment of "oppositional culture" on the part of a student whose demographic, after generations of being systemically denied success, has imbibed the belief that formal education will not serve him and so seeks ways to subvert academic routine. In Ogbu's interpretation, these beliefs, based on reality, become central to a people's "folk culture" and are thus absorbed routinely and subliminally in daily life. Elijah Anderson's *Code of the Streets* (1999) provides yet another lens through which we might gain some understanding of Justin. Anderson argues that poor Black youth often gain respect on the streets of their communities through loud, boastful, insulting and witty banter; this behavior, while it often protects them within their communities, leads to censure and punishment within schools; Anne Ferguson in her classic *Bad Boys* (2001), also makes this argument.

185

Anderson's and Ferguson's observations serve as evidence to support Pierre Bourdieu's (2003) theory that only the favored classes enter schools with the dispositions needed to succeed academically and that schools are unable to teach these dispositions – ways of speaking and interacting – to students coming from communities that manifest different interactive norms. Because educational institutions demand conformity to those norms but seem unable to teach them, African American students whose communicative patterns are non-normative are doomed to fail.

None of these theories is mutually exclusive, and each provides insight into what is taking place in the above vignette; together they offer ways of perceiving rationality in Justin's behavior rather than pathology or delinquency. They should all be understood as contributions to a multilectical interpretation of the events seen in the outtakes above. They illustrate the dialectical dynamic between macro structures of race and class and meso structures of school, family, and peer groupings in underserved communities.

Dickar, Bahktin, Ogbu and Anderson are all perceptive observers and researchers, and their analyses are richly multilayered, but their tendency is to reify macro structures of race and class and thus these structures appear as deterministic and enduring despite what individuals do in the spaces they produce together. Through their eyes, Justin and his teacher have little agency to transform the circumstances in which they find themselves. As in Marx's analysis in *Capital*, men and women are severely and predictably constrained by their class identity. Macro structures are indeed formidable and enduring, and as William Sewell Jr. (2005) and David Harvey (1996) point out, these structures often appear to control important aspects of what takes place on all other levels of social life. Multilectics, however, insists that what takes place on the meso and micro levels, and how individuals interact (even unconsciously) with each other, also transforms macro structures over time. Sewell's analysis of the French Revolution highlights the importance of contingency and agency, interactive on the meso and micro levels of social life, to topple a monarchy that had endured for centuries. In the United States, the recent revolution in consciousness regarding the rights of women and gays attest to the vulnerability of established systemic structures and the power of relationships forged in opposition to the status quo. These relationships often begin to emerge through unconsciously enacted culture; they are evidence of the fluidity of the transformative process across macro, meso and micro layers. They give us a vision of possibility without negating the power of systemic injustices.

Multilectics proposes that macro economic and social structures (class, race, gender) necessarily mediate what takes place on the meso level of social life within communities, schools, families and friendships. It also insists that what happens on the micro level of social life, on the level at which we unconsciously interact with each other (gesture, gaze, prosody) is part of the constantly evolving dynamic that fluidly merges with the meso and the macro. What individuals do together in-the-moment and reflectively necessarily emanates into other areas of social life beyond the particular contexts of their interaction.

A MULTILECTICAL APPROACH TO RESEARCH

RETURNING TO THE VIGNETTE

During the burst of classroom laughter that follows Justin's interruption, Mr. C., having been bumped, leans back into the Justin (frame 8) and then makes eye-contact with him. It is here that video analysis becomes useful as a tool to observe on micro-meso levels that are generally excluded from classroom analysis. On the video, after Justin makes contact with the teacher, you can see the teacher's body slowly leaning towards Justin and then turning towards him as Justin moves away.

In the 1.1 seconds that follow, the teacher repartees not with anger but with street savvy that generates twice the laughter that followed Justin's initial joke. The teacher's spoken retort is much lower in volume than Justin's initial comment (63dB v. 76dB), indicating his easy and unforced establishment of control. The laughter that embraces his comment comprises 60% of the entire event. Justin grins (not visible in the video), and takes his seat. Continuing the fencing analogy, the teacher was able to parry and riposte to Justin's socially needy interruption without harping on it, thus enhancing his own status in the eyes of Justin and the other students. The entire event lasted under ten seconds after which Justin was back in his seat and the class discussion continued where it had left off.

MULTILECTICS: SURROUNDING THE EVENT WITH MEANING

If we use multimodal and multilevel analysis to examine the vignette and surround it with meaning, we can learn about Justin's capacities and potentials beyond what transcripts, official ideologies, and the theories thus far discussed can tell us.

Though, as already mentioned, we cannot see motion in the above frames, we can tell something about the relationship between Mr. C. and Justin just from the C.'s facial expression and bodily stance. His glance (frames 4-6) is directed at Justin, so we know he sees him approaching. Nevertheless, Mr. C.'s body posture barely changes; he does not appear threatened by Justin or by the 1.4 seconds of classroom laughter that erupts after Justin's loud words and gesture. Mr. C., through the relationship he has built with Justin, has personal data, absorbed through months of interactions with Justin, that allows him to interpret what is taking place through a more multidimensional lens than those examined so far. The teacher has experience with Justin that facilitates seeing him as an individual rather than as a representative of a particular theory or ideological perspective however much Justin's identity is infused with constructs of race and class.

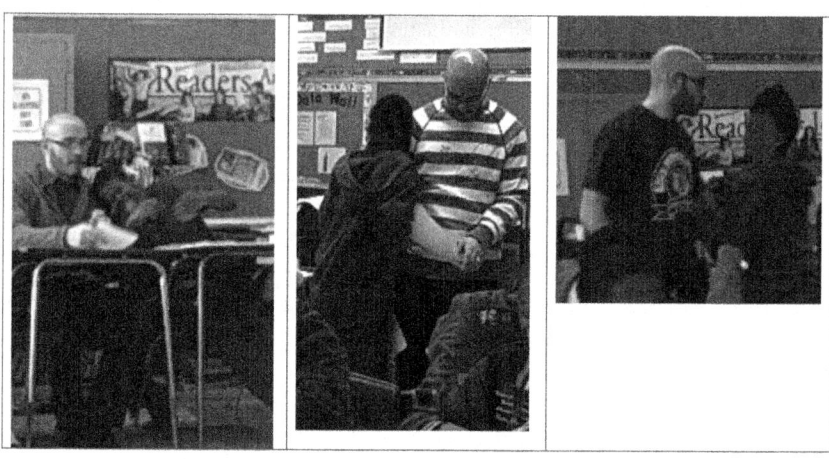

For example, Mr. C. knows that Justin's father was killed in a police chase a year earlier and that there is no strong adult male figure in Justin's life now. Mr. C. told me, "Justin is raising himself. He doesn't take his report card home because no one will read it. There's no one who tells him it's time to go to bed, no one to tell him it's time to take a bath." Knowing this, Mr. C. theorizes that the physical contact central to so many of Justin's disruptions (see below) are not intended to subvert the lesson so much as to affirm Justin's bond with him, to produce family and to make school less foreign. Justin is seeking favorable attention, trying to attain status in school that he cannot attain through grades, and creating an environment that is not defined by his academic deficits. These interruptions were always couched in a wisecrack or joke, additional evidence that could be used to support the theory of Justin's benign motives however they do not exclude Bakhtin's (1984) insight about laughter equalizing the playing field. Though not stated in theoretical terms, Mr. C. clearly recognized the multilectical relationship between macro economic and racial structures (that mediated involvement with the police, family dysfunction and academic weakness) and meso-level social interactions in school. Mr. C., raised in the same neighborhood as Justin, also was attuned to and adept with the type of banter critical to attaining street status. He understood Justin's mode of discourse not as a sign of disrespect or ignorance but as one of Justin using the resources he had at hand to forge relationships. Fred Erickson (1987) writes that "when teachers and students differ in implicit expectations of appropriateness in behavior, they act in ways that each misinterprets. Their expectations are derived from their experience outside school in what sociolinguists have called speech communities." Such misinterpretations can lead to "entrenched attitudes" (p. 4) that can suffuse classroom interactions with hostilities and mistrust. In the vignette of Justin and Mr. C., modes of communication, engaged in unconsciously and intuitively. Mr. C did not stop to think, "what is going on here?" He had internalized a disposition toward Justin that permitted him to meet Justin's interruption not as a breach in decorum but as a contribution to a decorum that bound learning with laughter, jest, and affection. Justin's interruption mediated positive rather than negative energy. Analyzing Justin's behavior only through official lenses of perception would not be able to illuminate the multilayered meanings that surge through the event illustrated above; such a monosemic approach would and does do Justin a great disservice.

From a multilectical standpoint, this event is evidence of the crucial role that micro level activity (the teacher's unthreatened and unthreatening gestures and prosody joined with mutual recognition of solidarity – visible in eye contact and body language) has on the meso level of classroom social life. The intuitive interaction between this teacher and student fostered a classroom environment in which Justin felt less alienated than in other classrooms. It is probable that Justin's interaction also eased the anxieties of many other students in the classroom who were in the same statistical category as Justin and who had also experienced "repeated failure and repeated negative encounters with teachers" (Erickson 1987, p. 348) that in turn fostered mistrust of the entire educational enterprise. The two episodes of laughter within the event represented classroom unity and comfort. A problem that might have been situated within Justin (he could have been identified as *the* problem) was transformed into a multifaceted dynamic that included what the teacher did, what the student did and what the class as a whole did together. The possibility of illuminating these complex dynamics and nuances is why I choose multilectics as my primary methodology to educational research and pedagogy.

That this engagement on the meso level mediated Justin's relationship with school is evidenced by the fact that this was one of the few classes that Justin regularly attended: Justin didn't show up in classes where teachers screamed at him; when he did, he often got suspended. If the event was only one of a series of disruptions that remained isolated within the narrow range of the relationship between teacher and student without any consequences for academic achievement it might be treated as a mere diversion from serious pedagogical theory. I argue, however, that these types of events within this classroom mediated officially unrecognized strides in academic achievement with the potential to disrupt the deterministic and enduring constraints associated with being poor and Black or Hispanic in the United States.

DISRUPTION, EPIPHANY, REFLECTION

Often Justin's interruptions were not attempts at demonstrating a personal bond with his teacher but were directed towards the class in general. What often stood out about these unsolicited performances was their relevance to what we were studying and their clear demonstration of learning even though they were often conveyed through speech that was frequently censured in schools. What was apparent, on a micro level, was the classroom solidarity that surrounded almost every such breach of academic language by Justin. Evidence for this classroom solidarity included the almost universal laughter that Justin's remarks generated followed by an almost immediate return to work. Because of the laughter and the language, the serious and perceptive threads that ran through Justin's remarks were often camouflaged. These pertinent threads often joined the experience of being poor and Black with the transformative powers of education, but the insights that Justin manifested in these situations are not part of the monosemic representation of his abilities as reflected in the official transcripts.

We are discussing the Bill of Rights, which none of the students had heard of before we introduced them. Justin turns toward the center of the class, the amendments held in his right hand as he points to them with his left, and he interrupts the teacher, "I'm gonna start carrying this shit around with me" (see image on left). He adds that the next time a police officer stops him in the street he'll take out the amendments, point them out to the cop and say, "I have amendment rights, bye bitch." His remark, made humorous through the prosody of his voice and his gestural actions, also reflected the realization that knowing his amendment rights was useful to him in his everyday life. A teacher could have diverted the conversation into a criticism of Justin's language, giving him negative feedback for his use of the word, "bitch," rather than positive feedback for the connection he was making. Especially in this community where the word itself was gender neutral that would probably have been a mistake.

A week later, Mr. C. and I met with Justin and showed him the video of him talking about the amendments. We wondered if he would discuss it with us in front of a group of university professors and graduate students. When we broached the subject, Justin's first remark was, "Why do you have to show me cursing?" evidence that Justin was aware of code switching – the appropriateness of language within different contexts, and also that he was concerned with the way in which others perceive him. Again, these are dimensions to Justin that are in no way reflected in the official record that implies a disdain for how authorities view him. We asked Justin why the amendments were so important to him. Justin then related a story of how he was walking through the complex in which he lived when the police came in searching for drug dealers. The police made Justin and many other Black youth lie down on the floor and they put a gun to his head. "I was scared!" Justin told us, "I didn't know about my amendment rights." Justin said that if he had known about his rights, he would have called upon them for protection. Without doubt, the lesson in class had taken root in Justin's consciousness because

he could apply it to the life he knew outside of school. Indeed the teacher and I believed that if the students had learned one thing during the year it was that they had rights enshrined in the Constitution.

The issue of cursing in class and the role of what is often considered vulgar language within a community brings up issues of comfort, alienation, judgment and the development of skills that students will need outside their own communities. Justin frequently curses in class, but this is indicative not of his ignorance but of his sense that he is among friends. Bahktin (1984) in his book about Rabelais writes that the use of vulgar language among intimates indicates comfort and a breaking down of hierarchies; if we interpret Justin from this Bahktinian perspective his offense is not inappropriate language but rather his determination to transform the class into a less alienating place. Justin's implicit critique is that in school he should be permitted to use the language he uses elsewhere. Clearly issues of race and class come to bear on the norms that Justin considers legitimate and those the schools seek to impose. The classroom then becomes a space where these values are contested. Negotiation, rarely embarked upon, is however possible when a polysemic and polyphonic methodology is embraced. Such an approach doesn't privilege the dominant lens that sees "vulgar language" as a manifestation of backwardness. If the gauntlet is thrown down over issues of language, the rigidity of borders between school and community can become unbridgeable, but given that Justin is conscious of the inadequacy of his formal language skills such an outcome need not be inevitable. Justin needs to learn academic speech and write formal academic papers, but when in the midst of classroom discussions applying judgment to the way students talk may be counter productive.

That issues of language and respect are important to Justin and not merely theorized by others as important to him can be surmised from an event in which another student suggested, before the whole class, that Justin try to improve his "diction." When the teacher supported the suggestion, Justin responded angrily, "I speak the way I speak. I ain't going to speak like no nerd. I ain't going to change up my speech for no one." From my vantage point, Justin seemed to be resisting Academic English, seeing its imposition as an act of symbolic violence. Justin, of course, didn't theorize his reaction in this way, but in the video, seeing him slouched and angry, I was certain he felt it viscerally. Mr. C. disagreed. From his standpoint, Justin was angry not at being criticized for the way he spoke but for being criticized publicly, an act of disrespect that he would never tolerate on the street and thus an analysis that resonated with Anderson's (1999). When we asked Justin about it over a year later, he tended to agree with the teacher's interpretation but said he would not respond so negatively to the critique now, maybe a realization of his need to broaden his language skills. What is important is that multiple lenses provide nuance to any interpretation of what is going on that one lens by itself is unable to provide. From the dominant lens perspective alone, Justin's resistance to being corrected might reflect hostility to education and an intransigent personality. From a multilectical perspective, this monosemic interpretation is challenged.

LANGUAGE SEEN MULTILECTICALLY

Justin's spelling and grammar errors and his limited vocabulary can be surmised from his test scores and official transcripts, but what can nowhere be found in these records is Justin's ability, through written language, to transport the reader into his world. Justin thus has abilities that many of the most *correct* writers lack. Because schools tend to reward standards and correctness rather than exploring and fostering talents and skills that manifest themselves in non-conventional ways, Justin's potential to excel as a writer and thinker go unrecorded; the language he speaks is not recognized as a viable foundation for achievement and as a resource that is rich on its own terms despite the limitations it imposes.

The first class assignment was to write about the most important event of the last three years. Clearly, this was the death of Justin's father, but Justin chooses not write about his father directly but about the dirt bike his older brother gave him shortly after his father was killed, a dirt bike similar to the one his father was riding when he was shot. In fact the theme of dirt bikes runs through the two major pieces of writing Justin did in the 7th grade though the second text acknowledges his father's death.

Justin begins his memoir with pure street, "Wow this dirt bike look mad good, who dirt bike is this I asked. It was a black white and red 50cc dirt bike. ... It had a fresh smell like if some one was cooking hot dogs on the grill." Justin's first draft of twenty-three handwritten lines (132 words) contained eighteen mistakes – ten grammatical mistakes according to Standard English and eight misspelled words. By the time Justin finished his third draft, his memoir had become a much more

polished product though it was still filled with errors. At the same time, however, Justin's street voice was vibrant and jubilant, giving the piece an integrity and a presence that mark a good writer. His text was a mixture of street and Standard English. With help, Justin made many of the required spelling and grammatical corrections, though it is important to note that many of his errors reflected the spoken language in his community. So Justin wrote "his self" rather than "himself" and "I was doing it perfect" rather than "I was doing it perfectly." When his uncle tells him, "Will, gest what it's yours" (Guess what, it's yours), Justin's spelling may well be a more accurate reflection of the way his uncle speaks than correct spelling. An essay that would probably have failed by official standards because of its many grammar and spelling errors and its use of street vernacular clearly established voice, setting, and character while simultaneously transmitting, through his writing, the exhilaration of the experience, "I was going so fast I looked like I was lightening striking across the sky. I felt like nothing could stop me."

None of the talent that Justin manifests in his memoir, that tell so much about race, class, and his life, is reflected in the official transcripts. Nor do the transcripts reveal the pleasure and pride that Justin felt after having reading his completed piece (see outtake above). The school transcripts represent a monosemic verdict from above and afar. They ignore the data that is evidence of Justin's pride in an academic product and the progress he has made, evidence that a multilectical methodology makes clear.

Later in the semester, writing an essay about "Ghost of the Lagoon," a story by Armstrong Sperry (2002) about Mako, a boy who overcomes his fears and kills a shark that threatens the community, Justin writes, "I too have had to conquer fears that were in my mind. It all started when my dad was riding his ATV and the cops hopped on him and pushed him and the ATV into a tree. I never got to see my father again. Then two weeks later my brother got an ATV and gave it to me. I was afraid to ride it because of what happened to my father. When he called me downstairs I had butterflies in my stomach and didn't know what to do. When I finally got to the back of my house my hands started shaking and my knees were throbbing." Justin concludes his essay, "This is why Ghost of the Lagoon impacted my life because I can relate to Mako just like when he came over his fear of the shark I came over my fear of that ATV." In this essay, corrected for spelling and grammar, Justin made the connections between literature and his own life that we wish all our students would do, and he used words like "throbbing" and "throttle," advanced vocabulary that Justin found useful for describing the events in his life.

Justin's writing demonstrated his *possibilities* for becoming a lover of literature, an accomplished writer and a more profound thinker.

These possibilities revealed themselves in a context in which he felt that the teacher and his peers were on his side. The classroom environment, mediated by micro- and meso-level interactions, made school a place that could facilitate learning for Justin and threaten the statistics that predict his future.

READING

The macro forces of class and race have much to do with the fact that Justin and most of his peers read below, often well below, grade level. Their dismal reading skills make it difficult for them, almost impossible for some of them, to successfully graduate from secondary school and matriculate into college despite their intelligence and their talents. In the United States, No Child Left Behind and Race to the Top demand that schools alone reverse academic failures that are deeply enmeshed in social, cultural and historical conditions. The idea that schools by themselves are supposed to reverse injustices deeply rooted in society ignores the multilectical understanding that what takes place on the macro level infiltrates every aspect of what takes place within schools. Making schools alone responsible for reversing academic failure is a convenient strategy used to avoid confronting systemic injustices that seep through every social interaction. But both failure and success are mediated not only by class and race but also by relationships that individuals form with one another. Just as macro conditions forcefully color possibilities for teaching and learning, micro and meso conditions can also transform macro forces. Where Marx is skeptical of individual capacities to transcend rigid class boundaries, multilectics envisions those boundaries as being stretched, redrawn, made permeable and even destroyed through the activism of human beings; agency and structure are dialectically interdependent.

That so many poor, middle school students read well below grade level and that most of them will probably never become grade-level readers (Cunha and Heckman 2010) is indicative of the formidable power of macro level forces. There are, additionally, almost certainly developmental obstacles to become a fluent reader as adolescence advances. Powerful emotional obstacles that discourage adolescents who can't read well – feelings of shame, lack of motivation, disinterest, self-doubt – are also part of the picture. It became clear to us that Justin's greatest impediment to achievement in school was not his reading ability per se but his reluctance to acknowledge and improve it. When we wanted to include videos of Justin in a presentation about education, Justin's first statement to us was, "Don't show me reading," though he had no problem with us showing videos of him charging his teacher, interrupting the class with his jokes, or arguing. As we continued to talk with Justin about his reading skills, he went from, "I just don't like reading. If I see a whole book of words, I'm just not going to read it" to "I don't struggle [with reading] like I used to struggle" to "You know I be struggling [with reading]." So through our conversations with Justin, he came to publicly admit, at least to us, that reading was a challenge for him though he would not admit it to even his peers who read at the same level he did.

We suggested to Justin that he work with a reading specialist but he adamantly refused saying it would be embarrassing to have an outsider come to the school and pull him out of class. After many conversations, however, he agreed to meet with me once or twice a week to read in the school library since I was not identified as an outsider and I met individually with many students. We read excerpts from books on dirt bikes, comic books, and short novels. It was often frustrating, but by the end of the year both Justin and I thought we had made progress though not enough progress to significantly improve his reading score on the standardized exams.

THE IMPORTANCE OF THEORY

There are many ways to tell the story of Justin. Maybe the most common story, one that is shaped by the dominant statistical framework, is that he is a student with few abilities and without the disposition to succeed in school. In this analysis, the fault for failure resides in Justin (classical deficit versions) or within his teachers, this latter analysis underlying the design of policies like No Child Left Behind and Race to the top (Ravitch 2012). Because the statistics correlate so strongly with the macro forces of class and race, it is maybe understandable that common discourse so often takes it for granted that being Black and poor automatically means failing in the public school system despite the small but far from negligible examples of success that challenge the deterministic aspects of that narrative.

More complex analyses, drawing on resistance theory, communication styles of various cultural networks, and economic market theories including the role of schools as designed to maintain and reproduce existing economies all offer important insights into educational dysfunction. They highlight the formidable mediating powers of macro forces on the trajectory of our most underserved youth (they of course also mediate the successes of our most privileged communities). Like the wall of statistics that are used to describe Justin, however, these theories tend toward imperviousness, giving little hope that we can pierce and even topple the foundations of inequity.

Multilectics, by embracing the multiple conditions that surround every event, confounds deterministic social theories. Its power rests in its refusal to reify macro forces over all other forces, its insistence that what we do at any level of society mediates all other levels, and its axiological drive to locate power in what we do with each other in the spaces we produce together. Multilectics facilitates seeing beyond the confines of what is prescribed and opens up multiple avenues for exciting change. It does not deny the imposing force of social and economic structures, of ideologies and hegemonic thought, but it gives us access to the possibilities that can emerge when our theories are broader, when they welcome the voices of all participants and are conscious of the contingency that accompanies multiple modes and contexts of engagement. From a multilectical perspective, any structure that is constructed by human beings can be transformed by human beings.

Through theoretical lenses that see poverty, race, linguistic background and immigrant status as deterministic, Justin's trajectory is predictable; the school transcripts confirm the enduring power of these conditions. They are challenged however, by the relationships that Justin, Mr. C. and I established with each other during Justin's 7th grade year. Evidence gathered from meso- and microlevel research depicts a Justin who is far more complex than the statistics would have you believe and far more agentic then most theories would predict. Multilectical data represents a Justin who is thoughtful, funny, insightful, self-aware, a Justin who is searching for way to successfully navigate conflicting worlds and expectations given the tools he has at hand. Justin gave us access to his world because he understood the need to acquire skills that were not native to the life he knows. Success seemed attainable when he embraced and was embraced by a community that pushed him forward without demeaning or judging him, and when theory and practice, dialectically interwoven, embraced his multidimensionality. Possibilities produced and visible on the meso and microlevels of social life comprise the cracks in the macro edifices that today seem so enduring.

REFERENCES

Anderson, E. (1999). *Code of the street.* New York: W. W. Norton & Company.
Bakhtin, M. (1984). *Rabelais and his world.* (H. Iswolsky, Trans.). Bloomington, IN: Indiana University Press.
Bourdieu, P. (2003). Cultural reproduction and social reproduction. In P. Jarvis & C. Griffin (Eds.), *Adult and continuing education* (pp. 173-185). New York: Routledge.
Collins, R. (1981). On the microfoundations of macrosociology. *American Journal of Sociology, 86,* 984-1014. doi:10.1086/227351
Cunha, F., & Heckman, J. J. (2010). *Investing in our young people* (Working Paper No. 16201). Cambridge, MA: National Bureau of Economic Research. Retrieved from http://www.nber.org/papers/w16201
Dickar, M. (2008). *Corridor cultures.* New York: New York University Press.
Erickson, F. (1987). Transformation and school success: The politics and culture of educational achievement. *Anthropology and Education Quarterly, 18,* 335-356.
Fellner, G. (2013). Toward a broader dialectic: Joining Marxism with Mailer to forge a multilectics that advances teaching and learning. *International Journal of Qualitative Studies in Education.* doi:10.1080/09518398.2013.825346
Ferguson, A. A. (2001). *Bad boys, public schools in the making of black masculinity* (1st ed.). Ann Arbor, MI: The University of Michigan press.
Gee, J. P. (1996). *Social linguistics and literacies* (second ed.). New York: RoutledgeFalmer.
Harvey, D. (1996). *Justice, nature & the geography of difference.* Malden, MA: Blackwell Publishing.
Marx, K. (1990). *Capital* (Vols. 1-3, Vol. 1). London: Penguin Classics.
Ogbu, J. U., & Matute-Bianchi, M. E. (1986). Understanding sociocultural factors: Knowledge, identity and school adjustment. In Bilingual Education Office, California State Department of Education (Ed.), *Beyond language: Social and cultural factors in schooling language minority students* (pp. 73-142). Sacramento, CA: California State University.
Sewell Jr., W. H. (2005). *Logics of history.* Chicago: The University of Chicago Press.
Sperry, A. (2002). Ghost of the lagoon. In *The language of literature* (pp. 124-131). Evanston, IL: McDougal Littell Inc.

Tobin, K. (2006). Qualitative research in classrooms: Pushing the boundaries of theory and methodology. In K. Tobin & J. Kincehloe (Eds.), *Doing educational research* (1st ed., pp. 15-57). Rotterdam, The Netherlands: Sense Publishers.

Valle, J. W., & Connor, D. J. (2011). *Rethinking disability: A disability studies approach to inclusive practices*. New York: McGraw-Hill Companies, Inc.

WOLFF-MICHAEL ROTH

10. CONVERSATION ANALYSIS

Deconstructing Societal Relations in the Making

"The university makes us go through all this," the secretary tells me after I complained about the paperwork associated with getting a student to graduate. I respond, "We all are the university, you, I and everybody else. The university only exists in and through our actions. Thus, we can change the university by changing our actions."

This or similar little episodes may be familiar to readers. It exhibits two very different attitudes about social life, social organization, and social relations. On the one hand, there is the belief that organizations and relations exist out there, independent of our actions and interactions. We are but dopes filling the slots provided in the collectivity (group, organization, or society) in and of which we are a part, made to operate by internal (psychological) laws and genes. We simply play the roles that someone else created – institution, teacher, administrator, or student – animated by some internal mechanism. What I told the secretary, on the other hand, is a very different orientation. Social organizations such as the university only exist in and through our actions and, relevant to the present chapter, to our interactions with the surrounding social and material world (Boden 1994). We best think of them as fields that provide resources and constraints to our actions. Without the structures constituted by resources and constraints, it makes little sense to talk about action; but without actions, it does not make sense to talk about structures that are both prerequisite conditions and outcomes of our actions. We continuously produce social life by interacting with others – thereby reproducing and changing it – not only as it pertains to the particular relationship with another person but also as it pertains to society at large. But how do we do this? To provide a gloss of this chapter's topic, we reproduce|change social structure in and through conversation.[1] This chapter is about conversation analysis, an analytic process that can be used to reveal how we continuously reproduce|change society and social relations in and through everyday face-to-face interactions.

A DEMONSTRATION

Event: Reading/Interpreting a Graph

To provide some concrete situation, which we can take as a form of ground against which theoretical and methodological considerations can be checked, let us take a look at the following fragment involving Anne and Dan. Dan has asked Anne to interpret a graph displaying birthrate and death rate of some population (the graph can be found in the offprints in Figure 10.1). As part of the arrangement that has brought them together, she is supposed to tell Dan how birthrates and death rates affect the population. (The transcription conventions are discussed in the text and are also available in Note 2.[2])

Fragment 1
```
01 A:    ((Fig. 10.1a)) SO [(0.43)  ]
02              [((puts paper down))]
03       (0.43) ((hits table hard with hand)) (0.54) HERe (0.21) we have the
04       ((Fig. 10.1b)) (2.11) ((Fig. 10.1c)) dEATh rate ((Fig. 10.1d))
05       increasing (0.68) an the BIRTHrate ((Fig. 10.1e)) increasing
06       ((traces birthrate)) and the birthrate is increasing (0.76) fA:Ster
07       (0.87) than the death rate. (1.80) So they are bOTh increasing but
08       the birthrate envi- increasing faster than the death rate so
09       preSUMmably that means that the population is increasing. ((Fig.
10       10.1f))
11
12
13       (0.93)
14       is that right then?
15       (0.96)
16 D:    u:m::
17       (0.44)
18 A:    [((Fig. 10.1f, circles))]
         [round [this] region?    ]
19 D:           [hhh ]
20       (0.78)
21 D:    um ((Fig. 1g)) YEAh if you take– (0.20) well shall I think I should
22       (stay out?)– if you took
23       [birth minus the death]
24 A:    [((Fig. 1h, circles ))]
25       (0.56)
26 D:    OR the birth plus the death (0.11) rate which is negative, you are
27       gonna get s:omething positive (0.78) u growth rate right?
28
29 A:    yea [I'M] looking at the slopes of the curves=
30 D:        [so ]        =oh, okay.
31
```

In this fragment, we notice how Anne signals in three ways that she is ready to start: first she says louder than normal "SO"; then, she lays the sheet with the graph and instruction flat on the table, which gets her ready to use the hand for pointing (Figures 10.1a–b); after a very brief pause, she hits the desktop with her palm. She then describes the two lines labeled death rate (line 05) and birthrate as "increasing" (line 06), stressing (see underline in transcript) or pronouncing certain syllables much louder than normal (see capital letters with or without underline). She then compares the two increases (line 07–line 08), notes that birthrate is increasing faster than the death rate (line 10), and draws the tentative ("preSUMably") conclusion that the population will increase (line 11–12). There is

200

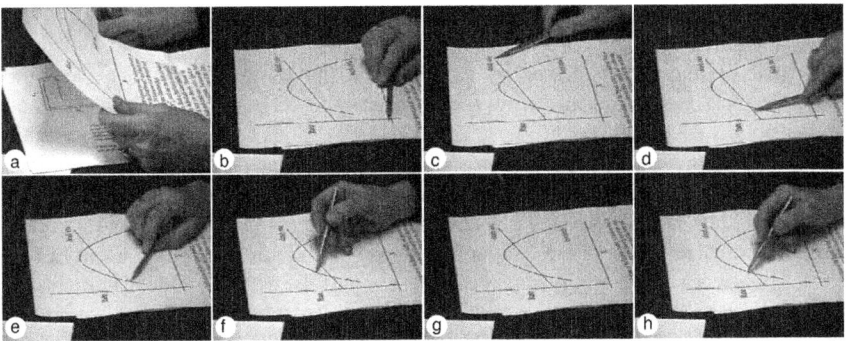

Figure 10.1. The video offprints feature Anne's hand(s) at different instances during a session in which she interprets a graph from biology.

a pause of nearly a second (line 13), after which one can hear Anne asking whether she is right (line 14). There is another pause of nearly one second, after which Dan gives off a drawn out (indicated by colons) ":m::," followed by another pause (lines 15–17). Does Dan not want to answer? Or has he not understood Anne's question? Or, have we been too quick in saying that Anne has in fact asked a question? Anne continues, "Round this region?" with a rising pitch at the end (indicated by question mark), which we tend to hear as a question. There is another pause before Dan begins to speak, hesitatingly at first as indicated by the "um," "YEAh," sudden stops (indicated by n-dash in "if you take–"), and hearable pauses (indicated by "(0.20)").

These emphases and louder than normal utterances give the talk a measured, rhythmic structure, which, as Anne has not and could not have prepared what she said, is an emergent and contingent phenomenon. The circling gesture can be seen as a signal that Anne wants to get into the conversation and say something (line 24); but Dan does not stop talking (line 23). Then, when he does stop, Anne does not begin, which leads to a pause, after which Dan eventually picks up again and continues his explanation (lines 26–28). Because the pause gives both an opportunity to talk, we may actually say more appropriately, "it is pausing" or "*the conversation* is pausing" and thereby mark that both speakers are subjects of the conversation as well as subject to and subjected to the collective phenomenon.

When Dan seemingly finishes his explanation, as indicated by the query "right?" (line 28), Anne weakly acknowledges uttering a "Yeah," which she immediately follows suggesting that she is looking at the slopes. She stresses her own focus ("I'M"), the slopes of the curves, which therefore can be heard as a contrast to something he just has explained. That there is a difference between Anne's looking at slopes and what he has explained can be seen from Dan's acknowledgment of the contrast evoked, "Oh, okay."

A First Analysis

Now that we have moved step by step through the transcript, we can *gloss* the event it represents in the following terms, where the verb "to gloss" is understood as the action of providing a coarse, everyday description of what has happened (Garfinkel and Sacks 1986). In response to Dan's request, Anne provides a tentative inference for a small section of the graph and then asks Dan whether she is correct. Dan initially hedges but eventually accedes, providing at least a partial answer about the relationship between birthrate and death rate. If we are told that one of the two is a university science professor and the other a student in the same department, we tend to bring our background knowledge to the situation to attribute these roles to the individuals. Who is who? Often in social life we use roles to explain what people do and say. In this situation, readers do not have this information beforehand and have to infer structure from the (verbal, gestural) actions. Let us take a look at the situation.

Dan has asked Anne to provide an interpretation of the graph from a second-year university ecology textbook. Anne begins the interpretation, then stops and asks whether she is right. Together, these pieces of information provide indications that Anne is not sure about the graphs; she is not knowledgeable about them. Dan does not want to answer, he hedges, like teachers hedge when students want to know how they are doing before actually completing the task. But Anne insists, both asking and leaving pauses rather than continuing with the task. Eventually, Dan responds. All of this seems to suggest that Dan knows how to read and interpret the graph; Anne, on the other hand, does not know it. Everything we know from the literature on graphing is that graphing is a general, generic skill scientists have. Knowing this leads us to infer that Dan is the professor and Anne the student. But let us look again.

The fact is that Dan is a student – and not even one of the top students – and Anne a professor, both from the same physics department. They know one another. Dan currently completes a co-op internship during which he recruits physics professors for a project concerning experts doing interpretations of graphs from their own and another field. In this situation, using the sociocultural roles two individuals take in society might have led us to an inappropriate prediction about who knows (something about) graphs and graphing and who does not. The psychology and cognitive science literature on science and graphing would have suggested, too, that Anne, qua scientist, should be the expert and Dan, qua student of science, the novice.

However, in this situation, the matter of who knows or is presumed to know is played out in a situated way. Anne displays uncertainty ("presumably," "Is that right?"), whereas Dan displays certainty. After hedging, to which societal actors may attribute after the fact the waiting of the person in the know in the face of a question by a student, he does indeed provide an answer. That is, the societal actors in this situation did not just enter a relation in the way we enter, or figure out, a concrete number in an equation such as $2x + 3 = 5$. Instead, the two together produce the unequal relationship to which they are subject and subject in the course of the unfolding event. Anne displays uncertainty about the graphs; Dan displays certainty. They display these different degrees of certainty to one another, but they also are displayed intelligibly for all those who overhear the situation or who, as we analysts, have the privilege to see the videotape or transcript. Here, they do not draw on their roles as a resource. As it happens, they draw on the particular situation as a resource to construct knowledge inequality in the reverse of what one might have expected on the basis of their social position and science experience. Here, Dan has invited Anne to the think-aloud session; he is the researcher and she is the one from which information is to be elicited. Anne shows that she expects him to know the answer to the question he asked.

This in itself is a reversal of many other interview situations where the interviewer does not know the answer – interviews journalists conduct with scientists, for example. Anne knows that the present situation is part of a scientific study, which involves tasks that cognitive scientists pose but to which they already have some standardized answer. Her query as to the correctness of her first inference makes sense against the background of the interview situation. But this alone would not *explain* the situation either. Dan is still the undergraduate, and the scientist has been invited qua expert, and as such, may know more about the topic than even the best cognitive scientist. One way out of the quagmire of wrong causal predictions is based on societal position, expertise, and so on is to assume the actors being involved in making assessments in the course of making a situation.

In this short fragment we also see that the content of interview responses cannot be taken as if it represented knowledge as such; rather, what is said during an interview (think-aloud protocol) is the outcome of an activity, the nature of which constitutes the background of which the societal actors are aware.[3] What they say is said given their awareness of the situation and cannot be separated (abstracted) from it. This constructive nature of talk characterizes all interview situations, even if they are conducted under the most strictly controlled conditions and protocols (Maynard and Schaeffer 2000; Suchman and Jordan 1990) and school examinations (Maynard and Marlaire 1992).

We see that in this situation Anne displays uncertainty with respect to knowledge and Dan displays certainty. This, however, is not always the case in the interaction over and about this particular graph. There are moments when both emerge as knowing something – including the moment when Anne responds positively after Dan has sought confirmation that she understands his elaboration (line 29). It is worthwhile here to take a closer look. Dan actually makes some contradictory statements. First he suggests that death rate should be subtracted from birthrate (line 23) and then he suggests they had to be added (line 26), but that death rate was to be taken as negative (lines 26–28). This may at first be quite confusing. However, to hear the two in the way they hear each other, we need to remember that both are members of a physics department; the meeting takes place in the locales of the department. In physics, quantities such as rates or forces are signed, that is, they are considered not only in their values (like 2 deaths/month) but also together with their direction. Here, death rate is a rate that decreases the population. Thus, a physicist would write death rate = –2 individuals/month. This is just what Dan says, and which Anne acknowledges. This example also shows us that we cannot get everything about the societal relation between the two from the transcript or videotape. We also need to do the ethnographic work that provides us with the understanding of *this* situation as well as what the interaction participants assume about the levels of intersubjectivity they bring, the sense that is common to them, what is truly their common sense. To research situations and to conduct reasonable analyses, we need to be competent societal actors so that we can hear the participants in a situation of interest – here physicists – in the manner that they hear each other.

We can see therefore that actors do bring background information and sensitivity to context to the societal situation. But this background information cannot be used to construct causal explanations about how events will unfold. Rather, both the professor-student and interviewer-interviewee relations are *resources* for the two participants in constructing their interaction. Whether and how this background knowledge is brought to bear on and therefore structures the unfolding event is a matter of contingency, depending on the situation itself, which, because of the contingent nature, neither the participants nor the analyst/theoretician can predict. In the approach described here, the participants themselves produce relevant resources to assist each other and themselves in producing the situation as an orderly and ordered event, recognizable as such to any one else from a similar cultural background. If the outcomes of interactions were known beforehand, there would not be any need to interact; there would be no need to conduct think-aloud protocols or interviews. There would be no need to have committee meetings to make decisions about tenure and promotion; there would be no need to have national parliaments or congresses. All we would have to do is construct an algorithm that takes individual knowledge, interests, or opinions and calculates some result. The fact that we do not do this hints at the fact that social relations are more than the sum total of the individual members. There is something new springing forth, both in terms of process and the products. Society is not just reproduced but continuously changed in and through societal relations. This is why dominant school activities may become the minor activities and marginal activities may become the dominant ones (Goulart and Roth 2006).

This then is a very productive way of approaching interactions that also allows us to understand other situations. For example, educators have long been familiar with the phenomenon of a gap between the lessons a teacher plans and the way a lesson actually unfolds – this gap is captured in the distinction between planned and enacted curriculum (Roth 2013c; Tobin and McRobbie 1996). Although a teacher might know her students, she can never foresee exactly how the curriculum will actually unfold. The enacted curriculum is always a *collective* achievement of teacher *and* students, emerging from their transactions in praxis, whereas the plans only involve the teacher, her understandings (students, subject matter) and expectations. This is why lessons, even when teachers have prepared these very well, still can turn out to be unsuccessful: even the best plans cannot (completely) control the events that they project. Conversation analysis constitutes an important tool (method) that allows us to analyze and understand how such events as the enacted curriculum emerges as the result of situated actions, themselves contingently drawing on the social and material resources available in the setting. Rather than being dopes, teachers, students, and all other societal actors who participate in our research are understood to be highly competent social actors who coparticipate in making societal structure emerge in and through their situated activity. Because participants act, societal structure is always in the making and, therefore, subject to change. But participants always draw on existing resources; therefore what emerges from their actions already exists as possibility in the situation. It is not completely new. Situated action therefore also reproduces societal structure. That is, conversation analysis allows us to get at the simultaneously occurring and in fact mutually presupposing reproduction and transformation of societal relations, societal structure, societal organizations, and society at large.

Itinerary

In this first part of this chapter, I present some basic ideas about how conversation analysis is conducted. Prior to the transcript and offprints, there already had to have been (a) the real-life event and (b) the recording activity. The association between the original event and the tape is an innocent, one-to-one relation – this is evident from the fact that the event only happened once, in real-time through, whereas the tape is iterable, it can be played over and over again (Ashmore and Reed 2000). The tape is then transcribed, which constitutes a translation into a different medium, and therefore cannot be taken innocently as a process of one-to-one matching (e.g., Latour 1999). The transcription makes use of a notation system, as seen in Note 2, designed to symbolize as many interesting elements as possible in the written medium that are present on the tape (Roth 2013b). As analyst, I then "work up" the transcript in elaborating and explicating what is and can be seen. My text is therefore both descriptive (what I have seen) and pedagogic – it teaches my readers how to see events they are familiar with in the transcript (Roth 2013c).

In the following sections, I first introduce conversation analysis (CA) and some of its key ideas and continue my analysis of the fragment to show how various aspects of conversation analysis are done. In attending to what I am doing and in verifying what I am saying, readers already engage in conversation analysis as praxis. I could have taken many other fragments from the same or other tapes involving the two participants to show the same phenomena, or other tapes featuring Dan and other professors, or another student interviewing professors and scientists. I stay with this transcript because readers are already familiar with it and because it allows me to limit the amount of background information that has to be provided for an insider's perspective.

CONVERSATION ANALYSIS: DISCIPLINE AND PHENOMENA

A Brief History

Conversation analysis emerged during the 1960s from the seminal efforts of Harvey Sacks and Emmanuel Schegloff who, influenced by Ervin Goffman and Harold Garfinkel, strived to study social structure through the analysis of commonsense activities. The then recent emergence of cheap audio recording technology provided a tool with which to capture natural phenomena produced in and through talk-in-interaction. These early researchers noted that the details of recorded talk have to be recovered during transcription; Gail Jefferson did, during the early days, a lot of the transcriptions for Sacks before becoming an important CA scholar in her own right. The seminal texts that founded the discipline include "A simplest systematics for the organization of turn taking for conversation" (Sacks, Schegloff, and Jefferson 1974) and *Lectures on Conversation* (Sacks 1992a, b), which began their life as widely circulated lecture notes.[4] Another text, "On formal structures of social action" (Garfinkel and Sacks 1986), articulated the theoretical commitments common to ethnomethodology and conversation analysis.

Over the years, conversation analysts have investigated numerous issues including four overlapping but analytically distinguished types of interactional organization: *turn-taking*, *sequence*, *repair*, and *preference* organization. In the following two sections, I discuss these four types of organization and then turn to describe *formulating*, a pervasive feature of everyday talk.

Turn-Taking and Sequencing

Turn-taking as an organizational feature of interactions is one of the fundamental ideas underlying conversation analysis. Normally, one person speaks at a time and change to the next speaker occurs with minimal overlap or gap. Change over generally occurs at the completion of a grammatical unit, which may be a sentence, clause, phrase, or lexical construction (Sacks et al. 1974). Thus, although there are lengthy pauses during Anne's articulation of an interpretation – here 2.11 (line 04) and 1.80 seconds (line 08), but lasting up to 10 seconds in other parts of the transcript – Dan does not begin to speak (see the 8.18 seconds in Fragment 2 below). The pauses are prior to the end of a unit. However, the events following the completion of the inference (line 12) show that Anne expects Dan to comment. When the comment does not come forth, we can hear Anne explicitly requesting it (lines 14, 18). Fundamental to the enterprise of conversation analysis and the understanding of the intersubjective nature of conversation is the phenomenon of *recipient design*. That is, utterances are designed for others. They therefore imply their own intelligibility and therefore intersubjectivity. Anything a person says in conversation to another is inherently assumed to be *for* the other and, therefore, understandable. Consequentially, *what* is said and *how* it is said therefore cannot be entirely new in its form or content. A particular form of recipient design leads us to sequencing and its realization in adjacency pairs.

Fragment 2
01 D: so start in region one and (0.71) talk about (0.68) conservation of the
02   species in that area.
03   (2.95)
04 A: WELL HERE the BIRthrate (2.32) the BIRth of RAte (0.31) in numbers
05   per year presumably (1.38) is still below the death rate (8.18) but it
06   (0.43) s:o (1.10) but it is rising– what I see is– there wa– this is
07   increasing.
08

The idea of sequencing is related to that of turn-taking and recipient design. Analytically, conversation analysts get at sequencing, among others, through the study of *adjacency pairs* – greeting-return greeting, summons-answer, question-answer, and invitation-acceptance/rejection. In Fragment 1, Anne twice formulates what can be heard as a question. According to the adjacency pair organization, we should expect a response. Similarly, in the following, Dan can be heard as uttering something like an invitation Anne to begin by talking about a particular aspect of the graph, "region one," that is, the area to the left of the left intersection (from Anne's perspective). According to the adjacency pair organization, we should be able to expect an acceptance or rejection. In Fragment 2, Anne accepts the invitation and began to describe the birthrate curve as lying below the death rate curve.

The two parts of a pair are connected by means of *conditional relevance*, not as a mere latching of the two parts, but as the "participants' prospective and retrospective production and calibration of joint understanding" (Lynch and Bogen 1996, p. 275). After the first part initiates the adjacency pair, the next utterance is heard as a second pair part. If it is absent or does not fit, the second speaker is accountable for it. Thus, when Dan does not answer Anne's question or Anne does not follow Dan's invitation, they have to account for the deviation from the expected organization. On the other hand, the speaker may take the non-occurrence of the second part of the sequence as an indication of trouble. Here, Anne may take the non-response as an indication that the question was unclear; this then calls for *repair*. From Dan's perspective, because he is supposed to generate a think-aloud/interview protocol, providing Anne with answers in the response is not the *preferred* course of action. We now turn to repair and preference.

So far we have looked at the conversation through the lens of a homunculus sitting in the brain of a participant, deciding on what to do next. However, conversation analysis is actually to be used to get at a collective, societal phenomenon *sui generis*. That is, conversation analysis takes conversation as a collective phenomenon in its own right that cannot be explained by adding up the intentions and interpretations of individuals. Rather, we need to take adjacency pairs as wholes with parts. If a part is changed, the whole changes; if the whole changes, each part changes. That is, whether something someone is saying is a question, an insult, an answer, and so on is a function of the pair, and, therefore, of the turns that precede and succeed the turn of interest. In a strong sense, therefore, we cannot say that Anne asks a question until we know the effect that the locution has had on the situation. That is, whether something Anne says is a question, from the perspective of the conversation, depends on the next thing Dan says or does not say. Conversely, what Dan will say is an answer, an expression of hurt feelings, or a reply to an answer is a function of what Anne has said and what she will say after Dan has finished talking.

Repair and Preference

Repair in conversation is both a well-studied phenomenon and an analytic concept in conversation analysis (Schegloff, Jefferson, and Sacks 1977). Fragment 1 exhibits several instances of conversational repair. After Anne has made her inference about the consequences of the relation between the slopes of birthrate and death rate, there is a pause. Such pauses are opportunities (resources) for anyone to take the conversational floor. The pause is the outcome of a collaborative effect: Anne does not continue to speak, perhaps because she expects or anticipates a response; Dan does not begin, perhaps anticipating or expecting that Anne will continue. Anne then asks the question, "Is that right then?"

Fragment 1 (excerpt)
```
12          increasing. ((Fig. 1f))
13          (0.93)
14          is that right then?
```

This question allows us to retroactively hear the pause from her perspective as waiting for a comment that would deal with the uncertainty she had articulated ("presumably" [line 12]). Her query would be understood as functioning as a repair: Anne anticipates or expects a comment and, as it is not forthcoming, articulates what she expects to happen. Dan does not comment, perhaps does not understand the cue that a comment is expected; the explicit articulation of a request for comment then constitutes a repair.

A repair move can also be discerned in Fragment 3. Dan has completed one of his tutoring moves (lines 01–02, 05–06), which ended with a question. Anne, however, does not respond but asks a question in turn, "if you=are in region two?" (line 08). Dan responds by saying, "Yea" (line 09).

Fragment 3
```
01 D:     now if you are in region two (0.86) your
02        [bIRthrate's lARger]
03 A:     [OH this is (mean?)]
04        (0.46)
05 D:     so your population's gonna go up s:o you're gonna increase until what time?
06
07        (1.83)
08 A:     if you=are in region two?=
09 D:         =yea
10        (1.19)
```

Let us work our way backward. We may gloss what happens in this fragment in this way: Dan responds with an affirmative to a question, which has taken up a particular region of the graph as the topic of the talk (line 02). Her query therefore seeks confirmation as to the nature of the region talked about, which Dan confirms. That is, Anne's question (line 08) seeks to repair an uncertainty about the current focus by proposing one of the three areas as candidate. Dan confirms the proposed candidate area as the one he was talking about (line 09).

In the end, we can ascribe to Anne to have done multiple things. That is, Anne does more than clarifying the region her question pertains to. At the end of her utterance, the pitch moves upward. Raised pitches at the end of an utterance are resources for hearing what has been said as a question. That is, Anne both repairs a possible misunderstanding or lack of understanding of the original question, and reiterates the question at the same time. The fact that Dan begins to respond indicates that he has heard Anne's utterance as a request to respond.

The fundamental ideas underlying preference organization are that (a) when alternative (discursive) actions are possible, the *preferred* one is generally expected and chosen and that (b) the difference between preferred and *dispreferred* is demonstrated in the way the turn is shaped (Pomerantz 1984). The preferred action is frequently made available by the first speaker in a turn and, if a rejection occurs, has to be (and generally is) accounted for by the respondent. For example, in Fragment 1, there is a moment in which repair is interactively made necessary and then achieved; it immediately follows the request to comment on the inference (line 14).

Fragment 1 (excerpt)
14   is that right then?
15   (0.96)
16 D: u:m::

After the fact we may gloss the situation in this way: Anne has asked explicitly for the comment, but a conversationally lengthy pause develops. Dan does not respond, although he is asked an explicit question. When he eventually does respond, it does not actually constitute the word but a drawn-out "u:m::." Preferred responses usually are given immediately. Pausing and delaying responses by producing verbal tokens such as "uh" or "um" indicate a *dispreferred* answer was called for. Teachers who do not want to reveal correct responses right away may act in this way. The same pauses and verbal tokens may be taken as an indication that the person queried does not have a pat answer or that the question was clear. Rather than selecting one or the other possible interpretation, analysts interested in the online production of societal structure look for the actions of other members in the situation. Here, after another pause, Anne comes to utter "Round this region?" and produces a circular movement near to and a little to the right of the left intersection point.

Fragment 1 (excerpt)
14   is that right then?
15   (0.96)
16 D: u:m::
17   (0.44)
18 A: [((Fig. 10.1f, circles))]
          [round [this] region?   ]

After the fact – i.e., after Dan's turn – we can say that Anne has asked whether her inference is right, and now indexes verbally and gesturally to a particular area on the graph. If Dan had not understood which area the question "Is this right then?" refers to, the actions in line 18 in Fragment 1 would have repaired his lack of understanding.

Formulating

A pervasive feature of talk in interaction is participants' attention to formulate what is going on (Garfinkel and Sacks 1986). Thus, the verbal contributions to interactions are not just about informational content regarding the current topic but also co-articulate what is being done or what has been done. *Whatever* a person says provides materials that others can use for *making out* what he or she means to say. This is particularly the case when trouble is apparent.

There is always more to a situation than participants can say in so many words. Thus, in the fragment, Anne provides her reading of the two lines, compares the two, and then draws an inference about the effect on the population for a case where "birthrate is increasing (0.76) fA:Ster (0.87) than the death rate" (Fragment 1, lines 07–08). Moreover, she formulates when she says "I'm looking at the slopes of the curves" (Fragment 1, line 29). That is, she is not just looking at the curves but she is stating, for the benefit of Dan, what she is doing at the moment.

Fragment 1 (excerpt)
```
07        birthrate)) and the birthrate is increasing (0.76) fA:Ster (0.87) than the death
08        rate. (1.80) So they
```

When she requests an assessment, Dan articulates the result of the comparison between the two rates when birthrate is larger than death rate. In response, Anne says that she has been looking at the slopes of the curves. Here, we can hear her contribution as *formulating* what she has done and still is doing – looking and talking about the slopes of the curves. That is, when Dan apparently does not understand what she has done – draw an inference from the fact that the slope of birthrate is larger than that of the death rate in the particular region – she formulates what she has been doing, that is, looking at (and talking about) the slopes rather than the values of the two curves.

Formulating is a pervasive feature. In other parts of their session, for example, Anne formulates long pauses and Dan's hedges as her having missed something. Just prior to the following fragment, Anne again requests a comment about whether she has been right with her inferences. After hedging in a manner almost identical to Fragment 1, Dan provides in Fragment 4 a hesitating assessment, "I think tha:t's correct?" and continues, "Is that what it says on the graph?" There is an ever lengthening pause without a response from Anne, which Dan interrupts with a token that invites Anne to respond "Or?" (line 05). After a brief pause, Anne initiates a repair move, "you mean here?" and, while moving her right hand until it points to the text, utters "that's what you say?" Dan overlaps this utterance, acknowledging her repair regarding the nature of the thing being talked about and pointed to (line 07) and, reiterating his earlier question, says "yea, does it say?" (line 08). While still pointing to the lower part of the caption, Anne queries, "You want me to look there?" (line 09).

Fragment 4

```
01 D:      yeah that- yeah (.) I think tha:t's correct. (0.32) Is
02         that what it says on the graph?
03         (2.75)
04         °Or?°
05
```

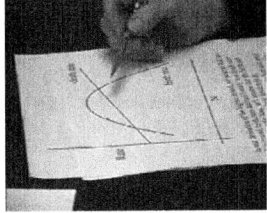

```
06         (0.39)
07 A:      you mean here?
08 D:      [that's what you say?]
09 A:      [((rH moves to text))]
           [yea, does it ] [say?]
                                      [you ] want me to
           look there? ((still pointing to text))
```

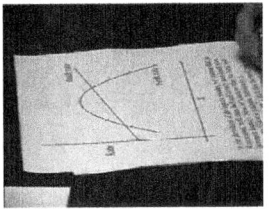

In this fragment, Anne twice formulates what she heard Dan to mean without that he had said this in so many words. Framed in question form, she articulated Dan to "mean" attending to a particular part of the instructions (line 07), which she immediately thereafter points to. She formulates a second time what he was doing, "that's what you say?" In line 09, again, she formulates hearing Dan as instructing her to look somewhere at the lower part of the instruction. Dan has not done so, but Anne makes available to Dan that she has heard him saying so, and in this, she also tells everybody else viewing the tape and reading the transcript.

A second aspect of formulating can also be found in this fragment. In saying, "is that what it says on the graph?," Dan is doing something. In line 09, Anne explicitly articulates what he is doing. Without saying it in so many words, Dan exhibits what he has been doing to Anne (and the analysts). *We* do not need to infer what he was doing. Anne articulates it for us: Dan is "doing [wanting me to look there]," where I have drawn on a recommended denotation practice to bracket the gloss of what is being done (cf. Garfinkel and Sacks 1986). That is, in the present situation *we* do not attribute intentions to actors or interpret what they have done; one of the participants, here *Anne*, has formulated for everyone to hear what is being done. This is important, for her subsequent actions take into account what she has seen and heard Dan to have done rather than what we, the analysts, might have seen him do and say. It is also important because attending to what participants say in this way gives us the actors' perspective rather than our own interpretation of what someone is saying or what someone is doing and how this is taken up in the situation (see also Roth 2013c).

PROSODY AS RESOURCE IN AND FOR INTERACTION

Educators and educational researchers are singularly focused on words and the language (discourse) they constitute. But at the origin, there are not words. Anyone who has tried to transcribe a video- or audiotape recorded under everyday, noisy classroom conditions knows that there are moments when intent and prolonged listening does not allow hearing *what* is being said; all one can hear are indistinct sounds. At the origin of utterances, words, and language therefore are sounds. As part of our cultural upbringing, we learn to hear sounds in particular ways, as motorcycles, musical instruments, or voices. Moreover, we learn to hear them as approaching motorcycles, musical instruments playing a tune rather than being tuned, and as voices articulating words. But words do not suffice in the constitution of interaction – the increased number of misunderstanding in email conversation, and the use of specific signs to put expressions in relief (e.g., smiley faces, typographic reproduction of faces) should alert readers that face-to-face communication has a variety of other symbolic means for producing conversational resources. A related familiar, folk-psychological notion is that of "body language"; that is, bodies as a whole or in part move, and these movements are seen as part of communication. One known but in education little studied communicational resource is prosody (intonation), which speakers use to indicate syntax, turn-taking, utterance type (question, statement), attitudes, affect, and feelings (e.g., Roth 2007a; Roth and Tobin 2010).

Prosodic features include speech intensity (a measure how loud someone speaks), pitch or frequency of the voice, and duration (words can be spoken fast or drawn out, between words there may be pauses). Changes in these features, individually or in combinations, produce stressed or emphasized syllables. Thus, a word spoken much louder or at a much higher pitch than the surrounding talk will be heard as having been emphasized or received stress. In a conversation analytic approach, these features are understood as resources that both speaker and listener use for making sense.

Prosody and Temporal Structuring

Time is often treated as a factor that conditions events and their unfolding in time; it is taken in the physicists' manner, an external and objective frame external to interactions. Yet numerous scholars in disciplines such as sociology (e.g., Bourdieu 1990) or organization science (Orlikowski and Yates 2002) view time as a resource for action, giving recognition to the fact that temporal structures are shaping and being shaped by ongoing human action. Time is therefore neither external and determining nor entirely shaped and determined by human action. As other resources, temporal structures restrain and enable the reproduction|transformation of culture and are both the medium and an outcome of cultural practices. Conversation analysis is a method that allows us to get at such phenomena as a brief look at an excerpt from Fragment 1 shows (lines 05–07).

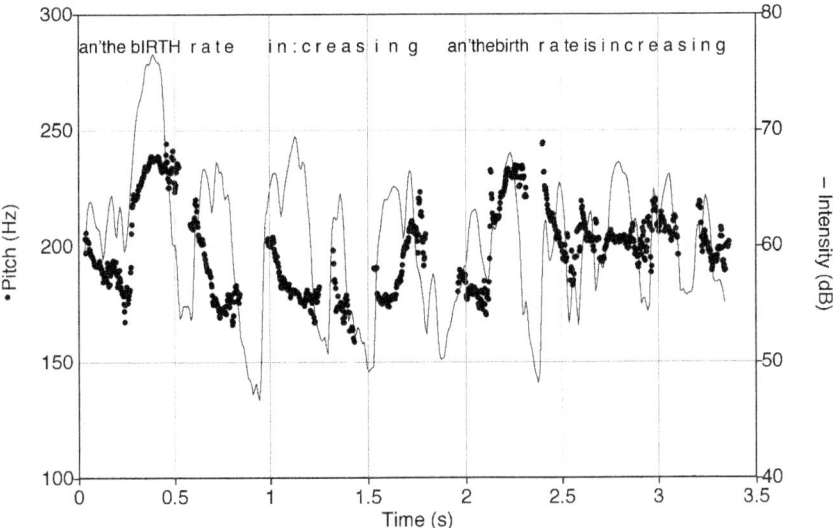

Figure 10.2. Speech intensity (dB) and pitch (Hz) for an excerpt from the episode (lines 05–07). That a part of the utterance "bIRTH" is much louder than normal is evident from the peak of intensity. The emphases usually fall where two or three of the variables intensity, pitch, and phoneme length are larger than in the surrounding talk.

Fragment 1 (excerpt)
05 A: dEATh rate ((Fig. 1d)) increasing (0.68) an the BIRTHrate ((Fig. 10.1e))
06   increasing ((traces birthrate)) and the birthrate is increasing (0.76)
07

Anne achieves the emphasis of "bIRTH" both by the greater speech intensity and a significant rise in pitch; the lengthening of the phoneme and a corresponding sudden rise in pitch are responsible for the emphasis on "ing" (Figure 10.2).[5] In the second occurrence of "birth," however, emphasis is due only to the rise in pitch. None of the phonemes making up "increasing" stand out in loudness, pitch, or length when compared to the pronunciation of the immediately preceding "rate is." This leads us to the transcript as provided, "an the bIRTHrate increasing and the birthrate is increasing" (lines 05–07).

One of the functions that this stressing of syllables has is similar to pointing; it is making salient current features in the setting or in the semantics of the utterance itself (Pozzer-Ardenghi and Roth 2005). Thus, Anne marks the words birth and death, which are thereby marked as the semantically important items. Throughout the transcript, Anne employs this device and thereby makes salient to herself and her audience what is the momentarily salient element.

A first look at the transcript reveals regular emphases that appear to structure the performance; these emphases are also related to the particular verbal tokens. For

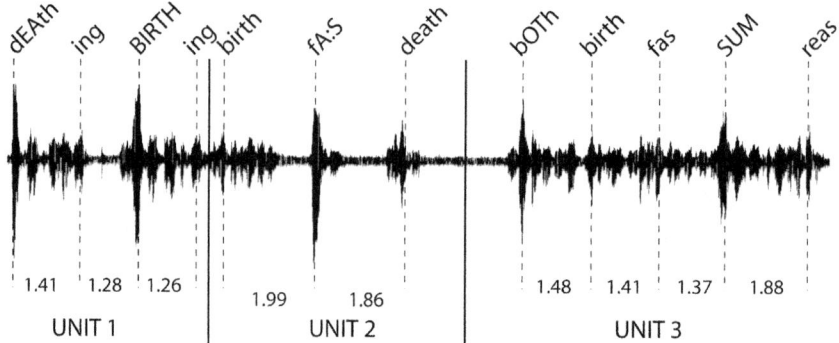

Figure 10.3. The emphasized syllables have been added to the waveform of the opening section of the episode; dotted lines mark the center of the emphasized syllables and numbers denote the time in tenth of a second between adjacent emphases within a speech unit.

example, in lines 05–06 of Fragment 1, corresponding items are stressed "dEATh rate increas<u>ing</u> (0.68) and the BIRTHrate increas<u>ing</u>." A plot of the waveform of her voice allows us to mark the stresses in time (Figure 10.3). We immediately see the rather regular temporal appearance of the stresses during the different sections of Anne's initial reading and interpretation of the graph. During the first descriptions, the temporal distances between stressed syllables are from 1.3 to 1.4 seconds, in the next part where Anne compares birthrate and death rate, the stressed syllables are separated between 1.9 and 2.0 seconds, and in the final section, all but one distance lie between 1.4 and 1.5 seconds.

Here, the emphases are on semantically similar items and occur in regular intervals. Both are resources for structuring the delivery. This delivery appears to serve Anne in pacing herself through this unknown thicket of the graph; her thinking aloud takes on structure, her thinking becomes structured in and through the delivery. It is also a resource to the person who is the intended audience; it is a resource for attending to those things that currently are to stand out.

Time and temporality are also of particular issue in and during interactions, that is, in the interval between the actions of the participants. It is in the mastery of the intervals that cultural competence plays itself out (Bourdieu 1990). For example, in the transcript there are two instances (lines 13, 15) where the pause after a completed sentence unit reaches what has come to be known as the *standard maximum silence* of about one second (Jefferson 1989).

Fragment 1 (excerpt)
```
12      incre<u>as</u>ing. ((Fig. 10.1f))
13      (0.93)
14      is that right then?
15      (0.96)
16      u:m::
```

A brief reflection shows that silences in interaction are always produced collaboratively. The fact that Anne asks whether she has been right in the as tentative marked inference suggests she is expecting a comment. Dan has not shown any indication that he understands this intent in the growing pause. There is another pause developing, followed by Dan's production of "u:m::" (Fragment 1, line 16), a signal that answering is the dispreferred action or that there is uncertainty about what the question is. Anne's uncertainty about whether Dan is aware of her expectation is heightened by the fact that another pause begins to develop again interrupted by Anne who now circles the region immediately to the right of the left intersection point and queries, "Round this region?" Another silence ensues, followed by semantically empty tokens before Dan begins to respond. From his perspective, responding when the task has been set up for Anne to provide a think-aloud protocol is the dispreferred action. He allows the pauses to develop. For Anne, these developing pauses are resources for inferring that the content of her question had not been clear.

There are other moments when the pauses in Anne's production exceed the one-second standard maximum silence (Fragment 1, lines 01–04, 04, 08; Fragment 2, lines 03, 04, 05, 06, 07; Fragment 3, lines 07, 10; Fragment 4, line 04). But in these moments, she has not yet reached a completion point from her own and Dan's perspectives. At other moments in this and other interviews, Dan encourages the participant to think/talk aloud. That is, in these situations, he takes Anne and other participants as not fulfilling their commitment to the research protocol and therefore reminds them of the task specification that requires thinking aloud.

We may summarize, therefore, that pauses are the outcome of a joint production that cannot be reduced to individual intentions. They are societal practices through and through, with substantial differences in how they play out across cultures. Thus, for example, the pauses between speakers are different for Hawai'ians and white residents of Hawai'i (Au 1980). As members of First Nations in the Pacific Northwest told me during graduate courses, they do not feel comfortable to speak unless there are long pauses, which may be of the order of 10 seconds or more between speakers. If students from such cultures take part in lessons characterized by typical white-middle class turn-taking routines and the temporality thereof, it does not surprise that they do not do as well as others.

Prosody, Interaction, and Emotion

In thinking aloud, Anne explicitly addresses the activity system; she is following the instructions, which have told her to think aloud so that the Dan and the social scientists he is working for t the time could learn about graphs and graphing, particularly about expertise.

Speakers have characteristic pitch ranges. These ranges may change as a function of the overall emotional state of the person (Roth 2007b). In the present situation, across the interview/think-aloud session, Anne's range lies between 175 and 200 Hertz (Hz), with occasional moments where her voices ranges between 200 and 235 Hz, particularly during the moments when a task was still unfamiliar

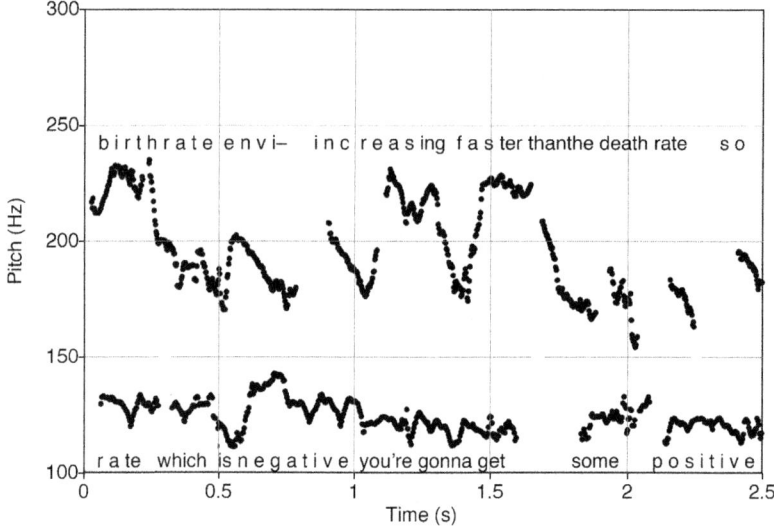

Figure 10.4. This representation of pitch levels characterizes Anne (top) and Dan (bottom) when they speak longer stretches. For Anne, the pitch varies between 175 and 200 Hz, with peaks reaching 235 Hz; Dan's voice is characterized by pitch levels between 115 and 135 Hz, with occasional peaks reaching to 145 Hz.

(Figure 10.4). The pitch range for Dan's voice lies between 115 and 135 Hz, with occasional peaks reaching to 145 Hz. Variations from the normal range are resources for speakers and listeners for making sense of what is being said and for the speaker's emotional coloring at the moment.

For Anne, too, asking whether she is right or wrong comes from and is associated with a particular affective state, which expresses itself in a high pitch (Figure 10.5). Every time she asks to receive a hint or an assessment, the pitch moves into the 300–350 Hz range. On the other hand, when the same utterance "right" is used in different contexts, for example, as a form of acknowledgment, the associated pitch was in or near her normal (or peak) range.

Figure 10.5 exemplifies the pitch ranges when Dan hedges ("umm," "hhh"), and when he accedes to Anne's query ("if you take– well"). In the former case, his voice stays within the pitch range (including the peaks), but in the latter case, he invariably moves into or above the pitch range normally occupied by Anne. Subsequently, his pitch descended until reaching its normal range between 115 and 135 Hz. This is a consistent pattern throughout the session and other female interviewees; it is more difficult to discern with the male participants, for their pitch ranges were similar to that of Dan.

Here, the pitch appears to articulate the express wish to meet up with the person making a request or asking a question. His voice not only matches the pitch range,

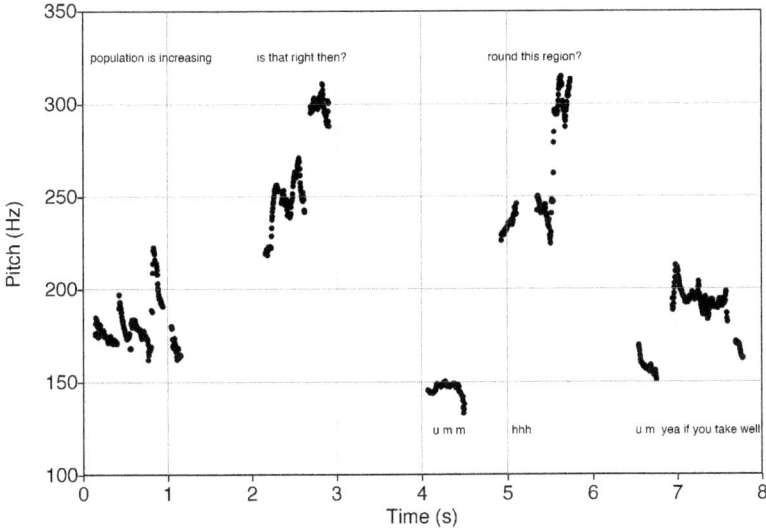

Figure 10.5. When Dan does not accede to Anne's requests, his pitch remains in his normal range. However, when he does respond, his pitch rises into Anne's range as if trying to meet her, not only metaphorically, but literally, at least with respect to the absolute pitch.

but also quotes the pitch contour, both of which are expressions of alignment (or intent thereof) between speakers of quite diverse cultural background (Müller 1996; Roth 2005). At another level, matching pitch and pitch contour are ways of expressing empathy and solidarity, which are therefore ways of making emotions available to others and to reproduce these emotions (Roth and Tobin 2010).

Prosody and Emotion

Stressed syllables can be heard. But, in many situations, the hearings can be crosschecked against the electronically produced measures of speech intensity and pitch. Stresses in speech produce a rhythm, and this rhythm together with pitch and loudness are expressions of emotions. Because these expressions are materially in the room, others notice them, who, in fact, are entrained not only into the same rhythm but also into the same emotion (Collins 2004). We have analyzed data that show that the rhythm in the speech of an agitated African American student engaged in an argument with her teacher, is the same that other students in the class display through tapping the desk, wiggling with the leg, and nodding with their heads (Roth and Tobin 2010). The more agitated the young woman becomes the more her pitch rises and the more her rhythm accelerates. But, interestingly, the rhythm of other students' movements accelerates as well. This acceleration is subsequently reversed through the "calming" talk of a fellow student, leading to decreases in rhythm, speech intensity, and pitch. Not only the student reduced the pitch levels, but also her teacher; and the rhythm displayed in the taping and wiggling of the legs also slow down. That is, the reduction of tension at the verbal level is also signaled through the return to normal levels at the prosodic level. Here, prosody and movements are a means to track not only the individual emotions and mood, but also the collectively enacted emotion and mood in the classroom. Rhythm appears to play such a tremendous role in the production of societal relations that it becomes one of the determining factor in learning as a whole (Roth 2011).

The changes in pitch can be associated with changes in the emotive aspects of the situation – for example, girls in disputes over a game of hopscotch displayed disagreements both semantically and emotionally through large changes in pitch (Goodwin, Goodwin, and Yaeger-Dror 2002). In the present fragments, Dan's hedging and resistance to responding, which can be seen at the temporal unfolding of the transcript, are also indicated at the prosodic level. As such, these forms of resistance are also available to Anne. Staying in his normal range when explicitly asked to answer a question may be heard as an indication that he resisted making a step toward her (Figure 10.5). On the other hand, every time Dan followed a request, his pitch moves way beyond his normal range into and above Anne's normal range. He was acceding, taking a step toward and empathizing with her, which was also expressed at the pitch level (Figure 10.5, right hand side).

Hand Gestures, Body Movements

Gestures with the hands and other body parts constitute resources to interaction participants for making sense of and communicating what is going on. By their very definition, gestures are understood to be symbolic movements designed to contribute to symbolic activities, thinking and sense making. (For a good introduction and overview of gesture research, particularly from a perspective consistent with a sociocultural approach see McNeill 1992.) There are many instances of gesture use apparent just in the brief fragments featured in this chapter. However, conversation analysis does not have to limit itself to gestures, that is, the explicit symbolic aspects of interactions, but also can turn up interesting phenomena of other body movements, which, as all aspects of a setting that participants make salient to each other, come to be resources in the ongoing, real-time sense-making of conversationalists. The movement or non-movement of entities in the setting can be resources in and for the constitution of participants' ongoing and developing sense, even when they do not speak a single word for long periods of time (Roth 2004b). In this vein, I

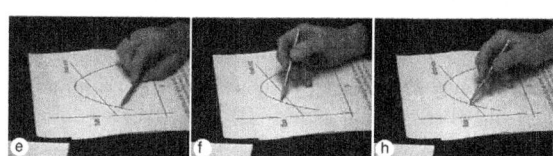

Figures 10.1 e, f, g. are illustrations of Anne's pointing, which orients both Dan and her own attention to particular

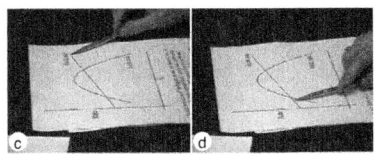

The movement from Figure 10.1 c to d constitutes an iconic gesture, that is, in its shape it reproduces the shape of the line.

describe above how Anne shifts her body position and orientation and how these shifts are associated with the division of labor in the responsibility for the task of completing the interview. But let us take a closer look at the deployment and function of gestures in the present corpus.

Anne's pointing to the graph as she thinks aloud orients Dan to particular locations of the graph that correspond in some way to her speech. As Anne progresses, in talking about the birthrate curve, for example, her hand is turning so that the pencil almost always stays perpendicular to the slope of the line where she was pointing (Figures 10.1e, f, h); similarly, when she talks about the death rate, the pencil is perpendicular to the slope of the line (Figures 10.1c, d). The pencil point marks the point of attention; the deictic gesture is a resource for attending to the point. Thus, from the speaker's perspective, pointing is both a resource for getting the work of attending done and an outcome, the result of attending. The pointing (deictic) gesture is a resource that allows Anne to orient and focus as well as tracking her own progression. Thus, at the time Anne talks about the death rate for the first time, describing it as increasing, her hand has already moved along the line on the paper. The perceptual image, the hand movement, and the utterance "death rate is increasing" are three different forms in which the same idea unit expresses itself. They are not just three forms that are additive. From a sociocultural perspective, the different forms of expression are mutually constitutive and presuppose one another; in other words, they stand in a dialectical relationship (McNeill and Duncan 2000).

It is clear, then, that when Anne is leaning forward and bringing her hand and pencil to the paper in front of her, this is an expression of the intention to attend to and talk about the graph, the part of the activity that she is responsible for. When she leans backward and takes her hands off the graph, this expresses, among other things, that she is not currently orienting to a specific aspect of the graph and to getting her part of getting the think-aloud session done (Roth and Middleton 2006). Thus, the body orientation and hand position have interactive function. They exhibit attention and focus, readiness to continue, and therefore also constitute resources for Dan concerning the interaction.

The hand gestures also have interactive function, which is made even more explicit in moments of trouble. Thus, when Dan does not respond to Anne's question about the correctness of her inference, Anne circles a particular region on the graph querying, "round this region?" (Fragment 1, line 18). At this moment, her hand gesture is the dialectical complement of the utterance, providing a perceptually (but not verbally) available specificity to "this region." Here, the gesture more than the utterance is a resource for directing the interlocutor's attention to a specific physical region.

Hand gestures (movements) have other interactive functions as well. Thus, hitting the desktop hard with the palm of her hand (Fragment 1, line 03) is a culturally recognizable sign for getting ready and starting an activity that has been set up in previous actions; it means something like "okay, let's get going." Here, Anne has completed reading the captions and instructions and now sets out to engage in that part of the task described in the text. In line 24 (Fragment 1), while Dan continues talking, Anne moves forward, then brought her hand to the graph and circles the same region as previously.

Fragment 1 (excerpt)
23 D: [birth minus the death   ]
24 A: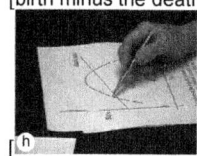
        [ʰ   ((circles))]

In this movement, she indicated readiness to talk, but she refrains, as Dan does not stop until uttering "death." At the same time, this gesture again means she reiterates the region that her question has been about; there is no need to reiterate the question verbally. Consequently, a pause begins to develop. From Dan's perspective, Anne appears to have indicated intent to speak; from Anne's perspective, she has expressed what she wanted to express and therefore she does not need to talk leaving the turn to Dan. He then takes the opportunity provided. The pause here is a resource that allows him to take the next turn, which in fact constitutes a continuation of the immediately preceding one.

This hand movement toward the graph as an instance of the intent to speak is further put in relief, for throughout the session, there is a clear division of labor with respect to the responsibilities for the textual and graphical part of the sheet (Roth and Middleton 2006). Anne is responsible for the graph, and Dan for the contents of the text. In their bodily, gestural, and verbal interactions, these different responsibilities are expressed in different modalities. Thus, Anne's forward movement and hand gesture to the graph not only point out something but also indicate that Anne is ready to act toward (talk about) something that falls within her realm of responsibility. When she leans back, taking her hands away from the graph (or pointing to the text), the salient issue pertains to Dan's part in the division of labor of researcher and researched. These actions are resources for making the event in the way we can witness it.

A MICROCOSMS OF SOCIETY AND SOCIAL RELATIONS IN THE MAKING

Members and Researchers

In much of the education literature on classroom interactions, intersubjectivity is treated as something that independent individuals have to achieve. From a traditional psychological and radical constructivist perspective, this is a difficult task given that these approaches treat human beings more or less as monads. However, it should be evident that human interaction generally and conversation in particular *presuppose* intersubjectivity to the same extent that it produces intersubjectivity. There would be no conversation possible if we could not assume there to be a considerable degree of common ground. Many language philosophers therefore have come to the conclusion that language constitutes that common ground: it always comes to us from the other, is produced for the other, and is returning to the other in every act of speech (e.g., Derrida 1998). In other words, it is language that speaks in conversation and we are as much subject of language in speech as we are subject to and subjected to language that never is our own but always already something alien, through and through bearing the marks of the Other.

Conversation analysis is both based on and allows articulation of the fundamentally intersubjective nature of human interaction. For example, it does not make sense for Anne to ask Dan in Fragment 1, "is that right then?," unless she can presuppose that Dan already understands the words she is and will be using. Moreover, she has to presuppose that Dan understands her to ask a question rather than to make a statement, to beg for something, etc. To intend asking a question, Anne has to presuppose that whatever comes from her mouth is understood as a question. Similarly, in responding at all, Dan not only has to assume that Anne hears the sounds he produces as words, but also that she already understands what he is saying. In this sense, he cannot say anything that is radically new; whatever he can usefully contribute to the interaction already is presupposed to be intelligible. It already is prefigured within the existing possibilities. Not only words, but also hand and arm movements used in pointing and iconic gesturing are presupposed as material forms that signify and denote. At the same time, these actions introduce new elements in the sense that they orient participants to particular locations in the setting. In summary, then, intersubjectivity is both the condition for and the outcome of the communicative interaction; intersubjectivity is continuously reproduced and transformed.

Intersubjectivity as a presupposed condition of the interaction is particularly important when we consider the emergent nature of the interaction. Frequently researchers formulate what their participants do in terms of intentions. This in itself is not inappropriate, for, as I show here, interaction participants make available to each other, in and through their actions, not only actions but also intentions. It would be inappropriate, therefore, to suggest that the intentions *predate* the actions observed. Anyone taking a little time out during a meeting and observing what is going on will note that events continuously unfold. There is generally too little time to articulate a response prior to speaking. What *exactly* a speaker wants to say is said *in* the moment of speaking. Just like Anne, human beings generally think as they go – *on their feet,* as the popular expression goes – their thoughts (and cognition) being *in* their actions, simultaneously made available to others and themselves. Human conduct is such that the actions themselves are such that they can be explained in terms of intents. Thus, Anne is able to provide a gloss of Dan's action: he is "doing [wanting (her) to look there]." Dan may still suggest otherwise, but the fact is that in his actions and talk, Anne finds sufficient evidence supporting her formulation (gloss) of what he has done.

The rapidity and efficiency of human actions in real time cannot be understood unless we take them as providing sufficient elements that can be used in accounts of what has happened. Extending this idea, I suggest that thinking does not have to precede the actions but is expressed in the (discursive) action as it unfolds.

With ethnomethodologists, conversation analysts explicitly recognize the role the researcher's cultural competence plays during the analysis. To be able to understand what is being said without saying so, the researcher, too, has to be a member in the cultural community under investigation (ten Have 2002). Here, *member* is not used to refer to a person but rather to the mastery of natural language used in the production and display of commonsense knowledge in and of everyday activities as observable, reportable, and accountable phenomena (Garfinkel and Sacks 1986). Thus, to articulate what is going on in talk, to understand what is being said and done in and through talk, analysts need to be members (of the community, culture, tribe) – lest they mishear what participants are saying and articulate structures that are irrelevant to the populations and situations studied. This became very clear to me during an extensive three-week eight-hour-per day effort during which David Middleton, a social psychologist experienced in the analysis of discourse (e.g., Middleton and Edwards 1990), collaboratively analyzed the present data corpus. It turned out that he misheard the interactions whenever the content concerned specialized knowledge of physics or advanced mathematics. For example, he was not attuned to the difference between Anne and Dan with respect to their foci of attention to slopes and values of birthrate and death rate, respectively; he also missed the point of Dan's adding rather than subtracting the two rates. In other parts of the transcript, Anne and Dan talk about first, second, and partial derivatives. Here again, David found himself at a disadvantage because he lacked the cultural understanding characteristic of the community of physicists. Whenever Dan and Anne presupposed specialized knowledge that remained unarticulated because it "went without saying," David missed the point of their interaction during his analysis.

Power/Knowledge

Conversation analysis is an ideal tool for analyzing how social positions and relations are reproduced|transformed in and through interaction. One way of getting at power in educational contexts is through the way in which questions of knowledge play themselves out, are negotiated or contested, and come to be settled for the purposes at hand (e.g., Roth 2013c). Who knows what and when and how this knowledge pertains to the issues at hand is an important aspect of positioning, maintaining existing knowledge/power gradients, and overturning these gradients, even if only for the moment.

In line 14 of Fragment 1, Anne asks Dan whether her inference is right; he eventually responds providing some elaboration. Interactionally, the authoritative knowledge is thereby attributed to Dan; in his response, he accepts. In Fragment 2, Dan operates as a tutor, inviting Anne to go about the task in a particular way (lines 01–02); Anne follows this invitation, thereby coproducing the tutor-tutee relationship. This difference in knowing constitutes a difference in power. This power is not some substance that people bring to their interactions with others. Rather, it is an effect, a quality and product of the interaction. Thus, Anne may be thought as having power that she could have played out in her interactions with Dan given that she is the professor. Furthermore, the latter is not in a more powerful situation inherently, for he depends on his participant to get his recording, and, as established in the consent agreement, Anne can stop her participation at any point. Yet it turns out that Anne makes a request for assessment and Dan eventually accedes to it. He is in the situation that he may or may not grant the request. The asymmetric positioning of the two is a result of their interaction, initiated by Anne, but co-produced by Dan.

In other parts of the session over and about the same graph, Anne asks Dan for hints, that is, she requests help. This articulated – at least in this situation – a difference with respect to who is presumed to be knowledgeable about the topic. Although the preferred action to questions and queries is responding, not responding is also a possible action. In fact, withholding a response can be a way of controlling the situation. For example, teachers withhold answers to encourage students to think their way through some issue. Withholding something one has and could give away without material loss – here knowledge/information – is a way of reproducing|transforming control and therefore power. Thus, when Anne does as what we gloss to be requesting a hint, Dan, after some more back and forth, eventually says, "so start in region one and (0.71) talk about (0.68) conservation of the species in that area." From the after-the-fact perspective, we can say that Dan yields the request for help, but he controls how this help unfolds. Both Anne and Dan act as if he knew the answer and as if he were in a position to grant or withhold the request. In the following brief exchange, for example, he does not provide what we can hear to be the requested answer but responds with his own questions in turn.

Fragment 5
01 A: so this is a stable point, is it?
02   (0.18)
03 D: y:– (0.20) well you tell me:hh (0.74) what do you: think?
04

Here, Anne first makes an assessment of the second point where birthrate and death rate intersected, and then seeks confirmation whether the situation is as she has described it (line 01). Dan appears to respond quickly, that is, in the preferred mode, but then suddenly stops the somewhat extended "y:" sound. There is a brief pause, followed by a request for her to tell him, which is, after a lengthening pause without response, followed by a question, "what do you: think?" (lines 03–04). Here, he does not respond directly, which would be the preferred action, but twice attributed the responsibility for providing a full assessment to the person making the original assessment request – this is a typical prerogative of teachers. To reiterate, he is in the know and, here, does not reveal this knowledge to the person asking, who nevertheless participates in attributing knowledge to him. But both contribute to conferring this special power to him.

We notice other features related to differences in position and positioning. For example, at one point in the fragment, Anne ends up "complaining" to or "chiding" Dan. This complaint is enacted in, arises from, and is acknowledged interactively through joint action. Anne has provided a description of the slopes of the two curves, and draws an inference. She then asks Dan whether what she has said is right. He gives a description of what to do – subtracting or adding the rates – then utters, "so" (line 30), as if expecting Anne to continue or draw her own conclusion from what has been said. Anne, however, suggests that *she* is looking at the "slopes of the curves" (line 29).

Fragment 1 (Excerpt)
```
29 A:     yea [I'M] looking at the slopes of the curves=
30 D:         [so ]    =oh, okay.
31
```

Here Anne stresses the personal pronoun "I" together with the truncated auxiliary verb "am." In this, Anne can be heard to emphasize what she has done, which Dan hears as a contrast with what he has said. The "oh" signals to everyone within hearing range the surprise, the novelty of the information that Anne just has provided. So in effect, Dan does not provide an answer to a supposed question, but in his response talks about something else. Anne says, "I'M looking at the slopes of the curves," which contrasts the curves that Dan has talked about. Anne not only provides information about the difference between their respective contributions, but she also does relational work – she chides him for not having responded to her question.

TECHNICAL ISSUES

Transcription

Many researchers collect their videotapes and then select some for transcription and analysis. In my research team, we proceed differently. We transcribe the tapes in their entirety as soon as possible after they have been recorded. This has the advantage that we can direct our cameras in subsequent recording sessions in order to extent our database concerning interesting issues. The first transcripts are done quickly and therefore rough, because we do not spend a lot of time trying to get every single word; we do not transcribe pauses and overlaps (e.g., Figure 10.6). The figure shows that there is little detail and even many missing element when the transcript is compared to Fragment 1 and Figure 10.1. Video offprints are added into the transcript, especially where participants make extensive use of gestures or where other aspects of the talk can be understood better (or only) with the image present. At this stage, a screen print of the video image is created, which is then directly inserted into the transcript.

A: ? here we have the death rate increasing (PICTURE 0.12.35) and the birth rate increasing (PICTURE 0.12.41) and the birthrate is increasing faster than the death rate ? presumably that means that the population is increasing (PICTURE 0.12.58) is that right then
D: Well ? birth + death your ?
A: I'm looking at the slopes of the curves ?

PICTURE 0.12.35   PICTURE 0.12.41   PICTURE 0.12.58

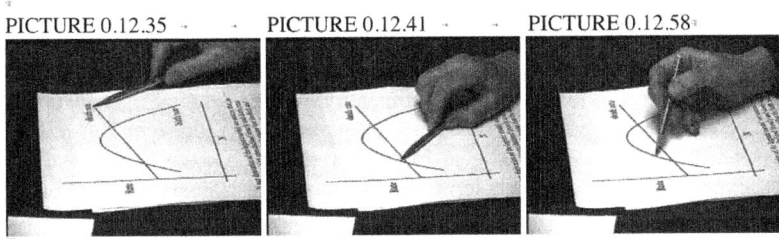

Figure 10.6. As soon as possible after recording, a rough transcript often including many passages marked as undecipherable. The video offprints is labeled using time into the tape (h:mm:ss) so that the exact moment can easily be found again in the Quicktime™ movie file.

In subsequent analyses, the transcripts are enhanced. Pauses are inserted, and transcription conventions are used. I also use a font that spaces letters equally. At this stage, programs that create a visual representation of the soundtrack – intensity or waveform – are useful because the pauses can be measured more quickly and more accurately. Also, overlapping talk can be isolated and the exact points of overlap determined. Video offprints are imported into a painting program such as Adobe Photoshop, changed to gray-scale, and, if necessary, elaborated and touched up. At this stage, I also produce the high-quality video offprints; publishers generally require a pixel density of 300 pixels per inch. Depending on the ultimate use of the image, I choose the specific size: about 1 inch (2.54 centimeters) wide when the image is inserted in the transcript (see Fragment 2), larger or smaller producing figures containing single or multiple off prints. The ultimate result is saved in the program specific file type as well as in JPG-compressed form. (This format can easily be shared across platforms and, most importantly, is acceptable to publishers.)

Generally, I do my own transcripts from the initial stages through all transformation to the most refined ones such as those featured in this chapter. Transcribing allows me to really get to know the tapes and their contents. Furthermore, while transcribing, I already annotate and comment on the transcript and salient fragments. The amount of time spent doing the rough and subsequent fine transcripts is more than returned in the detailed familiarity that I develop in and about the database. As I have said to many colleagues who have asked me about how I could pull together so much information from the large databases I create as part of my research, I become so familiar with the data sources that an analysis is like walking through a library. Whenever I feel like reading or needing this or that, I just go to the right shelf and pull the desired materials. This intimate familiarity with all aspects of the tapes and transcripts leads to the fact that I learn many different things, which can be reported to different audiences, leading to a number of publications rather than only one.

Listening and Hearing

While constructing the transcription, the conceptual differences between listening and hearing are quite evident. These differences actually allow me to develop a better appreciation of words in communication. In western cultures, words and language receive preferential treatment – the term (phal-) logocentrism highlights this (Derrida 1982).[6] Those who attempt to transcribe video- or audiotapes can easily experience the questionable nature of the central status words take in most analyses, which tend to forget that we *make* societal relations and *do* (rather than mean) *things* with the words we use. There are frequent moments during transcription, where listening does not allow me to make out what has been said (I then put question marks in parenthesis to mark those places). Even repeated listening may not help. But analysts experience time and again that when others tell what has been said or what they have heard, they too can hear it. All of a sudden, what has been but an undecipherable noise becomes a more or clear articulation. That is, sounds hit our ears; it is our long-time experience in a particular linguistic context that allows us to hear certain sounds *as* words rather than as noise. It is similar to other moments in everyday life: We hear a motorcycle approaching or receding rather than just noise.

We can draw from this the lesson that prosodic features are just as legitimate resources in collective sense-making activity as are the sounds we hear as utterances. Similarly, we use bodily configurations and gestures all of the time as resources for attributing intention and attitude (boredom, interest) to others who may "pick up" the same body movements and gestures so that we collectively express the same attitudes and intentions to one another. In a classroom, students express in the way they lean back, yawn, orient their bodies, and so forth their interests, emotions, and intentions. We may adapt to or do something about it, that is, use these displays as resources, and thereby reproduce and transform forms of culture.

From this we can learn that all communication involves *material* signs, which always appear in material contexts. There is no need for us to appeal to "meanings" (e.g., Roth 2013a). Culture, societal relations, and societal structure, which, as I suggest above, are the outcomes of human interactions, are therefore instantiated in material communicative forms. It is by interacting with such material forms that we come to know about and learn cultural forms, even emotions, both how they express themselves materially and the corresponding sounds that we hear as their names. There is no mysterious transmission of cultural practices and signification. Communication, in whichever form it occurs, is always materially available in the setting so that all participants, all those present, can access it and, qua resource, draw on it in subsequent action.

Analytic Process

Colleagues and graduate students frequently ask me how I do my analyses. Normally, my analytic process begins with some noticing, often while I transcribe. For example, when I started looking at the videotapes and rough transcripts of this database, in particular the session involving Anne and Dan, I went, "Wow, something is going on here." Contrary to what one might expect from a scientist invited to provide an expert reading of a series of graphs, Anne and some of her colleagues began to ask the interviewer about the "correct" interpretation. In some instances, the interviewer began to articulate such a reading or guide the interviewee to a standard reading. To better understand the interactions, I first transcribed an entire session in detail, that is, yielding about 30 pages of transcript as exemplified in the fragments presented here. In the process, I came to hear the tape over and over again, becoming attuned to the slightest change in the voice and became familiar with the recorded events. I became so familiar with the tape that I could replay it, in my mind, together with the particular prosodic features. As I listened to the tapes, an increasing amount of detail became apparent to me. I took notes and wrote small analyses as I went along working my way second by second through the tapes. It turns out that in such work, I come to hear what is being said in parts of the tape that previously I could not understand despite intent listening.

As I go along, I also use the PRAAT software, which allows me to check the accuracy of the transcript, and also to get an impression of the various prosodic features. I produce graphs of intensity and pitch, add the words matching them to the other physical features, and print them to be able to take rapid notes on the printed version. In working my way through the tape(s), I also check for the occurrence of the same or contradictory patterns to those I previously noted.

Conducting sessions involving others is helpful for noticing new types of events. This is so even when I have been very familiar with a tape. For example, less then a year prior to the reworking of this chapter, I took a 2-minute clip to a data analysis session with colleagues from four universities in Brisbane. Listening to what my peers had to say about the events shown in the tape, I realized a dimension that I had not attended to before. I then conducted a complete ethnomethodologically and conversation-analytically oriented re-analysis and, together with a colleague, published a paper on that feature that had become salient to me only while watching the tape with others (Roth and Gardner 2012). In my research group, we capitalize on such opportunities that arise from collective analysis. We often meet to collaboratively analyze a tape that someone brings to the session. These sessions are organized according to the principles of *Interaction Analysis* (Jordan and Henderson 1995). We play the tape, and whenever someone sees something of interest, we stop and begin to talk about what we have seen. We replay the fragment of interest as often as we deem necessary until we all feel to have said as much as we could. We then move on until someone calls for another stop. We usually do not get very far into the tape, and many times we did not get farther than 90 seconds or a few minutes; this is how rich even the shortest moments of human interaction can be.

Eventually I come to the point where I do not seem to have any more new insights. I then begin to go back through the notes, looking for patterns and organizing themes. I begin to write notes about my notes, leading to more comprehensive and encompassing statements about the events and the ways of participants to make sense of the situation they find themselves in. I also read related articles and books; new theoretical understanding and acquaintance with empirical research often lead me to new insights about what is going on in my own data. I usually work for many days, generating hundreds of typewritten pages of analysis, descriptions, theoretical commentaries, and worked-up transcripts.

Technologies and Tools

Conversation analysis began with audio recordings. As VCR and digital video technology became readily accessible and affordable, an increasing number of researchers not only used these means for doing research but also extended the analysis of interactions to include body movements and positions (e.g., Heath 1986). These recording means can be understood as part of the "estranging" task all anthropologists have to complete when they attempt making the familiar look strange (ten Have 2002). For many researchers, a digital camera will be a technology of choice. It allows recording in stereo, it is small enough to be taken into most places, and it is relatively unobtrusive. The stereo feature comes in handy during transcription, especially of multi-person talk. Using headphones one can hear the different directions of the voices, which aids in recovering who spoke and what was said. When using external microphones, depending on the make, the digital stereo feature may be lost.

For those using Macintosh computers, iMovie provides an ideal tool for digitizing video and for creating a variety of formats for self-contained movie files, which, because of their smaller size, are more easily stored on CD and shared. Self-contained movie files can be scanned rapidly, which is of great advantage for quickly finding fragments. For those who use archiving and analysis software to label fragments, they will need self-contained movie files. Finally, transcription programs require self-contained movies. A commercial version of Quicktime™ has been useful in our research. It permits the creation of shorter clips even after the production of self-contained movie files and the creation of self-contained sound tracks that are required for the analysis of prosody. This software also allows inserting captions, a nice feature when using video fragments during conference talks.

CLAN is one free, multi-platform piece of software developed at the University of Pittsburgh that I use for some purposes (http://childes.psy.cmu.edu/clan/). It can be operated both for transcribing and for conduction conversation analysis. Another transcription program designed to facilitate the transcription and analysis of video data is called *Transana*, and it is freely available (www.transana.org). Transana is available as both a single-user application and a multi-user version, which allows a local workgroup to share access to a single dataset. It provides a way to view video, create a transcript, and link places in the transcript to frames in the video. It provides tools for identifying and organizing analytically interesting portions of videos, as well as for attaching keywords to those video clips.

After having used a number of different software packages, I have found *PRAAT* (http://www.praat.org) the most useful and reliable across the voice ranges for which I conduct prosodic analysis – from seventh-grade students to practicing adult engineers, technicians, and scientists. Its multi-platform availability is of advantage to all those who collaborate a lot, which frequently has to occur across platforms. Furthermore, PRAAT allows creation of graphs in postscript and PICT formats (on the Macintosh platform), which can be shared between programs on the same machine and with collaborators.

POSSIBILITIES AND CONSTRAINTS

Conversation analysis has developed as, and continues to be, among others, a rather specific analytic endeavor concerned with the emergence of social relations and societal structure in and through *talk-in-interaction*. Over the decades, numerous researchers have found among its methods useful analytic tools to investigate a variety of phenomena not for the purpose of contributing to CA independent of the setting – the interests of "pure" CA (ten Have 1999) – but to contribute to understanding phenomena in their own disciplines, that is, applying CA to the problems and in the settings of interest. The concerns of these researchers have a decidedly applied character and perspective, concerned with various forms of institutional interactions. In this chapter, I exemplify a variety of concepts and procedures that educational researchers might find useful as resources in their own analysis of interesting societal and institutional phenomena.

Most generally, educators – even those who are not committed to social and cultural criticism – are in the business of contributing to change, for example, their students' knowledge and identity, and their and their students' world. Conversation analysis is a powerful tool as it allows us to explicate the ways in which conversationalists reproduce|transform societal order in ongoing, contingent, and highly efficient ways. That is, it is a powerful tool especially for the critical educator interested in how power/knowledge and social inequalities are brought about maintained in an ongoing manner. Its power arises from the fact that even if deconstruction is not part of a researcher's methodological agenda, it is a perspicuous factor of the ultimate descriptions a researcher arrives at (Lynch and Bogen 1996). Employed in concert with my video-based ethnographic efforts, CA has developed into my tool of choice.

Conversation analysis is, however, not a methodological panacea. CA does not provide us with the whole picture. Similar to the limitations that have been attributed to ethnomethodology (Chua 1977), CA allows us to get at how societal actors reproduce|transform societal relations, societal orders, and societal ideology; that is, it is concerned with the local organization of societal order. In this orientation, it does not allow us to understand the *external* determinations of structures that come from outside of the actors' point of view. That is, for example, CA can help us in explicating and understanding how Anne and Dan reproduce|transform societal relations in an interview/think-aloud-protocol situation, using a variety of cultural resources at hand, but it cannot get at the societal phenomenon of social scientists conducting interviews and think-aloud protocols; only a cultural-historical (Marxist) analysis of the division of labor leads us to the emergence of the phenomenon and its interpenetration with society as a whole. CA is, in a sense, loyal to the local and particularities of everyday life. It is a shopfloor perspective on the making of society. It therefore fails to move beyond the everyday and make connections with the macrolevel of society and imposes an ideological description on situations and people it studies (Smith 1999). That is, CA can get at the use and deployment of resources in the setting, but it cannot (normally) get us at the (external, structural) determination of (some of) these resources. Together with a critical (e.g., Marxist) theory, conversation analysis – as ethnomethodology (Freund and Abrams 1976), can be used to provide a critique of ideology and the production and dissemination of societal information. Both forms of research see societal knowledge inextricably linked to the situations in which and how it is produced. Critical educators, therefore, will want to appropriate CA into a critical theory that allows for and legitimates more activist stance to social life than is taken by CA and ethnomethodology.

NOTES

[1] In the work of my research group, we have found it helpful to unite pairs of mutually constitutive and presupposing mutually exclusive terms but to separate them with the Sheffer stroke "|." This creates a unit that embodies a contradiction, which in turn constitutes the motor of change (Goulart & Roth, in press).

[2] Conversation analysts make use of a transcription notation system that Gail Jefferson (e.g., 1989) developed over a period of years. Those listed below are the most commonly used. More complete discussion can be found in Heritage and Atkinson (1984), ten Have (1999), or Psathas and Anderson (1990).

A: [I'M] looking D: [Oh]	Brackets indicate the extent to which speech or actions overlap.
A: curves= D: =oh	Equal signs are used when there is no audible gap between two utterances next.
(0.56)	Pause measured in hundreds of a second are enclosed in single parentheses.
(.)	A dot in parentheses indicates a slight pause, less than 0.10 seconds long.
Faster	Underline indicates emphasis or stress in delivery.
YEA	Capital letters are used when a syllable, word, or phrase is louder than the surrounding talk.
A: S:o::	When a sound is longer than normal, each colon indicates approximately 0.1 of a second of lengthening.
A: Envi-	The n-dash marks a sudden stop in the utterance.
.,?	Punctuation marks are used to capture characteristics of speech rather than grammatical features.
.hh::	A dot prefixed "h" denotes inbreath; without dot, exhalation.
(stay out?)	The question mark following items enclosed in single parentheses denotes an uncertain hearing.
((circles))	Double parentheses enclose transcriber comments.
°Or?°	Degree signs enclose utterances produced with low speech intensity.

³ Throughout this chapter, I understand *activity* in the sense of cultural-historical activity theory (Roth, 2004a).
⁴ At the time of this writing (March 2013), Google Scholar lists at least 8835 citations for the "A simplest systematics." and over 4235 citations to the *Lectures*.
⁵ For the technical aspects of working with image and sound tracks, see the section below. Having tried out a number of different packages for working with the sound track, I have found PRAAT the most useful, versatile, and platform independent. The curves for the pitch and intensity graphs were produced within PRAAT and then saved in image format to receive further treatment in a graphics package (e.g., addition of text).
⁶ "Tympan" (Derrida, 1982) explicitly links the penetration of the ear by words, on the one hand, and the penetration of thought by a binary logic, on the other.

REFERENCES

Ashmore, M., & Reed, D. (2000). Innocence and nostalgia in conversation analysis: The dynamic relations of tape and transcript. *FQS: Forum Qualitative Sozialforschung/ Forum Qualitative Social Research* [Online journal], *1* (3). Available at URL: http://www.qualitative-research.net/fqs-texte/3-00/3-00ashmorereed-e.htm (Accessed December 17, 2004).

Au, K. H. (1980). Participation structures in a reading lesson with Hawaiian children: Analysis of a culturally appropriate instructional event. *Anthropology and Education Quarterly, 11*, 91–115.

Boden, D. (1994). *The business of talk: Organization in action*. Cambridge: Polity Press.

Chua, B. (1977). Delineating a Marxist interest in ethnomethodology. *The American Sociologist, 12*, 24–32.

Derrida, J. (1982). *Margins of philosophy*. Chicago: Chicago University Press.

Derrida, J. (1998). *Monolingualism of the Other; Or, The prosthesis of origin*. Stanford, CA: Stanford University Press.

Freund, P., & Abrams, M. (1976). Ethnomethodology and Marxism: Their use for critical theorizing. *Theory and Society, 3*, 377-393.

Garfinkel, H., & Sacks, H. (1986). On formal structures of practical action. In H. Garfinkel (Ed.), *Ethnomethodological studies of work* (pp. 160-193). London: Routledge & Kegan Paul.

Goodwin, C., Goodwin, M. H., & Yaeger-Dror M. (2002). Multi-modality in girls' game disputes. *Journal of Pragmatics 34*, 1621-1649.

Goulart, M.I.M., & Roth, W.-M. (2006). Margin|centre: Toward a dialectic view of participation. *Journal of Curriculum Studies, 36*, 679-700.

Have, P. ten (1999). *Doing conversation analysis: A practical guide*. London: Sage.

Have, P. ten (2002). The notion of member is the heart of the matter: On the role of membership knowledge in ethnomethodological inquiry. *FQS: Forum Qualitative Sozialforschung/Forum Qualitative Social Research* [Online journal], *3*(3). Available at URL: http://www.qualitative-research.net/fqs-texte/3-02/3-02tenhave-e.htm (Accessed December 21, 2004)

Heath, C. (1986). *Body movement and speech in medical interaction*. Cambridge: Cambridge University Press.

Heritage, J., & Atkinson, J. M. (1984). Introduction. In J. M. Atkinson & J. Heritage (Eds.), *Structures of social action: Studies in conversation analysis* (pp. 1-15). Cambridge: Cambridge University Press.

Jefferson, G. (1989). Preliminary notes on a possible metric which provides for a "standard maximum" silence of approximately one second in conversation. In D. Roger & P. Bull (Eds.), *Conversation: An interdisciplinary perspective* (pp. 166-196). Clevedon: Multilingual Matters.

Latour, B. (1999). *Pandora's hope: Essays on the reality of science studies*. Cambridge, MA: Harvard University Press.

Lynch, M., & Bogen, D. (1996). *The spectacle of history: Speech, text, and memory at the Iran-contra hearings*. Durham: Duke University Press.

Maynard, D. W., & Marlaire, C. L. (1992). Good reasons for bad testing performance: The interactional substrate of educational exams. *Qualitative Sociology, 15*, 177-202.

Maynard, D. W., & Schaeffer, N. C. (2000). Towards a sociology of social scientific knowledge: survey research and ethnomethodology's asymmetric alternates. *Social Studies of Science, 30*, 323-370.

McNeill, D. (1992). *Hand and mind: What gestures reveal about thought*. Chicago: University of Chicago.

McNeill, D., & Duncan, S. D. (2000). Growth points in thinking for speaking. In D. McNeill (Ed.), *Language and gesture* (pp. 141-161). Cambridge: Cambridge University Press.

Middleton, D., & Edwards, D. (1990). *Collective remembering*. London: Sage.

Müller, F. E. (1996). Affiliating and disaffiliating with continuers: Prosodic aspects of recipiency. In E. Couper-Kuhlen & M. Selting (Eds.), *Prosody in conversation: Interactional studies* (pp. 131-176). Cambridge: Cambridge University Press.

Orlikowski, W. J., & Yates, J. (2002). It's about time: Temporal structuring in organizations. *Organization Science, 13*, 684-700.

Pomerantz, A. (1984). Agreeing and disagreeing with assessments: Some features of preferred/dispreferred turn shapes. In J. M. Atkinson & J. Heritage (Eds.), *Structures of social action: Studies in conversation analysis* (pp. 57-101). Cambridge: Cambridge University Press.

Pozzer-Ardenghi, L., & Roth, W.-M. (2005). Photographs in lectures: Gestures as meaning-making resources. *Linguistics & Education, 15*, 275-293.

Psathas, G., & Anderson, T. (1990). The "practices" of transcription in conversation analysis. *Semiotica, 78*, 75-99.

Roth, W.-M. (2004a). Activity theory in education: An introduction. *Mind, Culture, & Activity, 11*, 1-8.

Roth, W.-M. (2004b). Perceptual gestalts in workplace communication. *Journal of Pragmatics, 36*, 1037-1069.

Roth, W.-M. (2005). Becoming like the other. In W.-M. Roth & K. Tobin (Eds.), *Teaching together, learning together* (pp. 27-51). New York: Peter Lang.

Roth, W.-M. (2007a). Emotion at work: A contribution to third-generation cultural historical activity theory. *Mind, Culture and Activity, 14*, 40-63.

Roth, W.-M. (2007b). Mathematical modeling 'in the wild': A case of hot cognition. In R. Lesh, J. J. Kaput, E. Hamilton, & J. Zawojewski (Eds.), *Users of mathematics: Foundations for the future* (pp. 77-97). Mahwah, NJ: Lawrence Erlbaum Associates.

Roth, W.-M. (2011). *Geometry as objective science in elementary classrooms: Mathematics in the flesh*. New York: Routledge.

Roth, W.-M. (2013a). *Meaning and mental representation: A pragmatic perspective*. Rotterdam, The Netherlands: Sense Publishers.

Roth, W.-M. (2013b). Translation in qualitative social research: The possible impossible. *Forum Qualitative Sozialforschung/Forum Qualitative Social Research, 14*(2).

Roth, W.-M. (2013c). *What more in/for science education: An ethnomethodological perspective*. Rotterdam, The Netherlands: Sense Publishers.

Roth, W.-M., & Gardner, R. (2012). "They're gonna explain to us what makes a cube a cube?" Geometrical properties as contingent achievement of sequentially ordered child-centered mathematics lessons. *Mathematics Education Research Journal, 24*, 323-346.

Roth, W.-M., & Middleton, D. (2006). The making of asymmetries of knowing, identity, and accountability in the sequential organization of graph interpretation. *Cultural Studies of Science Education, 1*, 11-81.

Roth, W.-M., & Tobin, K. (2010). Solidarity and conflict: Aligned and misaligned prosody as a transactional resource in intra- and intercultural communication involving power differences. *Cultural Studies of Science Education, 5*, 805-847.

Sacks, H. (1992a). *Lectures on conversation* vol. 1. Oxford: Basil Blackwell.

Sacks, H. (1992b). *Lectures on conversation*, Vol. 2. Oxford: Basil Blackwell.

Sacks, H., Schegloff, E., & Jefferson, G. (1974). A simplest systematics for the organization of turn taking for conversation. *Language, 50*, 696-735.

Schegloff, E., Jefferson, G., & Sacks, H. (1977). The preference for self-correction in the organization of repair in conversation. *Language, 53*, 361-382.

Smith, D. (1999). *Writing the social: Critique, theory, and investigations.* Toronto: University of Toronto Press.

Suchman, L. A., & Jordan, B. (1990). Interactional troubles in face-to-face survey interviews. *Journal of the American Statistical Association, 85*, 232-244.

Tobin, K., & McRobbie, C. J. (1996). Cultural myths as constraints to the enacted curriculum. *Science Education, 80*, 223-241.

WEB-BASED RESOURCES

Charles Antaki's website (Loughborough)—with practical guides to doing CA. URL: http://www-staff.lboro.ac.uk/~ssca1/sitemenu.htm

Many conversation analytic and ethnomethodological websites (individuals, resources) are indexed at a site for ethnomethodology and conversation analysis (ETHNO/CA NEWS) maintained by Paul ten Have URL: www.paultenhave.nl/EMCA.htm

Some readers may find Transana helpful for transcribing and linking video and transcript. It is available at URL: http://www.transana.org. Only the PC version is currently available (December 2004).

The downloadable files and manuals for the CLAN software can be found at URL: http://childes.psy.cmu.edu/clan/

PRAAT is a freely available program designed for linguists and has many features (http://www.praat.org/). I found it to give the best analyses of pitch, which depend both on the algorithm a program uses and the parameters chosen by the analyst.

Emmanuel Schegloff, a leading scholar and practitioner of conversation analysis, has made numerous papers available in PDF format on his website at URL: http://www.sscnet.ucla.edu/soc/faculty/schegloff/

Chuck Goodwin is an applied linguist who uses classical conversation analytic procedures, but also analyses body movements, body positions, and gestures as well as prosody. A number of his papers and chapters are available online at URL: http://www.sscnet.ucla.edu/clic/cgoodwin/

WIKIPEDIA provides some further introductory descriptions and resources at URL: http://en.wikipedia.org/wiki/Conversation_analysis

DAVID W. JARDINE

11. ON HERMENEUTICS

"Over and above Our Wanting and Doing"

> My real concern was and is … not what we do or what we ought to do, but what happens to us over and above our wanting and doing.
>
> Hans-Georg Gadamer, from *Truth and Method* (1989, p. xxviii)

I

> The hermeneutic phenomenon is basically not a problem of method at all. It is not concerned primarily with amassing verified knowledge, such as would satisfy the methodological ideal of science – yet it, too is concerned with knowledge and with truth. But what kind of knowledge and what kind of truth? (Gadamer 1989, p. xxii)
>
> I have retained the term "hermeneutics" … not in the sense of a methodology but as a theory of the real experience that thinking is. (p. xxxvi)

If hermeneutics is, as Hans-Georg Gadamer suggests, "basically not a problem of method at all," it would seem rather difficult to make a case for hermeneutics as a research method in education.

Hermeneutics may not provide us with a method, but it does give researchers and teachers and students an image of how human understanding operates in the world. It articulates how the world is a *living* world of *living* ancestry that perennially has to take up the task presented by the arrival of the new and the young into that living world. As such, it provides a way to re-think what we experience in our day to day lives as teachers, what we understand teaching to be, what we imagine about the relations between the young and the old, what we understand knowledge and tradition and language and conversation and art and play and imagination and words and images and the methods of the sciences to be. This by-no-means exhaustive array of topics are all dealt with in *Truth and Method*, Gadamer's profound, beautiful and terribly difficult work, originally published in German in 1960 and first translated into English in 1975.

In this chapter, I want to show how hermeneutics has a special affinity to education. It is not simply that hermeneutics is particularly well suited to education as an object of scholarly investigation. More than this, hermeneutics, as a way of conducting research, is educative in its intent. It wants to listen, to affect and to invite, not merely inform. But there is an even strong affinity between hermeneutics and education. Hermeneutics is also, I suggest, a way of conducting classroom life. My work has been focussed for several years now on classroom events–not only interpreting them using hermeneutics as a way of understanding, but showing how, in effective, intellectually stimulating classrooms, *teaching and learning themselves can be hermeneutic in character* (e.g., Jardine, Clifford and Friesen 2006). This itself is a hermeneutic point. Our choice of research methodologies is, of necessity, a choice regarding how understanding happens and what sort of voice is given to the "object" of such research. Therefore, our choice of research methodologies is a deeply pedagogical choice *at the outset*, before any research project has begun.

This case regarding the pedagogical character of hermeneutics can be made because hermeneutics has, at its heart, the belief that understanding occurs and can be properly cultivated and cared for only in the often contentious, often transformative, *relationship between* the young and the old, the new and the established, between ancestral bloodlines and what Hannah Arendt (1969, p. 177) called "the fact of natality." *"The true locus of hermeneutics is this in-between"* (Gadamer 1989, p. 295), as one might expect from a theory of experience named after a god of borders and boundaries who, sometimes trickster in intent (Jardine, Clifford and Friesen 2003), sometimes monstrous (e.g., Jardine 1998; Jardine and Field 2006; Jardine and Novodvorski 2006), shuttles messages between heaven and earth, between the gods and humanity.

II

For those who have struggled to find their way through the first part of Gadamer's *Truth and Method*, it is often very difficult to understand exactly why, in introducing hermeneutics, he begins by talking about "aesthetic experience." This seems very far away from anything that might help us understand the classroom, or the curriculum or how to do educational research.

Gadamer's talk of "aesthetic experience" is not about developing a theory of "art appreciation" (although it certainly has a profound relevance for such development). He is discussing aesthetic experience as an introduction to the nature of hermeneutics. He is pointing to a commonplace experience that any teacher knows about full well. Before we adopt any methodological stance, before we "do" any research, before we know it, we enter a classroom and something that a student says, some work that they have produced, something they have written, some question they ask, the look in one child's eyes, some sketch posted on a bulletin board–these simple things sometimes *strike* us, *catch* our fancy, *address* us, *speak* to us, *call* for a response, *elicit* or *provoke* something in us, *ask* something of us, *hit* us, *bowl* us over, *stop* us in our tracks, makes us *catch our breath*.

This initiatory phenomenon of hermeneutics must be thought about phenomenologically and experientially:

Things announce themselves, bear witness to their presence: "Look, here we are." They regard us beyond how we may regard them, our perspectives, what we intend with them, and how we dispose of them. (Hillman 1982, p. 77)

Rich and memorable experiences catch our attention and ask things of us. As such, the venture of coming to understand such things is characterizable as "more a passion than an action. A question *presses itself upon us*" (Gadamer 1989, p. 366, my emphasis) and places us and our being-in-the-world into question.

This is what Gadamer means by suggesting that, at the core of hermeneutics, at the core of "what happens to us over and above our wanting and doing," is something akin to an "aesthetic experience." Aesthetic experience, Gadamer suggests, is the experience of being drawn out of our subjectivity and into a teeming world of relations that lives "beyond our wanting and doing." The task posed to understanding at such a juncture cannot be simply one of corralling that teeming world back into the confines of our constructs.

In these aesthetic moments we are drawn out of ourselves and our constructions and our methods and our "our"-centeredness and get caught up by something, charmed by it, drawn into *its* sway, into *its* play, into *its Spiel*. (This is why, after exploring aesthetic experience, Gadamer then turns, in *Truth and Method* [1989, pp. 101-109] to the ways in which play is a clue to understanding what happens to us in understanding the world.) Such events–such moments of "opening" and of "venture" – "would not deserve the interest we take in [them] if [they] did not have something to teach us that we could not know by ourselves" (Gadamer 1989, p. xxxv). Like monsters in fairy tales, they wouldn't whisper to us or stop us in our tracks if they didn't have something to tell us.

Hermeneutics is, therefore, implicitly a critique of a particular way in which constructivism has been conceived. We can only suggest what is entailed here (e.g., Jardine 2005, 2006; Jardine, Fawcett and Johnson 2006).

There are some lines from a poem by Rainer Marie Rilke that Gadamer cites as the frontispiece of *Truth and Method*: "Catch only what you've thrown yourself, all is mere skill and little gain. But when you're suddenly the catcher of a ball thrown. – towards you, to your center – why catching then becomes a power – not yours, a world's." What addresses us does so from beyond our wanting and doing, beyond our constructs. We experience the limits of our experience by experiencing something that calls us to go beyond the limits of our experience. Less philosophically put, we live in the world and that world houses us and our thinking and experiencing. We do not house it in our constructs. This, of course, is an *ecological* and a *pedagogical* point as much as it is a commentary on research methodologies in education.

Gadamer (2001) put it so simply: "something awakens our interest–that is really what comes first!" (p. 50). "Understanding," Gadamer insists, "begins ... when something addresses us" (1989, p. 299). Hermeneutics goes further even than this. It wants to show that, within this beginning, originary experience of being addressed is some sort of "truth claim," (Gadamer 1989, p. xxii) although, of course, what is meant here will need the rest of the chapter and more to fill out.

III

In a chapter on hermeneutics as a "research method" in education, you might expect someone to tell you *how to do it*. But this way of proceeding towards understanding–starting with explicitly laying procedures on the "how to" of understanding – is a contentious matter in hermeneutics itself and understanding why this is so helps in our understanding of hermeneutics and its ways.

There is a brief, lovely, difficult passage from *Truth and Method* (1989, p. 21) that will help us here: "Youth demands images for its imagination and for forming its memory. Thus [Giambattista] Vico [b. 1668] supplements the *critica* of Cartesianism with the old *topica*." Gadamer is suggesting that anyone new to something ("youth," so to speak – Vico's *pedagogical* point is not necessarily or solely a *chronological* one) cannot begin the task of coming to understand through being told what *method* to use (*critica*, from Rene Descartes [b. 1596] *Discourse on Method* [1955]). A method has no face, no body, no memories, no stories, no blood, no images, no ancestors, no ghosts and spirits, no monsters, no familiars. It doesn't help us get our bearings and learn our way around, because there is no "place" to it. The young, as Jean Piaget so well attests, are imaginal, playful, bodily beings in their coming to understand (see Jardine 2005).

Hermeneutics does not begin its work by beginning with method. It does not begin by characterizing understanding as an action or set of actions we can marshal. It begins, rather, with *topica* – great image-filled, sensory, alluring *topics* that address us and draw us into their sway and ask things of us. To re-cite Gadamer's claims, "*something* awakens our interest" (2001, p. 50, emphasis added), "*something* addresses us" (1989, p. 299, emphasis added).

The first question in hermeneutics is "What is your topic?" because in pursuit of an answer to this question, memory is formed, images are entertained, thinking is enriched by traversing the terrain, the place, the topography, with all is shapes and ancestors and old stories and vital new arrivals. Hermeneutics begins substantively, with a topic that addresses us and draws us in. "*What* is being investigated itself holds part of the answer concerning *how* it should be investigated" (Smith 1999, p. 39). Part of the task of hermeneutics is learning how to "entrust ourselves to what we are investigating to guide us safely in the quest" (Gadamer 1989, p. 378).

This probably seems really odd on the face of it because this description of hermeneutics still has no face. Hermeneutics can only start to substantively and imaginatively appear in the face of "a case" (even though hermeneutics does not produce "case studies"). It is always *something* that happens that awakens our interest in pursuing interpretation.

There is always a story that happened once upon a time.

IV

A former student teacher phoned me in a panic late one August, excited that she had been offered a job in an Early Childhood Education classroom starting the next week and, of course, apprehensive about all that might entail. She phoned, I suspect, as much for reassurance as for advice. Eight weeks later, well into the school year, she phoned again and recounted the experience of going to her new school just days before the children were to arrive.

The principal was not available when she arrived, and she was instructed by the school secretary that her room was "down there, Room 10." She had walked down the hallway to what was to be "her room" and paused. The door was shut and she spoke of this shut door being "imposing," "as if something was going on in there already" that of which she was not yet part of, something to which she did not yet "belong." As she told it, she knew that when she opened that door, somehow, "everything would be different," things would be, in her words "turned around." She sensed that, once she "stepped in," she would be finally "crossing over" from student to teacher: "once I entered the room, I knew that would be *it*."

Here is where hermeneutics can start to work. This incident, in its very commonplaceness and simplicity, was full of address for me when it occurred. These new teacher's words sound familiar. "Something is going on" (*im Spiele ist*)," "something is happening" (*sich abspielt*) (Gadamer 1989, p. 104) (note how both these etymological twists in the German terms dovetail with *Truth and Method*'s interest in play, *Spiel* – a love of etymology gets cultivated as you become practiced in hermeneutics [Smith 1999, p. 39]).

I expect, at first blush, that we have all had similar experiences to the sorts of things this new teacher seems to be articulating or alluding to. In some sense, and to some degree, we all understand what this new teacher is talking about. On the face of it, we sort of "get" it. Her tale is familiar, familial, something with which we already have deep, unvoiced "kinship" (Wittgenstein 1968, p. 36), something to which our own lives and what we've experienced of the life of teaching somehow bear a "family resemblance" (p. 32). We live together in a world in which such things are not especially extraordinary to say.

In the face of this *prima facie* sense of kinship, the hermeneutic question is this: How are we to do justice to this particular episode that happened to a particular teacher at a particular time and place, while at once respecting the undeniable sense of kinship we experience in hearing this teacher's tale? Again, the moment of address occurs somehow "between" this new eruption of life and some older that is awoken.

Hermeneutics requires that we attempt to experience this happenstance incident as, so to speak, "speaking to us," having something to say to us beyond what we might be able, as yet, to say of it. Imagine this. I stood at the closed door and knew that when I walked through, everything would be different. This incident, taken up hermeneutically:

> draws us [*both* parties to that telephone call] – outside of ourselves [this is not "teacher narrative" owned by any one of us] and imposes its own

presence on us. [It] no longer has the character of an object that stands over against us; we are no longer able to approach this like an object of knowledge, grasping, measuring and controlling. Rather than meeting us in our world, it is much more a world into which we ourselves are drawn (Gadamer 1994, pp. 191-192)

Those new teacher's comments seem "surrounded" by living *worlds* of relations, worlds full of images, faces, concepts, rituals, bloodlines, invocations, spooks and sprits. They are "familiar." And those surroundings seem to already surround me, since it seems that I am already living in a familiarity with that world.

Hermeneutics is therefore pointing to something very commonplace, but also something very odd to articulate in the context of research methodologies: "a hitherto concealed experience that transcends thinking from the position of subjectivity" (Gadamer 1989, p. 100).

To cite again from Rilke's frontispiece "Not yours, a world's."

V

At this juncture, part of the work of understanding hermeneutics is to understand aspects of its reflections on the treatment usually given to such incidents in most research methodologies that we have inherited. Hermeneutics is, in part, a critique of the ways that the human sciences have methodologically, epistemologically and ontologically "aped" the natural sciences to terrible, damaging, effect. More bluntly put, hermeneutics provides a critique of how *education* has become spellbound by a weak and intellectually dull-minded version of the methodologies of the natural sciences. Differently put, the following ancestral exploration can be read as a description of the situation that teachers and students often experience at school. We can only untangle a few small threads of this inheritance in this context.

"A substance is that which requires nothing except itself in order to exist" (Descartes 1955, p. 275). This is a longstanding definition, cited here from Descartes (seventeenth century) but winding its way back into the work of Thomas Aquinas (thirteenth century) and from there, back into Aristotelian metaphysics (third century B.C.E.). I cite it here because for much work in educational research (quantitative and qualitative alike), the fundamental given (the root of the notion of "data" as "that which is given or granted") in research is *not* that original, ambiguously alluring familiarity that first strikes us when we hear this new teacher's words about going to her school for the first time. What is given in those methodologies for which this Cartesian idea of substance holds sway is *not* a world into which we are drawn. Rather, what is strictly given is this new teacher's words is an "isolated incident."

The literal text produced by this particular teacher at this particular time in this particular situation-this, severed from all its abundant familiarity, severed from our interest in it, severed from what we think it means or what worlds it reminds us of– this "that which requires nothing except itself in order to exist." This is the substance of (most forms of) research. In light of this pronouncement about the substance of this incident, all that compelling familiarity is henceforth understood to be *subjective*, an added, distortive, contaminating "extra" that we "bring" to the in-fact isolated, "in itself" thing and somehow lay over top of it as a layer of subjective response or the like. What was initially experienced as the address of something from beyond the confines of subjectivity is, in this way, rendered subjective (see Gadamer's discussion of the "subjectivization of aesthetics" [1989, pp. 42-80]; see also Jardine and Batycky 2006). Both quantitative and qualitative methodologies fall for this move.

Against this premise of isolated substances, we make this incident into something portioned off from anything else except itself. We have to rescue it from its familiarity, because the familiarity it evokes in us is, we presume, a *contamination* of its being what it in fact is. Therefore we must begin by systematic acts of severance aimed at retrieving the given ("the isolated incident") out of the amorphous web of interweaving meanings in which it was originally embedded and in whose abundant embrace it first appeared. We must sever any interconnections that are already at work before the methods of our inquiry are enacted. We must (ideally, at least) put out of play any understanding of or connection to this instance that we may have as researchers. We must suspend any spontaneous familiarity or sense of kinship that it evokes in us, any sort of aesthetic appeal or experiential reminders or reminiscences. We must also put out of play any interconnections we see or suspect between this instance and any other meanings or tales or stories or narratives. We must stop dreaming that the world has something to say to us.

These two acts of severance-this instance from us and our lived familiarity with and attraction to it, and this instance from any and all other instances-will allow it to become a self-identical substance, something that stands "without us" and without reference to any other incident. Thus severed, it no longer signifies or signals anything beyond itself. It becomes, as far as we know thus far, "an isolated incident," just itself and nothing more.

This is a fascinating process to which we subject both the instance and ourselves. It is, as we have alluded, akin to a sort of purification ritual (Bordo 1988, p. 108) that both we and the instance must undergo. Regarding the instance itself, ambiguous linkages and telltale signs and marks of potentially violating interconnectedness are systematically eliminated, producing of a sort of virginal, untouched instance. And regarding ourselves, we can no longer approach this instance with the moist and fleshy and playful and imaginative familiarity with which we began. We must now simply "behold" it with what Alfred North Whitehead named the "celibacy of the intellect" (cited in Fox 1983, p. 23). We must remain strictly within the parameters of the methods of severance we have enacted, for any other interconnection would despoil or defile the instance we have so carefully and methodically isolated and purified. Our connection to this instance thus becomes gutted. We understand it "from the neck up" and only within the bounds that our severing and isolating methodology allows. We deny that it is our kin. We begin our work with "abandonment" (Arendt 1969, p. 188) and "betrayal" (1969, p. 196).

"I don't know anything. I've never seen it before. It's not mine. It doesn't point to me. I'm not implicated." Severance has freed us from our kinships and dependencies. I'm just an anonymous, replaceable, controllable, predictable, method-wielder now. My only connection to this incident will be forged *after* and *as a consequence of* and *solely within the parameters of* my "methodology."

There is an aside here that is simply astounding. The researcher has been purged of dark and lingering familiarities and the incident, too, has been isolated from its world of relations.

This spins us back to Descartes and his Aristotelian notion of substance. Isolated, purified, self-identical substances – *objects*, one might say – *contain no contradictions*:

> Descartes' emphasis on clear and distinct ideas ... served to canonize the Aristotelian principle of non-contradiction. Since the Cartesian paradigm recognizes no self-contradictions in logic, and since logic (or geometry), according to Descartes, is the way nature behaves, the paradigm allows for no self-contradiction in nature. (Berman 1983, p. 23)

The clean and clearly isolated instance is what it is without reference to anything else (the principle of identity [A=A] that underwrites the principle of non-contradiction [it either is A or it isn't A]). The isolated incident is what it is only *without* all its relations. Individual, self-contained, autonomous, self-existing things come first.

A more direct and familiar way of putting this process is that, through these severances of the original familiarity in which we were immersed and which addressed and charmed us in the first place, we render this instance into *an object* and, correlatively, render ourselves into a *knowing subject* which has this object, not as something to which we belong and have a kinship or relation, but as something standing over against us and is allowed, now, to appear only within the confines of the methods that knowing subject wields. The instance as object now no longer draws us into a world. It no longer is experienced as fitting into a complex fabric of interrelations in which I ambiguously belong with it, but rather "stands out," isolated from what surrounds it.

From this original severance thus begins a long series of correlative purification movements between this instance and myself as inquirer. "Subject and object precipitate out simultaneously. Yet even while separate, they remain interdependent, because the breakdown in the world [i.e., the tearing of the instance out of the fabric of familiarity in which it originally lived] corresponds to a breakdown in understanding" (Weinsheimer 1987, p. 5). Once divested of the original, intimate knowing, I can no longer claim to understand this now severed object. That original allure never was *knowing the object*. It was just subjective. Although I might have experienced this original allure as a matter of the object drawing me into *its* orbit, in fact (according to the ontological assumptions of this way of proceeding) it was a matter of *me* drawing the object into *my* orbit.

In this way, "both subject and object are derivative and secondary, in that both precipitate out of the more primordial unity of being at home in the world" (Weinsheimer 1987, p. 5), a "being at home" bespoken by the fact that I somehow "already understood" what this teacher said before the specific work of rendering it an object of research even began. This precipitated subject and precipitated object "are [both] determined negatively: the knowing subject [now severed from our original senses of familiarity] no longer understands and the object [now severed from its living context of familiarity and kin] no longer fits" (p. 5).

Now "real research" can finally begin because we finally have an "object" to research. Before these severances, we had a *topica*. Now, as a consequence of *critica*, we no longer have a topic. We have an object-domain to which we do not belong and in relation to which "belonging" doesn't even make sense.

These fundamental acts of severance and the convoluted sequence of correlative purification transformations in both the object of inquiry and the inquirer, give subsequent research peculiar and deliberate anonymity and rootlessness. When we hear this new teacher's talk about the anxieties of opening the classroom door for the first time and entering in, all we can do is set up a research project in which we can collect a lot of new teacher's talk and then check whether or not a significant number of "respondents" will cite the same experiences, use the same words and concepts, speak in the same terms in their reports of their own experiences as beginning teachers. Because we have actively and intentionally reduced this instance to an isolated incident, it becomes essential to collect more and more incidents in order to raise this first incident out of its isolation. An interesting turn of events: we raise these incidents out of their isolation through first isolating them and then rescuing them (us?) from their (our?) isolation by finding frequently occurring themes.

Because we have actively and intentionally restricted ourselves to that knowledge produced methodologically, it becomes illegitimate to engage these instances in ways other than simply collecting them and looking for surfaces features. This first instance becomes significant (that is to say, it points to something beyond itself) only insofar as it can now be shown to reoccur in a (mathematically) significant number of other equally actively isolated incidents. Significance thus becomes intimately linked with *frequency*. This happens to the extent that, even in qualitative studies, some still ask how many people they should talk to in their research interviews and how many transcripts must mention some term before my qualitative understanding is adequately and warrantably "saturated."

The interest of such a mathematization of significance is not to better understand the world(s) into which this incident has drawn our attention. The purpose is not to cultivate a place of commiseration and conversation and reflection and thinking and scholarly investigation into this *topica* that has addressed us. Rather, the purpose is to be better able to control, predict, and manipulate the future reoccurrences of such talk (Habermas 1972). Obviously, however, we might be able to say with great assurance what the future statistical likelihood is of a beginning teacher using the terms we have coded and counted, without having considered for a moment *what is being said,* what worlds are being invoked by such terms.

Above, we mentioned that, following upon the methodical severances of our familiarity with the world, there is a correlative negative determination of both object (which now no longer fits) and subject (who now no longer understands):

> The cognitive remedies for these twin defects are likewise correlative. The object is disassembled, the rules of its functioning are ascertained, and then it is reconstructed according to those rules; so, also, knowledge is analysed, its rules are determined, and finally it is redeployed as method. The purpose of both remedies is to prevent unanticipated future breakdowns by means of breaking down even further the flawed entity and then synthesizing it artificially. Thus Gadamer speaks of "the ideal of knowledge familiar from natural science, whereby we understand a process only when we can bring it about artificially" [Gadamer 1989, p. 336]. (Weinsheimer 1987, p. 6)

Once these "cognitive remedies" are enacted, we can (within mathematically prescribed limits) predict the reoccurrence of such incidents and therefore we no longer are "taken aback" by such reoccurrence. Such incidents will not allure us again and catch us off guard, with all the disorienting and disturbing consequences that such allure can have. These remedies prevent the possibility of understanding being provoked by something unwittingly and without methodical anticipation. Thus, "objectification" protects us from dangerous unanticipated turns that the world might take. This is precisely the strength of this sort of research. It rules out of consideration unanticipated ("uncontrolled for") interchanges with the world.

Of course, the methodical attainment of such objectivity does not altogether prevent playful, risk laden, unanticipated interchanges. Things still happen. However, their happenstance occurrence is divested of any claim of or access to truth.

Truth and method become identified.

VI

Hermeneutics doesn't drag us through difficult terrain like this in order to "philosophize." It does so because this terrain is *one of the things that has happened to us.* Reflecting on such matters helps us think through what has happened to our ability to understand what comes to meet us in our experience. Doing a hermeneutic study requires this sort of work because hermeneutics contends that we have inherited a world full of images and assumptions and desires that affect how we might imagine the very existence and status and worth and place of those new teacher's comments.

Hermeneutics steadfastly holds that these incidents happen and have their meaning and significance *in the world.* Part of the real work of hermeneutic research is to let us deeply experience how deliciously and terribly difficult is the task of wanting to *understand* the great inheritances of human life in the midst of which this new teacher's words appeared. Hermeneutics isn't a psychology. The inner thoughts and feelings of this student's private interiority are not its topic. Her comments' arrival makes *the world* of teaching "waver and tremble" (Caputo 1987, p. 7). Her comments call ancient tales to account. And her comments do so "beyond [her] wanting and doing."

It is precisely the identification of truth and method that hermeneutics works against. The title of Gadamer's major work is not as simple as it seems. Hermeneutics suggests that there is a "truth" to be had, an understanding to be reached, an experience to be savoured in the provocative, unmethodical incidents of our lives that address us, a truth which is despoiled and thus left out of consideration by the methodical severances and isolation requisite of much qualitative and quantitative research work.

So, to begin again elsewhere. This new teacher's comments arrive. I've heard this before, somewhere. Something is going. "In this short passage, we have an embarrassment of symbolic riches" (Turner 1987, p. 18) – multiple meanings, "interweaving and criss-crossing" (Wittgenstein 1968, p. 32) (*textus* originally means "to weave," like textiles):

> The term "initiation" in the most general sense denotes a body of rites and oral teachings whose purpose is to produce a radical modification of the person to be initiated. Initiation is equivalent to an ontological mutation of the existential condition. The novice emerges from his ordeal a totally different being: he has become *another*. (Eliade 1975, p. 112)

Are this new teacher's words signs of initiation and transformation? Are they heralds of "becoming *another*?" The hermeneutic question at this juncture is not "Is this what is somehow 'really' going on in this teacher's words?" as if there was some objective template in the world against which such a claim could be measured. The hermeneutic question clusters like this: "What *difference* does it make if we read these words this way? What possibilities open up? What images and tales and ways of acting in the classroom become warranted? What dangers arrive? What dragons be here?"

We are not "amassing verified knowledge" (Gadamer 1989, p. xxii) here. We are playfully teasing out a territory and learning its ways and asking what relief might be found in allowing this new teacher's words to "world" (Heidegger 1962) in this way. This teacher's words can be heard to re-tell ancient and power-laden narratives of initiation and transformation, "insiders" and "outsiders," thresholds and boundaries, liminal spaces and monsters. They are full of images of rites of passage and moving from child to adult and back again (because, of course, once she "enters the room" and turns around, the child will be at the door wanting in). And let's add to the mix the offhand comments of an elementary school principal: "I enjoy having student-teachers in the school. It keeps things lively, keeps us on our toes. And anyway, it's our responsibility. The profession needs new blood." If these moments are allowed to "expand to their full breadth of illuminative meaning" (Norris-Clarke 1976, p. 188), this principal's words, along with that new teacher's words, echo down into a rich "implicate order" (Bohm 1983) of metaphors, mythologies and traditions. They contain images of education's relation to and responsibility for the young, as well as images of the mysterious "liminal period" (Turner 1969) indicated by the hyphenation "student-teacher." The movement through such "threshold times" (Mahdi et al. 1987, p. ix) is full of "ambiguity and paradox, a confusion of all customary categories" (Turner 1987, p. 7) and as such, the tales told of such times lend themselves to a discourse that is itself "incurably figurative and polysemous" (Clifford 1986, p. 5) – just the sort of thing that Vico suggests the young need for the cultivation of their memory and character. Just the sort of literature that might help a student-teacher understand the terrible ambiguity of her task.

Ok, here's a warning It is easy to have a hermeneutic meditation get out of hand. Hermeneutics is necessarily, not accidentally, prone to exaggeration (Gadamer 1989, p. 115) and hyperbole (Hargreaves 2005) – flights of over-abundant fantasy. We don't know yet if we are going too far, whether there is any truth to be had. But this much is true about doing hermeneutic work: it has *already begun*. The unfolding and exploring and articulating of and writing about the venture into these worldly possibilities *is* the work of "doing" hermeneutics. We have already started to lay out the shapes of a possible way to understand the experience of teaching and its manifestation in the ordinary talk of a new teacher and an old principal.

This much is true as well. Interpretive research begins with a different sense of the given. Rather than beginning with an ideal of clarity, distinctness, and methodological controllability–all consequences of the presumption of isolated substances – and then rendering the given in light of this ideal, hermeneutics begins in the place where we actually start in being granted or given (*datum*) this incident in the first place. Hermeneutics begins (and remains) with the evocative, living familiarity that this tale started to evoke in the first place–that address, that strange familiarity or weird seemliness, that old memory of having read words like this before, felt moments like this in the hallways of schools. The task of interpretation is not to clarify and straighten out this mess. It is, rather, to bring out this evocative given in all its tangled ambiguity, to follow its evocations and the entrails of sense and significance that are wound up with it and not "betray" it (see Caputo 1987) with promises of isolation and clarity and cleanliness.

Hermeneutics suggests that these striking incidents make a claim on us and open up and reveal something to us about our lives together and what it is that is going on, often unvoiced, in the ever-so commonplace and day-to-day act of being and becoming a teacher. In this sense, our unanticipated, unmethodical being in the world–this happenstance phone call from a former student and her tale of walking down a hallway and standing by a closed door – can, quite literally in certain instances, make a claim to some sort of truth.

Teachers are drawn to this story of this student-teacher because it "rings true" to the lives they have led, to moments they have faced, to monsters in education's closet.

Something is waking up here at the edge of familiarity.

VII

We need to ask here the inevitable question: How do I know that this reading I have given this instance is reliable? "What kind of truth" (Gadamer 1989, p. xxii) are we dealing here? How do I know I'm not just delusional, spooked by Descartes' demons or black biles?

Well, I don't know all by myself or in advance or through the assurance of having properly applied a particular method. I cannot separate out in advance which features of my reading of this incident reveal nothing more than idiosyncrasies of my individual experiences. "This separation must take place in the process of understanding itself" (Gadamer 1989, p. 296) and a hermeneutic study, in part, is the articulating of this process, not simply the articulating of the *end-product* of this process. I can only find out about the revelations and distortions that my life brings to the images haunting that phone call from a new teacher by *working such matters out*. And I have to work these matters out *in public*–in writing, in talking to colleagues, in reciting this incident to new student teachers and listening to the buzz that is created, in reading more and thinking more, and therefore in letting the potential distortions of my subjectivity work themselves out into a worldly territory that can comfort and contain and cultivate and limit and, sometimes, humiliate them.

This incident happened 15 years ago, and it still has me in its grip. I'm still "working on it."

Interpretation thus becomes a movement of shaping and making something of this instance and its human topographies, while, at the same time, shaping and making something of myself in the midst of this world in which I work as a teacher, a writer, a scholar, a parent, and so on. Differently put, I become someone in the process of coming to know about the world in which I live. This is why Gadamer (1989) links up hermeneutics, understanding, and the cultivation of character (*Bildung*). I have to let my pre-understandings and prejudices and presumptions fully engage this new teacher's words. I have to bring what I thought I knew about this world of teaching under the witness of these words and see what happens. Hermeneutics is thus not a form of methodological imperviousness but is, rather, precisely the opposite. I must let what I have come to know about this world be susceptible to being supplemented, enhanced, transformed, further-changed, embarrassed, perhaps even humiliated, in confronting what this teacher's text has to say (Gadamer 1989, p. 299) about this world of teaching. I don't get to say all by myself what will happen, how things will work out, how comments will be understood or whether the work will continue. Teachers know all about this.

Hermeneutics is therefore already operating in a pedagogical space. The fact that I happened to have read and vaguely remembered Mircea Eliade's work on initiation, the fact that I happened to have been called by this teacher and to have been struck by what she said – all of these "happenstances" make possible the interpretation that will then ensue (Weinsheimer 1987, p. 78). The interpretation that results is thus unavoidably linked to me. It is not something produced by an anonymously wielded method that anyone could wield and get the same results.

However – and here is the paradox – *what* the interpretation is henceforth *about*, is not "me" but that topography *of which* I have had certain experiences: initiation. Initiation and its kin form a world in which I am "housed." They are not housed inside of me.

This hermeneutic insistence is rooted in Edmund Husserl's (1970, pp. 12-13) phenomenological admonishment that "consciousness is always consciousness *of* something." Human experience is *intentional*, not psychopathological. Therefore, when students say that they are interested in children's experiences, the hermeneutically proper question is "Children's experiences *of what*? What is the topic, what is the terrain, in which you wish to meet children and understand their ways?" Hermeneutically conceived, people don't "have" experiences. They have experiences of something and therefore, "experience" does not delineate an interiority that has to be deciphered through matching up this new teacher's comments to her real, inner, private, individual, "moist gastric intimacy" (Sartre 1970, p. 4). Hermeneutically, we are *had* by experience. We suffer it or undergo experiences. We do not possess them. Experience, hermeneutically conceived, is something that happens to us over and above our wanting and doing. To re-iterate something that might now be a bit clearer, hermeneutics is concerned with "a hitherto concealed experience that transcends thinking from the position of subjectivity" (Gadamer 1989, p. 100).

Even though interpretive work is not possible without a living connection to its topic, it is *the topic* that is the centre of interpretive work. My experiences with such topics are not "interior states" that subjectivize the living phenomenon of initiation and rites of passage into something of *mine* (any more than I would subjectivize that new teacher's words into her property). On the contrary, for hermeneutic work, my experiences are best understood as ventures or journeys through something. In *Truth and Method*, this is why so much discussion occurs regarding the difference between the two German terms for "experience": *Erlebnisse* (1989, pp. 60-80) and *Erfahrung* (pp. 346-361). *Erlebenisse* is etymologically linked to the intimacies of one's inner life (*Leben*, to live). *Erfahrung* contains the roots both of a journey (*Fahren*) and of ancestry (*Vorfahren*).

This latter usage says that our experience is worldly and haunted by those who have journeyed before us. It suggests that, in the classroom, we do not meet students as isolated individual subjectivities. We meet them as worldly beings in the world, say, of poetry or mathematics or the like.

VIII

The question remains: What kind of truth is being proffered by a hermeneutic study? Clearly, the truth of a hermeneutic study cannot be that its claims match up to some objective state of affairs. The reliability of a hermeneutic study is not that it matches up to a world that existed "in and of itself" before that interpretation ensued. If this were the case, interpretation would be an overlay. Hermeneutics is not "objective research" in this dated sense. Its "truth" is not found in its correspondence to objective states of affairs.

Hermeneutics draws the pre-Socratic image of *alethia* for its understanding of the "truth" of hermeneutics. First, *alethia* means to open up what was previously shut, to show what was previously concealed, to uncover that which was covered over, to make present that which was absent, to say that which was silent. It was precisely this sense of "something opening up" that that new teacher's comments provoked. Something seemed to be an open question again, not a closed concept. To understand those ordinary comments as true is to cultivate in ourselves the ability to experience them as an opening into a heretofore closed or occluded field of relations and memories and ancestries and conversations and contestations. Initiation, it seems, is not a closed case. It is still "open for the future" (Gadamer 1989, p. 340) and these incidental comments of a new teacher have effected such opening into a world. These comments are, in this sense, "true." They are true because, insofar as it is part of the living human inheritance, "initiation" it is not isolated or fixed or finished but is, rather, open to being taken up anew in ways that are beyond our wanting and doing. When we are able to experience it this way, as "standing in a horizon of ... still undecided future possibilities" (Gadamer 1989, p. 112), we are able to experience its truth. When it is just a dead theme under which teacher's comments silently "fall," it is no longer true in this "hermeneutic" sense. There is nothing "true" about a "theme" under which instances fall except in those moments where some incident opens up to questions and susceptibility and risk what the theme might mean in ways that render it "in play" again, open, again, to the arrival of the new case and the difference that new case might bring.

But there is a fundamental caution here in hermeneutic work. Opening up, of necessity, closes off as well. These glimpses of the living human inheritance are susceptible to calcification, sedimentation. Opening up does not "amass" like verified knowledge. *Alethia*, as a privative term, always reminds us that truth, in this hermeneutic sense, is a dance between revealing and concealing, between opening up and closing off:

> One has to ask oneself whether the dynamic law of human life can be conceived adequately in terms of progress, of a continual advance from the unknown into the known, and whether the course of human culture is actually a linear progression from mythology to enlightenment. One should entertain a completely different notion: whether the movement of human existence does not issue in a relentless inner tension between illumination and concealment. Might it not just be a prejudice of modern times that the notion of progress that is in fact constitutive for the spirit of scientific research should be transferable to the whole of human living and human culture? One has to ask whether progress, as it is at home in the special field of scientific research, is at all consonant with the conditions of human existence in general. Is the notion of an ever-mounting and self-perfecting enlightenment finally ambiguous? (Gadamer 1983, pp. 104-105)

In making something of the vivid intersections between this new teacher's comments and the bloodlines of blood sacrifice and the like, we necessarily close off other possibilities, turn our backs on other options (options which a future voice may later open anew). Truth in this human inheritance is not to be had through full, final presence, but through the living inner tension between illumination and concealment. This makes hermeneutic truth very fragile, very mortal, very close to what happens to us. This initiation-venture regarding this new teacher's comments will not last forever; it will not be always and everywhere proper and appropriate. Its telling character is out of our hands because, after all, we do not and cannot know what will come of this moment of opening. Thus "truth has in itself an inner tension and ambiguity" (Gadamer 1977, p. 227). A hermeneutic study, therefore, doesn't get everything out in the open by the force of its methodical will. Rather, a hermeneutic study always alludes to concealment, unfinishedness, darkness, frailty and invalidity (e.g., Jardine 2000).

Second, *alethia* means to liven up, to enliven, to see the life in or breath life into what previously was dead (lethal), lifeless, boring, obvious, flat, deadly, deadening (great terms for teachers to consider when reflecting on classroom life). This is the most phenomenological characteristic of *alethia*. It is linked to the adrenaline rush of insight, the giddy breath of generativity and newness ("the new, the different, the true" [Gadamer 1977, p. 44]) and liveliness, the weird feel that something has *happened*. Opening (sense one of *alethia*) is a *movement*, an animation, a happening upon in which something seems to turn around and face me and demand, claim, address in a voice that is not my own. This means something very simple. The topic I've ventured into has *its own life* "beyond my wanting and doing."

There is a wonderful mythopoetic expression of this phenomenon in Clarissa Pinkola-Estes' re-citing of the tale of *La Loba*:

> The sole work of *La Loba* is the collecting of bones. She is known to collect and preserve especially that which is in danger of being lost to the world. ... [H]er speciality is said to be wolves.
>
> She creeps and crawls and sifts through the *montanas* ... and *arroyos* ... looking for wolf bones, and when she has assembled an entire skeleton, when the last bone is in place and the beautiful white sculpture of the creature is laid out before her, she sits by the fire and thinks about what song she will sing.
>
> And when she is sure, she stands over the *critura*, raises her arms and sings out. That is when the rib bones and leg bones of the wolf begin to flesh out and the creature becomes furred. *La Loba* sings some more, and more of the creature comes into being; its tail curls upward, shaggy and strong.
>
> And *La Loba* sings more and the wolf creature begins to breathe.

And *La Loba* sings so deeply that the floor of the desert shakes, and as she sings, the wolf opens its eyes, leaps up, and runs away down the canyon. (Estes 1992, pp. 27-28)

This can be read as an expression of the deep experience that hermeneutic writing and research entails. Sometimes those moments that address us – a child's comment, a passage read in a book – just lie there like dry bones. Sometimes we have to just collect them and protect them and wait. Sometimes we sing over them a bit and something stirs and then fails right in front of our eyes. Like I've already mentioned, that new teacher's phone call was 15 years ago, and I'm still carefully and patiently musing over it, hoping that it will come to life again, hoping that the song sung, this enchantment, this book chapter, will result in a re-enchantment (Berman 1983) and a reanimation of the world. *Part* of this is out of my hands because my work is on behalf of a life that is not my work, on behalf of a "topic" that lives "beyond my wanting and doing."

This sense of *alethia* as "enlivening" is therefore also privative, and it necessarily hides its inverse. By courting natality and life and liveliness, we necessarily concede mortality to understanding. Our explorations of initiation, our conversations with teachers and their mythic dreaming, our work, our insights, our writing, our lives – none of this will last forever and this not-lasting is not a failure. It is, rather, an insight. A hermeneutic study must not aspire to an ever-mounting enlightenment because, philosophically, hermeneutic experience and understanding are most fundamentally "an experience of human finitude" (Gadamer 1989, p. 357).

This links to Hannah Arendt's great and terrifying insight into the life and breath of education itself:

We are always educating for a world that is or is becoming out of joint, for this is the basic human situation, in which the world is created by mortal hands to serve mortals for a limited time as home. Because the world is made by mortals it wears out; and because it continuously changes its inhabitants it runs the risk of becoming as mortal as they. To preserve the world against the mortality of its creators and inhabitants it must be constantly set right anew. The problem is simply to educate in such a way that a setting-right remains actually possible, even though it can, of course, never be assured. Our hope always hangs on the new which every generation brings; but precisely because we can base our hope only on this, we destroy everything if we so try to control the new that we, the old, can dictate how it will look. Exactly for the sake of what is new and revolutionary in every child, education must be conservative; it must preserve this newness and introduce it as a new thing into an old world. (Arendt 1969, pp. 192-193)

Hermeneutic truth, therefore, does not progressively amass. In terms of humanity's efforts to understand itself – say, for example, this great movement from student to teacher – we are not getting anywhere. Even though many research methods have amassed great archives of verified knowledge, we still face, in our lives as students and teachers, the great, unfinished tales of such movement. To know of these matters "in truth" is to know that what such matters will turn out to be is necessarily "yet to be decided." There is an empty chair at the table (see Jardine and Batycky 2006). *This* is the truth of things.

Finally, a third sense of hermeneutic truth. After dying, *Lethe* was the river one's "soul" crossed when ferried into the underworld (parallel to the Roman River Styx) and such crossing involved forgetting what one had undergone or experienced. *Alethia*, as the privative of "forgetting," thus means remembering what was forgotten, recovering what has been lost. When I talked to this new teacher on the phone, when I recite this happenstance event to others and draw out the threads of thresholds and passages and the like, the first response tends to be "oh, yeah, right," as if something is quite literally *recognized*. This difficult sense of breath-intake is key to hermeneutics. A new piece of knowledge is not amassed. Rather, it is as if something lost has been found again, something old is remembered. And "re-membered"is triple here: "1. 'bringing back to memory' 2. 'gaining new members.' 3. 'putting back together'" (Jardine 1992, p. 14).

And, like senses one and two, this third sense, too, hides the seeds of its own demise. Things get forgotten or repressed or sublimated or lost, members arrive and die off, things put together fall apart. The centre does not hold forever. The living truth of things must "always must be renewed in the effort of our living" (Gadamer 1989, p. 100-111).

IN CONCLUSION

> The truth of [hermeneutic] experience always implies an orientation to new experience. "Being experienced" does not consist in the fact that someone already knows everything and knows better than anyone else. Rather, the experienced person proves to be, on the contrary, someone who ... because of the many experiences he has had and the knowledge he has drawn from them, is particularly well-equipped to have new experiences and to learn from them. Experience has its proper fulfilment not in definitive [amassed] knowledge but in the openness to experience that is made possible by experience itself. (Gadamer 1989, p. 355)

Amassed verified knowledge makes us less and less interested in what the new case might have to say. We become, not "experienced" but "experts" whose cynicism and condescension increases as that mass increases. Our understanding becomes "saturated" because we have seen enough that we feel able to close down the venture and end it. "Been there, done that," as the saying goes. As experts, we become less and less susceptible to the difference that the new case might bring. For example, living in a classroom where young children are learning to write or where young adults are learning to be teachers brings no exhilaration and pleasure because, as a consequence of our amassment, nothing can possibly happen that will speak to us from beyond the amassed consequences of our wanting and doing. Worlds become more and more of a closed case. We become more and more impervious to being interrupted. This is not a version of understanding that bodes well for pedagogy.

To become good at hermeneutics, you have to enter into the process, not of amassing verified knowledge and attaining "expertise," but the process of *becoming experienced*. Hermeneutically understood, the more experienced I become, the *more* susceptible I become to the difference that the next case might bring, the *more* susceptible I become to being addressed. Understanding, understood hermeneutically, means the cultivation of susceptibility in ourselves and others.

A good hermeneutic study opens up our ability to experience "the fecundity of the individual case" (Gadamer 1989, p. 38) that comes to meet us in the world. This, I suggest, bodes well for treating education as a hermeneutic endeavor.

REFERENCES

Arendt, H. (1969). *Between past and future*. New York: Penguin Books.
Berman, M. (1984). *The reenchantment of the world*. New York: Bantam Books.
Bohm, D. (1983). *Wholeness and implicate order*. New York: Ark Books.
Caputo, J. (1987). *Radical hermeneutics*. Bloomington, IN: Indiana State University Press.
Clifford, J. (1986). Introduction. In J. Clifford & G. Marcus (Eds.), *Writing culture: The poetics and politics of ethnography*. (pp. 2-11). Berkeley, CA: University of California Press.
Descartes, R. (1955). *Descartes selections*. New York: Scribners.
Eliade, M. (1968). *Myth and reality*. New York: Harper & Row.
Eliade, M. (1975). *The quest*. New York: Harper and Row.
Estes, C. P. (1992). *Women who run with the wolves: Myths and stories of the wild woman archetype*. New York: Ballantine Books.
Fox, M. (1983). *Original blessing*. Santa Fe: Bear and Co.
Gadamer, H.G. (1977). *Philosophical hermeneutics*. Berkeley, CA: University of California Press.
Gadamer, H.G. (1983). *Reason in the age of science*. Boston, MA: MIT Press.
Gadamer, H.G. (1989). *Truth and method*. New York: Continuum Press.
Gadamer, H.G. (1994). *Heidegger's ways*. Boston, MA: MIT Press.
Gadamer, H.G. (2001). *Gadamer in conversation: Reflections and commentary*. Edited and translated by R. Palmer. New Haven, CT: Yale University Press.
Hargreaves, A. (2005, October). Review of back to the basics of teaching and learning. *Education Canada*.
Hillman, J. (1982) Anima mundi: Returning the soul to the world. *Spring, 40*, 174-188.
Hillman, J. (1989). *Healing fiction*. Barrytown: Station Hill Press.
Hillman, J. (1991). *Inter/Views*. Dallas: Spring Publications.
Husserl, E. (1970). *The Paris lectures*. The Hague: Martinus Nijhoff.
Jardine, D. W. (1992). *Speaking with a boneless tongue*. Bragg Creek: Makyo Press.
Jardine, D. W. (1998). Student teaching, interpretation and the monstrous child. In D. W. Jardine (Ed.), *To dwell with a boundless heart: On curriculum theory, hermeneutics and the ecological imagination* (pp. 123-134). New York: Peter Lang Publishers.
Jardine, D. W. (2000). Learning to love the invalid. In D. W. Jardine (Ed.), *Under the tough old stars: Ecopedagogical essays* (pp. 193-200). Brandon, VT: Holistic Education Press.
Jardine, D. W. (2003). The profession needs new blood. In D. Jardine, P. Clifford, & S. Friesen (Eds.), *Back to the basics of teaching and learning: Thinking the world together* (pp. 55-70). Mahwah, NJ: Lawrence Erlbaum and Associates.
Jardine, D. W. (2005). *Piaget and education*. New York: Peter Lang Publishing.

Jardine, D. W. (2006). Cutting nature's leading strings: A cautionary tale about constructivism. In D. Jardine, S. Friesen, & P. Clifford (Eds.), *Curriculum in abundance* (pp. 123-135). Mahwah, NJ: Lawrence Erlbaum and Associates.

Jardine, D. W. & Batycky, J. (2006). Filling this empty chair: On genius and repose. In D. Jardine, P. Clifford, & S. Friesen (Eds.), *Curriculum in abundance* (pp. 213-225). Mahwah, NJ: Lawrence Erlbaum and Associates.

Jardine, D., & Field, J. C. (2006). Disproportion, monstrousness and mystery: Ecological and ethical reflections on the initiation of student-teachers into the community of education. In D. Jardine, S. Friesen, & P. Clifford (Eds.), *Curriculum in abundance* (pp. 107-119). Mahwah, NJ: Lawrence Erlbaum and Associates.

Jardine, D. & Novodvorski, B. (2006). Monsters in abundance. In Jardine, D., Friesen, S. & Clifford, P. (Eds). *Curriculum in abundance.* (pp. 103-5). Mahwah, NJ: Lawrence Erlbaum and Associates.

Jardine, D., Clifford, P., & Friesen, S. (2003). Whatever happens to him happens to us: Reading coyote reading the world. In D. Jardine, P. Clifford, & S. Friesen (Eds.), *Back to the basics of teaching and learning: Thinking the world together* (pp. 41-52). Mahwah, NJ: Lawrence Erlbaum and Associates.

Jardine, D., Friesen, S. & Clifford, P. (2006). (Eds). *Curriculum in abundance.* Mahwah, NJ: Lawrence Erlbaum and Associates.

Jardine, D., Johnson, B., & Fawcett, L. (2006). Further thoughts on cutting nature's leading strings: A Conversation. In D. Jardine, S. Friesen, & P. Clifford (Eds.), *Curriculum in abundance* (pp. 139-148). Mahwah, NJ: Lawrence Erlbaum and Associates.

Mahdi, L., Foster, S., & Little, M. (1987). *Betwixt and between: Patterns of masculine and feminine initiation.* LaSalle, IL: Open Court.

Norris-Clarke, W. (1976). Analogy and the meaningfulness of langauge about God: A reply to Kai Nielsen, *The Thomist, 40*, 176-198.

Sartre, J. P. (1970). Intentionality: A fundamental idea in Husserl's phenomenology. *Journal for the British Society for Phenomenology, 1*, 3-5.

Smith, D. G. (1999). *Pedagon: Interdisciplinary essays on pedagogy and culture.* New York: Peter Lang Publishers.

Turner, V. (1969). *The ritual process.* Chicago: Aldine.

Turner, V. (1987). Betwixt and between: The liminal period in rites of passage. In L. Mahdi, S. Foster, & M. Little (Eds.), *Betwixt and between: Patterns of masculine and feminine initiation* (pp. 3-41). La Salle: Open Court.

Weinsheimer, J. (1987). *Gadamer's hermeneutics.* New Haven, CT: Yale University Press.

Wittgenstein, L. (1968). *Philosophical investigations.* Cambridge: University of Cambridge Press.

REBECCA J. LLOYD AND STEPHEN J. SMITH

12. MOTION-SENSING PHENOMENOLOGY

> Sometimes I just have to see the ocean to gain inspiration. I want to get close and hear the water caressing the beach, the sound rippling through me. Today I stand for about 5 minutes of real time in what feels like an eternal moment. My heart rate is elevated from the run that brings me to the beach, pulsing into the freshness of the waves moving in my direction. My gaze stretches to the horizon, to the place where gravity plays with the wind, and back to the ripples inches from my feet. The sensory experience of being close to water affects the way I feel on many levels. The more I see and hear the natural flow of water, the more I feel at ease with the natural movement of thought. (Rebecca Lloyd's journal 2001)

This opening journal entry was written when I, Rebecca, the first author of this chapter, was first introduced to phenomenology. It was written on a particular day when I needed to take a break from academic readings and shift my attention to the topic of my first phenomenological inquiry (Lloyd 2004). As I re-visit this chapter in 2014, I realize that the ocean has never left my side. It continues to surge and ripple through me as I explore phenomenologically what it means to be more fluid than solid in moving through life. Flow and fluid movement is thus more than a topic that both Stephen and I explore through our writings (e.g., Lloyd 2011a, 2011b, 2011c, 2012a, 2012b; Lloyd and Smith 2009; Smith 2006, 2007, 2012, 2014). Sensing the motional ebbs and flows is a sensibility we have towards daily life, even during times of injury or heartache when the likelihood of flow seems emotionally out of reach (Lloyd 2015).

We are not alone in living our phenomenological inquires. Max van Manen (2014) suggests that phenomenology is more than a "philosophical perspective … it [is] the source for questioning the meaning of life as we life it" (p. 13). To become a phenomenologist, then, is no easy task, since it requires a commitment beyond that of following a procedure or a protocol. While phenomenology is a scholarly and methodological undertaking, as might be said of any other research endeavour, it is also a commitment to taking up the ways, both traditional and creative, of describing the meanings that lived experiences hold. Becoming a phenomenologist, however, is something yet again. It is about more than pursuing a research method, more than facility with the procedures and techniques that the phenomenological tradition makes available. Becoming a phenomenologist is a way of remaining in touch with lived experience just as one tries to apprehend its meanings. The phenomenologist considers how events and actions constitute lived experience, how researcher activity accesses the inherent meanings of lived experience, and how a research practice that is methodologically explicit can render these meanings accessible to others, all the while living in the midst of the experience.

"Phenomenology is a method; it could also be called an attitude" wrote Jan Hendrik Van den Berg (1972, p. 77). He went on to say how the phenomenologist adopts a way of observing life that differs from scientific protocols putting observers at objective distance from the things of interest. The phenomenologist mistrusts observational categories and any "opinions" that get in the way of an open, receptive sense-taking of the incidents, events or "phenomena" in question. The phenomenologist would have any interpretation "spring from this life."

> If he [sic] intends to write a discourse on swimming, he will want, first of all, to swim – and repeat his swimming until he knows and can express what swimming is. Only he who knows the sea, the river, the stream, the lake, physically can know what it is really like. (Van den Berg 1972, p. 77)

The requisite attitude is best expressed as a *disposition* in order to emphasize the level of physical attentiveness necessary. It is comprised dispositionally of postures, positions, gestures and indeed expressions, depending upon the degree of physical engagement and attentiveness that the subject matter requires. Martin Heidegger (1968) wrote:

> We shall never learn what 'is called' swimming, for example, or what it 'calls for,' by reading a treatise on swimming. Only the leap into the river tells us what is called swimming. (p. 21)

If we return to the opening to this chapter, note that it does not begin with a conceptual description of flow, a psychological state where perceived constraints and worries disappear as bodily action merges with awareness within the timeless nature of the present moment (Csikszentmihalyi 2008/1990). It begins instead with an orientation towards the movement of fluid itself, where water acts as invitation to leap into it and become immersed in the phenomenon of interest. To provide context, I wrote that journal excerpt when I was interested in the flow experience of exercise pedagogy, particularly in fitness classes and one-on-one training sessions when there are moments of joyful movement with others. I knew such moments of flow in these contexts as a fitness leader and trainer, and as an athlete and dancer I knew 'in my bones' the possibilities of experiencing flow with others. Still, I wanted to know more about the possibilities of flow, not just as a performer, and not simply as one who teaches fitness and is employed as personal trainer, but as a doctoral candidate in education with an interest in the pedagogical relation that is defined in moments of intense flow. Instead of putting my lived experiences of flow behind me, however, I needed inspiration for my doctoral study and a dispositional consciousness of how to approach it. I needed a sensory reminder of flow and its interactive possibilities. I recall wanting to loosen my stiffening 'academic' ideas of flow by literally running to a place where the reminder of flow is evident and where the prevailing flow motions kindle a phenomenological imagination of its interactive possibilities. Beginning a phenomenological inquiry of flow interactions required adopting the movements that activate a sense of flow. It required connecting actively with a waterscape where one can sense the moods, motions, and gestural formations of flow phenomena.

No research text suggested running to the beach and entertaining the elemental motions of the ocean. No research text suggests making soup, folding laundry, gardening, walking the streets, or any of the many 'diversions' that occupy researchers of all stripes. But those are precisely the activities that inspire writers of a phenomenological bent when there is a sensed connection between the postures, positions, gestures, and expressions that such activities require and the physiognomic aspects of the topic at hand. Flow, as a phenomenological topic, indicates a topology of being in flow motion. It recalls lived experiences of flow through the mediation of places where flow can be activated and where a sense of writing about flow can be enlivened.

I, Stephen, the second author of this chapter, had a related sense of my research topic. I focused initially on a physical education curriculum geared to flow experience (Smith 1982) and subsequently on how children's decision-making in physical activity enhances the possibilities of flow (Smith 1988, 1997a). Running was one of my lived flow experiences. I wrote the following account of running while contemplating my doctoral topic at the University of Alberta.

> Running is a good time for writing. Writing on the run. My thesis question of the educational significance of physical play preoccupies me, even as I think about running. But once up and running, unlike sitting at my writing desk where ideas of physical play shoot in all directions, there is a different, more agreeable questioning of the physicality of play. The agitated mood of the office, with its jabbing, niggling, galling incomprehensions, is massaged by the flow motions of the run. Running imposes its own feeling for the question that is ever on my mind. The question bounces around while running, up and down, in cadenced stride. It runs ahead, turns around, and waits until I catch its pulsations. It becomes heavy, weighing me down momentary, before a burst of speed pitches the question back into its rightful, energetic place.

> Writing is a little like running. I write with a running hand words that run together, around in circles, or off the page. I run into difficulties as I write, running around them, and often away from them. Running up against writer's block. I take a breather from my writing, time out to collect my thoughts. I run over what I've written and, in these pulsing motions, my writing is directed, enlivened, projected. I write over that which ran by me and in this writing the flow of running returns. Writing contains the flow motion I have experienced while running. Its prose fleshes out this lived experience of physical play. Writing engulfs my running, clearing a space where running finds its phenomenological place. (Stephen Smith's personal writing 1979)

Writers have long sought solace and recuperation in physical activity. Certain phenomenologists, with their interests in catching the salient aspects of lived experience, have taken to heart the physical affinities of writing and those somatic practices that bear the postural, positional, gestural and expressive features of their topics. David Abram (1996, 2010), David Levin (1985), Alphonso Lingis (2005, 2012) and Kenneth Shapiro (1985), for instance, follow the phenomenological admonition of returning to the things themselves, corporeally, physically, tangibly, palpably, kinaesthetically in texts "destined to bring back all the living relations of experience" (Merleau-Ponty 1962, p. xv). They follow a tradition of describing conceptually that which has been lived perceptually in the "flesh" and which carries the "flesh of the world" to phenomenological apprehension (Merleau-Ponty 1968). In fact, they follow a long tradition of "vocative" thinking that remains in touch with bodily motions. Berel Lang (1995) writes of Aristotle:

> Long after the immobility of death caught him, holding him to one place in the earth, we think of him still, first, as the Peripatetic, the teacher who walked as he taught, whose mind was so active that it seemed to grow feet. But here, too, most of us recall this feature as a quirk, an accident of posture or patience; thus we persist in keeping the body the captive of the mind, its servant, even – at some points – its symptom. Only a few obscure students, rarely heard, are willing to acknowledge their loss. These understand how much more they would have been able to learn from the master – if only they had the opportunity to watch, under the cloak of his words, that extraordinary walk. (Lang 1995, p. 14)

Recall also the European wanderings of Jean-Jacques Rousseau, the evening walks of Immanuel Kant in Königsburg, Søren Kierkegaard's on-foot explorations of Copenhagen, or Martin Heidegger's walks though his beloved Black Forest (Solnit 2000, pp. 15-29). How much more might we understand their ideas if we literally followed in their footsteps?

Our own topics of phenomenological inquiry take us a step farther. We regard this scholarly work as a necessary, ongoing blend of lived, living and still-to-be-lived experiences. Phenomenology that moves, emotes, and motions to the significance of its topic begins and ends in the register of movement appropriate to that topic. On the topic of flow, phenomenology is inherently moving, flowing, defining itself around the motions constitutive of flow. Elsewhere flow is variously turned into a cognitive construct, a behaviour, a quality of motion, an extra-human force, or a property of physical environments. Fragmentary views, these reductions fall short of the phenomenological reduction which would, in the silences of primary, movement consciousness, show "not only what words mean, but also what things mean: the core of primary meaning around which the acts of naming and expression take shape" (Merleau-Ponty 1962, p. xv).

Consider now the disposition of another phenomenological expert. Max van Manen (2002) describes the setting, position and sentience constitutive of his inquiry into the seemingly inactive phenomenon of writing phenomenologically. He begins:

> I am sitting at my keyboard, mulling over some last words. As I stare out of the window into the dark winter evening, I barely notice the lights of the cars

that are crossing the bridge spanning the banks of the river. In fact, I am scarcely aware that I am looking out of the window, until casually my son walks into the room. "Hi, what are you doing?" he queries. Awoken, as if from a daydream, I say, "I am writing." "Oh no, you aren't. You are just looking out of the window." He laughs, teasingly, and leaves.

It is true. I was staring out of the window. And yet, while I may have been observing the traffic, following some cars or trucks with my eyes, I did not really see them. My thoughts were elsewhere. More accurately: I was elsewhere. Where? One way to say it is that I was caught up in the words that I was writing, silently chewing them and then spitting them onto the keyboard, onto the computer screen. But is this writing? Am I writing? Well, yes and no. I am producing words, a text even. Yet, these are just words. This is not really writing. So my son was right. But when could I say that I am actually writing? I wonder if there is an actual moment that I can say: "Now. Now I am writing!" (van Manen 2002, p. 1)

Max van Manen's words on writing beg the question of how far removed the writer can be from the subject of writing and still be writing of its livedness. Alternatively, they ask: what experiential attunements, sensory awarenesses, kinaesthetic connections, in the writing process itself, make possible a moment of textual connection to the subject of writing? What, indeed, are the movements of dispositional attunement to the topic at hand when one can say "Now. Now, I am writing?" Max van Manen goes on to address the "writerly space" of phenomenological reflection where we step out of "the ordinary world of daylight [to] enter another, the textorium, the world of the text" (van Manen 2002, p. 3). The "textorium" we enter is a space of solitude, detachment from the practical tasks and responsibilities of the day, withdrawal to the office space or computer desk. A writer's retreat. We take leave of the immediacy of lived experience, its sociality and mimetic resonances, for the sake of discerning its portended meanings. But this leave-taking is no escape from reality. It is for the sake of lending greater reality to that which is lived, defining, through the licence of a textual methodology, the most salient, reverberating, touching aspects of the phenomena of daily living, and re-engaging life with a heightened awareness of its sensibilities. On the one hand:

> The phenomenologist as writer is an author who starts from the midst of life, and yet is transported to that space where, as Robert Frost once said, writing is "like falling forward into the dark." Here meanings resonate and reverberate with reflective being. (van Manen 2002, p. 7).

On the other hand, the phenomenologist as researcher is a "reflective being" thrown back into "the midst of life" to the lived spaces and times of the topic at hand. "One writes to make contact, to achieve phenomenological intimacy with an object of interest" (van Manen 2002, p. 245).

Motion-sensitive phenomenology (Lloyd and Smith 2006a) emphasizes the *transposition* of the actions of living into the activity of writing and the latter's capacity to not simply re-enact or represent times and events past but to rejuvenate the ongoing practice of living well. Phenomenology, as the study of lived experience, recalls the details of life; but, as the study of living and still-to-be-lived experience, it inspires and invigorates us in the lives we lead. It is not "passive" in the sense of simply being inactive; on the contrary, there is a "receptive passivity," a "pathic" register of activity, a dispositional attunement, in other words, a motion sensitivity, that phenomenology cultivates (van Manen 2002, pp. 250, 251). A study of flow must then connect us with the motions constitutive of that experience in a practice that flows back and forth between swimming and writing, running and writing, walking and writing, in fact, between any number of activities and the activity of writing phenomenologically that transposes the flux of life into a heightened understanding of flow motion.

DOING MOTION-SENSING PHENOMENOLOGY

As we update this methodological chapter, we have made a subtle shift from motion 'sensitive' to motion 'sensing' phenomenology in order to suggest even more strongly the motional resonances in writing. Highly influenced by Max van Manen's work, we framed our initial chapter as a variation on his action 'sensitive' approach to doing phenomenology for a number of reasons. First, Max van Manen is widely recognized as one of the foremost phenomenological scholars in North America (Pinar, Reynolds, Slattery, and Taubman 2000). Second, he has published a number of treatises on phenomenological method, in addition to the aforementioned text, which are widely used in education, health care and the human sciences (van Manen 1984, 1990, 1997). Third, Max van Manen has long concerned himself with the action reference of phenomenology, whether that be, say, the expressive "tone of teaching" (van Manen 1986) or its bodily expressed "tact" (van Manen 1991). Max van Manen's procedures for undertaking "lifeworld phenomenology" enable us to be sensitive to motion and to the active register of a flow consciousness.[1]

The practical steps of the inquiry process include: orienting to a phenomenon of interest; asking specific "what" questions that will bring one closer to the heart of the phenomenon; defining reflective modes that facilitate the answering of such questions; deepening understanding by consulting philosophical and phenomenological texts; re-grouping and organizing the inquiry through inherent theme structures; and lastly, re-writing the transition segments so the text appears to be seamless (van Manen 1990). To these steps we bring a motion-sensitivity needed in the phenomenological description of flow motion and, by this example, a sensitivity indicative of phenomenology writ large. Accordingly, we reframe Max van Manen's steps of inquiry as a practice, both actual and textual, of making sense of flow phenomena (i.e., sensing), discerning the essences of flow (i.e., essencing) and, in the process, cultivating a heightened flow sensitivity to the motions of others (i.e., sensitizing).

Sensing

The latitude of phenomenological inquiry enables us to "question something from the heart of our existence, from the center of our being" (van Manen 1990, p. 43). Even small phenomenological inquiries require "that we not simply raise a question and possibly soon drop it again, but rather that we 'live' this question, or better, that we 'become' this question" (p. 43). We must have a sense, from the outset, that the inquiry is significant and that the question is one that carries us to the heart of what moves us most deeply.

The question we asked in a study of interactive flow in exercise pedagogy (Lloyd 2004; Lloyd and Smith 2006b) was: "What is the nature of flow in exercise instruction and what makes such an experience pedagogically justified?" We were mindful, in asking this question, of flow as a motivational psychological theory of engaging activity that has been extensively researched by Mihaly Csikszentmihalyi (2000) for over 30 years. He characterised flow in terms of the intrinsic motivation of the participant, as a match between the level of inherent challenge in the experienced activity and the participant's skill level, as full immersion in activity such that self consciousness disappears, and as a lack of worry and anxiety on the one hand and boredom on the other so that all that exists is the merge of action and awareness. We can thus make psychological sense of flow, in Mihaly Csikszentmihalyi's terms, as an experience subject to certain defining characteristics. But what sentient properties does this experience hold? What is the sense of immersion and what are the feelings of fluidity? What sense of ourselves and of our relations to others do we have in flow motion? These questions prompt a participatory exploration of flow rather than the empirical detachment that Mihaly Csikszentmihalyi and his associates have adopted (Csikszentmihalyi 2000; Jackson and Csikszentmihalyi 1999). They require stepping into flow, immersing ourselves in flow motions, in order to sense and make sense of the bodily experience of fluid movement.

The data of flow need to take on a sensory quality indicative of flow consciousness. This is no easy task and requires not just a bracketing of assumptions, theories and conceptions of flow, or what the phenomenologists have called the *époche*, but also the textual practice of participatory consciousness. It requires learning to write in flow. My (Rebecca's) struggle with my former objective, behavioral mode of analysis, for example my masters thesis research (Lloyd and Trudel 1999), required dedicated time to a writing process that begins to express the incarnate intentionality, which is to say, the corporeal and intercorporeal feelings and sensations of flow consciousness. Here is one such textual reflection that oriented me toward the phenomenon of interactive flow.

> A drumbeat traveling into my watery glide to the shore from the red tide is pulling me away from the shower I so desperately need to rinse the slimy salt from my body. It draws me toward a small gathering of people. At the heart of the enclosed circle I see a demonstration of Capoeira – a Brazilian martial art based on interactive movements where each action or gesture has a specific reaction.

> The space between the martial artists is close although they always have enough room to finish a fully extended fan kick or an inverted one-arm supported kick. Every now and then they tap each other gently on the shoulder or back as if to say, "you're it." The tap lasts a moment with an immediate, almost seamless, exchange of positions. It is a game of two continuously moving bodies merging into one awareness with a specific set of rules. The pace is quick with little time to think of strategic moves. A rhythm of thrusts and parries, kicks and counters, is generated by these sweating bodies, sparkling in the sun.
>
> Later I do a trial class of Capoeira. I think that, as a dancer, I have the flexibility and body awareness to jump right into the moves, but as I begin to sense the interactive nature of the art and the rhythm of two people connecting I realize I need to be more aware of how my body moves in relation to my partner. I can't do the fancy kicks whenever I feel like it. I have to learn how to lunge and move from side to side to pick up the first phase of interactive rhythm. Still, I enjoy my introduction to Capoeira as it helps me recall the beauty, interactive awareness and holistic connection of the performers I observed at the beach last Sunday. (Rebecca Lloyd's Personal Journal 2000)

This writing sample indicates the movements of interactive flow in differing types of physical activity, whether they be spectacular transitions between one-arm supported postures, reaches or kicks in Capoeira, or the final glide to the shore in surfacing from the fluid, repetitive movements of swimming. It records my inclination to adopt the postures, positions, gestures and expressions of flow motion that can be observed and made kinaesthetically meaningful. I, Rebecca, was moved to experience interactive flow as I was moving in response to something, some action, some medium, and some body.

While orienting to interactive flow through observation, participatory consciousness and journal reflection, note is taken of Max van Manen's suggestion to make sure that the descriptions of lived experience articulate fully the meaning of the phenomenon, especially where "[o]rdinary language is in some sense a huge reservoir in which the incredible variety of richness of human experience is deposited" (van Manen 1997, p. 61). Becoming mindful of the words we use challenges us to think creatively and imaginatively of significant flow data. We immerse ourselves, through daily action, interactions and journal reflection, in waterscape words of flow,

"Waves" beckon to us, speak to us, and suggest to us some elemental sense that suffuses flow motion. They remind us of rhythms of life, oscillations of energy, pulses, circulations, ebbs and flows.

> Each time at the ocean I am mesmerized by the changing shapes, solicitous colors, and evolving atmosphere that ebb and flow with the tide. This is not simply human imagination or projection, but receptivity to an inherent expressivity of the waves.

It strikes me, particularly through the memory hints of previous connections, that the ocean speaks with some kind of primordial, amniotic power. Many of our gestures must surely originate in this briny wash, both as evolutionary fact and continuing natural affiliation. The wave of a hand draws its gestural power from the cresting of the sea; a caress traces the sensuous swell of a forming roller; while a kiss is a lapping of wetness that draws one into a fluid embrace.

Between the sitting on the beach and motions of the water, there is the beckoning of the sea toward a more intense connection with the world. I begin to wonder how separate the reality of the seascape is from our consciousness, from our perception of it. It beckons us and we participate, but this gesture of solicitation has an independence and a reality separate from us into which we enter, as into a relationship. Gesturing lies, as Rembrandt once said, "in the curtains," which is in the folds and creases of human habitation. It's in the pattern and form of the waves.

In the gesturing of the waves there is an absence of self-consciousness or, better still, a filling of the void that often marks our passage through everyday events. This elemental gesturing is not defined as an act of consciousness, but as an opening to the world which fills us with the world's flesh, as Merleau-Ponty might say, or with its fluid, which is more apt. It is a transcendence of self and an openness to the world beyond the narrow definition of the sensual or sexual. It is the critical moment of recognition of our being in the universe which is ironically reflected back in the form of touch by what we are actually able to truly see and feel.

The idea of 'flow motion' opens up a space for contemplating not only the gestures of human form – which include the constitutional gestures arising from birth and heredity, the habitual gestures arising from environment, custom, and simply growing up, and the fugitive gestures that spring from temporary emotion – but also gestures of rhythm and unity which are much more about world attunement and receptivity to the things of a supposedly more 'natural order' of living. Within this space one might think differently about those attunements and receptivities that have a physical basis to them and, instead of being confined to a de-natured sense of language acquisition, it might be possible to trace them out as full-blown gestures of form, rhythm and unity. Seascape gestures, waves, might provide, in other words, paradigmatic examples of a range of natural expressions. (Smith 2001, email communication)

We attend to waves and to other words of flow motion, such as rushes, ebbs, immersions, floats, pulses, runs and swims and dives, in order to sense something elementally constitutive of the phenomenon.

The senses of flow motion are further stimulated through literary and poetic texts. Max van Manen (1997) writes that poetry "allows the expression of the most intense feelings in the most intense form" and a poet "can sometimes give linguistic expression to some aspect of [non]human experience that cannot be paraphrased without losing a sense of the vivid truthfulness that the lines of the poem are somehow able to communicate" (p. 70). Poetic descriptions of fluid, seascape-formed gestures of flow draw us to "oceanic memories that continue among all humans who have landed. The pulsing waves of ancestral amphibians are recorded in every undulation of an organ, in every sweep of tissue, in every course of blood" (Conrad-Da'Oud 1995, p. 311; cf. Conrad 2007)). Poetry can evoke the sense of flow motion where there is "no inside, no outside, no up or down, no 'body,' only wave motions, many kinds – short waves – long waves – dancing waves" (Conrad-Da'Oud 1995, p. 309). Narrative, story, fiction, the novel, can likewise evoke flow motion and reveal gestural meanings otherwise hidden from phenomenal view. Milan Kundera's (1990) description of a wave between an elderly lady and a lifeguard captures well the duration of an interactive, fluid gesture.

> She walked around the pool toward the exit. She passed the lifeguard, and after she had gone some three of four steps beyond him, she turned her head, smiled, and waved to him. In that instant I felt a pang in my heart! That smile and that gesture belonged to a twenty-year-old girl! Her arm rose with bewitching ease. It was as if she were playfully tossing a brightly coloured ball to her lover. That smile and that gesture had charm and elegance, while the face and the body no longer had any charm. It was the charm of a gesture drowning in the charmlessness of the body. But the woman, though she must of course have realized that she was no longer beautiful, forgot that for a moment. There is a certain part of all of us that lives outside of time. (Kundera 1990, p. 3)

The poetics and prose of flow motion orient us to bodily senses, metaphors and meanings that are too often dulled in the arduous, painstaking work of objectifying experience (Markula and Denison 2000). These insights, having to do with waves and floats and flows, suggest motions of a lived body responding to the motions of another living being (Smith 2011, 2014a, 2015). They bring attention to a "structure of comportment" (Merleau-Ponty 1963) and a "bearing of thought" (Heidegger 1965) that resonate with the phenomenon of flow motion; in fact, they intimate how "each body's movements all day long form part of the skeleton of meaning that also gives any aberrant or spectacular bodily action its luster" (Foster 1995, p. 5).

It is with such phenomenological attentiveness that I, Rebecca, began to write about teaching fitness. The following journal entry illustrates the emerging focus on an interactive sense of flow motion.

> I have the pleasure of training Ben, an 80-year-old client, every Tuesday. Ben started personal training six years ago when he experienced a mild stroke which now limits his cardiovascular capacity and the use of his right arm. Physical activity, whether it be running, skiing or biking has always been a

part of his life, so Ben has hired me as his personal trainer to help monitor and guide his recuperation.

One of Ben's goals is to increase his aerobic endurance and capacity. We go for a 30 min light power walk/jog/run and look for small windows of opportunity where he can do intervals of increased intensity. We include natural inclines such as hills in the neighbourhood or landmark distances such as sprinting between benches in the park loop.

Today turns out to be one our special days….

Ben greets me warmly as I meet him in front of the garage door of our gym. It is his favourite spot and he is always 2 to 3 minutes early so I do my best to make sure our sessions start right on time if not before. Today Ben is wearing his red polar fleece jacket and looks quite cozy. We trek outside past the smiling front desk staff and Ben salutes them with his good arm. I don't know what it is about our outside walk/runs but everyone who walks or drives by immediately smiles when they see us together. I think our shared activity gives them a sense of connection to taking the time to appreciate the good things in life such as exercising and enjoying the fresh air. We wait for the first crosswalk patiently and enjoy the weekly update of what we've been up to. Ben tells me he went swimming twice, played tennis once, and saw Jane, his other personal trainer, last Friday. He is feeling good and we start our steady light jog.

As I turn my shoulders towards him and reach in the direction of his hips I ask, "Ben, can you hear the sound of your right foot? Listen to it as it rolls through and connects with the ground." Ben changes his heavy-footed impact and lightens up the motion. His upper body starts to soften but his hip flexors appear to be tight since his hip elevates slightly as his foot passes from a back extended position to a forward heel reach.

We approach another crosswalk. Ben just looks for a moment and then darts out before me. He likes to run out on the road. There are times when I have reached out and grabbed the back of his shirt in his moments of glee, watching the approaching traffic for fear we might not reach the other side in time. Ben even plays games with pedestrians. He likes to be the fastest person on the sidewalk. If there is another walker or jogger nearby, his focus is fixated ahead, pushing forward until we pass.

The sound of Ben's jog is a syncopated thud. The right foot often lands flat-footed and the left quickly passes through to complete the cycle. It changes a little when I point out the sound or cue ease in the hips, but it is something that requires specific thought to refine – until we get to the light on Broadway. There is something different between that traffic light and the quieter street crossings. It gives so little time to cross safely to the other side.

> Ben asks me to run ahead and get the light ready so we don't have to stop. I run up, press the button, and it changes immediately. Ben, who is 10 steps behind, seizes the moment and overtakes me in a joyous stride. I feel the presence of a young, eager boy, speeding by my side. He floats across. The only sound is the swoosh in the air as he zooms by. I look up and see both of his arms swinging and he continues to run until the loud breaths catch him. The strident exhales return us to our walk and his heart rate starts to slow down.
>
> Ben's sprint transcends time, his physical presence, the grounding reality of a heavy right foot, and the dysfunction of a right arm. His youthful energy catches him in a glide across the street to the other side and beyond. I push to catch up with him, laughing in the moment. It is not unlike Agatha's wave, in Kundera's (1990) *Immortality*, flowing though her body cultivating a sense of childhood youth in a motion that transcends old age. (Rebecca Lloyd's Personal Journal 2003)

Moments such as these happen from time-to-time, yet they need not be sheer happenstance. A kinaesthetic attentiveness, wherein our bodily motility brings about a physical communion with others, creates moments of vitality, energy and seemingly transcendent motions of flow beyond the repetitive drudgery of daily tasks or, in this case, beyond the heavy-footedness of running. When I shared my written description of the walk/run outings with Ben he explained that:

> Everything feels different when I run across the street. I feel energized in a way that just plain running doesn't. It's a liberating moment from what running usually is for me. Running up the street can be pretty boring ... When I ask you to run up and get the light it is no longer routine. I get incentive in taking a risk, like going down a steep ski slope, and that I can do it. Running becomes more natural because I suddenly get the feeling of freedom. The fact that I can't continue is age-related. The feeling of running at that point is tremendous. It's not an out-of-body experience, but something that approaches it .... Twenty years ago I could do a six-minute mile, now that's no longer possible. Any moment I can go back to that feeling and throw myself over the road, figuratively speaking, it feels good. It feels very good. (Client Response 2003)

Before writing about Ben's youthful run across the street and asking him to read it, he told me that he was unaware of any physical transformation. But after reading the passage, Ben became increasingly excited about moving as if he were a youth again and shortly after decided he would focus on increasing the motion and strength in his right arm in the gym. He and I started incorporating two-arm cable triceps extensions and biceps curls, along with range of motion active stretches. Ben's swinging arm motion in that fleeting moment of running across the street filled him with a sense of possibility in a part of him that he once thought was disabled.

Noticing and noting a flow motion allow one to experience it again with increased frequency and sensory awareness. We sense the motion aesthetically through writing up its duration in phenomenological notation, and we sense the motion kinaesthetically through running down, running over, running with the notation of that moment in an active register of flow motion. Phenomenological data draw attention to the rhythmical swing of arms and legs, to running together, to the full-bodied grace of youth, to fluid motion and wave-like surges of emotion that cultivate a deeper relation with the world at large. Phenomenology, in the givens of experience and the give and take of experiential description, begins to disclose a "primordial choreography" and "poetizing motility" (Levin 1985, p. 15).

Essencing

Ben's transition from doing a lop-sided run to a floating glide across the street provides but one example of flow motion. The point of motion-sensing phenomenology is not merely to generate further examples; it is to deepen the sense of motion that the example above contains. It is to catch the essential, sentient, sensible meaning of this evocative moment of flow motion. We thus pursue a phenomenological reduction that attends to its essential characteristics.

This is a method of "existential reflection" (van Manen 1997) in which attention is paid to the following aspects of lifeworld experience: to the sensing and essencing of body awareness or corporeality, spatiality, temporality and relationality. These experiential foci are the "fundamental existentials" of all conceivable experience (van Manen 1990, pp. 101-106) and, indeed, come close to the elements of movement first articulated by Rudolf Laban and since incorporated in a range of movement disciplines (Hodgson 2001). They refer to the conjunction of behaviour and attitude, motion and emotion, position and disposition, gesture and gists of meaning, expression and impression. Corporeality, spatiality, temporality and relationality are the general structures of lived experience indicative of what is essential to this and any other experience of flow motion. What characterizes a particular experience are the distinctive corporealizing, spatializing, temporalizing and relating motions involved.

We ask, in our focused exploration of interactive flow in exercise pedagogy, what is the particular and distinctive sense of the teaching body? Where and how does my body move, not just on the external surfaces of objective space and time, but in terms of the kinaesthetic registers of expansive and contractive spaces and the bodily feeling and muscular-skeletal sensing of physical effort (Cohen 1993; Laban and Lawrence 1974)? What is it to become aware of the movements of another body while teaching movement? How does somatic connectivity change, strengthening or weakening the teaching connection, not just in relation to spatial proximity and distance, but also in creating and giving space, standing back or making contact, reaching out, touching, and at times making deep contact with others? And in being not just on time but in time with another: What is the effect of teaching quick, effervescent movement over slow, penetrating movement? How do instructor movements of varying effort, whether forceful or light, staccato or sustained, jerky or flowing, influence client postures, positions, gestures and expressions?

In questioning the lived body, lived time, lived space, and the lived other as the existential heuristics of experiencing flow, we show flow motion to be essentially about pedagogical interaction. For example, within a walk-run routine, I, Rebecca, was able to see, feel and move with Ben's moment of flow motion as I ran by his side. I was able to do this because I was moving and predisposed to feel movement. I did not assume an objective distance, analyzing his gait through passive observation, in what Max van Manen describes as the phenomenological "gaze of wonder [that] sweeps us up in a state of passivity" (van Manen 2002, p. 251). I felt kinaesthetically the glide wash over her as I reciprocated Ben's joyous stride. I wasn't vicariously feeling his flow by imagining myself enjoying a youthful run across the street. I was able to step interactively into the time and space of her client's experience. I departed from the predominantly visual mode of observation in which though "the seer is caught up in what he sees, it is still himself he sees: there is a fundamental narcissism of all vision" (Merleau-Ponty 1968, p. 139). I observed synaesthetically and kinaesthetically, to which we can add the neologism "kinethically" as an indication of participatory observation that is now especially mindful of the quality of another person's movement experience.

Motion-sensitivity affords a multi-sensory, inter-subjective, inter-corporeal, intertwining of what moves and moves us. Phenomenological reflection seeks to catch this motion sensitivity, virtually, vicariously, reciprocally, in an essencing of the senses of flow motion. It is an agogic stress that phenomenology provides initially – a stress on momentary duration, a notation of sustainment, which is not so much a pause for thought as it is an extension of the lived experience by sensitive touch, contact and direction. Before there is a logic of the phenomenon of flow motion there is the phenomenagogic accent on the flow moment. Note is taken of what might so easily pass unnoticed. Phenomenology, as a reflective, textual practice, then brings the moment agogically and even pedagogically to mind.[2]

We pursue the agogic, phenomenogogic and phenomenologic essencing of flow motion in order to provide an alternative approach for athletic trainers and physical educators who are generally entrenched in technical, managerial and narrowly biomechanical representations of the human body. Richard Shusterman (1999) points out that enthusiasts of bodily training tend to "see the body as a moving mechanism, with joints as its components and flesh to cushion the skeleton" and objectify the body "as though they were already separated from it" (p. 7). To observe a client in this way affects how movement is understood and analysed. Personal trainers typically assume "the gaze of a coffin maker" in sizing up what is "tall, short, fat or heavy" and unfortunately "[l]anguage keeps pace with them. It has transformed a walk into motion and a meal into calories" (p. 7). But can we really learn what is essential "about the living body from a dead body" (Pronger 1996, p. 428)? Can knowledge of movement be based on bodies whose owners have "vacated the premises" (p. 438)? Even the movement terminology of physical education curricula has a tone of bodily detachment such that body awareness –

what the body can perform, space awareness – where the body can move, movement quality – how the body moves, and relationships – with whom or what the body relates (Pangrazi and Gibbons 2003), externalize the movements and motions of the lived body, severing them from the senses of moving bodily in concert with another.

Phenomenological inquiry, with its bracketing of the objective form and function of movement for the sake of attending to the corporeal, spatial, temporal and relational stresses of flow motion, deals essentially with the "vitality of the pedagogical relation" (van Manen 1992). It highlights an energy, aliveness, and "animate consciousness" (Sheets-Johnstone 2011) evident in motions that flow back and forth, to and fro, reciprocally, interactively, responsively. It divines an essence to flow motion that enlivens that motion, actively and interactively in the moment of flow and, let us say, hyperactively in that moment's textual duration. It is not necessarily the case that "every word kills and becomes the death of the object it tries to represent" (van Manen 2002, p. 244), nor is the opposite case necessarily so, that "we write to taste life twice, in the moment and in retrospection" (Nin 1976, p. 149). Writing with motion-sensitivity may breathe life into bodies that have been deadened to touch, contact and tactful engagement with other bodies. Textualizing flow motion may reclaim a sense of fluidity just when "as we walk upon the earth, drawn into clasping and grasping, and finding a purchase for ourselves through firm hands and erect, hardened bodies, we become deadened to 'our home.' We are no longer wet" (Conrad Da'Oud 1995, p. 311).

Essencing has us look with motion-sensitivity to further instances of interactive flow. We are mindful now of representations of motion that abstract the body, its space and time, and that distance it from other bodies. We are conscious particularly of the dispositions of movement that such texts represent – the transposed poses, postures, positions, gestures and expressions – which incline us not to sense flow motion. We look askance at the customary crossed-armed postures or arms akimbo positions of authority so evident in personal training and seek instances of more fluid, interweaving, interpenetrating, folding, enfolding, unfolding motions of responsiveness. The following excerpt from my (Rebecca's) doctoral thesis (Lloyd 2004) illustrates movement toward an essential connectivity.

> May is a client who responds well to managing gestures. As she is lying back on the leg press, she begins her descent and stays there a little too long. The weight stack clangs together and she starts to talk about her legs and the last time she did something like this. I ask May to keep going. Not with my words but with my hand. My arm sweeps down to the depth of her knee flexion and my wrist rolls up following the upward lift of my elbow into a complete arm and finger extension. My signal sends a message: Travel up and keep the pace. May pushes up and continues to bend her knees in a 30 to 40 degree angle. May is almost going low enough but is shying away from a depth that will challenge her gluteus maximus. Her knees show hesitancy and she is quick to get out of the compressed position. I gesture to May to come down lower by beckoning her with an in-coming wave, a gathering motion of

my hand. I call her knees to bend and they comply with an approximate 60-degree flexion. May's knees are responsive to my wave. My hands guide the depth and extension of the movement. As long as my hands continue to move, May repeats the motion. I see her legs start to quiver and I suggest that she take a break. We made it up to twenty. A set well done!!! (Rebecca's Personal Journal 2003)

My hands guide the path of May's motion with fluid motility. She attends to the tempo, pattern, and bodily signs of fatigue, her fingers showing the desired grace and pace of the exercise. My hands are not rigid or stiff as a pointing motion might be. They are alive, tracing a "primal sensibility" (Sheets-Johnstone 1999, p. 136) which is conveyed to May's movement. These hands that wave with the intentionality of flow motion are different than fingers that reach with managing intent. They have the capacity to touch and be re-touched. Like the extension of a dancer's hand in an arabesque, they are not stiff. There is animation in the way the fingers sweep away from the body as if gliding over the top of water. These hands make contact beyond the span of the limbs.

Michelangelo's painting of the Sistine Chapel shows fingers with such tactile dexterity. God's and Adam's fingers aren't stiff or connected across space in a straight line. The inter-connection is apparent in the flowing movement of flesh across sensitive space. David Levin (1985) picks up on the "awesome dimensions" of this gesture:

> In his depiction of "The Creation of Man," we see the hand of God reaching down from the heavens and the hand of Adam as it reaches up from the earth. Their arms are *stretched to the limit*, their fingers touch. The meeting of hands, that 'point' where they meet, initiating a binding contact, is even of awesome dimensions. It can move us with the might of a thunderbolt. It can shake us with the strength of an earthquake. The gesture extends the mystery of their communication across all generations of mortals and across the infinity of space which separates us from the Creator. The painting re-presents an experience of primordial presence as it is bodied forth in its archetypal gesture. (p.135)

God's and Adam's fingers reach toward each other with touching sensitivity. They are not stretched to the limit like managing hands. They are mutually interconnected with curvatures of fluid somatic sensibility and other-directed sensitivity. Accordingly, when we revisit my fluid hand reaching out to guide the pace and outer shape of May's leg press motion, we realize that even fluid, folding hands have the propensity to be 'one-sided.' The beckoning incoming wave followed by the rippling extension of my fingers and hand conducted May's motion. The pace did not come from May's desire to do just one more press; May moved in response to an external gesture. Helping clients respond to their own desires, sensations, and bodily awarenesses requires a shift from one-sided movement instigation to motion sensitivity to energy that flows in and out, and back and forth.

Sensitizing

The sensing and essencing of flow motion that we have described sensitizes us to further instances and pedagogical possibilities. Phenomenologically we write and re-write our reflections on movement experience in relation to inherent theme structures, meanings lifted from one example and related to another. We write, keeping in mind the test of high quality phenomenological writing as the "eureka factor" (Dukes 1984, as cited in Creswell 1988) or the degree to which the text resonates with readers' experiences. We organize this writing around themes that clear a path of understanding the phenomenon (van Manen 1997, p. 29). We indicate, thematically, the layers of emotive, kinaesthetic, synaesthetic, somaesthetic depth to the experience of interactive flow in exercise pedagogy, through continuing referral to water and its flow motions.

Let us begin with floating. It means to "go with the flow" of the currents and natural movements of water. Yet already we sense floating to be far removed from the phenomenon of interactive flow described so far. Mihaly Csikszentmihalyi (2000) reminds us that going with the flow is "an expression used by the counterculture of the 1960s" which is in "some ways antithetical to what flow means" (p. xviii). Susan Jackson and Mihaly Csikszentmihalyi (1999) explain that "going with the flow" implies "a laissez-faire attitude, where one is taken along as if on a ride that requires no effort of one's own" (p. 115). The sensing of flow motion happens when we move with and through the environment in which we are immersed. There can be effortless sensations, but these are a result of combinations of effort and relaxation, or what Moshe Feldenkrais (1980) called "pleasurable exertion" where "one is able to make contact with one's own skeleton […] muscles and […] environment practically simultaneously" (Feldenkrais 1980, p. 77). A sensitivity to flow motion does not mean to "stand outside oneself" (Ackerman 1999). It may be that teaching group fitness on a stage can be likened to floating on waves of energy from a sea of bodies moving to the pre-crafted and pre-choreographed sequences cued and managed by the presenter. But the flow motion we have explored indicates a greater *depth* of interaction.

Sensitizing to flow suggests swimming rather than floating. Here fluidity surrounds and supports the flesh as the body is propelled forward in bubbling, wake-producing strokes. Bodily experience dissolves in the inter-connection of one's flesh with the buoyant world, creating a "solidity, so to speak; which even water presents" (Bergson 1975, pp. 211-212). By immersing ourselves in the movements of others, whether they be the particular individuals within a group or personal training clients, we can adopt a similar solidity.

> I only started to feel specific responses, comparable to the way synchronized swimmers adjust their strokes, when I immersed myself in my personal training client's body. Motions that I taught with Platonic understanding, i.e., the 'ideal' way to demonstrate them, describe them, and perform them, were not uniformly or 'ideally' represented in the motions of my clients. Martha's squat differed from Leo's, Suzie's, Ben's, and Frank's squats. After I demonstrated 'set up' where I would ask my clients to assume the position I

just performed and continue the motion with a steady tempo, I learned that each person has a unique understanding of the motion, history associated with the motion, internal desire to repeat the motion, and level of somatic awareness and interest to refine the motion. (Rebecca's Personal Journal 2002)

Delving beneath superficial sensations creates bodily encounters that are lasting, life changing and life affirming. Jumping into a pool, off a dock, or into the ocean can be a quick, tingling burst if the intention is to re-surface and jump joyfully in again. It can also be the entry point to another place – a deeper dimension of the carnal world that lies below the surface and surrounds, immerses and embraces movement consciousness. The longer one sustains a plunge, the more time one has to become absorbed in everything the water-human merge has to offer. Time below the surface permits the aesthetic and emotional qualities of the moment to 'sink in.'

The deeper one goes into the ocean depths, the more one approaches the human limits of being alive. In fact, as dives go increasingly deeper[3] the parasympathetic and sympathetic nervous systems start to work in conjunction instead of opposition, a biological response similar to that found in reptiles. There is an incredible amount of bodily effort to sustain the pressures of the ocean depths and return to the surface. One must prepare diligently to survive such descents. One might wonder, if diving requires so much effort, then why take the plunge? Wouldn't it be more enjoyable to move within the shallows and observe radiant, tropical fish while breathing with the help of a snorkel? Divers think otherwise. A depth meter is an essential part of every deep-sea dive to counter the pull of wanting to go just a little deeper. Once one leaves the surface and glides downward, there is no natural feeling of how deep one should go. If a critical depth is passed, there may not be enough oxygen left to make the journey upward. Funnily enough, the journey to the surface is not the primary thought of a diver who feels 'at home' with the fish. Perhaps Freud was right in expressing the "oceanic feeling" we crave as an infant (Ackerman 1999) or in this case, what we crave as a child-like adult experiencing flow in depth. This bliss in merging with the ocean depths can either be attributed to connecting to a primordial state of being or to the early stages of nitrogen narcosis[4] and oxygen poisoning. If one has never plunged into the ocean depths can one have the sense of belonging that the water brings, "the embrace of the depths ... a deep immersion the ultimate gentle release, a homecoming in an element" that can bring "only joy" (Ecott 2001, p. 135)?

"The embrace of the depths" is a very fitting phrase for the joyful sensation of deep immersion. Any workaholic, artist, writer, or musician can relate to the feeling of complete intoxication with a project. Once the activity is begun, it is possible to be drawn so deeply into the experience that there is no longer a natural moment to surface, re-group, and reflect. The worry is that an individual may willingly delve into the bliss of prolonged deep activity knowing full well that there are potential physical or stressful hazards for overall wellness. What, then, are the ethical implications of engaging in deep pedagogical flow. Is the client ready for such deep penetration? What sensitivities are needed to the moods and feelings of the client?

Diving sensitizes us to the interactive motions of deep flow in exercise pedagogy. Reflections on gestural moments of flow motion, beyond moments of physical resonance, require a critical sensitivity. We ask: Are the hands of helpfulness guiding and affirming the other's motions? Do they nurture the others postures, positions, gestures and expressions? Do these hands respond to another living, breathing, moving body in holding, supporting, molding, shifting, shaping and so setting in place new patterns of exercise motion? Do they bring vitality to these movement patterns? Do they draw one into an "embrace of the depths" of human interaction where one can feel and guide the client's motions as if they were one's own? Do they express a "chiasm of the Flesh" (Merleau-Ponty 1968), criss-crossing motions, gestural reciprocity, where who moves and who is moved overlap and approximate one being?

Describing flow motion from the "surface" to the "depths" helps us discover how exercise pedagogy can move from an elevated stage of one-sided instruction to motions of deep, other-directed absorption (Lloyd 2004; Lloyd and Smith 2006b). Within this thematic structure we become sensitive to the "pedagogical tact and thoughtfulness" (van Manen 1991) pertaining to a particular region of lived experience and, in so doing, shed some light on what it means to move, be moved and sustain, textually and phenomenologically, the flow motions of pedagogical relationship.

CONCLUSION

Motion-sensing phenomenology, involving sensing of, essencing of, and sensitizing to, the potential depth of flow experience in exercise settings provides a guide for human science research into the larger realm of movement education. At a time when movement is more often that not observed mechanically as "motor skill" acquisition, when "[m]ovement research and movement education have been neglected in our time" (Rudolf Laban as cited in Moore and Yamamoto 1988), it is necessary to consider meaningful and thoughtful motion in meaningful and thoughtful ways. The Husserlian "I move" is central to human and other-than-human consciousness. Movement in all species of living things precedes its consciousness awareness such that, even the Merleau-Pontyean "I can do" is, in the first moment of awareness, a primal, animate consciousness (Sheets-Johnstone 1999, pp. 134, 135). What I think "I can do" is a conscious apprehension, a comprehension, of preconsciously thinking in movement. I move, therefore I am. To become motion-sensitive is thus to become attuned to "our wordless kinetic beginnings and our wordless celebrations of movement" (p. 225). It is to rediscover in movement a grounding of the phenomena of life, a preconsciousness of the pulses of living, a positioning and gesturing of ourselves within flow, certain motions, and agogic accent on moments of deep, interactive movement experience.

Motion sensitivity naturally lends itself to a phenomenology which is, as Maxine Sheets-Johnstone (2011) points out, "virtually nowhere to be found in phenomenological studies" (p. 269). The search for essences must take on a new dynamic, spatial, temporal and relational tone. We can no longer seek to elucidate an "end-state" (Sheets-Johnstone 2011, p. 269) as in determining the fixed nature, meaning or essence of "lived experience," but open the door to exploring the pulse of "living experience," its senses, incarnate essences and sensitive registers of meaning. The present chapter is but a step or stroke in this direction – a running step, a swimming stroke, a waving hand – amidst strokes of the computer keyboard that sustain certain moments of flow motion.

We have focused on particular instances of flow motion in this chapter with two sets of examples: those drawn from the flows of running, swimming and diving and those drawn from teaching the motions of flow to others. Our interest is sensuously, essentially and sensitively phenomenological *and* pedagogical. We began the chapter by blurring the boundaries between the flow motions of physical activity and the flow of writing phenomenologically. We conclude the chapter having blurred the divisions between lived experience, a textual practice, and a teaching relationship. Phenomenology and pedagogy are interwoven. The postures, positions, gestures and expressions of flow motion transpose to phenomenology and pedagogy though the durational accents that writing a text for others and being physically with others provide. Motion-sensing phenomenology is more than a research undertaking. It is a textual practice of moving kinaesthetically, aesthetically and ethically with others.[5]

NOTES

[1] The following discussion extends earlier methodological outlines of the applicability of "lifeworld phenomenology" to the phenomena of the play, game and sport regions of the world (Smith 1992, 1997b).

[2] The term "agogic stress" is the special accent given a note in music by slightly increasing its duration. It's about subtle, nuanced tempo and rhythm changes as a result of phrasing. It differs from the dynamic accent of loudness and the tonic accent of pitch. "Agogy" is the suffix for leading forth, guiding, or bringing, taking, promoting or stimulating that which any prefix names. Thus, we use the neologism "phenomenagogy" as sensitivity to movement duration, and "pedagogy" as sensitivity to the durations of moving with others (see Smith 2014b).

[3] In 1976, Jacques Mayol, the real-life hero who inspired the popular theatrical film production Big Blue, was the first to descend to 312 feet (100 meters), a depth once considered to be a physiological impossibility for humans. It was thought that pressure at that depth would cause the thorax surrounding the lungs permanently to collapse, but Mayol – sometimes admiringly referred to as *Homo aquaticus* – not only survived with his lungs and chest intact, but has continued to press the limits in competition with several others who aspire to be "the deepest man alive" (Earle 1995, pp. 16-17).

[4] Nitrogen under pressure causes a peculiar euphoric effect much like the dreamy state induced by laughing gas, nitrous oxide. At about 100 feet and deeper, divers get "high," often experiencing a tranquil, giddy "buzz." Some divers happily hallucinate, become forgetful or confused which way is up, or decide that the regulator is a nuisance and offer it to passing fish (Earle 1995, p. 53).

[5] Please see our website http://function2flow.ca/ for practical examples of our current motion-sensing phenomenological inquiries as well as a conceptual, curricular overview of the Function-to-Flow model.

REFERENCES

Abram, D. (1996). *The spell of the sensuous: Perception and language in a more-than-human world.* New York: Vintage Books.

Abram, D. (2010). *Becoming animal: An earthly cosmology.* New York: Pantheon Books.

Ackerman, D. (1999). *Deep play.* New York: Vintage Books.

Bergson, H. (1975). *Creative evolution.* Westport, CT: Glenwood Press.

Cohen, B. B. (1993). *Sensing, feeling, and action: The experiential anatomy of body-mind centering.* Northampton, MA: Contact Editions.

Conrad-Da'Oud, E. (1995). Life on land. In D. H. Johnson (Ed.), *Bone, breath, & gesture: Practices of embodiment* (pp. 297-312). Berkeley, CA: North Atlantic Books.

Conrad, E. (2007). *Life on land: The story of continuum, the world-renowned self-discovery and movement method.* Berkeley, CA: North Atlantic Books.

Creswell, J. W. (1998). *Qualitative inquiry and research design, choosing among five traditions.* Thousand Oaks, CA: Sage Publications.

Csikszentmihalyi, M. (2000). *Beyond boredom and anxiety. Experiencing flow in work and play.* San Francisco, CA: Jossey-Bass.

Csikszentmihalyi, M. (2008/1990). *Flow: The psychology of optimal experience.* New York: Harperperennial, Modernclassics.

Ecott, T. (2001). *Neutral buoyancy: Adventures in a liquid world.* New York: Grove Press.

Feldenkrais, M. (1980). *Mind and body. Your body works.* Copyrighted newsletter by Moshe Feldenkrais.

Foster, S. L. (1995). *Choreographing history.* Bloomington and Indianapolis, IN: Indiana University Press.

Heidegger, M. (1965). *On the way to language.* New York: Harper and Row.

Heidegger, M. (1968). *What is called thinking?* (J. G. Gray, Trans.). New York: Harper and Row.

Hodgson, J. (2001). *Mastering movement: The life and work of Rudolf Laban.* London: Methuen.

Jackson, S. A., & Csikszentmihalyi, M. (1999). *Flow in sports: The keys to optimal experiences and performances.* Champaign, IL: Human Kinetics.

Kundera, M. (1990). *Immortality.* New York: Perennial Classics.

Laban, R., & Lawrence, F. C. (1974). *Effort.* London: Macdonald & Evans.

Lang, B. (1995). *Mind's bodies: Thought in the act.* Albany: State University of New York Press.

Levin, D.M. (1985). *The body's recollection of being.* London: Routledge.

Lingis, A. (2005). Contact. *Janus Head, 8*(2), 439-454.

Lingis, A. (2012). The weight of reality. *Mosaic: A Journal for the Interdisciplinary Study of Literature, 45*(4), 37-49.

Lloyd, R. J. (2004). *Interactive flow in exercise pedagogy.* Unpublished doctoral dissertation, Simon Fraser University.

Lloyd, R. (2011a). Awakening movement consciousness in the physical landscapes of literacy: Leaving, reading and being moved by one's trace. *Phenomenology & Practice, 5*(2), 70-92. www.phandpr.org/index.php/pandp/article/download/93/142

Lloyd, R. J. (2011b). Teaching games with inner sense: Exploring movement consciousness in women's volleyball. *PHEnex journal/Revue phénEPS, 3*(2), 1-17.

Lloyd, R. J. (2011c). Running with and like my dog: An animate curriculum for living life beyond the track. *Journal of Curriculum Theorizing, 27*(3), 117-133.

Lloyd, R. J. (2012a). Hooping through interdisciplinary intertwinings: Curriculum, kin/aesthetic ethics and energetic vulnerabilities. *Journal of the Canadian Association for Curriculum Studies, 10*(1), 4-27.

Lloyd, R. J. (2012b). Breastfeeding mothers and lovers: An ebbing and flowing curriculum of the fluid embrace. In S. Springgay & D. Freedman (Eds.), *Mothering a bodied curriculum: Emplacement, desire, affect* (pp. 270-293). Toronto, ON: University of Toronto Press.

Lloyd, R. (2015). From dys/function to flow: Inception, perception and dancing beyond life's constraints. *The Humanistic Psychologist, 43*(1), 24-39. DOI 10.1080/08873267.2014.952416

Lloyd, R. J., & Smith, S. J. (2006a). Motion-sensitive phenomenology. In K. Tobin & J. Kincheloe (Eds.), *Doing educational research: A handbook* (1st ed., pp. 289-309). Rotterdam: Sense Publishers.

Lloyd, R. J., & Smith, S. J. (2006b). Interactive flow and exercise pedagogy. *Quest, 58*, 222-241.

Lloyd, R. J. & Smith, S. J. (2009). Enlivening the curriculum of health-related fitness. *Educational Insights, 13*(4). www.ccfi.educ.ubc.ca/publication/insights/v13n04/articles/lloyd_smith/index.html

Lloyd, R. J., & Smith, S. J. (2006). Motion-sensitive phenomenology. In K. Tobin & J. Kincheloe (Eds.), *Doing educational research: A handbook* (1st ed., pp. 289-309). Rotterdam: Sense Publishers.

Lloyd, R. J., & Trudel, P. (1999). Verbal interactions between an eminent mental training consultant and elite level athletes: A case study. *The Sport Psychologist, 13*, 418-443.

Markula, P., & Denison, J. (2000). See spot run: Movement as an object of textual analysis. *Qualitative Inquiry, 6*(3), 406-432.

Merleau-Ponty, M. (1962). *Phenomenology of perception* (C. Smith, Trans.). London: Routledge & Kegan Paul.

Merleau-Ponty, M. (1963). *Structure of behavior*. Boston, MA: Beacon.

Merleau-Ponty, M. (1968). *The visible and the invisible* (A, Lingis, Trans.). Evanston, IL: Northwestern University Press.

Moore, C-L., & Yamamoto, K. (1988). *Beyond words: Movement observation and analysis*. New York: Gordon and Breach.

Nin, A. (1976). *Letter to a young writer. The journals of Anais Nin* (G. Stuhlmann, Ed.), Vol. 5, 1947-1955. London: Quartet Books.

Pangrazi, R. B., & Gibbons, S. (2003). *Dynamic physical education for elementary school children* (Canadian ed.). Toronto, Ontario: Pearson Education Canada.

Pinar, W. F., Reynolds, W. M., Slattery, P., & Taubman, P. M. (2000). *Understanding curriculum*. New York: Peter Lang.

Pronger, B. (1995) Rendering the body: The implicit lessons of Gross anatomy. *Quest, 47*, 427-446.

Shapiro, K. J. (1985). *Bodily reflective modes: A phenomenological method for psychology*. Durham, NC: Duke University Press.

Sheets-Johnstone, M. (2011). *The primacy of movement* (Expanded second edition). Philadelphia, PA: John Benjamins.

Shusterman, R. (1999). Somaesthetics: A disciplinary proposal. *Journal of Aesthetics and Art Criticism*. Retrieved December 2003 from http://www.temple.edu/aesthetics/somaesthetics.html

Smith, S. J. (1982). *The phenomenology of play behaviour and its educational significance*. Unpublished M.Ed. dissertation, University of Queensland.

Smith, S. J. (1988). *Risk and the playground*. Unpublished doctoral dissertation, University of Alberta.

Smith, S. J. (1992). Studying the lifeworld of physical education: A phenomenological orientation. In A. Sparkes (Ed.), *Research In physical education and sport: Exploring alternative visions* (pp. 61-89). London: Falmer.

Smith, S. J. (1997a). *Risk and our pedagogical relation to children: On the playground and beyond*. Albany, NY: State University of New York Press.

Smith, S. J. (1997b). The phenomenology of educating physically. In D. Vandenberg (Ed.). *Phenomenology in education discourse* (pp. 119-144). Durban: Heinemann.

Smith, S. J. (2006). Gestures, landscape and embrace: A phenomenological analysis of elemental motions. *The Indo-Pacific Journal of Phenomenology, 6*(1), 1-10.

Smith, S. J. (2007). The first rush of movement: A phenomenological preface to movement education. *Phenomenology & Practice, 1*(1), 1-13.

Smith, S. J. (2011). Becoming horse in the duration of the moment: The trainer's challenge, *Phenomenology & Practice, 5*(1), 7-26.

Smith, S. J. (2012). Caring caresses and the embodiment of good teaching, *Phenomenology & Practice*, 6(2), 65-83.
Smith, S. J. (2014a). Human-horse partnerships: The discipline of dressage. In J. Gillett & M. Gilbert (Eds.), *Sport, animals, and society* (pp. 35-51). New York: Routledge.
Smith, S. J. (2014b). A pedagogy of vital contact. *Journal of Dance and Somatic Practices*, 6(2), 233-246.
Smith, S. J. (2015). Dancing with horses: The science and artistry of coenesthetic connection. In N. Carr (Ed.), *Domestic animals and leasure*. New York: Palgrave Macmillan, in press.
Solnit, R. (2000). *Wanderlust: A history of walking*. New York: Penguin.
van den Berg, J. H. (1972). *A different existence*. Pittsburgh, PA: Duquesne University Press.
van Manen, M. (1984). Practicing phenomenological writing. *Phenomenology + Pedagogy*, 2(1), 36-69.
van Manen, M. (1986). *The tone of teaching*. Richmond Hill, Ontario: Scholastic.
van Manen, M. (1990). *Researching lived experience: Human science for an action sensitive pedagogy*. London, Ontario, Canada: The Althouse Press.
van Manen, M. (1991). *The tact of teaching*. Albany, NY: State University of New York Press.
van Manen, M. (1992). The vitality of the pedagogical relation. In B. Levering, S. Miedema, S. Smith, & M. van Manen (Eds.), *Reflections on pedagogy and method* (Vol. 2, pp. 173-192). Montfoort: Uriah Heep.
van Manen, M. (1997). From meaning to method. *Qualitative Health Research: An International, Interdisciplinary Journal*, 7(3), 345-369.
van Manen, M. (2002). *Writing in the dark: Phenomenological studies in interpretative inquiry*. London, Ontario, Canada: The Althouse Press.
van Manen, M. (2014). *Phenomenology of practice: Meaning-giving methods in phenomenological research and riting*. Walnut Creek, CA: Left.

JOE L. KINCHELOE

13. CRITICAL HISTORIOGRAPHY

"Critical" is used in the critical theoretical sense of the term. Emerging in the work of the Frankfurt School in post World War I Germany, critical theory along with approaches to scholarship emerging from the work of W.E.B. DuBois addressed the frustration produced by positivist methods of studying social, cultural, political, economic, psychological, and educational phenomena and the oppression of unbridled capitalism. Critical scholars from diverse disciplines were impressed by critical theory's approach to the social construction of human experience (see Kincheloe 2004, for more insight into these issues of criticality).

Buoyed by critical insights, such scholars came to view their disciplines as manifestations of the discourses and power relations of the socio-historical contexts that produced them. The discourse of possibility implicit within the constructed nature of social experience suggested to these scholars that a reconstruction of the humanities and social sciences could lead to a more egalitarian and democratic social order. In such a context historical research took on a new usefulness, a new sense of what could be. In a critical modality history could escape a necrophilic concern with the past for its own sake and become a part of a contemporary conversation about social change and democracy.

Thus, critical theory revolutionized the notion of theory itself. In a critical context theory would not longer be viewed as a universal body of intractable truth but as a guide to the socio-cultural, political, psychological, and educational domains. In historiography critical theory does not determine how we see the world but helps historians gain new lenses for viewing educational phenomena and new strategies for exploring them. Critical theory is particularly concerned with issues of power and justice and the ways that the economy, matters of race, class, gender, sexuality, religion, and other forces shape both educational institutions and individual consciousness.

A critical historiography in education helps educators locate who they are, the goals of their pedagogy, and their political orientation to the educational act. In a critical historical context educators begin to learn the reasons for the multifaceted origins of public education. They find that schools were formed for competing purposes: the regulation of the poor, immigrants, and other "social threats" as well as for the democratic desire to educate an enlightened citizenry. Throughout history, education has served both causes concurrently. In this context educators can begin to make the choice as to which educational god they want to serve and build their pedagogies around their preferences.

In an essay (Kincheloe 1991) I published in the 1990s on educational historiographical methods, I addressed this issue of historian subjectivity and ways of seeing. The means by which power and culture shaped the perspectives of historians and thus the histories they produced were not deemed to be an important dimension of historiographical – especially educational historiographical – literature in the early 1990s. While strides have been made such concerns still are relegated to the periphery of historical scholarship. Even those deemed revisionists in the radical scholarship of the 1960s and 1970s were not especially concerned with issues of the subjectivity of the historian.

As Thomas Kuhn (1962) wrote over four decades ago, members of scholarly disciplines come to see themselves as responsible for the pursuit of common goals – objectives that form the core of so-called disciplinary matrixes. These disciplinary matrixes reflect their assumptions in the questions and methodologies employed in analyzing the concerns of a particular discipline of knowledge. What I then called a critical meta-analysis involves the myriad of ways that ideology, discourse, culture, and positionality shape this disciplinary matrix. In this context, I believe, that there are many engagements that are necessary to move educational historians and educational historiography to new insights into the limitations of the discipline and our ways of "doing historical research."

In this conceptual domain critical historians of education take an important cue from African American historians of education of the first half of the twentieth century: W.E.B. DuBois, V. P. Franklin, Carter Woodson, Horace Mann Bond, and many others. These historians saw no conflict between their scholarly goals of race uplift – the effort to improve the living conditions of people of African descent – and rigorous scholarship. They viewed themselves as scholars with profound connections to the black community. Critical historians, like these African American scholars, maintain close connections to marginalized individuals and communities and view their work as part of larger efforts to improve the lot of the oppressed (Alridge 2003). As the famous liberation theologian, Enrique Dussell has maintained, what meaning does scholarship have:

> For a Hindu beggar covered with mud from the floods of the Ganges; or for a member of a Bantu community from Sub-Saharan Africa dying of hunger; or for hundreds of thousands of poor marginalized in the suburban neighborhood like Nezahualcoyotl or Tlanepantla in Mexico .... (Dussell quoted in Mignolo 2001, p. 34)

Critical historians of education embrace a history that provides insight into problems that matter, that can help change the lives of those in need. Drawing upon the spirit of Paulo Freire, we proclaim a historiography for a pedagogy of the oppressed. Such an approach to history is grounded on an emancipatory reason that we referenced earlier as postformalism. As a form of emancipatory reason, postformalism is a multilogical alternative rationality (Aronowitz 1988) that employs forms of analysis sensitive to signs and symbols, the power of context in relation to thinking, the role of emotion and feeling in cognitive activity, and the value of the psychoanalytical process as it taps into the recesses of (un)consciousness. In the character of critical theory, postformalism attempts to democratize these ways of making meaning. In this effort postformal historians study issues of purpose, meaning, and value. Critical historians, thus, believe that the compelling interpretations that emerge from these purposes and scholarly processes can produce knowledges that provide a basis for just action in the present.

The knowledges that critical historians produce lead to action by working to decolonize the mind. Hegemonic, ideological, and discursive forms of power emanating from power centers in the Western world have worked to shape the consciousness of a wide range of individuals. The history of education that comes out of this mindset is many times blinded by the intense white light of dominant power. The result of such history is to exclude the experiences and insights of those who have not been well served by educational establishments. Historical knowledges produced by critical historians cannot predict the future or provide educators with a blueprint for the "correct" way of educating. Nevertheless, critical history of education can help us understand how situations came to exist in a way that informs our actions (Murphy 1997; Parker 1999). Thus, a critical history is a pragmatic history – a story of the past with consequences for the present and future.

Such a pragmatic history by nature connects the past, present, and future. History is changed by the events of the present. When we study histories written about gender and education in the late nineteenth century, we are amazed by the assumptions about gender that shaped such chronicles. The changing role of women in the last half of the twentieth century forced historians to rewrite earlier histories of the schooling and education of women. Thus, critical historians aware of the co-constructed relationship of past, present, and future and the role of power in shaping everyday events continuously gain new perspectives into old concerns. Such critical histories expose oppressive assumptions, the fingerprints of power on archival manuscripts, and the cultural logics of established historical interpretations. This critical expose opens a stargate to an alternative future, as it sheds a revealing light on the foibles of the old regime. Even in light of the critical historian's understandings of the complexities and ambiguities of reconstructing the past, she still insists that compelling historical interpretations can lead to social and educational change (Parker 1999; Barros 2004; Bentley 2005). A critical historical consciousness leads to enhanced human agency that helps individuals and groups navigate their way through a maze of socio-cultural, political, economic, and educational structures that too often serve to regulate and discipline.

To get to this point critical historians often start their research with a basic question: what groups and individuals are advantaged and what groups and individuals are disadvantaged by particular historical educational plans and organizations? Here critical historians begin to identify the power relations that shape educational issues. In this context a literacy of power becomes especially important. Such a literacy involves a complex understanding of a variety of the ways power operates to marginalize and oppress. Critical historians are thus obligated to understand hegemonic, ideological, discursive, disciplinary, and regulatory modes of power and the ways they affect human efforts to shape their own lives. Understanding such power dynamics does not make the critical historian's task any easier. Power in a critical complex sense does not play out in some paint-by-numbers formula. Every circumstance is different and while hegemony may exist, it may manifest itself in unique and perplexing ways.

Historians operating in the critical sense outlined here struggle for accuracy even when events elude their initial expectations. Many of us operating in this critical historical domain have often heard conservative critics argue that social theory informed history allows particular worldviews to dictate their interpretation and their narrative. This is the case only if one is an inept historian. Social theory in the critical sense of the term helps historians formulate questions, rethink what counts as a source, develop interpretive strategies, expand one's toolbox of methods, and develop unique narrative styles (Parker 1997; Gale 1999). Critical theory does not dictate what it is one finds in the process of historical research. In fact, if it works properly it expands the possibility of finding new sources and developing innovative ways of making sense of the past and its relation to the present. Any historian – no matter what his or her ideological/theoretical orientation who looks only for and uses evidence that supports some larger political point has committed an unnatural act against Clio (the Greek muse of history).

I have been confronted with these accusations of "cooking the research" so often in my career as a critical educational researcher that I feel it important to address these matters in more detail. Let there be no ambiguity about this tenet of critical historiography: dishonestly picking and choosing historical data to marshal support for a specific political, social, or educational agenda is bad history. Critical historiography is concerned with asking questions of the past – not dictating answers about it. These questions take us where they will, and we must have the courage to venture into these uncharted hermeneutic domains. In this interpretive netherland critical historians must avoid the deterministic sirens imploring us to view only macro-structures while ignoring the lived complexity of everyday life as well as the criticalists who would move us to see only the oppressive dimensions of schooling in lieu of expressions of education's democratic impulse.

Concurrently, critical educational historiography as it focuses on race, class, gender, sexual, religious concerns must not lose sight of the reformulation and intensification of the power of new twenty-first century forms of capital-driven global colonialism. Such structures exert new forms of regulation on peoples around the planet as they co-opt education for their own insidious designs. An exploration of these new phenomena must be carried out in diverse locales with concentrated attention paid to the ways particular individuals and groups have resisted their intrusions. The critical historiography here searches for new formulations and articulations of power and oppression, but always within a dialectic shaped by the interaction of individual and structure. Individual and structure simply cannot be considered as separate dynamics because of their co-constructive relationship. Structure shapes the individual, as the individual shapes the structure (Castro-Gomez 1998; Bentley 2005). One cannot study the history of schooling nor walk into a contemporary school without noting the omnipresence of this process. The dance of the subject and the macro-structure is a key dimension of the critical complexity referenced earlier.

A key dimension of doing historical research in education involves anticipating and addressing the complexity of history and historical research. Contrary to naïve objectivist assertions, history is much too complex to be known in some final, comprehensive, and intractable manner. Historians – no matter how brilliant they may be – cannot escape the blinders of her particular historical era. Our Zeitgeists shape us in ways we can never completely understand in our lifetime. Even the documents historians validate as "authentic" are soaked with dominant power and shaped by the subjective perspectives of their producers. Often when critical historians address such complicating factors, they are accused of relativism and the attempt to kill history. Understanding the ways that the construction of a historical narrative is in part a creative act, a feat of the imagination does not take away from the usefulness of historical scholarship. Indeed, it provides us with a more accurate picture of the historiographical process and how history may be either distorted or used in a socially beneficent manner.

All historical research is ensnared in this web of complexity, whether we like it or not. Historical narratives assume particular epistemological, ontological, political, ad infinitum positions – whether the historian is conscious of them or not. Based on these commitments historians choose to include particular data in their narratives while excluding other information. So much happened in the time and place about which one is writing that the historian is forced to use a set of subjective criteria to select what is and is not important. Critical historians attempt to make these criteria open for inspection by their readers. Objectivist historians often act as if they don't exist, arguing that they made no subjective choices – we're just telling the story as it really happened (Murphy 1997; Norkus 1999). Of course, no one can do that in some objective, disinterested manner, even when we're attempting to describe something that happened in the present. Human beings always see the world from a particular vantage point.

In light of the previously mentioned critical theoretical goals and issues of complexity, the history of education we are promoting here moves historical scholarship to a new level of scholarly rigor. We are not defining rigor here in some positivistic follow-the-standardized-procedure modality. Our definition of rigor involves an awareness of the influence of one's own subjectivity on historical research, the complexity of the past, the power dynamics at work in all phases of historical research, the dynamics of a useful history that promotes the social good, and the multiple dimensions of historical narratives. I have argued in many places that such rigor demands a multilogical approach to scholarship and social action.

As I mentioned earlier in this chapter, postformalism calls on historiography to bring multiple perspectives to its work. This concept of multilogicality rests at the heart of a critical multiculturalism and an evolving notion of criticality. I have expanded these notions in my description of the research bricolage (Kincheloe 2001, 2005; Kincheloe and Berry 2004). A complex mode of research is grounded on this multilogicality. This assertion is not some esoteric, academic point – it shapes social analysis, political perspectives, curriculum development, teaching and learning, and the field of educational history. Acting upon this understanding, critical historians understand that historical observations hold more within them to be analyzed than first impressions sometimes reveal. In this sense different frames of reference produce multiple interpretations and multiple realities. The mundane, the everyday and the historical dimensions are multiplex and continuously unfolding – while this is taking place, human interpretation is simultaneously constructing and reconstructing the meaning of what we observe. A multilogical educational history promotes a spatial distancing from reality that allows an observer diverse frames of reference.

Drawing upon this postformal multilogicality in this historiographical pursuit, critical historians, like liberation theologians in Latin America, make no apology for seeking the viewpoints, insights and sensitivities of the marginalized. The way to see from a perspective differing from that of the positivist guardians involves exploring an institution such as education from the vantage point of those who have been marginalized by it. In such a process subjugated knowledges once again emerge allowing historians to gain the cognitive power of empathy – a power that enables them to take pictures of reality from different vantage points. The intersection of these diverse vantage points allows for a form of analysis that moves beyond the isolated, decontextualized and fragmented analysis of historical reductionism.

Cognitively empowered by these multiplex perspectives, complexity-sensitive, multilogical historians seek a multicultural dialogue between Eastern cultures and Western cultures, a conversation between the relatively wealthy Northern cultures and the impoverished Southern cultures and an intracultural interchange among a variety of subcultures. In this way forms of knowing, representing, and making meaning that have been excluded by reductionist and often white patriarchal elitist history move us to new vantage points and unexplored perspectives. Understandings derived from the perspective of the excluded or the "culturally different" allow for an appreciation of the nature of justice, the invisibility of the process of oppression, the power of difference and the insight to be gained from a recognition of divergent cultural uses of long hidden knowledges that highlight both our social construction as individuals and the limitations of monocultural ways of meaning making.

In our critical historiographical use of multilogicality we begin to uncover the ways that race, for example, is embedded not only into the topics that historians of education traditionally chose to study but also in the construction of history as a discipline. By the seventeenth and eighteenth centuries race had emerged as a colonial construct characterized by white conquerors and the "colored" colonized. This hierarchy was built into a meta-philosophy of history that assumed hierarchical distinctions between diverse groups of people. Such inscriptions can be easily seen in the historical productions of the centuries following the advent of colonialism, yet they were often oblivious to the historians and their readers. A critical multilogical historiography of education seeks to identify and expose tacit assumptions such as these.

A multilogical historiography promotes a displacement of a monological perspective from the centers of various power blocs – racial, class, gender, sexual, religious, national, etc. In this way diverse ways of seeing and being are valued and employed in the historical topics chosen, interpretive strategies devised, and the historical research methods engaged. By recognizing the power of difference we begin to understand the limitations of the epistemological assumptions behind much Western historiography. In this context we discern that objectivist forms of history are built on an epistemological house of cards that collapses quickly when reductionist truth claims are seriously questioned. Thus, critical historiography's view from the bottom, its respect for subjugated knowledges moves educational historians to listen to colonized peoples, racially marginalized individuals, men and women who did not benefit from the promises of schooling, and other peoples occupying the lowest rung of the socio-economic ladder. In such a context such individuals' ways of seeing and making meaning can inform our understanding of the world, society, education, the construction of selfhood, and, thus, the study of history in dramatic new ways.

In this critical multilogical context educational historians enter a new domain of practice. In this zone of critical multilogicality such historians if they are operating in North America work in solidarity with Asians, Africans, Latin Americans, indigenous peoples, and subcultures within their own societies. In their "interracialism" and "interculturalism" they understand that there is far more to history than the socially constructed notion that civilization began in ancient Greece, migrated to Europe, and reached its zenith in the contemporary U.S. In histories that emerge in various fields, education included, this assumption exists in an influential and unchallenged state. Critical multilogical historians challenge this monological Eurocentrism and search for the ways it insidiously inscribes the "doing of educational history." At this point educational historians look for various forms of indigenous knowledge both as a focus for historical research and for their epistemological and ontological insights. Not only do we learn about such knowledges and the cultures that produced them, but we also use their ways of seeing and being to challenge Western monological perspectives. Here critical multilogical historians question reductionist notions of historical objectivity and superficially validated historical facts.

Historiographical multilogicality is a break from the class elitist, white-centered, patriarchal histories that have dominated Western historiography for too long. While many successful efforts have been made to get beyond elite, white, male histories, critical historians want to go farther – they want to understand the colonial impulses that work to exclude important histories of education from non-Western and subjugated domains and how these domains shape normalized history. Learning from indigenous knowledges, African, Islamic, Asian, and Latin American philosophies of history, critical historians learn new ways of practicing their craft. Those who have suffered under existing political economic and social arrangements are central to the project of critical historiography. Because those who have suffered the most may not have left written records – the bread and butter of traditional historiographical source material – critical historians employ oral history that grants voice to those peoples and perspectives lost to traditional educational history.

Critical oral history exerts a democratizing effect on educational history, as it welcomes the perspectives of those who have not been the beneficiaries of schooling (Parker 1997 1999; Mignolo 2001). In this context it opens new domains of inquiry to educational historians, moving the educational historian to look to sources of evidence previously dismissed. In my own interviews with students who were deemed to be failures in the schools they attended, I uncovered idiosyncratic ways of expressing their frustrations that would be overlooked by more traditional educational historians. For example, in studying the educational life histories of several school dropouts in Pennsylvania, I was allowed access to former students' personal writings that provided new insights into the ways they had been mis-evaluated in school. Their writings gave me profound insights into who these students were, what they suffered in school, and the compelling talents they possessed that were never uncovered by standard educational practice.

Critical Historiography: An Affirmative Presentism

A key dimension of a critical educational historiography involves what might be referred to as an affirmative presentism. In more traditional forms of historiography presentism is viewed as a venal sin. The fallacy of presentism, as it is labeled, occurs when a historian infuses the past into present – e.g., the U.S. is in the same shape of the Roman Empire and will fall just like it did if we continue our sinful ways. At the same time the charge of presentism can also be made when historians interpret the past using frameworks developed in the present – e.g., in the eleventh century the Iraqis knew that someday they would face threats from Russia. Obviously, in both of these cases a historiographical mistake is being made. A presentism that simply imports contemporary modes of understanding and frames of reference to the past produces anachronistic interpretations of history.

What historiographers have traditionally labeled historicism provides the grounding for the historical craft's disdain for mixing past and present. The key argument of historicism is that each epoch possesses its own unique *Zeitgeist* and, thus, must be viewed on its own terms, values and belief structures. In viewing the past historicism posits that all present-day values must be set aside. If such values are employed either consciously or unconsciously, then the historian has fallen into the briar patch of presentism. To stay out of such a briar patch, historicism maintains that the purpose of all history is to understand the mindset of people living in the past and to see the cosmos through their eyes.

Critical historians advocating an affirmative presentism discern many flaws in these anti-presentist and historicist arguments. While understanding that anachronistic judgments can be made by applying the ways of seeing of one era to another, an affirmative presentism understands the complexity of the historicist notion of seeing the past through the eyes of those historical figures who lived in it. No historical era is made up of one perspective – indeed, there are always multiple and conflicting viewpoints coming from a wide diversity of groups. If the objective historian is to examine a historical era from the perspective of those who lived during it, which group's perspective is chosen? Students? Teachers? Administrators? Defenders of the educational status quo? Critics? Given the nature of historical sources, historians will often unconsciously embrace the perspective of those who left written records. Of course, the authors of these sources tend to be the most privileged members of the social order under study.

This question of sources raises a whole new set of problems for historicists who seek to represent "the past as it really was." The historical sources to which historians have access are always subjective, idiosyncratic perspectives of particular groups of people viewed through the researcher's presently constructed interpretive lenses. What sources does a historian choose to include as part of her narrative? What sources does she choose to exclude? All of these questions make the historical research process much more complex than historicists and other groups of historians originally thought it was. In addition, we can never completely grasp a moment of the past in the way it was experienced by even one group of people because we know many things that happened in the following months, years, decades, and centuries. The consequence we assign such historical moments is always shaped by the historical hindsight not possessed by the historical participants (Parker 1997; Castro-Gomez 1998; Alridge 2003).

Thus, educational research – even some educational historical research – isolates past from present. The temporality of education, the time related processes of which educational processes are a part is often overlooked in educational research. One role of historical research in education – its place in the multiperspectival bricolage that Kathleen Berry writes about in this volume – is to help researchers understand the inescapable relationship between past and present in all knowledge production. One's socio-cultural, political economic location in the present will always influence one's research no matter if she is a historian, ethnographer, semiotician, or statistician in education. An affirmative historiographical presentism in this context understands that the present always affords the past with meaning. This should not make us give up the effort to produce great educational history but should make us better historians as we study this hermeneutic process. For example, the textbook battles in the mid-1970s led by right-wing religious conservatives take on a new type of historical importance after the political and educational victories of right-wing operatives in the subsequent thirty years.

Present events, thus, construct the importance of past events. An educational historian needs to know how this process takes place. Humans grant meaning to both present and past events by our decisions about which ones are important and by how we narratively position them. Processes such as the emergence of hyperreality and globalization demand a rethinking and rewriting of history. History, thus, changes history (Valdes and Hutcheon 1994; Barros 2004). After 9/11 the history of relationships between the Muslim world and Europe took on new importance. The point is made over and over again – many historians may want to pristinely separate present and past but such segregation is simply not possible. Critical historians in this context dismiss the segregationist effort and work to understand the complexity of the relationship.

Appreciating that our knowledge of the educational past is always partial – dependent upon what happens next – critical historians promoting an affirmative presentism understand the hermeneutic limits on any historical research. We all live and operate in a particular social, cultural, political economic (nb: political economic, not political and economic), discursive present and it is that spatial and temporal locale that creates the horizon on which we view the past. The better we understand our present situation, the more rigorous our historical scholarship will be. The more rigorous our scholarship, the more compelling our interpretations of historical moments will become. And the more rigorous our interpretations become, the greater use value they provide critical historians for informing critical action in the present. How did the present situation come to be? critical historians ask. What social, cultural, political economic situations induced individuals to make particular decisions about educational purpose, curriculum content, school policy, teacher prerogative, etc?

Embedded in these presentist oriented questions – and all historical questions for that matter – are projections of the future. Often without consciously understanding the teleology they embrace, Western historians have assumed a future dictated by Western epistemologies and ways of seeing the world. Critical historians with their study of the interaction of the past and present expose such Eurocentric/Amerocentric inscriptions that shape educational history and contemporary educational affairs. The process of engaging in an affirmative presentism is never easy, as critical historians must always search for what is not readily apparent to someone from a different era. If we are to produce a usable history that informs – not directs – contemporary emancipatory action, we must focus on historical disjunctions, naive attributions of cause and effect, the lost pathways of particular historical processes, forgotten options that seemed plausible to people of the historical era being studied, etc. Devoid of these complicating dynamics, the critical histories we produce may be too simplistic, too reductionist in the ways we think that they might inform present educational practices (Valdes and Hutcheon 1994; Murphy 1997; Parker 1997; Cooper 2005).

As critical historians we take on the challenge of engaging a historiography that is unafraid to address the relationships connecting the past, present, and future – even as we understand how complex such interconnections may be. Healing racial, class, gender, and religious divisions, for example, requires an understanding of the historical ways such conflicts oppressed and caused suffering among particular groups. Without such knowledge paths to an emancipatory future are much harder to forge. Thus, critical historians who embrace an affirmative presentism become brokers that work to connect past, present, and future. As time brokers critical historians don't predict the future, they do not gain access to some mystical crystal ball. The hermeneutic relationship connecting past, present, and future is much too complex for such a positivistic notion. As previously noted, critical educational historians gain insight via their historical work that helps guide their own actions as well as the actions of their readers in the present and future (Parker 1999; Barros 2004; Gresson 2004).

In this context of affirmative presentism critical educational historians pay close attention to the African concept of *sankofa* (Alridge 2003; Hotep 2003). *Sankofa* refers to going back to understand the past for the purpose of moving forward. In this African framework the past is not something lost to the ages but inseparable from the present and the future. In this context *sankofa* becomes a key historiographical concept as it provides compelling multilogical perceptions of how the present came to be and the possibilities the future portends. Employing this notion an affirmative presentism interrogates the cultural significance of the histories we produce. There is a profound difference between an anachronistic presentism that applies the tacit ways of seeing of the present to an interpretation of the past and its meaning and an affirmative presentism that understands the ways that present and past are intertwined in complex and often confusing ways.

Understanding this omnipresent entanglement, critical historians continuously study the ways that present forces shape their relationship to the past. This dynamic is a crucial aspect of a critical historiography. Indeed, critical historians maintain that it is important to not only understand these forces but to also let their readers know about them. This is where an understanding of a critical epistemology – an appreciation that knowledge is always a product of a particular vantage point – becomes extremely important in historical and other forms of educational research. It is in this context that we wish that contemporary devisors of standardized, allegedly value neutral curricula in Western schools had a greater historical consciousness of how past and present are intertwined. Such a perspective could help them discern the ways that historical and social forces continuously shape the nature of what we consider objective educational research. While a presentist-oriented history is always dangerous, it is inevitable. The point of our affirmative presentism is to acknowledge and study the relationship between past, present, and future in ways that can promote a more rigorous form of educational history that can be used in ways to promote the social and educational good.

REFERENCES

Alridge, D. (2003). The dilemmas, challenges, and duality of an African American educational historian. *Research News and Comment.* Retrieved March 30, 2006 from http://www.aera.net/uploadedFiles/Journals_and_Publications/Journals/Educational_Researcher/3209/3209_ResNewsComment.pdf

Aronowitz, S. (1988). *Science as power: Discourse and ideology in modern society.* Minneapolis, MN: University of Minnesota Press.

Barros, C. (2004). The return of history. In C. Barros & L. McCrank (Eds.), *History under debate: International reflection on the discipline.* New York: Haworth Press.

Bentley, J. (2005). Myths, wagers, and some moral implications of world history. *Journal of World History, 16*(1). Retrieved March 21, 2006 from http://www.historycooperative.org/journals/jwh/16.1/bentley.html

Castro-Gomez, S. (1998). Traditional and critical theory of culture: Postcolonialism as a critical theory of globalized society. Retrieved December 3, 2005 from http://www.javeriana.edu.co/pensar/sc5.html

Cooper, F. (2005). *Colonialism in question: Theory, knowledge, history.* Berkeley, CA: University of California Press.

Cuban, L. (1993). *How teachers taught: Constancy and change in American classrooms 1880-1990* (2nd ed.). New York: Teachers College Press.

Gale, T. (1999). *Critical policy methodology: Making connections between the stories we tell about policy and the data we use to tell them.* Paper Presented at the Joint Conference of the Australian Association for Research in Education and the New Zealand Association for Research in Education. Melbourne. Retrieved March 30, 2006 from http://www.aare.edu.au/99pap/gal99121.htm

Gresson, A. (2004). *America's atonement: Racial pain, recovery rhetoric, and the pedagogy of healing.* New York: Peter Lang.

Kincheloe, J. (1991). Educational historiographical meta-analysis: Rethinking methodology in the 1990s. *Qualitative Studies in Education, 4*, 231-245.

Kincheloe, J. (2001). Describing the bricolage: Conceptualizing a new rigor in qualitative research. *Qualitative Inquiry, 7*, 679-92.

Kincheloe, J. (2004). *Critical pedagogy.* New York: Peter Lang.

Kincheloe, J. (2005). On to the next level: Continuing the conceptualization of the bricolage. *Qualitative Inquiry, 11*(3), 323-350.

Kincheloe J., & Berry, K. (2004). *Rigor and complexity in educational research: Conceptualizing the bricolage.* London: Open University Press.

Murphy, R. (1997). Hayden White on facts, fictions and metahistory. *Sources: Revue d'Etudes Anglophones, 2*, 13-30. Retrieved March 30, 2006 from http://www.paradigme.com/sources/SOURCES-PDF/Pages%20de%20Sources02-1-1.pdf

Norkus, Z. (1999). Between philosophy and rhetoric, or historicizing postmodernism in meta-historical studies. Retrieved March 30, 2006 from http://www.crvp.org/book/Series04/IVA-26/chapter_vii.htm

Parker, L. (1997). Informing historical research in accounting and management: Traditions, philosophies, and opportunities. *Accounting Historians Journal.* Retrieved March 21, 2006 from http://www.findarticles.com/p/articles/mi_qa3657/is_199712/ai_n8781710/pg_2

Parker, L. (1999). Historiography for the new millennium: Adventures in accounting and management. *Accounting History.* Retrieved March 21, 2006 from http://www.findarticles.com/p/articles/mi_qa3933/is_199911/ai_n8865215/pg_6

Valdes, M., & Hutcheon, L. (1994). Rethinking literary history—comparatively. American Council of Learned Societies. Occasional Paper No. 27. Retrieved March 30, 2006 from http://www.acls.org/op27.htm

GLOSSARY

Critical theory: a theory oriented towards creating social change through the critique of political, cultural, social, and historical phenomena. This theoretical approach was developed by the Frankfurt School, a group of social theorists, who based their work on Marxism, Neo-Marxism, psychoanalysis, structuralism, and post-structuralism.

Epistemology: the branch of philosophy that studies knowledge and its production. Epistemological questions include: what is truth? Is that a fact or an opinion? On what basis do you claim that assertion to be true? How do you know?

Hermeneutics: the study of interpretation. Historically it was a method used only to interpret and understand religious texts, since, it has been utilized to study any text including lived experience, its layered meaning, and the relationship between the interpreter and the interpreted.

Historiography: the study and critical examination of history, historical methods, and historical writing. It employs a meta-analysis of the writing of the past using various literary methods (deconstruction, discourse analysis, textual analysis, hermeneutics, semiotics, and ideological contextualization) for interpretation.

Objectivism: the epistemological belief that disinterested knowledge can be produced about any phenomena simply by following the scientific method. If the method is followed rigorously no values, ideology, or other human perspectives will undermine the objectivity/validity of the knowledge produced.

Ontology: the study of the nature of being, existence, and reality, a branch of philosophy and metaphysics concerned with what it means to exist in a specific reality.

Positivism: an epistemological position that values objective, scientific knowledge produced in rigorous adherence to the scientific method. In this context knowledge is worthwhile to the extent that it describes objective data that reflect the world.

Praxis: central to liberatory education, it is the process through which critical analysis and action are simultaneously enacted. Praxis uses theoretical understandings, lived experiences, and pragmatic strategies to intervene in social, political, and cultural contexts.

Reductionism: a tendency in tradition Western research that assumes that complex phenomena can be best appreciated by reducing them to their constituent parts and then piecing the elements back together according to causal laws. This process typically involves forms of decontextualization and isolation of variables that work to undermine an understanding of the relation of phenomena under study to the world around them.

Zeitgeist: the German word for spirit of the times, commonly employed in historiography.

CAROLYNE ALI-KHAN

14. LIBERATION, MICE ELVES AND NAVEL GAZING

Examining the Ins and Outs of Autoethnography

THE DANGER OF BEING SURROUNDED BY MICE ELVES

"I want to thank you, falettinme, be mice elf, agin" (sic[1]) an old P-funk song[2] croons in my head as I start to write about autoethnography. Autoethnography – writing about "personal experience for the purpose of extending sociological understanding" (Wall 2006, p. 38) – is a scholarly version of 'being mice elf (myself) again.' It is also trusting that myself has something of value to say, and allowing the space for mice elves (the truths and distortions of my story) to resonate with others. I have found that autoethnography can open up for analysis a unique vantage point, one that is deeply valuable as a research and teaching tool. Yet I also believe that it is important to approach the reading and writing of autoethnography with a critical eye that acknowledges broader cultural contexts. I write this in the United States, in the second decade of the twenty-first century, at a time when TV reality shows, twitter feeds, blogs and selfies, have invaded public discourse and saturated the cultural landscape.

It seems as though I live in a world that is awash with self-adoring mice elves. My recent forays into Internet and media spaces have troubled me. Navigating cyberspaces I have had the distinct feeling that I have been immersed in a house of mirrors, a land where every 'I' is affirmed by "likes." It appears to me that many Internet spaces are as much forums for textual self-admiration as they are legitimate conduits for sharing ideas. Immersion in hyperspace, (as I have experienced it), currently entails being consistently bombarded with the notion that what I have to say *as an individual* is of paramount importance, *every opinion counts* and *I am the world*. Meanwhile every artefact of my daily life (from toothpaste tubes to newspapers) urges me to connect online and share, (share, share, SHARE) the minutia of my life. In this regard social network spaces seem little different from 'legitimate' news sites, or soda cans. Everyone everywhere (apparently) wants to know what 'I' think.

I am increasing unsettled. It seems that in our brave new information-age world nothing is too trivial and narcissism is never a concern. Of course I am not the first to point out that this landscape of 'me culture' and *(self)sharing as caring* is the new arena of bread and circuses (in that it is able to distract our attentions away from more serious concerns, and divert our energies into myopic and trivial pursuits). But in addition to my broad misgivings, I find 'me culture' to be additionally problematic as an educator and researcher who values narrative methods and believes that autoethnographies should be taken seriously in scholarly communities. Professionally I want to value the 'I' and honour the insights of the self in research, but I am forced to recognize that in current informational, social and media culture the word "I" is far too ubiquitous and in its ubiquity, is much abused.

As I wrestle with my disdain (on the one hand) and the seduction of (rather flattering) 'I' filled spaces on the other, I have begun to understand the complexity of using the self in research at this moment in time. I have also begun to understand the impact of a 'mice elf world' on teaching. Each semester I struggle to convince my students that *opinion* and *informed position* are neither the same nor of equal merit. I find it becomes increasingly difficult to push back against my student's belief that it is 'respectful' to unquestioningly treat all words and ideas as *equally valid.* My students initially (and sometimes persistently) find it difficult to critique a relativist stance that supports every position. An 'I' filled world has taught them to focus on individual stories rather than structural paradigms. As a result it has chewed away at the foundations for understanding critical theories and perspectives. It is therefore with trepidation that I approach autoethnographic work as a researcher and educator. So I begin this chapter by offering my personal list of cautions for myself, other autoethnographers, and those using this work to teach. I try to: 1. Be mindful of the way that this work is situated in the context of a broader selfie-infused world that has idolized individualism. 2. Worry about promoting unscientific thinking (such as the idea that personal beliefs are the same as scientific evidence). 3. Be careful to not encourage superficiality or the narcissism of simply spotlighting oneself. 4. Recognize that stories of the self can either illuminate structural realities *or* work against being able to see them. 5. Keep in mind that navel gazing is not always the best way forward.

Despite my concerns, I believe that autoethnographic research can facilitate valuable perspectives and that it has much to offer qualitative researchers, educators and students. In what follows I highlight why I believe autoethnography is a liberating rather than domesticating pedagogy, and I reflect on why it is worthy of serious scholarly consideration. In order to do this I provide examples of how (reading and writing) autoethnographies can enrich research and teaching. I intertwine personal autoethnographic moments to illustrate how and why I believe autoethnography matters. In conclusion I offer for analysis an annotated bibliography in which I group and highlight different types of autoethnographic texts. I present this work in the hope that readers will be inspired to teach from this literature and perhaps to craft their own mice elfs.

INS: AUTOETHNOGRAPHY IN RESEARCH.

Autoethnographies Can ... Push back on Regimes of Truth

Autoethnographies can support multiple ways of interpreting and sharing the world; in essence they can push back on oppressive regimes of truth. To reference a New York City phrase, there are '8 million stories in the naked city,' similarly there are many types of autoethnographies, each with its unique style and stance. Perhaps this should not be surprising; Roxanne Doty (2010) argues that there is no clear (agreed upon) methodology for creating autoethnographies.[3] A review of the literature confirms an enormous variety of autoethnographic texts. This range of different types of autoethnographies illustrates that it is an idiosyncratic, pliable and slippery genre, encompassing a multitude of different foci. For example: There is a heated debate between researchers who advocate for 'evocative' texts that pull readers into the emotional world of the authors (e.g., Ellis and Bochner 2006) and those who prefer traditional, ethnographic work presented as formal 'analytic' texts (e.g., Anderson 2006). In addition there are: Co-constructed autoethnographic texts (e.g., Barton and Darkside 2000) which move beyond a single or dominant voice to present separate but aligned and co-constructed realities. Multi-authored autoethnographic texts (e.g., Ellis, Adams, Ellingson, Bochner et al. 2009) that aim to honor the voices of multiple "I"s as they speak/write alone and together. Multimodal autoethnographic texts (e.g., Perira, Settlemas and Taylor 2005) which simultaneously work as art and text, disrupting the page visually and thereby pushing readers 'hear' different voices differently. Performative autoethnographic texts, (e.g., Blinne 2012), which pull readers into a rich narrative space by using literary techniques to encourage an experiencing of the text. Autoethnographic texts that work to convey the immediacy of physical sensations and reinsert the body into the act of reading and being (e.g., Carlass 2010). Autoethnographic texts which are more about others than the self, and use personal experience to shed light on the experiences of others (e.g., Snyder-Young 2011). Overtly political autoethnographic texts, which seek to inspire action by foregrounding the lived realities of structural oppression (e.g., Warren 2011). And autoethnographic texts that unite the intellectual and the spiritual, to challenge the notion that academia should be a secular world (e.g., Poulos 2010). These examples are by no means comprehensive,[4] but they begin to highlight the versatility, range and variety of autoethnographies. They also illustrate how autoethnography is an inherently postmodern research stance in that it balks at regimes of truth, refutes positivism and rejects conceptions of a single objective reality that can be measured and represented uniformly.

Autoethnographies Can ... Challenge Hierarchies

Autoethnographies can shed light on deficit orientations and subjugated positionings. In doing so they can create the space from which to challenge the idea that social hierarchies are natural and inevitable. I recall[5] my first tryst with autoethnography as a research method. Preparing to write a cultural studies essay (Ali-Khan 2009a) as a doctoral student, I was advised to write about what I knew. I was terrified. As a student, minority, and woman, I believed that I knew a whole lot less than nothing. The epistemological weight of traditionalist bifurcations had led me to believe that I had no option but to live in a world backslashed binaries, (e.g., professor/student, objective truth/subjective feelings, rational science/ emotional arts) and I knew that I was on the wrong side of every textual line. In addition to this I also believed (despite any evidence of success) that I was still *just*, a woman, a working class soul and an oddball minority. One who simply did not belong in the world of knowledge. Expressing this to my mentor I was advised to read the work of Valerie Walkerdine. Walkerdine (1990) powerfully describes the class and gendered nature of the imposter syndrome and the fear of being 'found out' as a fraud, despite professional success. As I read Walkerdine's autoethnographic notes, interpretations, and theorizing of her experiences, I realized how much they resonated with what I knew of the world. This then afforded me a vantage point from which to question the hierarchies that housed my own experiences. The insights of her work helped me to write about, politically contextualize and understand my struggles to overcome my insecurities and internalized beliefs about my raced, classed, gendered position in the world. I was able to apply this insight to my understanding of my own experiences. Both reading the autoethnographic work of others *and* writing my own pushed me into a critical space. From this space it was possible to question the inevitability of hierarchies and begin to resist my own internalized deficit orientations.

Autoethnographies Can ... Destabilize the Idea of Simple Truths

Autoethnographies challenge the idea that there are simple truths that can be distilled from lived experiences. Instead of simple clearly laid out truths, autoethnographies present messy, personal and complicated texts, which often leave the work of interpretation to the reader. Carolyn Ellis, Tony Adams and Art Bochner (2010) make the point that as a genre autoethnographies inherently embrace complexity. Although Ellis and Bochner argue that their evocative autoethnographies are substantively different from Andersons (2006) analytic ones, both types of texts embrace an understanding of experience as complex. Laurel Richardson and Elizabeth St Pierre (2008) believe that these two camps are not in fact dissimilar, they argue, "any dinosaurian belief that 'creative' 'analytical' (autoethnographies) are contrary and incompatible are standing in the path of a meteor" (p. 477). Whether analytic, evocative (or neither), autoethnographies tend to be personal, layered, messy and complex. To return to Walkerdine's work – which although not formally classified as autoethnography is writing (graphy) about the self (auto) – and is typical of a great deal of autoethnography in that it is complex in both form and content. This work nurtures contradictions: it is creative *and* analytical, rational *and* emotional, scholarly *and* personal, scientific *and* poetic. In addition to this it is written from the perspective of someone who is simultaneously an empowered academician *and* a woman struggling with structural patriarchy. It illustrates that there are no simple truths in social life. It also highlights how autoethnographic texts are methodologically able to allow for contradictions and multiple vantage points to organically emerge, and to present lived worlds that are full of intersectionality, contradictions and complexity. Such texts can encourage readers to understanding how we are *all* occupy multiple social positions. They can also create a space from which we can learn to refuse simple truths; critique master narratives; honor the complexity of personal experience; escape from binary thinking and challenge the backslash of separation between internal/external, self/other, personal/communal. They challenge us to see a more complex reality.

Autoethnographies Can ... Unite Scientific and Artistic Agendas

Autoethnographies can convey the world as a sensory space by utilizing methods beyond the scope of traditional academic texts. Stacy Holman Jones (2008) argues that autoethnographies are uniquely suited to cross the divide between science and art. I have found this important to my research. I think of myself as a contingent educational researcher. I question whether art holds more 'truth' than science and my scholarly existence is dependant on post-positivist paradigms. For me both reading and writing autoethnography have been affirming. This is not only because autoethnographies validate lived experiences, nor because they are therapeutic to write (e.g., Tillman 2009), although both of these are true. But rather because I have relished the creative and emotional space to try to become an 'artsy ethnographer' (Behar 2007) who might create a space in which work, play, science and art unite. For those who seek this space, creating autoethnographic text can be a way to engage in both serious and whimsical contemplation, and to rethink events in new ways. Balancing 'telling and showing' (Jones 2008) requires autoethnographers to move beyond being 'academic tourists' who visit a topic but can contemplate only the surface of things (Pelias 2003). Instead it necessitates "fall(ing) into a story" (Poulos 2010, p. 50). In my work this 'falling in' has allowed for new insights to emerge. For example writing about street skating (2009) forced me to understand my body as a reflection of political struggles in larger worlds; using Shakespeare to think about virtual educational learning environments (in press) connected me to historically important literary traditions and pushed me to think about the ontology of the body; examining my experiences in high school classrooms (2011) led me to create a fictional student who embodied and exemplified tropes and popular conceptions of teaching. These have been joyful writing acts. As I "narratively constructed life" (Owen, McRae, Adams and Vitale 2009, p. 187) I was able to seek truth in metaphor. I have found myself "wrapped up in a moment" (p. 49) in which I could legitimately use rhetorical devices (Owen, McRae, Adams and Vitale 2009). This quest to "produce aesthetic and evocative thick descriptions" (Ellis, Adams and Boucher 2010, p. 2) put to rest my fears that art and science, objectivity and truth, and emotional and rational knowledge are incompatible. Autoethnography was my place for scientific insights and artistic representations to meet. In addition to the way that *writing* autoethnographic texts can reconnect art and science, *reading* literary creativity in autoethnography can 'release the imagination' (Greene, 1995) and encourage readers to bring their artistic as well as their intellectual insights to the interpretation of texts. Autoethnographic writers such as Kristin Wilson (2011) and David Carless (2010), provide powerful examples of artistic and literary autoethnographic texts that invite close reading and facilitate intimate understanding.

Autoethnographies Can ... Encourage Us to Make Connections

Autoethnographies can encourage readers, authors and academicians to explore how our lives are connected to the lives of others and understand ourselves as relational (rather than individual) beings. As autoethnographies are narrative, reading autoethnographic texts encourages empathy in ways that more 'objective' traditional research texts do not. Although Carol Rambo (2007) insists that our stories are our own, I am not so sure. Not only is the world around the self populated with objects, ideas and other people, but Matin Tolich (2010) argues that our stories are *so* interconnected with those of others that they are inherently not ever our own; through his view "the self is porous" (p. 1608). In this porosity we are constantly absorbing the worlds of others and sharing ours, and so we are all, in effect, co-constructed. Paulo Friere (1998) would agree, he claimed that we inherently make ourselves with others (and further argues that we should never see our stories or our accomplishments as solely our own). I have found this perspective personally true as writing autoethnography has helped me understand my place in a populous universe and reflect on the ways in which the making of myself has been contextual and intricately bound to the lives of others. Autoethnographies inherently support this worldview as they often present a self as it exists in context and therefore in constant dialogue with the world. As a phenomenological approach it connects micro and macro discourses and can cement the personal to the political. As a reflexive method, autoethnography zooms in on the structure/agency dialectic and presents it as an embodied tale.

Autoethnographies Can ... Make Us Better Critical Teachers

If, as educators, we define good teaching as that which creates the space for critical reflection about power and justice (as I do), then reading and writing autoethnographies can help us to better our praxis. It is important to insert a caveat here: It is critical in writing teacher autoethnographies to be careful of the urge to "make ourselves look good" and instead "be reflexive" (Adams and Jones 2011, p. 113) so that we do not unwittingly write the type of 'savior' teaching narratives common in popular film. With that in mind, autoethnographies about teaching have much to offer. For example, Joe Kincheloe and Ken Tobin (2009) remind us of how important it is to fight positivistic and reductionist notions of teaching and being and to connect classroom struggles to broader political aims and impetus. Kincheloe brings these insights into specific pedagogical focus as he discusses the importance of critical (political) self-reflection for teachers (2005). Another salient example of this is John Warren's (2011) teaching autoethnography in which he highlights the importance of understanding teaching as a political act. Tricia Kress (2011) helps educators understand how to embark upon a journey of understanding their own social and political construction as she explains how and why to write autoethnographic teaching texts. My own forays into this method have clarified for me the extent to which autoethnography requires reflexivity. Writing a teacher autoethnography (2011) forced me peer closely and critically at who I am and what

I do professionally. It made me re-evaluate successes and failures in my teaching and helped me to see my students and myself as players in a larger sociocultural contexts. Writing an autoethnography that included my schooling experiences (2009b) helped me remove myself from the immediacy of experience and from this critical distance understand schooling differently. I believe that these insights are important for my quest to not unwittingly reproduce what was done to me in schools.

OUTS: THE AUTOETHNOGRAPHIC BODY IN TEACHING

Not Leaving Our Bodies at the Door

I now turn from examining autoethnography in research to further raise questions about the usefulness of autoethnography to understanding the way that bodies exist and are erased in schools. In the spirit of honoring autoethnographic methods, in this section I continue to intertwine snippets of my life story. My story is the story of a body: Like many young women, in my youth I was anorexic and also expended a great deal of my life energy working to try to be considered beautiful. Writing these words, I recognize how much these admissions are out of place in the rational world of education where we are first and foremost, brains-on-stems. As a professional educator I have felt encouraged to leave my body at the door. In schools and colleges over the past two decades I have had the distinct feeling that I have been expected to be above considering the value of my body; to speak of bodies has been (outside of feminist and queer literature) generally considered gauche (particularly as a school teacher). Perhaps I have internalized mores, but as an academician still I find that I am still implicitly encouraged to distance myself from myself by the clever use of articles. Pronouns provide distance. I often read "*the* self" and "*the* body" rather than "*my*" or "*our*" when "my" or "our" were clearly the subject. Micheal Humphreys (2005) argues that as academicians we should instead bring our bodies close to our texts. He argues that we should expose our bodies in our work, and write as fully fleshed and emotional beings who thereby expose our 'fragility.' But I believe we should be cautious in heeding this advice, there is a price for too much self-disclosure. Martin Tolich cautions budding autoethnographers to proceed with care and to remember that, "there are no future skin grafts for autoethnographic PhDs" (2010, p. 1605). We must live with the consequences of what we write. Speaking from the 12th century, Omar Khayyam (taken here both literally and metaphorically) would agree,

> The Moving Finger writes; and, having writ,
> Moves on: nor all thy Piety nor Wit,
> Shall lure it back to cancel half a Line,
> Nor all thy Tears wash out a Word of it. (1898)

These words should certainly give us pause. But although writing about hearts and bodies may leave us vulnerable, David Carless (2010) points out that *our bodies intrude on our lives* and the stories which our bodies wish to tell make demands on our attention.

My teaching story (typical of women in the West) was one of a body intruding on my life. As a young female teacher I felt the pressure of needing to be attractive and successful. I internalized dominant ideas about gender and although on some level I understood that in my quest to be a perfect I was contributing to my own oppression, I had no vantage point for structural critique. Like many women I took my quest to be a "good girl" a bit too far. I worked hard at being a successful and engaged teacher, while simultaneously I worked hard at lifting weights, pushing my body, and being very, very thin. Like so many women then and now I gutted myself on the altar of commoditized desirability. The personal and professional intertwined in my body. The hip-bones that I could feel through my trendy Gap pants assured me that I was a good teacher. Every one of my teenage students weighed considerably more than I did, this ironically assured me that I had great classroom management. I viewed my lack of physical presence as proof of substantive professional presence.

I am now an assistant professor in college of education in the United States. As teaching is primarily a female profession, every semester my undergraduate classes are filled with young women. They are mostly White, predominantly middle class, often strikingly thin and all hopeful. They walk through my classroom doors looking to do the right thing, and looking both too much and too little at themselves. In my classes they write analytic autoethnographies about their communities, their ideas and assumptions, and the ways that schooling influenced who they are and what they believe. I encourage them to look inward and read and write (to use Freire's term) 'the word and the world' (1987). Sometimes, catching a glimpse of *something* not quite right, I pull a student aside to ask a simple question, "Are you okay?" And time after time the short answer is "no." No, no, no, no, not okay at all. Time and again I am faced by a young, smart, outwardly successful woman, who is hanging by a thread. *Sometimes our bodies intrude on our lives.* These students tell me tales of struggles with bulimia and anorexia, poverty, mental illness, infidelity, domestic violence and despair. They pay the heavy price of patriarchy and they still try to be perfect. Their experiences are sadly far from unique. I view them and think back on how my own life was clawed at by ideas about what it meant to be good at being a woman, and by sexual and domestic violence. These experiences affected my grades (as a student) and my teaching (as a professional). They also impacted what I believe I am able sense in my students. Speaking with them I remember the feeling of isolation that is not bourn out by statistics. I was not alone in my experiences of my gendered body, but like my students now, I was in a world that silenced, shamed and isolated those experiences. Without the stories of others there was no place to understand structural contexts and patterns of shared experiences.

At their finest, what autoethnographic texts can do is, by inserting the body into narratives, stitch individuals back into the collective fabric of social contexts, making clear how our bodies and our stories are part of a social whole. An excellent example of this is the work of Murray Drummond (2012) in which he takes us inside his quest for a strong masculine body.[6] Texts such as this can un-silence and un-isolate experiences. They can demand that we acknowledge the physicality of being, insist that we hear individual stories and compel us to acknowledge the way that power is structured and how those structures impact lived experience. I believe that it is important to tell whole stories, address 'difficult knowledge' (Pitt and Britzman 2006) and bring controversial issues onto classrooms in order to fight against silencing and work towards empowerment, respect and understanding. Autoethnographic work can assist in this endeavour. Queer teaching autoethnographies (e.g., Hermann-Wilmarth and Bills 2010) in their refusal to ignore bodies, provide some of the most salient and powerful examples of how this can be done.

Becoming Mindful and Being Fully Present

I believe that educational research is in part about finding ways to be fully present and cognizant of the world. Using autoethnography in the classroom has encouraged me to try to be mindful and fully attuned to the unfolding research field. As such it has afforded me the space to also think about the role of emotions in teaching. Autoethnographies about teaching present the act of teaching as an embodied. These types of academic stories offer a portal through which readers can experience (through the words of others) not only the intellectual, but also the physical and emotional dimensions of being a teacher in a classroom. Visual theorist, John Berger (1972) argues that we always look at visual texts in relation to ourselves; I believe the same is true for autoethnographic narratives. They give us access to each other's lives and as we read these accounts, we are able to relate the experiences of others to a renewed understanding of our own.

Autoethnographies about teaching often highlight the ways in which the act of teaching is simultaneously intellectual, physical and emotional, and as they do so they push readers to think about the experiences of their own bodies and emotions in classrooms situations. Here are some examples: Ronald Pelias (2004) reinserts the body into pedagogy as he describes his teaching body by using memories, poetry and the metaphors of speech and heart. Kristin Wilson (2011) uses the metaphor of Pandora's box to describe her emotions while teaching and struggling to redress instances of structural inequity. Valerie Walkerdine (1990) highlights the importance of her female body as a child and as an adult to discuss the ways that being a girl and a woman impacted her understanding of teaching. Antonia Darder (2010) describes teaching as a whole body activity and reminds us to not ignore the bodies of youth we teach. Ken Tobin (2005) uses autoethnographic methods to pull readers in to his emotional and intellectual struggle to overcome the disconnect between his students lives and his own. Each of these texts creates the space for teachers and teacher educators to be able to consider their bodies and emotions and those of others as significant to their praxis and to examine their experiences and behaviors in this holistic light.

Living in Time and Space

Autoethnographies about teaching are also uniquely situated to remind readers to think about time and space as they operate in the physical worlds of school. I believe this focus is of particular urgency at this time (the second decade of the 21st century), as the bodies of children (and adults) in schools spaces are currently under attack. I write this a time where children in schools are being pushed to disconnect from their bodies and instead think of *being* (in school) as simply *being tested*. Time is conceived of as 'test prep' or 'on task.' Space is experienced as confined, allowing only certain movements and heavily under surveillance. Disciplines and practices that undermine these narrow definitions of time and space, such as those found in art, recess, music and theatre, are vanishing and being replaced by Common Core pedagogies. I believe that the reduction of time and space to instrumentalist ideals is nothing less than a sacrifice of children's bodies to brain-on-stem conceptions of childhood. In my two decades of high school teaching I worked in multiple school buildings in which children and adults were treated as criminals in waiting, in which metal detectors, surveillance cameras and police were as commonplace as book-bags and pencils. In the light of these contexts, and the inhumane disrespect of children's rights to their time and their space, it is deeply important to reinsert bodies tales into the stories we tell of school. Autoethnographies have the capacity to remind us that learning is lived. Teachers are not fleshy programmable robots, children are not test scores, and real learning is not measurable by a list of numbers and subcategories of objectives. They remind us that we are hearts, bodies, minutes and movement, even in school buildings.

Dancing with Mice Elves

I believe that it is time to embrace autoethnographic writing in educational research and in teacher education. If we are careful in how we do this we can reap the rewards of understanding ourselves and each other in all of our messy complexity. I hope that we embrace the risk, and that we choose to dance with 'mice elves' in the halls of academe.

AND THAT'S WHAT IT'S ALL ABOUT: AN ANNOTATED BIBLIOGRAPHY OF AUTOETHNOGRAPHY

In the annotated bibliography that follows I provide a sample of different types of autoethnographies and highlight issues in the field. I present these in agreement with Stephen Hartnett and Jeremy Engels who point out that for engaged scholars "the methodological conundrum is striving to balance itself with society, text with context, the existential delirium of the now with the scholarly rigor of analysis – all the while honoring the obligations to social justice" (2008, p. 598). Works are ordered alphabetically. The first section examines the field as a whole and presents a range of ways of doing and thinking about autoethnographies. The second section explores a wide range of ethical questions in autoethnography. The third section highlights autoethnographies that transgress boundaries and binaries. The last section examines the potential of autoethnography as political and liberating pedagogy. I hope that researchers and teachers are inspired to read these articles, write their own and to create textual spaces where we can be ourselves – each acknowledging the other and each trusting that we all have something of value to say.

Autoethnography How Shall I Call Thee?

Autoethnography is (like any other field) complex and contested. One rift in the field revolves around the debate whether autoethnography should embody a textual refusal to explain as it evokes reader responses (à la Ellis, Boucher, and Richardson), or be carefully analytical (à la Anderson). In the following section I highlight the debate between analytical (CAP) and evocative autoethnographers. I then present examples of a variety of different types of autoethnographies.

To CAP or to Evoke?

Anderson, L. (2006). Analytic autoethnography.
   Leon Anderson believes that autoethnography can and should be not only evocative but also analytical. In this work he acknowledges the importance of evocative autoethnography but then problematizes the rejection of realist epistemological assumptions that has been embraced by evocative ethnographers such as Carolyn Ellis and Arthur Bochner. He guides readers through a substantive history of autoethnography and then outlines the tenants of analytic ethnography. In contrast to radically non-traditional, poststructuralist evocative autoethnography, analytic ethnography is presented as a subgenre in the realist ethnographic tradition.

Atkinson, P. (2006). Rescuing autoethnography.
   Paul Atkinson supports Anderson's definition of analytic ethnography in addition to furthering the discussion. Atkinson reminds us not to succumb to overdrawn and often simplistic notions of an inherent divide between postmodern and positivist research. Atkins points out how much ethnographic work has been based in author's personal involvement in the area of study and is not written from the dispassionate distance that postmodernists claim. Ethnography is the interaction between the author and the word. With that in mind he supports Anderson's analytic stance and cautions against self-absorption and the aim of self-transformation in autoethnography.

Denzin, N. K. (2006). Analytic autoethnography, or déjà vu all over again.
   Norman Denzin uses the metaphor of 'apples and oranges' and uses multiple research examples to examine differences in autoethnographic approaches and describe why he parts ways with Anderson. Denzin usefully traces the research

traditions (e.g., the Chicago schools) behind different approaches as he discusses merit. He also connects autoethnography to critical pedagogy and reminds us that it should be a performance vehicle rather than an end unto itself.

Ellis, C. S., & Bochner, A. P. (2006). Analyzing analytic autoethnography an autopsy.

Carolyn Ellis and Arthur Bochner argue against Anderson's ideas. They describe the different orientations (theirs as evocative and Anderson's analytical) as the difference between thinking of autoethnography as a journey or destination, in the moment or in the theorizing, empathizing or abstracting. They argue that what they do is political and undercuts hierarchies whereas what Anderson does is support these.

Ellis, Carolyn, Adams, Tony E., & Bochner, Arthur P. (2010). Autoethnography: An overview.

With a postmodern passion, Ellis and Boucher argue that autoethnography is a response to the confines of epistemological, ontological and axiological positivist paradigms, master narratives and colonialist and sterile research impulses. Addressing the crisis in representation they make a case for writing that is value laden, evocative and 'closer to literature than physics.' They describe different autoethnographic styles and genres and go on to explain exactly what autoethnographers do, as well as why and how they do it. This is a valuable how-to guide for researchers wishing to explore evocative autoethnography.

Richardson, L., & St Pierre, E. A. (2008). Writing: A method of inquiry.

This chapter is comprised of two sections written by Laurel Richardson, and one section written by Elizabeth Adams St. Pierre. It offers a clear how-to for writing autoethnography. Explaining CAP (creative analytical process) autoethnography, this piece offers readers and researchers a complex yet easy-to-understand set of guidelines on how to write and review autoethnography. It includes both writing exercises and theoretical groundings.

Exploring the Field of Autoethnography

Cann, C. N., & DeMeulenaere, E. J. (2012). Critical co-constructed auto-ethnography.

Colette Cann and Eric DeMeulenaere write a fictionalized autoethnographic dialogue of their experiences. They present this as a co-constructed autoethnography "within the traditions of critical theory, critical pedagogy, and critical race methodology" (p. 147). This text reads more like a play than a traditional paper as it consists entirely of the authors' dialogue about their lived personal experiences connected to the writing of this text (e.g., picking up a phone and calling each other to discuss this article). Cann and DeMeulenaere bring to life the process of co-writing and the pragmatic concerns of academicians who do this type of writing (e.g., will this harm me for tenure, and is this *really* research?).

Denzin, N. K., & Lincoln, Y. S. (2003). The discipline and practice of qualitative research.

Norman Denzin and Yvonna Lincoln trace the history of qualitative research, describing how researchers have recently struggled to locate and represent themselves. They describe the value of postmodern sensibilities (that seek to not silence voices) and the methods and uses of multiple interpretive practices. They also explain process, genres, phases and paradigms in qualitative research. This text is valuable for researchers wishing to locate autoethnography within the broad field of qualitative research.

Holt, N. L. (2003). Representation, legitimation, and autoethnography: An autoethnographic writing story.

Nicholas Holt examines rigor and ethics in autoethnography by using peer review feedback to highlight potential issues and obstacles to the use of this method. He presents his writing story as a guide for others, as he examines the critiques against autoethnographies and then responds to them. This is an important text for those seeking to justify and publish this type of research.

Hughes, S., Pennington, J. L., & Makris, S. (2012). Translating autoethnography across the AERA Standards toward understanding autoethnographic scholarship as empirical research.

In this article in AERA's publication *Educational Researcher* Sherick Hughes, Julie Pennington and Sara Makris 'legitimize' autoethnography by framing and justifying it in empirical terms. They contextualize the place of autoethnography in qualitative research by tracing its epistemological and methodological history. They then use the standard 'AERA focus areas' to argue that autoethnography can withstand interrogation from empiricists. They create a rubric for evaluating autoethnography, which they see as a step toward "producing equitable, socially just, and transparent reviews of the autoethnographic research" (p. 217). This work is important for autoethnographic researchers who find themselves swimming against the tide in institutions mired in positivist paradigms.

Jones, S. H. (2008). Making the personal political.

Stacy Holman Jones shares her vision of evocative autoethnography that is able to engage in 'the business of music novels and film' by demanding and successfully eliciting audience/reader engagement and response to academic texts. She guides readers in thinking about how to balance 'telling with showing' as she connects knowledge, experience, meaning, text and narrative. Jones also provides lists of challenges, actions and accomplishments for performative writing. She offers a thought-provoking analysis of exactly how and why to create this type of text and how to analyse it.

Ngunjiri, F. W., Hernandez, K. C., & Chang, H. (2010). Living autoethnography: Connecting life and research.

This article is the introduction to a special issue in the Journal of Research Practice that is devoted to autoethnography. Faith Ngunjiri, Kathy-Ann Hernandez, and Heewon Chang discuss the range of different types of autoethnographies (including collaborative autoethnography) and offer detailed analysis of exactly how these works are different and why they are valuable. They include a brief discussion about the ways forward in autoethnographic research. Although intended as an introduction to subsequent texts, this is a good stand-alone piece that provides readers with a basic understanding of the lay of the autoethnographic land.

Pelias, R. J. (2003). The academic tourist: An autoethnography.

Ronald Pelias muses on the habits of academic life. He argues that academicians are tourists, constrained by internal and external forces that keep them always at 'the surface of things.' Pelias takes readers on a personal and evocative journey through the world of his contemplations about writing as he challenges researchers to refuse and refute superficiality and to use autoethnography to dig deeper.

Pereira, L., Settelmaier, E., Taylor, P. (2005). Fictive imagining and moral purpose. Autobiographical research as/for transformational development.

Les Pereira, Elizabeth Settelmaier and Peter Taylor offer examples of how to present multi-authored autoethnographies. They use multiple fonts, creative headings and subheadings, text boxes of 'asides' and the other graphic devices to present and represent intersecting and complex personal realities.

Roth, W-M. (2005). Auto/biography and auto/ethnography: Praxis of research method.

This edited volume offers twenty-one chapters from leaders in the field on autoethnography. These pieces are primarily drawn from and for educators at the k-20 level. The text is divided into six parts that together explain autoethnography and offer examples of different types of autoethnography.[7]

Wall, S. (2006). An autoethnography on learning about autoethnography.

Writing as a doctoral student, Sarah Wall walks readers through the landscape of autoethnography with clear and concise language. She catalogues names used describe this type of work, describes different styles of autoethnography (from rigorous to evocative) and examines the criticisms levelled against it. In addition she outlines how to begin autoethnographic work and analyse data as she reflects on her own experiences with this method.

Beyond Me, Myself and I

This section engages in reflections on ethics, conceptions of truth, implicating others and the secret lives of our stories. It highlights ethical guidelines, ethical dilemmas and some unintended consequences of researching self.

Adams, T. E., & Jones, S. H. (2011). Telling stories: Reflexivity, queer theory, and autoethnography.

Tony Adams and Stacy Holman Jones examine the connections between autoethnography, rigorous reflexivity and queer theory. They explain queer theory as that which, 'addresses harmful situations.' They describe rigorous reflexivity as a reflexivity that focuses on not only the self but also the way that *others* are implicated by writing about the self and they discuss challenges of representation (including the temptation to make oneself look good). Using sections of dialogues (about queerness) taken from interactions with their parents, siblings and children, they also question truth in autoethnographies.

Chatham-Carpenter, A. (2010). "Do thyself no harm": Protecting ourselves as autoethnographers.

How do we apply the ethics of harm to ourselves? Using italics to indicate her inner voice or thoughts, April Chatham-Carpenter makes visible the vulnerability of exposing oneself through autoethnography. In this work she walks readers through a spiral into anorexia that was triggered by her desire to write about it. Ultimately this work compellingly highlights the pressure to publish that junior scholars are subjected to as well as the multiple dangers of self-harm that can accompany self-disclosure.

Delamont, S. (2009). The only honest thing: Autoethnography, reflexivity and small crises in fieldwork.

Sarah Delmont includes in this work a six-point manifesto against autoethnography. Her critique provides interesting and well thought out food for thought for those wishing to be prepared to defend this type of work. Delmont argues that there is a substantive need for reflexive ethnography (in which authors reflect on the communities they study and their relationship to research subjects and topics) but little need for autoethnography, which she considers to be both inherently unethical and entirely about an obsession with self.

Guillemin, M., & Gillam, L. (2004). Ethics, reflexivity, and "Ethically important moments" in research.

Marilys Guillemin and Lynn Gillam offer a complex view of research ethics for autoethnography. They distinguish between procedural ethics (e.g., IRB board approvals) that involve formal checklists and standard responses to ideas of participant protection (developed from the biological sciences) and 'ethics in practice' that involve a more nuanced response to the many different types of ethical dilemmas that occur in situ while doing research. They argue that it is important to establish a strong link between these and describe how and why a robust reflexivity is the key to ethical autoethnographic research.

Owen, J. A. T., McRae, C., Adams, T., & Vitale, A. (2009). Truth troubles.

Using the controversy over Stephen Frey's fictional memoir "A million little pieces" as a familiar cultural text, Jillian Owen, Chris McRae, Tony Adams and Alisha Vitale argue that "truth" always an inherently unstable variable and should not be the criterion for evaluating life texts. They *trouble truth* as they contrast factual truths with ideas that are true. They challenge readers to think about the slippery nature of all social truth as they argue that "truth" in the scientific sense, may not be of paramount importance in the quest to understand personal (autoethnographic) experience or the larger world.

Rambo, C. (2007) Handing IRB an unloaded gun.

Carol Rambo writes about an autoethnography that was denied publication by a university IRB after having been accepted at a journal. The original autoethnographic manuscript (referred to in her text) examined a personal troubled history (incest and mental illness) and a sexual relationship between a professor and a student (a decade earlier). Rambo argues that professor-student trysts are far from unique and need to be discussed. She uses her own experiences, letters and transcribed conversations to allow readers to follow her arguments and her manuscript as she is denied IRB approval. Academic freedom of speech, harm to others and harm to authors' professional careers are addressed in this unique and troubling work.

Roth, W. M. (2004). Review essay: Autobiography as scientific text: A dialectical approach to the role of experience.

Wolff-Michael Roth damns Wolcott's book (see Wolcott 2002), in an article in which he critiques both the tools of analysis that Wolcott employs and the personal behaviors of the author. In order to "avoid an ad hominem" attack Roth creates two characters, the protagonist (whom he names Wally Haircut) and the author Harry Wolcott. Using Foucault, Bourdieu in his analysis and differentiating between social, cultural and symbolic capital, Roth examines the power relationships between Wally and Brad and the extent to which Wolcott benefited from his research.

Snyder-Young, D. (2008). "Here to tell her story'": Analysing the autoethnographic performances of others.

Dani Snyder-Young writes about the problematic nature of analysing autoethnographic performance as she reflects on 'the voice' of homeless actors in a community-based theatre project. This piece offers insightful reflections on power and distortions in re/presentation and assessment. It can be particularly helpful to researchers who are questioning ways to understand and appraise autoethnographies.

Strobel, Kara M. (2005). After the aftermath: A reply to Wolff-Michael Roth's review of Harry F. Wolcott's "Sneaky kid and its aftermath."

Kara Strobel takes on Michael Roth's review of Harry Wolcott's 'Sneaky Kid' (see Roth 2004 and Wolcott 2002). In a point-by-point discussion of both Roth's review and the original text, she refutes Roth's arguments, questions his standpoint and defends Wolcott.

Tolich, M. (2010). A critique of current practice: Ten foundational guidelines for autoethnographers.

In a 'must read' for autoethnographers, Martin Tolich addresses endemic problems in the ethics of autoethnography. He does this by first using examples to highlight the need for complex ethical guidelines and then outlines ten of these. Tolich makes the point that autoethnography often includes details on the lives of others. He goes on to illustrate how informed consent often is post facto and mired in messy relationships. The ten guidelines in this work offer novice and seasoned autoethnographers concrete strategies for about thinking about issues such as consent, vulnerability and consultation.

Wall, S. (2008). Easier said than done: Writing an autoethnography.

Sarah Wall offers insights on her previous autoethnographic work about being an adopting parent. She references a wide body of literature about the process of autoethnography. She explores the notion of "truth" in autoethnographic writing, addresses questions of ethics, and raises questions about the difference between good stories and good scholarship. Wall also touches on the vulnerability of autoethnographic writing and makes connections to larger feminist issues in research.

Wolcott, H. F. (2002). Sneaky kid and its aftermath: Ethics and intimacy in fieldwork.

This book, written by Harry Wolcott, started a firestorm about ethics in research and has been hailed as a both a tour de force and anathema to research. It is a compilation of articles about a "sneaky kid" who arrived and claimed residence on Wolcott's land. It describes the relationship between Wolcott and the kid and about the educational system that failed the sneaky kid, leading to his (in effect) squatting on Wolcott's land. The book also addresses the sexual relationship between author and subject and the trial of the kid who later burned down Wolcott's house. It includes the script of a play made about these events.

Wyatt, J. (2006) Psychic distance, consent, and other ethical issues: Reflections on the writing of "a gentle going?"'

In the genre of autoethnographies that are about therapeutic healing and opening wide trauma, Jonathan Wyatt writes about his writing about the experience of his fathers dying. He unpacks the inner conflicts and ethical dilemmas he faced in this project. This work prompts readers to think about the motivations for autoethnographic writing, the type of framing that it encourages, and the unintended consequences and independent life of published work.

One Love

In this section I offer samples of autoethnographies that inherently address issues of binaries and dualistic thinking. These works offer examples of how to use autoethnography to reconnect body/mind, self/other, internal/external, rational/emotional and other binaries.

Barton, A. C. (2000). Darkside: Autobiography in science education: Greater objectivity through local knowledge.
Angela Calabrese Barton (a professor at Teachers College) and dark side (a 17-year-old minority male) use parallel autoethnographic stories (laid out side-by-side on the page) to understand the social structures that shaped their lives and scientific understanding. In addition to this they use this type of autoethnographic text as an opportunity to make connections between (subjective) local knowledge and objectivity. They then dialogue about urban science education. In conclusion they reflect on the value of this type of multiple author ethnographic research to the participants themselves and to the field.

Behar, R. R. (2007). Ethnography in a time of blurred genres.
Ruth Behar argues that ethnography exists in a time of blurred genres when fiction and non-fiction are no longer distinct. She examines the history and uses of anthropology to remind us not to write boring books! Behar describes the fear in the sciences of good writing that might be perceived as too self indulgent and too emotional. Using multiple examples Behar shows us how to overcome this fear to read and write ethnographies like a writer and thereby produce rich, creative and evocative texts.

Blinne, K. C. (2012). Auto(erotic)ethnography.
Kristen Blinne explores herself and the topic of masturbation in this autoethnographic article written for the Sage journal *Sexualities*. In this work she fully takes on the challenge of reconnecting the public/private, as she reinserts her body into academic discourse. Pushing against dualisms and boundaries Blinne draws analogies between autoethnographic writing and masturbation as she reflects on acts that fully engage our creative and imaginative selves.

Carless, D. (2010). Who the hell was that? Stories, bodies and actions in the world.
David Carless presents seven short personal stories, each written from his standpoint as a gay man and each illustrating the way his body was significant to his lived experience. Carless uses his lived experiences to highlight the embodied nature of all research and question notions of propriety and acceptable story

material in academic discourses. He uses evocative prose to pull readers in to his thoughts and feelings and layers these texts with sections of formal writing about how autoethnography allows for a rich representation of lived experience. This work offers powerful insights as why the intrusions of the body into research should not be ignored.

Doty, R. L. (2010). Autoethnography – Making human connections.
In this short work Roxanne Lynn Doty highlights the importance of having a presence in writing. She illustrates how autoethnographies can bridge the distance between texts and the things in the world that texts seek to represent. She argues that accessible, personal and poetically moving texts are inherent to social justice as they refuse emotional distance and compel readers to be drawn in. Doty also argues that the concern for methodology can be an imposition and distraction that disconnects readers from the topic. She reminds us that 'connections to others' should be the point of all research.

Drummond, M. (2012). The natural: An autoethnography of a masculinized body in sport.
Murray Drummond uses autoethnography to describe his journey toward a strong body. By using details of his thoughts, physical sensations and life history Drummond provides a lens from which to understand the mores and habitus of sport (in particular triathlon) subcultures. He combines theory and a deeply personal (and at times heart wrenching) narrative to fully explore the meaning of becoming strong. Without focusing on methodology he nonetheless provides one of the most powerful examples of how to write compelling autoethnography. This work is both highly evocative and deeply analytical.

Ellis, C., Adams, T. E., Ellingson. L., Bochner, A. P., et al. (2009). Coda mentoring relationships.
Caroline Ellis, Art Bochner and their students and colleagues discuss the importance of mentoring relationships and the way that personal and professional lives can intersect through these relationships. Together these authors highlight how autoethnography enables and affords intimate and personnel relationships between those who conduct this kind of research and their professors and mentors. This work highlights how autoethnographic work can alter professor/student boundaries.

Poulos, C. N. (2010). Spirited accidents: An autoethnography of possibility.
Christopher Poulos argues that writing can be a spiritual quest through which one can cultivate the art of being open to understanding and experiencing the human condition. Through his view the process of writing involves tapping into a higher state of being, as meaning emerges from the creation of text. His description of a reflexive autoethnography inherently challenges the cool rationality of a disembodied positivism and connects product with process, and rational with spiritual.

Rambo, C. (2005). Sketching Carolyn Ellis, purple diva of autoethnography.
Carol Rambo presents a multimodal autoethnographic 'sketching' of the 'autoethnographic diva Carolyn Ellis.' Ellis is described in great detail presented through a collage of different types of autoethnographic moments. This text is highly emotional and almost performative and is at times more like spoken word than written text. It hovers on the edge of taboo as Rambo states, "Have you ever loved a teacher so much it hurt? ... I exist forever in relation to Carolyn Ellis" (p. 4). This text implicitly pushes readers to contemplate the boundaries between an autoethnographic self and others.

Sundén, J. (2012). Desires at play: On closeness and epistemological uncertainty.
Embracing the affective turn and confessional mode of autoethonography, Jenny Sundén describes falling in love while playing World of Warcraft. She explores the interconnectedness of sensing and making sense, as she challenges readers to think about the politics of emotions and about the security of believing mind body bifurcations.

Tillmann, L. M. (2009). Body and bulimia revisited: Reflections on 'A secret life.'
Lisa Tillmann uses autoethnography to walk readers through the trauma of her struggles with bulimia, her students' experiences with eating disorders, and her unraveling marriage. Tillman grants readers access to taboo topics through the intimate vantage point of her own thoughts and actions. This work illustrates how autoethnography can access social behaviors in layered and complex ways and how it can remove the distance between self and other, to instead "honor others' struggles, bear witness to others' traumas, and combat others' oppression without dismissing (one's) own" (p. 107).

Wilson, K. B. (2011). Opening Pandora's box: An autoethnographic study of teaching.
Kristin Wilson writes a compelling account of her politics, pedagogy and emotions as she struggles with ethical issues in teaching writing. This is a beautifully crafted essay melds field notes from teaching, reflection and mythology as it makes connections between, lived teaching moments, ethical struggles in schools and the metaphor of Pandora's box.

Fightin' Words!

This section explores the notion of autoethnography as a tool for political resistance. These works remind researchers and readers to use autoethnographies to question their own postionality and to use their insights to effect change in the classroom and in the world.

Ali-Khan, C. (2009a). Go play in traffic: Skating, gender and urban context.
   In this work, I use my experience of urban street skating to question the politics of urban space, gender norms, consumerism, notions of health, and the difference between sport and play. I lead readers through a day as a skater in the city. Through this journey I examine the meaning of my body as it moves in space and time in a quest to understand how our physical selves are sites for compliance or resistance against oppressive and hegemonic norms.

DeLeon, A. (2010). How do I begin to tell a story that has not been told? Anarchism, autoethnography, and the middle ground.
   Describing himself as a 'colonized man' Abraham DeLeon connects autoethnography, therapeutic writing, testimony and postcolonial theory to radical politics. He describes how he inhabited a 'middle ground' between White and indigenous identities as a Latino and (briefly) a teacher in the Southwest. DeLeon argues that autoethnography is 'anti-normative discourse' that is subversive, queer and anarchist. Although this work is far more descriptive than analytical it raises interesting questions about the political potential of autoethnography.

Hermann-Wilmarth, J. M., & Bills, P. (2010). Identity shifts: Queering teacher education research.
   Using a queer, critical, poststructural and feminist lens Jill Hermann-Wilmarth and Patricia Bills set out to queer teacher education research. They explain the subversive power of queer theory as its ability to destabilize multiple traditional binaries (e.g., Man/Woman, Black/White, Researcher/Researched). They describe their research experiences with LGBT pre-service teachers who did not always adhere to the script that they had laid out, but instead talked about their own issues. They document how they tried to hear and respond to their research participants and how using autoethnography enabled them to address issues of power, develop a collective subjectivity, to rethink flexibility and to deepen the research process.

Kincheloe, J. L. (2005). Critical ontology and auto/biography: Being a teacher, developing a reflective teacher persona.
   Building on his previous work on critical ontology (2003a) teachers as researchers (2003b) and post-formal psychology (1999) Joe Kincheloe discusses how autoethnographic insights can work to effect real change. He frames looking at ones own experiences as a way to develop an understanding about the construction of self and the world and argues that this encourages an 'ideological disembedding' from which critical insights about self, others and paths to agency are given the space to emerge.

Kincheloe, J. L., & Tobin, K. (2009). The much exaggerated death of positivism.
   Joe Kincheloe and Kenneth Tobin discuss how the culture of positivism continues to impact educational research despite numerous claims that 'positivism

is dead.' This article pushes back at assumptions that knowing is 'scientific' and 'neutral' and 'universal.' It describes the harm that can come from a research world that is populated only with dominant truths and explains how epistemological and methodological restrictiveness can squeeze the life out of research and silence the experiences of marginalized populations. Kincheloe and Tobin challenge researchers to diversify knowledge production and allow for personal, political, creative, situated and imaginative truths to emerge.

Kress, T. M. (2011). Critical praxis research.
Tricia Kress powerfully explains the situated nature of all research, while shedding light on the importance of interrogating the construction of self. In this text she uses a bricolage approach, as she connects personal experiences to theory. Kress utilizes metaphors (e.g the sins of gluttony, greed, sloth, and wrath), in addition she uses comic book formats, cites letters, and includes poems, vignettes and remembrances. She presents a 'how-to' for reflexive research methods that are supportive without being prescriptive and are heavily based in social justice concerns.

Miller, A. (2009). Pragmatic radicalism: An autoethnographic perspective on pre-service teaching.
Andrew Miller examines his journey of first becoming a teacher after hating school and then becoming a better teacher while struggling with pressures to conform. For Miller autoethnography is a means through which to overturn oppressive schooling discourses as he argues for a 'critical awakening' (which appears to be quite similar to Paulo Freire's notion of conscientization). Miller describes writing this autoethnographic article as a part of his awakening. He argues that autoethnography can help teachers question their socialization and thereby not reproduce inequities and their own childhood struggles in the classrooms they teach in.

Nelson, H. L. (2001). Damaged identities, narrative repair.
Although not directly housed in autoethnographic literature, Hilde Nelsons book offers an important contribution to understanding the power of personal stories told by oppressed and subjugated groups. She describes what she terms 'counter stories' which are stories that can do the work of resisting oppressive identities and replacing them with ones that demand respect. Counter stories work to shift the perspective of oppressors by challenging master narratives, and simultaneously shift the identity of the authors of these stories by giving them the opportunity to reframe their experiences and to understand broader sociopolitical contexts.

Sobre-Denton, S. (2012). Stories from the cage: Autoethnographic sensemaking of workplace bullying, gender discrimination, and White privilege.
In this work we follow Rachel (Miriam Shoshana Sobre-Denton) through the excruciating moments of her work place bullying. She divides her text on this into

thematic 'layers' (e.g., 'masculine identities' and 'gender discrimination') followed by a method section. Each layer is comprised of sections of 'then' (the description of lived events) and 'now' (additional contextual information and theoretical analyses). As she unpacks the workplace bullying she experienced, she highlights the complexity of her identity as a White woman who is both race privileged and gender subordinated. She implicitly challenges readers to examine the complex web of their own social positions and to investigate the impact that these positions may have on their social and professional interactions.

Tobin, K. (2005). Becoming an urban science educator.
Ken Tobin begins by describing the disconnect of being an urban science teacher while living in a suburban world. He explains the challenges he faced becoming comfortable with his urban school and community environment and the steps he took to fully engage with and understand it. As the piece progresses Tobin walks us through his relationships with staff and students at the school. His blend of analytical and descriptive text enables us to feel the struggles that take place in under-resourced schools and communities. He concludes with a discussion of how autoethnography and metalogues can clarify lived experiences and guide teachers and researchers.

Walkerdine, V. (1990). Schoolgirl fictions.
Valerie Walkerdine examines the politics of gender and class as she describes the experience of coming from the working class and becoming a middle-class researcher. She examines how her own identity was created and constructed and forces of socialization involved in the domestication of girls. Walkerdine uses vignettes, memories, inner dialogues and ethnographic research notes to acknowledge and address discomforting ideas about researcher/researched relationships vis-à-vis and class gender politics.

Warren, J. T. (2011). Reflexive teaching: Toward critical autoethnographic practices of/in/on pedagogy.
John Warren argues that teachers should seek to understand how their experiences as students shape their practice as teachers. In this article he describes the importance of "being accountable to the journey that has brought me to a critical moment of my body in the presence of others" (p. 140). He evocatively describes his journey as a teacher and a critical ethnographer while referencing Henry Giroux's ideas about the role of public intellectuals. This work creates multiple spaces for reflection for teachers interested in education for social justice.

NOTES

[1] I want to thank you, for letting me, be myself again.
[2] Sly and the Family Stone (1969).
[3] This idea is contested by some autoethnographic methodologists (see annotated the annotated bibliography section).

[4] See annotated bibliography for details and further reading.
[5] Ryan Snelgrove and Mark Havitz (2010) refer to my method here as "retrospective," Claudia Mitchell (2011) would call this "memory work." I include this as a footnote as I heed Roxanne Doty's advice by not letting an obsession with method interfere with the text. Ken Tobin (personal correspondence) also argues that method should be woven into texts, rather than front loaded.
[6] For additional readings on this subject please see the section "One love" in the annotated bibliography in this chapter.
[7] For further details consult Debra Pane's review of the book on www.academia.edu

REFERENCES

Adams, T. E., & Jones, S. H. (2011). Telling stories: Reflexivity, queer theory, and autoethnography. *Cultural Studies ↔ Critical Methodologies, 11*(2), 108-116.

Ali-Khan, C. (2009a). Go play in traffic: Skating, gender and urban context. *Qualitative Inquiry, 15*(6), 1084-1102.

Ali-Khan, C. (2009b). On being us and them: A voice from the edge. In Ö. Sensoy & C. D. Stonebanks, (Eds.), *Muslim voices in school: Narratives of identity and pluralism*. Rotterdam: Sense.

Ali-Khan, C. (2011). Shaken and stirred: On coming to critical praxis. In T. Kress (Ed.), *Critical Praxis Research (CPR): Breathing new life into research methods for teachers*. Netherlands: Springer.

Ali-Khan, C. (in press). 'More things in heaven and earth Horatio' – Seeing and believing in Second Life. In C. Milne, K. Tobin, & D. Degenero (Eds.), *Sociocultural studies and implications for science education: The experiential and the virtual*. Dordrecht, the Netherlands: Springer.

Anderson, L. (2006). Analytic autoethnography. *Journal of Contemporary Ethnography, 35*(4), 373-395.

Atkinson, P. (2006). Rescuing autoethnography. *Journal of Contemporary Ethnography, 35*(4), 400-404.

Barton, A. C., & Darkside. (2000). Autobiography in science education: Greater objectivity through local knowledge. *Research in Science Education, 30*(1), 23-42.

Behar, R. R. (2007). Ethnography in a time of blurred genres. *Anthropology and Humanism, 32*(2), 145-155.

Berger, J. (1972) *Ways of seeing*. London: Penguin.

Blinne, K. C. (2012). Auto (erotic) ethnography. *Sexualities, 15*(8), 953-977.

Cann, C. N., & DeMeulenaere, E. J. (2012). Critical co-constructed autoethnography. *Cultural Studies ↔ Critical Methodologies, 12*(2), 146-158.

Carless, D. (2010). Who the hell was that? Stories, bodies and actions in the world. *Qualitative Research in Psychology, 7*(4), 332-344.

Chatham-Carpenter, A. (2010). "Do thyself no harm": Protecting ourselves as autoethnographers. *Journal of Research Practice, 6*(1), Article M-1.

Darder, A. (2010). Schooling bodies: Critical pedagogy and urban youth. In S. Steinberg & J. L. Kincheloe (Eds.), *19 urban questions: Teaching in the city*. New York: Peter Lang.

Delamont, S. (2009). The only honest thing: Autoethnography, reflexivity and small crises in fieldwork. *Ethnography & Education, 4*(1), 51-63.

DeLeon, A. P. (2010). How do I begin to tell a story that has not been told? Anarchism, autoethnography, and the middle ground. *Equity & Excellence in Education, 43*(4), 398-413.

Denzin, N. K. (2006). Analytic autoethnography, or déjà vu all over again. *Journal of Contemporary Ethnography, 35*(4), 419-428.

Denzin, N. K., & Lincoln, Y. S. (2003). The discipline and practice of qualitative research. In N. Denzin & Y. Lincoln (Eds.), *The landscape of qualitative research* (2nd ed., pp. 1-45). Thousand Oaks, CA: Sage.

Doty, R. (2010). Autoethnography – Making human connections. *Review of International Studies, 36*(4), 1047-1050.

Drummond, M. (2010). The natural: An autoethnography of a masculinized body in sport. *Men and Masculinities, 12*(3), 374-389.
Ellis, C. S., & Bochner, A. P. (2006). Analyzing analytic autoethnography an autopsy. *Journal of Contemporary Ethnography, 35*(4), 429-449.
Ellis, C., Adams, T. E., Ellingson. L., Bochner, A. P., Denzin, N. K., Durham, A. S., Madison, D. S., Craft, R. A., Pelias, R. J., Defenbaugh, N., & Richardson, L. (2009). Coda mentoring relationships: Creating a future for qualitative inquiry. In N. Denzin & M. D. Giardina (Eds.), *Qualitative inquiry and social justice: Toward a politics of hope* (pp. 279-302). San Francisco, CA: Left Coast Press.
Ellis, C., Adams, T. E., & Bochner, A. P. (2011). Autoethnography: An overview. Forum: *Qualitative Social Research, 12*(1), 1-18.
Freire, P. (1998). *Pedagogy of the heart*. New York: Continuum International Publishing.
Freire, P., & Macedo, D. (1987). *Literacy: Reading the world and the word*. Westport, CT: Bergen & Garvey.
Greene, M. (1995). *Releasing the imagination: Essays on education, the arts, and social change*. San Francisco, CA: Jossey-bass.
Guillemin, M., & Gillam, L. (2004). Ethics, reflexivity, and "ethically important moments" in research. *Qualitative Inquiry, 10*(2), 261-280.
Hartnett, S. J., & Engels, J. D. (2008). "Aria in time of war": Investigative poetry and the Politics of witnessing. In N. K. Denzin, & Y. S. Lincoln, (Eds). *Collecting and interpreting qualitative materials* (2nd ed., pp. 578-622). Thousand Oaks, CA: Sage.
Hermann-Wilmarth, J. M., & Bills, P. (2010). Identity shifts: Queering teacher education research. *The Teacher Educator, 45*(4), 257-272.
Hesse-Biber, S. N., & Leckenby, D. (2004). How feminists practice social research. In S. Nagy Hesse-Biber, P. Leavy, & M. Yaiser (Eds.), *Feminist approaches to research as a process: Reconceptualizing epistemology, methodology, and method* (pp. 209-250). New York: Oxford University Press.
Holt, N. L. (2003). Representation, legitimation, and autoethnography: An autoethnographic writing story. *International Journal of Qualitative Methods, 2*(1), 1.
Humphreys, M. (2004). Getting personal: Reflexivity and autoethnographic vignettes. *Qualitative Inquiry, 11*(6), 840-860.
Hughes, S., Pennington, J. L., & Makris, S. (2012). Translating autoethnography across the AERA standards toward understanding autoethnographic scholarship as empirical research. *Educational Researcher, 41*(6), 209-219.
Jones, S. H. (2008). Making the personal political. In N. K. Denzin & Y. S. Lincoln (Eds.), *Collecting and interpreting qualitative materials* (2nd ed., pp. 205-246). Thousand Oaks, CA: Sage.
Khayyam, O. (1898). *Rubáiyát of Omar Khayyám*. (Vol. 2). LC: Page.
Kincheloe, J. L. (1999). Trouble ahead, trouble behind: Grounding the post-formal critique of educational psychology. In J. L. Kincheloe, S. R. Steinberg, & P. H. Hinchey (Eds.), *The post formal reader: Cognition and education* (pp. 4-54). New York, NY: Falmer.
Kincheloe, J. L. (2003a). Critical ontology: Visions of selfhood and curriculum. *JCT: Journal of Curriculum Theorizing, 19*(1), 47-64.
Kincheloe, J. L. (2003b). *Teachers as researchers: Qualitative inquiry as a path to empowerment*. Psychology Press.
Kincheloe, J. L. (2005). Critical ontology and auto/biography: Being a teacher, developing a reflective teacher persona. In W.-M. Roth (Ed.), *Auto/biography and auto/ethnography: Praxis of research method* (pp. 155-175). Rotterdam: Sense.
Kincheloe, J. L., & Tobin, K. (2009). The much exaggerated death of positivism. *Cultural Studies of Science Education, 4*(3), 513-528.
Kress, T. M. (2011). *Critical praxis research*. The Netherlands: Springer.
Mitchell, C. (2011). *Doing visual research*. London and New York: Sage.
Miller, A. (2009). Pragmatic radicalism: An autoethnographic perspective on pre-service teaching. *Teaching and Teacher Education, 25*(6), 909-916.

Nelson, H. L. (2001). *Damaged identities, narrative repair*. Cornell University Press.
Ngunjiri, F. W., Hernandez, K. A. C., & Chang, H. (2010). Living autoethnography: Connecting life and research. *Journal of Research Practice, 6*(1), Article-E1.
Owen, J. A. T., McRae, C., Adams, T., & Vitale, A. (2009). Truth troubles. *Qualitative Inquiry, 15*(1), 178-200.
Pelias, R. J. (2003). The academic tourist: An autoethnography. *Qualitative Inquiry, 9*(3), 369-373.
Pelias, R. J. (2004). *A methodology of the heart: Evoking academic & daily life*. Walnut creek, CA: Altamira Press.
Pereira, L., Settelmaier, E., & Taylor, P., (2005). Fictive imagining and moral purpose: Autobiographical research as/for transformational development. In W.-M. Roth (Ed.), *Auto/biography and auto/ethnography: Praxis of research method* (pp. 49-74). Rotterdam: Sense.
Pitt, A. J. & Britzman, D. P. (2006). Speculations on qualities of difficult knowledge in teaching and learning. In K. Tobin & J. L. Kincheloe (Eds.), *Doing educational research – A handbook* (pp. 379-401). Rotterdam: Sense.
Poulos, C. (n.d.). Spirited accidents: An autoethnography of possibility. *Qualitative Inquiry, 16*(1), 49-56.
Rambo, C. (2007). Handing IRB an unloaded gun. *Qualitative Inquiry, 13*(3), 353-367.
Rambo, C. (2005). Sketching Carolyn Ellis, purple diva of autoethnography. *Studies in Symbolic Interaction, 28*(1), 3-14.
Richardson, L., & St. Pierre, E. A. (2008). Writing: A method of inquiry. In N. K. Denzin & Y. S. Lincoln (Eds.), *Collecting and interpreting qualitative materials* (2nd ed., pp. 473-500). Thousand Oaks, CA: Sage.
Roth, W-M. (2004). Review essay: Autobiography as scientific text: A dialectical approach to the role of experience. *Forum Qualitative Sozialforschung/Forum: Qualitative Social Research, 5*(1).
Roth. W-M. (Ed.). (2005). *Auto/biography and auto/ethnography: Praxis of research method*. Rotterdam: Sense.
Sly and the Family Stone. (1969). *Thank you falletin me be mice elf agin*. Retrieved from https://www.youtube.com/watch?v=5YXPJOUD7G0
Snelgrove, R., & Havitz, M. E. (2010). Looking back in time: The pitfalls and potential of retrospective methods in leisure studies. *Leisure Sciences, 32*(4), 337-351.
Snyder-Young, D. (2011). "Here to tell her story" Analyzing the autoethnographic performances of others. *Qualitative Inquiry, 17*(10), 943-951.
Sobre-Denton, M. (2012). Stories from the cage: Autoethnographic sensemaking of workplace bullying, gender discrimination, and white privilege. *Journal of Contemporary Ethnography, 41*(2), 220-250.
Sundén, J. (2012). Desires at play on closeness and epistemological uncertainty. *Games and Culture, 7*(2), 164-184.
Strobel, K. M. (2005). After the aftermath: A reply to Wolff-Michael Roth's review of Harry F. Wolcott's "Sneaky kid and its aftermath." *Forum Qualitative Sozialforschung/Forum: Qualitative Social Research, 6*(3), Art. 6.
Tillmann, L. M. (2009). Body and bulimia revisited: Reflections on 'A secret life.' *Journal of Applied Communication Research, 37*(1), 98-112.
Tobin, K. (2005). Becoming an urban science educator. In W.-M. Roth (Ed.), *Auto/biography and auto/ethnography: Praxis of research method* (pp. 175-180). Rotterdam: Sense.
Tolich, M. (2010). A critique of current practice: Ten foundational guidelines for autoethnographers. *Qualitative Health Research, 20*(12), 1599-1610.
Walkerdine, V. (1990). *Schoolgirl fictions*. London: Verso.
Wall, S. (2006). An autoethnography on learning about autoethnography. *International Journal of Qualitative Methods, 5*(2), 1-12.
Wall, S. (2008). Easier said than done: Writing an autoethnography. *International Journal of Qualitative Methods, 7*(1), 38-54.
Warren, J. T. (2011). Reflexive teaching: Toward critical autoethnographic practices of/in/on pedagogy. *Cultural Studies ↔ Critical Methodologies, 11*(2), 139-144.

Wilson, K. B. (2011). Opening Pandora's box: An autoethnographic study of teaching. *Qualitative Inquiry, 17*(5), 452-458.

Wolcott, H. F. (2002). *Sneaky kid and its aftermath: Ethics and intimacy in fieldwork.* Rowman: Altamira.

Wyatt, J. (2006). Psychic distance, consent, and other ethical issues: Reflections on the writing of "A gentle going?" *Qualitative Inquiry, 12*(4), 813.

PETER WALDMAN

15. EDUCATING DESIRE

An Impressionist Tale of Alcoholics Anonymous

HOT FLASHES

I here present you, courteous reader, with the record of a remarkable period in my life: according to my application of it, I trust that it will prove not merely an interesting record, but in a considerable degree useful and instructive. In *that* hope it is that I have drawn it up; and *that* must be my apology for breaking through that delicate and honourable reserve which, for the most part, restrains us from the public exposure of our own errors and infirmities. – Thomas De Quincey, *Confessions of an English Opium-Eater*, (1822/1949, p. v)

I duck into the church basement feeling like a cliché.

It's my third day of sobriety. I've quit on my own, cold turkey, no detox. No, I'm not a tough guy; in fact I'm weak and quite stupid. In AA they recommend the alcoholic continue drinking until medical treatment, i.e., Librium, becomes available. Otherwise *you can die*. Not so with opiate withdrawal. You can get very sick, like the worst flu you can imagine, but you won't die.

The drug is gone from my body, flushed from my system via involuntary excretion processes of which I'm totally ignorant and unaware, but I'm not experiencing any withdrawal. No stomach cramps, no nausea, no headache, no vomiting. I imagine a gang of opioid molecules clinging to the desperate receptors of my oozy, cross-wired brain … and letting go. Still, my mouth is dry. My palms are like wet sponges. My heart is banging in my ears. I can't eat. I slept the first night, but last night I got two hours, tops. I feel like a raw nerve the world is scraping against.

A small foyer leads to a large, rectangular room with metal folding chairs arranged in columns and rows, four by eight on either side with a narrow aisle running down the middle. The black linoleum floor is spotless. The chairs slowly fill with talking, animated bodies. The stale smell of smoked tobacco lingers momentarily as the room settles. Nicotine is a tolerated addiction in AA.

Six bare light bulbs bulge from a high ceiling, fixtureless. Framed messages hang against fake wood-panelled walls the color of mud: "One Day at a Time," "Keep It Simple," "Easy Does It" (Mariana Valverde and Kimberley White-Mair 1999). These phrases might as well be in Cyrillic for all they mean to me.

I'm in the back row closest to the door with my coat on. Two rows in front of me a woman whispers in a man's ear and he laughs out loud like it's the funniest thing he's ever heard.

As usual I begin to perspire for no apparent reason, except for the effort of fixating upon my own emotional discomfort and obsessive mental processes, which results in a paralyzing self-consciousness. The flood begins at my scalp along the hairline and pours into my eyes and down the back of my neck from behind my ears. I'm drenched in seconds. I stand to find the bathroom leaving my coat hanging over the chair.

My damp shirt chills my skin and my glasses fog up in the cold air of the foyer. I repeat to myself: *idiot, idiot, idiot, idiot, idiot.* To my left at the end of a long hall I can make out a door that says, 'Toilet.' I race to it and jerk it shut behind me, jamming the hook through the eye in one blind motion. No paper towel, only toilet paper, but the cheap kind that crumbles into pieces when it gets wet. I pull a knot off and tamp it against my forehead. The sink spits scalding water. No mirror. I sit on the toilet to organize myself, swabbing my glasses with a shirtsleeve and picking bits of toilet paper off my forehead.

I walk back to my seat pretending to be at ease, but I'm fooling no one. The coat hanging over my empty chair is the perfect metaphor. I am nobody. I am nothing. An empty frame, a negative presence, I produce nothing, I merely consume.

A woman with braided brown hair and kind, curious eyes approaches me and introduces herself as Evelyn. She offers me a laminated sheet of white paper with a list typed across it and says, "Are you a newcomer? Would you mind reading this when I ask you to?" To my grinning, sweaty silence she nods her head approvingly and wanders off.

Wait a minute! I didn't sign up for this. People are less afraid of *dying* than they are of public speaking. This is too much. Way too much, way too early. Maybe I am in withdrawal. I shouldn't be this anxious. I grab my gut feeling for cramps. I swallow hard waiting for the bitter creep of nausea.

I scan the list. Across the top in bold caps it reads, "**THE TWELVE TRADITIONS OF ALCOHOLICS ANONYMOUS (SHORT FORM)**" Then, numbered one through twelve are the Traditions:

Our common welfare should come first; personal recovery depends on AA unity.

For our group purpose there is but one ultimate authority – a loving God as He may express Himself in our group conscience. Our leaders are but servants; they do not govern (AA World Services, Inc. 2002).

Evelyn's measured voice interrupts my perplexity at the God language. She sits in front of the group at a small blue desk upon which one daisy staggers from a thin glass vase. She's about to read from a laminated sheet that looks just like mine.

She says: "Hi, my name is Evelyn and I'm an alcoholic," and in unison the room greets her: "Hi Evelyn!" Collapsing into my seat I barely whisper it under my breath but my mouth moves dutifully.

She continues, hardly looking up from her script: "Welcome to the _____ group of Alcoholics Anonymous. This is an open meeting[1] of Alcoholics Anonymous. We are glad you are all here, especially newcomers."[2]

I smile, then cover my mouth embarrassed for having smiled, then smile embarrassed for having covered my mouth.

Evelyn says, "In keeping with our singleness of purpose, and our Third Tradition which states that 'The only requirement for AA membership is a desire to stop drinking.' We ask that all who participate confine their discussion to their problems with alcohol."

I've always thought of addiction as a grab bag of vice. Stick your hand in and take your pick. One's predilection for this or that substance – booze or barbiturates, codeine or cocaine – is less important than the phenomenon itself, which is insatiable desire, never enough, obsession, compulsion, a total loss of control. And yet, I tried a few NA meetings last year (Narcotics Anonymous), and felt completely out of place. All the talk was about freebasing and shooting up and skin-popping. I felt like a kindergartener with my clean white pills manufactured in a government approved laboratory. But I was no different than any of them, really. I could match anybody out there in my total lack of renunciation.

Evelyn's voice strolls along. She reads from the "AA Preamble":

Alcoholics Anonymous is a fellowship of men and women who share their experience, strength and hope with each other that they may solve their common problem and help others to recover from alcoholism. The only requirement for membership is a desire to stop drinking. There are no dues or fees for AA membership; we are self supporting through our own contributions. AA is not allied with any sect, denomination, politics, organization or institution; does not wish to engage in any controversy, neither endorses nor opposes any causes. Our primary purpose is to stay sober and help other alcoholics to achieve sobriety. (AA Grapevine, Inc. 2013)

Aside from the words 'alcoholics' and 'alcoholism,' which will require substitution, I feel I could get with all that. Sharing 'experience, strength, and hope'; of course I'm feeling short on strength and hope. I'll concentrate on *experience*. That's a start. Still, my experience has yet to be transformed. That's what AA does, it transforms you (Swora 2004).

Evelyn nods in the direction of a longhaired man with a brown ponytail and mustache who also holds a laminated text. He's sitting next to a large orange bear of a man with an orange wildfire beard. They're both smiling as if they've heard a joke; in fact they look high, and they're obviously friends. There's a comfort between them that's palpable in their body language. They lean into each other like conspiring kids, the way that flowers bend toward the sun, and I take an instant liking.

The guy with the ponytail says, "Hey, I'm Jeff and I'm an alcoholic and addict."
"Hi Jeff!"
OK. An alcoholic *and* addict. Maybe addicts aren't so rare after all.

Jeff has a velvety baritone voice like an anchorman. He says, "I'm going to read the fifth chapter in 'The Big Book' called, 'How It Works,' or part of it anyway." His buddy is *really* listening, eyes closed and nodding his head here and there as Jeff reads his part. And he has to have heard this pre-meeting stuff a thousand times before. They seem like old-timers even though they're barely in middle age; they look like they belong. Jeff's unnamed friend is wearing a maroon and gold vertically striped soccer jersey that matches his overall solar effect, and he's listening, and he seems very, very happy … or content, or whatever you want to call it. He seems like a man satisfied *in* and not merely *with* life. He must be a Buddhist. AA doesn't make you glow.

I remember Jack Klugman's black-clad, furrow-browed worrywart Jim Hungerford in *The Days of Wine and Roses,* the complete opposite of this guy, hounding poor Jack Lemon, the impressionable Joe Clay, at every dry-out tank he wound up in (Manulis and Edwards 1962). I must admit this particular AA stereotype makes me uncomfortable: the Brill-creamed hair, the dark, narrow suits and skinny ties, the Cold War black-and-white world. *But that's not the way it is now, Jeff's Day-Glo friend a case in point.* And maybe I'm the jerk. After all, Klugman's Twelfth Stepper was doing a good thing, he was 'working his Program,' doing his service work, which is the ultimate object of AA besides one's own sobriety, and one's own sobriety is maintained only by giving back to AA. In helping others stay sober, one helps oneself stay sober 'one day at a time.' AA is a collectivist ethics of care with an individualist rationale.

Jeff reads from his laminated card:

> Rarely have we seen a person fail who has thoroughly followed our path. Those who do not recover are people who cannot or will not completely give themselves to this simple program, usually men and women who are constitutionally incapable of being honest with themselves. There are such unfortunates. They are not at fault; they seem to have been born that way. They are naturally incapable of grasping and developing a manner of living which demands rigorous honesty. (Anon. 2001, p. 58)

Jeff takes a breath and so do I. *Born that way? Constitutionally incapable of being honest with myself?* What pessimism! What determinism! *Rigorous honesty?* About what? About drugs? Addiction? Every aspect of my waking life? I'm honest enough. I see myself as a character out of Dostoyevsky or Kafka. I'm the Underground Man, repulsive, wicked and sick. I'm a gigantic insect.

Jeff continues: "Our stories disclose in a general way what we used to be like, what happened, and what we are like now. If you have decided you want what we have and are willing to go to any length to get it-then you are ready to take certain steps" (Anon. 2001, p. 58).

Later I would come to understand from my research participant, Laura (pseudonym) that 'wanting what we have' is less an abstract collective yearning than a practical matter of one AA member identifying with another based upon the contents of his or her individual story, usually as it is told publicly (but anonymously) at meetings, and according to the temporal specifications listed above. I was also to learn that AA traffics in stories. Life stories, or 'qualifications' as I heard them described at meetings, are the currency of Twelve Step groups; they are the means of social exchange at the level of the open meeting. But only "appropriate" stories are acceptable (Cain 1991), stories whose temporal structures and substantive contents both generalize out – "our stories disclose in a general way" – and result in sustained sobriety through 'working the Steps,' or 'working one's Program,' which is the third and final part of AA's storied temporal logic, "what we are like now." My AA story is quite "inappropriate" by Cain's (and AA's) standards. In fact, at the time of the meeting my story is stuck in the past of "what we used to be like," i.e., addicted.

Laura told me the early AA members described the middle portion of the qualification, or, "what happened" ... that we found ourselves in AA, as a 'hot flash' experience, a moment of spiritual/religious enlightenment. In later editions of *Alcoholics Anonymous* ('The Big Book'), spiritual experiences of the "educative type" are described in which, according to William James, spirituality develops and adheres in one slowly over time (Anon. 2001, p. 567). AA cofounder Bill Wilson's spirituality 'developed,' it seems, all at once:

> Suddenly the room lit up with a great white light. I was caught up into an ecstasy which there are no words to describe. It seemed to me, in the mind's eye, that I was on a mountain and that a wind not of air but of spirit was blowing. And then it burst upon me that I was a free man. Slowly the ecstasy subsided. I lay on the bed, but now for a time I was in another world, a new world of consciousness. All about me and through me there was a wonderful feeling of Presence, and I thought to myself, "So this is the God of the preachers!" A great peace stole over me and I thought, "No matter how wrong things seem to be, they are all right. Things are all right with God and His world." (Anon. 1957 p. 63)

Quite a difficult act to follow. And this is discounting the other (Twelfth Step) "spiritual awakening," the one that happens "as the result of [working] these Steps" (Anon. 2001, p. 60). Any spiritual experience I have will be "educative" by definition and will pale in comparison because this kind of thing doesn't happen to me.

The third and final portion of the appropriate AA narrative, or "what we are like now," (p. 58), describes the ongoing process of recovery which involves 'working one's Program,' a process that is both unique and uniform, whose common activities include attending meetings, 'working the Steps,' sponsoring and other Twelfth Step work. "What we used to be like, what happened, and what we are like now" are the temporal markers in a narrative reconstruction project that leads from addiction/ignorance to sobriety/knowledge at the levels of ontology, epistemology and axiology, through the structured and deeply personal practice of a shared cultural and institutional form, the AA qualification, applied to what we might call the three-act life arc of the sober alcoholic in AA.

Jeff carries on: "Without help it is too much for us. But there is One who has all power-that One is God. May you find Him now!" (p. 59)

I knew this was coming, but I was told that God could be anything: the group itself, the ideals of honesty, compassion, and forgiveness, the Buddha, Shakespeare. I wasn't expecting this churchy feeling.

Klaus Mäkelä and colleagues (1996) contend, "most AA members resolutely deny" AA to be a religious institution or organization, preferring the label "spiritual" as more descriptive of their endeavor. But the authors also argue that this "ambiguity is an essential feature of AA [...] an ideology in which the religious and its denial exist in a state of dynamic tension" (p. 10).

The actor's *oomph* that Jeff puts into that last evangelical line, "May you find Him now!" (implied by the exclamation point) is, again, probably replayed thousands of times in thousands of meetings every day of the year, but for Jeff and his buddy it's as if it's being spoken and heard for the first time. I wonder if, like me, the God language ever leaves them perplexed, or unconvinced, or if they are disoriented at His ubiquitous masculine gender assignment. Maybe they take what they need and discard the rest, which is how Laura will describe her pragmatic approach to AA.

In *The Twelve Steps to Sobriety,* Bill Wilson reminds readers of "the common saying that holds well in meetings [...] 'Find the similarities and discard the rest'" (Anon. 1973/2013, p. 25). For Laura, the similarities refer to her recognition of and her identification with the stories and storytellers of AA at the meeting level.

Jeff continues: "Half measures availed us nothing. We stood at the turning point. We asked His protection and care with complete abandon. Here are the steps we took which are suggested as a program of a recovery:

We admitted we were powerless over alcohol – that our lives had become unmanageable.

Came to believe that a Power greater than ourselves could restore us to sanity.

Made a decision to turn our will and our lives over to the care of God *as we understood Him.*

Made a searching and fearless moral inventory of ourselves.

Admitted to God, to ourselves, and to another human being the exact nature of our wrongs.

Were entirely ready to have God remove all these defects of character.

Humbly asked Him to remove our shortcomings.

Made a list of all persons we had harmed, and became willing to make amends to them all.

Made direct amends to such people wherever possible, except when to do so would injure them or others.

Continued to take personal inventory and when we were wrong promptly admitted it.

Sought through prayer and meditation to improve our conscious contact with God *as we understood Him,* praying only for knowledge of His will for us and the power to carry that out.

Having had a spiritual awakening as the result of these steps, we tried to carry this message to alcoholics, and to practice these principles in all our affairs. (Anon. 2001, pp. 59-60)

In the research literature the Twelve Step process has been variously described as, "a rhetoric of transformation [...] which moves the alcoholic from drinking to sobriety by means of a rhetoric of predisposition, of empowerment, and of transformation" (Swora 2004, p. 187). More pragmatically Mäkelä and colleagues (1996) see the Steps as "a series of tasks and problems to be solved" and not "a code of conduct to be interpreted" (p. 118). Similarly, the cultural sociologists Jean Lave and Etienne Wenger (1991) liken AA to a "community of practice," and specifically, to a community of masters, or fully participating old-timers, and apprentices, or peripherally participating newcomers. But what is AA practice, I wonder, without the shared balm of spiritual belief?

EMPTY SIGNIFIERS

Dead air. The room has gone silent. Evelyn smiles at me, expecting big things. From behind her blue, daisy-topped desk her eyebrows are raised in...what? Confusion? Compassion? Consternation? She displays her laminated sheet for me to see as if it were a question mark in a game show, or a flare gun. *Oh!* The Twelve Traditions lie across my lap like a sick pet. Am I really to read from this thing, and out loud?

I'm reminded of my Hebrew school days when I learned to decode those ancient, vertebral symbols, and to sing my *haftorah* through an elaborate system of melodic tablature. I mumbled the *bruchas* over the bread and the lip puckering wine, but I never knew what any of it meant.

I lift the laminate to my face. I read aloud, quickly: "One, our common welfare should come first; personal recovery depends upon AA unity..."

"What's your name? What's your name? What's your name?" The question shoots at me from a sea of rubbernecking faces, and I'm in a sweat again. In a gesture of futility I wipe at my forehead with a bare, wet palm and shake it out like a dirty rag sending a mist of perspiration across the back row.

"Oh," I say. "My name is Peter, and I'm ..." I mumble something that sounds like 'alco-addict,' but no one, including myself, really knows what the hell I've just said. Still everyone responds with a cheerful, "Hi Peter!"

I rewind to the beginning of the Traditions list, and I recite:
1. Our common welfare should come first; personal recovery depends upon AA unity.
2. For our group purpose there is but one ultimate authority – a loving God as He may express Himself in our group conscience. Our leaders are but trusted servants; they do not govern.

3. The only requirement for AA membership is a desire to stop drinking.
4. Each group should be autonomous except in matters affecting other groups or AA as a whole.
5. Each group has but one primary purpose – to carry its message to the alcoholic who still suffers.
6. An AA group ought never endorse, finance, or lend the AA name to any related facility or outside enterprise, lest problems of money, property, and prestige divert us from our primary purpose.
7. Every AA group ought to be fully self-supporting, declining outside contributions.
8. Alcoholics Anonymous should remain forever nonprofessional, but our service centers may employ special workers.
9. AA, as such, ought never be organized; but we may create service boards or committees directly responsible to those they serve.
10. Alcoholics Anonymous has no opinion on outside issues; hence the AA name ought never be drawn into public controversy.
11. Our public relations policy is based on attraction rather than promotion; we need always maintain personal anonymity at the level of press, radio, and films.
12. Anonymity is the spiritual foundation of all our Traditions, ever reminding us to place principles before personalities. (AA World Services, Inc. 2002)

Bill Wilson wrote that the Twelve Traditions "are a guide to better ways of working and living. And they are to group survival what AA's Twelve Steps are to each member's sobriety and peace of mind [...] The group must survive or the individual will not" (in Rudy 1986, p. 11). The anonymous authors of *Twelve Steps and Twelve Traditions* (the '12 and 12') "hoped that this volume will afford all who read it a close-up view of the principles and forces which have made Alcoholics Anonymous what it is" (Anon. 1952, p. 18).

Laura told me she prefers the '12 & 12' to 'The Big Book.' She said the life stories (the qualifications) in 'The Big Book' bother her in a vague, unnameable way, and she usually tires of reading them. She much prefers listening at meetings. She finds the '12 & 12' more oriented toward practice than 'The Big Book,' and more concerned with the issues that alcoholics face in their everyday lives. Mäkelä and colleagues (1996) contend that in spite of the significance of both texts, "the program and the methods of work are mainly transmitted orally" (p. 121). Indeed, the authors describe an AA meeting as a "speech event." There is no 'crosstalk' in an AA meeting. The qualifications are dialogical to the extent that members respond to them with "second stories," or responses (Arminen 2003). Second storytellers seek to identify with various aspects of a qualification and with the qualifier herself. Again, this is the intersubjective phenomenon of identification and recognition that Laura finds so vital to her continual recovery.

"Thank you, Peter," Evelyn says with genuine exaggerated gratitude.

I mumble inaudibly, a stupid smile stretched across my face.

The group smiles back, a miasmic sea of disembodied faces. I feel like an idiot. No, I feel like *the* idiot. The schoolroom dunce with the cone shaped cap. I'm ashamed at what they must think of me behind those ambiguous smiles. That most of them are probably rooting for me never enters my mind. No. They are thinking bad thoughts. Somehow I've managed to stigmatize myself in a place where, by definition, 'normal' involves a life story of utter chaos.

Stigma is woven through the fabric of our social relations. We're all caught to some extent in the crosshairs of our imaginings of others' perceptions of us. But for those who possess a "deeply discreditable attribute" (Goffman 1963), like an addict or alcoholic, social relations are structured according to a normal/abnormal dualism and an internalized inferiority in the subject that continually reproduces itself by and through those relations.

But that's not why I'm here. I'm not here because of stigma. I'm here to get better, to quit using. "The only requirement for membership is a desire to stop drinking." A desire to kill desire? Substitute 'drinking' with 'popping painkillers' and I'm a member. But a member of *what* exactly? The meeting speeds along with the readiness of a military exercise.

THE ROLE OF A LIFETIME

Evelyn asks if there are any newcomers or people with thirty days or less. *Of what?*

Two hands go up.

"I'm Mike, I'm an alcoholic, I got twenty-seven days back today," says a head of thick salt and pepper hair in the front row.

The room explodes with applause. Then from the fourth row:

"Tessa, alcoholic, twelfth day back."

Back? More applause. I close my eyes and it sounds like rain.

"Thank you, Mike, thank you, Tessa," Evelyn says.

Tessa is beaming in profile. I imagine Mike is beaming, too, but I can only see the back of his head. Slips and relapses, it seems, are part of the AA program (Denzin 1987).

"Cold out there, isn't it?"

Darin Weinberg (2000) terms the use of spatial metaphors such as "out there," the "ecology of addiction in drug abuse treatment discourse." Such metaphors refer to sites of "degradation, dirtiness, solitude, and savagery," danger zones of addiction where a thin and wavering line separates life from chaos and death. The only 'cure' is a return back to the fold, as it were, as "addictions can be controlled through ongoing participation in a communal project of mutual-help" (p. 606).

Evelyn continues: "And I know I don't have to say it because you both already know, but please stay after to get reacquainted with everyone and maybe even to meet some new people, OK?"

I'm praying for her not to call on me.

She asks, "Is anybody from out of town? Is it anybody's first time here?"

Screw it! I'm not hiding anymore. Better to be executed by firing squad than drowned in a drainage ditch. I want my life to matter. I don't want to die without having lived. My hand shoots up like a second grader's but I'm too late. One row down and to the right a middle-aged man with curly blonde hair and an impish, curly grin has Evelyn's attention. Maybe she didn't see my hand up in the back.

"Hello everybody, I'm Paul, I'm an alcoholic. I'm from Glasgow, in Scotland."

As opposed to Eritrea? I rebuke myself. Enough with the one-liners and the cynicism. It's transparent. You're frightened. Sarcasm is the basest form of humor and the best defense. Let your guard down. Open up. Let it in. Breathe.

"I'm really happy to be here," Paul says. "The Rooms are my family, my life, and I think of all the Rooms in the world like One Big Room, if you get my meaning. One big family." *Wun beeg fam-ee-lay ...*

For Sean O'Halloran (2006), "the Rooms" is a "virtual synonym" and a "metonym" for the Program itself, as well as a "structural metaphor" that "frequently collates with terms like *safe* and *home*" (pp. 82-83).

But I'm stuck on Paul's accent. There's a singsong joy to it that gets me giddy. You can be the biggest jerk in the world and say the most awful things to the nicest people, but roll a few R's, elongate the long /i/ sound to its breaking point, and you've got a friend in me for life.

AA is indeed international in scope. According to information obtained from its website www.aa.org, as of January 2013, over two million AA members were reported in over 170 countries, with just under 115,000 individual groups (Service Material 2013). Mäkelä and colleagues (1996) describe an AA meeting as "a unique speech event defined by a specific combination of rules of talk" with "room for cultural variation" (p. 149). Their analysis of AA meetings in 'eight societies' reveals a great deal of variability in meetings across cultures – in attitudes towards positive vs. negative politeness, for example, in ritual elaboration, in openness and social visibility of meetings, and in equality of membership viz. newcomers and old-timers. Spiritual beliefs, or the belief in a 'Higher Power of our understanding' also differs across cultures. The authors find AA members professing Christianity as their Higher Power to be directly related to the corresponding strength of Christian belief in their respective regions (13% in Sweden vs. 56% in Poland, for example). Some AA members profess a belief in God *and* in the AA fellowship as their Higher Power. But "only a tiny minority openly acknowledge that the 'power greater than ourselves' means nothing to them personally" (p. 157).

The power greater than ourselves means nothing to me personally.

"I don't want to take up too much time," Paul continues, seems to incant. "I just want to thank everybody for being here. I've got sixteen years come March 5th." (Resounding round of applause.) "But I wouldn't have sixteen minutes if it weren't for all of you." *Al o'yee.* "Because you're never alone if you've got the Rooms." (Nods of assent, yeahs, yeses, and yeps.) "I'm feeling very grateful right now, grateful for my sobriety, and I just wanted to share that, to say hello, and to just give thanks. So, thank you."

"Thank you, Paul," Evelyn says, and "thank you for sharing."

"Thank you," says Paul.

The gratitude is overwhelming.

"Is there anyone else? Any newcomers?" She is seeking out my hand, but it's balled up in a fist in my lap. There's no escape.

I raise my hand limply. "Hi," I say, but in a volume and pitch reserved for nocturnal rodents. What am I doing here? I should be in bed. I should be in rehab or in detox at the very least because I am not well, and everybody here would probably agree with me.

Of course others will continue to describe alcoholism and/or addiction as a weakness of will. Perhaps the religious zeal will have faded from such a condemnation in comparison to America's early Temperance days when men of the cloth like Lyman Beecher described any use of alcohol as sinful. In fact, Harry Levine (1993) argues that AA shares its roots with Temperance. Beecher's "The Nature and Occasions of Intemperance," taken from his *Six Sermons on Intemperance* (1828), possesses the exuberant certitude of some of AA's rhetoric:

> No sin has fewer apologies than intemperance. The suffrage of the world is against it; and yet there is no sin so naked in its character, and whose commencement and progress is indicated by so many signs, concerning which there is among mankind such profound ignorance.

For Beecher, however, the will is free; and while AA cofounders Bill Wilson and Dr. Robert 'Bob' Smith were heavily influenced by William James's *The Varieties of Religious Experience* (1902), their admiration did not extend to James's notion of a free will, as that would obfuscate the disease concept.

Contradictions everywhere, but also hope. Because for me, at this moment, it doesn't matter what addiction *is*. What matters is what it *does*, and what it does is destroy my life.

"Hi, I'm Peter," I say, finding my voice somewhere in the hollows of my shame. No more cowering, no more lies. Laura will say as much, that honesty is key.

I say the words dutifully, as I'm expected to, as if the meeting were a performance and this was my part to play along with everyone else, provided I stick to the script.

"My name is Peter and I'm an addict."

METALOGUE: DIGGING DEEPER

Ken: I like the first person impressionistic tale. It really captures the phenomenological project. I felt your emotions and from a hermeneutic perspective I could understand the standpoint of different stakeholders you identified in the narrative. Can you provide some insights into the process you chose to focus the narrative?

The focus emerged over time. I have a few hundred pages of false starts. I did not want to write a traditional AA ethnography in the style of Denzin (1987) or Rudy (1986): empirical, symbolic interactionist participant/observation. I simply wasn't interested in doing that. And really, I couldn't have done it if I'd wanted because I already felt deeply implicated in AA, even though I was never a member.

I had a very strong personal point of view about it, based on lived experience, and I wanted to explore that using Van Maanen's (1988) "impressionist tale" as method and methodology, the epistemology of which is to "braid the knower with the known" (p. 102). Here he is on the 'standards' of the impressionist tale and on the 'obligation' of the impressionist writer:

> [...] standards [for the impressionist tale] are not disciplinary but literary ones, the main obligation of the impressionist is to keep the audience alert and interested. Unusual phrasings, fresh allusions, rich language, cognitive and emotional stimulation, puns, and quick jolts to the imagination are all characteristic of the good tale. (p. 106)

I think these criteria are quite different from Carolyn Ellis's (1999) notion of 'verisimilitude' in autoethnography, or the appearance of being 'real,' which she likens to 'validity' in more positivist-inclined social science research. But I disagree. I'm with Yvonna Lincoln who, still seeming to want it both ways, argues, "the silliest issues in such research [life history and narrative] would be traditional ideas of internal and external validity, replicability, and objectivity. It's not that these issues don't get done well in this form of research; they are simply not in the same universe" (in J. Amos Hatch and Richard Wisniewski 1995, p. 120). Besides which, I find impressionist tales to be more presentational than representational, which is my reason for using the somewhat awkward construction, '(re)presentation.' It is not the aim of the impressionist for a 'realistic' interpretation of the lifeworld – that's the job of the "realist" who "push[es] most firmly for the authenticity of the cultural representations conveyed by the text" (van Maanen 1988, p. 45). The impressionist tries for a subjective and interpretive phenomenology of a particular mode of being in a particular field. Also, my 'field' is an unorthodox one of memories and texts…I'm not doing empirical work and I'm only seeking generalizability at the theoretical and methodological levels, and that would have more to do with the storied aspects of self and identity than with anything involving AA, addiction, or alcoholism.

Once I decided on impressionist tales I had to find something to tell about, to narrate. And once I decided on an open AA meeting of my memoires and imaginings I was set. Everything really flowed from there. I always knew what was going to happen next. All I had to do was check the 'Suggested Open Meeting Format' PDF, ransack my memories, and apply what Van Maanen (1988) calls "dramatic recall" (p. 103) to the processes of rumination and write-up.

Let me explain how I came to tell about these stakeholders in the narrative. Following van Maanen they are 'impressions' of people I either met or observed in the dozen or so AA meetings I attended in earnest during the late 1990s and early 2000s. Jeff and his buddy, whose name becomes Buddy, both spoke to me directly but at different times and at different meetings. I brought them together to be friends. (Their names, like all the names used, except mine, are pseudonyms.) Evelyn is a sort of 'composite' of several meeting chairs that I observed. (By the way there were just as many male chairs as female; I made Evelyn female because my narrative was already crowded with men. And yes, one of these Evelyns gave me the Twelve Traditions to read out loud in front of 150 or so people…a huge meeting, the biggest I'd been to.) Mike and Tessa were also 'composites' of the many people I'd witnessed being welcomed back into the group after a slip or a full-blown relapse. Paul the Scot was actually an Irishman, and he was more charming than I could ever hope to describe.

All these stakeholders are filtered through the first person present lens of a quite unsettled narrator (I/me). In literature we might call him an unreliable narrator, but we won't here. We'll say he's as reliable as the next guy, but he's in a bit of a spot and it's affecting his conduct and the way he perceives/interprets the world, and a particular world of texts. The stakeholders are there, along with the narrator, to hold the thing up to a certain light. But when it comes to my actual research participant, Laura, the stakes are raised considerably. I have an ethical responsibility for her that I don't have for the other stakeholders in the narrative.

Ken: The narrative captures some history and provides facts about the tenets of AA. It also raises issues of the place of addicts whose addiction is not alcohol and the role of God and Judeo-Christian religion. As a person who is in some ways marginalized – how accurately do you feel this methodology allows you to represent your marginalization?

For me, the first person present is the most immediate experience one can have with a text. It allows the reader to walk in the shoes of the 'subject' being (re)presented, which is the phenomenological project in a nutshell.

Having said that, I think there are a couple of levels of marginalization in the narrative. There is the marginalization of the addict/alcoholic in general, which most of us think of as stigma (Goffman 1963), and there is the marginalization I (re)present as a non-believer encountering and mediating a spiritual/religious group. I realize you're referring to the latter since that's one of the main conflicts of the narrative, the problem of the nonbeliever in AA.

I try to (re)present what AA variously calls the Higher Power, the Higher Power of one's understanding, God, Him, He, as that concept is (re)presented at an open meeting. My perplexity is real as are my feelings of marginalization at being a nonbeliever in AA, and my desire for what I call the shared balm of spiritual belief. The 'dynamic tension' of AA either being or *not* being a religious institution that Klaus Mäkelä and colleagues (1996) write about is less dynamic, for me, than it is untenable, but in a functional sense this tension has helped to fuel the narrative in ways I never imagined. It gets even stickier further along.

Ken: Beyond getting the permission of the IRB, what are the main ethical issues that emerge when a decision is made to use impressionistic tales as a vehicle for dissemination?

I think here we get back to where we ended with the first question – the relationship I have with my research participant, Laura, which requires elaboration. But first I think it's important to say that she and I hold very different points-of-view regarding AA. If the first part of the project, the part we've read here, is a hermeneutics of suspicion, or an interpretation that seeks to disclose hidden meanings in texts and in social structures and relations, then the second part, Laura's part, is a hermeneutics of faith that seeks to disclose AA as *she* sees it

(Josselson 2004). Laura's involvement in AA is much more than tenable; it's a large part of what gives her life genuine meaning. It helps to keep her alive, quite literally, so part of the ethical project for me is respecting that, which really means respecting Laura.

I hope that the respect I have for Laura is evident in the work. As much as possible I tried to keep quiet during Laura's research interview and write-up so that she could tell her story for herself, in the first person, and uninterrupted. In this sense, perhaps, the impressionist tale is *the* ethical choice for dissemination because it can give historically marginalized research participants, i.e., addicts/alcoholics, more immediate access to readers than traditional forms of scholarship.

However, I think one of the most important things to remember is that no matter how unswerving and loyal a faithful hermeneutics is, it is still a hermeneutic, an interpretive tool that informs (re)presentation. There is no such thing as a neutral interpretation. In spite of my intended 'faithfulness' to Laura's story as she told it to me, I must be wary of the power I hold in telling her story for her, and of the symbolic violence I am capable of inflicting on her as the author of her tale, especially since I'm identifying her as marginalized not once but twice – both for being a (sober) alcoholic and for being a member of AA.

Gene Fellner: You broaden a discussion about the spaces where art and research meet. Your text is art, very much about sensing before making sense, which is the phenomenological core, at least it seems so to me. You present as legitimate research a move beyond the stating of facts or the positivist idea of what reality is. There are some parallels to some of Mailer's best work, to historical fiction and history as fiction (as Robespierre said it was).

I'm trying to produce something 'literary' with the dissertation as a whole, and I'm conscious of that, and of the fact that I'm dealing with history, capital and lower-case: the history of AA, and mine and Laura's personal histories. While I don't go very deeply into the specifics of my personal history, the piece is ultimately quite revealing because of the risky subject matter involved; and I think I reveal a relation to the self that is common amongst addicts/alcoholics in my angst-driven interactions with the meeting, with the people in the meeting, and with some of the AA texts, which is the relation of self-loathing.

But I do think there is some making-sense here, not just sensing. There is the other 'me,' the present/future educational researcher who comes to the front of the stage every once in a while to cite something or to give you his thoughts before rejoining the cast. (Thanks to Mitch Bleier for that analogy.) This is not an impressionist tale in the strict sense of the term. Sometimes I wonder if van Maanen would approve.

Gene: If the purpose of phenomenological research is to help us to understand each other on a deep sense-basis that generates understanding beyond difference, to make the strange familiar not merely on an intellectual plane but in ways that often elude factual narration and description, then you have been a successful phenomenologist. What's different is that you arrive at a truth through imaginative forays, through conscious manipulation and embellishment of what we generally think of as fact. Such means are usually not considered legitimate within the field of academic research; indeed they challenge the essential rules of research, though they are welcomed in art. Picasso said that "art is a lie that makes one realize truth," and you have played with the truth as it is commonly understood in order to make your truth resonate with the reader on a plane beyond reason. I think van Maanen gets all of this intellectually, but is less successful than you in transmitting the sense-feeling of the subject experiences. I wonder what your research means for Research. I also wonder what it means that the subject-object dichotomy is so thoroughly and beautifully blurred.

Yes, I think this sort of writing blurs the subject/object dichotomy; and obviously it's nothing that literature, beginning with the novel, hasn't done before. I was trying to avoid the idea of a grand narrative of addiction/alcoholism, which is implicit and unavoidable in the structured life storytelling of AA. Different people – indeed, different countries – approach addiction treatment and recovery differently. Eugene Raikhel and William Garriott (2013) remind us of this important fact in *Addiction Trajectories,* which has had a big influence on me lately. The editors and authors of this collection of anthropological essays try for a less deterministic notion of addicts/alcoholics than is commonly understood. "Addiction trajectories" are "the directed (yet contingent) movement of people, substances, ideas, techniques, and institutions along spatial, temporal, social, and epistemic dimensions" (Introduction, Section 1, para. 2). It's the most global vision of addiction I've yet encountered, and the critical and compassionate approach to its subjects and subject matter is very appealing. I see Laura and I as having travelled different addiction trajectories. If there's any suspense to these tales I suppose it exists in guessing what *my* trajectory will be, as we already know Laura's. (A suspenseful dissertation!) I agree with you that a broader discussion of the spaces between art and research would be invaluable and I would love to be a part of it. Appreciating that there's a place for this sort of work is important for legitimizing an epistemology of the imagination in education research, however marginal that place might be.

NOTES

[1] There are several types of AA meetings each with different formats and texts including meetings for Beginners, Open and Closed Discussion meetings, Step meetings, Big Book meetings, Tradition meetings, and Open meetings like the one (re)presented in this narrative (Inter-Group Association of AA 2010, p. 1).

[2] Most of Evelyn's 'lines' are taken from an undated 'Suggested Open Meeting Format' PDF file retrieved from San Diego's AA website, www.aasandiego.org.

REFERENCES

AA Grapevine, Inc. (2013). AA preamble. [PDF file.] Retrieved from www.aa.org

AA World Services, Inc. (2002). The twelve traditions of Alcoholics Anonymous (short form). PDF file.] Retrieved from www.aa.org

Anonymous. (1952). *Twelve steps and twelve traditions*. New York: Alcoholics Anonymous World Services, Inc.

Anonymous. (1957). *Alcoholics Anonymous comes of age: A brief history of AA*. New York: Alcoholics Anonymous World Services, Inc.

Anonymous. (1973/2013). *The twelve steps to sobriety and the history of how they work.* [Kindle Keyboard version.] Retrieved from http://www.amazon.com

Anonymous. (2001). *Alcoholics Anonymous: The story of how many thousands of men and women have recovered from alcoholism* (4th ed.). New York: Alcoholics Anonymous World Services, Inc.

Arminen, I. (2004). Second stories: The salience of interpersonal communication for mutual-help in Alcoholics Anonymous. *Journal of Pragmatics, 36*, 319-347.

Beecher, L. (1828). *Six sermons on intemperance*. Retrieved from http://utc.iath.virginia.edu/sentimnt/sneslbat.html

Cain, C. (1991). Personal stories: Identity acquisition and self-understanding in Alcoholics Anonymous. *Ethos, 19/2*, 210-253.

Denzin, N. K. (1987). *Treating alcoholism: An Alcoholics Anonymous approach*. Newbury Park: Sage Publications.

De Quincey, T. (1822/1949). *Confessions of an English opium-eater*. London: Oxford University Press.

Ellis, C. (1999). Heartful autoethnography. *Qualitative Health Research, 9*, 669-683.

Goffman, E. (1963). *Stigma: Notes on the management of spoiled identity*. New York: Simon & Schuster.

Hatch, J. A., & Wisniewski, R. (1995). Life history and narrative: Questions, issues, and exemplary works. In J. A. Hatch & R. Wisniewski (Eds.), *Life history and narrative* (pp. 113-136). Abingdon, Oxon: RoutledgeFalmer.

Inter-Group Association of AA of New York, Inc. (2010). [Brochure.] Meeting book: Greater New York City area.

James, W. (1902). *The varieties of religious experience*. [Kindle Keyboard version]. Retrieved from http://www.amazon.com.

Josselson, R. (2004). The hermeneutics of faith and the hermeneutics of suspicion. *Narrative Inquiry, 14*(1), 1-28.

Lave, J. and Wenger, E. (1991). *Situated learning: Legitimate peripheral participation*. Cambridge: Cambridge University Press.

Levine, H. (1993). Temperance cultures: Alcohol as a problem in Nordic and English-speaking cultures. In M. Lader, G. Edwards, & D. C. Drummond (Eds.), *The nature of alcohol and drug-related problems* (pp. 16-36). New York: Oxford University Press.

Mäkelä, K., et al. (1996). *Alcoholics Anonymous as a mutual-help movement: A study in eight societies*. Madison, WI: University of Wisconsin Press.

Manulis, M. (Producer) and Edwards, B. (Director) (1962). *The days of wine and roses* [DVD.] United States: Jalem Productions.

O'Halloran, S. (2006). Power and solidarity-building in the discourse of Alcoholics Anonymous. *Journal of Groups in Addiction & Recovery, 1/2*, 69-95.

Raikhel, E., & Garriott, W. (Eds.). (2013). *Addiction trajectories* [Kindle Keyboard version]. Retrieved from http://www.amazon.com.

Rudy, D. R. (1986). *Becoming alcoholic: Alcoholics Anonymous and the reality of alcoholism*. Carbondale, IL: Southern Illinois University Press.

Service Material from the General Service Office. (2013). Estimates of AA groups and members as of January 1st, 2013. [PDF file.] Retrieved from www.aa.org

Suggested open meeting format. (n.d.). [PDF file.] Retrieved from www.aasandiego.org

Swora, M.G. (2004). The rhetoric of transformation in the healing of alcoholism: The twelve steps of alcoholics anonymous. *Mental Health, Religion & Culture,* September 7(3), 187-209.

Valverde, M. and White-Mair, K. (1999). 'One day at a time' and other slogans for everyday life: The ethical practices of Alcoholics Anonymous. *Sociology, 33*, 393-410.

Van Maanen, J. (1988). *Tales of the field: On writing ethnography.* Chicago and London: University of Chicago Press.
Weinberg, D. (2000). "Out there": The ecology of addiction in drug abuse treatment discourse. *Social Problems, 47*(4), 606-621.

MALGORZATA POWIETRZYNSKA

16. TO YOUR HEALTH! HEURISTICS AND DEEP BREATHING AS MINDFULNESS PROMOTING INTERVENTIONS IN EDUCATIONAL CONTEXT

"FEEL THIS MOMENT"

I am sitting in a spacious, attractive, modern room on the 40th floor of the newly re-erected 7 World Trade Center which is the home for the New York Academy of Sciences (NYAS). Behind me a wall of floor-to-ceiling windows reveal a panorama of downtown Manhattan glittering with lights on this cold, crispy, and crystal clear February evening. I am here awaiting the beginning of a sold out event. As the audience members slowly fill the rows of seats, I can hear buzz of their muffled voices. With seemingly nothing else to do (I came alone and, unusually for me, I arrived quite early), I catch myself drifting with my thoughts. I think of another event I attended in the morning at yet another freshly minted building of John Jay College. I remember the speeches by the Chancellor of the Department of Education and the Chancellor of the City University of New York highlighting collaborative efforts between the City's educational giants. I think of the speakers' lack of genuineness when glossing over the many problems that continue to plague public schooling in the city. Then, I remember the reason for being where I am. I close my eyes and try to bring myself back; I try to be present; I try to be in the moment. I focus on my breath. "Breathe in, breathe out, in, out …" Someone is taking a seat next to me. I open my eyes and catch myself scrutinizing and judging the stranger. I notice the way he smells as the scent bothers me. I think to myself, "Oh, why did he have to sit next to me? Oh, how I wish they would start already." My thoughts take over again! I close my eyes and return to my breath … Moments later the speakers emerge and take seats on the podium at the front of the room. They are neuroscientists Richard Davidson and Amishi Jha and a clinical mindfulness expert Jon Kabat-Zinn. Their talk tonight, Becoming Conscious: The Science of Mindfulness, is the last in the series titled The Emerging Science of Consciousness: Mind, Brain and the Human Experience. As advertised on the NYAS's website, the speakers are here "to explore the role of consciousness in mental and physical health, how we can train the mind to become more flexible and adaptable, and what cutting-edge neuroscience is revealing about the transformation of consciousness through mindfulness and contemplative practice."

A mushrooming of similar events is a testament that mindfulness, as a special case of contemplative practice, has entered mainstream science. Labs in a number of distinguished colleges and universities across the United States have opened their doors to research involving meditative states. Curious scientists collaborate on projects that provide an insight into how in the fast-paced, technology-driven world of information overload our brains and lives may be impacted by a radical idea of pausing and being in the moment; in other words – being mindful. Often perceived as incongruent traditions, western and eastern thought finally come together in the hope of providing relief to human beings many of whom are victims of chronic stress. The ultimate teacher and relentless student of contemplative practice, the Dalai Lama, routinely meets with scientists in an unprecedented exchange of eastern and western epistemologies. Modern methodologies meet centuries old traditions when Tibetan monks perform their meditation practice in fMRI tubes providing invaluable data of what is happening in their mindfulness-trained brains (Davidson and Begley 2012). The data are revealing the effects of *neuroplasticity* – our brain's ability to modify its structure and functioning. It turns out that when we engage in contemplative practice (such as mindfulness meditation), we are in effect exercising our minds. An analogy may be drawn between exercising the mind and exercising the body: meditation has an analogous strengthening effect on our brain as doing physical exercises has on our muscles. Moreover, just like physical exercise promotes health, the same is true for effects of exercising the mind. Healthier brains translate into improvements in overall wellbeing including decreased levels of stress and depression. Commenting on his understanding of meditation, a participant in one of our studies noted:

> I think meditation is a process of concentration in order to clear the mind from unwanted thoughts. It is also a way to exercise our brain and mind. I practice meditation sometimes, and it always helps. Meditation increases mindfulness. (Edward, in-service science teacher, February 26 2012, Week 4 of the study)

The explosion in acceptance of mindfulness in scientific circles is relatively new. In the words of Arthur Zajonc (2009), for many years the mindfulness pioneers "felt alone in their stubborn conjunction of the scientific and the contemplative" (Personal Practice and Finding Fellowship, para.1). Richard Davidson often admits spending years of his early career as a "closeted meditator" while being feverishly discouraged by his academic colleagues from his interest in what is now known as contemplative neuroscience. A son of a painter and a biomedical scientist, Jon Kabat-Zinn links the pursuit of contemplative practice with his search for the unifying factor of the different ways of knowing (artistic and scientific). As a young professor at the University of Pennsylvania, Amishi Jha admits to being shocked when she first heard the word meditation uttered by Davidson in a scientific setting. Soon after, having experienced benefits of incorporating meditation practice into her busy life of an academic, she made mindfulness a focal point of her research program. Despite the skepticism of their peers and working against the grain of the privileged scientific paradigms, all these scholars have turned their passion into fruitful careers whose unifying theme is that of beneficence. They are among the pioneers whose work continues to provide a mounting evidence for the many benefits associated with contemplative practices. As a result there has been notable proliferation of applications of meditative practices in the most unexpected fields of social life ranging from the US military to pop-culture. In a recent film, a Danish director, Phie Ambo, documents a study conducted by Davidson and his research team that found positive effects of meditation and yoga on the returning war veterans suffering from the post-traumatic stress disorder (Dyekjaer and Ambo 2012). In its relentless search for a happier and thus more efficient workforce, corporate America (notwithstanding its often less than altruistic motivation) has jumped on the mindfulness bandwagon. David Gelles (2012) of the Financial Times reports how large companies such as Google, General Mills, and Green Mountain Coffee incorporate mindfulness training into their corporate practices. Politicians join in promoting mindfulness as a cure for the collective ills. In his book, "A Mindful Nation" congressman Tim Ryan (2012) explains "How a Simple Practice Can Help Us Reduce Stress, Improve Performance, and Recapture the American Spirit." In popular culture, the rapper Pitbull and a singer-songwriter Christina Aguilera encourage their young fans to "feel this moment" through their high-energy song about stopping to appreciate life. So how might we as individuals and collectives reap the benefits of contemplative practices? As an educator and a researcher, I join a growing number of enthusiasts who believe in the desirability of incorporating the practices into our educational system. In this chapter, I describe the logics we apply to our mindfulness-focused research work against the backdrop of the current state of the field in the educational settings. By "we," I refer to the research squad led by Kenneth Tobin. The members of this collective are students and doctoral candidates of the Ph.D. program in Urban Education at the City University of New York. Many of the ideas presented here have their genesis in Tobin's continually evolving research philosophy and practice. I also weave in my voice as well as the voices of other squad members and research participants.

MINDFULNESS-BASED INTERVENTIONS IN EDUCATION AND IN EDUCATIONAL RESEARCH

(…) social research is something much too serious and too difficult for us to allow ourselves to mistake scientific *rigidity,* which is the nemesis of intelligence and invention, for scientific *rigor,* and thus to deprive ourselves of this or that resource available in the full panoply of intellectual traditions of our discipline and of the sister disciplines of anthropology, economics, history, etc. In such matters, I would be tempted to say that only one rule applies: "it is forbidden to forbid," or watch out for methodological watchdogs. (Bourdieu and Wacquant 1992, p.227)

Consisting of contemplatives and contemplative scholars; neuroscientists; cognitive, developmental and educational scientists; and educational activists, the Mind and Life Education Research Network (MLERN 2012) frames *contemplative practices* in modern scientific terms as "forms of mental and behavioral training that are intended to produce alterations in basic cognitive and emotional processes, such as attention and the regulation of certain forms of negative affect, and to enhance particular character traits that are considered virtuous, such as honesty and kindness" (p. 146). To the group, applying contemplative practices to cultivate these shifts in cognitive skills and socio-emotional dispositions is central to the aims of education in the 21st century. In their recent review of research into K-12 mindfulness training programs, John Meiklejohn and his colleagues (2012) agree that both teachers and students can benefit significantly from enhancing attentional and emotional self-regulation and from promotion of flexibility. Indeed, an earlier report by the Garrison Institute (2005) found many commonalities among contemplative programs for K-12th grade students. Consistent with the MLERN description, the programs appear to train and refine attention, promote emotional balance, and help students develop a capacity for self-regulation. They also share a common set of "short-term" outcomes consistent with those of mainstream education which include enhancing students' learning and academic performance, improving the school's social climate as well as promoting emotional balance and pro-social behaviors. Among the "long-term" outcomes identified by the report are the development of noble qualities such as peacefulness, internal calm, compassion, empathy, forgiveness, patience, generosity and love. Looking beyond K-12, Shauna Shapiro, Kirk Warren Brown, and John Astin (2008) document similar findings: when applied to higher education, meditation can contribute to enhancement of cognitive and academic performance, management of academic-related stress, and development of the "whole person."

INVESTIGATING MINDFULNESS: THE QUESTION OF PARADIGM

While the extant literature points to the proliferation of mindfulness-based programs across the educational spectrum, there is agreement that research in this newly emerging field is in its infancy. One concern is that while there is support for the feasibility and acceptability of mindfulness-based interventions in educational settings, more "scientific" evidence of their effectiveness is needed (Meiklejohn et al. 2012). For example, Christine Burke (2009) notes that the existing studies conducted with children and adolescents are characterized by "weak" methodologies and designs. She concludes that there is a need for "a more rigorous course of gathering empirically-sound evidence of the efficacy of these interventions" (p. 143). Scientific rigor is often associated with following a positivistic paradigm that focuses on establishing causality through quantitative methodologies with the "gold standard" of randomized controlled trials. In an opening quote to this section, Bourdieu equates such reliance on a single paradigm with scientific rigidity which may be ill-suited for research in social sciences. Indeed, Shapiro and her colleagues (2008) note that due to their subtlety and complexity, meditation experiences may not easily lend themselves to quantification by existing measures. Therefore, they recommend that some research "may include qualitative reports of phenomenological changes" (p. 32). Members of the MLERN group (2012) appear to try to find a happy paradigmatic medium by pointing out that the field of mindfulness-based interventions would benefit from research drawing on quantitative data resources and experimental methods as well as "careful qualitative analyses documenting processes of change in a deep and rich way" (p. 151). Instead of dichotomizing research into qualitative and quantitative, Tobin (2012) recommends thinking of research "in terms of the logics used in arriving at conclusions and the manner in which conclusions are framed and nuanced" (p. 9). That Buddhist scholars and monks rub elbows with prominent cognitive scientists and psychologists in interrogating contemplative practices may in itself be a testament to the viability of suspension of dichotomies in favor of dialectical relationships and wholeness.

When considering suitable paradigms for researching the effects of mindfulness training on teachers and students, Robert Roeser and his colleagues (2012) advocate applying multi-method, multi-trait, and multi-informant measures to establish the empirical and practical significance of these programs. Methodological multiplicity is a lynchpin of studies conducted by Tobin and his research squad. More precisely, in our interpretive research (inspired by Frederick Erickson 1998) we employ multi-level, multi-method, and multi-theoretical approaches which we maintain are well-suited to examining multilectic (as opposed to one-dimensional) life experiences of our research participants (Tobin 2012). To that end, for example, we embrace and try to illuminate multiple voices (polyphonia) representing multiple meanings (polysemia) ascribed by study participants who may occupy different positions in social life. Gene Fellner (this volume) advances a compelling argument for applying the concept of multiplicity to the way of being in the world including the way we conduct research. In order to capture the multiple ways of being, we generate phenomenological accounts of what is happening in the classrooms and we develop their hermeneutic interpretations. In the process we strive to stimulate transformative shifts where such shifts appear desirable. Based on the research findings we generate a theory which is then available to others. We adopt Margaret Eisenhart's stance on theoretical generalizability (Eisenhart 2009). Accordingly, the decision whether the research is generalized depends on its user and not on the individuals who do the empirical or theoretical scholarship.

GETTING MY FEET WET IN THE POOL OF MINDFULNESS-BASED RESEARCH

Tobin's interest in the benefits of contemplative practices has its genesis in his work on the intersection of emotions, teaching and learning (Tobin and Richie 2012). Motivated by his conviction that there is desperate need for generating transformative shifts such as regulation of certain forms of negative affect, Tobin initiated a series of mindfulness-centered studies. One of the research projects was conducted with pre-service and in-service teachers in a graduate-level science teacher education program. This was my very first encounter with conducting an empirical study. It was a unique opportunity to learn from and with Tobin and Konstantinos Alexakos who, in his dual role of a principal investigator | instructor, welcomed us into his classroom. A follower of the interpretive research paradigm,

Alexakos had previously undertaken studies in his classroom with his students who often assumed roles of co-researchers as well as co-authors of research papers. He also was developing a research agenda that focused on the role of emotions in the classroom (Alexakos 2015). For me, participation in the research project was an opportunity to apply theoretical knowledge I gained only a few weeks earlier during the final course of my program taught by Tobin. I wondered if the recently ignited theory-driven romance with interpretive research would have the same appeal when tested "in the field." Working in the trenches and interacting with the study participants aligned well with my intuitive conception of the type of researcher I wanted to be. In addition, as Tobin comments in chapter 1 of this volume, I found working side by side with more experienced colleagues, as is the case in the Australian educational system, a preferred way of developing research skills. Such Deweyan *learning by doing* combined with being supported by a group of like-minded associates stands in contrast to the sense of loneliness felt by novice researchers as described by Alexakos (2015). Not only was I a novice in conducting interpretive research, I knew close to nothing about mindfulness and had absolutely no exposure to meditative practices. Through participation in the research, I was able to get familiar with the concept and to adopt its tenets. As I illustrate below, I was one of many who benefited from the research in a profound way.

"WE CAN DO BETTER" – CONDUCTING AUTHENTIC RESEARCH

Mindfulness-related investigations are often motivated by the researcher's desire to improve the human condition. This drive to "do better" is grounded in a belief that altering the status quo rather than merely documenting it should be the focus of social inquiry. One could frame this approach in terms of a social contract between the researcher and the society where research, as a privilege, is not merely to benefit an individual (the researcher) but ought to benefit a collective (the society). Following the principle of beneficence (The Belmont Report 1979), our major goal is for the research participants to directly benefit from our studies. When this happens, research is considered *authentic*, namely, it meets the standards associated with conducting social inquiry of high quality. It is this aim rather than rigidly conforming to any one methodological and/or theoretical framework that motivates our work. As outlined by Tobin in chapter 3 of this volume, we adopt and expand on the authenticity criteria as theorized and practiced by Egon Guba and Yvonna Lincoln (1989). Often, at the forefront of the study is accomplishing ontological authenticity which is manifested through changes in individual ontologies (the way life is experienced). For example, learning about and adopting mindfulness practices may impact teachers' relationship towards stress as they become more attuned to their emotional states. Learning from and with other members of the collective is essential for the ontological changes to occur. Educative authenticity is accomplished when opportunities are created for everyone to express their perspectives and when no particular standpoints are privileged. Mindfulness may help in increasing levels of acceptance of difference.

Through the increased present-moment awareness, teachers and students alike may be better equipped to recognize and adequately respond (rather than react) to the subtleties and nuances inherent in each individual.

One way to promote authenticity research is to develop and implement interventions that would catalyze improvements for all involved in the study. Based on the relevant literature and personal experience, it was clear that the in-service and pre-service teachers who participated in our studies, as did we (we consider it unreasonable to draw a demarcation line between the researchers and the researched), needed mindfulness-focused tools to assist in managing the stressors of the daily professional lives. Our approach was unique in that we did not develop a freestanding mindfulness-based course or program. Instead, we decided to weave our interventions into existing courses. The idea was to minimize interruption of what is often referred to as the "official curriculum." We theorized that if successful those interventions could become part of any course or class. Mindfulness heuristic and a three-minute deep breathing practice were two interventions we developed and enacted in our studies. Both interventions are central to the discussion in the sections below.

HEURISTICS, HERMENEUTICS AND REFLEXIVITY: GRASPING THE CONSTRUCT OF MINDFULNESS

How does one explain the concept of mindfulness? According to Kabat-Zinn (1994), to cultivate mindfulness is to "pay attention in a particular way: on purpose, in the present moment, and non-judgmentally" (p. 4). At the same time, mindfulness is one of the concepts that Pema Chödrön refers to as ineffable. Our Australian colleagues, Nichole Albrecht, Patricia Albrecht and Marc Cohen (2012) agree by saying that "capturing and defining mindfulness in words is complex as it requires similar consideration to defining human consciousness" (p. 3). Therefore, when writing about mindfulness, they aim at allowing the reader to experience "a taste of mindfulness" and to develop "his or her own understanding" of the concept. To that end they provide an experiential account of mindfulness from perspective of teachers who have been exposed to mindfulness-based training. Paul Grossman (2008) argues that mindfulness cannot be fully comprehended by discursive, theoretical, or intellectual thinking but primarily relies on practical introspective practices. Grossman is concerned that depending on the amount and type of meditation practice people may have different semantic interpretations of mindfulness.

In our hermeneutic approach to conducting research, we adopt Tobin's (2009) standpoint on definitions. For him, "definitions can comprise thick descriptions and be contingent on the circumstances of a study" (p. 507). Accordingly, rather than trying to formulate a definition of mindfulness, we attempt to surround the construct with meaning. One way to accomplish this is by generating a heuristic where the heuristic is a means of unpacking a construct. A heuristic may be a series of statements that describe different aspects of mindfulness. We call these statements *characteristics* where the characteristics are meant to give insights into what the construct is. For example, being able to pay attention in the present moment is one of the facets of mindfulness. *"I pay attention to my moment-to-moment sensory experiences"* is an example of a characteristic that describes this feature. Through a heuristic we attempt to create what Joe Kincheloe (2003) refers to as a hermeneutic cycle or interplay between a whole (the abstract) and parts (the particular). Hence, mindfulness may be understood through interpretation of its parts expressed through the characteristics. Unlike Grossman, we are not concerned with the convergence among the meanings people ascribe to the construct of mindfulness or its parts. Instead we acknowledge difference and nuance as typical, inescapable and, axiologically speaking, valuable aspects of social life.

Heuristic is an inherently malleable tool and thus it may take various forms and serve different functions. Tobin refers to it as a "shape shifter" since it is meant to change so as to be situationally relevant. Accordingly, one of our mindfulness heuristics is contextualized to an educational setting and includes characteristics reflective of the teaching-learning environment. For example, a characteristic, *"I can tell when something is bothering the teacher,"* refers to the ability to be aware of and sensitive to the class instructor's negative emotions. This characteristic encompasses awareness and compassion which are central to the construct of mindfulness. In its format, a heuristic may resemble a survey where each characteristic is accompanied by a rating scale. The rating scale is used to allow the respondent to make a personal connection with a particular characteristic in the heuristic. A student may read, *"During this class, I can focus my attention on learning"* and consider where on the continuum between "always" and "never" she might fall. This requires that she pause, even if briefly, think and make a judgment call. Since we strongly reject ontological realism, the point is not to gain an accurate assessment of how the person enacts social life but to draw her attention to the way mindfulness may be manifested (in this case through paying attention and focusing on the task at hand). The aim is to create an opportunity for self-reflection in relationship to a series of characteristics that describe what being mindful may mean. *Reflexivity* or becoming aware of what one may be unaware of is a big part of how the heuristic works. To Bourdieu, when applied to research in social sciences, reflexivity entails the systematic exploration of the "unthought categories of thought which delimit the thinkable and predetermine the thought" (Bourdieu and Wacquant 1992, p. 40). The following quotes by students of an undergraduate physics course who participated in one of our studies are examples of reactions to the heuristic. They appear to testify to the reflexive power of the heuristic:

> Many of the questions [characteristics] asked were of things that I unconsciously did and when my attention was brought to that aspect through a question, I had a realization that I did do many of these things.

> I never actually thought about any of these questions [characteristics] during class, but now that I am looking back, I am noticing more than I thought I did about my surroundings.

This heuristic made me think and reflect on my existence in the classroom/lecture hall more than I ever would have without it.

Since awareness and paying attention are at the core of mindfulness, the heightened awareness reported by the students may be indicative of an increased incidence of mindfulness in their practices. The quotes also confirm the realization that many of us go through daily life on autopilot, without being fully aware of our conscious experience even though attention and awareness are universal human qualities. Sadly, as noted by Albrecht and her colleagues (2012), we are often "trained out of mindfulness through fast paced and outcome driven lives" (p. 5).

Heuristics may be experienced in different ways: they may be completed on-line or using a more traditional paper and pencil format. We also use heuristic as tool to guide a conversation. To that end, we invite individual participants to meet with one or two researchers so that we may have a discussion about each of the characteristics in the heuristic. We avoid referring to these meetings as interviews since interviewing usually denotes working towards predetermined goals. Rather, we allow the conversation to unfold without privileging anyone's perspective. I find these conversations particularly rich and nuanced. The meaning making is aided through each person's ability to ask the other for clarifications and negotiate the flow of the conversation. Naturally, each of the conversations is unique in that the respondents have distinctive interpretations and commentaries regarding mindfulness. Embracing multiple ontologies and difference is consistent with the multi-perspectival way of doing research. At the same time, unifying themes may emerge. Such was the case during my mindfulness-heuristic-centered conversations with three student-participants. Even though each may have found a different set of characteristics salient to their lives, they all expressed a desire to "improve" some aspect of their conduct reflective of those characteristics.

In addition to acting as a vehicle for obtaining first-person self-reports, heuristics may be used as tool for structuring an observation. The observation may be conducted in real-time or using video files to determine what happened in terms of each characteristic and to gage the extent to which the practices in the classroom are mindful. There is also emerging evidence that heuristics maintain their appeal when translated into other languages or when used with school-aged children. As of this writing, a Polish version of the heuristic was incorporated into a mindfulness-based study at one of Poland's public universities. In New Zealand, Joanna Higgins and her colleagues (2013) used an age-appropriate version of the heuristic in a school-based study conducted with 11- to 13-year-old students. The preliminary results of the two studies point to the applicability of the heuristic to those environments. At the same time, in both these studies we experienced pushback when our colleagues tried to apply psychometrics to the way they thought about heuristic. It is important to acknowledge that at early stages of our mindfulness studies, we experienced a fleeting temptation to construct and validate a psychometrically sound instrument. However, since our focus is never on generalizing from sample to population but rather on illuminating nuance and difference, heuristic emerged as a more appropriate alternative to a survey. Even though it may appear similar, heuristic does not possess the psychometric qualities of a questionnaire. Paul Grossman (2008) points to a number of issues inherent in investigations driven by the psychometric assessment and attempting to quantify of the construct of mindfulness. When speaking of bridging the Eastern and Western paradigms, he warns, "haste toward an understanding of mindfulness may limit a genuine opportunity to expand perspectives beyond the familiar" (p. 408).

"I BREATHE TO LIVE, NOT TO MANAGE MY EMOTIONS." BREATHING MEDITATION AS MEDICATION?

The program of observation and analysis through which it is affected is not a blueprint that you draw up in advance, in the manner of an engineer. It is, rather, a protracted and exciting task that is accomplished little by little, through a whole series of small rectifications and amendments inspired by what is called le métier, the "know-how," that is, by the set of practical principles that orients choices at once minute and decisive. (Bourdieu and Wacquant 1992, pp. 227-228)

Contingency is a big part of our methodology. When Tobin was planning one of his studies on emotions in the classroom, he encountered literature that connects emotions with breathing patterns. Therefore, he imagined that breathing practice would be one of the emotion-regulating interventions enacted in our study. However, as we were embarking on the study, we did not have an a priori plan of what form intervention would take. I learned that there is no need to be uneasy about prearranging all aspects of the study. After all, social life is complex and to a large extent unpredictable. It is characterized by what William Sewell (2005) refers to as "thin coherence" and ever-present contradictions. Our methodological commitment to providing phenomenological description of what is happening and to hermeneutically figuring out why it is happening rests on embracing instability. Thus it is quite impossible and unrealistic to plan for all aspects of the study. When referring to research work in progress, Bourdieu speaks of "fermenting confusion" full of mishaps and misfirings, false starts, wavering, impasses, renunciations, and so on (Bourdieu and Wacquant 1992, pp. 219-220). Our research was often like that. At times, we realized that our research agenda was in direct conflict with the goals of the instructor. Whenever that happened, we engaged in negotiating a course of action that would be acceptable to all stakeholders. Student-participants were also involved in the decision-making regarding what would or would not be done. When they protested against an aspect of a study, it got suspended immediately. Conversely, there was a time when our suggestion to discontinue a particular practice was struck down by the student-participants. As I noted in the previous section and discuss elsewhere (Powietrzynska 2015), contingency played a major role in the development of the mindfulness heuristic; we generated four versions in response to the shifting circumstances and foci of the study.

Enacting a Breathing Intervention

Since we were among science teachers, we wanted our intervention to focus on physiological aspects of breathing meditation. One of the student-participants noted that breathing exercise could be thought of as a medical intervention. Indeed, when speaking to the class, Tobin experienced a comic slip of tongue when he referred to *breathing meditation* as *breathing medication*. When considering the benefits one may reap from engaging in breathing meditation, another participant compared it to brushing one's teeth – you do not particularly care for doing it but you do it because you know it is good for you. A clinical professor of psychiatry and a mindfulness expert, Daniel Siegel, considers reflective practices (such as focusing on one's breath) a brain hygiene technique. He promotes engagement in a daily *brain-brushing* routine toward developing well functioning brain as well as what he refers to as an *integrated brain* (Siegel and Hawn 2009).

Since two of the master's program students on the research squad, Natasha and Parvathy, had prior experience with breathing meditation, they volunteered to model the technique to the class. Alexakos considered it beneficial that the practice was introduced to his students by their peers. He believed that this way the intervention would not be seen as part of the required activities and students who felt reluctant to participate would feel less pressure to do so. The collective three-minute breathing practice was done right before the class started. The facilitator(s) asked the students to sit comfortably, to close their eyes (if they wished) and to take slow and deep breaths in and out. Since breathing was meant as an intervention to mediate negative emotions, we emphasized diaphragmatic (abdominal) as opposed to thoracic (chest) breathing. Participants were asked to place hands on their abdomens to monitor how their stomachs expanded with each in-breath and how they collapsed with each out-breath. In studies conducted by the Belgium-based researchers Pierre Philippot and Gaetane Chapelle and their Canadian colleague Sylvie Blairy (2002), slow and deep regular breathing through the nose was associated with production of happiness/joy. As noted by these authors, their studies offer support to theories of emotion stating that the quality of emotional feelings are, at least in part, modulated by body feedback. More precisely the alteration of respiration is sufficient to induce emotion. Therefore, we had the empirical and theoretical grounds confirming that the breathing exercise in our study might translate into production of positive emotional states right before the class, which in turn could catalyze improved learning.

We discovered that awareness of the link between physiology and emotions is not universally shared among students preparing to become teachers. A number of the characteristics in our mindfulness heuristic referred to this connection. For example, one heuristic item stated, "*During this class, I am aware of the relationship between my emotions and breathing pattern.*" When responding to this characteristic, over 65% of 174 physics course students answered *rarely*, *hardly ever* or *never*. One of the students commented: "It never appeared to me that we have different breathing patterns as our emotions change therefore I haven't ever been aware of this change." When the connection between breathing and emotions was made by the study participants, it was usually salient for intense, negative emotional states such as being nervous, stressed, angry, upset, frustrated and anxious. These states were often associated with exams and being graded or with difficulties in grasping the course content. Our heuristic pointed to the bi-directionality of the connection between breathing patterns and emotions. Responses to the characteristic, "*I use breathing to manage my emotions*" revealed that only 35% of the study participants did so at least occasionally in the physics class. Among the other 65% was a student who commented that she "breathed to live, not to manage her emotions."

Figure 16.1. Natasha (at the front of the classroom) leads deep breathing practice.

Breathing is such a natural and "automatic" function that it usually goes unnoticed. Bringing attention to the breath is often at the center of mindfulness training. Kabat-Zinn (1994) notes that as we begin befriending our breath, we see immediately that unawareness is everywhere (p. 20). At least one of the study participants noted that with each practice she was able to increase her focus. For her, taking deep breaths not only assists in releasing stress but also helps concentration. Amy Salzman (n.d., para. 2) notes that "one of the primary ironies of modern education is that we ask students to 'pay attention' dozens of times a day, yet we never teach them *how*." Maintaining focus on the present moment may be challenging because of our brain's natural tendency to wander. It turns out that *mind wandering* is the default network of the brain causing our mind to always be preoccupied with thoughts. A neuroscientist and representative of scientific skepticism, Sam Harris refers to the phenomenon as an "incessant" "cascade of thoughts" (Wood 2013, p. 7). Jha (2012) explains that to the brain the state of *REST* translates into *Rapid, Ever Present, Self Related Thinking*. Engaging in mindfulness-based training helps in taming the inclination for always being engulfed by thoughts as beautifully expressed by Alexakos' student, Nashia:

> I think of it [meditation] as trying to clear my thoughts, to focus on my breathing and nothing else, to allow the outside world to blow through me without disrupting. (Nashia, in-service teacher, March 3 2012, Week 5 of the study)

One misconception around mindfulness practice is that it involves repressing our emotions or thoughts. Harris explains:

> The goal is not to be without thought, but to be aware of the character of your experience in each moment and not suffer unnecessarily. Almost all our suffering is the product of our thoughts. We spend nearly every moment of our lives lost in thought, and hostage to the character of those thoughts. You can break this spell, but it takes training just like it takes training to defend yourself against a physical assault. (Wood 2013, pp. 6-7)

Mindfulness practice allows us to recognize that we are not our thoughts or emotions; it is meant to change our relationship towards our thoughts and emotions. That is where the ontological shifts are meant to occur. Our lives may still be characterized by negative thoughts or emotions but we are able to accept them for what they are – negative thoughts or emotions. In that sense mindfulness is about allowing thoughts and feelings without engaging in them in any way. It is about allowing thoughts to come and go without trying to stop them, without chasing after pleasant thoughts or trying to get rid of unpleasant feelings. It is about stepping back and resting in the space of awareness. The following characteristics in one of our mindfulness heuristics are reflective of these ideas: "*I recover quickly when I am unsuccessful*," "*When I produce strong emotions, I easily let them go*," and "*I identify distracting thoughts but let them go (without them influencing future action)*."

HEALTHY TEACHING AND LEARNING

Examining how contemplative practices might affect quality of instruction, stress and immunological reactivity, burnout within profession, and health are among goals of teacher-centered mindfulness research (MLERN 2012, p. 151). Nichole Albrecht and her colleagues (2012) recognize stress in school system as "a catalyst stimulating the proliferation of wellness promoting programs" (pp. 1-2). The scholars report that mindfulness practice has been shown to help teachers reduce their stress levels, assist with behavior management strategies and improve self-esteem. At the onset of our study, a pre-service teacher-participant seemed to grasp a connection between stress, contemplative practice and health when he said:

> Unfortunately I don't practice meditation. Although, from the crazy classroom stories I've been hearing lately, I think I might need to master this art form in order to keep my sanity! From what I understand, meditation involves a breathing regime and moments of silence in order to reflect on your inner self and to find some sort of inner peace. Personally, it seems like we stress ourselves from the everyday grind and the hustle and bustle of life. I think it would be beneficial for everyone to partake in meditation or just some sort of inner reflection, not necessarily through meditation. It should be any form of relaxation that allows a moment to reflect. (Brad, pre-service science teacher, February 28 2012, Week 4 of the study)

Indeed, Roeser and his colleagues (2012) characterize teaching as uncertain, emotional and attentionally demanding work. They hypothesize that mindfulness training may promote development of teachers' habits of mind which "include tendencies to gather data through all of the senses, to be aware of and reflect on experience in a non-judgmental manner, to be flexible when problem solving, to regulate emotions and be resilient after setbacks, and to attend to others with empathy and compassion" (p. 167).

Not unlike us, they consider emotion regulation especially important because when stressed, teachers must be able to self-regulate in the presence of the class and the stressor itself. In our research we were able to capture increased emotional states experienced by the in-service and pre-service teachers as they were making presentations to their peers. These emotionally charged states manifested themselves through teachers' physiology such as fluctuations in heart rate and in levels of oxygenation in blood as recorded by *oximeters* worn on instructors' wrists and emitting Bluetooth signals to a computer. Roeser et al. agree that when doing mindfulness-related research with teachers, we need measures of biological factors (such as cortisol, inflammatory cytokines, or heart variability) to assess outcomes such as teachers' stress, burnout, and general health.

Often, unless their attention is brought to it, teachers and students do not make a connection between emotions and learning. Responding to the heuristic, one of our study participants commented:

> I don't think emotions play a huge role in a physics class, but if this was in a psychology class, I feel like a majority questions [characteristics] would be more relevant.

At the same time, as is evident from a quote by another student, a heuristic might be an effective way for igniting this awareness:

> I never completed a survey [referring to the heuristic] with these kinds of questions. But I feel like the questions [characteristics] are very important. Emotions are big part of our lives. This survey is good one because it connects our emotions to other crucial aspects in class.

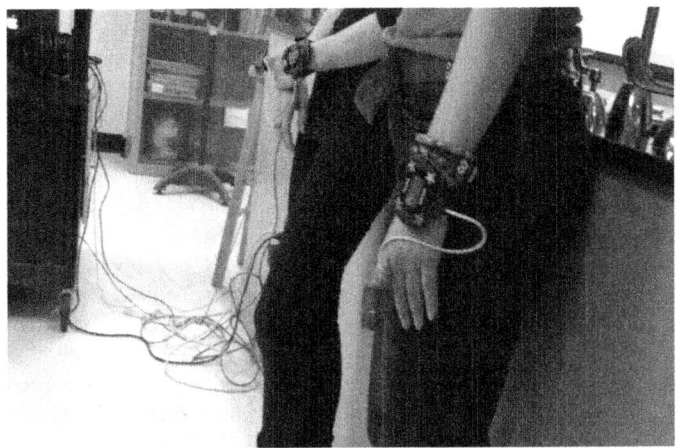

Figure 16.2. Student-presenters wearing oximeters.

According to some students, the heuristic may assist in gaining awareness of emotion-mediating interventions that they already have and use:

> The questions [characteristics] really made me think about my emotions during class. They made me understand that I do things during class to try and improve my frustrated emotions and make me realize what I do when I get emotional. It has helped me realize that breathing is one of the techniques I use and before this survey [heuristic] I was not aware of this as I am now.

The idea is for more students and teachers to incorporate mindfulness interventions into their hectic lives. We found that the three minutes of the collective breathing practice we enacted in Alexakos' class were characterized by a profound silence and a sense of tranquility. Those who chose to participate (not everyone did) often commented on the calming effect the practice had on them. They also reported noticing desirable changes in their physiology. Having recognized the benefits of breathing meditation, a number of participants adopted the practice into their lives that stretched beyond the professional realm. Aimee is one of the students who embraced and gained benefits offered through our research. Below is her brief story.

ONE HUNDRED SEVENTY ONE BEATS PER MINUTE

It is week seven of the study and it is Aimee's turn to make a presentation in class. The topic is charter schools, assessment, and accountability. Aimee is new to the program and unlike her co-presenter she has no teaching experience. She is nervous and eager to wear the oximeter to monitor her heart rate and level of oxygen in her blood – the physiological manifestations of her emotional state.

Knowing that a deep breathing activity is planned for the class this evening, she approaches the researchers and wants to practice breathing with them even before her classmates arrive. Her heart rate is elevated at 98 beats per minute (bpm). She and the researchers briefly discuss some of the benefits of mindful breathing in regulating emotions. Aimee admits to being a smoker and that she is increasingly concerned about her health. Subsequently, during the group breathing exercise, Aimee's heart rate drops notably. However, when she starts presenting, her heart rate increases dramatically reaching 171 bpm only a few minutes into the presentation. The class instructor decides to intervene. He approaches Aimee and encourages her to regulate her breathing and to refocus. Aimee's reaction is that of surprise – she has no idea that her heart rate is off the charts – record high among the class presenters to date. After the intervention, Aimee's heart rate drops to 148 and then further to 139 bpm. Throughout the remainder of the presentation, Aimee's heart rate fluctuates between 107 and 130 momentarily jumping to 158 bpm.

Figure 16.3. The monitor at the left displays Aimee's heart rate at 171 bpm. Aimee and her co-presenter (both wearing oximeters) are at the front of the room next to the screen.

This vignette is not atypical of what we witnessed during our research. Here, when faced with a stressful situation, Aimee experiences what some might consider dangerously elevated levels of heart rate. More importantly, she is unaware of the powerful effect the emotions have on her physiology. An analysis of Aimee's responses to an early version of the mindfulness heuristic reveals that she often struggles with separating herself from her emotional states. She chooses "*often true*" in response to the following four characteristics: "*When I have distressing thoughts or images, they tend to consume me,*" "*I feel the need to judge how I feel,*" "*I make judgments about whether my thoughts are good or bad,*" and "*I tend to react strongly to distressing thoughts and/or images.*" In our conversations, Aimee does confirm that she considers herself a very emotional person who often exhibits strong reactions to those she interacts with. What works to Aimee's advantage is her curiosity and love for science. Therefore, once she becomes aware of a potential problem (the negative impact of unmediated emotions) as well as a scientifically sound solution (such as breathing meditation), she seeks to enact ontological changes as evidenced in the following quote:

> I can be very passionate about issues that concern humanity or the world at large. Sometimes my emotions in relation to such things can get me a little flustered and I lose my pace in the teaching/learning sphere. I am trying to learn how to talk myself into slowing down my thoughts and breathing before speaking. Sometimes I get upset when people are unkind or disrespectful. I used to react very strongly in these instances but am learning not to take that behavior personally. I am in control of my emotions when I feel like I am being treated fairly. (…) I think meditation frees a person of as much "thought" as possible. In doing so, he/she will feel more at peace. I would like to become more in touch with the act. So far, I stick with breathing exercises and burning sage on occasion.

Figure 16.4. Aimee (and other participants) engaged in deep breathing practice.

Both our mindfulness interventions had a profound impact on Aimee's way of being in the world. She often comments on her appreciation of the heuristics (see the text box). As we witnessed in the vignette and may see in the photograph above, Aimee was also an eager participant of the breathing practice in class. The practice extended to other fields of her life including the oft-stressful work as a buyer for a high-end health food store. Subsequent to our study, Aimee joined our research squad and has written reflective pieces regarding her participation in research and its transformative effects. She also shared her experiences at presentations we made for other researchers. Aimee continues to monitor her heart rate as she embarks on her teaching career through completing her student-teaching assignment in one of New York's public high schools. At times, Aimee feels powerless as a student teacher. For example, when she tried to introduce breathing meditation to the students she co-teaches with the class instructor of record, she got discouraged by their lack of enthusiasm towards it. Indeed she often comments on the students' dismissive attitude towards most of what goes on in school. Therefore, she practices breathing when in the classroom and says that it helps in coping with the daily challenges she encounters there. In our recent meeting, Aimee used an interesting metaphor to describe her way of "intervening" whenever she experiences intense emotions, "I always imagine that through breathing I'm taking my hands and I'm holding my feelings [makes a holding gesture with her hands] as opposed to my arms just flapping widely [flaps her arms vigorously] while my emotions take over. So I'm learning to hold it and keep it there." Aimee and I became good friends and we continue to exchange mindfulness-focused wisdom. A few days ago, we celebrated a special anniversary – during our research squad meeting Aimee proudly announced that it had been a year to the day since she quit smoking. Aimee's journey exemplifies the principles guiding achievement of ontological and educative authenticity through participation in research.

> *The concept of mindfulness was first introduced to me through a heuristic during my first graduate course in science education. I was so excited to see the type of material the heuristic addressed because I have always had a strong interest in the notion of self-improvement practices for the sake of good mental health. I particularly enjoyed the free response components because I love having the opportunity to express the details in my thinking. When I first completed the heuristic, I thought back on the huge strides I have made since high school with regard to my self-esteem and outlook on the world. Completing the heuristic each week encouraged me to deeply see that my personal process of bettering my health (both for me and those around me) is far from complete.*

Figure 16.5. Aimee commenting on the mindfulness heuristics.

ETHICAL CONSIDERATIONS IN MINDFULNESS-BASED RESEARCH

My main interest is promoting ethics without touching religion. Ethics are universal values. We must find a way to promote the basic human values in a secular way without touching religion. In order to do this, the scientific findings are very convincing and Richard Davidson's work is very helpful in this field. Sometimes I call him Guru of Science! (His Holiness the Dalai Lama as cited in "The Dalai Lama's Madison Connection," 2013, para. 11)

In light of church-state separation governing our public school system, one concern is that forms of meditation might be perceived as an attempt at infusing Buddhism or Hinduism into school curricula. Addressing similar fears, Kabat-Zinn (Davidson et al. 2013) points to fundamental principles of mindfulness and asks, "Paying attention, awareness – how Buddhist is that?" Elsewhere, he also states emphatically that "mindfulness will not conflict with any beliefs or traditions – religious or for that matter scientific – nor is it trying to sell you anything, especially not a new belief system or ideology" (Kabat-Zinn 1994, p. 6). Tobin (personal communication, February 26 2013) maintains that appropriating ideas with roots in spiritual practices and applying them in the field of education does not constitute indoctrination of religious practices. He argues that the tenets of mindfulness and breathing meditation are not saturated with Buddhist doctrine. On the contrary, he points to a burgeoning research in social science that supports health benefits associated with these practices.

We were very much aware of a possibility that mindfulness might be seen as "spiritual" even though our intent has always been to frame and present it as a secular construct. To that end, our early version of the mindfulness heuristic did not include loving-kindness and compassion. By excluding these dimensions of mindfulness we were partly responding to the class instructor's initial reservations about them as well as the fact that many of the existing mindfulness surveys we modeled our heuristic on did not incorporate this element of mindfulness. The practitioners of the ideas of contingency and emergence, as the study progressed, we felt that there was no escaping of incorporating the concept of compassion into the heuristic. We believe that cultivating qualities such as caring, kindness, compassion and other altruistic qualities could be among the purposes of secular education rather than being relegated to the realm of spirituality. In other words, in addition to cultivating *habits of mind,* mindfulness could assist in the development of *habits of heart* or what Kabat-Zinn (1994) refers to as "heartfulness" (p. 7). In her article exploring aggression among students in Bogota, Carolina Castano (2012) argues that by encouraging compassion based on understanding the emotional and social lives of others, science education could serve as a special place for interrupting violence. When discussing the issue of bullying so pervasive in classrooms across the United States, participants in our study identified mindfulness as a possible way to ameliorate hostility and to assist teachers in identifying and intervening when faced with cases of physical and emotional violence. An intersection of awareness and compassion as well as replacing reacting with responding – all components of mindful conduct – could contribute to a more peaceful and harmonious school environment. Much of current aggression and violence that spills over to schools is attributed to computer games. As part of their mindfulness-based projects, Davidson's research team entered into collaboration with developers of electronic games to create and investigate the effects of apps cultivating loving-kindness and compassion in children and youth (Davidson et al. 2013).

To gain an understanding of student assumptions regarding the intersection of spirituality and meditation, as part of the early version of the mindfulness heuristic, we invited 18 participants of our study to respond to two relevant questions. Following the conclusion of the study, I met with two participant-researchers (Aimee and Aga) and our colleague, Gene Fellner, to collectively analyze the responses. We discovered that to the question exploring understandings of spirituality, about half respondents, particularly those who appeared to consider themselves spiritual, saw a connection between spirituality and religion or some form of a higher being/power. Students who did not make that connection considered spirituality in ethical terms as a relationship of self to other living organisms including humans and as a peace of mind. One person actually equated spirituality with what might be perceived as mindfulness describing it as the "awareness of the universe, yourself and your thoughts." We noted that when answering the question on their understanding of meditation and the extent to which they practiced meditation, the vast majority of the students described meditation in secular terms. In addition, we agreed that the respondents framed meditation in positive or neutral terms. Some of the words and expressions they used included: *mindfulness, self-reflection, relaxation, concentration, clearing the mind, getting rid of anxious energy, centering yourself, calm, inner thoughts, peace, balance, tranquility.* Two students appeared to link meditation to praying or religious practices and another (a practicing Christian) favored "filling mind with God's word" over meditation. Aga explained that to Catholics meditation may be the opposite of prayer because in prayer you want to fill yourself with god whereas with meditation you're clearing your mind and letting go of everything. In that sense, meditation may be contradictory to Christian practice. We noticed that many students perceived meditation as an intervention: *it can be relaxing; a stress-coping technique; practice that can adjust or improve your feeling through breathing technique; a way that person can calm her/him self down and push away bad or stressful thoughts; helps people to feel at ease and to be relaxed.* We concluded that understanding meditation as "medication" is separate from spirituality. Gene explained the difference in the following way:

> If it works as intervention, it's fantastic – it doesn't cost anything; you can get your blood pressure down; it makes perfect sense, why wouldn't you do it. If you practice it [meditation] spiritually, you're practicing it ontologically. It's understanding reality and your role as being organically intertwined with everything else. That your breath is not just your breath, but it's everybody's breath. That we live in a connected world.

During our meeting, when reflecting on her participation in the study, Aga joined the voices of her peers regarding the secular dimension of the practice we enacted:

> We didn't talk about meditating together, we talked about breathing together [referring to what was done during the study]. Breathing is physiological; it's a thing we do all the time anyway. And just breathing in a certain way may be thought of as similar to saying, "Guys, we will be doing jumping jacks right now." How is that different from taking gym? You don't have to meditate, nobody's telling you to meditate. We are getting in touch with our

bodies, we are listening to our bodies; I would think of it as a biological function almost. It's like doing sports together.

One of the student-participants voiced having her initial misconception about the nature of mindfulness and meditation resolved when she stated during one of the class discussions:

> I think by basically doing the open-ended questions [in the heuristic] it kind of widened my whole thinking as to what mindfulness and meditation is really about because it ties in to what we're currently doing. I was seeing it as a spiritual thing. And what Parvathy is talking about, the yoga thing and deep breathing, all that ties in because it's more of your own inner personality coming out, your own beliefs and stuff like that. So it may be good for research to answer these questions because I was thinking just religiously but then it goes further out. (Laura, in-service science teacher, Week 4 of the study)

These findings may point to a relatively weak link between mindfulness and religion or religious practices as perceived by participants in our study. To the majority of them, meditation does not appear to be a philosophical or religious notion but a medical intervention – an emotion-ameliorating, focus-enhancing, awareness-increasing technique.

WHERE TO FROM HERE?

> Mindfulness is like clothes. Not everyone can fit in the same dress. You have to have it tailored. A lot of it is learning about yourself. It's something that we cannot form into a pill and have everyone swallow it. (Aga, an in-service biology teacher, study participant-researcher, March 3 2013)

Should mindfulness be part of education in public schools? Roeser and his colleagues (2012) recognize that current concerns about teacher stress and health care costs as well as concerns about enhancing student engagement and achievement represent a way mindfulness training can enter school systems. Shapiro and her colleagues (2008) suggest that it might be useful to expand the traditional definitions of education to include the development of social, emotional and other valuable forms of intelligence relevant to occupational accomplishment, life satisfaction, ethics, and pro-social engagement. Indeed, Davidson considers attending to the development of emotional intelligence as more important than development of cognitive intelligence (Dyekjaer and Ambo 2012). To Tobin, fostering wellness should become a priority for science curriculum reform. We believe that potential benefits of mindfulness to well-being and moral growth of those involved in education is reason enough for promoting mindfulness-based interventions similar to those presented in this chapter. To that end, we have been engaged in actively incorporating the practices into our immediate environments. At the Graduate Center, Tobin was successful at introducing an elective course on mindfulness and contemplative practices within the Ph.D. program in Urban

Education. He also started incorporating breathing practice into the courses he teaches where he models the practice and then invites his students to take turns in leading the meditation with their peers. At our sister institution, Brooklyn College, some faculty members monitor their pulse rate during departmental meetings and adjust their breathing patterns to mediate their emotional states. Heuristics are used routinely as part of the graduate teacher-education courses taught by Alexakos. Led by our study participants, middle school students perform deep breathing practice before exams. Those among us with administrative appointments make mindfulness part of teachers' professional development. My sleeping patterns have largely improved when I realized that I did not need to engage emotionally in or "take home" work-related issues. We call on others in the education community to consider incorporating mindfulness into their practice. Existing models are plenty. Just like Janet Etty-Leal, the author of Meditation Capsules program offered in Australian schools, we encourage educators to listen to their own intuition and wisdom when cultivating mindfulness in education (Albrecht, Albrecht, and Cohen 2012).

HEURISTICS REVISITED – A METALOGUE WITH KEN TOBIN

Ken: Our work on the development of mindfulness heuristics has been continuous and, based on what we have learned from respondents, we have begun to expand the heuristics we have developed in the methods we have employed to lay out the characteristics. Can you provide some insights into our current thinking regarding the use of a Likert scale to afford respondents making a strong connection to each of the characteristics – or to put it another way, to enhance reflexivity and expand the possibilities for changing practices with respect to each of the characteristics included in the heuristic?

Malgorzata: Your question appears to be alluding to heuristics functioning as an intervention. In my view, this application of heuristics has gained prominence in our studies mainly because we (at least I) have grown to privilege principles of authentic inquiry over other methodologies. When a heuristic is meant to act as an intervention (i.e., its application is to translate into benefits for study participants), a Likert scale may be a relatively unobtrusive medium to possibly "hooking" a respondent on a particular characteristic or a set of characteristics. As reported by many participants in our studies, that is what happens when they are asked to link the way they believe they enact social life to a point on a frequency spectrum (e.g., from *never* to *always*).

Inclusion of a Likert scale in heuristics may also become a source of some confusion. Since a Likert scale is typically used in social sciences towards generating numerical data for statistical analyses, more often than not, those unfamiliar with the way we theorize heuristics tend to mistake them for surveys or questionnaires and expect us to apply them accordingly. When trying to differentiate between heuristics and surveys, a member of our research squad and a close collaborator, Karim Gangji, recently argued that while the main purpose of surveys is to *rank and rate*, heuristics are meant to *bring a sense of awareness* about a particular construct and to possibly *transform* the way participants enact social life. In this case, a Likert scale serves the purpose of making the connection with characteristic(s) and once such connection is made (consciously or unconsciously), changes that are consistent with the ideas presented in the heuristic may occur in the study participant. How do we know if that happens? Since we are not behaviorists, we do not search for visible manifestations of the changes in the participants' conduct; we do not place much value on the numerals they circle either; we do not try to establish whether there are statistically significant differences between two or more occasions of heuristic administration. Rather, we ask the participants to describe their experience with and following the completion of the heuristic and they provide us with oral or written renderings of such. These "testimonials" rather than numerical representations are our data which by definition is saturated with polyphonia and polysemia. This approach is consistent with the contingent and emergent study designs that do not set up a priori assumptions or hypothesis to be tested. To be sure, how heuristics (and the associated Likert scale) are used depends to a large extent on the set of logics (i.e., theoretical frameworks and methodologies) one is applying. When research design is grounded in contingency/emergence and authentic inquiry, the validity or reliability of the numerals participants circle is of little significance to the researcher. Indeed, Konstantinos Alexakos' students admitted to him they were "upgrading" their rating by circling higher numbers in coteaching heuristics when "evaluating" their peers. Of course, it might be that a researcher applies an event-oriented methodology or she wishes to engage in a landscape study. In these cases, a Likert scale may become a useful tool to generate statistical data that will help in identifying patterns and contradictions (such as spikes in the curve). Admittedly, we did "commit" studies in which statistical procedures were used. However, at this point, we are much more drawn to designs that assist in capturing reflexivity and uniqueness of experience. Perhaps the shape a Likert scale takes could be rethought in order to avoid the "numbers' trap." I remember a recent discussion about the use of Likert scales during one of the research squad meetings. The members of the collective suggested replacing the numerals with letters (A, B, C, etc.) or icons or forgoing a Likert scale altogether. We are yet to test these recommendations.

Ken: Do you envision changes in the mode of presenting characteristics? For example, what if we learned about the optimal number of characteristics included in the heuristic and the rate of presenting characteristics to respondents? Would it make sense to present characteristics one a day for example? Obviously there is a maximum number we should not exceed, but is there an optimal rate of interest using respondents to different characteristics associated with a heuristic?

Malgorzata: The beauty of heuristics lies in their shape-shifting quality. Unlike surveys or questionnaires (particularly those that have been statistically validated and are thus permanently fixed), heuristics may be manipulated in virtually all possible ways (feel free to bend, twist, stretch or shrink them) as long as they serve a specific purpose (such as possibly increasing the incidence of mindful practices) and appeal to its intended audience. As noted, we have had our share of twists and turns in our effort to generate what we naively hoped to be an ideal, or close to an ideal, mindfulness heuristic. I believe it would be equally naive to claim that it is possible to arrive at an "optimal" number of characteristics – such an assertion would fly in the face of our ontological stance that celebrates difference rather than sameness. What I mean is that depending on the circumstances, different length of a heuristic may prove adequate and acceptable to its respondents (both as collectives and individuals). An analogy may be drawn to teaching | learning. In-service teachers learn relatively quickly that there is no one "perfect" lesson plan since the structures (e.g., who the students are, what day of the week or time of the day it is, whether it is scorching hot or bitterly cold, what furniture surrounds you and your students, what color are the walls, what class or activity preceded yours, to name a few) that come into play when one enacts the curriculum vary to a considerable extent.

Having said that, there is no denying that careful consideration is in order when one tries to determine the characteristics "dosage" level. What we appear to be learning through this ongoing hermeneutic project is that indeed *less is more*. As you remember our early version of heuristic contained a relatively high number of characteristics. Of course, our initial and, as it turned out, unrealistic ambition was to capture an exhaustive (or close to it) number of characteristics of a multifaceted construct. Based on the protests from study participants we realized that long heuristics might be counterproductive by creating negative emotional reactions in respondents. Consequently, we gradually cut back on the heuristic length. We seem to have relapsed recently when we inflicted a combined 35-characteristic-long *Mindfully Listening and Mindfully Speaking* heuristic upon a group of pre-service elementary education teachers. Again, the data analysis revealed that the respondents were progressively "running out of steam" as they were going through the heuristic, i.e., the further into the heuristic, the fewer comments each characteristic received.

To date all our heuristics were expected to be completed in one sitting usually once, twice, or three times a semester. I am very much interested in and curious about trying to launch smaller doses of characteristics but at more frequent intervals. Let's say we would email to participants a single characteristic to ponder over on a daily basis. Would such practice possibly increase the level of reflexivity? Indeed, Karim Gangji and I, as part of our ongoing heuristic-grounded collaboration (Powietrzynska, Tobin, Alexakos 2014), are considering breaking a heuristic into clusters of characteristics and sending individual clusters to Karim's students on a weekly basis. We are determined to test and report on reactions to this approach by Karim's upcoming cohorts of pre-service elementary education teachers.

Ken: Mauricio Pietrocola and Carolina Souza have explored heuristics that have utilized only iconic representations of characteristics. They have varied the number of characteristics and the extent to which text is incorporated into them. To what extent do you think this work can frame future developments associated with mindfulness heuristics?

Malgorzata: I believe it was our colleague Helen Kwah who first suggested that we consider incorporating into our heuristics non-textual representations of characteristics. Indeed, since then Helen has begun collaborating with Gene Fellner on research projects involving various non-verbal forms of expression, which, as noted by Fellner in this volume, while being welcomed in art, are usually not considered legitimate within the field of academic research. In their "sensing before making sense" work, just like Kwah and Fellner, Pietrocola and Souza push the boundaries towards legitimizing alternative research methodologies. If our research participants (and we) are to describe and make sense of lived experience, it only follows that we attempt to employ into this phenomenological-hermeneutic project an expanded array of non-discursive representation. It seems to me that mindfulness-related work in particular lends itself to doing just that. Adopting mindfulness practices promises to expand the way we experience life (i.e., we become more aware of and attuned to our sensory experiences–the sense of smell, touch, vision, and so on). Therefore, heuristics could take forms that would appeal to different senses through inclusion of visual and possibly auditory (e.g., musical) representation of mindfulness characteristics. Consequently, such re-imagined heuristics may prove more inviting and accessible for individuals with artistic/creative sensibilities including young children for whom text may not be a preferred way of experiencing, processing, embracing, and transforming life.

Ken: Our recent work together has addressed Mindfully Speaking and Mindfully Listening. Which topics do you consider to have the highest priority for the development of new heuristics? For example, do you see topics such as harmony and wellness as priorities for mindfulness heuristics?

Malgorzata: By all means! As you are well aware, what appeals to me as a researcher is the principle of authentic inquiry. Accordingly, I see research as necessarily leading to potential improvements in practice (as defined by study participants), be it teaching | learning or enhancing one's or the planet's wellbeing. As we argued in our recent co-authored manuscript

(Powietrzynska, Tobin, and Alexakos 2014), the issues of wellness and sustainability occupy a prominent position as our research foci. To that end, for example, knowing that adopting mindfulness practices has been linked to improved health, the mindfulness heuristics we generated to date aim at addressing potentially unhealthy states such as sustained stress. Having witnessed a number of study participants (students, teachers, and family members) fall victim to the modern disease of unawareness (such as that of mind-body connection) that often led to highly undesirable outcomes in physical (e.g., a heart attack) and mental (e.g., deep depression) health, we offer mindfulness heuristics as part of a wellness tool kit potentially assisting in ameliorating modern-world inflictions. What needs stressing, however, is that it is the research participant rather than the researcher who decides the utility of a heuristic. In other words heuristics will work for those who are attracted to the concepts they address and find them useful to their daily practices. It is only then that (through a reflexive process) shifts in practices with respect to characteristics included in the heuristic are likely to occur as you note in the opening question of this metalogue. If what we offer in a heuristic does not rank high in the participant's axiology, our efforts have failed.

REFERENCES

Albrecht, N. J., Albrecht, P. M., & Cohen, M. (2012). Mindfully teaching in the classroom: a literature review. *Australian Journal of Teacher Education*, *37* (12), 1-14.

Alexakos, K. (2015). Being a science educator | researcher: a personal narrative from the sociocutural perspective. In C. Milne, K. Tobin, & D. Degenero (Eds.), *Sociocultural studies and implications for science education: The experiential and the virtual*. New York: Springer.

Bourdieu, P., & Wacquant, L. J. (1992). *An invitation to reflexive sociology*. Chicago, IL: The University of Chicago Press.

Burke, C. A. (2009). Mindfulness-based approaches with children and adolescents: A preliminary review of current research in an emergent filed. *Journal of Child and Family Studies*, *19*, 133-144.

Castano, C. (2012). Extending the purposes of science education: addressing violence within socio-economic disadvantaged communities. *Cultural Studies of Science Education*, *7*, 703-718.

Davidson, R. J., & Begley, S. (2012). *The emotional life of your brain: How its unique patterns affect the way you think, feel, and live – and how you can change them*. New York: Hudson Street Press.

Davidson, R. J., Jha, A. P., & Kabat-Zinn, J. (2013, February 6). *Becoming conscious: Uncovering the science of mindfulness*. Panel presented at the New York Academy of Science. New York.

Dyekjaer, S. (Producer), & Ambo, P. (Director). (2012). *Free the mind: Can you rewire the brain just by taking a breath?* [Documentary]. Denmark: Danish Documentary Production.

Eisenhart, M. (2009). Generalization from qualitative inquiry. In K. Ercikan & W.-M. Roth (Eds.), *Generalizing from educational research: Beyond qualitative and quantitative polarization* (pp. 51-66). New York: Routledge.

Erickson, F. (1998). Qualitative reserach methods for science education. In B. J. Fraser & K. G. Tobin (Eds.), *International Handbook of science education* (pp. 1155-1173). Kluwer Academic Publishers.

Garrison Institute Report. (2005). *Contemplation and education: A survey of programs using contemplative techniques in K-12 educational settings: A mapping report*. New York: The Garrison Institute.

Grossman, P. (2008). On measuring mindfulness in psychosomatic and psychological research. *Journal of Psychosomatic Research, 64*, 405-408.

Guba, E., & Lincoln, Y. S. (1989). *Fourth generation evaluation*. Newbury Park, CA: Sage Publications.

Higgins, J. (2012, November 28). *Report from New Zealand: Investigating the emotinal climate of an elementary school classroom*. Presentation at the Research Squad meeting at the Graduate Center of the City University of New York. New York.

Jha, A. P. (2013, March 16). *Improving attention and working memory with mindfulness training*. Keynote address at the Mindfulness in Education Network's Fifth Annual Conference. Bryn Mawr.

Kabat-Zinn, J. (1994). *Wherever you go, there you are: Mindfulness meditation in everyday life*. New York: Hyperion.

Kincheloe, J. L. (2003). *Teachers as researchers: Qualitative inquiry as a path to empowerment* (2nd ed.). New York: RoutledgeFalmer.

Meiklejohn, J., Phillips, C., Freeman, M., Griffin, M., Biegel, G., Roach, A., et al. (2012). Integrating mindfulness training into K-12 education: Fostering the resilience of teachers and studnets. *Mindfulness, 3*(4), 291-307.

Mind and Life Education Research Network (MLERN). (2012). Contemplative practices and mental training: Prospects for American education. *Child Development Perspectives, 6*(2), 146-153.

Philippot, P., Chapelle, G., & Blairy, S. (2002). Respiratory feedback in the generation of emotion. *Cognition & Emotion, 16*, 605-627.

Powietrzynska, M. (2015). Heuristics for mindfulness in education and beyond. In C. Milne, K. Tobin, & D. Degenero (Eds.), *Sociocultural studies and implications for science education: The experiential and the virtual*. New York: Springer.

Powietrzynska, M., Tobin, K., & Alexakos, K. (2014). Facing the grand challenges through heuristics and mindfulness. *Cultural Studies of Science Education*. Advance online publication. doi:10.1007/s11422-014-9588-x

Roeser, R. W., Skinner, E., Beers, J., & Jennings, P. A. (2012). Mindfulness training and teachers' professional development: An emerging area of research and practice. *Child Development Perspectives, 6* (2), 167-173.

Ryan, T. (2012). *A mindful nation: how a simple practice can help us reduce stress, improve performance, and recapture the American spirit*. New York: Hay House, Inc.

Saltzman, A. (n.d.). *Education Resources: K-12*. Retrieved from The Center for Contmepmplative Mind in Society: http://www.contemplativemind.org/resources/k-12

Sewell, W. H. (2005). *Logics of history: social theory and social transformation*. Chicago: The University of Chicago Press.

Siegel, D., & Hawn, G. (2009, October). Goldie Hawn and Dan Siegel at TEDMED 2009 [Video file]. Retrieved from https://www.youtube.com/watch?v=1OdBXGHwNCk

The National Commission for the Protection of Human Subjects of Biomedical and Behavioral Research. (1979, April 18). *The Belmont report: Ethical principles and guidelines for the protection of human subjects of research*. Retrieved from U.S. Department of Health and Human Services: http://www.hhs.gov/ohrp/humansubjects/guidance/belmont.html

Tobin, K. (2012). Interpretive approaches to multi-level, multi-method, mulit-theoretical research. In S. R. Steinberg & G. S. Canella (Eds.), *Critical qualitative research reader* (Vol. 2, pp. 116-128). New York: Peter Lang Publishing.

Tobin, K. (2009). Turning into others' voices: Radical listening, learning from difference, and escaping oppression. *Cutlural Studies of Science Education, 4*(3), 505-511.

Tobin, K., & Richie, S. R. (2012). Multi-method, multi-theoretical, multi-level research in the learning sciences. *The Asia-Pacific Education Researcher, 21*(1), 117-129.

Wood, G. (2013, April 24). *What martial arts have to do with atheism*. Retrieved from The Atlantic: http://www.theatlantic.com/national/archive/2013/04/what-martial-arts-have-to-do-with-atheism/275273/

Zajonc, A. (2009). *Meditation as contemplative inquiry: When knowing becomes love* [Kindle version]. Retrieved from http://www.amazon.com

MARISSA E. BELLINO

17. USING PHOTOVOICE AS A CRITICAL YOUTH PARTICIPATORY METHOD IN ENVIRONMENTAL EDUCATION RESEARCH

MY EVOLVING EPISTEMOLOGY

Over the last three years I have shifted from teaching a more disciplined and traditional environmental science class to a more critical, local, participatory course focused on the lived experiences of youth. It is difficult to tease apart the methodology from my pedagogical practice since the two are so intertwined. Accordingly, I regard it as important to explore my personal shift as well as attempt to explicate the resulting methodological shifts, which played out in the classroom, and how the outcomes of the classroom informed my teaching. My reflexive praxis has evolved in response to my own growth as a critical educator and through this chapter I want to share how my own growth opened up spaces for my students' growth. Within this space my ideas about teaching and learning, research, and environmental education, three constructs I view as inextricably linked, evolved.

Photovoice was a teaching and research methodology I used to explore what it means to be a young person living in New York City. The evolution of the photovoice methodology over a two-year period shows how the process, products, and outcomes of research looked different as my thinking about research shifted. My experience in the classroom through the use of photovoice contributed to my developing a critical educator identity. Parallel to my transformation, my students developed their own criticality, and this combined phenomenon made the classroom more collective and critical in all aspects of learning and research. The new ways we began to think about research fostered deeper connections between experience and theory and a more dialogic learning space emerged.

My personal transformation is remarkable to me and caught me, every step of the way, by surprise. There were growing pains, like when Bruce Banner turns into the *Hulk*. I could feel the shifts in my thinking and in my heart, and I could feel myself fighting with internal, conflicting ideas. Beliefs I always held about research were crashing against new ideas that I was exposed to in my doctoral program and continually challenged my thinking. I come from a background where positivism was the dominant paradigm for research and science education. I never thought about my epistemological stance as a decision I made. I was uncritical because I never knew that being critical existed. I was never given the opportunity to challenge these ideas having not been exposed to any critical or sociocultural theory in education. Research was only and always hypothesis driven, quantitative in nature, involved the writing of literature reviews, and knowledge was shared through scientific papers.

The first exposure I had to critical and social theory was in my early doctoral courses. The readings, Freire, hooks, Giroux, McLaren, Harvey, Lipman, Fine, challenged my whole way of thinking about education and research. The classes were dialogic, discussing assumptions about young people and education, and we together tried to uncover some semblance of truth in the messiness of ideas, experiences, power, hegemony, and ideology. I was frightened. I sat in my classes and didn't speak the entire semester. But I listened and felt myself, my thinking, my beliefs, changing. During this time my ways of thinking about education were most challenged by reading *Pedagogy of the Oppressed* (Freire 2000), and connecting Freire's ideas on the banking model of education to my own experiences in the classroom. Reading about neoliberalism and its agenda for public schooling helped me to see our current education system as a vehicle for socializing and reproducing our capitalist society. The hidden messages young people were internalizing by constantly being measured and sorted were working to create an uncritical citizenry. I imaged a classroom that challenged this dominant ideology, a place that empowered young people by drawing on their realities and experiences and connecting these to larger systems of power.

The learning environment, as I re-imagined it, was a classroom where individual and collective life experiences were privileged and valued. I conceptualized an environmental science class that was not dictated by the chapters of a textbook or a test but encompassed the places that young people spend their time. These places would be investigated and phenomena observed would be interpreted and connected to social and environmental theory. By moving away from the traditional ways environmental education is presented, this new course could open up a more inclusive definition of environment that encompassed the natural, social and built spaces that surround youth. I believed this could be accomplished by creating a space in school for young people to explore their identities in relation to the places and people that they were interacting with and by reflecting on how their experiences connected to research and theory. I felt that classes like this were lacking; learning in science was not connected to the lived experiences of students but driven by the memorization of information. I imagined a more dynamic experience where learning and knowledge emerged from students, challenged their views of school, and fostered a more local environmental and critical consciousness.

I was exposed to the research methodology of photovoice in the first semester of my doctoral program and was drawn to its participatory and visual nature, as well as its adaptability. Photovoice is a form of action research in community development and education, where marginalized social groups capture images and voice their concerns in the hopes of creating awareness for themselves and others to spark change (Wang and Burris 1997). I thought that young people would be drawn in by photovoice's use of technology and storytelling. Photovoice has been incorporated into community and educational research with youth and has been modified in many ways to meet the goals of individuals and projects (Strack et al. 2004). I latched onto photovoice and saw it as the perfect vehicle to support my re-imagined environmental science class.

In preparation for using photovoice I filled a notebook with ideas about how students would investigate their local environments. Before the class knew about photovoice, I had determined the project goals, the questions students were going to discuss and write about, and the overall purpose of our project. This first year I reduced photovoice to a method, a series of steps that were to be followed in order to reach a specific outcome. The limitations I placed on the class through my thorough planning undermined the participatory nature embedded in photovoice. Through reflection on the first year I came to a deeper understanding of photovoice as a methodology, a means of allowing many voices to come together to tell the experiences of youth in New York City. In the second year of photovoice I allowed the project to be more unstructured and students were better able to analyze their worlds as they saw and experienced them. While the project goal was always to encourage critical thinking about local environments, the second year of photovoice allowed for a more emergent and participatory experience.

PHOTOVOICE YEAR 1

In the spring semester of 2012, I introduced photovoice to a group of 24 students in my college-credit, environmental science course. The students were a mix of high school juniors and seniors who were historically the more academically oriented students at my school. As the course was an elective, the students self-selected into the class after completing their state required science courses and passed the requisite exams. This created a community of students who were more academically driven, college bound, and on the surface had benefited from the traditional model of public schooling.

There were two major tasks planned for the semester, photovoice and an original research project. The photovoice project attempted to discover how young people make meaning from their observations of and interactions with the local environment. Students gathered images from their environments, discussed them in small groups, wrote individual narratives based on a small selection of their pictures, and in groups created a collective presentation about shared themes. This experience was used as a vehicle for students to develop a research question that they investigated, write a research proposal, and collect data to answer their question. The end product, defined by me from the start, was to write a scientific style research paper of their study.

The photovoice project began with students gathering relevant images. During the winter break each student was asked to take approximately 100 pictures and organize them into four folders. The folders included (1) Definition of environment (2) Interactions with your environment (3) Strengths of your environment (4) Areas in need of improvement in your environment. Students returned with mixed results, some had many pictures while others had only a few. Students described a sense of confusion about the different categories of pictures, as they had trouble conceptualizing what was meant by each category and where certain pictures belonged. There was also technical difficulty with uploading pictures and many poor quality photos. Overall, the students seemed more concerned about the photograph as an artistic expression than as a representation of their way of seeing.

Students shared their photos in randomly assigned groups of four using the SHOWED method (Wang and Burris 1999). This method is aimed at generating conversation around the images and includes the following questions:
- What do you see in this image?
- Why did you take this picture?
- What is really happening here?
- How does this relate to our lives?
- Why does this condition exist?
- What can we do about it?
- How could this image educate others?

It is important to allocate time and space for dialogue, but most of the research on photovoice does not address the challenges of implementing this in a classroom environment where students are rarely asked to be so open with their thinking. These questions challenged the students and they found it difficult to maintain conversations about their photos without my presence prompting them to go further. Not surprisingly they lacked the language and skills that are developed through dialogue and explored in critical and social theory.

I filled this gap by introducing some of the critical theory that photovoice draws from and by sharing example photovoice projects. But my knowledge was limited and I constantly felt inadequate and ill prepared. As much as I tried to support the goals of the project by building in the time and space for collaborative work, the students could sense my inexperience and the tasks seemed repetitive. Many students had difficulty engaging their peers in conversation and often, all four group members shared their images in one 90-minute class period. This was an indication that students were not having the critical conversations that are inherent in the photovoice methodology and that I had not implemented the structures to allow them to do so. These types of critical conversations are not experienced much in schools (especially in science) where so much of the learning is disembodied from the lived realities of learners.

Through the process of sharing photos, students selected a set of images to write a personal narrative. In the narratives students explained why they selected each image, the context of the image, and how they connected the images to larger themes in their lives and to ideas discussed in class. Student themes included the replacement of natural places with new development, the abandonment of buildings, and the obvious disparity between places like Manhattan and the Bronx. Students shared their narratives with me, not in their groups or with the class, and many saw these as a waste of time.

Groups combined ideas and images into one final presentation for the class. Students told the story of their images and included two discussion questions. Presentation themes included the clash of nature and the city, the possibility of a utopian New York City, the changes of space in the city, community tolerance and diversity, and stereotypes of boroughs. The presentations were one-sided, not dialogic, and the discussion questions were used as writing prompts that were not shared with the class. While many of the issues that students raised in their presentations and through their questions were deeply critical, "What stereotypes exist in your neighborhood and how do you break them?," "What is one change in your community that has affected you either negatively or positively?," and "Throughout the city, why do we see differing access to green space?," these questions were never explored as a collective. Each group posed questions that reflected their concerns as young people. Potentially these questions could have generated ideas about the lived experiences of youth, informing how young people see themselves in relation to their neighborhoods and the greater city. But the class as I had structured it, did not open up the space for these conversations, reinforcing the ideology that we, in schools, in research, work and think alone.

The photovoice process this first year moved students from their images, to personal narratives, to group presentations, and then to research projects. I was fixated on the students conducting a research project the way I had always thought about research. While I had given them opportunities to explore their perspectives using photovoice, I quickly pulled them right back into a positivist model of research where they had to go through the "steps of research." Reading the literature, developing a proposal and obtaining approval, writing consent forms, collecting data, analyzing data, and writing a final scientific paper.

The final research papers varied in their criticality. Some emerged directly from the photovoice images and discussed issues of power, race, gender and class, (e.g., Youth Perceptions of New York City Boroughs). Other final papers were closely tied to positivistic, causal models of research utilizing more quantitative data collection methods (e.g., Preferences for Nature Based or Recreational Activities in Central Park). All of the final papers were uploaded to a course website in an online journal format which I believed represented the epitome of authentic research. The variation in the projects reflected my own tensions with research, especially questions about who research is for and how it should be disseminated. Many students struggled with the quantitative/qualitative divide, themselves the product of years of schooling that privileged the scientific method and quantifiable data.

There were many moments for critical reflection during the photovoice phase of the research, particularly the student narratives and group presentations. The students asked many critical questions but few were ever discussed collaboratively or used as springboards for further collective research. I was so focused on using photovoice to get to what I believed was "real" research that I did not allow the time for the narratives to be shared with the class or for lengthy discussions of the presentation themes. As a class we did not capitalize on the concerns and observations raised and as a result I moved us back into the positivistic paradigm of "real" research. All of the critical issues that emerged, diversity, comfort, abandoned space, lack of care for neighborhoods in different parts of the city – all were lost. I take the blame for this. I was unable to see photovoice as an inherently critical research methodology in and of itself and I was afraid of engaging young people in discussions about their identities and how these inform their ideas about race, equity, and power. I was scared of the discomfort that I believed would be generated when conversations moved into difficult territory. I was unprepared to allow the class to go where they wanted to go or to allow for more collective and participatory research to emerge from the photovoice project. I felt pressured by my students and myself to complete a research project because that was the "final product" I had envisioned and they continually questioned how photovoice helped achieve this.

One student wrote a critique of photovoice highlighting many of the assumptions held about research.

> Photovoice might be a technique to add your voice, but it does not mean we should devote time to such a technique in class. The process is not natural to my classmates and I. The project is in reality so sincere and artistic that it seems wrong. It would almost be like asking students to rap ... Students in the class have already been taken away from the purpose (of photovoice) by having to do it on demand. What are we trying to convince the public of if we did not wish to tell them anything in the first place? What we appear to be doing is making up possible answers based on our opinions. This is not good enough for me and what my fellow classmates will say, will quite frankly not educate me. I personally will not influence people in power through this process. I do not believe I could even influence my peers or neighbors. I feel like my photovoice has *no purpose* and I do not know how to stress that enough. (Candice, Spring 2012)

My role as the teacher during this first year of photovoice felt fixed as I maintained my authority in the classroom. I framed the project, selected the research groups, facilitated the discussions, dictated the research process, and demanded the final product be a traditional research paper. This goes against the tenets of participatory action research where the research questions are meant to be a product of the participants, coming out of their needs and experiences (Reason 2006). I was scared to give up the power and comfort in the classroom for fear of difficult conversations and discomfort. I knew critical conversations were lacking in schools and believed that schools needed to create space for them, but my fear of having these conversations in the classroom was very real and prevented them. I was doing a disservice to my students by not allowing them to engage in critical dialogue but I felt like I was doing it for the greater good of teaching research skills. In my teaching journal I wrote, "I must create the space for students to express themselves without fear" and "Have students direct the conversation, not be so involved in asking the questions" (Spring 2012). It was clear that as much as I wanted to create a critical space for students, I did not know how and I was not ready.

I ended the first year of photovoice with mixed feelings. Many students outright rejected the process while in it, but came to see it as something that helped develop their research question. Other students were turned off to research the way I presented it, finding it inaccessible and rigid. Reflecting on the year I see how the entire structure of the photovoice project resisted collaboration, participation, a deepening of critical lenses, a critique of traditional research methods, the development of new data collection methods, or an awareness of who has the right to do research. I tried to address many of these issues the following year.

PHOTOVOICE YEAR 2

Throughout the first year of photovoice, I was constantly learning, reflecting on the process, my practice, and what I was reading in my doctoral courses. I was developing my own critical educator identity and was determined to improve the photovoice project for the next year. I strongly believed that photovoice was a way for me to guide my students in their own critical awakening. I introduced critical, social, and environmental theory throughout the year and used photovoice as a critical research method, with no additional research and no scientific paper requirement. I knew my own criticality evolved through exposure to readings and conducting research and so I created similar opportunities for my students.

The goals of the course and the photovoice project had not changed. I was still determined to create a space for learning that was relevant to young people and I was still interested in reimaging environmental education as more local places that hold meaning. The investigation into local environments began with students completing a community reflection. Participants described their communities in terms of behaviors, environments, strengths, improvements, and ideal communities. Each student completed his or her community reflections on the course website. The first year the website was a space to share the final research paper, but the second year, the website and blog became a shared place for documenting the research process. Community reflection data was collected, shared, and analyzed on the blog and students spent time reading each response, writing about their overall impressions, and collectively generating cross cutting themes. The themes that the students identified were community identity, community access, high school community and diversity, segregated communities, integrated communities, dominant cultures and identity, nature, safety, crowding, housing and alternative spaces. Many days were spent conceptualizing each theme in large and small group discussions and the collective ideas were continually documented on big chart paper (Figure 17.1).

Each student chose a theme based on their interest, formed a research group, and designed a photovoice project through the lens of their research theme. Over a two week period students photographed their various communities and brought photos to class each day to share with their group. Images were discussed using the SHOWED method and for each image students explained how it was connected to their research topic. When students wrestled with ideas or experienced tensions in what they thought about their neighborhoods and what they saw through their pictures, I supported thinking with films and reading. We read, learned, and shared about critical pedagogy, inequality and diversity in New York City, social class,

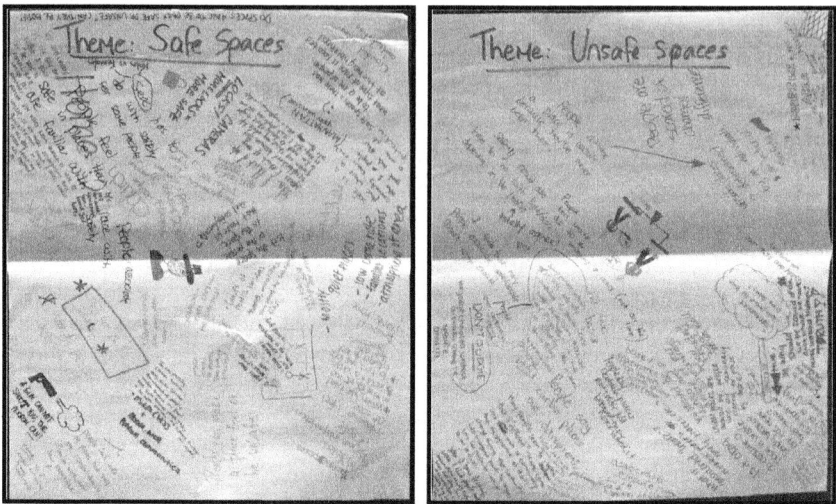

Figure 17.1. Student generated ideas about safe and unsafe places, a common theme which emerged from the community reflections.

participatory action research, stop and frisk, right to the city, critical media literacy, social norms, stereotypes, race, and gentrification. The infusion of theory helped build a new, common vocabulary to explain and make sense of what students saw in their images. Connections between experience, language, and theory, allowed critical conversations to emerge during the photovoice discussions.

Students used a subset of their images to write a photovoice narrative through the lens of their research theme. Some students wrote from the perspective of diversity and how they experienced it in their own lives. Some wrote through the lens of community identity and explored how their connection to their community influenced their sense of belonging or not belonging. Each student was given a page on our research website to share their narrative and images. Unlike the first year, I allowed time for the students to read and learn from one another. As a class we looked across the photovoice narratives for big ideas, which we documented on the course blog. The collective analysis of the narratives revealed that young people critically interpret the physical and social spaces in their local environments and their interpretations of place is tied to their developing personal and social identities. Many students highlighted the impacts of globalization on local communities and discussed the tension experienced from the benefits of globalization and the reality that these forces are changing communities in ways that are homogenizing and displacing populations (Figures 17.2 & 17.3).

The image shows a wall that divides the park from the elevated street to the right. The wall is often scattered graffiti consisting of vulgar language, and names of graffiti writers. This graffiti is then covered up with black paint, which is equally heinous against the red wall. There are some communities where walls such as this one would have been painted over with a lovely mural. Graffiti artists will appreciate the art on the wall and children would enjoy the drawings as they play. Unfortunately there are no individuals willing to take on this task in my community. There are little to no situations in which people come together to better the community. This is what the wall looks like when people graffiti over the black paint intended to cover graffiti. The wall displays a hopeless cycle of repainting and graffitiing.

Source: Chloe, April 2013

Figure 17.2. Chloe, describing the wall in a park in her neighborhood. Her research topic was community identity.

For the final research product each group created a presentation of their images and thinking for the class. These presentations highlighted the ways students connected experiences to social and environmental theory we had read and discussed. During presentations the entire class built on the research themes and added interpretations around issues of gentrification, diversity, homelessness, privatization, loss of funding for parks, and housing. These dialogic presentations allowed students to make connections to their own research and for me to see how theory had assimilated into their thinking. Each group presented to the class for 90-minutes, facilitated the class discussion and shared their new knowledge (Figure 4). After each presentation, a short blog post was created to continue discussions and allow for further reflection.

Starbucks is one of the main sites of gentrification in my neighborhood. This and Whole Foods, which also came into my community recently. The Starbucks brought in new types of people, the business class. Right above the Starbucks is a daycare. There is already a daycare right across the street, but this new one seems different. It doesn't seem open to the public and looks more exclusive. On this one block alone there is Starbucks, Verizon, Petco, Duane Reade, Crumbs Cupcakes, and a Chase Bank. That very same block used to have a park that neighborhood kids used to go to after school and more affordable housing for the community, a C-TOWN (grocery store), and local businesses. Where have those people gone?

Source: Amber, April 2013

Figure 17.3. Amber, describing the changes she has seen in her community. Her research topic was community access.

After all groups presented, each student reflected on the entire photovoice process on the course blog. Reflections highlighted the cumulative impact of the photovoice research and demonstrated connections between all of the research topics. Four larger themes emerged for students at the end of the photovoice process. Community identity was a concept that many students struggled with, specifically in how communities are defined and bounded. The ways students define their community varied and there seemed to be a shift from thinking about community as a physical geographic space to a more socially constructed and dynamic space.

Figure 17.4. Final student presentations structured to allow an ongoing dialogic process of the research topics.

> I never gave much thought to community before this class; I saw community as where I live, but I've realized that you can take your community with you. Community includes the people you hang out with and where you feel most comfortable. (Aurora, June 2013)

The relationship between community identity and the emerging personal and social identities of students were constantly being negotiated. Many students expressed shifts in their own identity in relation to youth, race, and culture and struggled with the influence community had on personal identity or personal identity had on how they perceived their community.

> I've noticed many of us struggle with race identification ... I found myself questioning who I was and how that shaped my view of community? Or was it my community that shaped me? (Samara, June 2013).

Almost all students observed changes in their neighborhoods, specifically related to gentrification. Changes included the increased presence of new buildings catering to a different social class than currently is living in the community and an increase in chain stores. Students observed how this paired phenomenon homogenize communities, displace local people and places, and remove a sense of community identity.

> And that these big chain stores like Chipotle, Starbucks, and Pinkberry are being put into neighborhoods that did not have them, it's changing the whole ambiance of that community. I don't know if that is a good thing because if every neighborhood becomes gentrified and looks like every other neighborhood then everything is going to look the same and have the same feel and that in itself takes away from our communities. (Angel, June 2013)

Safety, comfort, transportation, quality housing, and parks were all cited by students as aspects (physical, social and psychological) that all communities deserve equal access to but, as was represented by student photos and experience, was not the case. A general observation was that places deemed more "desirable" had greater access to these resources than other "less desirable."

> We deserve to have access to parks, stores that one might find in financially sound neighborhoods, hospitals and even green spaces for the nature lovers in the city. We may not find these things in every neighborhood because that place may be classified as "unsafe" or because they are not in a prime real estate location ... But even so, that should not justify the lack of accessibility to these necessities in neighborhoods. (Gene, June 2013)

Throughout the second year of using photovoice I constantly questioned, "what was happening?" If my students' knowledge and ways of seeing the world were being constructed in the moments of dialogue and reflection, how could I find out what they were taking away from the research as a learning experience? I asked students to write a critical reflection discussing their learning and growth throughout the year. Student reflections demonstrate an emerging critical identity,

> The way I think has changed because I've realized so many things about myself ... The way I used to think was the generalized story of what the news media says. I learned that there is more to that. I think more in depth and critically. (Rose, June 2013)

> I am more vocal, I question why I think, or someone else thinks something and I now see how our experiences shape our thinking. (Rachel, Spring 2013)

> I look at the world through new eyes. Nothing is what it used to be and this couldn't be better. (Lourdes, Spring 2013)

Student reflections also express a desire to share knowledge with others and a deeper consciousness about the world they inhabit.

> I believe that even spreading knowledge through conversation can make a difference. Having as many individuals know about the issue as possible is a great start. That is my start. (Lourdes, Spring 2013)

> I want to use what I have learned to help educate people around me so that they too can educate people, a domino effect. I do not want what I learned to stop in the classroom, but want it to continue to blossom. (Marionette, Spring 2013)

Many students also expressed how different this learning experience was compared to previous classes. They highlighted the classroom community and relationships as well as the relevance of the class to their own lives, as key points in their experience.

> Listening to what others had to say and having others listen to what I had to say made me feel comfortable with sharing my ideas. This class created a sense of community with class discussions, blogs, and group work. (Ariel, June 2013)

I had many self-realizations in this class and I think many people did as well. I realized how biased I am to my own community and how I have separated myself because of my grades (or priorities) and the stereotypes I have. This class was a good place for having realizations and working things out in my mind. (Chloe, June 2013)

I think my biggest change was the way I think of my environment and the places around me. We once had a discussion about an increase in pawnshops in the Bronx and how an increase in pawnshops can show how that industry is taking advantage of the economic situations that the people in the Bronx are going through. This way of thinking has helped me see the underlying problems that affect my neighborhood. (Damien, June 2013)

PHOTOVOICE AS A TOOL TO (RE)CONCEPTUALIZE RESEARCH

There are three interrelated themes about research that emerged out of these two years of working with and modifying photovoice. These insights are related to the evolution of photovoice in the classroom from a purely research method to a research methodology. Firstly, when the end product of research is a scientific paper something stagnant is created that does not allow research to live on. During the first year, we built a website to share the final research papers, and I thought this represented a truly intellectual endeavor, but the papers and the site were inert. The scientific paper is the symbol of a dominant idea of research and its prescriptive nature turned many students off and shut down their ability to be critical. The end product of the first year photovoice research was cloaked in a positivist representation of research, and embodies all of the dominant ideas about what "good" and "scientific" research should look like. This formulaic nature of sharing new knowledge turned off many students to research as it represented the tools of science and research students did not connect with. When we introduce these tools to our students by saying research looks this way we are indoctrinating them into a particular way of thinking about research that negates all other ways of doing research. While our second year end product may not look like "traditional" research, it allowed everyone to be a part of the knowledge production and connect and discuss themes young people wrestle with in a globalized city. Papers can't evolve after they are finished but conversations, thinking, websites, and blogs can.

Secondly, during the first year of photovoice my role as teacher in the classroom created a divide between me – the keeper of research knowledge, and my students – the beneficiaries of my knowledge. The burden was on me to push them into critical spaces of thinking, to help them build their topics, to help them unearth what they were interested in. Their critical lens was restricted to my interactions with them, not them pushing one another to go deeper and be more. The dialogue was between me and one or two students, not between all of us. What I learned from the second year of photovoice is that youth leading youth in the research process decenters the research enterprise from me by putting them in a position where they are learning from themselves and learning from one another. In dialogue we all pushed each other, moved our thinking together, and I was able to step back from my role as keeper of knowledge and we opened up a space for new roles of teacher as student and students as teachers (Freire 2000). This allowed me to be a part of the students' emerging knowledge as much as they were a part of mine. In this way, the entire class was able to learn and, while messy, the photovoice images, narratives, and presentations were expansive. For example, in the first year gentrification came up for some individuals, but not everyone was able to learn from or connect gentrification to their own experiences. In the second year, when looking collectively, students could see how the forces of gentrification were playing out across neighborhoods in New York City, and the concept became more complex and relevant.

Finally, in the first year the class touched criticality during photovoice and then shied away from it during the research. The research moved from the collective to the individual and I believe this was a step backward. On the verge of touching upon difficult knowledge, I defaulted to my comfort areas and went back into my assumptions about research. In contrast to the first year, the second year began with students thinking about community at an individual level and then building more critical understandings, from theory and collective experiences. The class website has since become a storehouse of thinking about social theory, environment, and identity containing photographs, narratives, data analysis, and critical reflections. The site has evolved into a space that has documented the process of research as opposed to the product.

Photovoice as a youth participatory action research (YPAR) method has given me a new perspective on research. I have come to view YPAR as a powerful tool for teaching an interdisciplinary curriculum, incorporating multiple literacies, and connecting to the lived experiences of youth. YPAR democratizes the skills of research allowing youth to learn their own truths, to challenge what they have been told are truths, and to challenge the dominant assumptions about them as youth, minorities, and students (Cammarota and Fine 2008). Once students have the skills to conduct research they can contribute to the discourse, no longer being controlled by those who have power or privilege in education or universities. YPAR privileges the perspectives of youth and allows for polyphonia (multiple voices) and polysemia (multiple meanings) of their lived experiences and their stories. This kind of research by and with young people moves past a single view of what research looks like, allowing it to be truly a participatory and emancipatory tool for young people to investigate their own lives.

PHOTOVOICE AS A TOOL TO (RE)CONCEPTUALIZE ENVIRONMENTAL EDUCATION

Our classroom photovoice research created an opportunity to re-imagine an environmental science class. I used to think that environmental education was all about global issues that happened very far from home like deforestation, the hole in the ozone layer, climate change, and food production. These topics dominate the chapters of every environmental science textbook. With these assumptions so deeply embedded in my thinking, I taught environmental science as content, lectures of information, the science of what was happening. This way of thinking about "the environment" is irrelevant for many urban students and ignores the economic and political causes of environmental problems as well as the social implications of these problems.

Throughout the photovoice experience my students and I created an environmental science class that does not use a textbook or follow a structured curriculum. Our class was guided by principles of social justice and ecological justice and was rooted in the lived experiences of the students in the classroom. As a class, we re-conceptualize environment as dynamic and changing, as immediate and constant, as impacted by and impacting on individuals and communities. Environmental science was no longer about issues faced in some far away place but issues young people face locally, and experience in their neighborhoods. Photovoice as a tool allowed us to investigate local communities in a classroom context, and led to a deeper consciousness for the well being of people, communities, and ecosystems.

An environmental science class can become the class of everything. The disciplines are not siloed the way we teach them in schools and by adopting a disciplinary focus we mask the deeper connections between, for example, science, history, and economics. We are doing a disservice in schools by not allowing students to make interdisciplinary connections, and especially in relation to their own lived experiences. What happened in the critical classroom was a filling in of many of the gaps in education and students made new connections between local environmental phenomena and larger economic and social processes.

INCORPORATING RESEARCH INTO TEACHING AND LEARNING PRACTICES

I had held ideas about what traditionally research was and throughout the two years of developing photovoice, I started to have ideas about what research could be. Wrestling through the messiness of photovoice over the past two years I have found ways to introduce students to discourses about what counts as research, lenses through which to look at the world in different ways, and methods to collect data about what young people see in their local environments. By reflecting on the different ways I thought about research through conversations, and alternative research products, I was able to step back, tweak methods, and create new research opportunities that made research relevant and fresh.

The overall purpose of the photovoice work has been to use, modify and develop participatory methods for young people to explore their experiences and relationships in and with place. I believe that through thinking about these experiences and relationships, young people can critically investigate their local environments as places that embody many global and local environmental issues, issues that imprint on their personal and social identities. Utilizing these methods in our environmental science classroom has allowed students to develop research skills including developing research questions, collecting data, analyzing data, and sharing new knowledge. This challenges assumptions about who has the right to research and where knowledge is situated.

REFERENCES

Cammarota, J., & Fine, M. (2008). Youth participatory action research: A pedagogy for transformational resistance. In *Revolutionizing education: youth participatory action research in motion*. New York, NY: Routledge.

Freire, P. (2000). *Pedagogy of the oppressed* (30th anniversary ed.). New York: Continuum.

Reason, P. (2006). Choice and quality in action research practice. *Journal of Management Inquiry*, *15*(2), 187-203.

Strack, R. W., Magill, C., & McDonagh, K. (2004). Engaging youth through photovoice. *Health Promotion Practice*, *5*(1), 49-58.

Wang, C. (1999). Photovoice: A participatory action research strategy applied to women's health. *Journal of Women's Health*, *8*(2), 185-192.

Wang, C., & Burris, M. A. (1997). Photovoice: Concept, methodology, and use for participatory needs assessment. *Health Education & Behavior*, *24*(3), 369-387.

MARK VICARS

18. ARTS-BASED EDUCATIONAL METHODOLOGY

An Impossible Possibility?

Troubling the normative epistemic educational research landscape can be a risky endeavour and such endeavour has the potential to unsettle how research into teaching and learning gets done. Kuhn (1962/1996) argued it is the emergence, through experimentation, of unanswered or unanswerable question(s) that provides the impetus to shift the paradigms of a particular scientific belief to a newer paradigmatic and discursive sense and as Smith and Brown (2011, pp. 263-264) have noted about the resurgence of the paradigm wars:

> There is talk again in journals, at conferences, in university corridors and over coffee in cafes of 'paradigm wars' … we cannot hide from the fact that something is going on in our scholarly community that is aggressive, is combative and is causing harm. … 'wars' are going on across countries and within numerous university departments over funding social scientific qualitative work … Qualitative researchers are too attacked for publishing their work in journals that, in comparison to the natural sciences, have low impact factors. They are forced out of institutions because their work is critical or grounded in the political. They are verbally shot at in conferences, in tenure review panels and in job interviews for being 'unscientific' … And lastly, but by no means least, qualitative research done by sociologists or psychologists are bullied out of departments as they no longer fit into the 'new direction' a university suddenly is taking. This 'new direction' is, it might be said, not taken always for intellectual, moral or pedagogical purposes, but instead for reasons tied to money and the concentration of executive power.

The 'new direction' does not tell the whole story or adequately provide in-depth understandings of the complexities of the lifeworlds of students and their teachers. Knowledge of and about pedagogy, is, increasingly being constructed in the context of the disappearance of what lies beneath and beyond the surface of classrooms and methodological research practices that participate in this rich discursive and 'textual space' are a necessary, critical, resistant form of world and self-making.

Throughout my educational career, as student, teacher and now a university lecturer in a College of Education, I have learned to embrace the familiar signs of misrecognition upon faces when articulating hitherto un/imagined significances of 're/imagining' the effects of being between 'proper' and 'improper' pedagogies. In my insistent rebuttal of method, of the totems of validity and reliability et al, the pedagogy of discomfort (Zembylas and Vrasidas 2004) I routinely experience is that of colleagues discombobulated by postmodern claims of persuasive verisimilitude and my belief in how situatedness in research can rework performative prohibitions into unprecedented freedoms.

In this chapter, my exploration of my available freedom draws on artful praxis as a way of un/knowing and un/doing methodological certainty. It is a consciously ethical stance in my endeavour to speak back to the power of method in educational research, of putting my preaching into practice. After all: *It's no good running a pig farm badly for thirty years while saying, "Really I was meant to be a ballet dancer." By that time, pigs will be your style.* Quentin Crisp (http://www.crisperanto.org/memories/Mem5/human.html)

In this chapter I explore the tensions that arose between my professional identity as a teacher of English and Drama in a international school, with my choice to live as an openly gay man. I draw on the concept of artful praxis (McKenna 2012) to narratively authorise how my embodied, and culturally situated pedagogical experiences interplayed with the cognitive and emotional sources of my private self and how these were made the scene and setting for my professional identity at work.

ARTISTIC PRAXIS RE/MAKES THE UN/IMAGINABLE

Grasping at images from the past, I selectively revise scenes and reorder fragments in an attempt to make sense of those critical, defining transitional moments.

☐ *un/imaginable 1*: I never wanted to be a teacher. I based my perceptions of the profession on the grey suited, pallid-faced disciplinarians of my youth. They embodied the substance of control that was my secondary educational experience.☐

I reorganize the space at my desk in order to begin writing. Does the coffee pot need refilling? Do I have another packet of cigarettes? Have I remembered to switch on the answer phone? I start to tap away at my keyboard scouring experience, aware that it already exists as an 'interpretation' and is in need of interpretation' (Scott 1992). As I settle down in front of the computer screen, the taste of bitter coffee is blended with cigarette smoke and I reach for the mediating forces of memory and language and wait for them to assert authority on my unconscious. I am getting lost in past imaginings and struggle to find the language to share and interpret my world. How do I start to give a form to a narrative that will reveal how my identity as a teacher and my educational practice has been constituted through 'material, cultural and inter-psychic relations' (Smith and Watson 2001, p. 25).

☐ *un/imaginable 2*: The tacit pedagogies of schooling have habitually made me uneasy about speaking up, out of, from and about experiences. I am wary of the performative re/articulation of reinscribing the Other. And yet the personal in the professional keeps urging:

> you must go on, I can't go on, you must go on, I'll go on, you must say words, as long as there are any, until they find me, until they say me, strange pain, strange sin, you must go on, perhaps it's done already, perhaps they have said me already, perhaps they have carried me to the threshold of my story, before the door that opens on my story, that would surprise me, if it opens, it will be I, it will be the silence, where I am, I don't know, I'll never know, in the silence you don't know. (Beckett 1997, p. 418)

I light another cigarette and draw deeply, pulling the nicotine-laced smoke deep into kippered lungs. I observe my yellowed fingers. I light another cigarette and think about my father who lay dying from emphysema in a flock-wallpapered room for 13 months.

☐ *un/imaginable 3*: *What order can I start to impose on the illusions of myself and of others that claim to be truthful expressions? I am aware how the events I select are constantly up for negotiation. With each churned and filtered motion, they recoil from immediate analysis. Hesitantly, they emerge into words, phrases, sentences and paragraphs that require structure and 'emplotment' (Ricoeur 1995). It is in the writing that I find the craft of interpretation and locate the threads of meaning for my story.*

Twenty years ago I had arrived at a strange airport with no job, nowhere to live and as the pungent aroma of spices blended with eye-watering carbon monoxide fumes infused through my outer defences. I embraced its toxicity. Three months after arriving, I had applied for a job teaching English and drama at an international school and I could not believe my good fortune when I got the job.

SCENE 1: WELCOME TO THE SMOKERS BALCONY!

Sue, a formidable Geordie (origin in Newcastle, UK) who taught special needs, took me immediately under her wing.

We're not really allowed to smoke but the head turns a blind eye if we are discreet.

Dipping in and out of conversations, she maintained a constant dialogue and was the lynch pin that kept everything and everyone together.

> You canne hav any secrets on the balcony pet. I love it here, been here for three years now. The head is a good un and we're like one big family. Great place to work, kids are wonderful, staff is best I've ever worked with. Now tell me 'bout you.

SCENE 2: WHAT TEAM ARE YOU ON?

Steve, the newly appointed Head of English, in a department of two, had recently allotted himself the role of captain for the newly formed staff football team and set about establishing his order on and off the pitch.

I've decided to start an English Speaking Club. The little bastards keep talking their own language and I've got to do something to stamp it out. Here is how it works, every time one of the little fuckers uses ***** put their name on the board. At the end of each week the names will be collected and if a name appears more than once it will be published in the school magazine that is sent home to the parents. Naming and shaming tiger, that is what it's all about.

And so it continued, aggression seemed to characterize his every act. I had grown accustomed to his commentary on my sexuality in terms of

Had a good weekend? Are able to sit down? Had it up the arse?

My resistance to what Steve represented, personally and professionally, was making my position within the school increasingly vulnerable. I had a feeling that my days were increasingly numbered because I persistently remained skeptical of the changes that an effective teacher should only: deal with the part of the child that is above the neck. As our differences became more pronounced, it was apparent that at best Steve tolerated me. Using the status of Head of Department, he asserted authority and I was informed of departmental decisions as opposed to being involved in creating policy. He increasingly started to question and regulate my classroom. With each confrontation, it became clear that his need to win was driving the encounter. Agreeing to disagree was not an option. Metaphors of football, of playing on the same team, were drawn upon and it was made abundantly clear to me that in 'playing offside' I was disrupting 'his game.'

SCENE 3: TESTING TIMES

Examinations approached: the time of year when timetables are suspended and there is a sense of the daily life of school shuddering to a stop. It had been decided by the Principal that subject teachers would invigilate their own exams. Steve and I were thrust together for a week in the claustrophobic assembly hall.

Look at em, a couple of shittas.

Eh?

Returning from giving out extra sheets of paper, I did not have a clue to what he was referring.

Them, a couple of shittas!

What are you on about now?

Them!

He gestured to where two Year 11 lads were sitting industriously working through the question paper.

For crying out loud, stop it, they're kids.

They're a couple of pussies. You know what they said 'bout me?

I knew that he was annoyed. The students had asked to be transferred to my class two terms previous. Having to produce a valid reason for their wanting to move from what was the top set down to the bottom set, the Principal had demanded to know the reason. A meeting had been organized where their parents had explained that the two lads were uncomfortable and fed-up with being made fun of by Steve.

SCENE 4: BALLS TO IT ALL

It was at the annual sports day that the situation finally came to a head.

You're on shot-putt with Steve.

I inwardly groaned and made my way over to where a bunch of the less able and less physically streamlined kids were lining up.

Duuur, are you stupid or what, I told you to line up over there.

I was not quite sure if he was talking to me, or the kids. I looked around to check and spied Pete, the music teacher, lurking in the shade eating an ice cream and resplendent in a specially purchased, and it has to be said, rather camp red ensemble. Pete was not in the least sporty but felt that he should at least look the part. The lucky so-and-so had been given crowd control and, as there was not that much of a crowd to control, had found a quiet spot to observe the proceedings.

That fat queer cunt!

Oh leave it out; what has he ever done to you?

He makes me want to spew. You know what I want to do? I wanna tie that fat

queer fucker down to a chair and stuff my fist down his throat till he gags.

I want to ram it down so hard that his teeth break and he starts to choke.

How very sexual! What phallic imagery! It sounds like you want to fuck him?

Maybe that's it, you secretly fancy a bit of cock?

Fuck off, that's disgusting! Uurgh, is that all you think about?

I had had enough and walked away to join Pete and have a lick of his ice cream. As it was the time of year when contracts were up for renewal, I had decided enough was enough. My decision had just been made. In between mouthfuls of vanilla whip, I told Pete.

You're doing what?

I'm leaving.

Why?

Pete could not understand.

Look, I've had two years working with Steve and let's face it this is not the place it used to be. It is virtually unrecognisable from the school we started at four years ago. I don't look forward to coming in any more. The kids are still great but it's the rest of it that is a nightmare. Steve has re-signed for another two years and I have had enough.

Four years later and my leaving day approached. In the interim, there had been a change of leadership and the incoming Head had established a regime that reminded me of those tortuous times I had spent under the disciplining gaze of former PE masters. Increasingly, I felt I had nowhere to turn and just as I had aimlessly floundered on the football pitch I had for the past 12 months questioned whether I could sustain the humiliations that resulted from not being one of the lads. There had been a plethora of new appointments, all men and the emphatic performances of masculinity that I had believed secured them jobs in the first place had a dramatic impact across the school. Steve, the newly appointed Head of English, in a department of two, had recently allotted himself the role of captain for the newly formed staff football team and set about establishing his order on and off the pitch.

SCENE 5: FLEE SKIRTS BILLOWING

The last day of term arrived and I was running late for the ritual line up for the school photograph. Making my along the bleachers, I shouted out my apologies to the sweating bodies bunched together in a forced pose of institutional togetherness. We were anything but one big happy family.

Sorry I'm late, sooorrry!

Watch yer back boys, Vicars is coming through!

I had made the right decision. I felt such a sense of relief knowing that I would no longer have to put up with any more of it. I returned to my classroom to finish off packing up my things.

☐ *un/imaginable 4*: To re/present that particular unspeakable truth was a professionally transformative experience. Faced with a similar situation, I am now better prepared to articulate the conditions of my shameful silencing.

SCENE 6: SURPRISE!

Dahhhhling!

Karla the art teacher announced herself, bounded into my room and gave me a hug. I was bustled out of my classroom to an awaiting taxi. I demanded to know what was going on. I had come to hate surprises considering the amount I had had to accommodate during the previous couple of years.

ARTS-BASED EDUCATIONAL METHODOLOGY

Now, close your eyes.

Clutching onto Karla I made my way up the narrow winding stairs.

Surprise!

Opening my eyes I found myself in a small restaurant packed with year 10 and 11 students. A buffet was laid out and ominously a karaoke machine was buzzing on a raised platform stage. Isn't it fabulous! They organised it all. Happy leaving!

The next couple of hours were spent eating, drinking, saying goodbye and swapping email addresses. I was surprised to see Bank there, for the last two years he had been visibly reluctant to have anything at all to do with me. I had taught him at the beginning of year 10, he was in my English IGCSE set and we had always got on well. Steve had decided that those students who did not stand a chance of passing the exam would not be entered, as it would look bad on the department's pass rate. They would be taken out of mainstream English classes and would have to do extra EFL. I had argued against the decision but, as it was supported by the senior management, I had to tell Bank that he would be leaving the class.

But I don't want to, I will try harder, I really will.

I'm sorry, it has already been decided.

What if I got my parents to pay?

I'm sorry, there is nothing I can do.

I knew as well as he did that his departure from my class would be read by his peers that he was not that bright as only the less able kids were being creamed off and separated into the sink category.

Hello Bank, how are you?

I wasn't going to come. I hated you, you know! Why did you throw me out of your class? I was trying hard. …

As I explained to him what had happened and that it had not been my decision, he started to cry.

I'm sorry, I didn't know …

How could I explain?

Why didn't you tell me at the time?

Visibly upset and crying harder, he went to put his arms around me.

Karaoke Time

Saved by a song, I felt uncomfortable about being physical with Bank. I knew it was not appropriate behaviour for a teacher. I understood what he was trying to tell me and regretted not being totally honest with him at the time. Amid cheers and shouts of my name I was dragged to the microphone just in time to launch into Gloria Gaynor's Gay disco anthem I will survive. The whole room erupted with the refrain, Karla was being encouraged to join me on the stage and the amassed throng on their feet dancing and singing at the top of their voices. Suddenly, Bank jumped on to the stage and started to take off his tie, then his shirt. Dancing around me to the cheers of onlookers, he flung his arms around my waist and planted a kiss on my cheek. What on earth was happening now? What did he think he was doing? What did I think I was doing?

SCENE 7: I WILL SURVIVE

Dramatis Personae

SEXUALITY, an unconscious force

PEDAGOGY, a conscious force

PROFESSIONAL ETHICS, a controlling force

MINOR CHARACTER, a 17-year-old boy

A composite set represents the spaces of classroom and bar.

(Minor Character and Pedagogy are off stage. Professional Ethics is centre stage keeping control of sexuality who is walking slowly up stage out of sight of the audience. Suddenly music starts and sexuality moves down stage centre, Professional Ethics is unsure what to do and stands watching, helpless to intervene.)

PROFESSIONAL ETHICS: Stop it now!
SEXUALITY: (In a stage whisper) Relax it will be fine. (Starts to sing to the stoic figure of Professional Ethics) First I was afraid, I was petrified, kept thinking I could never live without you by my side.
PROFESSIONAL ETHICS (Glaring): This will end in tears, I'm warning you, behave!
SEXUALITY: But I spent all so many nights thinking how you did me wrong and I grew strong, I knew that I would get along.
PROFESSIONAL ETHICS: You are making a spectacle!
(Minor Character enters and walks over to Sexuality; Professional Ethics becomes increasingly agitated and concerned.)
PROFESSIONAL ETHICS: (Direct address to Sexuality) Enough is enough, it's time you made an exit.
(Minor Character starts to undress; Sexuality watches on bemused;
Professional Ethics is furious.)
PROFESSIONAL ETHICS: I'm warning you.
(Sexuality continues to move to the music. Sexuality stops dancing for a moment, looks at Professional Ethics and turns to face the audience who are on their feet

cheering, clapping, shouting encouragement and singing. Sexuality stands centre stage and is embraced by the Minor Character, the audience erupts once again. Sexuality and Minor Character look at each other and burst out laughing. They put their arms around each other and turning to face the audience they both start to sing.)

SEXUALITY/MINOR CHARACTER: And now you're back from outer space I just
walked in here to find you with that look upon your face.
PROFESSIONAL ETHICS: Look at yourself, think what other people are going to say, think of your position.
SEXUALITY: I should have changed that stupid lock; I should have made you leave your key
PROFESSIONAL ETHICS: For Christ's sake!
SEXUALITY: But I grew strong I learnt how to get along.
PROFESSIONAL ETHICS: You shouldn't be here doing this, I don't know why you were invited?
SEXUALITY: But I grew strong I learnt how to get along.
PROFESSIONAL ETHICS: You shouldn't be here doing this, I don't know why you were invited?

(Minor character moves towards Sexuality and starts to remove his school tie, which he swings around his head and flings into the audience. He then begins to slowly unbutton his shirt whilst dancing. He then removes his shirt and throws it over the head of Sexuality who all the time has been looking at Professional Ethics. Sexuality holds the shirt that had been draped over his face in his left hand and tries to replace the microphone on its stand. He starts to exit the stage only to be pulled back by the Minor Character who is now simulating a striptease act much to the delight of the audience. Minor Character sidesteps Professional Ethics who has run on to the stage and is attempting to stop the performance. Sexuality is momentarily transfixed unsure whether to comply with Professional Ethics' attempt to restore order or to go to the rescue of the Minor Character. He turns and walks towards the two characters who are grappling centre stage and his presence arrests the struggle. Professional Ethics glares at Sexuality who then turns to face Minor Character, they look at each other, both start to laugh and dancing they turn to face the audience.)

PROFESSIONAL ETHICS: STOP!!!!!

(Sexuality, invites members of the audience on-stage and as the music gets louder the stage begins to fill-up with an assortment of figures who are swaying in time to the music, Professional Ethics is hidden from view but is still audible. Sexuality, Minor Character and assembled figures all start to sing)

SEXUALITY: I will survive!
MINOR CHARACTER: I will survive!
AUDIENCE ON STAGE: I will survive!

(The song finishes, Sexuality walks off stage followed by a defeated
Professional Ethics. Pedagogy enters dressed in a Police uniform and walks around the set inspecting it as if were a crime scene. Note pad and pencil in hand,

Pedagogy scribbles on the pad and moves down stage right. There is a prolonged silence.)

PEDAGOGY: (To the audience who have returned to their seats) What did you witness? Come on who will be the first to speak, I demand to know! What is your understanding? Really, I am interested. What, you think I won't listen, that I have already made up my mind. How hard can it be to tell me what has been going here? You ask what I am going to do with the information. (To the audience) That sir/madam is none of your business. (Pedagogy stands waiting as the house lights are brought up and remains standing as the audience leave their seats and exit the auditorium. As the last person exits through the doors, Pedagogy can be heard beginning to talk.)

PEDAGOGY: Well, I'm waiting!

☐ *un/imaginable 5: Do not negate the problematics of proximity or choose to ignore the tacit dialectic of intimacy/detachment of psychological, social and emotional closeness to comfort/discomfort. Remember and revisit these pedagogical moments of transition.*

SHALL WE DANCE?

My collisions with the heteronorming situatedness of educational institutions and the actors within has made me wary of rearticulating the 'uniterrogated norm' (Lorber 1996). The capital of the academic field makes claims to and believes in a method of producing truth and authority. I have eschewed the un-problematical and in making choices about how best to represent the actions and language of those who to whom I have given a voice, I have struggled in interpretation to construct scenes where lifeless data is transformed into a landscape of flesh, blood and emotions. It was impossible to produce a neutral account veiled in objective language. Each and every articulation was imbued within a situated moral purpose and this knowledge helped me to re/know and re/understand my processes of my un/becoming teacher. Through my artful, trickly crafted acts of reinvention, the descriptive accounts of the past become tactical performative sites to subvert, defamilarise and jolt habitual perception of what educational inquiry and narrative might be or look like. De Certeau (1984) considers tactical-discursive forms as a means to re-imagine the effects between the 'proper' and 'improper' and an artful methodological praxis can be a willing resource to renovate the past in the present, to re-write, re-animate, re-shape and reconfigure voice and, in the process transform the stories we tell of ourselves and more significantly ourselves in the story.

If William's (2003) assertion that, "all propositions about the world are only meaningful if we can show how they can be verified" (p. 12) then I suggest, as educational researchers, we do not negate the problematics of proximity, or choose to ignore the tacit dialectic of intimacy/detachment of psychological, social and emotional closeness to comfort/discomfort. Nias (1996) has investigated the significance of emotions in the lives of a range of teachers and suggests that emotions are rooted in thought, that separation of feeling from perception is not possible. Emotional reactions to the task of teaching, it is proposed, are connected to views of the personal self, self-esteem, and professional efficacy and are influential in the construction of a social role/identity. She comments how:

> ... emotions are not simply *in* teaching. They are also a response to the conditions under which it takes place and especially to the increasing frequency with which individual teachers have to defend their sense of who and what they are. (Nias 1996, p. 305)

It may well be the case that as a reader you have an emotional response and find problematic my use of language that some my regard as offensive, but these were the words that were frequently used. I carefully suggest how a reaction to them is indicating a position to a research narrative that is critically and ideologically situated, located in epistemic landscapes of practice. There is always something at stake in research inquiry and re/presentation and we need to start to come-out about how our discursive practices and interactions are ideologically situated as no story of a life or an aspect of a life, can be any thing other than an interpretation, a re-presentation of questions about the relationship between life as lived and life as presented in research are, fundamentally, questions about the relationships between subjectivities, epistemologies and methodologies. How to reconstruct ideological and institutional conditions in which the lived experience is the defining feature of schooling relies on acknowledging the range of critical interpretative positions that can and should be foregrounded to give more of a methodological voice for 'improper' ways of seeing. Berger (1972, p. 1) has noted:

> Yet this seeing which comes before words, and can never be covered by them, is not a question of mechanically reacting to stimuli ... We never look at just one thing; we are always looking at the relation between things and ourselves. Our vision is continually active, continually moving, continually holding things in a circle around itself, constituting what is present to us as we are. (Berger 1972, p. 1)

Feminist, anti-racist, postcolonial and queer theories have all played a role in expanding and transforming and shifting focus on how race, gender, sexuality, ethnicity and dis/ability are productive sites of pedagogical resistance and can narrate generative possibilities for change. The process of showing artful praxis in this chapter involved reconstructing identities within stories of movement,. In the dialectic between order and disorder, the identity of each person remains open to revision.

REFERENCES

Beckett, S. (1997). *Trilogy*. London: Kalder.
Berger, J. (1972). *Ways of seeing*. London: Penguin Books.
Crisp, Q. (2012). http://www.crisperanto.org/memories/Mem5/human.html
De Certeau, M. (1984). *The practice of everyday life* (S. Rendell, Trans.). London: University of California Press.

Kuhn, T. S. (1962/1996). *The structure of scientific revolutions* (3rd ed) Chicago: The University of Chicago Press.

Lorber, J. (1996). Beyond the binaries: Depolarizing the categories of sex, sexuality, and gender. *Sociological Inquiry, 66*(2), 143-59.

Luke, A., & Carrington, V. (2002). Globalisation, literacy, curriculum practice. In G. Brooks, R. Fisher, & M. Lewis (Eds.), *Raising standards in literacy* (pp. 231-250). London: Routledge.

Nias. J. (1996). Thinking about Feeling; the emotions in teaching. *Cambridge Journal of Education, 26*(3), 296-306.

Ricoeur, P. (1995). *Figuring the sacred: Religion, narrative, and imagination.* Minneapolis, MN: Fortiss Press.

Mckenna, T. (2012). To begin the day. *Creative Approaches to Research, 5*(3), 7-20.

Scott. J. W. (1992). Experience. In J. Butler & J. Scott (Eds.), *Feminists theorize the political.* New York: Routledge.

Smith, B., & Brown, D. (2011). Editorial. *Qualitative Research in Sport, Exercise and Health, 3*(3), 263-265.

Smith, S., & Watson, J. (2001). *Reading autobiography: A guide for interpreting life narratives.* London: University of Minnesota Press.

Williams, M. (2003). *Making sense of social research.* London: Sage.

Zembylas, M., & Vrasidas, C. (2004). Emotion, reason, and information and communications technologies in education: Some issues in a post-emotional society. *E-Learning, 1*(1), 105-127. Retrieved from http://vrasidas.com/wpcontent/uploads/2007/07/elearnvol1no1.pdf

ALICE J. PITT AND DEBORAH P. BRITZMAN

19. SPECULATIONS ON QUALITIES OF DIFFICULT KNOWLEDGE IN TEACHING AND LEARNING

An Experiment in Psychoanalytic Research

Our research project wavers between two questions and the theoretical issues prompted by each: What makes knowledge difficult, and what is it to represent and narrate "difficult knowledge"? Whereas the first question resides in the content of knowledge, the second foregrounds issues of encountering the self through the otherness of knowledge. Moreover, if the first question takes its inspiration from psychoanalytic theories of trauma, it is the second question that moves us unequivocally into the more general realm of the psychical dynamics that animate teaching and learning. These questions and the oscillations between them characterize what Britzman (1998) has called "difficult knowledge," a concept meant to signify both representations of social traumas in curriculum and the individual's encounters with them in pedagogy.

Our project centred difficult knowledge as intersecting philosophical, pedagogical and methodological dilemmas. Philosophically, we were drawn to discussions of postmodernity that question the status of knowledge, authority and power in the university (Lyotard 1987; Code 1991; Readings 1996; Martin 1997). These were brought into tension with pedagogical discussions on what learning means when knowledge references incommensurability, historical trauma, and social breakdowns (Felman and Laub 1992; Caruth 1996; Ellsworth 1997; Britzman 1998; Cheng 2001). Both philosophical and pedagogical views of "difficult knowledge" question the relationship between education and social justice because they assume, albeit differently, a kernel of trauma in the very capacity to know. Contemporary efforts in critical, feminist, and gay-affirmative pedagogies elaborate some of these breakdowns in understanding. They focus on understanding the interests of learners to engage critically both with narratives of historical traumas such as genocide, slavery, and forms of social hatred *and* questions of equity, democracy and human rights (McCarthy and Crichlow 1993; Pinar 1998; Simon et al 2000). For pedagogical theorists, "difficult knowledge" also signifies the problem of learning from social breakdowns in ways that might open teachers and students to their present ethical obligations (Britzman 2000; Pinar 2001; Todd 2001).

Our second question, what it means to represent and narrate "difficult knowledge," also draws some of its urgency from contemporary methodological discussions in education on the uses of poststructuralism in qualitative research raised by Bloom (1998), Lather (2000, 2001), Laws and Davies (2000), Rhedding-Jones (2000), St. Pierre and Pillow (2000), Talburt (2000), and Yon (2000). Poststructuralist method heightens the problem of the verisimilitude embedded in such foundational concepts in qualitative studies as voice, identity, agency, and experience while still expecting to offer some contingent observations about how individuals – including the researcher – make knowledge in and of the world. This methodology offers a new tension to educational studies by bringing to bear on participant narratives the very problem of narrating experience and by asking what conditions or structures the narrative impulse. This linguistic turn in qualitative research is now known as "the crisis of representation" in that the adequacy of language to capture experience is considered an effect of discourse rather than a reflection of that experience.

Yet if we consider psychical dynamics as influencing and being influenced by encounters with knowledge, there is, working in our research questions, a further problem. If the crisis of representation is made from the logical priority of expression over experience (Volosinov 1986), psychoanalytic research (Felman and Laub 1992; Young 1994; Phillips 1998; Appel 1999; Chodorow 1999) adds another dimension to this crisis, making the sum of our philosophical, pedagogical, and methodological concerns into a complex. Significant psychoanalytic concepts – namely the unconscious, phantasy,[1] affect and sexuality – all work to unseat the authorial capabilities of expression to account exhaustively for qualities of experience, to view history as a causal process, and to separate reality from phantasy. In other words, psychoanalytic inquiry begins with the problem of resistance to discourse, and, as Laplanche reminds us, "must take account of the fact that the human subject is a theorizing being and a being that theorizes itself" (1989, p. 10). Socially-sanctioned discourses play a role in self-theorizing activities but do not exhaust the material. Psychoanalytic research posits education as an exemplary site where the crisis of representation that is outside meets the crisis of representation that is inside (Britzman 1998; Pitt 2000). Freud (1914a, p. 154) called this unexpected meeting "the playground of transference," where the means of knowing cannot be separated from one's own libidinal history of learning. We have come to believe that traces of this representational crisis, conveyed through the transference, can be theorized from attempts to narrate teaching and learning.

In this chapter we speculate on the various resonances that the crisis of representation leaves in narration by way of three psychoanalytic concepts: deferred action, transference, and symbolization. Because knowledge is lost and found in these psychical dynamics, they leave traces in narratives about knowledge. We are calling these traces "difficult knowledge." We consider constructions of difficulties in teaching and learning from the vantage of psychoanalytic writing and our own attempts to interview university teachers and students on how they think about difficult knowledge.[2] Throughout this paper, we elaborate a constitutive difficulty educational research confronts, namely representing teaching and learning. Thinking about this constitutive difficulty challenges us to rethink what counts as data and what data counts as. Thus, in this chapter, we move from being preoccupied with the content of our inquiry – that is with considering "data" as a property of what participants produce and as the culmination of research – to what we can learn about theory and narrative by working psychoanalytically.

We begin with a conceptual archaeology of our project. This is followed by discussions of three contexts where difficulties are elaborated, each of which is a resource that orients us toward our speculations on the qualities of difficult knowledge in teaching and learning. We first offer some clinical discussion written by psychoanalysts on the difficulties of narrating teaching and learning. We then provide some constructions of difficulty proposed in a "thought experiment" we designed as the basis for interviews with university teachers and students. Finally, we turn to further research constructions of difficulty in our interviews. We conclude with the claim that research cannot be immune from crises of representation in education and that the very design of narrative research enacts the crisis of representing teaching and learning.

THREE METAPHORS FOR RESEARCH: A CONCEPTUAL ARCHEOLOGY

To understand something about what makes knowledge difficult, our first research question, we turned to Steiner's (1980) essay, "On difficulty," on reading poetry and then to psychoanalytic theories of trauma. We wondered about metaphors of learning that might serve as an index for cataloguing "difficult knowledge." Poetry, the focus of Steiner's study, is a useful metaphor for inquiry in that the evocative qualities that language conveys resist interpretation, and this struggle is an important aspect of experiencing the strange demands of the poem. There is, in the reading of a poem, a felt tension between idea and affect and questions about the very nature of representation and understanding. There is a gap between experiencing the poem and recounting its meaning. Steiner offers four categories for grasping the individual's struggles with the elegiac text: contingent difficulties require homework to fill in the reader's gap of knowledge; modal difficulties concern the problem of constructing relevance; tactical difficulties draw attention to conflicts within the poem between innermost meaning and public statements; and, finally, ontological difficulties are met when the poem calls attention to the very possibility of understanding and communication as we know them (pp. 22-47). Steiner's categories did seem pertinent to relations between text and reader; they did not, however, illuminate for us the pushes and pulls in social relations that also compose the psychical landscape of teaching and learning in classrooms. Nor could Steiner's model address the work of phantasy, a concept to which we return in the next section.

Contemporary uses of psychoanalytic theories of trauma in the humanities (Felman and Laub 1992; Caruth 1996) offered a second metaphor for thinking about difficult knowledge as a complex event. The event of trauma is characterized by a quality of significance that resists meaning even as the affective force of the event can be felt. Caruth (1996) uses the term "unclaimed experience" to suggest the paradox of having painful experience but being unable to know just what has happened or why it is important to one's present. Originally, theories of trauma were useful to us because they centre the quagmire of insufficiency of knowledge, primal helplessness, and the incapacity to respond adequately. These dynamics, we believe, characterize one's early experiences in having to learn and later return as anxiety when one faces new knowledge that requires something significant of the learner.[3] And yet, the metaphor of trauma for our inquiry was not so useful in a key way: it occluded our own consideration of what happens when experience is merely conflicted, not elided. We began to wonder if our interest in the relation between historical knowledge that emerges in the wake of profound social traumas and learning from such knowledge foreclosed a curiosity toward the ways in which people do construct, through the transference and from their narratives of teaching and learning, emotional significance.

Our first question, "what makes knowledge difficult in teaching and learning"?, one that emerged from our early work with Steiner's index and with psychoanalytic theories of trauma, transformed into our second question, now refined as follows: How do difficulties interfere with the coherence of narrative construction as part of the complex of difficult knowledge alluded to earlier? Now we are able to consider, not only our own experiences of difficulty in writing this chapter, but, more generally, what our psychoanalytic research has come to be about: tracing the difficulties of representing teaching and learning in research itself.

Our research story, then, is told in the strange time of deferred action, a psychoanalytic concept that heightens the problem of how emotional significance and new ideas are made from past and present experiences. The supposition is that settling on significance is delayed for two reasons: the force of an event is felt before it can be understood, and a current event may take its force and revisions from an earlier scene. While the notion of deferred action is closely tied to Freud's theory of trauma, it can also signal more ordinary phenomena and therefore be used as a bridging concept between traumatic crises and thinking about them. In the time of deferred action, old experiences can be revised, and new psychical significance to current and past events can be constructed (Laplanche and Pontalis 1973, p. 111). The new event, however, bears the traces of the dynamics of earlier experience even as the earlier experience can be revised. Conceptualizing the strange time of deferred action brings us to the intimacy of the psychoanalytic dialogue and the third metaphor for our inquiry: clinical experience. Such experience serves, not only as the grounds of therapy, but also as the laboratory for psychoanalytic research into its own theories and practices.

While we will suggest, over the course of this paper, what it means for us to do psychoanalytically-informed research, here we want to provide a brief sketch of some qualities that distinguish this approach. As we have just suggested, emotional significance is constituted in the time of deferred action (Bollas 1999). Understanding, then, is not a feature of experience but a problem of symbolization. This leads to another quality of psychoanalytic research: the strange and conflictive interplay between data and theory. Both are narratives, yet neither is beholden to empirical claims nor confirmed through observation (Freud 1900; Green 2000). They gain their currency through speculation and belief because narratives are not the culmination of experience but constructions made from both conscious and unconscious dynamics. Data and theory, therefore, are like dreams in that they work at two levels, the manifest and the latent (Kohon 1999; Kristeva 2000a). While a narrative is made from a specific context, the affective force of what precisely is represented in narrative may derive from other scenes and from unresolved psychical conflicts. This is the dynamic of transference where one makes sense of new situations through the imperatives of older conflicts. In this view, representation is a compromise, an attempt to ward off crisis, because constructions are made from an argument between the wish for coherence and the anxiety over what coherence excludes (Little 1990; Kristeva 2000b; Bass 2001; Kristeva 2000b). All of these qualities suggest an interpretive paradox at the heart of psychoanalytic inquiry: interpretation makes narrative, but there is also something within narrative that resists its own interpretation. There can be no original moment in research that gives birth to interpretation even as we must use narratives as the force of interpretive research. The next section illustrates this dilemma.

SOME CLINICAL EXAMPLES OF DIFFICULTY IN NARRATING TEACHING AND LEARNING

In the clinical setting something of the intimacies of narrative in terms of its surprising associations, or the things furthest from one's mind, are reconstructed through the analytic dialogue by means of the push and pull of interpretations. This is slow work. Freud (1937, p. 261) named any encounter with interpretation "a preliminary labour performed by constructions" because narrative for Freud is inaugurated by a confusion of time, and this makes reasoned persuasion futile. Indeed, because both agreement and disagreement are also constructions, for any construction to matter, it must bear the cumulative weight of an event's emotional significance. When presentation and representation meet, symbolization emerges. But emotional significance is not something one makes once and for all because of the confusion of time that is narration. Where does one situate the event that is experience, in the past that is narrated or in the presence of its interpretation? For Freud both positions of time are embodied in the transference. We believe that construction as a problem of time and place opens a new question for the work of representing teaching and learning: how does one distinguish between obstacles to teaching and learning and obstacles to representing teaching and learning? As we will see, there is something utterly difficult about our recollections in terms of our capacity to locate them in the past and understand what they can mean for the present. What makes recollections of our educational history a form of difficult knowledge is that obstacles to learning become entangled with obstacles to representing learning.

Freud's (1914b, p. 241) efforts to recollect his own schoolboy days suggests this difficulty:

> It gives you a queer feeling if, late in life, you are ordered once again to write a school essay. But you obey automatically, like the old solider who, at the word 'Attention!,' cannot help dropping whatever he may have had in his hands and who finds his little fingers pressed along the seams of his trousers. It is strange how readily you obey the orders, as though nothing in particular had happened in the last half century.

Originally written for a celebration of the 50th anniversary of a school Freud attended as an adolescent, today "Some reflections on schoolboy psychology" is read less as an affirmation than as a reminder of the difficulties one confronts when trying to reflect upon and remember experiences of learning and teaching. One key difficulty is that school memories invoke not just relations with authority but also repeat one's own childhood helplessness, dependency, and desire to please. This strange combination means that reflecting on one's learning seems necessarily to pass through these unbidden repetitions of love, hate and ambivalence that make the transference, reminding us of the very earliest scenes of education, learning for love, even as we encounter ideas and selves that seem far removed in time.

But an earlier problem is also significant here. What happens when school experience cannot be recollected? Psychoanalyst Milner (1993) offers a description of her work with an eleven-year-old boy who was "suffering from a loss of talent for school work" (p. 18). She explores the force of these conflicts prior to their symbolization and narrates one game the boy devised for her in the analytic setting:

> [H]e himself became the sadistic punishing schoolmaster, and I had to be the bad pupil. For days, and sometimes weeks, I had to play the role of the persecuted schoolboy: I was set long monotonous tasks, my efforts were treated with scorn, I was forbidden to talk and made to write out "lines" if I did; and if I did not comply with these demands, then he wanted to cane me. (p. 21)

Milner assures us that the boy knew that he had never been treated as badly as he was treating his analyst. Even though the school made efforts to "adapt to his difficulties" (p. 21), she also suggests that memories of learning are closely tied to phantasies of refusing to learn, an insight that helped us think about the paradox of research discussed in our introduction. Phantasies of refusing to learn can take the form of reversing positions where the helpless learner becomes the demanding teacher. Then, not learning is symbolically equated with having to be punished. This little boy's distress was impervious to the demands of reason, and Milner's sense of frustration in her role as powerless schoolboy testifies eloquently to the boy's emotional reality. The boy's transference of an imagined education onto his present conflicts represents, for Milner, "difficulties in establishing the relation to external reality as such" (p. 21). As the boy's capacity to play creatively with the toys provided by the analyst increased, so too did his ability to symbolize his school experience with greater fluency, less as an equation where the symbol becomes collapsed with the object it represents, and more as construction (see also

Segal 1997). He began to tolerate the inevitable frustrations of learning while also being able to enjoy his engagements with knowledge. If transference is an obstacle to representing learning in the present, symbolization allows one to return the obstacles to the archaic conflicts they represent.

The work of symbolization, clearly at stake in both producing knowledge and reflecting upon learning, provides a route out of the tensions of childhood helplessness alluded to in Freud's narrative and enacted in the game Milner must play. Milner speculates that symbolization cannot be confined to the developmental task of adapting to external reality. For adapting to reality, at least in psychoanalytic views, may be akin to closing the gap between the symbol and that to which it refers. This is compliance, and it is justifiably experienced as coercion. Symbolization, she suggests, does not merely name the world and its objects; it also reflects the capacity to express emotional significance within a symbolic language (see also Mannoni 1999). That is, in symbolization, the idea and the affect influence one another. This relation is, for Milner, the grounds of creative thought. But because symbolization flows from the oscillations between the necessity to search for substitutes for original objects and "the emotional experience of finding the substitute" (p. 17), its rational quota can become undone by an excess of affect. Here too, between the agony of losing beloved (though also often feared) objects and the ecstasy of finding beautiful substitutes, questions of knowledge are made and broken.

These two stories of clinical experience, one from the vantage of maturity and the other more firmly anchored in the time of dependence, testify to the difficulties of representing our most meaningful encounters with knowledge and learning. This brings us to an intimate problem: learning is uncannily organized by repetition of past investments and conflicts – or, in short hand, new editions of old conflicts – projected onto present experiences, people, and events. Transference poses intimate problems for representing learning (Britzman and Pitt 1996, 2004) because presentations of learning are still imbued with phantasies and are not yet representations. Our focus on the transferential qualities of learning works against the idea that the grounds of knowledge are made rationally and that rationality will somehow win out, provided that the knowledge is persuasive enough, that the teacher creates sufficient scaffolding, and that the learner is able to use what is provided.[4] Instead, the transference represents both the obstacles and promise made from emotional ties consisting of love, hate, and ambivalence toward both new and old events. Transference is the signature we make upon histories of learning, but it writes in invisible ink. If learning begins with efforts to sustain one's continuity – through familiarity – the transference represents something of one's unresolved conflicts that remain obscured until acknowledgement of the emotional experience of knowledge itself can be symbolized. These are the problems that our protocol invoked both for the participants and for us.

SOME RESEARCH CONSTRUCTIONS OF DIFFICULTY

We created a "thought experiment" to help university teachers and students talk about the emotional significance of their encounters with "difficult knowledge." The document (see Appendix A) did become the basis of conversation, and at first we thought of the interviews as our "research data." This formulation and the chronology it assumes are, however, at odds with our theory. Our "thought experiment" is already both interpretation and data, and we asked participants to make a relationship to it. But here is precisely where narrative loses its referent: just as there is no original moment to interpretation, there is no original thing as "data." While we had hoped that participants could make coherent narratives of teaching and learning, one inaugural difficulty that we failed to appreciate is just how utterly difficult it is to represent teaching and learning. What we came to understand, long after the interviews were over, was that our research document became, for our participants, a metaphor for difficult knowledge.

The document lists affective experiences in constructing knowledge and therefore invites reflections on how individuals conceptualize knowledge when meaning breaks down and when they attempt some sort of repair, with what comes to count as difficult for them in teaching and learning, with how they describe the qualities of knowledge in difficulty, and with how they characterize and perhaps work through problems of emotional significance in pedagogical encounters with others or with texts. Divided into fifteen topics, all of which begin with the heading "Thinking About," the document asks for discussion on the following kinds of experience: breakdowns with others, fights with knowledge, experiences of influence, aloneness, hostility, anxiety, and confusion in teaching and learning, encounters with authority, insufficient knowledge, and promises of knowledge, desires for relevance, privacy, and hiding, and views on obstacles to learning, writing, and speaking. Our "thought experiment" is rich in negativity, in the insistence that conflict provokes learning, and in the view that acquiring knowledge is a transferential relation characterized through the dynamic of resistance – an odd combination of new editions of old conflicts, of relations and fights with new and old forms of authority, as ambivalent and partial, and as charged by tonalities of love and hate.

Participants received the document a few days prior to the hour-long interview so that they could consider the project's interests as they reflected on their own experiences. Their thoughts on what they had read structured the discussion, and individuals were invited to comment upon, in any order, whatever aspects of the document they found interesting, and including the structure and contents of the "thought experiment." Only now do we understand this difficulty. While we had hoped to move people from discussing obstacles to teaching and learning to discussing obstacles to representing teaching and learning, the experiment was also, for everyone involved, an experience[5] that presented two kinds of obstacles: it was an obstacle to interpret and an obstacle to interpretation.

We asked participants to set their emotions and intellect side by side as they considered experiences of difficulty in knowledge. What they produced was a blend of plot-driven narratives and something akin to what Julia Kristeva (2000b, p. 3) calls 'pre-narrative envelopes': "This pre-narrative envelope amounts to an emotional experience, both physical and subjective based on the drives in an interpersonal context. In other words, it is a mental construct that emerges from the real world: an 'emerging property' of thought." Individuals tried to grapple with emotions that came first on their way to knowledge, but they were caught as well in trying to articulate this coherently. They often met an obstacle made from a collision between the force of their affect and the insistence of the idea itself. Frequently, talk about affective attachment to knowledge could not create enough distance for this knowledge to have an existence outside of the force of the emotional response. While knowledge did not cause their affective response, it surely became entangled in it. We attribute this to a constitutive difficulty of that other scene: what it means to create a narrative and consider narrative as both construction and as resistance to construction.

If the crisis of representation plays out during our efforts to narrate teaching and learning, our research on how difficult knowledge is encountered and made significant continues this dilemma. In reading our interview transcripts, we at first wondered who and what are represented in these stories. At the manifest level, individuals were offering stories of their identity and experience. And yet many of the narratives resisted the coherence brought by their identity claims because, in stories of breakdown, the ideal self cannot be represented. That is, while the content of the story tried to settle the meaning, the structure and dynamics of the story hinted at the intrusion of another time: when meaning had lost its valency and when phantasy both propelled and impeded the construction of knowledge. Here, language becomes implicated in the communicative performance: there may be no words or too many words. Kristeva's notion of the pre-narrative envelope suggests this dilemma: the force of conflict bothers the narrative's attempt to make closure.

When individuals narrate experience, they also express their affective investments in knowing and being known, in new editions of old educational conflicts, and in their fragile work of reconsidering what shall count as worthy and worthless in teaching and learning. These dynamics, as we have tried to show, also transformed and refined our research questions. We now offer fragments from five interviews and ask the following question: What can we learn about the crisis of representing teaching and learning from reading conflicted stories about encounters with knowledge?

PARTICIPANTS' CONSTRUCTIONS OF DIFFICULTY MADE FROM THE PROTOCOL

An undergraduate student expresses strong feelings in all of her narratives. Her relations to knowledge are described as marked by a strange combination of fear, hostility, and excitement. Early on in the interview, she offers an example of how she understands the transformative force of knowledge as a danger to the self:

> there's a lot of books I'm afraid to pick up because I am afraid it's going to shake my entire foundation. ... I believe in evolution ... and Darwin's theory of natural selection, and there's a book now which is called Darwin's Black Box, and it's in direct conflict with you know, and I'm afraid to pick it up cause now where's that going to leave me? ... A lot of things would just fall out from under me ... where would I be?

Conflict, in the stories this student tells about knowledge, is a vibrant force that animates her interest in learning and her ambivalence toward the power of knowledge to influence. Even though several of her stories take up knowledge as something to be warded off or something that might be pulled out from under her, she also expresses anger at those who withhold knowledge that she has come to deem important (such as knowledge about the cruel treatment of animals that we use for food). She recounts times when her own impatience and anger interfered with her capacity to make use of knowledge and classroom experience. She worries about using her knowledge to create crises of belief in others while at the same time remaining convinced that others need access to her point of view. Knowledge seems propelled by two phantasies. It might be a magical weapon that bestows control and power upon her when she is the one who possesses it. At the same time, being in possession of knowledge can leave her vulnerable: others might steal it away. If knowledge seems almost magical in its capacity to transform the self, it may be because knowledge returns to the self as belief that threatens to crumble. Belief may locate the self, but knowledge can make it disappear. Influence rests uneasily between knowledge and belief, threatening both.

Some of these dynamics repeat with another undergraduate student who begins to discuss "Times when an idea or a viewpoint prompted you to reconsider previous views." In creating this prompt, we had assumed that individuals would already be in a position of having worked through initial difficulties with contradictory ideas. But this narrative suggests the difficulties of trying to settle, once and for all, the place new knowledge occupies when old beliefs persist. This psychology major enrolled in a feminist course on mothering and motherhood and was surprised to encounter perspectives that called into question her previous theories of child development. Her old theories had not addressed the possibility that the child makes the parent: "... a lot of theories ... in psychology always tend to, well, how it's affecting the child, but little is there ever talked about how the parent is affected by the child." She came to value a feminist perspective but worried about what that would do to her old knowledge of psychology.

This student articulates two kinds of worries, both of which continue her anxiety over influencing others or being influenced. She has the impression that she would have to abandon all psychoanalytic theory, which she enjoys, in order to pursue new lines of inquiry made from feminist critique. While she views feminism as holding great relevance for her life and thought, she also finds value in the Freudian concept of the unconscious. She answers her unspoken question, "Must I choose?," with an anxiety that anticipates the consequences of fighting openly with the traditions of psychology. Is it the case that one can revise received ideas without also running into the received self?

> I'm beginning to think perhaps ... my imagination I know could run wild but just maybe little things like not, well not little things, but not getting grants for particular research ... "no, no, sorry, we can't ... give you money for that research or it's not going to be easy to publish." Even if I did get the money, it may not be published or received very well, and even though I know that I shouldn't really necessarily care what others think, I could see that opening me to a lot of scrutiny.

At the level of manifest content, we see an undergraduate quite puzzled about the daily work of academics. In a certain way her over-populated phantasy does contain what Freud (1937) observed as "a kernel of historical truth" with punishing institutions and arbitrary decisions. If at the manifest level, she may be intimating the dilemma between theoretical integrity and institutional recognition, at the latent level, the workings of knowledge are not easily discerned. As the conversation proceeds, her struggles with knowledge become ever more difficult to untangle from obstacles to learning. Just as the boy in Milner's story became the punishing teacher in order to deflect his own feelings of being misunderstood, this student rehearses the punishments of having to learn by insisting that her intuition is devalued; that if texts are difficult, they hold no meaning; and teachers bore her with their knowledge. At first glance, the influence of others is refused in all of these turns, yet her statement," I know that I shouldn't necessarily care what others think" may be a negation of the conflict. For if the thoughts of others mattered, what would happen to hers?

When she discussed her strategies for working through dense texts, the difference between obstacles to learning and obstacles to representing learning collapses:

> Don't give me that schmancy fancy kind of stuff. Give me, just give me the idea. And from there I like to work with a method. I don't like working with ideas.

As each kernel of her narrative suggests, one never just gets the idea at two levels: ideas are not transmitted, nor are they immediately available for use. But there is something more, and this returns us to what the protocol was asking. While the notion of influence appears throughout the protocol, we are beginning to appreciate just what a pervasive and threatening force it is to imagine the self as influenced by knowledge. Just as there is no original moment to interpretation, there is no original moment of influence. This student tries to divide knowledge as a means to control the force of influence. Perhaps if knowledge cannot be put in its proper place, it can return as a threat that divides the learner.

A professor of religious studies at the end of her career speaks eloquently of her own strategies for managing conflict and ambivalence made from influencing others and being influenced. While the professor began the interview by noting that many of the conflicts articulated in the protocol were once preoccupations for her as a beginning teacher and wondered if she had anything to offer our project, her use of the protocol moved from viewing the items as concrete events to recount to speculating on the difference between her and her students and her own self-difference as a scholar.

Towards the end of the interview she began to muse on her pedagogical strategies with students:

> I've been dealing with the Bible for a long time, and I do say to them, right at the beginning, in the introductory lectures, that I'm not dealing with this as a foundation of belief. I'm not dealing with it as the word of God at all. I'm dealing with it as a document that can be analysed from a mythic point of view, an anthropological point of view, a literary point of view, or whatever. And the fact that we analyse it in this way doesn't undermine it as a document that can underpin belief.

In this pedagogical encounter, the use of knowledge can temper and draw attention to the force of influence. She went on to define religious belief as "absolute knowledge" but qualified her scholarship as "relative," as "always in question." This allowance is made from her own revisions of herself in knowledge:

> I find it's hard when you've got this lovely theory and you have to give it up. I mean, I have been working through, and I do it all the time, slowly, slowly, on coming to a conclusion that something I wanted to prove very much, and I'm using the word believe, as a feminist I can no longer believe. I had to abandon, for instance, my idea, when I first started, [that] goddess stuff was the original. In the Palaeolithic times, there was once an original great goddess who was all over the place. Now I certainly abandoned that one, but it took me a long time, and now I'm coming to the conclusion that actually most religion is based in male/female complementarity. I'd have preferred not to have that either.

If we make a division between "lovely knowledge" and giving that up, and if we can hold in tension our preferences for what we want with what we find, we also see that a working distinction between belief and knowledge opens one to accept the losses that compose the force of learning. This professor brings us close to Milner's (1993, pp. 16-18) observations that scholarly creativity requires times when what is real and what are phantasies are allowed to mingle. The risk of siding with one to the exclusion of the other, as we saw in the previous interview, is to forget that both phantasy and reality organize our relation to knowledge and thus allow knowledge its affective force. In this narrative, difficult knowledge is what one makes from the ruins of one's lovely knowledge.

If lovely knowledge is knowledge that one loves, what does one love when lovely knowledge is lost? A recently-graduated PhD, about to begin her first university post, came to the interview with the protocol well underlined. She wanted to discuss her breakdowns in meaning experienced while constructing knowledge. These breakdowns concerned her thesis topic, her theoretical framework, and her relations with people in and outside the academy. As the narratives unfolded, distinctions between scholarship and people could not be maintained. This, in fact, is a feature we have noticed across the interviews. Part of their blurring had to do with questions of love. Her dissertation was an oral history with female members of a political and military separatist organization in Europe that has been fighting actively for territory and political autonomy for many years. Originally conceived as a feminist inquiry into women's experiences of civil war, the longer she interviewed for her dissertation project, the more she questioned the veracity of the study's framework:

> I guess if you want to think about people, in a way – how they were forcing me to re-evaluate constantly what I considered to be my own, the knowledge that I was coming with to the project – in a way that was constantly challenging. And I often asked myself what my theoretical framework and indeed what my kind of background as a academic, how that was relevant to the topic. One example, quite early on, maybe it was about a year into it actually, was a woman who said, "I don't think we're ready to listen to women's stories because men's stories haven't been told yet." And I thought, well, there are lots of books talking about men's experiences in this organization. … And she said, "no, I've never, I haven't read anything really that talks about my husband's experience, for example." Her husband had been killed by [state] authorities. And I really kind of got into a little exchange with her about her being an insider and me being an outsider, but it wasn't in any way an accusation at all. She just said straight out, "Well, you have an outside perspective and that's good, and I have an inside perspective and *that*'s good." But she was one of the few people who put that in a way, but not in a way that was about being politically correct, or me having to lay out my identity, but just a kind of way of saying, 'we have different perspectives, my knowledge is inside knowledge, and you are coming from the outside, and we need that, too.' And so I feel that my own idea about what had been written previously and whose voices need to be heard was actually being questioned by the very people I was interviewing who were not only saying, "Yes, we want our voices heard." They were also saying, "We actually want the men's voices heard too, and somebody's got to do that." It really hadn't actually occurred to me before I started talking to the women – because in most cases, they were very close to the men. They were.

This historian was surprised to confront the wishes of her (lovely) knowledge and its adequacy to bridge what these women had to say with what she imagined they should say. This confusion between wish and external reality, we are suggesting, is also a dilemma for our own research and may well be a constitutive feature of any research project. What is uncommon is not the observation but how one elaborates its specificity.

Our historian could appreciate the fact of difference in whose voice needs to be heard, but, as we shall see, voice is never monolithic and is only represented as such if it can be reduced to the difference that is standpoint. Left over when perspectives are exchanged, and what makes one voice more than it can say, is the residue of sexuality. Self-difference, that is, the difference within made from sexuality, is neither easily exchanged nor stabilized through standpoint:

> When I wanted to talk about prison experiences and [the women's] relationships [when they were] in prison, I thought, do I now come out? Is that a good thing to do? Is that relevant to the interview? Will that help draw something out of someone that maybe they wouldn't normally want to admit that they'd had sexual relationships with other women in prison. ... I do remember a couple of times thinking, Is this a strategy? ... And then of course this repeats itself when I'm teaching often.

In trying to speak about women in prison, our narrator presents her own phantasy of being in prison. The phantasy is erotic, but she disrupts it through her question, "Is this a strategy?" In the previous excerpt, the women forced her to rethink; in this excerpt, her phantasy provoked the thought of the otherness of the women. If research returns to the researcher the startling question of how to use one's own subjectivity – even as the method claims intersubjectivity – part of that work requires confronting the phantasies that render one's own knowledge so lovely and so demanding. The question that shadows her narratives might go something like this: what good is my knowledge here, to you? Differences in perspective may not turn the researcher away from lovely knowledge toward difficult knowledge. It takes a move from presentation to symbolization to allow the first question its affective force: As to my difference, if my knowledge is no good to me, what good am I to you? Difficult knowledge is made from the ruins of erotic ties.

We conclude our discussion of participants' construction of difficult knowledge with one interviewee's comments about the protocol. For this advanced doctoral student, there is something quite wrong with the distinction we have made between knowledge and teachers: she believes that the most important experience in learning is the relationship one has with the teacher and not with the knowledge. At first glance, her insistence seems close to Freud's (1914b, p. 242) question as to whether he was affected more by "a concern with the sciences that we were taught or with the personalities of the teachers."

> Part of what I noticed when I was reading [the protocol] was what prompts or what questions were particularly evocative of emotional responses and questions. Like number 12, 'Times when an encounter with knowledge made you feel ashamed, or guilty or fearful,' it is like or, 'when knowledge betrayed.' It is like part of what is at stake in the construction of knowledge is a kind of authority that is not always a positive authority. So that knowledge will betray you, that knowledge will make you feel bad about yourself or knowledge will make you feel alone. Or like the stranger in the classroom, or whatever. Just that, you know, they struck me as interesting frames, interesting ways of setting up knowledge as, at the same time, something outside the individual, outside of the subject, outside of the person. But also completely not outside of that either. So, infused with or over determined by

the people who actually participate in knowledge, therefore figure as teachers.

A bit later on, she tried to clarify for the interviewer her interest in what actually happens in classrooms, particularly English literature classrooms:

> We all supposedly read the book, and now we are going to talk about the relationship between all of those things and why the book is in the course and what is actually in the text that relates back to the sort of structuring mechanism of the course ... the sort of purpose that we are all there for. But that is separate from what ... actually happens. And so I would want arbitrarily and strategically to set those two processes up as quite different and bring the teacher back in, which ... the [protocol] questions don't do. They sort of reify knowledge and separate it from an individual or subjects in a classroom. And yet personify that at the same time, which I thought is a kind of interesting contradiction.

We read this narrative with Kristeva's (2000b) theme of the "pre-narrative envelope." Perhaps it cannot be otherwise because representing learning returns one's own ambivalence in learning. This individual returns to the protocol its own questions. Where does authority come from in learning? Is authority found in the epistemological framework of the course or the teacher who represents the framework for students? There is also a question about symbolization: Should knowledge be personified and accorded with such casual force? Does knowledge stand on its own, creating its own effects on students? Or, does the teacher personify both knowledge and pedagogy?

These questions, as we have tried to show in our interview extracts, represent something of the difficulty of trying to determine the difference between obstacles to learning and obstacles to representing learning. If obstacles to learning are made from all that impedes from the outside, obstacles to representing learning return us to the inside. Conflicted stories about learning enact this distinction on their way to becoming stories about conflict, desire and ambivalence in learning. The detour, as we have tried to suggest, is in the movement from presentation to symbolization.

RESEARCH AS PRELIMINARY LABOUR

Laplanche and Pontalis's (1973, p. 112) entry on 'deferred actions' notes three characteristics: an experience that cannot be assimilated into lived experience; a revision of the first event because of a second event; and uneven development. The term suggests a revision and a repetition of time because of a quality of experience itself: events are not and cannot be immediately assimilated into meaning, and this aspect disrupts the possibility that the meaning of an event is set by its chronological order. Indeed, chronology is lost and found through an affective logic, and experience may emerge from a kernel of incomprehensibility. Caruth (1996, p. 11) suggests that 'unclaimed experience,' can only be reclaimed via a confrontation "with the possibility of a history that is no longer straightforwardly referential (that is, no longer based on simple models of experience and reference)." We bring this insight to our research project to suggest that narratives and data work in a similar fashion. From the vantage of deferred action, we might also begin to reconsider the problem of how experiences or practices in the human sciences become the "preliminary labour" for both insight and blindness.

Indeed, as researchers we learn something of our own knowledge when we stumble in the face of our own persistent blind spots, and we collude with interviewees in their production of satisfying narratives that dance around the surprise of self-implication. We are reminded of the various ways in which Freud conceptualized resistance in his work with his early patients. Over time, he became dissatisfied with his earliest formulations that resistance to his treatment emanated from the unconscious, thus preserving intact repressed material. Instead, he began to understand resistance as a defence mounted by the ego so that the ego might continue to enjoy its carefully crafted and, in many ways, useful symptoms. He learned that treatment itself provoked resistance. We bring this clinical insight to the problem of representing research. Fink (1997, p. 9), a Lacanian analyst, names the stakes of learning in analysis when he argues that "in therapy, the analyst sidesteps the patient's demands, frustrates them, and ultimately tries to direct the patient to something he or she has never asked for." On this view, we might consider the time of our research as organized by the pull of mastery against the threat of fragmentation and the push to destabilize old forms of mastery and allow new thought. But for this to occur, research must be understood as provoking, not representing, knowledge. We have called this provocation "symbolization," itself a quality of difficult knowledge.

Our "thought experiment" may indeed ask everyone involved what no-one can be prepared to offer. Our efforts to frustrate the linear, cohesive narrative are paradoxically familiar and strange, desired and unasked for. But if the crisis of representation is to become a central dynamic in any research endeavour, then the argument over the difference between obstacles to research and obstacles to representing research becomes part of the preliminary labour of constructions in research, a labour that is also a symptom of the crisis in representation. The paradoxical qualities of obstacles ushered into play by our "thought experiment" and the difficulty of deciding what shall count as an obstacle to experience and what might be better described as an obstacle to narration have also had a curious effect on this chapter. The metaphor of trauma turns out to be very difficult to hold in abeyance notwithstanding our earlier efforts to abandon it. Trauma returns, however, with a difference. The kernel of trauma that we have encountered in our theoretical investments, our stories of clinical experience, our protocol, and our interviews is not tied to models of pathology. Rather it emerges as a metaphor for the pushes and pulls between knowing and being known, between phantasy and reality, between one's early history of learning and one's haunted present of learning, and between experience and its narration. Our three psychoanalytic concepts – deferred action, transference, and symbolization – have helped us symbolize the experience and event of our research in ways that exceed identity as they move us towards these new kinds of relations to characterize this more ordinary yet ubiquitous trauma of having to learn.

NOTES

[1] We adhere to a spelling of fantasy that is close to its German origins in 'Phantasie' to signal the range of modes of fantasy that are worked with in psychoanalysis and that exceed the associations common to the English 'fantasy.' See Laplanche and Pontalis (1973, pp. 314-319) for a discussion of the distinctions among "conscious phantasies or daydreams, unconscious phantasies like those recovered by analysis as the structures underlying a manifest content, and primal phantasies" (p. 314). It is with the second mode we are primarily concerned in this essay.

[2] We conducted, with graduate students associated with our project, fifty in-depth interviews with faculty and students.

[3] Hermstein Smith's (1997) model of cognitive dissonance comes close to describing the disorganizing features of encounters with new knowledge we are suggesting here:

> an impression of inescapable noise or acute disorder, a rush of adrenalin, sensations of alarm, a sense of unbalance or chaos, residual feelings of nausea and anxiety. These are the forms of bodily distress that occur when one's imagined, taken-for-granted sense of how certain things are – and thus presumably will be and in some sense *should* be – is suddenly or insistently confronted by something very much at odds with it. Perceptually, it is the wave of vertigo one may experience at an unexpected sight. (p. xiv)

Where we depart from this model of cognitive dissonance is in highlighting uncanny qualities, when one attempts to make sense, not just of the unexpected, but what was, in fact, anticipated through the lens of anxiety. In bringing the concept of the uncanny to cognitive dissonance, we can begin to consider how even the familiar can become a source of difficulty. For some other approaches to emotional conflict in learning, see also Bogdan et al. (2000) and Sedgwick and Frank's (1995) introduction to the psychological theories of Sylvan Tomkins.

[4] If transference organizes and disorganizes experience at the same time, Gallop's (1997) discussion of how she came to be accused of sexual harassment suggests the difficulty of institutional efforts to make sense of it. Gallop, too, has trouble because her story can only be narrated in the time of deferred action: "But I won't be telling what happened chronologically; the story will appear broken into pieces and out of order" (p. 6). One piece of her story concerned whether there can be pedagogical uses of the transference. Gallop's argument to university officials is that the transference is a central quality of her pedagogical relation to students, but their response to her has no sympathy: "In the official report on my case, the university recommends that in the future I should stop working with any student who has such a transference unto me. Which means I would not work with any student who really believed I had something important to teach her" (p. 56).

[5] Laplanche, in his discussion of the human being as a self-theorizing or self-symbolizing being, argues that "all real theorizing is an experiment and an experience which necessarily involves the researcher" (1989, p. 12-13). He is thinking here of Freud's use of his own dreams and observations as the basis from which to develop psychoanalytic theory. We had not anticipated the ways in which our experiment not only inquired into experience; it also constituted its own experience.

REFERENCES

Appel, S. (Ed.). (1999). *Psychoanalysis and pedagogy*. Westport, CT: Bergin & Garvey.
Bass, A. (2001). *Difference and disavowal: the trauma of eros*. Stanford, CA: Stanford University Press.

Bloom, L. (1998). *Under the sign of hope: Feminist methodology and narrative interpretation.* Albany, NY: State University of New York Press.

Bogdan, D., Cunningham, J. E., & Davis, H. E. (2000). Reintegrating sensibility: Situated knowledges and embodied readers. *New Literary History: Philosophical and Rhetorical Inquiries, 31,* 476-507.

Bollas, C. (1999). *The mystery of things.* London: Routledge.

Britzman, D. P. (1998). *Lost subjects, contested objects: Toward a psychoanalytic inquiry of learning.* Albany, NY: State University of New York Press.

Britzman, D. P. (2000). If the story cannot end: deferred action, ambivalence and difficult knowledge. In R. I. Simon, S. Rosenberg, & C. Eppert (Eds.), *Between hope and despair: Pedagogy and the remembrance of historical trauma* (pp. 27-56). Lanham, MD: Rowman & Littlefield.

Britzman, D. P., & Pitt, A. J. (1996). Pedagogy and transference: Casting the past of learning into the presence of teaching. *Theory Into Practice, 2,* 117-123.

Britzman, D. P., & Pitt, A. (2004). Pedagogy and clinical knowledge: Some psychoanalytic observations on losing and refinding significance. *JAC: A Quarterly Journal for the Interdisciplinary Study of Rhetoric, Writing, Multiple Literacies and Politics, 24,* 353-374.

Caruth, C. (1996). *Unclaimed experience, trauma, narrative, and history.* Baltimore & London: John Hopkins University Press.

Cheng, A. A. (2001). *The melancholy of race: Psychoanalysis, assimilation, and hidden grief.* Oxford: Oxford University Press.

Chodorow, N. J. (1999). *Power of feelings: Personal meaning in psychoanalysis, gender and culture.* New Haven: Yale University Press.

Code, L. (1991). *What can she know?: Femininity in the construction of knowledge.* Ithaca, NY: Cornell University Press.

Ellsworth, E. (1997). *Teaching positions: Difference, pedagogy and the power of address.* New York & London: Teachers College Press.

Felman, S. (1992). Education and crisis, or the vicissitudes of teaching. In S. Felman & D. Laub (Eds.), *Testimony: Crises of witnessing in literature, psychoanalysis, and history* (pp. 1-56). New York: Routledge.

Felman, S., & Laub, D. (Eds.). (1992). *Testimony: Crises of witnessing in literature, psychoanalysis, and history.* New York: Routledge.

Fink, B. (1997). *A clinical introduction to Lacanian psychoanalysis: Theory and technique.* Cambridge, MA & London: Harvard University Press.

Freud, S. (1953-1974). *The standard edition of the complete psychological works of Sigmund Freud* (J. Strachey in collaboration with A. Freud, assisted by A. Strachey & Alan Tyson, Eds.& Trans.). 24 Vols. London: Hogarth Press & Institute for Psychoanalysis.

Freud, S. (1900). Interpretation of dreams (2nd part). *Standard Edition, 5,* 339-610.

Freud, S. (1914a). Remembering, repeating and working through (Further recommendations on the technique of psycho-analysis II). *Standard Edition, 12,* 145-156.

Freud, S. (1914b). Some reflections on schoolboy psychology. *Standard Edition, 13,* 241-244.

Freud, S. (1937). Constructions in analysis. *Standard Edition, 23,* 255-269.

Gallop, J. (1997). *Feminist accused of sexual harassment.* Durham: Duke University Press.

Green A. (2000). *Chains of eros: The sexual in psychoanalysis* (L. Thurston, Trans.). London: Rebus Press.

Herrnstein Smith, B. (1997). *Belief and resistance: dynamics of contemporary intellectual controversy.* Cambridge: Harvard University Press.

Kohon, G. (1999). *No lost certainties to be recovered.* London: Karnac Books.

Kristeva, J. (2000a). *The sense and non-sense of revolt: The powers and limits of psychoanalysis* (J. Herman, Trans.). New York: Columbia Press.

Kristeva, J. (2000b). From symbols to flesh: The polymorphous destiny of narration. *The International Journal of Psychoanalysis, 81,* 771.

Laplanche, J. (1989). *New foundations for psychoanalysis* (D. Macey, Trans.). Oxford: Basil Blackwell.

Laplanche, J. & Pontalis, J.-B (1973.) *The language of psycho-analysis* (D.Nicholson-Smith, Trans.). New York: Norton.

Lather, P. (2000). Drawing the line at angels: Working the ruins of feminist ethnography. In E. St. Pierre & W. Pillow (Eds.), *Working the ruins: Feminist poststructural theory and methods in education*, (pp. 284-311). New York: Routledge.

Lather, P. (2001). Postbook: working the ruins of feminist ethnography. *Signs, 27*.

Laws, C., & Davies, B. (2000). Poststructuralist theory in practice: working with "behaviorally disturbed" children. *International Journal of Qualitative Studies in Education, 13*, 205-221.

Little, M. I. (1990). *Psychotic anxieties and containment: a personal record of an analysis with winnicott*. Northgate, NJ: Jason Aronson Inc.

Lyotard, J.-F. (1987). *The postmodern condition: A report on knowledge* (G. Bennington & B. Masami, Trans.). Manchester: Manchester University Press.

Mannoni, M. (1999). *Separation and creativity: Refinding the lost language of childhood* (S. Fairfield, Trans.). New York: The Other Press.

Martin, B. (1997). Success and its failures. *Differences: A Journal of Feminist Cultural Studies, 9*, 102-131.

McCarthy, C., & Crichlow, W. (Eds.). (1993). *Race, identity and representation in education*. New York: Routledge.

Milner, M. (1993). The role of illusion in symbol formation. In P. L. Rudnytsky (Ed.), *Transitional bjects and potential spaces: Literary uses of D. W. Winnicott* (pp. 13-39). New York: Columbia University Press.

Phillips, J. (1998). The fissure of authority: Violence in the acquisition of knowledge. In L. Stonebridge & J. Phillips (Eds.), *Reading Melanie Klein* (pp. 160-178). London & New York: Routledge.

Pinar, W. (Ed.). (1998). *Queer theory in education*. Mahwah, NJ: Lawrence Erlbaum Associates.

Pinar, W. (Ed.) (2001). *The gender of racial politics and violence in America: Lynching, prison rape, and the crisis of masculinity*. New York: Peter Lang.

Pitt, A. J. (2000). Hide and seek: The play of the personal in education. *Changing English: Studies in Reading and Culture, 7*, 65-74.

Readings, B. (1996). *The university in ruins*. Cambridge: Harvard University Press.

Rhedding-Jones, J. (2000). The other girls: Culture, psychoanalytic theories and writing. *International Journal of Qualitative Studies in Education, 13*, 263-279.

Segal, H. (1997). On symbolism. In *Psychoanalysis, literature and war: Papers 1972-1995* (pp. 41-63). London & New York: Routledge.

Segwick, E., & Frank, A. (Eds.). (1995). *Shame and its sisters: A Silvan Tomkins reader*. Durham & London: Duke University Press.

Simon, R., Rosenberg, S., & Eppert, C. (Eds.). (2000). *Between hope and despair: Pedagogy and the remembrance of historical trauma*. Lanham, NJ: Rowman & Littlefield.

St. Pierre, E., & Pillow, W. (Eds.). (2000). *Working the ruins: Feminist poststructural theory and methods in education*. New York: Routledge.

Steiner, G. (1980). On difficulty (1978). In *On difficulty and other essays* (pp. 18-47). Oxford: Oxford University Press.

Talburt, S. (2000). *Subject to identity: Knowledge, sexuality, and academic practices in higher education*. Albany: State University of New York Press.

Todd, S. (2001). Bringing more than I contain: Ethics, curriculum, and the pedagogical demand for altered egos. *Journal of Curriculum Studies, 33*, 431-450.

Volosinov, V. N. (1986). *Marxism and the philosophy of language* (L. Matejka & I. R. Titnuk, Trans.). Cambridge: Harvard University Press.

Winnicott, D. W. (1972). *Playing and reality*. London & New York: Routledge.

Yon, D. (2000). *Elusive culture: Schooling, race, and identity in global times*. Albany, NY: SUNY.

Young, R. M. (1994). *Mental space*. London: Process Press.

APPENDIX A: INTERVIEW PROTOCOL: DIFFICULT KNOWLEDGE PROJECT

*Designed by Professors Deborah Britzman and Alice Pitt,
Faculty of Education, York University*

As described in the letter of informed consent, we are providing you, prior to the actual interview, a copy of our interview protocol. Our purpose is doing so is to familiarize you with the conceptual geography of the project and to allow you to think about your learning and teaching prior to the actual interview. At the time of the interview, you will be asked to describe yourself in any way you choose and then begin by discussing any of the "thought prompts" discussed below.

This interview is organized around the large question, what sorts of knowledge and what kinds of experiences are difficult in teaching and learning in university classrooms. We are also interested in times when learning is rehearsed in preparing for the classroom and times when knowledge is reflected upon after classroom encounters. We are interested in how people currently involved in university settings describe and narrate their difficulties with knowledge. Most generally, what counts for you as difficult knowledge? What happens to knowledge in times of difficulties? We are also exploring the question, what makes knowledge difficult in teaching and learning. We are interested in having you explore times in your university studies or teaching where you noticed difficulties for yourself. We are also interested in your narratives of times when meanings have broken down in learning and teaching and times where you attempt some sort of repair in making meanings.

To help you consider the sorts of experiences we are interested in, we offer the following "prompts" for you to think about prior to the interview. During the interview we will ask you to select and speak to whatever prompt that allows you to narrate experiences on difficult knowledge for you. At the end of the interview, we will also ask for your thoughts about the prompts for your experiences.

1. Thinking about breakdowns in encounters with others:
Times when you felt misunderstood in the classroom
Times when you felt let down or disappointed by others
Times when someone's response felt disappointing
Times when you tried to persuade others and were not successful

2. Thinking about fighting with knowledge:
Times when you encountered ideas that initially and perhaps still bother you
Times when you worried about knowledge
Times when your ideas and your feelings were at odds with each other
Times when you could not separate the good from the bad in knowledge

3. Thinking about reconsidering knowledge:
Times when an idea or viewpoint prompted you to reconsider previous views

Times when you questioned the ways you were seeing things
Times when you fell out of love with an idea or theory
Times when your identity as a teacher or student became irrelevant
Times when you created new conditions for learning and teaching

4. Thinking about experiences of influence:
Times when you misunderstood others
Times when empathy was tried and failed
Times when the advice of others felt meaningless
Times when you decided you needed to ask for help
Times where you wanted to explain something but words failed you or when you could not find the right words
Times when you received criticism that was difficult to listen to
Times when you felt overly susceptible to the influences of others
Times when you tried to help others
Times when your intuitive response failed
Times when the help you gave proved unhelpful

5. Thinking about experiences of aloneness with others:
Times you felt alienated in the classroom
Times when you needed help but could not ask
Times when you felt lonely in the classroom or in learning
Times when you felt like a stranger in the classroom

6. Thinking about experiences of confusion:
Times when you realized you were mistaken but could not turn back
Times when you felt lost or were falling behind
Times when learning about the world seemed to ask a great deal from you
?Times when you worked through confusion
Times when you felt you were on the wrong track
Times when knowledge felt too exciting
Times when you felt ambivalent about knowledge
Times when knowledge overwhelmed you

7. Thinking about encounters with insufficient knowledge:
Times when knowledge felt insufficient
Times when knowledge seemed suspicious
Times when knowledge seemed absurd
Times when knowledge betrayed you
Times when knowledge felt empty
Times when knowledge did not seem to count
Times when the purposes of your knowledge lost focus
Times when you had difficulty using knowledge
Times when an idea felt threatening or incomprehensible
Times when you were bored by knowledge

8. Thinking about encounters with the promise of knowledge:
Times when your returned to read a book and found something unexpected in the second reading
Times when you fell in love with an idea or theory
Times when knowledge felt promising
Times when you felt represented in learning and teaching
Times when you did not care whether you were represented
Times when you discovered you were deceiving yourself
Times when you have been asked a question that surprised you and pushed you to consider something about yourself that you had not previously considered

9. Thinking about encounters with the promise of learning:
Times when difficulties could be tolerated and learned from
Times when you were excited in the classroom
Times when you felt the force of surprise in learning or teaching
Times when you dramatically changed your mind
Times when your practices of learning dramatically changed
Times when you rethought your own self knowledge

10. Thinking about experiences of hostility:
Times when you felt attacked or when you wished you could express hostility
Times when you used knowledge to shock others
Times when you refused to read a particular text or participate in a particular discussion
Times when you wished for the teacher's or student's removal
Times when the present felt repetitious
Times when you could not attach to ideas
Times when books made you angry
Times when you became defensive toward ideas or others
Times when you had nothing to say

11. Thinking about encounters with authority:
Times when you recognized the constraints of the institution upon your learning and teaching
Times when you became aware of the history of your learning practices
Times when your identity as student and or teacher became irrelevant
Times when authority could not be located
Times when you questioned authority
Times when your own authority was questioned by others
Times when evaluation felt meaningless or inadequate

12. Thinking about encounters with anxiety:
Times when you felt remorse in teaching and learning
Times when you disappointed yourself

Times when knowledge embarrassed you
Times when an encounter with knowledge made you feel ashamed
Times when an encounter with knowledge made you feel guilty
Times when an encounter with knowledge made you feel fearful

13. Thinking about encounters with relevance:
Times when it was difficult to distinguish the important from the unimportant
Times when theory and practice seemed in profound conflict
Times when you noticed that your ideas were irrelevant
Times when what you thought was important was considered trivial
Times when something you learned altered other knowledge you held
Times when you discovered you had been deceived by the absence of knowledge
Times when you became dissatisfied with school knowledge

14. Thinking about experiences of time in learning and teaching:
Times when you felt as if your response in the present was really about something that happened in the past
Times when your learning occurred much later than the lesson
Times when your fantasies or rehearsals about teaching or learning failed you
Times when you began to question what you were learning
Times when you began to question why you were learning
Times when teaching or learning felt fragmented

15. Thinking about encounters with obstacles:
Times when your writing was blocked
Times when your reading was blocked
Times when your speaking with others was blocked
Times when you lost your interest
A different kind of question: Thinking about your story, how would you describe the qualities of knowledge and where would you put the difficulty?

III REFLECTIONS: AFTER DOING THE RESEARCH

PHIL FRANCIS CARSPECKEN

20. LIMITS OF KNOWLEDGE IN THE PHYSICAL SCIENCES

This chapter is an excerpt from a longer essay I have written on the limits of knowledge in both the physical and human sciences (Carspecken, forthcoming). The longer essay itself is a preliminary articulation of findings from what is a large on-going project. What the reader will find here is my initial investigation of physical science, oriented specifically toward revealing conditions that simultaneously make physical science *possible* and *limit* the type of knowledge it can produce.

The arguments developed and the conclusions made in this excerpt are further expanded within the larger essay. We will find, by the end of this excerpt, that transcendental argumentation and the concept of reflection are of interest to us. But we will not have fully explored what these two related things are. That exploration occurs in the next major portion of the larger work. Reflection and the transcendental inference turn out to be features of the conditions within which *human* sciences operate. They are features of intersubjectivity, in my developing a theory of that. Yet another section of the larger work explores intersubjectivity itself more fully. Kantian insights that one will find in use within this excerpt are there explained in ways that differ very much from Kantian philosophy. The exploration of intersubjectivity reveals conditions that enable and yet constrain *human* sciences in ways analogous to the enabling and limiting conditions discussed in this excerpt. But the limiting and enabling conditions of the human sciences have a different ontological and epistemological status from those in play with physical science. Finally, the longer essay concludes with a section on "what lies beyond the narrative horizon": a look at the implications that limits to knowledge in both physical and human science entail. Once the full essay has been read various points and arguments made in its different sections, including this section on physical science, take on additional significance and meaning. Obviously that circling / spiralling feature of the full essay's structure is lost with the publication of one section in isolation.

The exploration of limits to knowledge in the physical sciences that we have below stands on its own in many respects. Its relevance to today resides in the recent growth of a particularly virulent form of scientistic ideology. Scientism is the belief that all knowledge must take the form it has in the physical sciences if it is to be knowledge at all. This ideology has been around for a long time, but for approximately eight years now, in the United States and other nations as well, we have seen new and growing efforts to suspend funding for any social research that does not use experimental methods. The argument is that only experimental methods can determine "what works," and thus only this sort of research produces genuine "knowledge." An examination of the limits to knowledge in physical science should be at least helpful in the battle against scientism. In my longer work the critique of physical science to be found below leads directly into an elucidation of what is distinctive about inquiry in the social sciences – including what it can tell us that scientistic methods cannot.

THE "THEORY OF EVERYTHING"

A special issue of *Scientific American*, published in September of 2004, had on its cover:

Beyond Einstein
Toward a theory of everything
Energy that expands the cosmos
Different physics, infinite universes
And more ...

It is the blurb, "toward a theory of everything," that most captures the concerns of this chapter. The theory of everything, or T.O.E., has acquired slogan status in recent writings and television programs on string theory, oriented to the general public. It is used frequently by Brian Green in his three-part Nova program on strings, and crops up many times as well in his very popular book, *The Elegant Universe* (Green 2003). T.O.E. has been referred to by physicists and other scientists in their more technical publications for about twenty years (e.g., see Davies 2004, p. 17, and Ellis 2004, p. 632). Now it is a phrase known to many outside the physics community as well. Brian Green writes:

> For the first time in the history of physics we ... have a framework with the capacity to explain every fundamental feature upon which the universe is constructed. For this reason string theory is sometimes described as possibly being the "theory of everything" (T.O.E.) or the "ultimate" or "final" theory. These grandiose descriptive terms are meant to signify the deepest possible theory of physics—a theory that underlies all others, one that does not require or even allow for a deeper explanatory base. (2003, p. 16)

Methodological Naturalism and Reductionism

If a theory of everything really could explain *everything*, then could it explain its own production as a theory? In other words, would it form the basis at least of a theory of knowledge? An answer of "yes" would commit one to the philosophical stance of methodological naturalism which is the idea that the methods and logic of physical science exhaust all methods and logic for attaining knowledge of any kind. Knowledge of any type will be fundamentally the same with respect to how it is gained or produced, with respect to its basic form, its principles of acquisition, and its principles of verification. An answer of "yes" would also entail a commitment to reductionism whereby sociology, psychology, ethics, and other domains of inquiry into human phenomena would be proved reducible to biology, biochemistry, chemistry and finally physics. An answer of "no," on the other hand, would entail challenges to the concept of knowledge that we find in methodological naturalism, and put reductionism into doubt.

This question of whether a physical theory of everything could explain itself has much relevance to the so-called human sciences: social and cultural inquiry, and psychology. If a theory of everything, which is from start to finish a physical theory, could explain itself then methodological naturalism would be vindicated and social science really should go in the direction that many funding and government agencies are currently trying to push it (see Delandshere 2002, 2005). Experimental methods should then indeed be the "gold standard" for social and psychological science (Delandshere 2005). Research should be focused solely on "what works," or at least on what can be predicted given certain measurable initial conditions and a measurable intervention. Qualitative social research would no doubt have a place in the picture but as something to use in exploratory and descriptive ways. Qualitative research would ask questions, collect data, and suggest answers in a way that could in principle always be translated into the vocabulary of measurable initial conditions, treatments, and outcomes. Values, morals, states of awareness, intentions and the like would become things to study in forms analogous to physical systems, once they are objectivated in observational terms. They would take their place within the language of inquiry solely in the position of references rather than as terms intimately bound up with forms of inference and reasoning distinguished from those used in the natural sciences.

Scientism

Of course, there is some tongue-in-cheek at play when physicists speak or write about the T.O.E. However, the mild sense of facetiousness we find in uses of the phrase do *not* allude to doubts about methodological naturalism and reductionism. What is alluded to is rather such things as the question of whether any physical theory could provide its own initial conditions – a question that could eventually be answered "yes" or "no" solely *within* the framework of inquiry used by natural science. And when it comes to popular works on science for the "lay person" there isn't even this slight sense of the facetious. Most practicing scientists who write for the general public today appear to believe in methodological naturalism and the possibility of reducing all the sciences, level by level, to the principles of physics. The philosophical stances of naturalism and reductionism are ideologies when they are simply assumed to be true. Taken together we have the belief that all knowledge must have the form of knowledge it has in the physical sciences. Anything else will not be knowledge at all. This belief has often been called "scientism" and it pervades our culture today with potentially dire consequences for the social sciences (see for example, Schwandt 2002).

LIMITS TO EMPIRICAL KNOWLEDGE

There are many good reasons for doubt when it comes to a scientific theory of everything and the most significant of these reasons have to do with the idea of *necessary* limits to types of knowledge. These are limits that work in two ways: 1) they *enable* a method of inquiry with respect to an associated domain of phenomena; 2) they set aside other domains of phenomena which they *depend upon* and yet which cannot be studied with the method of inquiry they enable. In other words, limits of this type simultaneously make a domain of inquiry *possible* and *prohibit* it from accessing other domains.

This understanding of limits to knowledge, as both enabling and constraining conditions, is apparently lost on most physicists and other scientists writing about their field for the general public. The physicist and Nobel Laureate Steven Weinberg has given lectures and written articles about the limits to scientific knowledge which will be helpful to our explorations in this essay. His book of 2001, *Facing Up; Science and its Cultural Adversaries,* is a collection of such essays, many of them originally published in the *New York Review of Books* to answer challenges made by postmodern and critical theorists to the ideology of scientism. His article on the Sokal Hoax is probably well known to many readers of this paper (for the hoax, see Sokal, 1996a, 1996b). Weinberg's articles have served an excellent purpose by correcting a number of misunderstandings of contemporary physics, and invalid inferences that have been made from contemporary physics to the social sciences, by people working in our own field of social and methodological theory.

Reading Weinberg is illuminating both for an initial grasp of where limits to knowledge present themselves in theoretical physics and for gleaning an idea of how the scientific community (in so far as Weinberg is representative) tends to understand "limits." I have found three categories of limit within Weinberg's writings. One is a large category that has already been mentioned; a category pertaining to initial conditions for the theory of the expansion of the universe. Another category concerns the question of whether a physical theory could explain consciousness. And a third category concerns the observer-observed relation as this manifests in quantum physics. All three categories are related to the question of whether a theory of everything could explain itself. I will take them one at a time in an effort to find what they may tell us about limits to knowledge.

1. Could Initial Conditions Be Derived From a Fundamental Theory of Physics?

The problem of initial conditions is of interest to us here only because it illuminates more general issues about physical theories. First let's understand the problem. Certain initial quantities and ratios between quantities in our universe must be as they are or our universe would be radically different. The ratio of matter to antimatter soon after the big bang is an example. In big bang theory, at about 10^{-12} second after the "nominal moment of infinite temperature":

> The temperature of the universe had dropped by then to about 10^{15} degrees, cool enough for us to apply our present physical theories. At these temperatures the universe would have been filled with a gas consisting of all the types of particles known to higher energy nuclear physics, together with their antiparticles, continually being annihilated and created in their collisions. As the universe continued to expand and cool, creation became slower than annihilation, and almost all the particles and antiparticles disappeared. If there had not been a small excess of electrons over antielectrons, and quarks over antiquarks, then ordinary particles like electrons and quarks would be virtually absent in the universe today. It is this early excess of matter over antimatter, estimated as one part in about 10^{10}, that survived to form light atomic nuclei three minutes later, then after a million years to form atoms and later to be cooked to heavier elements in stars, ultimately to provide the material out of which life would arise. (Weinberg 2001, pp. 72-73)

There are other quantities and other initial conditions and "input parameters" (Green 2003, p. 143) to proposed fundamental theories of physics that are hard to explain though they are essential for the existence of the universe as we find it. Most can be calculated but not *derived* from the standard model of particle physics and other scientific theories. String theory is considered a strong possible candidate for the Theory of Everything because many of these initial conditions and quantities *can* be derived from it. And in addition, string theory seems capable of combining general relativity theory and quantum theory which is something that the standard model in particle physics cannot do. Brian Green, in his book *The Elegant Universe*, explains that string theory already makes deductively derivable many constants that the standard model of particle physics had to simply use as inputs. In terms of a full cosmological theory Green admits:

> We don't know whether the question of determining the initial conditions is one that is even sensible to ask or whether – like asking general relativity to give insight into how hard you happened to toss a ball in the air – it is a question that lies forever beyond the grasp of any theory. Valiant attempts by physicists such as Hawking and James Hartle of the University of California at Santa Barbara have tried to bring the question of cosmological initial conditions within the umbrella of physical theory, but all such attempts remain inconclusive. ... our cosmological understanding is, at present, just too primitive to determine whether our candidate 'theory of everything' truly lives up to its name and determines its own cosmological initial conditions, thereby elevating them to the status of physical law. (2003, p. 366)

As string theory is further developed it *could* perhaps become the Theory of Everything such that it does explain all initial quantities and conditions we find in the universe and, as we see, there is work being done at this time toward this end. What is philosophically of interest is the *idea* of a theory of everything – of what would have to be accomplished to arrive at one and what such a theory would look like in general terms.

The quest for ultimate substance: Scientific models and transcendent postulates
Now let's look a little closer at what this idea of a final theory could mean. The standard model of particle physics has to use specific quantities, such as the mass of twelve fundamental particles (see Green 2003, p. 9) as in-puts that come from outside the model itself. Part of the impetus to develop string theory is to reduce twelve to one:

> String theory alters this picture radically by declaring that the 'stuff' of all matter and forces is the *same*. Each elementary particle is composed of a single string – that is, each particle *is* a single string – and all strings are absolutely identical. Differences between the particles arise because their respective strings undergo different resonant vibrational patterns. What appear to be different elementary particles are actually different 'notes' on a fundamental string. The universe – being composed of an enormous number of these vibrating strings – is akin to a cosmic symphony. (Green 2003, p. 146)

Strings can be thought of as the ultimate "stuff" from which everything else comes and to which everything else can be reduced for explanatory purposes. It is the idea of an ultimate *substance*, despite modifications made to everyday notions of "stuff" in scientific models. One way to have a theory of everything would be to provide evidence for the claim that all things are really just different forms and states of a single substance that underlies them. There must then also be a way to explain different forms and states as well as changes between them. String theory in fact conforms well to the basic idea of the substance/accident or substance/property distinction that has long been discussed in philosophy. Strings occupy the position of substance and the 12 fundamental particles of the standard model occupy the position of the most basic sorts of properties, because these 12 fundamental particles are interpreted in terms of different resonances of the same material: strings.

What is significant about this? Well, is it possible to produce an ultimate theory, a fundamental theory of physics that could explain its own initial conditions (and also in some way explain itself, through reductionism as explored below) *without* invoking a concept of substance? "Substance" is a metaphor that is extended and abstracted from in physics to produce such concepts as matter, fields, energy, and elementary particles. The *sense* these concepts have to us intuitively depend upon a concept of substance, even though it has undergone various refinements and extensions to guide the formulation of mathematical models. Substance is something like a conceptually necessary concept for trying to produce a theory about anything objective.

We really don't have to emphasize "substance" too much because there are other basic concepts at work in the very idea of a fundamental theory. There is the concept of "sameness" and the concept of "difference," for example. There is of course "space" and "time" which seem to be conceptually necessary for any physical theory even though they can be altered from traditional conceptualizations to a great extent as has happened with general relativity theory (I discuss this more in the longer essay).

But let's take substance as our example here because strings certainly suggest it. Now, some readers may already be thinking that the concept of "string" in physics is not tied to its metaphor of origin because all that physicists are really interested in are the mathematical models that represent strings and the measurements and predictions they make possible. But I will soon argue against this objection in the section on realism versus positivism. Meanwhile, where did the idea of "substance" come from? "Substance" underlies concepts that are postulated as *transcendent entities* in scientific models. We cannot perceive strings, quarks, fields and the like but we conceive of them as small bits of substance (strings) or particles of substance (quarks) or as something that has spatial spread without having material (fields: an abstraction from "substance") and in each case we have concepts whose sense in some way depends upon one basic idea: substance.

The case of the concept of "field" is particularly illuminating here. It was first used very consciously as a metaphor for magnetic and electrical phenomena. When magnetically active substances were placed in proximity to each other it was apparent that attractive and repulsive forces were in play, following an inverse square law similar to that of gravitational force. The "lines of force" studied form in a shape that resembles a "field." But physicists believed that the phenomena were analogous to Newton's theory of gravity whereby forces form only when the entities that so interact are placed in proximity. "Field" was used consciously as a metaphor to help with keeping track of where objects would align but not as something that "really existed." Then Maxwell's work, building on work of Faraday, suggested that fields did have a physical reality to them such that one field could sort of "push" another field into being – that is what led to the idea of light being an electromagnetic wave requiring no other medium than the fields that propagate by creating new fields progressively in one direction, in a vacuum. A concept that began as simply a model to help with record keeping ended up being a full transcendental postulate. Fields were thought of as a sort of "substance" as soon as they were accorded physical reality (see Penrose 1989, p. 184-5). Prior to that, substance was an implicit metaphor underlying that of "field," but "field" was employed consciously as only a metaphor to aid in producing mathematical models.

Kant's idea of *a priori* concepts could be involved in this situation [by drawing attention to metaphors in my analysis I will depart from Kant in some important ways. For Kant on substance see (Kant 1965, p. 113, A 80 / B 106)]. Where did the idea of substance come from, and could it be something like an *a priori* category, which is to say a category that is necessary for experience but not given through experience?

Initially we would not be too attracted by an *a priori* category in the case of substance because "substance" has a *history* in philosophy that we can trace back to Plato and Aristotle and follow forward through Locke, Berkeley, Spinoza, and

Kant. When examining the history of the concept its basis in metaphor seems clear. For Aristotle, substance (*ousia*) referred to things that exist in themselves: particular beings. This is related to the notion of *persistence*. After Aristotle substance acquired the meaning of that which exists and persists behind appearances (Hamlyn 1984, p. 60). The Latin etymology of the word suggests something existing behind the properties and accidents that appear in perception. This was the sense that Locke gave to the term: it is more like external being-in-general than particular being; that which stands beneath the properties of particular things that we experience. We are used to thinking of the *a priori* as concepts and conditions that are prior to experience and hence a history that displays the evolving metaphorical basis for a concept would seem to run counter to the idea of *a priori* concepts. What is suggested is perhaps that experience is simply always interpreted and in the course of time certain interpretative metaphors become sedimented as features of common sense.

Yet, Kantian insights are in fact relevant here. Kant distinguished between the transcendental, as in "transcendental logic," and the transcendent. The latter are postulated supersensible entities and processes that Kant found illegitimate in the quest for valid knowledge. Knowledge must be based on experience, both Kant and the empiricists agreed on this. Transcendent entities are never items within experience and yet, he believed, they are constructed with categories that *are* applied to experience legitimately. Hence transcendent metaphysics for Kant was the result of improperly employing categories of the human understanding; using them without sensory input. These categories were *a priori* for Kant, but with a careful appropriation of Kantian insights we could argue that certain concepts are unavoidable in efforts to model objective reality *and* many of them have metaphorical roots. The full significance of that idea will gradually unfold.

In Kant's account the transcendental, as opposed to the transcendent, consists of conditions and concepts that can be found to be necessary for experience in general to be possible. These can be discovered by reflecting upon something certain, like "there is experience," in order to find out what would have to be the case *for* this certainty to be. It is a form of reflective inference. Kant illustrates this form of making inferences when he discusses the idea of *a priori* concepts in *The Critique of Pure Reason*:

> If we remove from our empirical concept of a body, one by one, every feature in it which is empirical, the colour, the hardness or softness, the weight, there still remains the space which the body (now entirely vanished) occupied, and this cannot be removed. Again, if we remove from our empirical concept of any object, corporeal or incorporeal, all properties which experience has taught us, we yet cannot take away that property through which the object is thought as substance or as inhering in a substance (although this concept of substance is more determinate than that of an object in general). Owing, therefore, to the necessity with which this concept of substance forces itself upon us, we have no option save to admit that it has its seat in our faculty of *a priori* knowledge. (Kant 1965, p. 45, B 6)

Contemporary versions of transcendental argumentation and modified understandings of what *a priori* can mean are discussed in my longer essay, not here. What captures our interest now is the question of whether fundamental concepts and categories can be found to be already presupposed and in play when we engage in scientific research. Scientific research on the physical world has to begin with ideas about objects and events in general. These ideas have then become refined as research has progressed, but those processes of refinement, further abstraction, could be limited with respect to how far they may proceed. "String" is a highly refined concept but one that still has something like a concept of substance behind it, which makes it intelligible. "Substance" in turn has something about "objectivity-in-general" behind it, which makes *it* intelligible. Perhaps the explicit concepts used to produce the transcendent postulates used in scientific models all are foregrounded notions that depend upon backgrounded and implicit concepts; horizons of intelligibility. The conceptual relations here are ones of implication: foregrounded concepts *implicate* backgrounded ones in that the foregrounded concepts are not intelligible – have no sense – without the backgrounded concepts implicitly understood along with them. Perhaps these background concepts recede toward a limit, a limit of what *objectivity* is in general. Transcendental forms of thinking could help in an investigation of this possibility because reflection is a process that helps to reveal what was already presupposed. Peter Strawson (1966) expresses the basic idea here in terms of the questions that a transcendental-style investigation would seek to answer:

> How in general must we conceive of objects if are to make empirical judgements, determinable as true or false, in which we predicate concepts of identified objects of reference? Or: What in general must be true of a world of objects of which we make such judgements? (1966, p. 82)

If it is the case that general concepts associated with the very notion of objectivity, of objects that can be perceived, measured and manipulated – are unavoidable then we must ask whether these general concepts could still somehow be explained with the methods of physical science. If we could show that there *are* fundamental concepts that do tell us what has to be true of a world of objects and events and yet cannot be studied with the methods of physical science (because they must be already presupposed as true as soon as one begins a scientific investigation), then we might still be able to explain them in a more roundabout way by trying to explain consciousness and thought empirically. Or we might be forced to conclude that the nature of the concepts must be studied in some way other than through the use of the methods of physical science.

For example, we might be able to show through conceptual argumentation alone that *in some manner* space and time will have to be included in any physical theory simply because the general domain explored in all possible physical theories *must* have spatial and temporal structure. Well, then maybe these structures, space and time in this case, perhaps substance and accident as well, have to be studied and explained in some other way than through physical models. Or maybe these categories and structures we find through transcendental forms of thinking can indeed be explained empirically but in a sort of circular way. This circularity would amount to being able to produce a fundamental physical theory to which all other sciences can be reduced: from philosophy to neuropsychology to biochemistry right down to physics.

So let's begin with the idea of categories or concepts or structures or conditions that cannot be grounded as valid for knowledge through measurements and predictions but that can be shown to be necessary for having physical knowledge. In the transcendent postulates of scientific models is there a framework that limits the direction in which all possible models can go? Do the entities postulated in the models presuppose something that applies for all possible physical models and that cannot itself be modelled?

We will actually make progress in exploring this issue by considering an objection to it from the start. That objection is the argument that scientific models do nothing more than guide measurements and make predictions. They are bookkeeping devices, not ontological representations. It does not matter whether the models depend upon metaphors or anything else because metaphors are simply metaphors and not to be taken literally. The meaning of "string" in string theory is not its *sense* but its *reference*. Let's examine this idea through the realism versus positivism debate in the philosophy of science.

Realism Versus Positivism
The relation between theory and measurement becomes important here. On the side of theory in fundamental physics we find postulated transcendent entities and events – things that are supersensible, that exceed direct sense experience but that are postulated as existing "behind" sense experience such that they provide correct predictions of what does come directly through the senses, usually as mediated by instruments. The validity of such models pertains to the measurements they direct and the predictions they provide. Thus one philosophical question that arises immediately when considering the role played by models in scientific explanations is whether the entities referred to in the models really exist or not. A number of practicing scientists argue that this is basically not an interesting question. Measurements are the heart and soul of science. So long as a model gives accurate predictions we have the knowledge we seek, and we cannot expect to have any more knowledge than this. Stephen Hawking (Hawking 2001) writes:

> Any sound scientific theory, whether of time or of any other concept, should in my opinion be based on the most workable philosophy of science: the positivist approach put forth by Karl Popper and others. According to this way of thinking, a scientific theory is a mathematical model that describes and codifies the observations we make. A good theory will describe a large range of phenomena on the basis of a few simple postulates and will make definite predictions that can be tested. If the predictions agree with the observations, the theory survives that test, though it can never be proved to be correct. On the other hand, if the observations disagree with the predictions, one has to discard or modify the theory. (At least, that is what is

supposed to happen. In practice people often question the accuracy of the observations and the reliability and moral character of those making the observations.) If one takes the positivist position, as I do, one cannot say what time actually is. All one can do is describe what has been found to be a very good mathematical model for time and say what predictions its makes. (2001, p. 31)

Hawking does not have things quite right here in that Karl Popper was *not* a positivist and even regarded his philosophy of science to be a refutation of positivism, particularly in its logical-positivist form. Use of the term "positivism" by Hawking and Green should be understood to refer to a very strict form of empiricism with all realist claims bracketed out of the picture and endorsing Popper's critique of verificationalism. But because Hawking and Green write primarily in realist terms, as if all the supersensible entities and geometries of space-time *exist*, and then appeal to "positivism" when some of the models do raise problems for realism, the expression "quasi-positivism" seems appropriately applied to them.

Here then, is another exemplary passage from Hawking regarding his quasi-positivist position:

From the viewpoint of positivist philosophy, however, one cannot determine what is real. All one can do is find which mathematical models describe the universe we live in. (2001, p. 59)

And one more:

From a positivist viewpoint, one is free to use whatever picture is most useful for the problem in question. (Hawking 2001, p. 118)

Brian Green, whose philosophical position is actually not precisely clear from what he writes in *The Elegant Universe*, makes an appeal to positivism at least with respect to one particularly important issue. One of the difficulties that string theory seems able to solve has been the relation between general relativity theory and quantum theory. According to general relativity theory, space is a continuum – it is smooth though it will bend with gravity. According to quantum physics at very small distances space is not continuous. It is rather characterized by "quantum foam." But strings have a size that is larger than the distances at which quantum foam effects occur. That means that *measurements* would in principle be impossible to make when the distances between whatever it is we wish to measure are smaller than the size of a string. Positivism therefore seems to make certain problems simply vanish because the nature of these problems cannot be formulated in measurement terms:

In a universe governed by the laws of string theory, the conventional notion that we can always dissect nature on ever smaller distances, without limit, is not true. There *is* a limit, and it comes into play before we encounter the devastating quantum foam. Therefore, ... one can even say that the supposed tempestuous sub-Planckian quantum undulations *do not exist*. A positivist would say that something exists only if it can – at least in principle – be probed and measured. Since the string is supposed to be the most elementary object in the universe and since it is too large to be affected by the violent sub-Planck-length undulations of the spatial fabric, these fluctuations cannot be measured and hence, according to string theory, do not actually arise. (2003, pp. 156-157)

The quasi-positivist position that Green and Hawking appeal to from time to time seems to be motivated only when transcendent postulates become too counter-intuitive or even raise contradictions if taken as real. Otherwise their writings on science definitely take the form of claims about what the universe is "really like," what actually exists and so on. It is basically extremely difficult to actually *practice* science, believing all the time that one is simply coming up with useful fictions that for some reason produce accurate predictions. The tendency is to think in terms of *what really exists* outside sense experience, but measurable with instruments or having effects that can be measured by instruments.

In the philosophy of science efforts to *completely* reduce scientific theories to measurements and predictions of measurements, a project that logical positivism deemed possible, produced such things as a tight distinction between the "observation language" and the "theory language" of scientific discourse. The observation language was the language in which all terms are defined by measurements. The grounding of all claims made with theoretical language had to reside in the translation of its terms to the observation language. This effort did not succeed in winning broad consent for very long. "Semantic realism" currently has won wide consensus in the philosophy of science. This is a more modest form of realism than "metaphysical realism" because it focuses on language as it is used in science and argues that such language use will always exceed strictly measurement terms. Psillos (2003) writes of semantic realism as follows:

Semantic realism is no longer contested. Theoretical discourse is taken to be irreducible and assertoric (contentful) by all sides of the debate. Making semantic realism the object of philosophical consensus was by no means an easy feat, since it involved two highly non-trivial philosophical moves: *first*, the liberalization of empiricism, and the concomitant admission that theoretical discourse has 'excess content,' that is, content which cannot be fully captured by means of paraphrase into observational discourse; and *second*, a battery of indispensability arguments which suggested that theoretical terms are indispensable for any attempt to arrive, in Carnap's words, at 'a powerful and efficacious system of laws' and to establish an inductive systematization of empirical laws. (p. 61)

We can say that the tension between the quasi-positivist perspective and the realist perspective is simply that: a *tension* that science works within. Semantic realism shows us that scientific language cannot be reduced purely to measurements. It has "excess content" of a realist nature; references to objects and object-like entities that are not completely captured by measurements and use of language-embedded categories that make induction possible (but cannot themselves be induced). Metaphors are a case in point. But at the same time, the use of metaphors and other terms with objective referents in scientific models is under great pressure to strip down towards measurements and observations. Operational definitions and "coordinate definitions" (Reichenbach 1991) strip linguistic references down toward observations and instrument readings. This direction is an important enabling condition for progressive research in the physical sciences. The limit case presupposed by this direction is that of a language in which only human-to-physical-world relations become represented. The operational definition is a definition in which the only meaning to be taken seriously for a term is the *act* of taking a measurement. Measurements in turn use a vocabulary ("length," "velocity," etc.) that are defined through "coordinate definitions":

> Defining usually means reducing a concept to other concepts. In physics, as in all other fields of inquiry, wide use is made of this procedure. There is a second kind of definition, however, which is also employed and which derives from the fact that physics, in contradistinction to mathematics, deals with real objects. Physical knowledge is characterized by the fact that concepts are not only defined by other concepts, but are also coordinated to real objects. This coordination cannot be replaced by an explanation of meanings, it simply states that *this* concept is coordinated to *this particular thing*. (Reichenbach 1991, p. 473)

Thus, argues Reichenbach, terms used as part of measurement practice take on coordinate definitions that refer to physical objects paradigmatic for certain measurement concepts: e.g., "length" is coordinated with "measuring rod." Whatever there is about language that deals specifically with human-to-human relations, the social world, as well as human-to-self relations would be absent in scientific language were its limit case to ever be reached. Semantic realism, however, draws attention to the fact that language is essentially a human-to-human medium. It will have "excess content" both in its use of terms for scientific models (giving us an unavoidable realist presupposition) and its use in communications between members of a scientific community.

When the excess content of scientific language starts to challenge intuition too far (e.g., a two dimensional model of time with imaginary numbers on one of its axes: see just below) or suggest contradictions (e.g., the wave *and* particle nature of elementary particles in quantum mechanics, the concept of space as a continuum *and* as something with discrete units) one can always appeal to quasi-positivism so as to ignore the philosophical issue. Thus Hawking writes of the two-dimensional model of time, having an imaginary axis as well as a real-number axis, and also of models of time in which there is a minimum or maximum value *without* it being intelligible to ask what happened "before" or "after" them (just as with respect to the surface of the earth – curved two-dimensional surface – it does not make sense to ask what is "north of north"). He then explains that the apparent conceptual difficulties of such models are resolved when one defines concepts in terms of measurements:

> In general relativity, on the other hand, time and space do not exist independently of the universe or of each other. They are defined by measurements within the universe, such as the number of vibrations of a quartz crystal in a clock of the length of a ruler. (2001, p. 35)

The debates between realist and "positivist" interpretations of scientific theories leave us with more clarity on the nature of scientific models. They are dependent on a language that *exceeds* measurements but scientific language has moved in the direction of defining terms as exclusively as possible as acts of measurement, and will no doubt continue to do so without ever being able to fully subsume language to measurement. It is this dependency on language with its "excess content" that is important in the quest for limits on scientific knowledge.

Restrictions on Language, Practice and Experience
As Reichenbach says, definitions of concepts in scientific language use both other concepts and measurements which are themselves coordinated with physical objects. It is the fact that *other concepts* are still part of the picture that is important, and that the language in general retains excess content. Excess content enters into scientific language at least partially through the processes of metaphorical extension and abstraction. Even a strictly empiricist interpretation of string theory would acknowledge that the metaphor of "string" serves the function of a *guide* to the construction of mathematical models.

There are some qualifications to be here in so far as the foregoing might imply that scientific language uses metaphors rather simply. It doesn't. There is a lack of intuitively available metaphors to represent some phenomena in particle physics – for example, the wave *and* particle characteristics we find within the domain of the very small. There is also the constructive process in mathematical knowledge, the expansion of the idea of dimensions so that spaces can have any number of them, the introduction of imaginary numbers with physical interpretations, and so on. But it seems that incompatible metaphors are juxtaposed when a single one will not capture what is meant to be modelled (wave *and* particle; continuity *and* discreteness), and new ideas developed by abstracting yet more from common metaphors ("quantum superposition" instead of just "position").

Either with a realist claim that strings really *are* existing ultimate substance or a quasi-positivist claim that this idea of "string" is to be taken as a metaphorical guide to the production of mathematical models, or something in-between, we have a philosophical issue of immense importance. A "string" is a kind of *object* in its sense, either in aiding record-keeping or as a postulated real entity, and like all objects it cannot be understood entirely on its own. Now, it is true that modern physics *abstracts* from ideas we find used commonly in ordinary language to produce counter-intuitive results, mathematical models that do not conform to ordinary ideas about objects and events. But the process of abstraction is limited by the material upon which it is worked. We can add greater dimensionality to the concept of object so as to have objects of more than three dimensions. We can model objects (containers) that have finite volumes but infinite surfaces and perhaps get accurate predictions of measurement from such things. The concept of "object," is connected to the concepts of space and time but the normal way we intuit this relationship can be surprisingly altered as in relativity theory. But each of these modifications is worked upon a background of concepts possessing excess content. These feats in modern physics are feats in taking the concept of objectivity as we find it in normal everyday communication and then, through abstractions and extensions, producing new counter-intuitive or just plain surprising models *without ever being able to escape the framework of objectivity-in-general.*

Scientific language has grown in this direction of greater objectivity through restricting attention to other referential functions of ordinary language and making the act of measurement more fundamental to the referents of key concepts. Everyday language use is essential for the metaphors, coordinate-definitions, and operational definitions of scientific models. Ordinary language is never completely abandoned in this process but rather accounts for the excess content we find in scientific discourse. Scientific discourse would not be possible without ordinary language.

The strict operationalization of meaning for the use of these models, such that a limit case is approached whereby the meaning of all referential terms in a scientific language would be entirely absorbed in the practice of measurement, suggests another restriction, this time placed on the large range of actual human *actions* or practices. Measurement is a subset of one kind of human action, instrumental action, which itself is a subset of human action in general. In each case, that of restricted language use and that of restricted practice, explicit rules have been generated to formalize both language use and action. Neither this explicitly restricted use of language nor this explicitly restricted form of practice could exist without something upon which the restrictions were made: the full range of human practices and the complete use of language as occurs in everyday life.

Restrictions on language use and practice correlate with restrictions on human experience. Third person, observational or perceptual experience becomes paradigmatic for experience in general. The restriction on experience is discussed more in the next section.

One more point needs to be made. The specialized language of scientific inquiry cannot, in an important sense, *itself* be a feature of the object domain to be studied. Language and measurement are *externally* related, such that language *use* can never be examined internally as a part of scientific method. The sorts of semantic investigations that semantic realism is based on are *not* investigations using the methods of physical science. If language use were to be studied with scientific method, then it would be objectivated into something that can be *observed* (measured) and a new specialized and restricted language, with "excess content," will be formed to produce models of it (as is done in empiricist linguistics). In the empirical sciences like physical science (and like empirical-only investigations of social life) the language of theory always comes from the *outside* in order to model observations.

In summary, we can make a preliminary statement about scientific models with Figure 20.1.

The idea that concepts might be presupposed as soon as a project to take measurements begins, concepts that cannot themselves be grounded in their validity in terms of measurements, has led us to notice a set of restrictions that characterize scientific explanations. It is possible to explore more in the direction indicated by Strawson to try to find, "what in general must be true of a world of objects," but doing so would require a close look at *what has been restricted* to produce scientific explanations and practice: ordinary language use, the full range of human practices, the full range of human experiences. From *within* this restored position we would then need to investigate communicative structures in ordinary language for how objective references are related to other types of references and how instrumental actions are related to other types of actions. This would aid us in seeking specific internal limits or boundaries to the process of specializing in the study of objectivity.

Scientific Models Involve:

1. A restriction on human experience to make experiences of objects and sense-experiences in general epistemologically primitive and exclusive,
2. Postulated transcendent entities interpreted in either a realist or quasi-positivist manner,
3. Explicit rules to restrict language use,
4. Explicit rules to restrict practice, or human action,
5. An external relation between language and practice, theory and action.

Fig. 20.1. Scientific models.

To seek specific limits in this way would actually be a large project. Kant basically took the first person position associated with observation and perception in order to discover transcendental conditions. We would have to examine first, second and third person positions together to explore the nature of internal limits that arise conceptually, when only the fpirst person plural position is allowed. In sections below a very small part of this work is begun, but it isn't necessary to go further with such a project to demonstrate limits to knowledge in the physical sciences. The discovery of restrictions alone provides evidence for such limits but raises new questions which are to be investigated next.

Section Summary
The question of whether a theory of everything can explain initial conditions and quantities for the universe as we find it has been interesting by guiding our explorations toward the nature of scientific explanations – modelling reality with an emphasis on measurements and predictions. Categories and concepts, like substance, space, and time are encountered that seem to pertain to the notion of objectivity-in-general necessarily and in way that removes them from being

possible objects of measurement themselves. A theory of everything might one day be produced in the sense that initial conditions and quantities can be derived from it, but we have found that such a theory would seem to depend upon a set of restrictions already introduced, at the start, on full human experience, language use, and practice. Core concepts involved in *any* such model can be found through reflective thinking.

Now our second two questions become foregrounded because we can ask whether or not these reflective inferences and the fundamental conceptual-metaphorical nexus underlying scientific models in general can be explained empirically in other ways. Can we start with a totalizing physical theory, for example, and then wrap it around, so to speak, to explain the process of producing theories? That would require a physical theory of consciousness. Or can we examine the relation between consciousness and the process of observation (taking measurements) more directly so as to somehow include consciousness in our theory of everything? Problems in interpreting quantum physics at the level of the measurement/measured relation are suggestive for this question. Both issues are entailed in another point made by Steven Weinberg in his exploration of the boundaries of knowledge:

> Much as we would like to take a unified view of nature, we keep encountering a stubborn duality in the role of intelligent life in the universe, as both the observer of nature and part of what is observed. (2001, p. 77)

2. Can a Theory of Everything Explain Consciousness?

Reductionism
Despite Weinberg's admission that we have a "stubborn" duality when it comes to a universe containing observers that are both the subject and part of the object of knowledge, he fully believes the duality can eventually be resolved through the success of a project of reduction:

> There are well-known problems in the description of consciousness in terms of the working of the brain. They arise because we each have special knowledge of our own consciousness that does not come to us from the senses. But I don't think that this means that consciousness will never be explained. The fundamental difficulties in understanding consciousness do not stand in the way of explaining the *behavior* of other people in terms of neurology and physiology and, ultimately, in terms of physics and history. When we have succeeded in this task, we will doubtless find that part of the explanation of behavior is a program of neural activity, that we will recognize as corresponding to our own consciousness. (2001, p. 76)

Weinberg and many others express confidence that one day consciousness will indeed be explained with a physical theory through reducing the phenomena studied by all the various scientific disciplines right to the most fundamental level of particle physics. If full reductionism were possible, then all phenomena could be ordered hierarchically in terms of its level of complexity. Ellis (2004, p. 608) presents a traditionally conceived form of reductionism in one hierarchical list, all disciplines being reducible to the discipline below it because all of the phenomena studied in one discipline will be reducible to the phenomena studied by those underneath. I reproduce this in Figure 20.2.

- Sociology/Economics/Politics
- Psychology
- Physiology
- Cell biology
- Biochemistry
- Chemistry
- Physics
- Particle Physics

Figure 20.2. Traditional version of reductionism.

Subtle Methodological Naturalism: Emergence
The theory of emergent properties has been touted as an alternative to pure reductionism that yet preserves methodological naturalism. There are many positive and promising features of emergence theory but also large problems when it comes to trying to explain subjectivity as an emergent property. Since the problems we can identify with emergence theory as used in arguments to support methodological naturalism are *also* problems with versions of traditional reductionism, and since the converse is not immediately obvious, I will regard emergence theory as the best candidate for an effort to explain consciousness with a physical theory, seeking to cast doubt on methodological naturalism as a whole in the process.

The basic idea here is the familiar one that a whole can be greater than the sum of its parts. John Wheeler explains the idea simply as follows:

> When you put enough elementary units together, you get something that is more than the sum of these units. A substance made of a great number of molecules, for instance, has properties such as pressure and temperature that no one molecule possesses. It may be a solid or a liquid or a gas, although no single molecule is solid or liquid or gas. (Wheeler 1998, p. 341)

Perhaps phenomena that we study in the human sciences – like meaning and values and morality and subjective states – cannot be strictly reduced to physics because as we ascend from one level of complexity to the next we must introduce new properties, new causal entities, new processes with their own laws and so on and so forth. The laws of physics cannot be used, if this were the case, to *deduce* laws that operate on higher levels. This would still be a version of reductionism because we would wish to find "laws" to explain the emergence of new properties, entities and processes. And the ontological status of these laws would have to be retained within the basic framework of physical science. Ellis presents a modified version of reductionism which includes emergence. I reproduce it in Figure 20.3.

The upper column on the right involves phenomena with emergent properties. The reference to metaphysics at the very bottom and at the top left column will not be discussed here. But readers should note that use of this term in both places is relevant to arguments I will soon make regarding Strawson's conceptualization of non-transcendent metaphysics – in ways that Ellis does not consider.

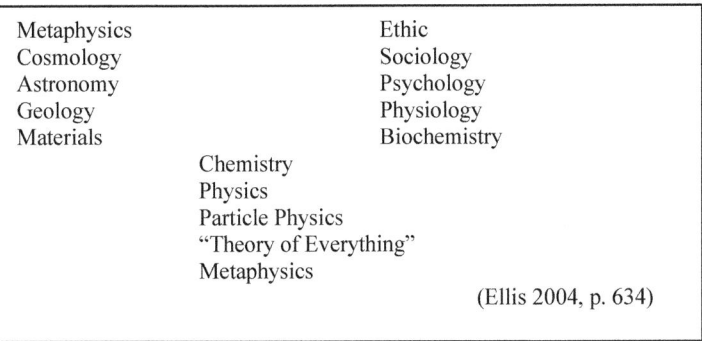

Figure 20.3. Reductionism with emergence taken into account.

Emergence theory is currently under much debate. Critics of emergence theory argue that "emergence" is simply shorthand for a group or cluster of discrete phenomena. The concepts of solid, liquid and gas, for example, could easily be understood this way, and so could the fact that temperature and pressure do not apply to a single molecule but rather to the behavior of a collection of them. These critics argue against emergence theory to favor a traditional version of reductionism.

A further problem for emergence theory at this time concerns all the different versions of emergence we can consider. Given a fairly large list of types of emergence we must wonder which might be grouped together into a single type, which are valid forms of emergence and which are not. Clayton summarizes these versions of emergence as follows:

- temporal or spatial emergence
- emergence in the progression from simple to complex
- emergence in increasingly complex levels of information processing
- the emergence of new properties (e.g., physical, biological, psychological)
- the emergence of new causal entities (atoms, molecules, cells, central nervous system)
- the emergence of new organizing principles or degrees of inner organization (feedback loops, autocatalysis, 'autopoiesis')
- emergence in the development of 'subjectivity.' (Clayton 2004, p. 597)

Of course, it is the last type of emergence that we are most interested in here. Can subjectivity and consciousness be regarded, explained even, as forms of emergence? This type of emergence is the one regarded as most problematical by Clayton and other writers on emergence. I think there is a very good reason why this last type of emergence, emergence of consciousness or subjectivity, has posed the greatest challenge. The reason is that emergence theory, as it is currently being explored and expounded, is located firmly within the framework of a physical scientific theory. Clayton's list of strictures for the study of emergence is very revealing and worth quoting in this regard. I present three of his strictures below:

1. Emergence studies will be scientific only if emergence can be explicated in terms that the relevant sciences can study, check, and incorporate into actual theories.
2. Explanations concerning such phenomena must thus be given in terms of the structures and functions of stuff in the world. As Christopher Southgate writes, 'An emergent property is one describing a higher level of organization of matter, where the description is not epistemologically reducible to lower-level concepts' (Southgate 1999, p. 158).
3. It also follows that all forms of dualism are disfavored. For example, only those research programs count as emergentist which refuse to accept an absolute break between neurophysiological properties and mental properties. 'Substance dualisms,' such as the Cartesian delineation of reality into 'matter' and 'mind,' are generally avoided. (Clayton 2004, pp. 579-580)

What we see here are the boundaries of natural science articulated acutely about the concept of "substance" once more. If subjectivity is to be understood as an emergent property in this way, then it is to be understood as a type of "stuff" – substance (point #2 in the quotation). Not only is subjectivity to be a type of stuff, but rather a form of the *same* stuff that ontologically is believed to underlie everything from the perspective of this realist version of scientism. Now, there are good reasons for the claim here that Cartesian dualism is something to avoid when trying to understand subjectivity (point #3). But the emergence theorists we find here (Clayton and Southgate) seek to avoid the problems of dualism by appeal to a single substance rather than two radically different substances. The main problem with Cartesian dualism is *not* that two substances were proposed by Descartes, but rather that *subjectivity was regarded as a substance in the first place*.

Can Subjectivity be Modelled?
From a roughly Kantian perspective we can say that the effort to think of subjectivity as a form of emergence in the sense given above makes the mistake of using a category of understanding employed (necessarily, for Kant) when we experience something through the senses – the category of "substance" in this case – to trying to understand something that we do *not* have access to through the senses. Subjectivity is ultimately not a sense phenomenon at all, but is rather presupposed whenever we experience something. Hence subjectivity cannot be

modelled in the same way that objectivity can. In the case of objectivity, all models have the conceptual *possibility* of representing something physical, such that terms in the model do not differ by conceptual type from what they represent, even though what they represent escapes experience. In the case of subjectivity, no model could actually be constructed with this congruency between conceptual types. It is true that models of subjectivity can and have been produced to predict behaviors under certain conditions, but in this case subjectivity *itself* has been dislocated to the interpretive processes of the model-maker and to the subject modelled in so far as she will be able to change her behavior as soon as she learns of the model that supposedly predicts it. A model of, for example, the relation between an "attitude" and behavior in certain situations treats "attitude" like a physical object by calling it a "variable" and locating it within a set of external relations (correlational or causal relations between attitude, measurably defined situation and behaviour). An "attitude," however, is ontologically not a discrete entity. Nor is it a shorthand term for a behaviour pattern – few people are still convinced by behaviorist doctrines and for good reasons.

Now, there are different layers of subjectivity that have to be taken into account when making an argument like this. Subjectivity pertains to what Kant called the phenomena of "inner sense" as distinguished from the phenomena of "outer sense." And in addition, subjectivity has to do with the "I" – the ultimate *subject* of both kinds of experience ("inner," and "outer").

The Inner/Outer Distinction
On the inner-sense/outer-sense distinction, we have experiences of trees, rocks and air as things somehow outside ourselves and we experience emotions, desires and thoughts as somehow inside. Kant pointed out that all objects of outer experience are framed both spatially and temporally but all objects of inner experience are framed only temporally, not spatially. An emotion has no spatial position, only a position in the temporal flow of experience (as in, I feel happy now but did not feel happy ten minutes ago). Recognizing an experience as one of the inner variety will *not* employ a category like that of "substance" whereas recognizing an experience as one of an object "outside" the self will require a category like substance. Hence if there is anything right about Kant's phenomenological description of the inner / outer distinction, subjectivity cannot be modelled in any way that involves the concept of "stuff." This is one argument to make against reductionism. Its full force is only grasped when we understand that to locate some objects of experience within space *and* time depends upon the possibility of having experiences of states and events that are *not* in any way possible to locate in space, and vice versa. In fact, the temporal orders of the objects of inner sense and outer sense themselves have to be distinct for any intelligible concept of experience-in-general (this is expanded in the longer essay). That means that to model subjectivity as a kind of "stuff" existing in some sort of special organization is to actually introduce an implicit contradiction to the situation. Let's examine this a little more carefully.

Wilhelm Dilthey modified Kantian arguments in his efforts to distinguish the sciences of nature (*Naturwissenschaften*) from the human sciences (*Geistes-*

wissenschaften). His argument was that the categories of understanding used for studying objects in the physical world are produced by a truncation of experience through the process of objectivation. Human experience is very multifaceted and does not consist primordially of mere experiences of objects in a physical world, mere perceptions of the outer-sense variety. But natural science has progressed by restricting full human experience to that which is most objective, most stripped of any subjectivity. Dilthey thus modifies Kant to argue that the categories he considered to be transcendental categories of consciousness, necessary for *all experience*, are actually categories produced by a truncation of experience (at least in many cases – this need not be true in all cases of the Kantian categories as I show in the longer essay).

> ... this idea of the world based on spatial extension is the original source of all knowledge of uniformities, and we are advised from the start to reckon with them. We gain control of this physical world by the study of its laws. These laws can only be discovered insofar as the lived character of our impressions of nature, the connection we have with nature to the extent that we are ourselves part of it, and the lively feeling in which we enjoy it recede ever more behind the abstract comprehension of it according to the relations of time, space, mass, and motion. All these moments work together to ensure that man effaces himself in order to construct – on the basis of his impressions – this great object, nature, as an order governed by laws. It then becomes the center of reality for man. (Dilthey 2002, p. 104)

From the "lived character" of holistic full experience we obtain the objective world studied by natural science through a sort of self-effacement. There are two senses to this idea of a self-effacement: one is the reduction of experience to observational experience, the other is something I will discuss shortly – the "I" of experience becomes set aside and presupposed as a purely anonymous subject without any properties whatsoever. In terms of the first sense of self-effacement, we construct an objective world by giving meaning only to the *most* objective portions of experience. This means, among many other things, that what Kant called "outer-sense" experiences now are taken to be the paradigm for *all* experiences. This world we access through outer-sense prioritizes the third person position over the first person position. It results in *abstractions* used to explain the physical world in the form of those transcendent postulates we have discussed already, which are brought to *explain* regularities in experience *from outside experience itself*. Hence Dilthey called these transcendent postulates that characterize scientific models "auxiliary constructions":

> The formation of the natural sciences is determined by the way in which their object, nature, is given. Images emerge from a continual flux, they are referred to objects, these objects fill and occupy empirical consciousness, and they form the object of descriptive natural science. But even empirical consciousness notices that the sensory qualities exhibited in images are dependent upon the standpoint of observation, upon distance, and upon

illumination. Physics and physiology show ever more clearly the phenomenality of these sensory qualities. Thus the task arises of thinking of objects in such a way that both their phenomenal changes and the uniformities emerging ever more clearly amidst these changes become intelligible. The concepts through which this happens are auxiliary constructions that thought creates for this purpose. Thus nature is foreign to us, transcending the apprehending subject, is elaborated by auxiliary constructions based on the phenomenally given. (Dilthey 2002, p. 111)

The role of metaphors in scientific models that we discussed earlier is hence further clarified here. Auxiliary constructions are *based* on the phenomenally given, in all its richness, but metaphorical extensions and abstractions from full experience produce transcendent entities that we do not and cannot experience. Natural use of language not only references more than objectivity, not only references everything within lived full human experience, but is a *part* of this experience. So we see once again, from a slightly new perspective here, that the formal languages of science are another domain in which we can find the employment of restrictions to enable the workings of physical science.

There is nothing wrong about this feature of the physical sciences *unless* the metaphors used to make sense of the physical world, metaphors that originated through a process that had to pull meaning away from a context of full lived experience toward only the objective side, are *next* used to try to explain subjectivity. Refinements introduced on third person experience already presuppose a dependence on, and distinction from, first person experience. First and third person modes of experience are in fact mutually dependent. Neither differentiated domain of experience can produce the conceptual basis for explaining the other.

Hence at this point we can argue that inner experience cannot be modelled at least in the way that outer experience can be. Clayton, in his fine discussion of emergence theory, expresses strong doubts about the possibility of explaining consciousness in terms of emergence for similar reasons. He quotes the consciousness theorist Chalmers:

The really hard problem of consciousness is the problem of experience. When we think and perceive, there is a whir of information-processing, but there is also a subjective aspect. As Nagel has put it, there is something it is like to be a conscious organism. This subjective aspect is experience. When we see, for example, we experience visual sensations: the felt quality of redness, the experience of dark and light, the quality of depth in a visual field. Other experiences go along with perception in different modalities: the sound of a clarinet, the smell of mothballs. Then there are bodily sensations, from pains to orgasms; mental images that are conjured up internally; the felt quality of emotion, and the experience of a stream of conscious thought. What unites all of these states is that there is something it is like to be in them. All of them are states of experience. (Chalmers 1995, p. 201, in Clayton 2004, p. 601)

Chalmers' point is better expressed by the quotations I have supplied from Dilthey in this section, but Chalmers' insight is precisely where Dilthey's was. Reductionism, using emergence or not, will not work when it comes to subjectivity, in part because a whole category of phenomena, with its own ontological significance, is shaved from experience. Neural science and its sister disciplines can be expected to produce *correlations* between first person experience and third person observations of neural activity. But reductionism would have it that the relation between the objective and subjective sides of such correlations is one of identity (e.g., thoughts simply *are* the neuro-physiological states they correlate with). And that proposition is in the end contradictory.

Subjectivity as the "I"
The second sense in which a type of self-effacement occurs in the enabling of physical science is linked to Kant's theory of the "I." Kant provides us with a great insight here that is progressively referred to, developed and finally modified within the longer essay. Kant argued that an "I think" (potentially, to be more accurate) accompanies all experiences and we are invited to notice this in the fact that all experiences can in principle be understood as "my" experiences. In section III of the longer essay I take a closer look at this idea of an "I" that accompanies all experiences but that is not itself an object of experience, because in this notion we find not only a precondition for natural science that cannot be studied by natural science, but also a special type of effacement that depends upon a fuller sense of the self, one which is deeply and essentially non-empirical but that includes more than the effaced "I." The distinction between inner-sense and outer-sense is worthy of attention but requires refinements when examined carefully because it is a distinction that is *produced* through intersubjectivity and can vary culturally in its specifics. It is not precisely as Kant would have it. But the "I" is something that can be argued for quite rigorously, as a type of *a priori* condition which cannot be explained empirically.

However, here we are simply exploring objections to the project of reductionism. And all we need to note is that experience includes an "I" that is yet not an object of experience. No experience could be possible if *some* experiences didn't have the accompaniment of the "I" within them. Experiences are always experiences *of* something. With the "I" in this most primordial and effaced sense we do not have something that is ever the "of" in an experience, but rather its counter-part: that which makes use of the term "of" intelligible when we say we have an experience of this or that. In Hegelian terminology we have the negative, or negation, in experience with the "I." The "I" is there whenever we find ourselves aware of something as something *else*, something other to us. The "I" is at first the *elseness* of any object of experience (whether an inner or an outer experience). The *elseness* of the object of experience is rather like finding a mirror in the object without finding what it reflects. It is in this sense the negative.

This is a more profound reason for rejecting reductionism in all its forms. The "I" of experience, we shall soon see (but only in the longer essay), is implicated by the distinction between inner and outer, by the concept of an objective world as well as a subjective world. The "I" will form a bridge for us to arrive at the full self and land firmly with the framework of the human sciences as those that study a domain presupposed and yet barred by the physical ones precisely through such things as this "I."

Emergence and Reductionism Do Not Work
It is for these reasons that the reductionistic project cannot work. Emergence theory is primarily an effort to shore-up the traditional version of reductionism and present a new argument in favor of methodological naturalism. Many things in emergence theory are exciting and will no doubt be fruitful. But the theory has so far been confined to the framework of physical science, as we see in the strictures that Clayton applies to it. Physical science has been enabled through a series of restrictions made on full human experience and full natural language use. Everything left out in this process of restricting cannot be explained by the resulting methodology. Emergence theory tries to keep everything within the boundaries of causal relations between entities, with entities conceptualized just in the way Dilthey elucidates: a process of abstraction that is bounded by basic concepts of objectivity-in-general. For example, Clayton writes about emergence theory as applied to the concept of subjectivity by casting the problem in terms of the "mind" and "brain" distinction:

> … research programs in emergence tend to combine sustained research into (in this case) the connections between brain and 'mind,' on the one hand, with the expectation that emergent phenomena will not be fully explainable in terms of underlying causes on the other. (Clayton 2004, p. 580)

Causation remains the fundamental category. But within the domains of meaning, culture, inner experience and understanding another human subject we do not find causal relations. We find other sorts of relations such as logical relations, semantic relations, illocutionary relations and much else. We must reject reductionism and emergence theory when the line is crossed from physical phenomena to those phenomena that were set aside in order to give the clearest most precise access possible to physical phenomena. Once that line is crossed we find entirely new categories within which to pursue inquiry. We must agree with Dilthey when he says:

> No real category can claim the validity it has in the natural sciences for the human sciences as well. If the abstract procedure expressed in a natural science category is transferred to the human sciences, then the natural sciences transgress their limits." (2002, p. 219)

3. The Observer-Observed Relation as it Arises in Quantum Mechanics

Reductionism and emergence are not viable ways for a theory of everything to explain consciousness, subjectivity and other things that are definitive for the human sciences (meaning, culture, etc.) because these things cannot be made objects of study. They are non-objective, yet necessary conditions for objectivity itself.

But perhaps consciousness could be included within a physical theory of everything in some other way. Anything objective is something that can be measured. What if the subject/object distinction were brought into play within the concept of a measurement such that they could be understood as dependent upon one another ontologically and not just epistemologically? This would change the traditional distinction made between ontology and epistemology, putting them together in some way `as yet to be elucidated. It would remove the notion of ontology from dependence on a backgrounded concept of the purely objective, like "substance." In philosophy we already have had proposals to change our understanding of ontology in ways like this. Hegel famously claimed that "substance is subject," and he developed an ontology which consists of the dialectic between forms of knowledge and the sorts of subjectivity related to each form, the whole process of which is explained as a movement of something (*Geist*) to know itself, importantly involving reflection. Heidegger included the hermeneutic circle (something that is most readily grasped as an epistemological process) into his *ontology* of human-being, and altered traditional notions of being as substance. Both Heidegger and Hegel, whose philosophies nevertheless differ very importantly from each other, alter our common sense understandings of time in the course of their work with ontology. They show us that there are *possibilities* for understanding substance, subject, existence, being, time and so on that differ from the more commonsense ways in which these concepts are understood.

Measurements in Quantum Mechanics
In physical science, quantum mechanics has forced philosophical issues similar to these, hovering about the relation between epistemology and ontology. There are experimentally demonstrated problems in the relation between measurement and what is measured when it comes to very small entities like photons and electrons. Quantum mechanics is a formal mathematical system that provides extremely accurate predictions between measurements of initial states and final states of physical systems following an intervention. There are no problems with its uses for making predictions. But there are very large problems when it comes to providing a physical interpretation of quantum mechanics. Weinberg summarizes the situation as follows:

> In quantum mechanics the state of any system is described by a mathematical object known as the wave function. According to the interpretation of quantum mechanics worked out in Copenhagen in the early 1930s, the rules for calculating the wave function are of a very different character from the principles used to interpret it. On the one hand, there is the Schrodinger equation [the wave function], which describes in a perfectly deterministic way how the wave function of any system changes with time. Then, quite separate, there is a set of principles

> that tells how to use the wave function to calculate the probabilities of various possible outcomes when someone makes a measurement. ...
>
> ... before a measurement the wave function of a spinning electron is generally a sum of terms corresponding to different directions of the electron's spin; with such a wave function the electron cannot be said to be spinning clockwise or counterclockwise around some axis, however, [when taking a measurement] we somehow change the electron's wave function so that the electron is definitely spinning one way or the other. Measurement is thus regarded as something intrinsically different from anything else in nature. And although opinions differ, it is hard to identify anything special that qualifies some process to be called a measurement, except its effect on a conscious mind. (2001, p. 77)

This is one of a number of things about quantum mechanics that has captured the imagination of the public and has resulted in the play, *Copenhagen*, by Michael Frayn. Is physical reality dependent, *ontologically*, on having an observer? In the famous two-slit experiment we have hard core data that is extremely hard to interpret with any ontology of the physical world. Roger Penrose's summary of the two-slit experiment is concise and clear:

> Here we have a source of particles and a detector screen, where there is a barrier with a pair of narrowly separated parallel slits in it, situated between source and screen. We suppose that one particle at a time is emitted, aimed at the screen. If we start with one slit open and the other closed, then a haphazard pattern of dots will appear at the screen, forming one at a time as individual particles from the source hit it. The intensity of the pattern (in the sense of the greatest density of dots) is most extreme in a central strip close to the plane connecting source to slit, as is to be expected, and it falls off uniformly in both directions from this central strip. This pattern is effectively the same if the experiment is repeated with the other slit being the open one. No puzzle here. But if the experiment is run once more when both slits are now open, then something extraordinary happens. The particles still make dots on the screen one at a time, but now there is a wavy *interference* pattern of parallel bands of intensity, where we even find that there are regions on the screen that are never reached by particles from the source, despite the fact that when just one or the other of the slits was open, then particles could reach those regions perfectly happily! Although the spots appear at the screen one at a time at localized positions, and although each occurrence of a particle meeting the screen can be identified with a particular particle-emission event at the source, the behaviour of the particle *between* source and screen, including its ambiguous encounter with the two slits in the barrier, is like a wave, where the wave/particle feels out both slits during this encounter.

If the particles (e.g., photons or electrons) were indeed particles, then having both slits open would simply result in a pattern on the screen that would be the sum of the two patterns obtained with first having one slit open, then closing it and opening the other. Instead we get a new pattern, a wave-interference pattern, that would be expected if the emissions were waves rather than particles. Yet experimenters see particle-like impacts on the destination screen *one at a time* with both slits open. If we really had waves we would see several places on the destination screen record an impact at once!

That is odd, but it gets even odder! If one tries to get more information about this puzzling result by placing another photographic plate at the side of the barrier when both slits are open in it, in order to sort of "see" (by recording) what happens when the particles reach the two slits, then the interference pattern on the original photographic plate (the destination screen) completely washes out and what one finds at the screen is what one would expect if the particles were truly and unambiguously particles. It is as if the particles (e.g., photons or electrons) "know" that we have tried to catch them as something between waves and particles, and change their behavior accordingly.

Here is a case in which no single transcendent postulate based on metaphors ("particle," "wave") can account for measured physical phenomena. Moreover, the act of taking a measurement appears to be in some way connected with what *exists* and even what *existed* in the past. Davies writes: "…the experimenter not only can participate in the nature of physical reality that is, but also in the nature of physical reality that *was*." (2005, p. 9) It is therefore extremely difficult to provide a physical interpretation for the formal mathematical model of quantum mechanics.

The concept of a "physical state" in classical physics is such that a state will be described through specifying the values of its variables. In quantum mechanics the term "state" was given a different meaning. The state of a physical system in this case is defined with the wave function Ψ which changes deterministically with time. From Ψ we can calculate the probability of getting various values for the variables of the system at a certain time if a measurement is taken. Once a measurement has been taken the value of the state, Ψ, changes in a way that can be calculated by taking the measurement value into account. But this change in Ψ is "sudden." It is non-continuous, and it is very difficult to understand such changes ontologically.

The values of variables in a physical system are not given an ontological status prior to the taking of a measurement. The position of a particle, for example, can be thought to "exist" simultaneously with different values (normally a contradiction) and hence the term "quantum superposition" is used. Position is, so to speak, "spread out" over a range. A measurement "collapses the wave function" so that a single value manifests. This is not a matter of simply "not knowing" which real value a variable has at any one time, it is a matter of there *being* no single existing value to the variable when measurements are not made.

Some have consequently argued for a new understanding of the universe that makes it dependent upon consciousness in some way. But this is a large leap to make from the puzzles of quantum mechanics which are at first appearance a matter of *measurements* in relation to the question of *what is measured*. It is not at first obvious that the measurer need be conscious. What is really involved, at first appearances, is the relation between a micro physical system (the particles) and a macro physical device that responds to it. Hence there have been efforts to argue for *observer*-independent interpretations/explanations of quantum mechanics (e.g., see *Physics Today*, March 1998, March 2000, September 2000 for some fairly technical arguments).

In the relational theory of quantum mechanics, the wave function is regarded as a sort of bookkeeping system rather than an ontological representation and the actual measurements taken are regarded as "real." This resolves the difficulty of trying to think of reality in terms of multiple but incompatible values of variables existing all at once: a particle spread out in a discontinuous way, for example. Thus in this interpretation there is simply no meaning to the idea of the variable having any sort of value when a measurement is not taken. But it raises a new problem which becomes apparent when we notice that the instrument used to measure a physical system is another physical system, and the measurement is an interaction within a larger physical system containing the original system of interest and the observation system (instrument). Once this is noticed then the meaning of a value obtained through a measurement becomes "relational":

> The core idea is to read the theory as a theoretical account of the way distinct physical systems *affect each other* when they interact (and not of the way physical systems 'are'), and the idea that this account exhausts all that can be said about the physical world. (Laudiser 2005, p. 2)

But then we can have a measurement of the original physical system of interest made by the initial observation system that produces a value for the original physical system (from the perspective of this measurement system) *and* have an interpretation of the observer-observed system from the perspective of another measurement system that does not yield this value but only a correlation between the physical system and the original observation system – a correlation without any outcome. Those who argue for relational quantum theory have relativized core concepts of "event," "position," "spin" and so on to having meaning only in terms of correlations – taking an observing apparatus into account and defining fundamental terms relationally.

However, a total physical system inclusive of all possible interactions with measuring systems would have to measure *itself* and this is not possible. Weinberg writes:

> At present, we do not understand even in principle how to calculate or interpret the wave function of the universe, and we cannot resolve these problems by requiring that all experiments give sensible results, because by definition there is no observer outside the universe who can experiment on it. (2001, p. 79)

What seems to be endemic to the situation is the inevitable transcendence of the "final" observer from all possible descriptions of physical systems. Marisa Dalla Chiara has related the debates over the significance of the observer in quantum mechanics to the self-reference issue in logic, first brought to the attention of the world by Godel with his incompleteness theorems. Chiara writes:

> If the apparatus observer O is an object of the theory, then O cannot realize the reduction of the wave function. This is possible only to another O', which is 'external' with respect to the universe of the theory. In other words, any apparatus, as a particular physical system, can be an object of the theory. Nevertheless, *any apparatus which realizes the reduction of the wave function is necessarily only a metatheoretical object.* (Dalla Chiara 1977, p. 340)

When a system to be studied includes *both* a physical system and an observer (another physical system) of it, quantum equations *can* describe the resulting complex system entirely, but only from the point of view of a new observer taking measurements – an observer who transcends what is described.

Similarly, Thomas Breuer published an independent proof for the impossibility of any physical system, whether conceptualized in quantum *or* classical terms, to measure itself (Breuer 1993). Hence:

> If one is interested in the quantum theory of the entire universe, then, by definition, an external observer is not available. Breuer's theorem shows then that a quantum state of the universe, containing all correlations between all subsystems, expresses information that is not available, not even in principle, to any observer. In order to write a meaningful quantum state ... we have to divide the universe in two components and consider the relative quantum state predicting the outcomes of the observations that one component can make on the other. (Laudisa 2005, p. 6)

In terms of conceptualizing knowledge of the universe, then, one can include observer positions by taking a third person position with respect to them. Any description of the whole universe has to make at least one division of it to produce an observation system and the physical system that remains. The universe is then relativized to a "second observer" position not included in the resulting description: the position from which choice of the division is made.

Quantum mechanics, like relativity theory, has pushed physical science forward by relativizing yet another set of terms that were thought to be absolute and unproblematical. In this case the terms are extremely basic – going right to the concept of "existence." The resemblance of the results of this work to the classical problem in philosophy that was raised to awareness most markedly by Kant is remarkable – the presupposition of subjectivity in all objective claims, with subjectivity presupposed in such a way to make it impossible for it to ever become an object of experience. We can choose observational systems conceptualized in purely physical terms and produce correlations between them and the rest of the universe, but *doing* this presupposes a second observer position that is not captured in physical terms and cannot be without presupposing yet another observer position.

Of course, many discussions of this topic do not refer to "consciousness," subjectivity or the "I," but rather to "observer" and mean by this a physical system that correlates with the physical system "observed." However, the bottom line seems to me and others who have contributed to discussions in this area that for a physical system to be an instrument-observer makes sense only through the fact that it is *read*. It delivers meaning. Hence some scientists have been toying with the idea of information theory in order to suggest a new ontological picture. The "it" of the universe is dependent on the "bit" – the unit of information that must have meaning, must not be strictly formal like a physical object or process but have semantic properties.

John Wheeler urged investigations into the question of whether or not we live in an "it from bit" universe, referring to the origins of the "bit" concept in computing:

> In the universe ... chance plays a dominant role. The laws of physics tell us only what *may* happen. Actual measurement tells us what *is* happening (or what *did* happen). Despite this difference [between computers and the universe], it is not unreasonable to imagine that information sits at the core of physics, just as it sits at the core of a computer.

> Trying to wrap my brain around this idea of information theory as the basis of existence, I came up with the phrase "it from bit." The universe and all that it contains ("it") may arise from the myriad yes-no choices of measurement (the "bits"). Niels Bohr wrestled for most of his life with the question of how acts of measurement (or "registration") may affect reality. It is registration—whether by a person or a device or a piece of mica (anything that can preserve a record)—that changes potentiality into actuality. I build only a little on the structure of Bohr's thinking when I suggest that we may never understand this strange thing, the quantum, until we understand how information may underlie reality. Information may not be just what we *learn* about the world. It may be what *makes* the world (Wheeler 1998, pp. 340-341).

Two Options?

I will not speculate more on this fascinating intersection of philosophy with physics. Let us end this chapter by noting that we *seem* to have two options facing us here, both of which emphasize necessary limits to physical knowledge.

One option is to acknowledge that we find ourselves within a universe in which everything is relational right down to the most core of all our fundamental concepts for acquiring knowledge of it, such that "a theory of everything" is really not possible because it runs into the idea of a whole universe without an observer.

The other option is to work the "it from bit" hypothesis towards an ontology that finds subject-object fusion at the heart of our most fundamental concepts: concepts of being, existence and so on. In this latter case we might have something like a dialectical concept at the far reaches of purely objectifying exploration. We might have a universe that contains "loops of meaning" as Wheeler expressed it. Meaning is something that cannot be reduced to physical states unless reductionism was possible, which I have argued is not the case.

Of relevance to both options is a now famous picture drawn by John Wheeler. This consists of a "U" standing for "universe" with an eye at the top of one of its columns, staring at the other column. The universe, he was suggesting, consists of both what is observed and the observer. A good reproduction of the diagram is given in Clayton's article (2004). Lucien Hardy modified Wheeler's drawing by adding a hand to the eye, a hand touching what the eye gazes at (Hardy 2004, p. 45). Measurement is not a passive affair, it is active and its central concepts have developed in relation to human action, or rather one subset of it: actions orientated toward the physical world in expectation of consequences.

The enabling conditions for the physical sciences limit the knowledge it can produce in ways that can easily be forgotten, unnoticed, hidden from view. They are restrictions on something else that physical science cannot itself study directly nor completely because its acts of measurement, its formalization of language and its restrictions on human experience only have the meaning they possess by already presupposing this other domain. This other domain can only be accessed in ways prohibited by the methodology of physical science. It is the core domain of the human sciences even though scientistic ideology has hidden this from even many social scientists. It is the subject of the next sections in the longer essay where its own key enabling conditions are explored and a new set of limits to knowledge uncovered.

REFERENCES

Breuer, T. (1993). The impossibility of accurate state self-measurements. *Philosophy of Science, 62*, 197-214.
Carspecken, P. F. (forthcoming). *Can a theory of everything explain itself? An essay on limits to knowledge in the physical and social sciences*. Rotterdam: Sense Publishers.
Chalmers, D. (1995). Facing up to the problem of Consciousness. *Journal of Consciousness Studies, 2*(200).
Clayton, P. D. (2004). Emergence: Us from it. In J. D. D. Barrow, C. W. Paul, & C. Harper, Jr. (Eds.), *Science and ultimate Reality* (pp. 577-606). Cambridge: Cambridge University Press.
Dalla Chiara, M. L. (1977). Logical self-reference, set theoretical paradoxes and the measurement problem in quantum mechanics. *Journal of Philosophical Logic, 6*, 331-347.
Davies, P. C. W. (2004). John Archibald Wheeler and the clash of ideas. In J. D. D. Barrow, C. W. Paul & C. Harper, Jr. (Eds.), *Science and ultimate reality* (pp. 3-26). Cambridge: Cambridge University Press.
Delandshere, G. (2002). Assessment as inquiry. *Teachers College Record, 104*, 1461-1484.
Delandshere, G. (2005). "Scientific" research in disguise and the threat to a spirit of inquiry. In B. H. M. Doecke, & W. Sawyer (Eds.), *'Only connect': English teaching and democracy*. Kent Town, Australia: Wakefield Press.
Dilthey, W. (2002). *Selected works, volume III; The formation of the historical world in the human cciences* (Vol. 3). Princeton and Oxford: Princeton University Press.
Ellis, G. F. R. (2004). True complexity and its associated ontology. In J. D. D. Barrow, C. W. Paul & C. Harper Jr. (Eds.), *Science and ultimate reality* (pp. 607-636). Cambridge: Cambridge University Press.
Green, B. (2003). *The elegant universe; Superstrings, hidden dimensions, and the quest for the ultimate theory*. New York: Vintage Books.
Hamlyn, D. (1984). *Metaphysics*. Cambridge: Cambridge University Press.
Hardy, L. (2004). Why is nature described by quantum theory? In J. D. D. Barrow, C. W. Paul, & C. Harper Jr. (Eds.), *Science and ultimate reality* (pp. 45-71). Cambridge: Cambridge University Press.
Hawking, S. (2001). *The universe in a nutshell*. New York: Bantam Books.

Kant, I. (1965). *Critique of pure reason* (N. K. Smith, Trans. Unabridged ed.). Boston; New York: Bedford/St. Martin's.

Laudisa, F. a. R., Carlo. (2005). Relational quantum mechanics. In E. N. Zalta (Ed.), *The Standford encyclopedia of philosophy*.

Penrose, R. (1989). *The emporor's new mind; Concerning computers, minds, and the laws of physics*. New York: Penguin Books.

Penrose, R. (2005). *The road to reality; A complete guide to the laws of the universe*. New York: Alfred A. Knopf.

Psillos, S. (2003). The present state of the scientific realism debate. In P. C. a. K. Hawley (Ed.), *Philosophy of science today* (pp. 59-82). Oxford: Clarendon Press.

Reichenbach, H. (1991). The philosophy of space and time; Selections. In R. G. Boyd, Philip, & J. D. Trout (Eds.), *The philosophy of science* (pp. 473-484). Cambridge, MA: MIT Press.

Schwandt, T. (2002). *Evaluation practice reconsidered*. New York: Peter Lang.

Sokal, A. D. (1996a). A physicist experiments with cultural studies. *Lingua Franca*, May/June, 62-64.

Sokal, A. D. (1996b). Transgressing the boundaries; Toward a transformative hermeneutics of quantum gravity. *Social Text*, Spring/Summer, 217-252.

Southgate, C. et al. (1999). *God, humanity, and the cosmos: A textbook in science and religion*. Harrisburg, PA: Trinity Press.

Strawson, P. F. (1966). *The bounds of sense; An essay on Kant's Critique of Pure Reason*. London and New York: Routledge.

Weinberg, S. (2001). *Facing up; Science and its cultural adversaries*. Cambridge, MA: London: Harvard University Press.

Wheeler, J. A. w. K. F. (1998). *Geons, black holes and quantum foam; A life in physics*. New York, London: W. W. Norton and Company.

CHERYL HOLZMEYER AND JOHN WILLINSKY

21. FROM *SCIENTIFIC RESEARCH IN EDUCATION* TO THE "OPEN SCIENCE" MOVEMENT

Science as Touchstone and Buzzword

The publication of the National Academy of Sciences' report *Scientific Research in Education* (2002) catalyzed a spectrum of critical commentary on the meanings of "scientific" research, among education scholars and beyond. Simultaneously, new online publication infrastructures and the open access movement suggested possibilities for more direct public engagement with education research. However, these possibilities remained inextricable from fraught epistemological and ethical questions about the terms of access to and engagement with research by broader publics, situated in a range of social contexts. Given the new infrastructures of scholarly communication enabled by digital platforms in recent years – including not only the inroads made by the open access movement, but also the emergence of a broader "open science" movement – this point is even more valid today than when earlier versions of this chapter appeared nearly ten years ago.[1] Though framed in capacious and universal terms, many contemporary open science initiatives are devoted to epistemological projects that embody narrow, particular, positivist approaches to "scientific" and "evidence-based" research – to the exclusion or marginalization of many other kinds of evidence and knowledge. These include qualitative, interpretive and community-based participatory research, as well as different kinds of local knowledge.

In this updated version, we reflect on current possibilities and challenges of scholarly communication by revisiting that earlier historical juncture. We tack back and forth between past and present, with an eye to speculations and eventualities at the intersections of: 1) discourses of "science" and "evidence" in educational research; 2) open access publishing initiatives and trends; and 3) broader scholarly communication initiatives enabled by the Internet and digital platforms, especially "open science" initiatives. Examining discourses of "science" both in educational research and in transdisciplinary scholarly communication and publishing illuminates the complex territory that contemporary education scholars must navigate. The landscape is particularly challenging for those emphasizing interpretive, non-positivist analytical frameworks and without "quick fixes" to offer those eager for such apparent solutions.

The principal argument of this chapter is that research dissemination practices and scholarly communication infrastructures, which were the focus of the earlier version, are constituted together with knowledge hierarchies. Examining discourses of "science" and "evidence" in educational research, including contestations of these terms, suggests how diverse scholarship may articulate with new digital systems of academic publishing and "open science" initiatives. These initiatives are simultaneously technical *and social*; they are inevitably value-laden, in ways that do not serve all types of scholarship equally. This point underscores the ultimate interdependence of academic publishing with other research issues, including epistemological questions. It points to the need to foster critical interventions and collaborations on behalf of public, democratic scholarship from multiple vantages, alongside publishing and beyond new information technology infrastructures, as suggested by the work of the other contributors to this volume.

RESEARCH AND PUBLIC SCRUTINY

Research in many traditions, for centuries if not millennia, has appeared in public meetings, journals, and other forms accessible to review – or rather, accessible to review by particular publics, who sometimes grant and sometimes deny its legitimacy as scholarship. In Western scholarship, key dimensions of the contemporary peer-reviewed research article were institutionalized through a history that includes public scrutiny of Isaac Newton's only published article, on optics, in the January 3, 1671 edition of the *Philosophical Transactions*. This was during the first decade of the new genre that has come to be known as the scientific journal (Willinsky 2006, pp. 234-244). Readers of Newton's article raised critical questions in letters to the *Transactions* that forced Newton to further clarify his research design and method, as well as the scope of his results. The back and forth between Newton and his critics in the pages of the *Transactions* continued until, after four years, Newton said, "No more," to the journal's editor, Henry Oldenburg. This exchange amounted to the setting of a standard for making research public; this standard placed *Transactions* readers in a position to not only think about replicating the experiment, but to check the sources, scrutinize the analysis, and challenge the conclusions (Kuhn 1978). Today, further complicating this picture, are proliferating disciplinary fields of research; new and ongoing debates over research methodologies and evidence; ever-expanding digital publication and data-sharing platforms; and the many potential scholarly and public research stakeholders, not only as research audiences, but as potential research collaborators. "Public scrutiny" is not singular but multiple, and becoming more so.

DISCOURSES OF "SCIENCE" AND "EVIDENCE" IN EDUCATION SCHOLARSHIP

The more recent past – the historical juncture from which this chapter first emerged – further illuminates the importance and complexity of relationships between public scrutiny and the status of education research. In 2002, the U.S. National Research Council (NRC) published one of the most important statements on education research in years, *Scientific Research in Education*, which addressed how to foster a "scientific" culture within a federal education research agency

(Shavelson and Towne 2002). The report's stated rationale was for the National Academies to weigh in on the scientific quality of education research, given what the authors describe as widespread skepticism over its cumulative value. In their estimation, this skepticism had led to explicit requirements for "scientifically based research" in the No Child Left Behind (NCLB) Act of 2001 (p. 1), which contained at least 111 references to this phrase (as noted by Feurer, Towne, and Shavelson 2002, p. 4). Ironically, without presenting any evidence on the current quality of education research, the authors of *Scientific Research in Education* appear to have accepted the supposedly widespread skepticism of the value of education research, while referencing the "rising enthusiasm for evidence-based education policy and practice" (p. 1). NCLB's emphasis on "scientifically based research" was also pivotal to institutionalizing and advancing the movement for "evidence-based practice" in education – following the "evidence-based practice" movement in medicine (Willinsky 2001b).

At what conclusions did the report arrive? The executive summary of *Scientific Research in Education* features six "scientific principles" said to "underlie all scientific inquiry, including education research" (Shavelson and Towne 2002, p. 2). These are directed at researchers not so much as principles, but as prescriptions:

SCIENTIFIC PRINCIPLE 1: Pose Significant Questions That Can Be Investigated Empirically
SCIENTIFIC PRINCIPLE 2: Link Research to Relevant Theory
SCIENTIFIC PRINCIPLE 3: Use Methods That Permit Direct Investigation of the Question
SCIENTIFIC PRINCIPLE 4: Provide a Coherent and Explicit Chain of Reasoning
SCIENTIFIC PRINCIPLE 5: Replicate and Generalize Across Studies
SCIENTIFIC PRINCIPLE 6: Disclose Research to Encourage Professional Scrutiny and Critique
(Shavelson and Towne 2002, pp. 3-5)

Next comes a section with six "Design Principles" to guide implementation, particularly the work of those responsible for setting up the U.S. Department of Education's Institute of Education Sciences, created in 2002 as "a resource for informed education decision-making." These include "DESIGN PRINCIPLE 1: Staff the Agency with People Skilled in Science, Leadership, and Management" to "DESIGN PRINCIPLE 2: Create Structures to Guide the Research Agenda, Inform Funding Decisions, and Monitor Work" to "DESIGN PRINCIPLE 6: Invest in Research Infrastructure" (Shavelson and Towne 2002, pp. 7-9). Laying out the principles in this way suggests that significant numbers of researchers are not posing significant questions, are not linking their work to relevant theories, and so on. In this way, the report's principles suggest a divide between its research criteria and existing education research. The issues raised continue to animate debate, in academia and beyond. For example, these principles continue to inform the U.S.

Department of Education's Institute of Education Sciences and its What Works Clearinghouse.

The chapter you are reading is part of the history of public scrutiny of the report. The first version of this chapter[2] was published in a volume devoted to exploring the implications of the NRC report for different types of education research and practice, from the vantage of a range of scholars. This earlier version focused specifically on the limitations of the NRC report's sixth and final scientific principle, focusing on research dissemination ("Disclose Research to Encourage Professional Scrutiny and Critique"). In particular, that version discussed the possibilities of the Internet and open access models of scholarly publishing to enable more direct public engagement with education research.

Below, we turn again to the report's sixth principle, this time in the context of the other principles that attempt to define "scientific" research in education. We elaborate on the main, updated argument of this chapter – that research dissemination practices, including online publication infrastructures and "open science" initiatives, are constituted together with knowledge hierarchies. These issues cannot truly be separated. In making this argument, we discuss open access publishing trends[3] since the report's publication, as well as broader scholarly communication and "open science" initiatives enabled by online, digital platforms (Willinsky 2005). We look at critical perspectives on "scientific" and "evidence-based practice" discourses in education research, both contemporary scholars' critiques of the 2002 *Scientific Research in Education* report and more recent analyses. These sources point to the need to examine systems of academic publishing together with sociologies of knowledge – especially the complexities of demarcating "scientific" from "non-scientific" research, or establishing hierarchies of research deemed more or less "scientific" or "evidence-based." Such an examination suggests ways in which new scholarly communication infrastructures, which some deem revolutionary, may perpetuate or even exacerbate long-standing disciplinary and methodological hierarchies, especially within and across the social sciences. This analysis highlights the interdependence of academic publishing and other dimensions of research, both social and epistemological. Alongside publishing and beyond new information technology infrastructures, there is a need to foster critical interventions and community-based collaborations on behalf of public, democratic scholarship underpinned by multiple social epistemologies (Longino, 2002).

EDUCATION RESEARCH DISSEMINATION AND OPEN ACCESS PUBLISHING TRENDS

The sixth and final scientific principle of the NRC's *Scientific Research in Education* (2002), reads: "Disclose research to encourage professional scrutiny and critique." It is followed by this elaboration:

> Scientific studies do not contribute to the larger body of knowledge until they are widely disseminated and subjected to professional scrutiny by peers. This

ongoing, collaborative, public critique is an indication of the health of a scientific enterprise. Indeed, the objectivity of science derives from publicly enforced norms of the professional community of scientists, rather than from the character traits of any individual person or design features of any study. (p. 5)

Yet, the sense that research is something disclosed for "professional scrutiny by peers" implies that it is a professional secret that should only be shared with those who can be trusted with it. Against such a notion, we argue that research is something to be publicly circulated in as wide a fashion as is feasible – based particularly on the input and interests of research subjects and non-academic research collaborators, alongside the new academic publishing possibilities enabled by the Internet. The Internet has proven itself a powerfully transformative publishing medium for research and scholarship, especially at the level of the journal article. As publishing has moved online, the Internet has opened a new world of access to the forms of knowledge that are recorded in journals, if less so for scholarly books at this point.[4] Meanwhile the open access movement has gradually leveraged these technological and publishing transformations on behalf of wider, free public access to academic articles for anyone with an Internet connection.

Prior to this open access movement, scholarly publishing was heading down a road of increasing corporate concentration, with publisher mergers and acquisitions, as well as corporate acquisition of scholarly society journals. The resulting price increases were leading to a declining state of access to research, including journal subscription cancellations that trimmed collections even at the best university libraries, while decimating those of less privileged institutions. The introduction of open access models through online publishing offered another path – toward wider circulation, sharing, and public scrutiny of academic research. In the years since the NRC report's publication, the open access movement has accelerated and helped to articulate the means, as well as the public value, of greater access to research for diverse stakeholders, from scholars to federal agencies. This goal was the impetus behind the founding of the Public Knowledge Project (PKP) in 1998, a project with which both authors of this chapter are involved. PKP has advanced research access efforts through the development of open source software platforms for online academic publishing, as well as through research into the use and reach of scholarly publishing. At the time of this writing, over seven thousand journals around the world and across disciplines are using PKP's open source software "to publish independent journals on a peer-reviewed and open access basis, greatly increasing the public and global contribution of research and scholarship" (MacGregor, Stranack, & Willinsky 2014).

In the field of education research, the Directory of Open Access Journals lists 380 journals that make their content free to read online, among them *Educational Researcher*, *Educational Policy Analysis Archives*, and *Theory and Practice in Language Studies*. Open access to research is being implemented through a number of different publication funding models, which include using entirely volunteer labor and publishing only online; relying on article processing fees to fund open access publishing; providing open access to articles after a period of embargo or subscription-only access; and offering open access options to those in developing countries, while charging fees elsewhere. To give a further example, the American Education Research Association (AERA) announced in 2014 its launch of a new open access journal, *AERA Open*, which will charge $400 dollars as an article processing fee for AERA members, with reduced fees for students and no charge for scholars from developing countries. In the face of the growing popularity of "gold" open access, based on authors or institutions paying fees to journals for open access article publication, it is good to remember that the majority of publishers of education journals, such as AERA, Sage, Blackwell, and Taylor and Francis, have policies in place that enable "green" open access. These journals permit authors to deposit their final, peer-reviewed drafts in their libraries' institutional repositories or make them available via personal websites, according to the SHERPA/RoMEO (Rights Metadata for Open Archiving) project, which provides authors with a database of such policies.

The implications of open access across research fields, including varied methodological and theoretical approaches to "science" and "evidence" within broader fields such as education, was recognized as important in the earlier version of this chapter:

> The privileging of one form of research can only end up obscuring the contribution, as well as diminish the funding and support, for other kinds of research. What then, one wants to ask, of critical pedagogy (e.g., Kincheloe and Steinberg 2006) to name one of so many different ways of doing education research, which help us to make sense of schooling through no less an application of rigorous and systematic methods, apart from the methods celebrated under the rubric of 'scientifically based research.' Surely, the full spectrum of research needs to be made freely available to teachers, administrators, parents, the press, and the public through open access, so that it can demonstrate its value to education, so that it can easily play a part in decision-making and deliberation over the quality of the child's educational experience, in the nature of the lessons learned, in the democratic contribution of schooling, in the shaping of the curriculum.

That earlier version went on to emphasize that if researchers focused only on publishing in academic journals while neglecting to attend to the wider potential readerships of their publications enabled by open access, "then only this narrowly defined range of scientifically based research is going to play a public and legislated part in education." It underscored researchers' responsibility for their work's public circulation and participation in public deliberation and decision-making, while also stressing that increased access, via open access journals and institutional repositories, "can have the fortunate side-effect of advancing researchers' careers, even as they increase their contribution."

Since the NRC's 2002 report and the earlier version of this chapter, both open access and broader "opens science" initiatives have had more time to play out, alongside initiatives on behalf of "scientific" education research and companion "evidence-based" education reforms. This period of more than a decade has helped illuminate not only the possibilities but also the probabilities and eventualities enabled by the Internet, online publishing, and digital platforms for academic scholarship, across different types of research. In what ways do new "open science" initiatives and information technology infrastructures of academic publishing dovetail with the prescriptive Scientific Principles of the NRC report and present-day discussions of "evidence-based" education? Or, conversely, how do they foster engagement with critics' analyses of narrow, particular, positivist discourses of "science" and "evidence" in education scholarship? How might they facilitate engagement with more qualitative, interpretive and community-based participatory research, as well as with different kinds of local knowledge?

FROM OPEN ACCESS TO OPEN SCIENCE: SCHOLARLY COMMUNICATION INITIATIVES IN A DIGITAL ERA

As the open access movement made inroads in increasing the free, online availability of peer-reviewed articles, other initiatives to "open" scholarship via digital means unfolded as well – including open source, open data, and open science initiatives. This proliferation of (often interconnected) initiatives has created a complex terrain in which the same "open" initiatives may be used to serve multiple and sometimes conflicting agendas, while obscuring the broader landscape of research politics.[5] Though emphasizing transparency and "openness," these initiatives, like other social projects, are also inevitably value-laden and often at least partially opaque, in terms of the epistemological or other values served. The "open science" movement is the most encompassing and arguably most fraught example of all. It comprises initiatives devoted not only to greater online access to peer-reviewed research (i.e. open access initiatives), but also to epistemological projects that embody particular approaches to "scientific" and "evidence-based" research – arguably, to the exclusion or marginalization of other social epistemologies and forms of research. As discussed further below, especially fraught are open science initiatives oriented toward and failing to problematize: 1) a unitary framing of "science," 2) the reproducibility (or replication) of research; and/or 3) altmetrics (i.e. alternative metrics) to evaluate research "impact," without attention to the contexts of research production and broader politics of knowledge. Too often, these elements combine to constitute a de facto positivist epistemology of "open science" that is not attuned to socially contextualized and interpretive approaches to empirical – and arguably *scientific* – investigation.

UNITARY "SCIENCE"?

As other commentators have also noted, the use of "science" as a unitary term, in open science initiatives and in the NRC's report, is arguably problematic in itself. Such a unitary term and conception of "science" is limited in its capacity to facilitate more capacious, critical public dialogues and approaches to research, from the perspective of both present and past interlocutors. It may too easily devalue both the wide spectrum of empirical inquiry warranting the designation "scientific," as well as the contributions of other types of inquiry and knowledge, including the arts and humanities, to public deliberation. For example, in Michelle Sidler's recent article "Open Science and the Three Cultures: Expanding Open Science to All Domains of Knowledge Creation," she proposes that open science advocates use the term knowledge instead of science, to more clearly include and engage with scholars in the social sciences and humanities:

> Scholars of language, rhetoric, and writing (like myself) are keenly aware of the power of words and their associations, and the word 'science' carries associations of division and inequality for some humanities and social science scholars. Either the movement will have to create and foster a broader definition of 'science' or it will have to replace the term altogether. (Sidler 2014)

Sidler mentions the Open Knowledge Foundation as an organization that already uses this more inclusive phrasing, while the Public Knowledge Project is another. Sidler also proposes adapting digital tools developed for "open science" initiatives for social sciences and humanities research, again while framing such efforts in terms of exploring "the potential impact of networked technologies on all fields of knowledge." She argues that this more multidisciplinary, cross-field appropriation of digital tools would lead not only to a more inclusive "open knowledge" movement, but could also be "the most pragmatic strategy for bridging the 'three cultures.'" Sidler's emphasis on the empirical and interpretive insights of all fields of knowledge parallel points made by earlier critics of the NRC's *Scientific Research in Education*. As Frederick Erikson summarized his critique of the NRC's report:

> [T]he current promotion by the federal government of 'science' as a unitary paradigm for educational research is a mistaken effort...[R]egardless of intentions, the consequences of this promotional effort are likely to be negative for educational research as a whole, because the promotion of the 'scientific' not only misrepresents science itself, but it also undervalues and marginalizes the contributions of the arts and humanities to our understanding of educational aims and practices. (Erikson 2005)

However, compared with Sidler's emphasis on science as one of "three cultures" that then need to be bridged, Erikson more explicitly problematizes the notion of a distinct and unitary "science," by discussing how promotion of the "scientific" in such monolithic terms leads to a distorted picture of science, or narrow scientism. Erikson's observations also problematize claims that digital tools, however adapted and reappropriated, are sufficient to foster interdisciplinary dialogue and engagement, without more deeply questioning the assumptions, values and claims to generalizability in different fields of inquiry. These include assumptions and values pertaining to generalizability itself.

FROM *SCIENTIFIC RESEARCH IN EDUCATION* TO THE "OPEN SCIENCE" MOVEMENT

REPLICATION AND REPRODUCIBILITY INITIATIVES

In this regard, another point of connection between the 2002 NRC report and present day open science initiatives is the emphasis on the replication, or reproducibility, of research. When the NRC report appeared, the fifth principle ("SCIENTIFIC PRINCIPLE 5: Replicate and Generalize Across Studies") was among the elements that some educational scholars found most problematic, indicative of a wider web of problematic assumptions about the supposedly unified, decontextualized nature of science. As Pamela Moss wrote, singling out this element among the six principles: "The word 'replicate' is the only term that seems to raise immediate concerns for researchers who privilege the stance that meanings are situated in social contexts" (Moss 2005, p. 22). Moss goes on to discuss how the report privileges particular types of research, including on the basis of replicability, as more "scientific" than other types – namely, qualitative and interpretive research. She also associates these research hierarchies with a unified conception of "science," pointing to the positivist elective affinities among these "open science" elements. As she puts it, "Consistent with a unified approach to social science, the report privileges programs of research that culminate in the establishment of replicable causal effects (idealized in randomized experiments), and it positions 'descriptive studies' as preliminary or supplementary to this task" (Moss 2005, p. 22). Moss also highlights how such criteria then influence the types of research produced in the first place, by guiding policymakers and the formation of peer review panels, including those charged with funding allocation. From this vantage, "open science" initiatives that emphasize reproducibility, especially those doing so in a way that suggest the neutrality and universality of reproducibility as a scientific touchstone, are actually undermining the "opening" of dominant discussions to the types of research highlighted by Moss.

Within the open science movement and open access publishing, one of the foremost initiatives emphasizing reproducibility (or replication) is the Public Library of Science (PLOS)'s Reproducibility Initiative, launched by PLOS One in 2012 with the aim "to help scientists validate their research findings by providing a mechanism for blind, independent replication by experts from Science Exchange's network of more than 1,000 providers at core facilities and contract research organizations" (Pattinson 2012). Though PLOS publishes an array of research through its open access journals, including studies that draw on qualitative methods and community-based research, this Reproducibility Initiative is most tailored to the methods, norms and criteria of clinical biomedical research. As the PLOS announcement continued, speaking of "the scientific community" in unitary terms:

> Reproducibility, or the lack thereof, is a known issue in the scientific community, but few have the time or resources to fully address it. The Reproducibility Initiative is intended to encourage authors to validate their work by facilitating collaboration with an unbiased expert, and offering a Certificate of Reproducibility upon completion. This project will benefit stakeholders from across the research spectrum, including research scientists,

drug companies, publishers, funders, and patient groups, all of whom agree that independent confirmation of results improves science and speeds discovery.

The announcement goes on to explain that, since its founding in 2006, PLOS hoped to be a publication that would not only advance "open access" to existing research to anyone with an internet connection, but also a venue for types of studies and findings that have tended not to appear in print at all. While "findings that historically did not make it into print" might conjure a range of images and types of research for different scholars, PLOS' Reproducibility Initiative specifies these as "the negative results, the replication studies, the reanalyses of existing datasets." In other words, the initiative is oriented toward clarifying and correcting a body of research of a certain type – especially, clinical biomedical research and randomized controlled trials (RCTs) that, for example, seek to answer questions about the efficacy of particular pharmaceuticals to treat particular patient symptoms. Research that does not fall under this umbrella, which may be less likely to be published for other reasons, is not addressed by this nor similar reproducibility initiatives in the "open science" movement. This includes, for example, research with less potential for commercialization that has a lower likelihood of being funded and carried out in the first place.

ALTMETRICS

Likewise, another multifaceted initiative in the broader open science movement is the altmetrics movement – a push for new, alternative metrics to track research dissemination and "impact," especially via social media and other Web publishing platforms, from Twitter and blogs to social networking sites. Its status as a movement is accentuated by having its own manifesto (Priem, Taraborelli, Groth, Neylon 2011), which begins with the observation that "No one can read everything," and continues to discusses the importance of filters and how "the growth of new, online scholarly tools allows us to make new filters" – or altmetrics. It seeks not only to "expand our view of what impact looks like, but also of what's making the impact." As the manifesto continues, "expressions of scholarship are becoming more diverse," including not only articles and citations of articles in non-traditional venues, but also "'raw science' like datasets, code, and experimental designs," and "Semantic publishing or 'nanopublication,' where the citable unit is an argument or passage rather than entire article." Altmetrics, then, becomes a catch-all term for attempts to measure this burgeoning digital world of scholarly communication. It comprises both metrics to help scholars filter this universe in new ways in conducting their research and metrics to help them demonstrate their research's "impact" and status within it – whether to fellow participants, university decision-makers, or funders.

Again, especially insofar as "raw science" and the publication of datasets – "open data" – are emphasized, the altmetrics movement also tends to articulate with reproducibility and replication initiatives such as PLOS' efforts.

Reproducibility itself can be considered an altmetric. These initiatives then constitute the terms in which scholars attempt to demonstrate their "impact" and the value of their research, shaping incentives and, arguably, laying the groundwork for new forms of individually-oriented careerism rather than publicly-oriented scholarship and critique of status quo power relations, in academia and beyond. As altmetrics analyst Martin Fenner writes in the introduction to a recent article, "Altmetrics and Other Novel Measures for Scientific Impact":

> Impact assessment is one of the major drivers in scholarly communication, in particular since the number of available faculty positions and grants has far exceeded the number of applications. Peer review still plays a critical role in evaluating science, but citation-based bibliometric indicators are becoming increasingly important...Altmetrics use indicators gathered in the real-time Social Web to provide immediate feedback about scholarly works. (Fenner 2014)

So while Fenner begins by making passing reference to key structural problems of academia, including a dearth of secure academic jobs and declining research funding, he does not delve further into these problems nor their possibly complicated relations to altmetrics and assessments of "research impact." Instead, Fenner presents a detailed discussion of altmetrics and the Social Web. He acknowledges the need to further address issues of metrics gaming, the Web's complex flux, and putting research *"metrics into context."* Yet, he includes no further analysis of the social and institutional *contexts of research*, particularly the relative investment, roles, and benefits received by the public versus private sectors. Nor does Fenner analyze how new metrics movements may simultaneously alter public and epistemological dimensions of these contexts of research production, including by obscuring the contributions of different types of research serving an array of public ends. Thus in many respects, the altmetrics movement is fraught with the conflict between different epistemological projects as well as tensions between public versus private agendas. Ironically, without attending to contexts of research production and a broader vision of the politics of knowledge, altmetrics can end up reinforcing quite conventional social relations, epistemologies and narrowly positivist approaches to "science," rather than more deeply alternative paradigms.

TOWARD A BROADER POLITICS OF KNOWLEDGE: STREET SCIENCE AND SOCIAL MOVEMENTS IN A NEOLIBERAL ERA

These public versus private valences and the multiple, conflicting epistemological projects within the "open science" movement all bear on possibilities for research dissemination, whatever the new publishing possibilities enabled by digital technologies. The epistemological projects described above are significant, in particular, for how they shape the institutionalization of research and knowledge in disciplinary fields and funding agencies as well as public norms of credibility. Public norms of credibility, in turn, bear on both public reception of and engagement with academic research (or lack thereof), as well as with claims by particular communities in the larger public sphere. They have consequences for how different types of research and knowledge claims are initially evaluated, then disseminated, and continue to fare upon wider circulation – perhaps characterized as "expert" and "legitimate," or "merely anecdotal," or in some other way. What happens, for example, to the scholarly contributions of thinkers such as Paulo Freire and Myles Horton, and the legacies of institutions such as the Highlander Center in Tennessee, in an era of the Education Sciences Reform Act (2002), which led to the formation of the Institute of Education Sciences?

From the vantage of the present, the lens of scholars' individual responsibility seems increasingly inadequate to address the challenges of public research dissemination in the face of methodological and research hierarchies such as those described above – hierarchies institutionalized under the rubrics of "scientific" and "evidence-based" by powerful public agencies and funders. For researchers who are devoted to relatively marginalized research agendas, such as critical pedagogy, including by reports such as *Scientific Research in Education*, often just pursuing such research and maintaining a foothold in contemporary universities is an accomplishment. While new open access publishing options are significant and helpful to wider research dissemination, by themselves they do not address the research hierarchies institutionalized under the rubrics of "scientific" and "evidence-based," nor the challenges these hierarchies pose to ensuring that the fullest spectrum of research is tapped and mobilized in public policy discussions. Here the challenges of research dissemination meet the possibilities of greater public engagement and democratic governance. At this nexus, the limitations of the NRC report's sixth principle, focusing on research dissemination, overlap with the epistemological and democratic limitations of the report's other five principles, in their prescriptive and narrow framing of the "scientific." As the earlier version of this chapter observed:

> [G]uiding policymakers and collaborating with teachers is not necessarily the same thing as fostering a more democratic approach that might better inform public deliberations over educational matters … [T]here is nothing inherently democratic about policymakers following research evidence in arriving at the most effective strategies for implementing specific policy goals (2001a). What is scientific is far more about the open and free inquiry into these educational phenomena. What is scientific is the systematic and imaginative ways in which education researchers seek to contribute to the very quality of public deliberation over education's ends and means. Rather than think about disclosing education research for the purpose of affording sufficient scrutiny from other researchers, researchers need to consider these new ways of expanding the circulation of this knowledge. Doing research today means testing the potential of new publishing technologies for opening research to greater scrutiny and impact, *as well as to greater integration with other forms of knowing*. (emphasis added)

So how might critical, progressive approaches to research dissemination (the sixth principle of the NRC report) be more fully engaged with the other principles pertaining to different types of research and knowledge, rather than suggesting that scientific research – especially in an area of such pressing public concern as education – operates apart from the world that it observes and pronounces on? What might be the key elements of a broader politics of knowledge?

Other commentators have noted these contradictions and limitations of "open science" initiatives as well, while suggesting key elements of a broader politics as knowledge. These include attention to the increasing privatization of education and, more generally, the overweening emphasis on market-driven, "neoliberal" policy-making throughout society. For example, Eric Kansa's recent piece, "It's the Neoliberalism, Stupid: Why Instrumentalist Arguments for Open Access, Open Data, and Open Science Are Not Enough," discusses how "open" initiatives focused primarily on cutting costs and speeding up research dissemination need to ask additional questions about the public value of this research and how it might be used to advance more inclusive and democratic societies. For those focused on commercial possibilities, Kansa writes:

> I don't have a problem with wealth creation as an outcome of greater openness in research. Who doesn't want more wealth? However we need to ask about wealth creation *for whom* and *under what conditions*? Will the lion's share of the wealth created on newly freed research only go to a tiny elite class of investors? Will it simply mean a bit more profit for Google and a few other big aggregators? Will this wealth be taxed and redistributed enough to support and sustain the research commons exploited to feed it? (Kansa 2014)

These questions are currently not central to and relatively neglected by most initiatives on behalf of altmetrics, reproducibility, and the "open science" movement. This may be understandable, given the larger and more difficult political and economic issues at stake. Yet neglecting to ask these questions means not being able to discuss the forces shaping contemporary universities where many "open science" advocates are situated. It means not asking about the trend toward universities serving commercial interests (Popp Berman 2012) that do not necessarily grow wealth or opportunity in society more generally, particularly relative to public investments in research (Mazzucato 2013). Not asking these questions itself becomes an indicator of the difference and distance between tenured, university-based "open science" advocates and those advocating for the *democratization* of research and knowledge from other locations.

These latter advocates often articulate their arguments in less positivist and more value-laden languages that do not pretend to a "view from nowhere," but recognize knowledge as situated in particular social locations and perspectives (Haraway 1988). Within the academy, such positions and discourses tend to articulate most of all with scholars whose conceptions of science include qualitative, participatory and interpretive approaches to research, including feminist and postcolonial science studies scholarship (Harding 2011) and historical scholarship on the educational legacies of colonialism and imperialism (Willinsky 1998). These are precisely the forms of inquiry that have tended to be marginalized both by dominant discourses of the "scientific" and "evidence-based practice" as well as by emerging technological infrastructures of scholarly communication. Here the public health field, specifically those approaches to public health research that emphasize community-based participatory research (CBPR), "street science" (Corburn 2005, 2009), and engagement with health social movements (Brown, Morello-Frosch, and Zavestoski 2011), is arguably a more helpful touchstone for the wide array of education scholars than the clinical biomedical research that has tended to shape "evidence-based practice" discourses and many open science initiatives. Drawing on many of the same reference points as critical pedagogy, these approaches to research underscore the potential contributions of academic and professional knowledge as well as non-academic local knowledge and "street science" to "co-produce expertise" (Corburn 2007) by shaping research agendas, carrying out research, developing analyses and interpretations, and arriving at practical implications and proposals for action. Such health research often points to the social and environmental dimensions of illness, beyond the individualizing lens of clinical medicine. It highlights the need to address inequalities of power and resources, while tapping local social and cultural knowledge, rather than only seeking more rigorous evidence or adopting new standards of "scientific" research and hoping for meaningful change to remedy health inequities on that basis.

Social movements and organizing are often vital to such community-based approaches to research, which are also emphasized by critical education scholars. For example, Donna Riley's recent paper (2014) "What's wrong with Evidence? Epistemological Roots and Pedagogical Implications of 'Evidence-based Practice' in STEM education," critiques the assumptions and trajectory of "evidence-based" initiatives in education research and practice, focusing on engineering education. She discusses the "Roots and Contexts for emergence of evidence based practice" not only in the No Child Left Behind Act of 2001, but also the Outcomes Based Education movement of the 1980s and the Taylorist scientific management movement of the early twentieth century. Riley notes the education community's concerns about "the over-reliance on experimental design and positivist epistemologies, and the loss of other ways of knowing …" both in the past and present. She observes that federal definitions of "scientific research" in education expanded only minimally in response to criticisms of the 2002 NRC report, such that "many of the critiques continue to hold a decade later" (Riley 2014, p. 3). As she reflects on the need for alternatives:

> It was a deliberate strategy our community set a decade or more ago – to enact chance in engineering education – to generate "hard data" that would convince engineering deans and high level university administrators – even our peers who teach engineering – that we need to change engineering education. Some thought they would listen to the data. But we are finding, with Dewey, that it is not that simple; research has not dictated practice. The causal theory that rigorous data causes change was wrong … can we draw on

social movements that have succeeded in creating widespread cultural chance to devise new strategies (based on experience rather than evidence) for change in engineering education? (Riley 2014, p. 5)

Riley highlights the need for broader approaches to "science" and "evidence"[6] as well as broader social movement strategies for change, to achieve engineering education that highlights the political, normative and organizational contexts of engineering and STEM education. While Riley does not address the open science movement directly, she does critique Massive Online Open Courses (MOOCs) as "hyped as the solution to budgetary crisis," while looking beyond technologies of "information transfer" for alternatives to "evidence-based practice" initiatives in education. Rather than looking to the altmetrics or open science movements, she quotes Cesar Chavez on the spirit and tactics of organizing: "The name of the game is to talk to people." Even open science initiatives and digital infrastructures designed to be more embracing of multiple types of knowledge are no replacement for attending to the social relations of research and community-based knowledge. Like public health scholars emphasizing CBPR, street science, local knowledge, the co-production of expertise, and collaborations with social movements, Riley turns to the organizing traditions of Cesar Chavez, Myles Horton and the Highlander Center as more promising touchstones for "effective strategies for cultural and institutional change" (Riley 2014, p. 5).

Taken together, these developments suggest that the current possibilities and challenges of scholarly communication in the field of education research (and beyond) cannot be addressed by research dissemination alone nor by emphasizing the individual responsibility of researchers, while disregarding the structural and neoliberal policy contexts of research, including research funding and criteria of research evaluation. Open access publishing environments and policies can make crucial contributions to more direct public engagement with research – yet they are insufficient. In addition, while new online publishing platforms and "open science" digital tools, including altmetrics, have emerged and continued to grow, even claiming to be revolutionary, other dimensions of education research remain deeply entrenched and removed from public engagement. New "open science" initiatives that embody unproblematized, positivist epistemological projects in many ways dovetail with the prescriptive Scientific Principles of the NRC report and present-day discussions of "evidence-based" education, rather than further opening discussion of the analyses and values of critics of those relatively narrow discourses of "science" and "evidence." Hence, trends in open science initiatives suggest that narrow discourses of "science" and "evidence" remain not *despite* but, in part, *because of* their further institutionalization in new scholarly communication infrastructures. For this reason, this chapter has argued that research dissemination practices and scholarly communication infrastructures are constituted together with knowledge hierarchies. This point underscores the ultimate interdependence of academic publishing with other dimensions of research, including issues of epistemology. It points to the need to foster critical interventions and collaborations on behalf of public, democratic scholarship underpinned by multiple social epistemologies, particularly in dialogue with academic labor movements and other longstanding social movements. These movements include, for example, the civil rights and labor movements that Cesar Chavez, Myles Horton and so many others have advanced, nurturing broader democratic politics alongside more democratic notions of knowledge.

NOTES

[1] This article was originally published, in a somewhat altered form, as "Scientific research in a democratic culture: Or what's a social science for?" Teachers College Record, 107(1), 2005, pp. 38-51, and builds on arguments presented in Willinsky (2001a, 2002) with the specific context of the National Research Council report, Scientific Research in Education (Shavelson & Towne 2002). A second version was published in an earlier edition of this Handbook. This chapter represents the third version.

[2] For critical reviews of other aspects of the Scientific Research in Education report (Shavelson & Towne 2002), see Erickson (2005), Gee (2005), Moss (2005), and Walker (2005), available at: https://www.tcrecord.org/library/Issue.asp?volyear=2005&number=1 &volume=107

[3] These trends include the National Institutes of Health (NIH)'s 2008 adoption of a Public Access Policy, which set a precedent for open access policies at the U.S. federal government level. This policy also provided the impetus for a research collaboration between the authors, investigating the implications of the NIH policy for a wide array of stakeholders, including those conducting different types of health research. In many respects, this diversity of health research parallels the array of educational research that contemporary critics argued was not adequately addressed by the NRC's report.

[4] In terms of the *open access* book, the National Research Council's publications, including *Scientific Research in Education*, discussed in detail in this chapter, are available in open access on its website, as well as for sale in other formats.

[5] Some of these ambiguities and tensions are highlighted in a recent book on "opening science": http://book.openingscience.org/

[6] Riley's distinction here between "experience" and "evidence" highlights the fraught status of the empirical in contemporary education scholarship, including the importance of interpretation to critical scholars such as herself and the limitations of positivist epistemologies.

REFERENCES

Bartling, S., & Friesike, S. (Eds.). (2014). *The evolving guide on how the internet is changing research, collaboration and scholarly publishing*. SpringerOpen (http://book.openingscience.org/).

Brown, P., Morello-Frosch, R., & Zavestoski, S. (2011). *Contested illnesses: Citizens, science, and health social movements*. Berkeley, CA: University of California Press.

Corburn, J. (2005). *Street science: Community knowledge and environmental health justice*. Cambridge, MA: The MIT Press.

Corburn, J. (2007). Community knowledge in environmental health science: Co-producing policy expertise. *Environmental Science & Policy, 10*, 150-161.

Corburn, J. (2009). *Toward the healthy city: People, places, and the politics of urban planning*. Cambridge, MA: The MIT Press.

Education Sciences Reform Act of 2002. H. R. 3801. Retrieved July 2014, from http://www.ed.gov/policy/rschstat/leg/PL107-279.pdf

Erickson, F. (2005). Arts, humanities, and sciences in educational research and social engineering in federal education policy. *Teachers College Record, 107*, 4-9.

Fenner, M. (2014). Altmetrics and other novel measures for scientific impact. In S. Bartling & S. Friesike (Eds.), *The evolving guide on how the internet is changing research, collaboration and scholarly publishing*. SpringerOpen (http://book.openingscience.org/).

Feuer, M. J., Towne, L., & Shavelson, R. J. (2002). Scientific culture and educational research. *Educational Researcher, 31*, 4-14.

Gee, J. (2005). It's theories all the way down: A response to scientific research in education. *Teachers College Record, 107*, 10-18.

Haraway, D. (1988). Situated knowledges: The science question in feminism and the privilege of partial perspective. *Feminist Studies, 14*, 575-599.

Harding, S. (Ed.) (2011). *The postcolonial science and technology studies reader*. Durham, NC: Duke University Press.

Kansa, E. (2014). It's the neoliberalism, stupid: Why instrumentalist arguments for open access, open data, and open science are not enough. Retrieved July 2014, from http://blogs.lse.ac.uk/impactofsocialsciences/2014/01/27/its-the-neoliberalism-stupid-kansa/

Kincheloe, J., & Steinberg, S. (Eds.). (2006). *Cutting class: Social class and education*. Lanham, MD: Rowman and Littlefield.

Kuhn, T. S. (1978). Newton's optical papers. In I. Bernard Cohen (Ed.), *Isaac Newton's papers and letters on natural philosophy and related documents* (pp. 27-45). Cambridge, MA: Harvard University Press.

Longino, H. (2002). *The fate of knowledge*. Princeton, NJ: Princeton University Press.

MacGregor, J., Stranack, K., & Willinsky, J. (2014). The public knowledge project: Open source tools for open access to scholarly communication. In S. Bartling & S. Friesike (Eds.), *The evolving guide on how the internet is changing research, collaboration and scholarly publishing*. SpringerOpen (http://book.openingscience.org/).

Mazzucato, M. (2013). *The entrepreneurial state: Debunking public vs. private sector myths*. Anthem Press.

Moss, P. (2005). Toward "epistemic reflexivity" in educational research: A response to scientific research in education. *Teachers College Record, 107*, 19-29.

Pattinson, D. (2012). PLOS one launches reproducibility initiative. Retrieved July 2014, from http://blogs.plos.org/everyone/2012/08/14/plos-one-launches-reproducibility-initiative/

Popp Berman, E. (2012). *Creating the market university: How academic science became an economic engine*. Princeton, NJ: Princeton University Press.

Priem, J., Taraborelli, D., Groth, P., & Cameron, N. (2011). Altmetrics manifesto. Retrieved July 2014, from http://altmetrics.org/manifesto/

Riley, D. (2014). *What's wrong with evidence? Epistemological roots and pedagogical implications of 'evidence-based practice' in STEM education*. Paper presented at the annual meeting of the American Society for Engineering Education (ASEE). Retrieved July 2014, from http://www.asee.org/public/conferences/32/papers/9995/view

Shavelson, R. J., & Towne, L. (Eds.). (2002). *Scientific research in education*. Washington, DC: National Academy Press.

Sidler, M. (2014). Open science and the three cultures: Expanding open science to all domains of knowledge creation. In S. Bartling & S. Friesike (Eds.), *The evolving guide on how the internet is changing research, collaboration and scholarly publishing*. SpringerOpen (http://book.openingscience.org/).

Walker, V. (2005). After methods, then what? A researcher's response to the Report of the National Research Council. *Teachers College Record, 107*, 30-37.

Willinsky, J. (1998). *Learning to divide the world: Education at empire's end*. Minneapolis, MN: University of Minnesota Press.

Willinsky, J. (2001a). The strategic education research program and the public value of research. *Educational Researcher, 30*, 5-14.

Willinsky, J. (2001b). Extending the prospects of evidence-based education. *IN>>SIGHT, 1*, 23-41.

Willinsky, J. (2005). The unacknowledged convergence of open source, open access, and open science. *First Monday, 10*(8). Retrieved July 2014, from http://firstmonday.org/issues/issue10_8/willinsky/index.html

Willinsky, J. (2006). *The access principle: The case for open access to research and scholarship.* Cambridge MA: MIT Press.

CONTRIBUTORS

Carolyne Ali-Khan is an assistant professor of Foundations and Secondary Education University of North Florida. Carolyne has extensive international experience, including research on photo-elicitation in a project with students in Pakistan, and collaborative activities in Japan and Ghana. She taught in urban schools in New York City and has a PhD in Urban Education from the Graduate Center of CUNY. Carolyne is co-editor of Bold Visions with Sense Publishers.

Marissa E. Bellino is a doctoral candidate in Urban Education at the City University of New York, The Graduate Center. Her interests include critical youth participatory research in urban science classrooms.

Kathleen S. Berry is professor of education at the University of New Brunswick in Fredericton, New Brunswick. She has published extensively in the field of critical studies, drama education, and social justice. She has received the Allan P. Stuart Award for Excellence in Teaching.

Deborah P. Britzman, FRSC, is Distinguished Research Professor at York University in Toronto and the author of numerous books and articles on psychoanalysis and education.

Phil Francis Carspecken is Professor of Education at Indiana University and author of numerous books and articles about social theory and research.

Gene Fellner is an assistant professor of education at the College of Staten Island, part of the City University of New York. His research explores the range of student strengths that are often not visible in the public transcripts that represent them, and the ways in which these strengths can be illuminated. In the service of this project, he seeks to find and understand spaces where art and research meet.

Cheryl Holzmeyer is a postdoctoral fellow at Stanford University Graduate School of Education and a Research Associate of the Public Knowledge Project.

David W. Jardine is Professor of Education at the University of Calgary. He is the author of numerous books and articles on hermeneutics and education, curriculum theory, and teaching.

Joe L. Kincheloe died from coronary artery disease, on December 19 2008, while on vacation in Jamaica. Joe was the Canada Research Chair in Critical Pedagogy in the Department of Integrated Studies in Education at McGill University. His research/teaching involved devising and engaging students in new, more intellectually rigorous, socially just ways of analyzing and researching education.

He developed an evolving notion of criticality that constructed innovative ways to cultivate the intellect as it worked in anti-oppressive and affectively engaging ways. With Shirley Steinberg, Joe founded the Paulo and Nita Freire International Project for Critical Pedagogy (http://freire.mcgill.ca/), which aims to improve the contribution that education makes to social justice and the democratic quality of people's lives.

Tricia M. Kress is an associate professor of Leadership in Urban Schools at the University of Massachusetts Boston. Her publications focus on the use of critical pedagogy and qualitative research as tools for improving urban education.

Rebecca J. Lloyd is an associate professor in the Faculty of Education at the University of Ottawa. Her interdisciplinary phenomenological research, framed by the 'function2flow' (http://function2flow.ca/) model, facilitates curricular and pedagogical understandings of becoming physically educated in alternative and mainstream activities.

Diana Moyer is a member of the Faculty Development Team in the Office of Research and Engagement at the University of Tennessee. She facilitates interdisciplinary research collaborations and proposal development for external funding.

Alice J. Pitt is Vice Provost of Academic Affairs at York University in Toronto. Her publications focus on the implications of psychoanalytic theory for teaching and learning in feminist classrooms and studies of policy, language, and autonomy.

Malgorzata Powietrzynska earned her Ph.D. in Urban Education at the Graduate Center of the City University of New York. She works at the Brooklyn Educational Opportunity Center of the State University of New York where she coordinates grant writing and grant administration activities. She is currently involved in research focusing on emotions and Mindfulness in Education.

Wolff-Michael Roth is Lansdowne Professor of Applied Cognitive Science at the University of Victoria. He studies knowing and learning across the life span, in in/formal educational settings and in the workplace, most recently in the context of the continuing assessment of aviation pilots.

Christina Siry is professor for Learning and Instruction at the University of Luxembourg. She researches the learning and teaching of science at the elementary level, with a particular focus on the complexities inherent in multilingual classrooms.

Stephen J. Smith is Academic Associate Dean in the Faculty of Education at Simon Fraser University and has written on curricular and instructional practices in physical and health education, the somatics of teacher education, and the phenomenology of cross-species relations.

Shirley R. Steinberg is Research Professor of Youth Studies at the University of Calgary. She is the founder of The International Institute of Critical Pedagogy and Transformative Leadership (freireproject.org), and the author and editor of numerous books and articles. Her recent book is the award winning Critical Qualitative Research Reader. She is a CTV Newschannel columnist on the Culture Shock weekly segment.

Barbara Thayer-Bacon is a professor in philosophy of education, program coordinator for the Cultural Studies in Education masters program and the Learning Environments and Educational Studies doctoral program, University of Tennessee. Her primary areas of scholarship as a philosopher of education are feminist theory and pedagogy, pragmatism, and cultural studies in education.

Kenneth Tobin is Presidential Professor at the City University of New York Graduate Center and is the author of numerous books and articles on science education, urban education, and research.

Mark Vicars is a teaching and research academic in the College of Education at Victoria University, Melbourne. His main research interests are literacy education, practitioner inquiry, teacher education and qualitative research methodology (narrative methods) with a focus on inclusion and diversity.

Peter Waldman completed a PhD in Urban Education at the Graduate Center of CUNY in 2014. A book (Sense Publishers 2015), based on his dissertation research, employs impressionistic narrative research draws on the author's experiences of addiction and Alcoholics Anonymous (AA). Peter is an adjunct lecturer at the College of Staten Island and has been a special education teacher with the Department of Education in New York City.

John Willinsky is Khosla Family Professor of Education at Stanford University and Professor (Part-Time) of Publishing Studies at Simon Fraser University, where he directs the Public Knowledge Project.

Photo: Joe Kincheloe and Kenneth Tobin.

INDEX

A

absolute truth, 94
accent, 58, 330
  agogic, 268, 273, 274
accountability, xix, 149, 353
achievement gap, 172
acting white, 52
action research, 85, 87, 97, 152, 156, 175, 368, 372, 374, 380
activity
  physical, 257, 262, 264, 274
  running, 256, 257, 260, 264, 266, 267, 274, 321, 362, 384, 388, 405
  swimming, 256, 260, 262, 265, 271, 274, 305
addiction, 323, 324, 327, 329, 331, 333, 335
adjacency pairs, 206, 207
adolescence, 156, 194, 342, 400
aesthetic experience, 236, 237
affirmative presentism, 286–289
African American scholars, 280
agency, xvii, xxi, 7, 8, 13, 23, 28, 41, 45–47, 52, 58, 61, 62, 64, 67, 68, 71, 86, 94, 98–100, 186, 194, 281, 313, 396, 456, 457
agency|structure, 47, 62, 298
Alcoholics Anonymous (AA), xli, 321–335, 475
alcoholism, 321–330, 333, 334
alethia, 249–252
alignment, 69, 217
Ali-Khan, Carolyne, xli, 157, 293, 295, 313, 473
Alridge, Derrick, 280, 287, 289
alternative rationality, 280
altmetrics, 464, 465, 471
amplitude, 42, 69–71
analytic memoranda, 48, 72
analytic philosophers, 138

Aquinas, Thomas, 240
archeological genealogy, 87, 101
archival manuscripts, 281
Arendt, Hannah, 19, 24, 236, 242, 251
Aristotle, 137, 258, 427, 428
artful practice, xlii, 92, 162, 383, 384, 393
assent, 35–40, 330
assimilate, 94
audiencing, 115
Austen, Jane, 143
Australian Educational Researcher, 12, 344
authenticity criteria, 34, 43–46, 73, 344
authority, 18, 82, 93, 109, 113, 121, 124, 136, 183, 185, 269, 322, 327, 372, 384, 386, 392, 395, 400, 402, 408, 409, 416
autobiography, x, 59, 61, 308, 310
auto/ethnography, 34, 44, 293–315, 332
autonomy, 29, 36, 62, 66, 104, 407
awareness, xxx, xxxv, 4, 10, 16, 38, 113, 123, 126, 175, 203, 256, 259, 261, 262, 267–270, 272, 273, 283, 345–347, 349, 351–353, 357–359, 361, 368, 373, 423, 450
axiology, xli, 169, 170, 195, 304

B

Bakhtin, Mikhail, 185, 189, 196
banking system, 105, 171, 172, 174, 368
behaviorism, 17–20
Bellino, Marissa, xlii, 367, 473
Belmont Report, xiii, 29, 36, 344
beneficence, 29, 36, 340, 344
benefits, xii, xxxix, 3, 4, 8, 29, 30, 36, 38, 41, 43, 45, 46, 51, 56, 111,

479

INDEX

112, 140, 142, 210, 285, 308, 340–344, 349, 353, 354, 357, 359, 360, 369, 374, 463, 465
Berger, Peter, 111, 112, 126, 127, 129
Berry, Kathleen, xiv–xviii, xxii, 6, 79–109, 114, 283, 287
bias, 392
bifurcations, 82, 91, 295, 312
Bildung, 247
binarisms, 98, 99
blurred genres, 84, 85, 91, 97, 109, 274, 310
body movement, 42, 62, 69, 218–220, 226, 228
Bond, Horace Mann, 280
Bourdieu, Pierre, 44, 186, 212, 214, 308, 341, 342, 346, 348
bricolage, xiv–xxii, xxiv, xxv, xxxix, 6, 13, 79–110, 113–116, 118–123, 130, 283, 287, 314
bricoleur, xiv, xv–xxii, xxxii, 79–93, 95–105, 107, 108, 113, 114, 119
Buddhism, 324, 343, 357

C

canonical knowledge, 66
capital, 10, 23, 71, 200, 282, 308, 334, 392
capitalism, 109, 279
Carr, E. H., 145
Caruth, Cathy, 395, 397, 409
case studies, xlii, 42, 84, 86, 238
causal explanations, 204
causal relationships, xxxi, 13, 17, 441, 445
causality, 11, 342
change, xxx, 44, 73, 74, 101, 153, 162, 163, 176, 205, 212, 225, 245, 266, 303, 327, 339, 367
chaos and complexity, 82, 109
character, 64, 182, 193, 229, 236, 240, 246, 247, 250, 281, 324, 326, 331, 342, 351, 390, 391, 431, 442, 446, 459
children's rights, 151
chronology, 402, 409
Clapp, Elsie Ripley, 144, 146, 147
class, x, xi, xxiii, xxv, 4, 6, 7, 9, 15, 21, 29, 33, 35, 37–40, 42, 43, 46–50, 52, 54–56, 59, 61, 63, 68–70, 73, 83, 89, 91, 94, 99, 102, 104–107, 109, 113–115, 119–121, 127–129, 143, 146, 168, 172, 173, 181, 183, 184, 186–195, 215, 217, 262, 279, 282, 285, 288, 296, 300, 315, 345, 346, 349, 350, 352–357, 359, 362, 367–375, 377–381, 387, 389, 467
coding, xx, 127
cogenerative dialogues, 37, 42, 50, 57
cognitive abilities, xxi, xxviii, 11
coherence, 40, 43–45, 48, 50, 51, 71, 72, 141, 145, 348, 398, 399, 403
collaborative methods, xiii, 31, 34, 51, 74
collectivity, 199
Collins, 61, 184, 217
colonialism, xix, xxiii, xxxv, 15, 21, 87, 90, 109, 120, 282, 284, 468
commitment, xvi, xvii, xxii, 49, 215, 255, 283, 348, 423
theory, 206
common sense, xvii, xxxvii, xl, 91, 101, 104, 111, 168, 173, 177, 204, 206, 222, 428, 446
community based, 152
compassion, xvii, 89, 326, 335, 342, 346, 352, 357
complexity, xii, xiv, xvi, xix, xxv, xxvi, xxix–xxxv, 4–11, 22, 24–26, 79–83, 85, 86, 89, 91, 94–103, 105–109, 122, 123, 153, 173, 282–284, 286, 288, 294, 296, 302, 315, 342, 438, 456
Compte, Auguste, 17

480

INDEX

conceptual analysis, xviii, 44, 125, 226
conceptual archaeology, 397–399
conceptual history, 82–84, 134, 280
conditional relevance, 207
consciousness, x, xv, xxi, xxv–xxxi, xxxv–xxxvii, 3, 5, 8, 18, 21, 27, 113, 121, 123, 128–130, 186, 191, 256, 258, 260–263, 272, 273, 279, 281, 289, 325, 339, 345, 368, 378, 381, 424, 429, 437, 438, 440, 442, 443, 445, 446, 480, 450
 animate, 269, 273
consent, 29, 34–40, 43, 223, 309, 371, 414, 432
constraints, 27, 161, 183, 190, 199, 229, 230, 256, 416
constructivism, 8, 237
constructivist, 8, 9, 117, 220
contemplate practices, 341, 343, 351, 359
content analysis, 113, 116, 117
context, ix–xviii, xx, xxi, xxv–xxx, xxxii, xxxiii, xxxv–xxxviii, 4, 5, 7, 9–12, 15, 20, 21, 23–28, 30, 33, 39, 56, 57, 60, 72, 80, 82–84, 100, 103, 112–117, 120–126, 128, 129, 136, 138, 146, 148, 154, 157, 160, 170–172, 174, 181, 185, 194, 204, 226, 240, 243, 256, 279–281, 285–289, 291, 294, 298, 302, 313, 339–364, 370, 381, 384, 399, 403, 443, 458, 465, 470
contextual embeddedness, 7
contextualization, 9–12, 83, 100, 101, 114, 125, 291
contingency, 348
contingent, 35, 40, 89, 122, 201, 204, 205, 229, 297, 335, 345, 361, 396, 397
contradictions, 35, 40–46, 48, 50–52, 57, 60, 62, 71–73, 93–96, 98, 106, 109, 115, 123, 167, 176, 183, 230, 242, 296, 331, 348, 361, 409, 432, 433, 441, 448, 467

conversation analysis, 199–231
coordinate definitions, 433, 435
corporatization, 3
coteaching, 35, 37, 48, 56, 57, 60, 61, 361
coursework, 12, 169
credibility, 34, 465
credible voice, 57
crisis of representation, 85, 90, 109, 396, 403, 410
critical bricoleurs, xviii, xix, 82, 96
critical consciousness, 128, 368
critical discourse, 52
critical discourse analysis, 101
critical epistemology, 289
critical ethnography, 34, 61, 62, 114–116, 120
critical hermeneutics, 113, 119, 120, 123–130
critical history, 144, 281, 282, 285, 286
critical history of education, 281, 282, 285, 286
critical interpretation, 114, 116, 123–128, 393, 470
critical meta-analysis, 280
critical pedagogy, 128, 168, 169, 170, 171, 177, 304, 373, 460, 466, 468
critical perspectives, xii–xxxix, xli, xlii, 3–5, 7–11, 13, 20, 26, 28, 31, 34, 35, 44, 48, 50, 52, 56, 58–62, 74, 79, 82, 87, 92, 95, 96, 101, 111–117, 119–132, 149–151, 154, 155, 158–163, 167–171, 174–178, 189, 229–231, 263, 272, 273, 279–286, 288–291, 293, 294, 296, 298, 304, 313–316, 335, 367–374, 378–381, 383, 384, 393, 395, 424, 455, 456, 458, 460, 461, 465–470, 473, 474
critical reflection, 298, 371, 378, 380
critical reflexivity, 307, 308, 345–348, 363

481

critical research, 11, 92, 111–130, 167, 176–178, 371, 373
critical theorist, 87, 116
critical theory, 19, 80, 95, 114, 123, 125, 230, 279, 281, 282, 290, 304, 370
critical tradition, 3, 129
criticality, 5, 6, 108, 279, 283, 367, 371, 373, 380
Cross, 19, 62, 69, 80, 104, 135, 265, 297, 321, 373, 462
crypto-positivism, x, xii–xx, xxii, xxiii, xxv, xxvii–xxxv, xxxviii, xl, 16, 19, 22, 26–28, 30, 31
Cuban, Larry, 148
cultural misunderstandings, 11, 138
cultural pedagogy, 111, 113, 114, 129, 130
cultural perspectives, 24, 170
cultural pluralism, 8, 104
cultural production, 44, 73, 123, 129, 130
cultural reproduction, 44
cultural studies, 4, 19, 111–113, 125, 130, 133, 135, 146, 153, 159, 295
culturally responsive teaching, 56, 57, 59, 130
culture, x, xvi, xxvi, xxviii, xxxi, 9, 11, 15, 16, 20, 22, 41, 44, 46–48, 52, 58, 61, 69, 73, 79, 80, 86, 88, 98, 102, 104, 111–115, 117, 122, 125–129, 137, 140, 146, 147, 170, 185, 186, 212, 215, 226, 249, 280, 284, 285, 293, 313, 330, 341, 445, 456, 462, 470
curriculum, 7, 8, 10, 15, 25, 58, 59, 60, 99, 104, 113, 114, 122, 127–129, 133, 134, 159, 204, 205, 236, 257, 284, 288, 345, 359, 362, 380, 381, 395, 460
cyberspace, 11, 12, 293

D

Dalai Lama, 340, 356

Darwin, Charles, 404
data analysis, 48, 227, 362, 380
Davidson, Richard, 339, 340, 356, 357, 359, 364
decentering, 101–103, 106, 379
decision-making, xi, 152, 153, 161, 172, 257, 348, 457, 460
decontextualized, x, xx, 5, 9, 10, 11, 20, 21, 24, 26, 85, 124, 174, 284, 463
decontextualized knowledge, 85
deferred action, 396, 398, 409–411
deficit perspectives, 57
dehumanization, 172
deictic, 219
democracy, 17, 123, 128, 140, 142, 161, 279, 395
democratic reconceptualization, 6, 8, 169
Derrida, Jacques, 6, 79, 146, 221, 226, 231
Descartes, Rene, 5, 17, 238, 240, 242, 247, 440
descriptive observation, 85
deskilling practices, 27
determinism, xxxiii, 324
Dewey, John, 17, 18, 125, 126, 138, 139, 144, 344, 468
dialectic, 31, 113, 186, 196, 231, 282, 298, 308, 392, 393, 446, 451
  dialectical relationship, 34, 219, 343
  dialectically, 46, 48, 72, 194, 196
  dialectics, xli, 183
dialogue, xii, xl, xli, 16, 37, 42, 50, 57, 89, 91, 115, 118, 122, 155, 156, 158–163, 169, 172–176, 178, 284, 298, 304, 307, 310, 315, 370, 372, 378–380, 385, 398, 399, 461, 462, 470
dichotomous thinking, 26, 183, 295, 303, 310, 313
difficult knowledge, 301, 380, 395–411, 414–417
digital technologies, 81, 88, 107, 465

disability, 393
discourse analysis, 42, 90, 101, 291
discourse of possibility, 279
discourses of emancipation, 81
discursive formation, 124, 281, 392
disposition(s), xlii, 7, 9, 61, 123, 177, 186, 189, 195, 256, 258–260, 267, 269, 327, 342
diversity, xxxii, xlii, 9–12, 22, 81, 83, 87, 89, 94, 95, 114, 122, 286, 371, 373–375, 470
domestication, 315
dominant ideology, 20, 172, 368
domination, 112, 113, 121, 123, 129, 171
dualisms, 138, 310, 329, 440
DuBois, W.E. B., 279
Dussell, Enrique, 280

E

Early, Margaret, 239, 403
Education Sciences Reform Act (2002), 466
educational psychology, 4, 17, 18, 61, 84, 202, 244, 313, 352, 400, 404, 405, 423
Educational Researcher, 4, 5, 7–9, 11, 13, 15, 22, 26, 30, 116, 122, 146, 212, 229, 282, 297, 305, 334, 392, 459
educative authenticity, 45, 344, 356
eidetic, 101, 107
Eisenhart, Margaret, 343, 364
Eisenstein, Zillah R.
Eliade, Mircea, 245, 247
Elkins, Stanley
emancipation, 81, 125, 129
emancipatory, xvii, xxi, 130, 280, 288, 380
emancipatory practices
emergence theory, 438–440, 443, 445
emotion(s), emotional, 16, 25, 29, 61, 69, 121, 127, 130, 137–139, 156, 170, 182, 194, 215–217, 226, 272, 280, 295–297, 299, 301, 310–312, 322, 324, 331, 332, 342–344, 346, 348, 349, 351–357, 359, 360, 362, 384, 392, 393, 398–403, 411, 441, 443, 474
emotional energy, 66, 189, 358
emotional experience of knowledge, 401, 403
emotional state, 215, 344, 349, 350, 352, 353, 355, 360
empathy, 70, 121, 217, 284, 298, 342, 352, 415
empirical science, 6, 435
empiricism, xxviii, 17–20, 29, 305, 428, 431, 432
environmental science, xlii, 367–369, 373, 380, 381
epistemic, 135, 335, 383, 393
epistemology, xii–xxix, xxxii–xxxiv, xxxvii, xl–xlii, 3–5, 8–10, 13, 15–17, 20–22, 25–28, 30, 31, 41, 91, 96, 114, 122, 127, 128, 146, 169, 170, 240, 283, 285, 288, 289, 291, 295, 303–305, 312, 314, 325, 332, 335, 340, 367, 393, 409, 421, 440, 446, 455, 456, 458, 461, 465, 466, 468–470
    epistemological, 3–5, 8, 10, 41, 122, 127, 128, 146, 283, 285, 291, 409, 421, 446
    epistemological assumptions, 10, 285
equity, 33, 45, 98, 104, 372, 395
Erickson, Frederick, 189, 343, 470
essence, 38, 128, 152, 156, 260, 269, 274, 294
    essencing, 260, 267–271, 273
essentialism, xii, xix, xxiv, xxvii, 7, 19, 25, 30, 45, 111, 117–119, 137, 183, 243, 267–269, 272, 326, 335, 344, 425, 435
essentializing, 94, 118, 119, 161

INDEX

ethics, xiii, xxii, xxiv, xxxvii, xl, 92, 161, 305, 307, 309, 324, 356, 359, 390, 391, 423
ethnocentrism, 21, 23, 24
ethnography
    ethnographic research, 47, 87, 294, 305, 306, 308, 310, 315
    ethnographic work, 175, 204, 294–296, 301, 303, 306, 309, 311
ethnomethodology, 206, 229, 230
Eurocentrism, 23, 24, 285
evaluation, 8, 92, 99, 111, 123, 141, 142, 157, 416, 469
event oriented inquiry, xii, xxvi, 25, 27, 41, 117, 187–189, 192, 195, 202–205, 220, 231, 252, 328, 330, 339, 361, 397–399, 409, 410, 447, 449
evidence-based research, 7, 455, 461
exclusion, 96, 98, 99, 121, 140, 406, 455, 461
exercise, 29, 36, 94, 256, 261, 267, 270, 271, 273, 304, 329, 340, 349, 354, 355
expansive research, 393
experience
    living, 255, 256, 258–260, 263, 264, 268, 273, 274
    reflection on, 190, 193, 240, 259, 261, 262, 267, 268, 271, 375, 378, 380, 396, 400, 402,
extraneous perturbations, 6

F

far-from-equilibrium conditions, 82, 91
fecundity, 253
feedback looping, 82, 91
Fellner, Gene, xli, 181, 183, 196, 334, 343, 358, 363, 473
feminism, 87, 114, 120, 121, 122, 404
feminist research, 87, 90, 120–122
feminist theory, 120, 121
Feurer, Michael J., 457
fiction, 304
Fine, Michelle, 380
Fink, Bruce, 410
fitness, 256, 264, 271
focus groups, 85, 87, 155
Foucault, Michel, 87, 92, 96, 101, 108, 109, 146, 308
Fox, S., 241
Frankfurt School, 19, 20, 116, 123, 125, 279, 290
Franklin, V.P., 280
freedom, 293
Freire, Paulo, 128, 170–172, 175–178, 280, 300, 314, 368, 380, 466
Freud, Sigmund, 272, 396, 398–401, 405, 408, 410, 411

G

Gadamer, Hans-Georg, 127, 158, 235–241, 244–253
Gee, James, 182, 470
gender, 4, 6, 7, 15, 42, 43, 65, 83, 94, 99, 102, 109, 113, 120, 129, 146, 163, 172, 186, 190, 279, 281, 282, 285, 288, 300, 313–315, 326, 371, 393
genealogy, 87, 92, 101
generalizability, 29, 34, 332, 343, 462
generalize, 325, 343, 378, 457, 463
genre, 19, 84, 85, 91, 92, 94, 97, 109, 114, 119, 120, 173, 175, 295, 296, 303–305, 309, 310, 456
geographical place, 113
gesture, 42, 64, 66, 68–70, 74, 183–186, 188, 189, 201, 218–220, 224, 226, 256, 257, 261–264, 267–270, 273, 274, 327, 356, 386
Giroux, Henry, 20, 171, 315, 368
God, xviii, xxxv, 16, 18, 148, 270, 322, 325–327, 330, 333, 358, 406
Goffman, Erving, 206, 329, 333

Google, 231, 241, 467
grain size, 34, 72
Gramsci, Antonio, 133, 134, 139
Gresson, Aaron D., 116, 289
grounded theory, 33-74

H

habitus, 59, 60, 311
hand gestures, 218-220
Harding, Sandra, 22, 26, 467
Hegel, Georg, 147, 446
hegemony, 19, 111, 133-136, 139, 143, 170, 282, 368
    hegemonic, 26, 79, 109, 126, 134, 135, 161, 195, 281, 313
Henry Oldenburg, 456
hermeneutic phenomenology, 86, 235
hermeneutic(s), xi, xx, xxi, xxx, 8, 27, 86, 95, 109, 113, 114, 116, 119, 120, 123-130, 153, 154, 160, 235-253, 282, 287, 288, 290, 291, 331, 334, 343, 345-348, 362, 363, 446, 473
Herrnstein, Richard, 411
heuristic, 52, 339, 345-349, 352-354, 356, 357, 359-364
Himmelfarb, Gertrude, 145, 146
historical knowledge, 146, 281, 398
historical moments, 83-87, 89, 92, 98, 287, 288
historical research, 97, 133, 142-148, 279, 280, 282, 283, 285, 287, 288
historiography, 145, 146, 149, 279-289, 291
history, x, xvi, xvii, xxii, xxiii, xxv-xxvii, xxxi-xxxiii, 20, 23, 24, 27, 30, 58, 83-87, 89, 92, 96-100, 102, 104, 107, 114, 123, 125-127, 129, 133-135, 138, 142-147, 149, 170, 183, 185, 194, 230, 231, 279-291, 334, 395, 398, 405, 452, 455-457
Holzmeyer, Cheryl, xlii, 455, 473

homosexuality, 104, 105
Horton, Myles, 466, 469, 470
human subjects, 29, 34-43, 130, 396, 445
Husserl, Edmund, 248, 273
hyperreality/hyperrationalism, 5, 7, 8, 111, 117, 127, 287
hypertexting, 11, 80, 82, 87, 91, 96, 100, 105-108

I

iChat, 51, 58, 74
identity, xv, xli, xlii, 11, 52, 113, 128, 130, 140, 145, 149, 163, 178, 186, 188, 196, 229, 242, 313-316, 332, 367, 368, 372-378, 380, 381, 384, 393, 396, 403, 407, 410, 415, 416, 444
ideology, 4, 17, 19, 20, 28, 30, 111, 117, 120, 128, 129, 172, 229, 230, 280, 291, 326, 347, 368, 371, 421, 424, 452
    critique, 129, 230, 373
imagination, 26, 130, 137-139, 235, 238, 256, 262, 283, 297, 332, 335, 405, 447
iMovie, 50, 54, 62, 69, 117, 228
impressionistic tale, xli, 321, 332, 334
inclusiveness, 81, 83, 87, 94
indigenous knowledge, 8, 16, 23, 24, 92, 110, 178, 285, 313
individual case, 253
inequity, 45, 52, 195, 301
informed consent, 29, 34, 36, 39, 40, 43, 309, 414
insider perspective, 27
Institute of Education Sciences, 457, 458, 466
institutional repository, 147, 460
Institutional Review Board (IRB), 29, 30, 34-39, 41-43, 307, 308, 333
intentionality, 248, 261, 270

INDEX

interaction, 6, 17, 18, 25, 33, 35, 36, 42, 47, 50, 61–64, 66–70, 72, 112–115, 120, 127, 130, 153, 158, 181, 183, 185, 186, 188, 189, 194, 199, 203, 204, 206, 210, 212–223, 226–229, 257, 262, 268, 271, 273, 282, 288, 303, 307, 315, 334, 369, 379, 393, 449
interaction analysis, 227
interconnectivity, 96
interculturalism, 285
interdisciplinary studies, 84, 88
internet, 12, 59, 63, 88, 92, 93, 108, 147, 293, 455, 458, 459, 461, 464
interpretation, 4, 7, 12, 27, 47, 50, 53, 54, 57, 67, 84, 94, 95, 99, 101–103, 107, 111, 114, 116–121, 123–130, 144–146, 153, 154, 157–159, 161, 167, 173, 174, 185, 186, 192, 202, 206, 207, 209, 211, 214, 227, 238, 246–248, 256, 281, 282, 284, 286, 288–291, 296, 297, 332–334, 343, 345–347, 374, 375, 384, 385, 392, 393, 397, 399, 402, 405, 434, 446, 448, 449, 468, 470
interpretive, xii, xvi, xvii, xx–xxiii, xxvi, xxx, xxxiv, xliii, 7, 26, 33, 40, 48, 50, 53, 67, 82, 84, 92, 95, 97, 99, 101–103, 114, 116–119, 123–130, 144, 145, 154, 158, 159, 161, 174, 185, 186, 192, 202, 206, 209, 211, 214, 227, 238, 246–248, 253, 256, 282, 284, 285, 287, 289–291, 296, 297, 305, 332–334, 343, 346, 384, 385, 392, 393, 397, 399, 402, 405, 434, 441, 446, 448, 449, 455, 461–463, 467, 470
interpretive bricolage, 82, 92, 95, 97, 101–103, 107, 118–120
interpretive research, 40, 46, 48, 246, 343, 344, 399, 463
interracialism, 285
intersubjective, 206, 221, 268, 328

interventions, xlii, xliii, 339, 341, 343, 345, 348, 353, 355, 359, 456, 458, 469
interview, 37, 38, 40, 41, 51–53, 58, 72, 84, 86, 100, 101, 105, 107, 113, 115, 133, 138, 155, 167, 203, 204, 207, 215, 219, 230, 243, 286, 334, 347, 383, 396, 397, 402, 403, 405–411, 414–417
intuition, 118, 121, 137–139, 360, 405, 433
iPod, 47
iTalk, 47

J

Johnson, P., 237
Jones, Susan R., 396
journal, 15, 19, 59, 88, 105, 107, 133, 144, 255, 256, 262, 264, 306, 308, 310, 371, 372, 383, 456, 459, 460, 463
justice, 7, 29, 36, 81, 83, 87, 94, 95, 96, 98–100, 104, 108, 114, 123, 128, 167, 169, 173, 177, 239, 279, 284, 298, 302, 311, 314, 315, 381, 395

K

Kabat-Zinn, Jon, 339, 340, 345, 350, 357
Kant, Immanuel, 258, 427, 428, 436, 440, 441, 442, 444, 450
Kincheloe, Joe L., 3–13, 15–31, 45, 74, 80–82, 87, 92, 94, 96, 107, 108, 167, 170, 172, 176, 279–289, 298, 313, 314, 346
knowing, xli, 152, 154, 159, 162
knowledge, 3, 15, 53, 79, 111, 133, 151, 167, 202, 235, 268, 280, 296, 325, 344, 368, 383, 395–411, 421–452, 455

Kress, Tricia, xli, 167–172, 175–178, 298, 314, 316, 474
Kristeva, Julia, 103, 403, 409
Kuhn, Thomas, 19, 82, 280, 383

L

language, 6, 7, 9, 18, 21, 29, 30, 44, 79, 87, 109, 111, 116, 128, 138, 156, 189–194, 212, 221, 222, 226, 235, 262, 263, 306, 322, 323, 326, 332, 347, 370, 374, 384, 386, 392, 393, 396, 397, 401, 403, 423, 432–437, 443, 445, 452, 459, 462, 467
Laplanche, Jean, 396, 409, 411
Lather, Patti, 45, 149, 396
laughter, 185
learning, x, xiv, xv, xviii, xix, xxvi, xxvii, xxxi, 4–7, 10, 15, 21, 22, 24, 27, 28, 30, 178, 287, 314, 379
learning environments, 33–35, 42, 44, 46, 58, 61, 62, 169, 172–176, 297, 346, 368
Leben, 248
legitimization, 117
legitimized research, 85, 86, 93, 99, 102, 335, 363
Lethe, 252
Levis-Strauss, Claude, 79
Lewin, Kurt, 152
liberal democracy, 140
liberation, 280, 284, 293–316
liminal period, 246
listening, 54, 67, 154, 155, 158, 159, 177, 212, 226, 227, 247, 324, 328, 359, 362, 363, 378
literal method of interpretation, 117
literature review, 82, 88, 104
lived experience, xli, 107, 110, 123, 130, 170, 171, 175, 255–260, 262, 267, 268, 273, 274, 291, 296, 297, 301, 310, 315, 332, 363, 367, 368, 371, 380, 381, 393, 409, 443

local knowledge, 310, 455, 461, 468, 469
Locke, John, 17, 140, 427, 428
logics of inquiry, ix, xl, 22
Longino, Helen, 458
loving-kindness, 357

M

magnetic resonance, 340
marginalization
    marginalized groups, 169
    marginalized individuals, 280, 285
    marginalized voices, 368
Marx, Karl, 183, 186, 194, 196
Marxism, 290
Marxist, xli, 86, 87, 95, 97, 103, 183, 230, 231
mass culture, 112
McLaren, Peter, 45, 167, 168, 177, 368
meditation, xlii, 246, 327, 339, 340, 342, 345, 348–360
member checking, 50
mentor, 89, 296, 311
meta-analysis, 280, 291
metalogue, 315
metaphor, 72, 73, 82, 96, 97, 126, 160, 245, 264, 297, 301, 303, 312, 314, 322, 329, 330, 356, 386, 397, 398, 402, 410, 426, 427, 428, 430, 433–435, 437, 443, 448
Mexican Americans, 140
Milner, Marion, 400, 401, 405, 406
Mindfully Listening, 362, 363
Mindfully Speaking, 362, 363
mindfulness, xlii, 155, 261, 262, 268, 269, 294, 301, 339–360, 362–364, 474
monosemia, 189, 190, 192, 193
Morgan, Bill, 136
Morland, Catherine, 143
Morris, Marla, 147

INDEX

Moss, Pam, 158, 159, 162, 463, 470
multiculturalism, 283
multilectical, xli, 181–183, 185, 186, 188, 189, 192–196, 343
multi-level, xi, xiii, xx, xli, 25, 33, 34, 56, 62, 72, 73, 85, 93, 112, 118, 120, 126, 183, 186–190, 194–196, 282, 283, 298, 343, 449
multilogical, 280, 283–285, 289, 343
multilogicality, 283, 284, 285
multi-method, 157, 343
multiperspectival, 8, 114, 287
multiple theories, 83, 87, 92, 96
Murray, Charles, 23

N

Narcotics Anonymous, 323
narrative, x, xxvi, xlii, 8, 51, 60, 85, 87, 88, 92, 94, 102, 108, 126, 130, 145, 156, 158, 185, 241, 245, 283, 296, 298, 300, 301, 304, 314, 369–371, 374, 380, 395, 396, 398, 402, 403, 407, 408, 410, 414
National Institute of Health, 470
National Research Council, 148, 456, 470
native, xxxviii, 115, 140, 196
Native Americans, 140
nature of science, 26
Nazi Germany, 279
neoliberalism, 368, 467, 471
neuroplasticity, 340
New York Times Magazine, 16
Newton, Isaac, 21, 97, 427, 456
No Child Left Behind, 194, 195, 457, 468
Nussbaum, Martha, 139

O

ontology, x–xxii, xxiv–xxxxxii, xxxv, xxxvi, xl, xli, 4, 5, 8, 9, 13, 18, 20–30, 41, 44, 45, 60, 82, 84–87, 94, 99, 101–103, 107, 109, 110, 121, 123, 124, 128, 145, 148, 149, 159, 169–172, 174, 177, 212, 242, 244, 245, 248, 256, 261, 267–269, 283, 285, 286, 289, 291, 295, 297, 298, 304, 310, 316, 332, 344, 346, 347, 351, 355, 356, 362, 392, 397, 421, 426, 428, 429, 430, 433, 435, 436, 439, 441–452, 459
ontological, 4, 5, 41, 44, 45, 60, 128, 148, 242, 245, 283, 285, 397, 421, 430, 439, 444, 448, 449, 451
ontological assumptions, 20, 242
ontological authenticity, 41, 44, 45, 344
open access, 455, 458–461, 463, 464, 466, 467, 469, 470
operational definitions, 433, 435
oppression, 8, 19, 23, 45, 120, 121, 129, 171, 172, 279, 282, 284, 295, 300, 312
oral history, 286, 407
outsider perspectives, 27
overlapping speech, 67, 68, 70

P

paradigms, 96, 97, 152, 173, 242, 294, 297, 304, 305, 340, 342, 343, 348, 367, 371, 383, 442, 462, 465
participant observation, 46, 331
participatory research, xvii, xxix, xxxv, xl, xlii, xliii, 10, 12, 17, 29, 33, 36, 38–40, 47, 59, 63, 67, 91, 112, 151–156, 158–163, 175, 223, 231, 261, 262, 268, 329, 344, 356, 358, 367–369, 372–374, 380–382, 455, 460, 461, 467, 473
part-whole dichotomies, 34
pathologize, 94
pedagogical, xii, xiv, xviii, xix, xxii, xxiii, xxvii, xxx, 7, 8, 11, 111, 112, 117, 127, 130, 157, 273, 395, 406, 411,
attentiveness, 256, 264, 266

488

pedagogy, 10, 15, 111–114, 117, 125, 126, 128–130, 152, 153, 168, 169, 170, 171, 172, 177, 182, 189, 253, 256, 261, 267, 271, 273, 274, 279, 280, 294, 301, 303, 304, 312, 315, 368, 373, 383, 384, 390, 391, 392, 395, 409, 460, 466, 468
peer debriefing, 50, 51, 58, 60, 61
peer-review, 456, 459, 460, 461
personal narratives, 87, 102, 370, 371
perspectives
  multiple, xli, 4, 7, 10, 107, 145, 148, 159, 283
Peters, Frederick, 128
phenomenological, 86, 88, 107, 236, 248, 250, 255–261, 264, 267–269, 271, 273, 274, 298, 331, 333, 334, 342, 343, 348, 363, 441
  essences, 269, 274
  reflection, 259, 268
photovoice, xlii, 156, 162, 163, 367–374, 376, 378–382
physiological expression, 274, 349, 353, 358, 444
Piaget, Jean, 238
Pinkola-Estes, Clarissa, 250
pitch, 69–71, 201, 209, 212, 213, 215–218, 227, 231, 257, 331, 385, 388
Plato, 17, 19, 137, 139, 427
plurality, 81, 83, 87, 89, 94, 95, 98, 104
pointing, 43, 70, 200, 211, 213, 218, 219, 220, 221, 236, 240, 270, 343, 463
polyphonia, xi, 34, 102, 110, 153, 158, 191, 343, 380
polysemia, xxxix, 158, 343, 361, 380
positionality, 4, 94, 95, 100, 119, 153, 280
positivism, 13, 15–31, 84, 87, 98, 101, 102, 106, 107, 109, 170, 291, 295, 311, 313, 367, 427, 430–434

postcolonial, 88, 102, 103, 108, 313, 393, 467, 471
postdiscourses, 81, 96
postmodern, 80, 82, 87, 88, 91, 108, 114, 117, 121, 124, 127, 129, 130, 149, 295, 303–305, 384, 424
poststructuralism, 87, 88, 103, 114, 115, 117, 121, 122, 303
power
  power blocs, 21, 123, 171, 285
  power relations, 9, 87, 128, 158, 161, 168, 279, 281, 308, 465
Powietrzynska, Malgorzata, xlii, 339, 348, 363–364, 474
PRAAT, 42, 69, 227, 229, 231
practices|schema, 47
praxis, 6, 47, 60, 85, 169, 176–178, 204, 205, 291, 298, 301, 306, 314, 367, 384–385, 392, 393
producers of knowledge, 28
progressive education, 144, 146
proof, 82, 88, 124, 300, 450
prosody, 184, 186, 189, 190, 212–220, 228
pulse rate, 255, 266, 352–354, 356

Q

qualitative data, xvi, 13, 74, 84, 86, 87, 110, 117, 124, 134, 136, 143–146, 290, 294, 305, 316, 383, 395, 474, 475
quantitative data, xxvi, xxxix, xli, 13, 21, 26, 42, 80, 84–86, 90, 116, 133, 134, 136, 139, 240, 241, 245, 342, 364, 368, 371
quasi-experiments, 33
QuickTime, 50, 54, 62, 69, 225, 228

R

race, 4, 6, 7, 15, 43, 83, 94, 99, 102, 113, 121, 129, 146, 172, 184, 186, 188, 191, 193, 194, 195, 196, 279,

489

280, 282, 284, 304, 315, 322, 371, 372, 374, 377, 393
racism, 140, 149, 393
radical listening, xxxiv, xxxv
randomness, 82, 91
rationalism, 6, 8
realism, 346, 427, 430–435
reductionism, 4, 6, 21, 104, 107, 109, 111, 284, 291, 422, 423, 426, 437–441, 444, 445, 451
reflection, 21, 176, 190–193, 215, 240, 243, 259, 261, 262, 267, 268, 271, 273, 297, 298, 307, 308, 309, 312, 315, 352, 358, 369, 371, 373, 374, 375, 376, 378, 380, 396, 400, 402, 421, 429, 446
reflexivity, 145, 175, 298, 307, 308, 345–348, 360, 361, 363
relational methods, xxx, 97, 140, 142, 151–153, 159, 161, 170, 224, 269, 274, 289, 449, 451
relationality, 84, 101, 104, 106, 107, 108, 267
repair, 97, 206–210, 314, 402, 414
representation, 11, 85, 94, 99, 109, 113, 127–130, 155–158, 181–183, 190, 216, 225, 268, 269, 297, 304, 305, 307, 311, 332, 361, 363, 370, 379, 395, 396, 397, 399, 401, 403, 410, 430, 449
repression, 121
research quality, 332, 384, 396
resistance, 5, 53, 55, 86, 94, 96, 98, 123, 128, 192, 195, 218, 312, 313, 386, 393, 396, 402, 403, 410
respect, xi, 4, 11, 22, 29, 36, 37, 58, 61, 63, 91, 137, 162, 185, 192, 203, 220, 222, 223, 285, 301, 314, 334, 360, 364, 421, 422, 424, 429, 431, 433, 450, 465, 470
right-wing religious conservatives, 287
rigor, 3, 7, 10, 11, 12, 16, 20, 26, 28, 103, 117, 142, 170, 177, 280, 283, 288, 289, 291, 302, 305, 306, 307, 324, 341, 342, 444, 460, 468
Rilke, Rainer Marie, 237, 240
Rousmaniere, Kate, 146
Rousseau, Jean Jacques, 140, 258

S

Santayana, George, 143, 147
Sartre, Jean-Paul, 248
schema, 17, 47, 48, 72
Schroeder, T. V.
Schutz, Alfred, 18
scientific method, 5, 16, 17, 19, 20, 97, 107, 109, 170, 174, 178, 291, 371, 435
scientific research, xxiii, xlii, 148, 455–458, 462, 466, 470
  in education, 148, 455–470
scientism, xxiii, xxviii, xxx–xxxiv, 16, 17, 422–424, 440, 462
Scott, Bell Patricia
Scott, Joan, 145, 146, 384
Sedgwick, Eve Kosofsky, 411
self-organization, 82, 91
semantic realism, 432, 433, 435
semiotics, 87, 95, 113, 116, 120, 122
Sewell, William (Jr), 44, 48, 61, 186, 348
sex, 43, 64
sexual, 6, 41, 263, 282, 285, 300, 308, 309, 387, 408, 411
Shavelson, Richard J., 457, 470
Simpsons, The, 139
Siry, Christina, xl, 156, 157, 163, 474
situated action, 205
situatedness, 384, 392
situating, 101–103, 126–128, 152–153, 155
Smith, Barbara, 383, 411
social change, 279, 290
social inequality, 172

social justice, xviii, xxxvii, 81, 83, 87, 94–96, 98, 100, 104, 167, 169, 302, 311, 314, 315, 381, 395, 473
social life, xxxix, 17, 25, 33, 44, 62, 72, 73, 153, 183, 186, 189, 196, 199, 202, 230, 296, 341, 343, 346, 348, 360, 361, 435
social organization, 199
social relations, xxxi, 199, 204, 220, 229, 329, 397, 465, 469
social reproduction, 49
social structure(s), 186, 199, 206, 310, 333
social theory, xi, 7, 8, 122, 126, 176, 282, 368, 370, 380, 473
socialization, 129, 314, 315
sociocultural, xxxix, 22, 27, 30, 33, 34, 60, 61, 185, 202, 218, 219, 299, 367
  theory, xxxix, 33, 34, 60, 61
sociology, xix, 4, 19, 61, 84, 112, 212, 423, 438, 439
sociopolitical, xv, xviii, xix, xx, xxvi, xxx, 12, 15, 20, 27, 30, 112, 114, 115, 121, 129, 314
solidarity, 70, 71, 189, 190, 217, 285
South Park, 139
Southern Illinois University, 144, 147
spatio-temporal relationships, 25
standpoint, xxx, xxxix, xl, 28, 31, 49, 85, 183, 189, 192, 309, 310, 331, 345, 407, 443
speech intensity, 212, 213, 217, 218
spontaneity, 82, 91
standpoint theory, 26
Steinberg, Shirley, 6, 8, 28, 87, 111–130, 460, 471
Steiner, George, 397, 398,
Stenhouse, Lawrence, 19
stories, 157
storytelling, 85, 88, 159, 335, 368
structure, xxv, xxvi, 17, 25, 83, 84, 86, 107, 135, 142–149, 206, 280–289, 334, 396, 428

structural history, 82, 83, 121, 127
student researchers, 26, 51–57, 70
subjective, xi, xxix, xxxiii, 26, 84–86, 102, 144, 171, 183, 206, 221, 241, 242, 268, 283, 287, 295, 310, 328, 332, 403, 438, 443–445
subjectivity, xi, xv, xxv, xxvi, xxix, xxx, 7, 27, 85, 103, 122, 129, 130, 145, 153, 169, 170, 171, 237, 240, 241, 247, 248, 280, 283, 313, 393, 408, 438, 440–446, 450, 451
subjugation, 121
subordination, 171, 315
substainability, 364
symbolization, 126, 369, 398–401, 408–410
synchrony, 42, 64, 67, 68, 271

T

tacit, xxxiii, xxxix, 9, 30, 115, 117, 119, 126, 170, 284, 289, 384, 392
Taubman, Peter, 260
teacher research, 42, 52
Teachers College Record, 470
technology, 12, 48, 63, 107, 133, 134, 147, 206, 228, 340, 368, 456, 458, 461
teleology, 288
temporal issues, 288, 429, 439, 441
theoretical bricolage, 88, 92, 96, 103, 114
theoretical framework, 50, 61, 72, 122, 145, 176, 344, 361, 406, 407
theoretical generalizability, 343
theoretical tools, 8
thick description, 60, 72, 73, 124, 297, 345
thin coherence, 44, 48, 71, 72, 348
think aloud, 203, 204, 215, 219, 230
Thomson, Pat, 154
Thorndike, Edward, 17
Tobin, Kenneth, 3–31, 33–74, 313, 341
totalizing frameworks, 82, 110

Towne, Lisa, 457, 470
transcription conventions, 74, 200, 225
transdisciplinary, 4, 455
transference, 396, 398, 399, 400, 401, 410, 411
triple quandary, 61
truth, 4, 8, 17, 19, 22–24, 27, 30, 79, 80, 94, 97, 100, 107, 109, 110, 121, 127, 128, 144, 148, 168, 170, 171, 174, 175, 235–239, 244–252, 264, 279, 285, 290, 293–297, 307–309, 314, 334, 335, 368, 380, 385, 388, 392, 405
Turner, David, 245, 246

U

unconscious, 384, 390, 396, 399, 404, 410, 411
universalise, 94
University of Tennessee, 135
urban education, xi, xlii, 39, 51, 57, 59, 335, 341, 474, 475
utterance, 42, 64–69, 74, 201, 206, 207, 209, 210, 212, 213, 216, 219, 226, 230

V

validity, 9, 24, 141, 250, 291, 332, 361, 384, 430, 436, 445
Vicars, Mark, xlii, 383, 388, 475
Vico, Giambattista, 238, 246
video analysis, xiii, 35, 37–40, 47, 50, 51, 58, 62, 187, 203, 204
voice, xli, 30, 42, 52, 57, 69, 71, 104, 121, 154, 158, 160, 162, 163, 178, 183, 190, 193, 195, 212, 214–216, 227–229, 236, 250, 286, 295, 305, 307, 308, 316, 322–324, 331, 339, 341, 358, 368, 369, 372, 390, 392, 396, 407
Voltaire, 143
von Ranke, Leopold, 144

W

Waldman, Peter, xli, 335, 475
Walker, V., 470
Washington, Mary Helen, xliii, 74
ways of seeing the world, 3, 16, 91, 122, 288, 378
wellness, xi, 133, 151, 152, 156, 163, 260, 272, 313, 339, 340, 351, 352, 354, 356, 357, 359, 363, 364, 382, 459, 468–470, 475
Western Modern Science, xxxvii, 24, 170
Western perspectives, x, xix, xx, xxvii, xxxv–xxxviii, xli, 5, 6, 9, 15, 21–26, 83, 120, 168, 170, 173, 281, 284, 285, 288, 289, 291, 348, 456
What Works Clearinghouse, 458
White, Hayden, 74, 290
Whitehead, Albert North, 25, 241
Willinsky, J., 455–470
Woodson, Carter, 280

Z

Zeitgeist, 3, 16, 26, 283, 286, 291
Zinn, Howard, 143
zooming, 36, 73

CPSIA information can be obtained at www.ICGtesting.com
Printed in the USA
LVOW04s1048300815

452091LV00005B/53/P